W. W. Norton & Company

With the purchase of *Western Civilizations* you get a FREE registration code to access online documents from the StudySpace student website.

W. W. Norton & Company
500 Fifth Avenue / New York, NY 10110
wwnorton.com

TO ACTIVATE YOUR REGISTRA

1. Go to the *W Civilizations* student web wwnorton.c Navigate to *Civilizations* StudySpace site.

2. Choose a chapter. Select "Documents" from the "Connect" section of the menu.

3. Select the document and choose "Register as a First-Time User."

4. Enter the registration code printed below. You will be asked to provide an e-mail address so we can send you an initial password. You will be able to change both your e-mail address and your password later.

XPXU-YAHV

Please visit our technical support website at
wwnorton.com/web/HelpDesk
if you have any difficulties or need assistance.

WORLD · POLITICAL
NATIONAL BOUNDARIES

Winkel Tripel Projection

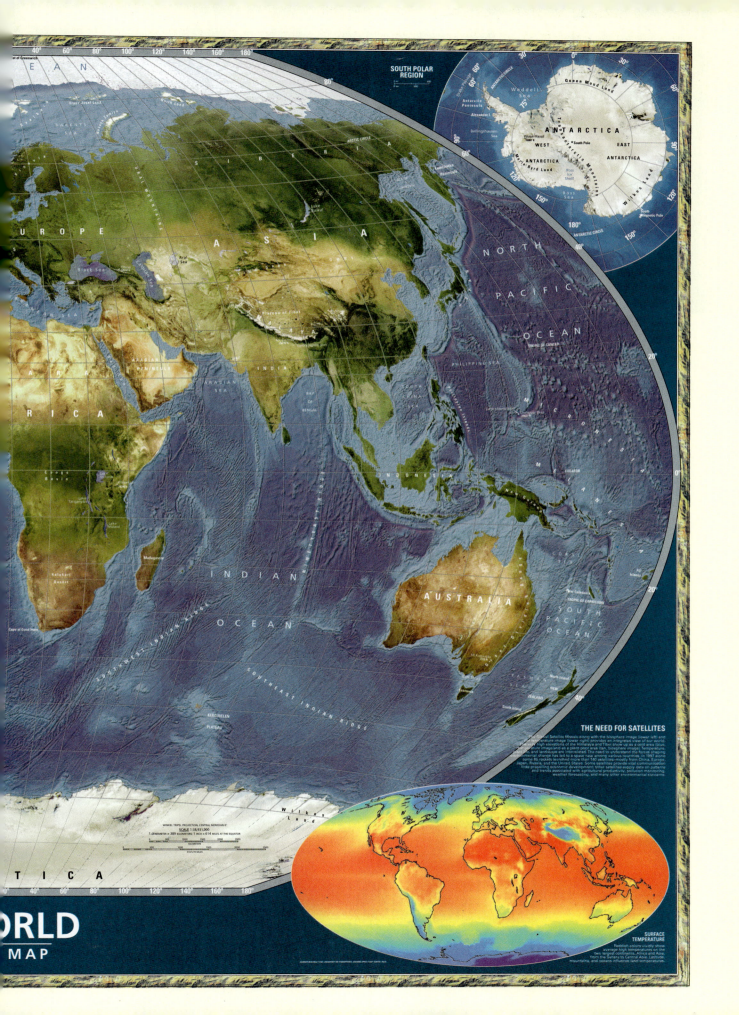

Volume B/Sixteenth Edition

Judith G. Coffin

Robert C. Stacey

Based on *Western Civilizations*
by Edward McNall Burns

Robert E. Lerner

Standish Meacham

W · W · Norton & Company · New York · London

WESTERN CIVILIZATIONS

THEIR HISTORY
& THEIR CULTURE

W. W. Norton & Company has been independent since its founding in 1923, when William Warder Norton and Mary D. Herter Norton first published lectures delivered at the People's Institute, the adult education division of New York City's Cooper Union. The Nortons soon expanded their program beyond the Institute, publishing books by celebrated academics from America and abroad. By mid-century, the two major pillars of Norton's publishing program—trade books and college texts—were firmly established. In the 1950s, the Norton family transferred control of the company to its employees, and today—with a staff of four hundred and a comparable number of trade, college, and professional titles published each year—W. W. Norton & Company stands as the largest and oldest publishing house owned wholly by its employees.

Copyright © 2008, 2005, 2002, 1998, 1993, 1988, 1984, 1980, 1973, 1968, 1963, 1958, 1954, 1949, 1947, 1941 by W. W. Norton & Company, Inc.
All rights reserved
Printed in the United States of America

Composition: TSI Graphics
Manufacturing by R. R. Donnelley & Sons—Willard Division
Book design by Antonina Krass
Layout artist: Paul Lacy
Production manager: Ben Reynolds
Editor: Karl Bakeman
Associate Director, Electronic Media: Steven S. Hoge
Copy Editor: Candace Levy
Project Editor: Lory A. Frenkel
Editorial Assistants: Rebecca Arata, Kate Feighery

The Library of Congress has cataloged the one-volume edition as follows.

Coffin, Judith G., 1952–
    Western civilizations: their history & their culture / by Judith G. Coffin and Robert C. Stacey.—16th ed.
       p. cm.
    Includes bibliographical references and index.
    ISBN 978-0-393-93099-3 (hardcover)
     1. Civilization, Western—Textbooks. 2. Europe—Civilization—Textbooks. I. Stacey,
  Robert C. II. Title. III. Title: Western civilizations, their history and their culture.

CB245.C65 2008
909'.09821—dc22
                                          2007042776

ISBN 13: 978-0-393-93101-3 (pbk.)
W. W. Norton & Company, Inc., 500 Fifth Avenue, New York, N.Y. 10110
www.wwnorton.com

W. W. Norton & Company Ltd., Castle House, 75/76 Wells Street, London W1T 3QT
1 2 3 4 5 6 7 8 9 0

To our families—Robin, Will, and Anna Stacey, and Willy, Zoe, and Aaron Forbath—for their patience and support. They reminded us that books such as this are worth the work, and also that there are other things in life.

To Robert Lerner, Standish Meacham, Edward McNall Burns, and Marie Burns, our predecessors who successfully guided *Western Civilizations* for thirteen editions, spanning six decades.

About the Book

Used by over 1,000,000 students *Western Civilizations* is renowned for its balanced presentation, clear prose, and exceptional treatment of cultural history. Originally published in 1942, the book began as an outgrowth of Edward McNall Burns's Western civilizations course at Rutgers University. Robert Lerner (Northwestern University) and Standish Meacham (University of Texas at Austin) took over authorship in the ninth edition and extended the book's traditional strengths to include the new social history. Beginning with the fourteenth edition, Judith Coffin (University of Texas at Austin) and Robert Stacey (University of Washington) debuted as the third generation of authors to lead this book. While Coffin and Stacey maintain the balanced presentation of *Western Civilizations*, they have enlarged the conception of "Western Civilization" to take in the diversity of the European world.

About the Authors

JUDITH G. COFFIN received her Ph.D. in modern French history from Yale University. She has taught at Harvard University and the University of California, Riverside, and is currently associate professor of history at the University of Texas at Austin, where she won a 1999 University of Texas President's Associates' Award for Teaching Excellence. Her research interests focus on the social and cultural history of gender, mass culture, slavery, race relations, and colonialism. She is the author of *The Politics of Women's Work: The Paris Garment Trades, 1750-1915*.

ROBERT C. STACEY is Dean of Humanities and Arts and Professor of History and Jewish Studies at the University of Washington in Seattle. A long-time teacher of western civilization and medieval European history, he has received Distinguished Teaching Awards from both the University of Washington and Yale University, where he taught from 1984 to 1988. The author or coauthor of four books, he is a Fellow of the Royal Historical Society and has held awards from the American Council of Learned Societies and from the Guggenheim Foundation. His current research deals with the history of Jews in medieval England.

Maps   xi

Chronologies   xii

Documents   xiii

Preface   xiv

Part IV From Medieval to Modern

Chapter 10 The Later Middle Ages, 1300–1500   370

Changes in the Land   372
The Black Death and Its Consequences   373
Social Change in the Later Middle Ages   380
War and the Development of the Late Medieval State   384
Kievan Rus and the Rise of Muscovy   395
Trials for the Church   398
The Pursuit of Holiness in the Late Medieval Piety   403
Thought, Literature, and Art   406
Advances in Technology   410
Conclusion   413

Chapter 11 Commerce, Conquest, and Colonization, 1300–1600   416

The Mongols   418
The Rise of the Ottoman Empire   422
Mediterranean Colonialism   427
Europe Encounters a New World   434
Conclusion   438

CONTENTS

CHAPTER 12 THE CIVILIZATION OF THE RENAISSANCE, C. 1350–1550   440

The Renaissance and the Middle Ages   442
The Renaissance in Italy   443
The Italian Renaissance: Painting, Sculpture, and Architecture   451
The Waning of the Italian Renaissance   459
The Renaissance in the North   462
Conclusion   469

CHAPTER 13 REFORMATIONS OF RELIGION   472

The Lutheran Upheaval   474
The Spread of Protestantism   482
The Domestication of the Reformation, 1525–1560   487
The English Reformation   490
Catholicism Transformed   495
Conclusion   499

CHAPTER 14 RELIGIOUS WARS AND STATE BUILDING, 1540–1660   502

Economic, Religious, and Political Tests   504
A Century of Religious Wars   506
Divergent Paths: Spain, France, and England, 1600–1660   513
The Problem of Doubt and the Quest for Certainty   522
Literature and the Arts   526
Conclusion   532

PART V EARLY MODERN EUROPE

CHAPTER 15 ABSOLUTISM AND EMPIRE, 1660–1789   538

The Appeal and Justification of Absolutism   540
Alternatives to Absolutism   542
The Absolutism of Louis XIV   546
The Remaking of Central and Eastern Europe   553
Autocracy in Russia   557
Commerce and Consumption   561
Colonization and Trade in the Seventeenth Century   564
Colonialism and Empire   570
Conclusion   575

CONTENTS xiii

Chapter 16 The New Science of the Seventeenth Century 578

The Intellectual Origins of the Scientific Revolution 580
The Copernican Revolution 582
Tycho's Observations and Kepler's Laws 583
New Heavens, New Earth, and Worldly Politics: Galileo 585
Methods for a New Philosophy: Bacon and Descartes 589
"And All Was Light": Isaac Newton 594
Conclusion 600

Chapter 17 The Enlightenment 602

The Foundations of the Enlightenment 604
The World of the *Philosophes* 606
Internationalization of Enlightenment Themes 609
Empire and Enlightenment 612
The Radical Enlightenment 617
The Enlightenment and Eighteenth-Century Culture 621
Conclusion 630

Part VI The Age of Revolution

Chapter 18 The French Revolution 636

The French Revolution: An Overview 638
The Coming of the Revolution 639
The Destruction of the Old Regime 642
A New Stage: Popular Revolution 650
From the Terror to Bonaparte: The Directory 658
Napoleon and Imperial France 658
The Return to War and Napoléon's Defeat: 1806–1815 663
Conclusion 670

Chapter 19 The Industrial Revolution and Nineteenth-Century Society 672

The Industrial Revolution in Britain, 1760–1850 675
The Industrial Revolution on the Continent 683
The Social Consequences of Industrialization 688
The Middle Classes 696
Conclusion 705

CONTENTS

RULERS OF PRINCIPAL STATES   A1

GLOSSARY   A6

TEXT CREDITS   A24

PHOTO CREDITS   A26

INDEX   A28

Maps

The Progress of the Black Death, Fourteenth
   Century   374
France During the Hundred Years' War   390
The Expansion of Muscovite Russia to 1505   396
The Great Schism, 1378–1417   400
The Spread of Printing   412
The Mongol Successor States   419
The Growth of the Ottoman Empire   426
Overseas Exploration in the Fifteenth and Sixteenth
   Centuries   429
The States of Italy during the Renaissance,
   c. 1494   461
The Empire of Charles V, c. 1550   479

Religious Situation in Europe, c. 1560   486
Map of the Netherlands   508
Europe at the End of the Thirty Years' War   512
Europe after the Treaty of Utrecht (1713)   552
The Growth of the Russian Empire   559
Population Growth, c. 1600   563
The Atlantic World   566
The Seven Year's War, 1756–1763   573
The Atlantic Revolutions   638
France and its Sister Republics   656
Napoleon's European Empire at its Height   666
The First Industrial Nation   676
The Industrial Revolution   686

Chronologies

Famine, Plagues, Rebellion, and Warfare, 1300–1450 378
Hundred Years' War, 1337–1453 387
The Rise of Muscovy, c. 1200–1505 396

Rise of the Mongol Empire, 1206–1260 418
Rise of the Ottoman Empire, 1300–1571 423
Portuguese Maritime Expansion, 1420s–1515 430
Encountering the New World, c. 1000–1545 436

Lives of Italian Renaissance Scholars and Artists 459
Lives of Northern Renaissance Scholars and Artists 469

Origins of the Reformation, 1450–1529 482
Spread of Protestantism, 1520–1560 490
The Counter-Reformation, 1534–1590 499

Religious Wars, 1540s–1648 509
Origins of the English Civil War, 1603–1660 521
The Search for Authority, 1572–1670 525

The Spanish Succession 550
Absolutist Rulers in Central Europe 556
Seventeenth- and Eighteenth-Century Wars 575

The Scientific Revolution, 1543–1637 581
Major Figures of the Scientific Revolution 593

Major Publications of the Enlightenment, 1734–1792 621
Lives of Enlightenment Thinkers 624

Periods of the French Revolution Era, 1789–1815 639
Origins of the French Revolution, 1788–1789 641
The First French Revolution, 1789–1792 648
The Second French Revolution, 1792–1794 657
Reign of Napoleon, 1799–1815 670

The Industrial Revolution in Great Britain, 1733–1825 680

Documents

Froissart on the English Peasants' Revolt, 1381   381
The Condemnation of Joan of Arc by the University of Paris, 1431   389
The Conciliarist Controversy   402

Marco Polo's Description of Java   421
Ottoman Janissaries   425
The Legend of Prester John   432
Enslaved Native Laborers at Potosí   437

The Humanists' Educational Program   444
Some Renaissance Attitudes Toward Women   447
Machiavelli's Italian Patriotism   450

Marriage and Celibacy: Two Views   489
The Six Articles   492
Obedience as a Jesuit Hallmark   498

The Destructiveness of the Thirty Years' War   511
Cardinal Richelieu on the Common People of France   516
Democracy and the English Civil War   520
Montaigne on Skepticism and Faith   524

Absolutism and Patriarchy   541
Mercantilism and War   549
The American Declaration of Independence   574

Galileo on Nature, Scripture, and Truth   587
Two Reactions to the "New Philosophy"   590
Newton on the Purposes of Experimental Philosophy   596

The Impact of the New World on Enlightenment Thinkers   613
Slavery and the Enlightenment   615
Rousseau's *Social Contract* (1760)   618
Rousseau and His Readers   622

What Is the Third Estate? (1789)   643
Declaration of the Rights of Man and of the Citizen   647
Social Grievances on the Eve of the Revolution (1789)   649
Olympe de Gouges, Declaration of the Rights of Women and of the Citizen   642
Debating the French Revolution: Edmund Burke and Thomas Paine   652
Two Letters from Napoleon   667

The Factory System, Science, and Morality: Two Views   678
Thomas Malthus on Population and Poverty   689
The Irish Famine: Interpretations and Responses   691
Marriage, Sexuality, and the Facts of Life   700

Since the 1920s, the western civilization survey course has held a central place in the curricula of American universities and high schools. Yet the concept of "western civilization" remains both elusive and controversial. It seems appropriate, therefore, that we begin by defining our terms. How do we, as authors, conceive of our subject?

During much of the twentieth century, "western" civilization meant "the civilization of western Europe," to which the history of the Ancient Near East was somewhat arbitrarily attached. Western civilization was therefore presented as beginning at Sumer, developing in Egypt, and then flowering in Greece. From Greece it spread to Rome, then made its way to France, Germany, England, Italy, and Spain, whose emigrating colonists brought it to the Americas after 1492. Rather like a train passing through stations, western civilization was thus conceived as picking up "cargo" at each of its stops, but always retaining the same engine and the same baggage cars.

This vision of western civilization was not only selective, it was often tied to a series of contentious assumptions. It cast the worldwide dominance of the European imperial powers between roughly 1800 and 1950 as the culmination of several thousand years of historical development, which it was the obligation of historians to explain. It also tended to presume that European global dominance in the nineteenth and twentieth centuries reflected and demonstrated the superiority of western European civilization over the African, Asian, and Native American civilizations the Europeans conquered during the heyday of their imperial expansion.

Historians today are keenly aware of how much such an account leaves out. It slights the use of force and fraud in European expansion. It also ignores the sophistication, dynamism, and humanity of the many cultures it sidelines. By neglecting the crucial importance of Byzantium and Islam, it even gives a misleadingly narrow account of the development of European civilization. It also misleads us about the civilizations created in North and South America after 1492, which were creole, or hybrid, cultures, not simply European cultures transplanted to other shores. This is not to argue that a study of western civilizations must give way to a study of world civilization. It is merely to insist that understanding the historical development of the West requires us to place our subject in a geographical and cultural context that is wider than western Europe alone; and that, shorn of its triumphalism, the history

PREFACE

of these various and differing western civilizations becomes vastly more interesting.

Therefore, we mean for the plural in our title, *Western Civilizations*, to be taken seriously. The West cannot be understood as a single, continuous historical culture. Rather, there have been a number of western civilizations whose fundamental characteristics have changed markedly over time. We treat "western" as a geographical designator referring to the major civilizations that developed in and around the Mediterranean Sea between 3500 B.C.E. ("Before the Common Era," equivalent to the Christian dating system B.C., "Before Christ") and 500 C.E. ("Common Era," equivalent to the Christian dating system A.D., "Anno Domini," "the Year of the Lord"). We also treat as "western" the civilizations that emerged out of the Mediterranean world in the centuries after 500 C.E., as the Greco-Roman world of antiquity divided into Islamic, Byzantine, and Latin Christian realms. The interdependence and mutual influences of these three western civilizations upon each other will be a recurring theme of the first half of this book. We take the same approach to describing the complex relationships between Europe and the other world civilizations with which it came into contact after 1500.

Western Civilizations rests on the efforts and learning of three generations of historians. Edward McNall Burns, Robert Lerner, and Standish Meacham constructed a textbook that combined a vigorous narrative style with attention to the diverse ways in which ordinary people responded to changing environments, societies, and cultures. In building upon their work, we have tried to retain these traditional strengths by remaining attentive to narrative, by aiming for clarity and accessibility without compromising on accuracy or ignoring complexity, and by presenting politics and culture as part of a single, shared world of historical experience.

We have also made significant changes to the book that reflect the changing historical interests of teachers, students, and scholars. In keeping with our broadened understanding of western civilizations, we devote much more attention to the world outside western Europe. We continue to integrate new scholarly work in social and cultural history and the history of gender into our narrative, but we have also substantially increased the attention we pay to economic, religious, and military history. We also pay particular attention to the varying ways in which these different western civilizations sought to govern themselves and the territories they conquered. "Empire" has been a consistent

theme in the history of the West for more than four thousand years. In revising this book, we have tried to do justice to its importance.

CHANGES TO THE SIXTEENTH EDITION

Throughout, we have worked to integrate the text, visual material, and pedagogy. That has meant bringing in different images, rewriting focus questions, and adding study questions to the documents as well as updating the text. These changes make the text more user-friendly while still allowing professors and students alike to tailor it to their particular course and interests.

Part I, "The Ancient Near East," was completely reorganized and rewritten for the fifteenth edition. However, we have made a number of changes to the text as well as to the artwork and document selections. In Chapter 1, the discussion of prehistory and the emergence of the earliest towns and villages have been updated, with particular attention to the exciting archaeological work currently underway at Çatal Höyük. We have also revised the presentation of Sumerian religion and added a discussion of Enheduanna, high priestess and daughter of Sargon I of Akkad. In Chapter 2, we have revised the discussion of Hatshepsut's role as a female pharaoh and added many new illustrations, including Hatshepsut's mortuary temple, one of the glories of ancient Egyptian architecture.

In Part II, readers will find a much-improved program of illustrations in all the chapters. Chapter 4 includes a revised account of Hellenistic religions, especially the so-called "mystery cults." Reflecting the consensus of recent scholarly work, Mithraism is now discussed only in Chapter 5, as an example of the new religious devotions that swept through early imperial Roman society. Readers will also find in Chapter 5 a new treatment of the economy of the Roman empire. Chapter 6 offers a completely new account of the fall of the western Roman empire during the fifth century C.E., emphasizing the suddenness of Rome's collapse and the profound consequences this collapse had for the Roman economy and for standards of living within the western Roman empire. Here too, as throughout the book, we are trying to reflect the current balance of scholarly opinion.

In Part III, "The Middle Ages," Chapter 7 now includes a separate section on the Vikings with several new accompanying illustrations. This chapter also features a revised explanation of the split between Shi'ite and Sunni Islam, a revised assessment of the influence of early Islamic civilization on Europe, and a new document box pairing passages from the Qur'an on Jews and Christians with the "Pact of Umar." Chapter 8 features another new document box, on the summoning of the First Crusade in 1096. A number of new illustrations have been added to Chapter 8 to give more students a better sense of daily life during the high middle ages. Readers will also find an improved discussion of climate change during this period. Chapter 9 includes a new document box on kingship as a religious office, which we hope will make it easier for students to grasp the issues at stake in the Investiture Conflict.

Part IV, "From Medieval to Modern," begins with a completely new chapter (10) on the later middle ages, which emphasizes the remarkable resilience and creativity that characterized European responses to the Black Death. The far-reaching consequences of the plague upon social, economic, and religious life are the central themes of this chapter. Interestingly, however, there is now considerable doubt among historians and epidemiologists as to whether the Black Death was in fact an outbreak of bubonic plague, or whether it may have been some other disease entirely. This new chapter includes an up-to-date discussion of this controversy, which remains unresolved as this book goes to press.

In Chapter 13, "Reformations of Religion," readers will find a new section on "Reform and Discipline," and a new selection of paired documents, contrasting Lutheran and Catholic positions on marriage and celibacy.

In Part V, we have rewritten Chapter 16, "The New Science of the Seventeenth Century," to make it clearer and more accessible. It emphasizes the transformation of scientific knowledge, practice, and institutions. Here as in all our discussions of intellectual history, we foreground the context in which new ideas emerged and how those ideas came to matter for a range of people, from philosophers, rulers, and bureaucrats to explorers, artists, and artisans.

In Part VI, we have expanded discussion of Napoleon's empire and its legacy to Europe and the world. We have added to Chapter 21 an extended discussion of slavery and its abolition in the Americas which follows up on the treatment of the Haitian revolution in Chapter 18. Coming as it does before the section on the American Civil War, it places developments in the United States in a larger, comparative perspective. No course can be comprehensive, especially one dealing with a topic as hard to define as the West, but we have chosen to touch down on a few topics, like the politics of abolition, with an eye to highlighting comparisons and global connections. We have expanded the treatment of U.S. imperialism in Chapter 22 for the same reason.

Part VI continues to be organized thematically. Chapter 19, on industrial society, focuses on the relationship between social, economic, and cultural change—or on industry as a way of life. Chapters 20 and 21 break the tumultuous history of the mid-nineteenth-century revolutions into two parts, to make themes easier to follow. Chapter 20 goes from the reaction against the French Revolution of 1789 to the renewed outbreak of revolution in 1848, and includes a discussion of nineteenth-century political ideologies and cultural movements. Chapter 21 begins with the revolutions of 1848 in central and eastern Europe and then focuses on the issues those revolutions raised, nation and state building, as they played out elsewhere.

In Part VII, we have revised Chapter 24, on World War I. Readers will find more material on the long-term evolution of warfare and the emergence of total war. We have also expanded the treatment of the Paris Peace Conference, another important global moment. The new scope of war summoned global institutions to contend with the war's ramifications. Whether or not those international concerns could be compatible with national interests was an open question, and would become a theme of the history of the twentieth century. So would other issues central to the Peace of Paris, such as the expansion of empire, the mobilization of movements for national self determination, and the protection of minorities within new nation states.

In Part VIII, which was almost entirely rewritten for the previous edition, we added discussion of the history of human rights to conclude the chapter on globalization. Why, suddenly, is the language of human rights so familiar? The change highlights the dramatic political transformation wrought by the end of the cold war; it also reflects the new horizons of a rapidly globalizing world, with all their potential and peril. Finally, a history of human rights provides the occasion to review some of the central debates of the Western political tradition.

INNOVATIVE PEDAGOGICAL PROGRAM

Western Civilizations, Sixteenth Edition, is designed for

PREFACE

maximum readability. The crisp, clear, and concise narrative is also accompanied by a pedagogical program to help students study while engaging them in the subject matter. Highlights of this innovative program include:

- **New "Transformations" feature provokes students to consider the implications of major historical events.** Throughout the Sixteenth Edition, we have inserted new material on important "transformations" in the history of western civilizations. Highlighted with an icon, these sections ask students to reflect on the larger political, social, or cultural consequences of major turning points in history. Frequently, they draw on cutting-edge scholarship that has transformed our understanding of these events. New "Tranformations" include:

- Chapter 1: "The Origins of Food Production in the Ancient Near East." This rewritten and expanded section focuses on the disadvantages and the advantages of agriculture.

- Chapter 6: "The German Invasions and the Fall of the Western Roman Empire." The new material on the German-Roman relations elaborates on the economic collapse of western Rome in the fifth century, and explains how aspects of Roman life—the tax and administrative system, agricultural systems, and city life—persisted.

- Chapter 10: "The Black Death." The effects of the plague rippled across Europe. It affected every aspect of life. For example, fewer people were available to work the fields, but there were also fewer people to feed. Prices of grain went up, but because there were fewer people competing for jobs, wages did, too. Consequently, ordinary people could now afford not only to buy more bread, they could also purchase dairy products, meat, fish, fruits and wine on a more regular basis. As a result, the people of Europe in the later middle ages ate a more balanced diet, and were consequently better nourished than they had been for centuries, or than some are today.

- Chapter 16: "Science and Cultural Change." This new "transformation" section deals with the cultural shifts that arose from the Scientific Revolution. Beginning in the 17th century, embracing science and the scientific method was at the heart of what it meant to be "modern." This has implications for the Enlightenment, but it also became the justification for new technologies and for new empires.

- Chapter 24: "The Peace Settlement at Versailles."

The Treaty of Versailles marks the emergence of the United States as a world power. But it also represents the first time so many countries were involved in a peace settlement and marks the scope of the war, the growing national sentiments and aspirations, and the tightening of international communication and economic networks.

- **NEW Document Questions.** Professors requested questions for the documents in the book. We have added questions at the bottom of each box that ask students to engage the primary source or connect it to the larger issues in the chapter.

- **End-of-Chapter Key Terms.** In response to requests from professors, each chapter includes a list of key terms to help students focus on the key ideas, events, or people in the chapter.

- **In-Text Documents.** To add depth to the more focused narrative of *Western Civilizations*, each chapter contains an average of four primary sources, two of which are paired to convey a sense of historical complexity and diversity.

- **Map Program with Enhanced Captions.** Over 130 beautiful maps appear throughout the text, including twenty-five new maps, each accompanied by an enhanced caption designed to engage the reader analytically while conveying the key role that geography plays in the development of history and the societies of the world.

- **In-Chapter Chronologies.** Several brief chronologies built around particular events, topics, or periods appear in each chapter and are designed to provide road maps through the narrative detail.

- **Focus Question System.** To ensure that students remain alert to key concepts and questions on every page of the text, focus questions guide their reading in three ways: (1) a focus question box appears at the beginning of each chapter to preview the chapter's contents; (2) relevant questions reappear at the start of the section in which they are discussed; and (3) running heads on the righthand pages keep these questions in view throughout the chapter.

- **Pull Quotes.** Lifted directly from the narrative, pull quotes appear throughout each chapter to highlight key thoughts and keen insights while keeping students focused on larger concepts and ideas.

RESOURCES FOR STUDENTS

StudySpace

wwnorton.com/studyspace

This student website provides a rich array of multimedia resources and review materials within a proven, task-oriented study plan.

Each chapter is arranged in an effective *Organize, Learn, and Connect* pedagogy:

Organize

In this section, students can work through Focus Questions, print out Chapter Outlines and summaries, or check in with Progress Reports that help them focus their studies.

Learn

This section encourages active learning with:

- **iMaps and GeoQuizzes that engage and test students' geographic knowledge** with map review worksheets and maps with zoom functions, highlighting, and labels.
- **Multiple-choice quizzes for each chapter.**
- **FlashCards** with audio pronunciations.
- **Interactive Chrono-Sequencers** that challenge students to reassemble sequences of events, reinforcing their understanding of the flow of history.
- **NEW! Document Quizzes** provide a form for students to answer the questions about the in-text documents.

Connect

In this section, students are reminded to connect to additional resources that include:

- **250 additional primary source documents**
- **Research Topics** that combine a writing prompt, documents, headnotes and sample questions.
- **NEW Interactive MapPlayer** with audio introductions, transitions, and conclusions, along with a suite of interactive functions to examine individual maps as they are presented in a progressive sequence.
- **Audio Glossary**

Study Guide

Margaret Minor and Paul Wilson, *Nicholls State University*

The *Study Guide* gives students a comprehensive means for review and self-assessment. Each chapter contains a chapter outline, identifications, multiple-choice questions, matching, and true/false questions, chronologies, and short-answer and essay questions.

RESOURCES FOR INSTRUCTORS

Norton Media Library

This newly expanded resource for multimedia lectures offers:

- PowerPoint presentations for each chapter
- Hi-resolution maps and graphics files from the book
- Art from the book
- Questions for Classroom Response PowerPoints (Clicker Questions)

Instructor's Manual

Steven Kreis, *American Public University*

Each chapter in the *Instructor's Manual* includes lecture outlines, key lecture topics, suggested films, and suggestions for integrating media into the classroom and using media as homework assignments.

Test Bank

April Harper, *State University of New York, Oneonta*

This vastly expanded test bank includes 60% more questions, including true/false and essay questions. It is available in *ExamView® Assessment Suite*, WebCT, and Blackboard formats.

Blackboard and WebCT Coursepacks offer study plans that integrate review materials for each chapter, as well as ready-to-use test banks, maps, PowerPoint lecture presentations, and practice quizzes.

Map Transparencies

ACKNOWLEDGMENTS

The drafts of the manuscript have benefited from careful reading by and suggestions from a group of professors to whom we are greatly indebted. Our sincere thanks to:

- Eric Ash, Wayne State University
- Sacha Auerbach, Virginia Commonwealth University
- Ken Bartlett, University of Toronto
- Benita Blessing, Ohio University
- Chuck Boening, Shelton State Community College
- John Bohstedt, University of Tennessee– Knoxville
- Dan Brown, Moorpark College
- Kevin Caldwell, Blue Ridge Community College

WESTERN
CIVILIZATIONS

FROM MEDIEVAL TO MODERN

FOR MOST OF THE TWENTIETH CENTURY, historians portrayed the Italian Renaissance and the Protestant Reformation as marking a dramatic break in European history, which brought the Middle Ages to an end and ushered in the modern world. To be sure, the sixteenth and seventeenth centuries saw decisive transformations in European life. For the first time, European sailors, soldiers, and merchants forged worldwide trading networks that brought the mineral and agricultural riches of the Western Hemisphere into their Atlantic ports. The Protestant Reformation shattered the religious unity of Europe, and a century of religious wars served only to cement those divisions. Meanwhile, new trends in cultural and intellectual life, many of which had begun in fourteenth- and fifteenth-century Italy, began to spread widely throughout the rest of Europe.

It is increasingly clear, however, that most of the new developments of the sixteenth and seventeenth centuries had deep roots in the later Middle Ages. The voyages that took sixteenth-century Europeans around the globe began in the thirteenth century with the conquest of the "Atlantic Mediterranean." The intensive study of classical Roman and Greek literature that characterized the Italian Renaissance developed out of the classical revival in the twelfth and thirteenth centuries. Even the theological doctrines of the Protestant reformers had roots in the theological controversies of the later Middle Ages. And all these developments took place in the context of continuing cultural and economic exchange between Europe, the Islamic world, and Byzantium.

FROM MEDIEVAL TO MODERN

POLITICS	SOCIETY AND CULTURE	ECONOMY	INTERNATIONAL RELATIONS
Chingiz (Genghis) Khan rules over Mongol clans (1206–1227)		Silk Road connects Europe with India, China, and Indonesia (1200s) Polo brothers travel to China (1200s)	Mongols conquer southern Russia (1237–1240) Mongols annihilate Hungarian army at River Sajo (1241) Mongol forces withdraw from Europe (1241)
Yuan dynasty in China (1279–1368) Rise of Ottoman Dynasty (1300) Babylonian Captivity of the church (1305–1378)	Civic humanism begins in Italy (1300s) Francesco Petrarch (1304–1374) Giovanni Boccaccio (1313–1375)	Development of mechanical clocks and compasses (1300) Explorers reach Azores and Cape Verde Islands (1300s) Over a tenth of Europe dies during the Great Famine (1316–1322)	
	John Wyclif, Oxford theologian (1330–1384) Geoffrey Chaucer (1340–1400)	Heavy cannons first employed (1330) Silver shortage begins in Europe (1340s)	Hundred Years' War (1337–1453)
Jacquerie rebellion in France (1358) Ming Dynasty in China (1368–1644) The Great Schism, ended by Council of Constance (1378–1417) Florentine Ciompi uprising (1378) English Peasants' Revolt (1381)	Leonardo Bruni (1370–1444) Jan van Eyck (1380–1441) University of Heidelberg founded (1385)	Onset of the Black Death, from which half of Europe dies (1347)	
		Medici family, originators of modern banking, flourishes (1397–1494)	Poland and Lithuania united (1386) Ottomans defeat Serbian empire at battle of Kosovo (1389)
Italian territorial papacy (1417–1517)	Giovanni Aurispa returns with classical manuscripts (1423) Sandro Botticelli (1445–1510) Neoplatonism in Italy (1450–1600) Leonardo da Vinci (1452–1519)	Portugal establishes Atlantic colonies (1400–1460)	Rise of Grand Duchy of Moscow (1400s)
			Turks conquer Constantinople (1453) England loses Bordeaux (1453)
Edward, duke of York dethrones Henry VI after War of the Roses (1461) Reign of Ivan III, the Great, tsar of all Russias (1462–1505) Ferdinand of Aragon marries Isabella of Castille, forming modern Spain (1469)	Desiderius Erasmus (1469–1536) Niccolò Machiavelli, author of *The Prince* (1469–1527) Albrecht Dürer (1471–1528) Sir Thomas More (1478–1535) Raphael (1483–1520)	Invention of movable type; the Gutenberg Bible (1454)	
		Explorers round the Cape of Good Hope (1487) Dias rounds southern tip of Africa (1488)	French monarchy absorbs Burgundy (1477)
	The High Renaissance begins (1490) The Catholic Reformation begins (1490)	Portugal founds slave-based plantation in St. Thomas (1490) Columbus lands in West Indies (1492) Disease kills much of Native American population (1492–1538) Vasco da Gama reaches India (1498)	Christian monarchs expel Jews (1492) and Muslims (1502) from Spain
	Roman Inquisition begins (1500) Saint Peter's Basilica erected in Rome (1500–1520) Papacy of Julius II (1503–1513) Saint Francis Xavier, missionary in Asia (1506–1552) Andrea Palladio (1508–1580) John Calvin (1509–1564)	Grain prices in Europe increase five-fold (1500–1650)	
Reign of Charles V, Holy Roman emperor (1506–1556)			

FROM MEDIEVAL TO MODERN

POLITICS	SOCIETY AND CULTURE	ECONOMY	INTERNATIONAL RELATIONS
	Papacy of Leo X, son of Lorenzo de Medici (1513–1521)	Portuguese ships reach Spice Islands and China (1515)	Cortes conquers Aztec Empire (1519–1522)
	Luther posts Ninety-Five Theses (1517)		Ottomans conquer Syria, Egypt, and Hungary (1510–1540)
	Emergence of Zwinglianism, Anabaptism, and Calvinism (1520–1550)		
	Edict of Worms (1521)		
	Peter Brueghel, painter of *Harvesters* and *Massacre of the Innocents* (1525–1569)		Charles V, Holy Roman emperor, sacks Rome (1527)
	Baldassare Castiglione's *Book of the Courtier* (1528)		Francisco Pizarro topples Incas (1533)
	Michel de Montaigne (1533–1592)		
	Henry VIII becomes head of the Church of England (1533–1534)		
	Calvin's *Institutes of the Christian Religion* (1536)	Rapid inflation marks the Price Revolution (1540s)	
	St. Ignatius Loyola publishes *Spiritual Exercises* (1541)	Silver found in Mexico and Bolivia (1543–1548)	
	El Greco, painter of *View of Toledo* (1541–1614)		
	Council of Trent (1545–1563)		
	Edmund Spenser, author of *The Faerie Queen* (1552–1599)		Peace of Augsburg (1555)
Reign of Philip II of Spain (1556–1598)			
Reign of Elizabeth I of England (1558–1603)	First *Roman Index of Prohibited Books* established (1564)		
	William Shakespeare (1564–1616)		
	Papacy of Pius V (1566–1572)		Ottomans defeated by Habsburgs and Venetians at Lepanto (1571)
	St. Bartholomew's Day massacre (1572)		Philip II annexes Portugal (1580)
English navy defeats the Spanish Armada (1588)		New World silver production peaks at 10 million ounces per year (1590s)	
Reign of Henry IV, first of the Bourbon Dynasty in France (1589–1610)			
Edict of Nantes (1598)			
Reign of James I, first of the Stuart Dynasty (1603–1625)	John Milton (1608–1674)		Thirty Years' War (1618–1648)
		Spanish economy collapses when silver imports drop (1620–1640)	
	Blaise Pascal (1623–1662)		
Cardinal Richelieu, first minister of France (1624–1642)			
Reign of Charles I of England (1625–1649)			Gustavus Adolphus of Sweden enters Thirty Years' War (1630)
English Civil War (1642–1649)			
The Fronde, a series of French aristocratic revolts (1648–1653)			Peace of Westphalia (1648)
Oliver Cromwell rules England (1649–1658)			
Louis XIV of France comes of age (1651)	Thomas Hobbes's *Leviathan* (1651)		
Charles II and the Restoration (1660–1685)			

Chapter Ten

Chapter Contents

Changes in the Land 372

Transformations: The Black Death and Its Consequences 373

Social Change in the Later Middle Ages 380

War and the Development of the Late Medieval State 384

Kievan Rus and the Rise of Muscovy 395

Trials for the Church 398

The Pursuit of Holiness in Late Medieval Piety 403

Thought, Literature, and Art 406

Advances in Technology 410

Conclusion 413

The Later Middle Ages, 1300–1500

TEXTBOOK ACCOUNTS OF THE LATER MIDDLE AGES generally make for grim reading. The period is traditionally seen as one of disintegration and crisis, in which the high medieval world collapsed in chaos and violence, producing social and political upheaval, religious disillusionment, and widespread psychological anxiety. During these disastrous centuries, epidemic disease cut the European population in half, crops failed, and the economy shrank. The shortcomings of the church brought a storm of criticism, but few reforms in religious life resulted. Even the weather got worse. It is all enough to make the sensitive reader shudder, turn the page, and pass on to the sunnier atmosphere of the Italian Renaissance, the chapter that usually follows this late medieval litany of disaster, death, and decay.

There can be no doubt that the fourteenth and fifteenth centuries were indeed an age of adversity for Europeans. Famine and plague cut fearful swaths through the populace; war was a recurrent fact of life across most of the continent; the economy shrank; and the papacy spent seventy years in continuous exile from Italy, only to see its prestige decline even further after it returned to Rome. But to characterize these centuries as simply ones of doom and gloom would profoundly misrepresent the courage and resilience that the people of Europe displayed in the face of famine, war, and plague. It would also cause us to miss many of the fundamental transformations that shaped European society for the next 400 years. Despite the challenges it faced, European civilization did not collapse during the later Middle Ages. Instead, this was a period of creativity and innovation that preserved and extended the most enduring features of high medieval European life into the early modern era.

FOCUS QUESTIONS

- How did climate change affect early fourteenth-century Europe?

- What were the economic consequences of the Black Death on Europe?

- To what extent were the social changes of the later Middle Ages a consequence of the plague?

- Why was warfare such a constant feature of late medieval life?

- Why did Russia develop differently from other late medieval European states?

- Why did late medieval efforts to reform the institutions of the Catholic Church fail?

- Were late medieval people disillusioned with their church?

- What accounts for the remarkable creativity of late medieval cultural life?

- How did technological advances affect everyday life?

10 THE LATER MIDDLE AGES, 1300–1500

Changes in the Land

> How did climate change affect early fourteenth-century Europe?

By 1300, the high medieval expansion of the European economy was reaching its limits. Between 1000 and 1300, the European population tripled in size. To feed its growing numbers of people, Europe transformed itself into a continent of grain fields that stretched, almost unbroken, from Ireland to Poland and on into Ukraine. Even within the agricultural heartlands of western Europe, where wheat, barley, rye, and oats had been grown for centuries, the pressures to produce more grain brought dramatic changes to the landscape that undermined the long-term sustainability of European agriculture. Forests were cleared, marshes drained, and pastureland reduced, all to grow more grain. Expanding urban populations offered lucrative markets for European grain producers, and the increasing size of European ships made the transport of grain more efficient than it had ever been before. But still Europe was barely able to feed itself. By 1300, the continent was reaching the ecological and technological limits of its capacity to support its population.

Until the early fourteenth century, agricultural conditions generally favored the intensive cultivation of the cereal crops on which European civilization increasingly depended. During the twelfth and thirteenth centuries, a gradually warming climate lengthened the growing season in northern Europe, making it possible to grow grain even on thin or boggy soils better suited to pasturing animals or planting fruit trees. Starting in the Arctic at the end of the thirteenth century, however, this warming trend reversed itself, and from the middle of the fourteenth century, the mainland of Europe became progressively colder. This change was not cataclysmic—we are talking about a change of perhaps one to two degrees centigrade in average annual temperatures, spread across 500 years—but it was sufficient to cause substantial changes in rainfall patterns, to shorten growing seasons, and to lessen the productivity of cereal agriculture in northern Europe, especially in marginal areas such as Greenland, where European settlements disappeared entirely during the fifteenth century.

The vulnerability of the European economy to such long-term climate changes was dramatically revealed in 1315, when a great famine struck northern Europe that would last for seven years. Warfare contributed to the suffering, but the root causes of this great famine were climatic. For reasons we do not understand (but which may have to do with massive volcanic explosions in Indonesia darkening the atmosphere with ash), the winters in northern Europe between 1310 and 1330 were exceptionally harsh, and the summers unseasonably cold and wet. Then, starting in 1315, torrential spring and summer rains washed away sown fields, while the cold summer weather prevented the remaining crops from ripening. Europeans could generally ride out a

Peasants Harvesting Grain. Harvesting with sickles was backbreaking work, as this illustration of English serfs working under the direction of a reeve indicates. By the early fourteenth century, Europe had become a continent of grain fields.

year or two of such conditions with only modest loss of life. But between 1315 and 1322, these adverse weather conditions were nearly continuous. The result was starvation on a very large scale. Weakened by malnutrition, people and domestic animals also fell victim to epidemic diseases. By 1322, when conditions at last began to improve, 10 to 15 percent of the European population north of the Alps and the Loire had perished. Even after 1322, however, growing conditions did not return entirely to normal. Cold winters continued until 1330. In Italy, floods swept away the bridges of Florence in 1333, and in 1343 a tsunami destroyed the port of Amalfi. Earthquakes and comets added to the sense of alarm and uncertainty.

And then a disaster struck that was so horrifying it seemed to many to portend the end of the world.

The Black Death and Its Consequences

What were the economic consequences of the Black Death for Europe?

The *Black Death* is the name given since the sixteenth century to a deadly illness that spread from Mongolia to China, northern India, the Middle East, and the Crimea during the 1330s and 1340s. By 1346, the disease had reached the Black Sea. From there, in 1347, Genoese galleys brought it, inadvertently, to Sicily and northern Italy. From Italy the plague (as contemporaries called it, from the Latin word *plaga*, "a blow") spread throughout western Europe along the trade routes, first striking the seaports, then moving inland. It moved with astonishing rapidity, advancing about two miles per day during 1348 and 1349 in both summer and winter. By 1350, the plague had reached Scandinavia and northern Russia, from which it then spread southward until it linked up with the earlier waves of infection that had brought it from Central Asia to the Black Sea.

After this initial pandemic outbreak, the Black Death continued to erupt in local epidemics for the next 300 years. Across most of fifteenth-century Europe, localities could expect a renewed outbreak of plague every decade. Gradually, however, the attacks of plague became less frequent and less deadly. The last European-wide plague outbreak occurred between 1661 and 1669, striking London in 1665 with particular severity. After 1720, however, the Black Death disappeared from western Europe, although it continued to afflict Poland and Russia until the end of the eighteenth century.

Mortality from the Black Death was on an almost unimaginable scale. At least a third, and probably half, the population of Europe died in the initial outbreak of 1347–1350. Thereafter, the population continued to decline. By 1450, the combined effects of plague, famine, and war had reduced the total population of Europe by at least 50 percent, and perhaps by as much as two thirds, from its high point around 1300. The European population did not fully recover to its pre-plague levels until the end of the seventeenth century.

This massive population decline also had dramatic effects on the landscape of Europe. In Germany alone, more than 40,000 villages attested before 1348 had disappeared by 1500. And even when villages survived, the fewer workers forced changes in agricultural practice. Around Paris, for example, more than half the farmland under plow in 1348 had been turned into pastureland by 1450. Elsewhere, abandoned fields and villages reverted to woodland, increasing the forested areas in parts of Europe by as much as one third over their pre-1348 levels. Better crop rotation systems and less intensive exploitation of marginal lands also helped restore the ecological balance of European agriculture in the aftermath of the plague.

Burying Plague Victims at Tournai, 1349. This contemporary illustration shows the dead being buried in wooden coffins. Despite the high mortality rates, survivors strove to bury their dead with dignity whenever possible.

10 THE LATER MIDDLE AGES, 1300–1500

Initial reactions to the Black Death ran the gamut from frenzied panic to supine resignation. Observers quickly realized that the plague was contagious, but how precisely it spread remained a mystery. At the time, most medical experts believed that the plague was spread through bad air and so urged people to flee from stricken areas (thus spreading the disease even faster) or to cover their noses with sweet-smelling

THE PROGRESS OF THE BLACK DEATH, FOURTEENTH CENTURY

Where did the Black Death come from, and where did it enter Europe, generally speaking? Why was the onslaught of the disease so devastating; and what agricultural, economic, and demographic factors helped make Europeans around 1350 so vulnerable to the disease? Note the rapid spread of the Black Death. Would such a rapid advance have been likely during the early Middle Ages or even in the ancient world? How did the growth of towns, trade, and travel contribute to the spread of the Black Death?

What were the economic consequences of the Black Death for Europe?

Plague Doctor Wearing Bird Beak Mask. Sweet-smelling herbs and flowers were placed in the masks' noses to counteract the bad air through which the plague was believed to travel.

flowers to counteract the miasma (as the "bad air" was known). Some people locked themselves in their houses, refusing to admit anyone until the threat had passed. Others did nothing, surrendering themselves to their fate; while still others (or so at least it was alleged by moralists) abandoned themselves to their desires, declaring, "Let us eat, drink, and be merry, for tomorrow we may die."

Others looked for scapegoats. When rumors began to circulate that Jews had caused the plague by poisoning the wells, scores of Jewish communities were attacked and thousands of their inhabitants massacred in the Rhineland, southern France, and Christian Spain. No such attacks on Jews are known from the Muslim areas of Spain or from elsewhere in the Muslim world, despite the fact that these areas suffered from the plague no less than did Christian Europe. Pope Clement VI (1342–1352) tried to halt these attacks, sending letters throughout Europe pointing out that Jews were dying from the plague in the same numbers as were Christians and ordering Christians to protect their Jewish neighbors from violence. But the letters did little good, and by the time they were received much of the damage had already been done.

A Procession of Flagellants, 1349. Participants scourge themselves with whips as they march in procession through Tournai. Their white clothing and black hats are symbols of penance.

THE LATER MIDDLE AGES, 1300–1500

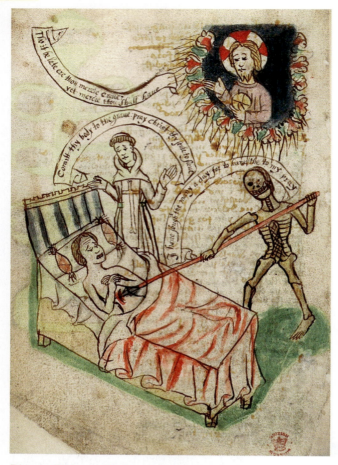

Plague Claims a Victim. An English priest gives the last rites to a bedridden plague victim, as a smiling devil pierces the victim with his spear and Christ looks on from heaven. In some English dioceses, two thirds of the priests died of the plague.

Perhaps the most famous response to the plague was the Flagellant movement, so called from the whips (*flagella*) with which these traveling bands of penitents beat themselves bloody in hopes of appeasing the wrath of God, which had brought the plague down on a sinful world. Such whips were first used in penitential demonstrations around 1260, but the practice was revived and extended in 1348 and 1349, when it seemed to many that the end of the world might be at hand. But the unruly and sometimes hysterical mobs that gathered around the flagellants aroused the concern of both ecclesiastical and secular authorities, and the movement was suppressed by papal order at the end of 1349.

In focusing on the flagellants, however, we should not overlook the vastly larger number of ordinary churchmen who stayed at their posts, ministering to the dead and dying until the plague claimed them too. A few priests may have fled, but where we can count them, the huge numbers of priests who died in the plague suggest that those who fled were a small and unrepresentative minority. On the whole, the clergy of Christian Europe acquitted themselves with courage in the face of this fearsome disease. There is no evidence to suggest that their response to the plague was contemptible or that it led to religious disillusionment on the part of their parishioners.

WHAT CAUSED THE BLACK DEATH?

Until very recently, most historians were confident that the Black Death was the result of a pandemic outbreak of *Yersinia pestis*, the microbe responsible for bubonic plague and for its even deadlier cousins, pneumonic and septicemic plague. In its bubonic form, *Y. pestis* is carried by fleas that travel on the backs of rats; humans catch it only if they are bitten by an infected flea or rat. Bubonic plague attacks the lymphatic system, producing enormous swellings (*buboes*) of the lymph nodes in the groin, neck, and/or armpit and causing boils and carbuncles to erupt on the skin. Pneumonic plague results when *Y. pestis* infects the lungs, allowing the contagion to spread in the same ways as the common cold. Septicemic plague occurs when an infected flea introduces *Y. pestis* directly into the human bloodstream, causing death within hours, often before any symptoms of the disease can manifest themselves.

This traditional explanation of the Black Death may still be proved to be correct. But doubts about this explanation have arisen in recent years from an entirely unexpected direction. Studies of HIV/AIDS have shown that among European populations only, a genetic mutation (known as the CCR5-delta 32 mutation) occurred 2,000 to 3,000 years ago. This mutation renders people who carry it either entirely or substantially immune to HIV infection by blocking the T receptors through which HIV enters the cells. Like all such mutations, this one was a random occurrence, and it conveyed no particular evolutionary advantage when it first occurred. Approximately 700 years ago, however, and lasting for the next 300 years or so, some epidemic event took place that selected for this particular mutation, driving up its frequency in the overall European populations to about one in ten individuals, but ranging from a low of 4 percent in Sardinia to a high of around 16 percent in Scandinavia and northern Russia.

This epidemic event can only have been the Black Death; and if the CCR5-delta 32 mutation did impart a substantial or complete immunity to the Black Death, then this would also explain why the disease gradually disappeared from Europe, whereas it has continued

What were the economic consequences of the Black Death for Europe?

periodically to ravage other parts of the world into the twentieth century. *Y. pestis*, however, does not enter human cells through the T receptors. How then could this particular genetic mutation have provided an immunity to the Black Death, if indeed the Black Death was caused by *Y. pestis*?

Two possible explanations suggest themselves. First, *Y. pestis* itself may have mutated; although the modern form of the microbe does not enter cells through the T receptors, perhaps the medieval form of the microbe did. The second possibility, however, is that the Black Death was not caused by *Y. pestis* at all; it was caused by an as-yet-unknown infection that could be either bacterial or viral and that we have not yet identified. At the moment, we do not know which of these explanations is correct or, indeed, whether some other explanation entirely will prove to be the answer to the puzzle of what caused the Black Death. Research is continuing but already provides a striking example of the contributions to historical understanding that are emerging from modern microbiology and the genetic sciences.

THE IMPACT ON THE COUNTRYSIDE

The economic and social consequences of the plague were profound. During the plague years of 1348–1350, harvests rotted in the fields, manufacturing ceased, and trade was disrupted. Basic commodities became scarcer and prices rose, prompting efforts by governments to enforce, through legislation, a return to preplague prices and wages. By 1375, however, the new demographic realities were beginning to alter the underlying patterns of the European economy. By 1400, Europe had entered a new economic world.

In the countryside, grain production declined after 1350 from its preplague levels; but the overall population declined much more. With so many fewer mouths to feed and grain relatively more abundant, the price of grain fell; but with many fewer workers competing for employment, wages rose and work became more easily obtainable. With wages high and bread prices low, ordinary people could now afford not only to buy more bread but also to purchase dairy products, meat, fish, fruits, and wine on a more regular basis. As a result, the people of Europe in the later Middle Ages ate a more balanced diet, and were consequently better nourished, than they had been for centuries or than some are today. A recent study of the contents of fifteenth-century rubbish dumps has concluded that the people of Glasgow, Scotland, ate a healthier diet in 1405 than they did in 2005!

A healthier ecological balance between arable land, pastureland, and woodland was also reestablished in the wake of the plague. Faced with declining prices for cereal crops, many small farmers reduced their grain fields and expanded their sheep and cattle herds. By turning arable land into pastureland, they reduced their labor costs, increased the overall profitability of their farms, and improved the fertility of the soil through better manuring. With land so easily available, small farmers were also able to increase the size of their landholdings, which led to further efficiencies of scale. And with the lessened demand for fuel, forests too began to recover and expand.

Great lords were slower to adjust to the changed economic circumstances created by the plague. Some lords responded to rising wage costs by demanding additional unpaid labor from their peasant tenants. In eastern Europe, many peasants were actually forced into serfdom for the first time during the fifteenth century, as lords expanded their grain fields to supply the growing Baltic grain trade. In Castile, Poland, and Germany also, late medieval lords succeeded in imposing new forms of serfdom on the peasantry, which would last

A Cured-Meat Merchant's Shop. Prepared foods, including smoked and cured meats, became increasingly popular and affordable in the later Middle Ages.

until the sixteenth and seventeenth centuries. In Iberia and Italy, even outright slavery became more common after the plague, after nearly disappearing during the twelfth and thirteenth centuries (on the growing late medieval slave trade, see Chapter Eleven).

In France, by contrast, where the peasantry was already relatively freer than in most other European countries by 1300, the later Middle Ages brought few changes in peasant freedom. Rents declined, but lords made up these losses by imposing other fees on them. In England, however, where serfs in 1300 were much more burdened than they were in France, serfdom declined and ultimately disappeared altogether during the later Middle Ages. In the new world of social mobility and economic opportunity created by the plague, English serfs found it relatively easy to vote with their feet, either by moving to the lands of a less demanding lord or by becoming town dwellers. To retain serfs on their estates, English lords were forced to offer them more favorable terms: lower rents, more animals, fewer work requirements, and greater personal freedoms. As a result of such accomodations, serfdom had effectively disappeared from England by the early sixteenth century.

For the unfree peasant farmers of late medieval Europe, the improved economic circumstances of their lives thus did not necessarily lead to greater personal freedom with respect to their lords. Except in England (and to a lesser extent in Catalunya), most serfs were not substantially freer of lordly control in 1500 than they had been before the plague. For free peasants and town dwellers, however, the economic conditions produced by the plague brought significantly increased social mobility and a wealth of new opportunities. The result was a widening gap between the rich and the poor at all levels of rural society, from peasants to the greatest lords.

The Impact on Towns

Towns were especially sensitive barometers of the changing economic climate of the later Middle Ages. After reaching their demographic peak around 1300, some towns were already experiencing declining populations and economic difficulties even before the Black Death struck. The plague, however, made the existing situation very much worse. Overcrowding, combined with the generally unsanitary conditions of medieval urban life, made Europe's cities particularly vulnerable to the plague. But warfare and local economic crises also contributed significantly to the population declines that afflicted so many late medieval cities. At Florence, for example, the population of the city rebounded quickly from the initial onslaught of the plague. By 1427, however, the population of Florence and its surrounding region had dropped from around 300,000 in 1338 to only about 100,000. At Toulouse in southern France, the population held fairly steady until the end of the fourteenth century, but then dropped from 26,000 to about 8,000 people between 1385 and 1430, largely as a result of devastation caused by the Hundred Years' War. London and Paris, by contrast, suffered only short-term declines as a result of the plague; their population losses to the plague were quickly made up by the large-scale immigration of new workers from the countryside. Many of these new workers were women, whose economic opportunities were greatly enhanced by the urban labor shortages resulting from the plague.

After 1450, however, Europe's towns and cities were once again growing; and by 1500, approximately 20 percent of the European population lived in urban areas, a larger percentage than had been the case two centuries before. Fueling this late-fifteenth-century urban growth was the increasing specialization of the late medieval European economy, made possible by the combined effects of plague and trade. With farmers now under less pressure to produce grain, they were

English Soldiers Setting Fire to St. Lo. When a town fell after a siege, both the town and its inhabitants were at the mercy of the besiegers, who were generally entitled to loot, rape, and plunder at will. The devastation from such attacks could be horrendous.

WHAT WERE THE ECONOMIC CONSEQUENCES OF THE BLACK DEATH FOR EUROPE?

Merchants Unloading Their Wares. From an early-fifteenth-century French manuscript.

freer to turn their lands to producing the agricultural products to which their lands were best suited. As a result, more specialized and efficient regional economies began to emerge. Sweden produced butter, which it traded for German and Baltic grain; England produced wool, which it traded for French wine and Italian cloth; Castile produced leather, which it traded for silks, fruits, grain, and spices; and so on in almost endless variety.

Towns with links to these networks of regional exchange benefited particularly from the new economic circumstances of the later Middle Ages. In northern Germany a group of cities and towns under the leadership of Lübeck and Bremen formed the Hanseatic League, whose members transported German and Baltic grain to Scandinavia and eastern England in exchange for dairy products, fish, furs, and (from England) wool and wool cloth. In northern Italy, the enhanced demand for luxury goods brought new wealth not only to the spice- and silk-trading city of Venice but also to the fine cloth producers of Milan and to the bankers and jewelers of Florence. Milan also prospered from its armaments industry, which supplied the warring states of Europe with armor and weapons, while Genoa profited from its trade in bulk goods, especially grain.

Not all late medieval towns prospered—the Flemish cities in particular suffered through a serious economic depression—but on the whole, European urban centers profited from the new economic circumstances created by the plague. Had this not been the case, these cities would not have been able to participate in the remarkable extension of European commercial networks to Africa, Asia, and ultimately the Americas that began in the fifteenth century and would continue, without interruption, until the end of the nineteenth century. (For further discussion of European commerce, colonization, and conquest during this period, see Chapter Eleven.)

The economic world of the late Middle Ages also stimulated the development of new business, accounting, and banking techniques. New forms of business partnerships, together with the development of insurance contracts, helped minimize the risks associated with long-distance trading voyages. Double-entry bookkeeping, widely used in Italy from the mid-fourteenth century on, gave merchants a much clearer

The Banker and His Wife, by Quentin Massys.

picture of the debts they owed and the debts that were owed to them—and hence of their profits and losses—than had been possible before. Banks too altered many of their earlier methods of doing business. The Medici family of Florence established branches of their bank in each of the major cities of Europe but were careful to organize these branches so that if one branch failed, it would no longer drag down the rest of the firm with it, as previous branch-banking arrangements had done. Banks also experimented with advanced credit techniques. Some even allowed their clients to transfer funds between bank branches without any real money changing hands. Such book transfers were at first executed only by oral command, but after 1400 they started to be carried out by written orders. These were the earliest ancestors of the modern check.

Social Change in the Later Middle Ages

To what extent were the social changes of the later Middle Ages a consequence of the plague?

Famine, plague, and war put extraordinary pressures on social order in later medieval Europe. It is perhaps surprising that revolutionary changes were avoided. Nonetheless, by 1500 European society was different in important and lasting ways from what it had been 200 years before. Not all of these changes were directly a result of the plague, but the plague's influence can be discerned behind most of them.

Revolts and Rebellions

The economic consequences of the plague were ultimately beneficial for those who survived it. But European society did not adjust easily to the new world created by the plague. Between 1350 and 1425, hundreds of popular revolts shook later medieval Europe. In 1358, for example, French peasants in the countryside around Paris rose up against their lords in an orgy of arson, murder, and rape, in a rebellion known as the Jacquerie (by their social superiors, all French peasants were caricatured as being named "Jacques"). In England too, a massive rising of peasants, artisans, and town dwellers (known misleadingly as the Peasants' Revolt) marched on London in 1381, demanding an end to serfdom, fixed rents for landholdings, and the more effective prosecution of the ongoing war with France. In Florence, workers in the wool cloth industry (known as the Ciompi, pronounced *chee-OM-pee*), beset by high unemployment and frequently cheated by their masters who controlled both the wool industry and the Florentine government, seized control of the city, demanding tax relief, full employment, and political representation in city government. Six weeks later, however, the Ciompi lost their hold on power, and a new government of masters revoked their reform measures.

The local circumstances that lay behind each of these revolts are unique, but certain general features do stand out about these and the hundreds of other similar revolts that occurred during these years. Most important, these revolts were not bread riots. Those who took part in them were not destitute, and their demands were almost never for the necessities of life. Some, like the English Peasants' Revolt and the 1408 rebellion at Lübeck in Germany, were touched off by resistance to new and higher taxes. Others, like the Jacquerie and the revolt of the Ciompi, took place at moments when unpopular governments were weakened by factionalism and military defeat. But as the historian Samuel Cohn Jr. has written, "politics, betrayal, and abuse were the sparks of rebellion, not conditions of misery or increased feudal exactions. It was

The Suppression of the Jacquerie, 1358. Although their initial attacks caught the lords off guard, the peasant rebels were no match for well-armed soldiers, who suppressed the rebellion with savage brutality.

FROISSART ON THE ENGLISH PEASANTS' REVOLT, 1381

Jean Froissart (1337?–1410?) is best known as the author of a lengthy history of the Hundred Years' War. He was not an eyewitness to the events of the Peasants' Revolt, but he had excellent English connections from whom he presumably derived his information. Froissart's perspective is entirely that of the aristocrats whom he served and with whom he associated. This fact makes his modest sympathy for the rebels of 1381 all the more interesting, particularly compared with his earlier, entirely negative portrayal of the 1358 Jacquerie rebels in France.

While these negotiations and discussions were going on, there occurred in England great disasters and uprisings of the common people, on account of which the country was almost ruined beyond recovery. Never was any land or realm in such great danger as England at that time. It was because of the abundance and prosperity in which the common people then lived that this rebellion broke out, just as in earlier days the Jack Goodmans rose in France and committed many excesses, by which the noble land of France suffered grave injury....

These bad people ... began to rebel because, they said, they were held too much in subjection, and when the world began there had been no serfs and could not be, unless they had rebelled against their Lord, as Lucifer did against God; but they were not of that stature, being neither angels nor spirits, but men formed in the image of their masters, and they were treated as animals. This was a thing they could no longer endure, wishing rather to be all one and the same; and, if they worked for their masters, they wanted to have wages for it. In these machinations they had been greatly encouraged originally by a crack-brained priest of Kent called John Ball ... who had the habit on Sundays after mass, when everyone was coming out of church, of going to the cloisters or the graveyard, assembling the people round him and preaching thus:

"Good people, things cannot go right in England and never will, until goods are held in common and there are no more serfs and gentlefolk, but we are all one and the same. In what way are those whom we call lords greater masters than ourselves? How have they deserved it? Why do they hold us in bondage? If we all spring from a single father and mother, Adam and Eve, how can they claim or prove that they are lords more than us, except by making us produce and grow the wealth which they spend? They are clad in velvet and camlet lined with squirrel and ermine, while we go dressed in coarse cloth. They have the wines, the spices, and the good bread: we have the rye, the husks and the straw, and we drink water. They have shelter and ease in their fine manors, and we have hardship and toil, the wind and the rain in the fields. And from us must come, from our labor, the things which keep them in luxury. We are called serfs and beaten if we are slow in our service to them, yet we have no sovereign lord we can complain to, none to hear us and do us justice. Let us go to the King—he is young—and show him how we are oppressed, and tell him that we want things to be changed, or else we will change them ourselves. If we go in good earnest and all together, very many people who are called serfs and are held in subjection will follow us to get their freedom. And when the King sees and hears us, he will remedy the evil, either willingly or otherwise."

These were the kind of things which John Ball usually preached in the villages on Sundays ... and many of the common people agreed with him.

Geoffrey Brereton, ed. and trans., *Froissart: Chronicles* (London and New York, 1968), pp. 211–213.

QUESTIONS FOR ANALYSIS

1. Why might Froissart have been more sympathetic to the uprising of the common people in England than he was to the French Jacquerie?

the nobles' political failures that led to the Jacquerie: their failure to protect their villagers from assaults by the English or by the regent of France and their collusion with the enemy in warlike pillaging of peasant property." Similarly, it was the failures of English armies in France and the rebels' belief that corruption on the part of those ruling in the name of the fourteen-year-old King Richard II caused the defeats that lay behind the Peasants' Revolt. The same point has been made about the urban rebellions of the period. As Cohn pointed out, "seldom did the revolts of artisans or workers directly attack their employers. Instead, their riots turned on politics. . . . [The revolts were] assaults against the arrogance, violence, and corruption of ruling aristocrats and merchant oligarchies."

Behind the social and political unrest of the period lay, therefore, not poverty and hunger but the growing prosperity and self-confidence that village communities and urban workers felt in the changed economic circumstances that arose from the plague. For the most part, the rebels' hopes that they could fundamentally alter the social and political conditions of their lives were frustrated. Kings, aristocrats, and urban oligarchs sometimes lost their nerve in the middle of an uprising, but they were almost always successful, after a time, in restoring their control and reasserting their dominance. After 1425, the number of such popular rebellions diminished. But they did not end; and this tradition of popular rebellion, established during the the later Middle Ages, would remain an important feature of European life for the next 200 years.

complex and uncertain, at a time when the costs of leading an appropriately noble style of life were continuing to escalate rapidly. As a result, the nobility of later medieval Europe felt themselves to be less secure in their wealth and social standing than they had been before the plague. These insecurities color almost all aspects of late medieval aristocratic life.

Across Europe, most noble families continued to derive the bulk of their revenues from their vast landholdings, just as they had done in the high Middle Ages. But many late medieval lords also tried to increase their nonagricultural sources of income. In Catalunya, Italy, Germany, and England, it was relatively common for nobles to invest in trading ventures. In France and Castile, however, direct involvement in retail commerce was regarded as socially demeaning and was, therefore, avoided by established noble families. Success in commerce could still be a route into the nobility, even in France and Castile. But when successful merchants were "ennobled" by kings or princes, they were expected to abandon their old employments and to adopt an appropriately noble way of life: living in rural castles or urban palaces surrounded by lavish households, embracing the values and conventions of chivalry (including a family coat of arms), and serving their prince at court and in war. Service to a king or great lord was an increasingly important expectation for the late medieval nobility, whose fortunes came to depend heavily on the gifts and favors (including tax exemptions and profitable marriages) that only rulers could bestow.

ARISTOCRATIC LIFE IN THE LATER MIDDLE AGES

Some late medieval lords failed to adapt to the new world created by the plague. As grain prices fell, rents stagnated, and wages for laborers and servants rose, the fortunes of these lords declined significantly. For the most part, however, the later Middle Ages was not a period of aristocratic crisis. Quite the contrary—the great noble families of fifteenth-century Europe were almost certainly wealthier, on average, than their counterparts had been 200 years before. Nor did the plague undermine the dominant position the nobility had established in European society during the high Middle Ages. It did, however, make their world substantially more

A Noble Hunting Party. This fifteenth-century illustration shows an elaborately dressed group of noble men and women setting out to hunt with falcons, accompanied by their servants and their dogs. The castle at Étampes, on the Loire, can be seen in the background.

Nobility remained, however, an uncertain and difficult status to maintain. What made a man or woman noble? In countries where nobility entailed clearly defined legal privileges (such as exemption from taxation or the right to be tried only in special courts), proven descent from noble ancestors, together with a recognized coat of arms, might be sufficient to qualify a family as noble in the eyes of the law. Legal nobility of this sort was, however, a somewhat less exclusive distinction than we might expect it to have been. In fifteenth-century Castile and Navarre, 10 to 15 percent of the total population had claims to be recognized as noble on these terms. In Poland, Hungary, and Scotland, the legally privileged nobility was closer to 5 percent; whereas in England and France, only 1 to 2 percent could plausibly claim the legal privileges of noble status.

Fundamentally, however, nobility was a marker of social rank, expressed and epitomized by an individual's noble style of life. Chivalry, courtliness, political influence, deference from social inferiors, and the ostentatious display of wealth—all combined to constitute a family's honor and hence to mark it off as noble. In practice, however, the lines of social distinction between noble and non-noble families were often fuzzy. The newly wealthy might live like nobles, even though they had no noble ancestors. Men from obscure families might rise through royal service into the ranks of the nobility, while long-established noble families might disappear through failure of heirs or simply their own political miscalculations. Even on the battlefield, the supremacy of the mounted noble knight was being threatened by the growing importance of lower-class soldiers, archers, and artillery experts in late medieval armies. There were even hints of a more radical critique of noble claims to innate social superiority. As the English rebels in 1381 enquired, "When Adam dug and Eve spun, Who then was the gentleman?"

Precisely because nobility was so contestable during the later Middle Ages, those who claimed the status took elaborate measures to assert its exclusivity and social distinctiveness. Late medieval aristocrats hosted lavish banquets, with table decorations forty-six feet high and hundreds of courses served over several days. They dressed in rich and extravagant clothing: close-fitting doublets and hose with long pointed shoes for men, multilayered silk dresses with ornately festooned headdresses for women. They maintained enormous households (in France around 1400, the Duke of Berry had 400 matched pairs of hunting dogs and 1,000 servants) and took part in elaborately ritualized tournaments and pageants, in which the noble participants pretended to be the chivalric heroes of thirteenth-century romances. Aristocrats also emphasized their cultural taste and refinement by supporting authors and artists and sometimes by becoming accomplished poets themselves. Nobility existed only if it was recognized; and to be recognized, noble status had to be constantly reasserted.

Rulers contributed to this process of noble self-assertion; indeed, they were among its principal supporters and patrons. Kings and princes across Europe competed with each other in founding chivalric orders,

The Duke of Berry's Banquet. Uncle of the mad king Charles VI, the Duke of Berry left politics to his brothers, the Duke of Burgundy and the Duke of Anjou. In return, he received enormous subsidies from the royal government, which he spent on sumptuous buildings, artworks, and feasts. Here, the duke interrupts his feasting to dispense alms to the poor. Some of his famous hunting dogs can be seen dining on scraps from his table.

CHAPTER 10

THE LATER MIDDLE AGES, 1300–1500

such as the Knights of the Garter in England and the Order of the Star in France. These orders honored knights who had demonstrated in an extraordinary way the idealized chivalric virtues of knightly prowess, loyalty, bravery, generosity, and courtesy on the battlefield. But although membership in these orders was strictly limited, the virtues they celebrated were seen as characterizing the nobility as a whole. By exalting the nobility as a class, chivalric orders helped cement the links that bound the nobility to their kings and princes. So too did the fees, pensions, offices, and marriages that kings and princes could provide to their noble followers. In a world in which the agricultural revenues of noble estates were declining, such rewards of princely service were critically important to maintaining noble fortunes.

It is easy to dismiss the elaborately performative aspects of late medieval aristocratic life as mere play acting—in the historian Johann Huizinga's words, as "a wholesale attempt to act the vision of a dream." To do so, however, would be a mistake. Late medieval rulers depended on the service—military, diplomatic, and political—that the nobility alone could provide, just as the nobility depended on the offices, revenues, prestige, and social affirmation that could be acquired only through service to a royal or princely court. The alliance that was forged in the fifteenth century between kings and their nobility was a response to these mutual needs and would become one of the most characteristic and enduring features of old regime (*ancien régime*) Europe. In France, this ancien régime alliance between crown and nobility lasted until the French Revolution of 1789. In England and Germany, it would last until the outbreak of World War I.

WAR AND THE DEVELOPMENT OF THE LATE MEDIEVAL STATE

> Why was warfare such a constant feature of late medieval life?

The ancien régime alliance between crown and nobility was in part a response to the new social and economic world created by the plague. But it was also a product of war and of the impact of war on the development of the late medieval state. The fourteenth and fifteenth centuries saw almost constant warfare at all levels of European society. To fight these wars, governments claimed new powers to tax their subjects and to control their subjects' lives. Armies became larger and military technology became deadlier. Wars became more destructive and society became more militarized. As a result of these developments, the largest and most successful European states (in particular, the national monarchies of Portugal, Spain, and France) were stronger and more aggressively expansionist by 1500 than they had been two centuries before. In 1500, the impact of these newly powerful states was still felt mainly in Europe. By 1600, however, their impact would be felt around the globe.

ENGLAND, FRANCE, AND THE HUNDRED YEARS' WAR

The Hundred Years' War was the largest, longest, and most wide-ranging military conflict of the later Middle Ages. England and France were its principal protagonists, but at one stage or another almost all of the major European powers became involved in it. Active hostilities between England and France lasted from 1337 until 1453, interrrupted by truces of varying lengths. The roots of the conflict, however, reach back into the 1290s, when King Edward I of England attempted to conquer the neighboring kingdom of Scotland, thereby provoking the Scottish kingdom to ally itself with France. And the threat of war continued until 1558, when Calais, the last piece of English-held soil in France, passed into French hands. Arguably, therefore, the Hundred Years' War might more accurately be called "The Two Hundred and Sixty Years' War."

The war had several causes. The most fundamental source of conflict, and the most difficult issue to resolve, was that the kings of England held the duchy of Gascony in southern France as vassals of the French king. In the twelfth and thirteenth centuries, this fact had seemed less of an anomaly. But as the conviction grew in the later Middle Ages that kingdoms were territorial entities, within whose borders only a single king should rule, the English presence in Gascony became more and more intolerable to the French crown. That England also had close commercial links, through the wool trade, with the French king's rebellious subjects in Flanders added further fuel to the fires of Anglo-French hostility. So too did the continuing French alliance with the Scots, who had been resolutely resisting English attempts to conquer their kingdom since the 1290s.

Greatly complicating all this, however, was a succession dispute over the French crown itself. In 1328, the last of King Philip IV's three sons died without leaving a son to succeed him. A new dynasty, the Valois, thereupon replaced the Capetians on the throne of France. Only by prohibiting inheritance through women, however, could the Valois kings claim to be the closest heirs to the Capetians. Otherwise, the rightful heir to the throne of France was King Edward III of England, whose mother, Isabella, was the only daughter of King Philip IV of France. In 1328, Edward was only fifteen years old, and he did not protest the succession of his Valois cousins. In 1337, however, when war erupted between France and England over Scotland and Gascony, Edward III responded by claiming to be the rightful king of France—a claim all subsequent English kings would uphold until the eighteenth century.

The Hundred Years' War itself can be divided into three main phases. In the first phase, from 1337 until 1360, the English won a series of startling military victories, most famously at Crécy (1346), Calais (1347), and Poitiers (1356). Although France was richer and more populous than England by a factor of at least three to one, the English political system was more effective in mobilizing the entire population behind the war effort. Taxes poured into King Edward's coffers, enabling him to hire and maintain a professional army of seasoned and well-disciplined soldiers, nobles, and longbowmen. The huge but poorly led feudal armies assembled by King Philip VI of France and his son, King John II, proved no match for the tactical superiority of the smaller English armies on the battlefield. English armies pillaged the French countryside at will; civil wars broke out between individual French lords; and when King John II himself was captured in 1356 at the Battle of Poitiers (*pwah-TYAY*), the French kingdom dissolved into chaos. Mercenary bands of French and English soldiers, known as "Free Companies," roamed the countryside, attacking and looting peasant villages and holding towns to ransom, at a time when France, like the rest of Europe, was struggling to recover from the initial devastation of the Black Death. In 1358, peasant frustration with the inability of both the crown and the French nobility to protect them boiled over in the savage rebellion of the Jacquerie.

In 1360, the Treaty of Bretigny brought the first phase of the war to an end. In return for renouncing his claims to the throne of France, Edward III of England received full sovereignty over a greatly enlarged duchy of Gascony (to be ruled over by Edward's son and heir, the Black Prince) and the promise of a huge ransom for the captive king of France. But the terms of the treaty were never honored by either side. The French crown continued to treat the duke of Gascony as a vassal, and the kings of England never surrendered their claims to be the rightful kings of France. The treaty brought

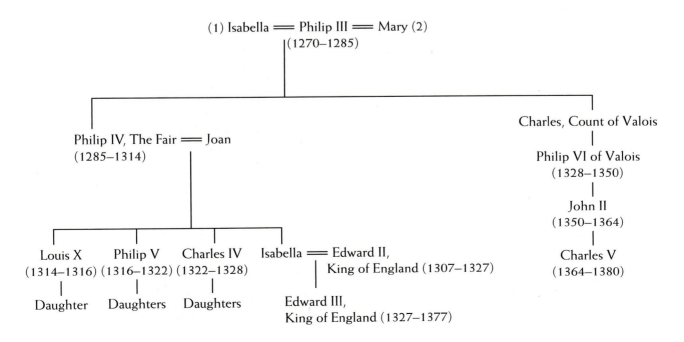

THE FRENCH SUCCESSION IN 1328

10 THE LATER MIDDLE AGES, 1300–1500

Soldiers Pillage a Parisian House. Looting was an accepted part of late medieval warfare. Here, soldiers are shown ransacking a fine house for valuables. Silver plate and bedding are tossed from the windows, while other soldiers break open a wine barrel. Elaborate rules governed the division of such spoils of war.

sixteen years of peace between France and England, allowing France a breathing space during which to recover from the devastation of war. It also brought England a large influx of cash from King John's ransom. But it did not resolve the underlying issues that had led to the war itself. Instead, a proxy war developed during the 1360s and 1370s, in which English and French troops fought in support of rival claimants to the throne of Castile and hired themselves out as mercenaries in the service of the warring city-states of northern Italy. By 1376, when formal war resumed between England and France, the Hundred Years' War had become a European-wide conflagration.

After 1376, the tides of war quickly shifted in favor of France. In England the Black Prince died, leaving a ten-year-old son, Richard II (1377–1399), to succeed the aging and senile Edward III. Meanwhile, the new king of France, Charles V (1364–1380), used the peace created by the Treaty of Bretigny to his advantage. By imposing a series of new national taxes on the common people of France, King Charles was able to restore order by ridding the countryside of the Free Companies. And by hiring the leader of one of these Free Companies, Bertrand du Guesclin, as the commander of the king's own army, Charles was able to create a professional military that could match the English in discipline and tactics. By 1380, when King Charles V died, English territories in France had been reduced to small areas around Bordeaux and Calais.

Unlike his father and grandfather, the new king of England, Richard II, had no interest in the French war. In 1394, he even married the French king's daughter. Under Edward III, however, the war had become extremely popular in England, not only as a matter of national honor and security but also as a reliable source of profit for those who fought in it. Richard's failure to prosecute the war therefore undermined his relationship with the country and especially with his nobility. When, in 1399, he attempted to confiscate the inheritance of his cousin, Henry Bolingbroke, Bolingbroke turned the tables, deposed Richard, and seized the throne as King Henry IV (1399–1413), the first of the Lancastrian kings of England.

As a usurper, Henry IV struggled to maintain his authority as king against a series of rebellions. Frequently ill, he was in no position to renew the French war. When his son Henry V succeeded him in 1413, however, the new king immediately began to prepare for renewed war with France. A brilliant diplomat, Henry sealed alliances with both the emperor Sigismund in Germany and with the dissident Duke of Burgundy, who was locked in a struggle with his rivals to control the French royal government, which had been left rudderless by the growing insanity of the French king, Charles VI

WAR AND THE DEVELOPMENT OF THE LATE MEDIEVAL STATE

King Richard II of England.

(1380–1422). When Henry V invaded France in 1415, he therefore faced only the army of the then-dominant faction around the royal court. The Duke of Burgundy stayed home. At Agincourt, Henry V won another crushing victory over a vastly larger, but badly disciplined French military force, just as Edward III had done at Crécy and the Black Prince had done at Poitiers. By 1420, Henry V had conquered most of France north of the Loire. By the Treaty of Troyes, signed in that year, the aged and infirm King Charles VI recognized Henry V as his heir to the throne of France, thus dispossessing his only surviving son, known as "the dauphin," the future King Charles VII.

Unlike Edward III, who used his claim to be king of France largely as a bargaining chip to secure sovereignty over Gascony, Henry V honestly believed himself to be the rightful king of France. His astonishing success in capturing the French kingdom seemed to the people of England to put the stamp of divine approval on that claim, raising English nationalism to new emotional heights. But Henry's successes in France also transformed the nature of the war, from a profitable war of conquest to an extended and expensive military occupation. It thereby sowed the seeds of eventual English defeat.

Henry himself died in 1422, still actively engaged in extending English control south, toward and across the Loire. King Charles VI died only a few months later. The new king of England and France, Henry VI (1422–1461), was an infant when his father died; but under the leadership of his uncle, the Duke of Bedford, English armies continued their slow push southward, while their ally, the Duke of Burgundy, controlled the northeast. The dauphin, meanwhile, withdrew to the extreme southwest of the country. His confidence in his right to the throne of France had been shatttered by his own mother's declaration that he was not the legitimate son of Charles VI. But as time went on, it also seemed increasingly unlikely that English forces would ever succeed in dislodging him from the territories south of the Loire.

This apparent stalemate was broken by the heroic figure of Joan of Arc. In 1429, Joan, an illiterate peasant girl, made her way to the dauphin's court to announce that an angel had told her that the dauphin was the rightful king of France and that she, Joan, should drive the English out of France. It is a mark of the

CHRONOLOGY

THE HUNDRED YEARS' WAR, 1337–1453

Valois Dynasty begins	1328
Edward III claims French throne	1337
Battle of Crécy	1346
Battle of Poitiers	1356
Battle of Agincourt	1415
French Burgundy allies with England	1419–1435
Joan of Arc commands French troops	1429–1430
Capture of Bordeaux ends war	1453

CHAPTER 10: THE LATER MIDDLE AGES, 1300–1500

The Murder of the Duke of Burgundy, 1419. This act of treachery, perpetrated by followers of the French dauphin (the future King Charles VII), made the new Duke of Burgundy into an outright military ally of King Henry V of England, paving the way for the English capture of Paris the following year.

hopelessness of Charles's position that she even got a hearing—much less that he then gave her a contingent of troops, with which she promptly lifted the English siege of Orleans. A series of further victories followed, culminating in 1430 when Joan brought Charles to Reims, the traditional coronation site for the French monarchy, where he was crowned king of France. But despite her victories, Joan remained an embarrassment: a peasant leading nobles, a woman leading men, and a commoner who claimed to have been commissioned by God. When, a few months later, the Burgundians captured her in battle and handed her over to the English, King Charles VII did nothing to try to save her. Accused of witchcraft and tried for heresy, Joan was burned to death in the market square at Rouen in 1431.

The French forces whom she inspired, however, continued on the offensive. In 1435, the Duke of Burgundy withdrew from his alliance with England; and when the English king Henry VI proved first to be incompetent and then to be insane, a series of French military victories during the 1440s finally brought the war to an end, with the capture of Bordeaux in 1453. English kings would threaten to renew the war for another century, and Anglo-French hostility would last until the final defeat of Napoleon in 1815. But after 1453, English control over French territory would be limited to the port of Calais, which would finally fall in 1558.

The Hundred Years' War was the most dangerous challenge to its existence that the French kingdom ever faced. The disintegration of that kingdom, first during the 1350s and 1360s, and again between 1415 and 1435, glaringly revealed the fragility of the bonds that tied the crown to its nobility and Paris to the outlying regions of Burgundy, Brittany, and Gascony. Nonetheless, the monarchy demonstrated remarkable resilience, and in the end the war strengthened the crown's

Joan of Arc. A contemporary sketch, drawn in the margin of the register of the English-controlled Parlement of Paris in 1429.

THE CONDEMNATION OF JOAN OF ARC BY THE UNIVERSITY OF PARIS, 1431

After Joan's capture by the Burgundians, she was handed over to the English, who put her on trial for heresy. Paris was at this date in English hands, so the verdict of the Parisian masters should not be considered unbiased. On the other hand, there is no evidence that it was extracted by force. Learned theologians were not inclined to approve of peasant women who claimed to hear the voices of angels, who dressed in men's clothes, and who led aristocrats into battle. Joan was condemned for heresy and burned at the stake.

You, Joan, have said that, since the age of thirteen, you have experienced revelations and the appearance of angels, of St Catherine and St Margaret, and that you have very often seen them with your bodily eyes, and that they have spoken to you. As for the first point, the clerks of the University of Paris have considered the manner of the said revelations and appearances. . . . Having considered all . . . they have declared that all the things mentioned above are lies, falsenesses, misleading and pernicious things and that such revelations are superstitions, proceeding from wicked and diabolical spirits.

Item: You have said that your king had a sign by which he knew that you were sent by God, for St Michael, accompanied by several angels, some of which having wings, the others crowns, with St Catherine and St Margaret, came to you at the chateau of Chinon. All the company ascended through the floors of the castle until they came to the room of your king, before whom the angel bearing the crown bowed. . . . As for this matter, the clerks say that it is not in the least probable, but it is rather a presumptuous lie, misleading and pernicious, a false statement, derogatory of the dignity of the Church and of the angels. . . .

Item: you have said that, at God's command, you have continually worn men's clothes, and that you have put on a short robe, doublet, shoes attached by points; also that you have had short hair, cut around above the ears, without retaining anything on your person which shows that you are a woman; and that several times you have received the body of Our Lord dressed in this fashion, despite having been admonished to give it up several times, the which you would not do. You have said that you would rather die than abandon the said clothing, if it were not at God's command, and that if you were wearing those clothes and were with the king, and those of your party, it would be one of the greatest benefits for the kingdom of France. You have also said that not for anything would you swear an oath not to wear the said clothing and carry arms any longer. And all these things you say you have done for the good and at the command of God. As for these things, the clerics say that you blaspheme God and hold him in contempt in his sacraments; you transgress Divine Law, Holy Scripture and canon law. You err in the faith. You boast in vanity. You are suspected of idolatry and you have condemned yourself in not wishing to wear clothing suitable to your sex, but you follow the custom of Gentiles and Saracens.

Carolyne Larrington, ed. and trans., *Women and Writing in Medieval Europe* (New York and London, 1995), pp. 183–184.

QUESTIONS FOR ANALYSIS

1. Why was Joan of Arc condemned for heresy?
2. In what ways does Joan of Arc highlight the major characteristics and preoccupations of the intensified popular piety of the later Middle Ages?

10 THE LATER MIDDLE AGES, 1300–1500

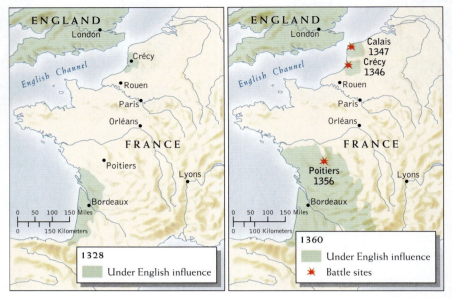

France during the Hundred Years' War

Here we see three snapshots of the political geography of France during the Hundred Years' War between France and England. In what areas of France did England make its greatest territorial gains before 1360? How and why did this change in the period leading up to 1429? What geographic and strategic advantages did the French monarchy enjoy after 1429 that might help explain its success in recapturing the French kingdom from the English?

capacity to rule France. To fight the war successfully, the Valois kings imposed new national taxes that would be the mainstays of French royal finance until 1789. With these new revenues, the Valois were able to create and maintain a standing national army whose size, sophistication, and expensive armaments (including, most important, its artillery) overwhelmed the forces that dissident nobles and regions might bring against it.

Although personally unimpressive, King Charles's victory in the Hundred Years' War laid the foundations on which the power of early modern France would be built. After 1453, the growing power of the French crown became quickly apparent. In 1477, Charles's son, King Louis XI (1461–1483), absorbed the duchy of Burgundy after the last Burgundian duke fell in battle at the hands of the Swiss. In 1485, King Louis XII helped topple King Richard III of England, whose alliance with Brittany had threatened to renew the English war with France. When, a few years later, Louis XII acquired Brittany through marriage, the French kings gained control over the last remaining independent principality within the borders of their kingdom.

The Hundred Years' War also had dramatic effects on the English monarchy. When English armies in France were successful, as they were under Edward III and Henry V, the Crown rode a wave of popularity and the country prospered from the profits of booty and ransoms. When the war turned against the English, however, as it did under Richard II and Henry VI, defeats abroad undermined support for the monarch at home. Of the nine English kings who ruled England between 1307 and 1485, no fewer than five were deposed and murdered by their subjects.

The particular propensity of the English for murdering their kings (a subject of comment across Europe) was a consequence of England's peculiar political system. As we have seen, England was the most tightly governed kingdom in Europe, but the strength of its political system depended on the king's ability to mobilize popular support for his policies through Parliament, while maintaining the support of his nobility through successful wars in Wales, Scotland, and France. This was a delicate task, at which incompetent or tyrannical kings could not succeed. At the same time, however, unsuccessful kingship was even more destabilizing in England than it was elsewhere in Europe, because of the power of the English state itself. In France, the nobility could endure the insanity of Charles VI because his government was not powerful enough to threaten them. In England, neither the nobility nor the larger political nation could afford to allow the incompetent kingship of King Henry VI to continue.

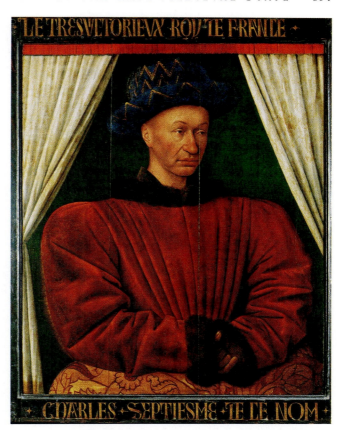

King Charles VII of France. The king's bulbous nose, bowed legs, and generally misshapen figure fed rumors that he had been conceived in adultery and so was not the legitimate heir to the throne of France. This portrait, done after his victory over the English, flatters him considerably.

The result was an aristocratic rebellion against Henry VI's government known as the Wars of the Roses, so called (by the nineteenth-century novelist Sir Walter Scott) from the emblems of the two competing factions: the red rose of Henry's family of Lancaster, and the white rose of Henry's cousin, the rival Duke of York. In 1461, after a six-year struggle, Edward, Duke of York finally succeeded in ousting Henry VI. He then ruled successfully until his death in 1483. But when Edward's brother Richard seized the throne from Edward's own young sons, political stability in England collapsed once again. In 1485, Richard III was in turn defeated and killed in the battle of Bosworth Field by the Lancastrian claimant, Henry Tudor, who then resolved the dynastic feud between Lancaster and York by marrying Elizabeth of York, the only surviving child of King Edward IV. As King Henry VII, Henry Tudor systematically eliminated potential rivals for the throne. He avoided expensive foreign wars, asked for little by way of taxation, built up a financial surplus by carefully managing Crown lands, and exercised a tight

King Richard III of England, 1483–1485. Richard deposed his nephews and seized the throne for himself. He was defeated and killed by Henry Tudor (King Henry VII) at Bosworth Field in 1485.

Henry VII. A 1505 portrait by M. Sittow.

(but largely welcome) control over the aristocracy. When he died in 1509 the new Tudor Dynasty was securely established on the throne, and English royal power was fully restored.

Despite the turmoil caused by war and rebellion, late medieval English political life had an essential stability. Local institutions continued to function; Parliament became increasingly important as a point of contact joining Crown, nobility, and local communities; and the political nation itself became steadily larger as prosperity brought new social groups into prominence. Most important, there was never any fundamental challenge to the power of the English state itself. When rebellions broke out, whether led by nobles or peasants, the rebels always sought to control the central government rather than to destroy or break away from it. Despite England's ultimate defeat, the Hundred Years' War strengthened this characteristically English equation between national identity and the power of the state. During the fourteenth and fifteenth centuries, mounting anti-French sentiment contributed to the triumph of English as the national language and to a patriotic vision of England itself as a country uniquely chosen by God. Having lost its continental possessions, England after 1485 became an island nation that looked to the sea as its first line of defense. This too would prove to be an advantage. England in the sixteenth and seventeenth centuries would be well positioned to take advantage of the new world of overseas commerce and colonialism opened up by Columbus's discoveries in the Americas.

Germany and Italy

Elsewhere, the consequences of late medieval warfare were more uniformly destructive. In Germany, armed conflict among the territorial princes who dominated the country, and between these princes and the German emperors, weakened all the principal combatants significantly. Periodically a powerful emperor would emerge to play a major role on the European scene. But the trend was toward the continuing dissolution of central power in Germany, as princes divided their territories among their heirs and as free cities and local knights strove to shake off the rule of the princes. Between 1350 and 1450, near anarchy prevailed across much of Germany. In the east, however, the rulers of Bavaria, Austria, and Brandenburg were able to strengthen their authority by supporting the efforts of local nobles to subject their peasantry to serfdom and by conquering and colonizing new territories, particularly on the frontier between Prussia and Lithuania.

The gains these rulers made during the later Middle Ages would make the Habsburg rulers of Austria and the Hohenzollern rulers of Brandenburg-Prussia the dominant powers in early modern Germany.

In northern and central Italy also, the last half of the fourteenth century was marked by incessant conflict. With the popes living at Avignon from 1309 until 1377, their control over the papal states collapsed. Warfare between city-states erupted throughout the northern half of the peninsula, further complicated by a rash of urban rebellions in the wake of the plague. By around 1400, however, Venice, Milan, and Florence had succeeded in stabilizing their own differing forms of government. Venice was now ruled by an oligarchy of merchants; Milan by a family of despots; and Florence was ruled as a republic, albeit one dominated by the influence of a few wealthy families, especially, after 1434, the Medici banking family. Having settled their internal problems, these three cities then began to expand their territories. By 1454, Venice, Milan, and Florence had subordinated almost all the other northern Italian cities and towns except Genoa, which remained prosperous and independent but gained no new lands. The papacy, meanwhile, now restored to Rome, reasserted its control over central Italy; while in the south, the kingdom of Naples continued to rule unchallenged by the other Italian powers, despite endemic local warfare and persistent maladministration.

A treaty in 1454 brought forty years of peace between these "five great powers." This peace was maintained by a form of "balance of power diplomacy," in which frequently shifting alliances among these five states checked the ambitions of each for further expansion. In 1494, however, a large-scale French invasion of Italy destroyed the diplomatic and military balance between the Italian powers, revealing in the process that the Italian city-states were no match for the powerful national monarchies that had developed during the fifteenth century north of the Alps. French control of the Italian peninsula would be short-lived, however. The ultimate beneficiary of the French invasion of Italy would be the newly united Spanish kingdoms of Aragon and Castile.

THE EMERGENCE OF SPAIN

Spain too had seen incessant strife during the later Middle Ages. Wars between the two principal Spanish kingdoms, Castile and Aragon, had weakened both combatants, while in Castile, a disastrous civil war during the fourteenth century was followed by a period of incompetent kingship and economic hardship during the mid-fifteenth century. In Castile, noble families took advantage of royal weakness to secure greater control over the peasantry on their estates and greater independence from the crown. After 1450, noble factions struggled for control over the Castilian court as feuds between noble families tore the kingdom apart.

The Aragonese crown preserved its authority rather better, benefiting from its alliance with the merchants of Catalunya, who were busily extending their commercial influence throughout the Mediterranean world. After 1458, however, Aragon too fell prey to civil war arising from a succession dispute, in which both France and Castile became involved. By 1469, however, King John had established his son Ferdinand as the unquestioned heir to the throne of Aragon. When, in that year, Ferdinand married Isabella, the heiress to Castile, their union became the basis on which a united Spanish kingdom would eventually be built.

In 1474, Isabella ascended to the throne of Castile; in 1479, Ferdinand became King of Aragon when his father died. Aragon and Castile continued to be ruled as separate kingdoms until 1714; even in contemporary Spain, tensions between the two former kingdoms continue. But the marriage of Ferdinand and Isabella ended the warfare between the kingdoms, and after 1479 the Catholic Monarchs (as Ferdinand and Isabella came to be known) were able to embark on united policies. Vast increases in royal revenues quickly followed. Much of this new revenue was devoted to building up Spanish military forces, which by 1500 were the most powerful in Europe. These forces were first employed to conquer Grenada, the last remaining Muslim principality in Spain, which fell in 1492. A decade later, Spanish armies intervened in Italy, eventually turning all of Italy into a Spanish protectorate. But this new army also played an important role within Spain, providing honorable employment and royal service to the fractious nobles of Castile and Aragon, while overawing any nobles who might be tempted to rebel against the growing power of the Catholic Monarchs.

The conquest of Granada was a turning point for the emerging Spanish monarchy. Both Castile and Aragon had been shaped for centuries by their involvement in the reconquest of Muslim Spain. But the victory of 1492 sealed a vision of Castile in particular as a country uniquely devoted to crusading. That vision of Castile's world mission might not have been so consequential, however, had it not been for the fact that only a few months after the conquest of Granada, Queen Isabella granted three ships to a Genoese adventurer named Christopher Columbus who promised to reach India by sailing westward across the Atlantic Ocean. He failed,

Ferdinand and Isabella Honoring the Virgin. A contemporary Spanish painting in which the royal pair is shown with two of their children in the company of saints from the Dominican order.

of course; but by landing in two new continents, which he claimed for Spain, Columbus extended the Castilian crusading tradition to the New World, with consequences that have lasted to the present day.

The year 1492 also saw the expulsion of the entire Jewish community from Spain, the culmination of a process of Jewish exclusion from Christian Europe that began in the late thirteenth century with the expulsion of the Jewish communities of southern Italy and England, continued with the expulsion of the Jews from France in 1306, and continued during the fourteenth and fifteenth centuries with a series of Jewish expulsions from the towns and cities of the Rhineland. The Spanish expulsion stands out, however, both for the total number of Jews involved (at least 100,000 and possibly as many as 200,000) and because of the rich cultural legacy the Jews of Spain had developed in the 1,000 years during which they had resided on the Iberian Peninsula.

Historians continue to debate why Ferdinand and Isabella ordered this expulsion. Between 1391 and 1420, tens of thousands of Spanish Jews had converted to Catholicism, many as a result of coercion but some from sincere religious conviction. Until around 1450, it seemed possible that these converts (*conversos*) might successfully assimilate into Spanish Christian society. Thereafter, however, the *conversos* became the targets of discriminatory legislation and popular suspicion that they remained secretly Jews. To make proper Christians out of the *conversos*, the Catholic monarchs may have concluded that they needed to remove the "bad influence" posed by the continuing presence of a practicing Jewish community in Spain.

Beyond such practical considerations, however, there may also have been a desire to create a new and explicitly Christian identity for the newly united country over which Ferdinand and Isabella ruled. Spain, per se, did not exist in 1492. Its creation would be the work of centuries, work that continues today. But the need for some common identity that would transcend the rival regional identities of Castilians, Aragonese, and Catalans (not to mention Galicians, Navarrese, Valencians, Basques, and Murcians) may already have been apparent. Certainly it is implied in the title Ferdinand and Isabella took to themselves as the Catholic Monarchs. Like other monarchs in late medieval Europe, Ferdinand and Isabella may have sought to strengthen their emerging nation-state by constructing a newly explicit and exclusively Christian identity for its people and by attaching that new identity to the crown. In such a Christian nation, however, there could be no place for Jews or Muslims.

THE GROWTH OF NATIONAL MONARCHIES

In France, England, Scotland, Portugal, and Spain, the later Middle Ages saw the emergence of markedly more powerful European states than had existed in 1300. But despite the impact of war and plague in reshaping European political life, many of the basic political patterns established during the High Middle Ages endured. Germany and Italy were politically divided by 1300 and remained divided in 1500. England and France, the two most powerful monarchies of the High Middle Ages, remained powerful states in 1500, although the combined kingdoms of Aragon and Castile, together with the kingdom of Portugal, had now emerged as a powerful rival to both. Only the position of Sicily had been fundamentally transformed. Economically exhausted by the demands of its high medieval rulers, Sicily became in the later Middle Ages the impoverished land it has remained until the present day.

Behind these continuities, however, lies one of the most notable developments in later medieval politics: the growing strength of national monarchies. By 1500, the kings of Iberia, England, France, and Scotland were all actively engaged in constructing a sense of national identity among their people and in focusing that identity on themselves. This fusion of nationalism and kingship was a product of the later Middle Ages. Forged by the fires of war and fueled by the growing cultural importance of vernacular languages, this fusion of national identity with kingship produced by 1500 a new type of political organization, the national monarchy, which was stronger and more powerful than anything Europe had seen since the heyday of the Carolingian Empire.

The superiority of these new national monarchies to older forms of political organization such as the empire and the city-state is most clearly visible in Italy. Until 1494, the Italian city-states had appeared to be well governed and powerful. But when the armies of France and Spain invaded the peninsula, the Italian political order collapsed like a house of cards. Germany would suffer the same fate only a few generations later; it would remain a battleground for the competing armies of France and Spain until the end of the seventeenth century.

The new national monarchies were not an unmitigated blessing. They were not only more powerful, they were also more intolerant and exclusionary than their high medieval predecessors, as the expulsion of Jews (and Muslims) from later medieval Europe reveals. But for better or worse, these newly powerful national monarchies would dominate Europe and the wider world for the next 500 years.

KIEVAN RUS AND THE RISE OF MUSCOVY

Why did Russia develop differently from other late medieval European states?

The fourteenth and fifteenth centuries also witnessed the consolidation of the state that would become the dominant power in eastern Europe. Russia, however, developed very differently from the national monarchies of western Europe. Unlike Spain or France or even Germany, Russia by 1500 had taken decisive steps toward becoming the largest multiethnic empire in the Eurasian world.

This development was not inevitable. Had it not been for a combination of late medieval circumstances, one or several east Slavic states might well have developed along the same lines as did the national monarchies of western Europe. As we saw in Chapter Eight, Swedish Vikings (known as Rus) had played a key role in establishing the principality of Kiev in modern-day Ukraine. During the tenth and eleventh centuries, Kiev maintained diplomatic and trading relations with both western Europe and Byzantium. But after 1200, several epoch-making developments combined to separate Russia from western Europe.

The first was the conquest of most of the eastern Slavic states by the Mongols. Commanded by Batu, a grandson of the great Chingiz (Genghis) Khan, the Mongols cut such swaths of devastation through Russia as they advanced westward that, according to one contemporary, "no eye remained open to weep for the dead." In 1240, the Mongols overran Kiev. Two years later they created their own state on the lower Volga River—the khanate of the Golden Horde—which exercised superiority over most of Russia for the following 150 years. During the thirteenth century, the Mongols ruled Russia directly, carrying out censuses, installing their own administrative officials, and requiring the native Russian princes to travel to Mongolia to secure permission from the great khan to rule their territories. After around 1300, however, the Mongols changed course. Rather than rule Russia directly, they instead tolerated the existence of several native Slavic states from which they demanded obedience and regular tribute payments.

THE RISE OF MUSCOVY

Kiev never recovered the dominant position it had enjoyed before the Mongol invasions. The native principality that finally emerged to defeat the Mongols and unify much of Russia was instead the grand duchy of Moscow. Moscow rose to power in the early fourteenth century as a tribute-collecting center for the Mongol khanate. Moscow's alliance with the Mongols did not necessarily protect it from Mongol attacks: the city was destroyed once at the time of the Mongol invasions and again in 1382. But despite these setbacks, Moscow was able, with Mongol support, to absorb the territory of the grand principality of Vladimir and so gradually to become the dominant political power in northeastern Russia.

Moscow also had the advantage of being far removed from the Mongol power base on the lower Volga. Its remote location made Moscow a valuable

CHAPTER 10: THE LATER MIDDLE AGES, 1300–1500

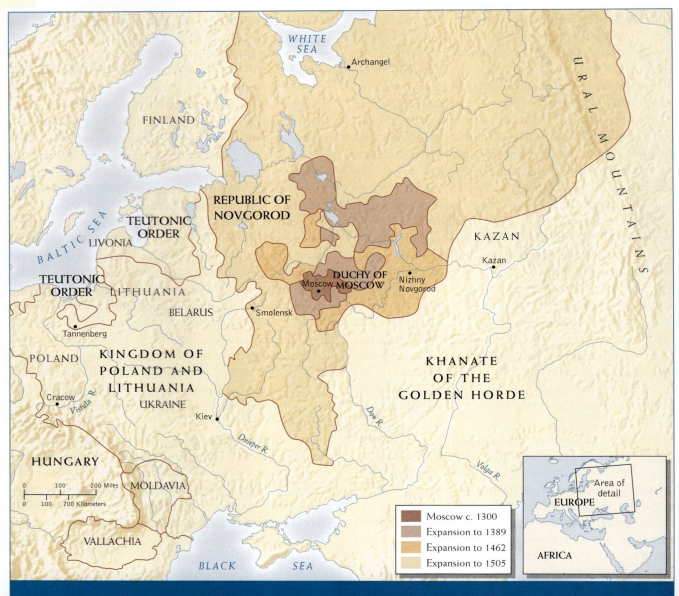

THE EXPANSION OF MUSCOVITE RUSSIA TO 1505

The grand duchy of Moscow was the heart of what would soon become the Russian Empire. How did the relative isolation of Moscow compared with Kiev allow for the growth of Muscovite power on the one hand and Moscow's distinctively non-Western culture on the other? Why did the Muscovite Russians identify so closely with the Byzantines, and why did they reserve such pronounced hostility for the West and Latin Christianity? What role did the Kingdom of Poland-Lithuania play in the development of this Russian attitude? How did the natural direction of the expansion of Muscovite power until 1505 help encourage attitudes often at odds with those of western European civilization?

ally for the Mongol khanate, while allowing the grand dukes of Moscow to consolidate their strength without attracting too much attention from the khans. Despite Moscow's remote location, however, the grand duchy maintained commercial contacts with both the Baltic and the Black Sea regions throughout the Mongol Period. What really distanced Moscow from western Europe was not, therefore, the fact that it was under the thumb of the Mongols. Rather, it was the enormous religious hostility that existed after 1204 between the Orthodox Christian world (to which Moscow adhered) and the Latin Christian world of

Europe. Hostility between these two great branches of Christianity had deep historical roots but became much more pronounced as a result of the Latins' capture of Constantinope, the capital of the Orthodox world, during the Fourth Crusade. During the fourteenth and fiteenth centuries, however, what particularly excited the religious animosity of Moscow toward western European Christianity was the growing strength of the Catholic kingdom of Poland and the fall of Constantinople to the Ottoman Turks in 1453.

THE RIVALRY WITH POLAND

During the High Middle Ages, Poland had been a second-rate power, usually on the defensive against German encroachments. During the fourteenth century, however, Poland's situation changed dramatically, partly because German strength was declining, but above all because the marriage in 1386 of Poland's reigning queen, Jadwiga, to Jagiello, Grand Duke of Lithuania, more than doubled Poland's size, enabling the newly combined kingdom to become a major expanionist state. Even before 1386 Lithuania had begun to carve out an extensive territory stretching from the Baltic Sea into modern-day Belarus and Ukraine. This expansionist momentum increased after its union with Poland. In 1410, at the Battle of Tannenberg, combined Polish and Lithuanian forces inflicted a stunning defeat on the Teutonic Knights, the German military order that ruled neighboring Prussia. Poland-Lithuania then began to push its borders eastward toward Russia. Although many Lithuanian nobles were Orthodox Christians, the established church in Lithuania was Roman Catholic. So too, of course, was the Kingdom of Poland. Thus when Moscow took the offensive against Poland-Lithuania in the late fifteenth century, its campaigns appealed to religious as well as national loyalties. Prolonged warfare ensued, greatly increasing Russian antagonism not only toward Poland-Lithuania but also toward the Latin Christian tradition it represented in the eyes of Muscovites.

MOSCOW AND BYZANTIUM

The growing alienation of Moscow from Latin Christian Europe was further increased by events leading up to the fall of Constantinople to the Turks in 1453. Connections between Byzantium and the Rus went back to the tenth century, when Byzantine missionaries had converted the Kievan Slavs to Orthodox Christianity. Thereafter, the Russian church gradually came to see itself as a special ally of Constantinople in de-

fending and maintaining Orthodoxy, an attitude embraced by the Muscovite church also. In 1438, however, Orthodox Church authorities in Constantinople agreed to submit to papal authority and unite with the Latin Christian church, in the hope that this might bring them western military support to withstand the Turks, who were by now knocking at the gates of the besieged city. The Russian church refused to follow Byzantium in this religious submission to Rome, regarding it as a betrayal of Orthodoxy; and when Constantinople fell to the Turks without any help from the west having arrived, Muscovite churchmen regarded the Turkish victory as divine punishment for Constantinople's religious perfidy. After 1453, the Muscovite state declared itself to be the divinely appointed successor to Byzantium, adopting in the process a particularly zealous anti-Catholic ideology, which was reinforced by the military threat from Poland-Lithuania. The Muscovite ruler took the title of *tsar*, which means "caesar," and Russians declared Moscow both "a second Jerusalem" and "the third Rome." "Two Romes have fallen," said a Russian spokesman, "the third is still standing, and a fourth there shall not be."

THE REIGN OF IVAN THE GREAT (1462–1505)

This Byzantine-derived ideology of divine election underlay both the later growth of Russian imperialism and the sacred position ascribed to the rulers of the Muscovite (and later Russian) state. Behind these developments, however, lay also the steadily growing power of the grand dukes of Moscow. Moscow itself achieved effective independence from the Mongols at the end of the fourteenth century, when a rival Mongol ruler named Timur the Lame (Tamurlane) destroyed the Mongal khanate of the Golden Horde. But it was the grand duke Ivan III, known as Ivan the Great, who transformed Moscow into a true imperial power. Declaring himself the White Tsar (and so the legitimate successor to the Mongol Golden Horde), Ivan launched a series of conquests between 1468 and 1485 that annexed, one by one, all the independent Russian principalities that lay between Moscow and the border with Poland-Lithuania. After invading Lithuania in 1492 and 1501, Ivan also succeeded in bringing parts of Belarus and Ukraine under his control. Battles between Russia and Poland-Lithuania would continue for several centuries, but by 1505, when Ivan died, he had established Muscovy as a power to be reckoned with on the European scene.

THE LATER MIDDLE AGES, 1300–1500

Ivan the Great.

Under Ivan III, Muscovy evolved rapidly in the direction of political autocracy and imperialism. In 1452, Ivan married the niece of the last Byzantine emperor, giving substance to his claims to be the Orthodox successor to the Byzantine emperors. He would later adopt, as his imperial insignia, the double-headed eagle of Rome. To display his imperial splendor, he also rebuilt his fortified Moscow residence, known as the Kremlin, in magnificent Italian Renaissance style. As tsar, Ivan presented himself as the autocratic ruler not only of Moscow but of all Russians everywhere, and potentially of Belarussians and Ukrainians also.

After Ivan's death, Russian expansionism was principally directed south and east, against the small successor states to the Mongol Golden Horde. From the mid-seventeenth century on, however, Muscovite pressure against Ukraine and Belarus would escalate, leading to the enormous Russian land empire Peter the Great would create in the early eighteenth century. We cannot draw a direct line from Ivan III to Peter the Great. But Peter would appeal to the foundations Ivan laid as justification for his own claims to incorporate both Russians and a wide variety of non-Russian peoples into what would become Europe's largest land-based empire. As they were for the states of western Europe also, the late Middle Ages were thus a decisive period in the political evolution of the Russian state.

Trials for the Church

> Why did late medieval efforts to reform the institutions of the Catholic Church fail?

The later Middle Ages were a challenging and difficult period for the institutions of the Catholic Church. Like other large landowners, monasteries suffered from the economic changes brought about by the Black Death. So too did bishops, who confronted the same price scissors (declining revenues and rising costs) as did the secular nobility. No ecclesiastical institution suffered more severe trials, however, than did the late medieval papacy, which endured almost seventy years of continuous exile from Rome—an exile that was followed first by a forty-year schism and then by a protracted battle with reformers who sought to reduce the popes' authority to govern the church.

THE LATE MEDIEVAL PAPACY AND CONCILIARISM

Following the humiliation and death of Pope Boniface VIII (1294–1303) at the hands of King Philip IV of France (see page 343), the late medieval papacy entered into a long period of institutional crisis. After four years of wandering in exile from Rome, the papacy resided continuously from 1309 until 1378 at Avignon, a small papal territory on the southwestern border of France. Here they built up a large and efficient bureaucracy, principally devoted to raising money to fund the reconquest of the papal states in Italy.

When the popes first settled in Avignon, they had not intended to remain there. But Avignon soon proved to have a number of advantages over Rome. It was closer to the major centers of power in fourteenth-century Europe, it was far removed from the tumultuous local politics of Rome and the papal states, and it was safe from the aggressive attentions of the German emperors. All the popes elected during the Avignon period were natives of southern France, as were nearly all the cardinals whom they appointed; for them, Avignon felt like home. As the papal bureaucracy grew in size, it too became more difficult to move. Nor could the wishes of the king of France be ignored. The French king was the principal secular supporter of the Avignon popes, and he liked having them on the borders of his kingdom, where he could browbeat them as necessary.

But despite Avignon's advantages, the papacy never abandoned the hope of returning to Rome. To do so, however, the popes first had to win back military control over the papal states in central Italy. This effort took decades. To finance these wars, the Avignon popes imposed new taxes and obligations on the churches of France, England, Germany, and Spain. Judicial cases from the church courts also brought large revenues into the papal coffers. More controversially, the Avignon popes also claimed the right to appoint bishops and priests directly to vacant church offices. Such appointments (known as papal provisions) were not necessarily abusive. Although they bypassed the rights of the local clergy to elect their own officials, the men appointed were often of outstanding ability. But all such appointees had to pay large fees to the papacy in return for their appointments, fees that critics declared to be simony (the purchase of church offices for cash).

By these and other measures, the Avignon popes strengthened their administrative control over the church. But this did not make them loved. Clergy and laity alike were alienated by the papacy's insatiable demands for money, and stories quickly spread about the unbridled luxury of the papal court. In fact, most of the Avignon popes were morally upright and personally abstemious; the cash they collected went overwhelmingly to pay the costs of war in central Italy. One, however, Pope Clement VI (1342–1352), was notoriously corrupt and immoral. Clement openly sold spiritual benefits for money, boasted that he would appoint a jackass as bishop if political circumstances warranted, and defended his incessant sexual transgressions by insisting that he fornicated on doctors' orders. His cardinals led equally luxurious and dissolute lives, feasting on exotic birds and drinking from sculptured fountains that spouted the finest wines.

In 1367, Pope Urban V tried to return to Rome but found his way blocked by the troops of King Charles V of France. In 1377, however, Pope Gregory XI succeeded in returning the papacy from Avignon to Rome. But when he died only a year later, disaster struck. Fearful that if the new pope were a Frenchman he might return to Avignon, the Romans rioted, demanding that the cardinals (who were mainly southern

Papal Palace at Avignon. This great palace was begun in 1339 and symbolizes the apparent permanence of the papal residence in Avignon.

Chapter 10 THE LATER MIDDLE AGES, 1300–1500

French) elect a Roman as the new pope. Fearing for their lives, the cardinals quickly obliged, electing an Italian who took the name Urban VI. Urban, however, immediately began quarreling with the cardinals, revealing what were probably paranoid tendencies. Fearing for their lives once again, the cardinals fled Rome, declared Urban VI's election invalid, and elected as the new pope a French cardinal who took the name Clement VII. Clement and the cardinals then marched on Rome with an army, but they could not dislodge Pope Urban from the city. Urban VI thereupon named a new, entirely Italian college of cardinals, while Clement VII and his cardinals withdrew to Avignon.

The result was the Great Schism, a nearly forty-year period during which the church was ruled first by two and ultimately by three competing popes, each

THE GREAT SCHISM, 1378–1417

During the Great Schism Europe was divided by religious allegiance. What common interests united the supporters of the Avignon pope? The Roman pope? Why did areas like Portugal and Austria find it so difficult to choose which side to support?

claiming to be the legitimate successor to Saint Peter. Europe's religious allegiances fractured along the lines of political division established by the Hundred Years' War. France, Scotland, Castile, Aragon, and Naples recognized the Avignon pope, while England, Germany, northern Italy, Scandinavia, Bohemia, Poland, and Hungary recognized the Roman pope. Nor was there any obvious way to end this embarrassing state of affairs. Both popes had been elected by the same group of cardinals; and thereafter, whenever one of the popes died, his supporters quickly elected a successor, thus prolonging the Schism. Finally, in 1409, some cardinals from both camps met at Pisa, where they deposed both popes and named a new one. But neither the Roman nor the Avignon pope accepted the council's decisions. As a result, after 1409 there were three rival popes excommunicating each other, instead of only two.

The Great Schism finally ended in 1417 at the Council of Constance, the largest ecclesiastical gathering of the Middle Ages. The council had strong support from several European princes, including King Henry V of England and the emperor Sigismund of Germany, and took care to depose all the other papal claimants before naming its own new pope, an Italian who took the name Martin V. This, however, took three years of effort, and so the council was unable to proceed with its larger goal of reforming the religious life of the church. That task was left for future councils.

The election of Pope Martin V restored the ecclesiastical unity of Europe. It did not, however, end the struggle over how the church should be governed in future. To end the schism, the Council of Constance had declared that supreme authority within the church rested not with the pope, but with itself and all future such general councils. It also ordered that general councils should meet regularly thereafter to oversee the governance and reform of the church.

These conciliar decrees were a revolutionary challenge to the traditions of papal monarchy. It is not surprising that Pope Martin V and his successors did all they could to undermine them. In 1423, when the next required general council met at Siena, Pope Martin sent its representatives back home almost immediately. Constance had specified that a council must meet, but it had not specified for how long that meeting must last! In 1431, however, when the next general council met at Basel, its members immediately took steps to ensure that the pope could not dismiss it. A lengthy struggle for power then ensued, in which the popes and the conciliarists competed for the support of Europe's kings and princes. Finally, in 1449, the Council of Basel dissolved itself in abject failure, bringing to an end this radical experiment in conciliar government over the church and dashing the hopes of those who thought it would lead to a thoroughgoing reform of religious life "in head and members."

THE GROWTH OF NATIONAL CHURCHES

The papacy's victory over the conciliarists was a costly one. To win the support of Europe's kings and princes against the conciliarists, the popes negotiated a series of treaties, known as "concordats," which granted these rulers extensive authority over the churches within their territories. The popes thus secured their own theoretical supremacy over the church at the cost of surrendering their real power to rule it. Under the terms of these concordats, kings now received many of the revenues from local churches that previously had gone to the papacy. They also acquired new powers to appoint candidates to church offices within their kingdoms.

As papal authority over local churches diminished, and the spiritual prestige of the papacy declined, kings and princes became the primary figures toward whom even churchmen looked to reform the religious and moral lives of their people. Many secular rulers responded aggressively to such expectations by closing scandal-ridden monasteries, suppressing heretics, punishing women accused of witchcraft, regulating prostitution, and prohibiting the lower classes from dressing

Joan of Arc drives Prostitutes from Her Army. This illustration, from a 1484 manuscript, tells one of the many legends that grew up around Joan after her death. It also shows the efforts that many late-fifteenth-century rulers made to present themselves as champions of moral reform within their lands.

THE CONCILIARIST CONTROVERSY

The Great Schism produced a fundamental and far-reaching debate about the nature of authority within the church. Arguments for papal supremacy rested on the traditional claims that the popes were the successors of Saint Peter, to whom Jesus Christ had delegated his own authority over the church. Arguments for the supremacy of a general council had been advanced around the University of Paris throughout much of the fourteenth century; but it was only in the circumstances of the schism that these arguments found a wide audience. The documents here trace the history of the controversy, from the declaration of conciliar supremacy at the Council of Constance (Haec Sancta), to the council's efforts to guarantee regular meetings of general councils thereafter (Frequens), to the papal condemnation of appeals to future general councils issued in 1460 (Execrabilis). Note, however, the limitations on Execrabilis. Even this condemnation does not go so far as to actually contradict Haec Sancta. It merely condemns appeals from papal judgment to future general councils that have no specified meeting date. The conciliar ideal was still powerful at the end of the fifteenth century; and in the sixteenth and seventeenth centuries, it would have a profound impact on European political thought about kings.

HAEC SANCTA SYNODUS (1415)

This holy synod of Constance . . . declares that being lawfully assembled in the Holy Spirit, constituting a general council and representing the Catholic Church Militant, it has its power directly from Christ, and that all persons of whatever rank or dignity, even a Pope, are bound to obey it in matters relating to faith and the end of the Schism and the general reformation of the church of God in head and members.

Further, it declares that any person of whatever position, rank, or dignity, even a Pope, who contumaciously refuses to obey the mandates, statutes, ordinances, or regulations enacted or to be enacted by this holy synod, or by any other general council lawfully assembled, relating to the matters aforesaid or to other matters involved with them, shall, unless he repents, be . . . duly punished. . . .

FREQUENS (1417)

The frequent holding of general councils is the best method of cultivating the field of the Lord, for they root out the briars, thorns, and thistles of heresies, errors, and schisms, correct abuses, make crooked things straight, and prepare the Lord's vineyard for fruitfulness and rich fertility. Neglect of general councils sows the seeds of these evils and encourages their growth. This truth is borne in upon us as we recall times past and survey the present.

Therefore by perpetual edict we . . . ordain that henceforth general councils shall be held as follows: the first within the five years immediately following the end of the present council, the second within seven years from the end of the council next after this, and subsequently every ten years forever. . . . Thus there will always be a certain continuity. Either a council will be in session or one will be expected at the end of a fixed period. . . .

R. L. Loomis, ed. and trans., *"Haec Sancta Synodus"* and *"Frequens"* in *The Council of Constance* (New York, 1961), pp. 229, 246–247.

Execrabilis (1460)

An execrable abuse, unheard of in earlier times, has sprung up in our period. Some men, imbued with a spirit of rebellion and moved not by a desire for sound decisions but rather by a desire to escape the punishment for sin, suppose that they can appeal from the Pope, Vicar of Jesus Christ; from the Pope, to whom in the person of blessed Peter it was said, "Feed my sheep" and "whatever you bind on earth will be bound in heaven"—from this Pope to a future council. How harmful this is to the Christian republic, as well as how contrary to canon law, anyone who is not ignorant of the law can understand. For . . . who would not consider it ridiculous to appeal to something which does not now exist anywhere nor does anyone know when it will exist? The poor are heavily oppressed by the powerful, offenses remain unpunished, rebellion against the Holy See is encouraged, license for sin is granted, and all ecclesiastical discipline and hierarchical ranking of the Church are turned upside down.

Wishing therefore to expel this deadly poison from the Church of Christ, and concerned with the salvation of the sheep committed to us . . . with the counsel and assent of our venerable brothers, the Cardinals of the Holy Roman Church, together with the counsel and assent of all those prelates who have been trained in canon and civil law who follow our Court, and with our own certain knowledge, we condemn appeals of this kind, reject them as erroneous and abominable, and declare them to be completely null and void. And we lay down that from now on, no one should dare . . . to make such an appeal from our decisions, be they legal or theological, or from any commands at all from us or our successors. . . .

Heiko A. Oberman, Daniel E. Zerfoss, and William J. Courtenay, eds. and trans., *Execrabilis: Defensorum Obedientiae Apostolicae et alia Documenta* (Cambridge, Mass., 1968), pp. 224–227 (with modifications by R. C. Stacey).

QUESTIONS FOR ANALYSIS

1. How might the conciliar movement be seen as a subtle challenge to the authority of the medieval papacy?
2. Why would a pope fear the decisions of a general council?
3. Why was it important to guarantee regular meetings of general church councils?

---

as if they were nobles. By these and other such measures, rulers could present themselves as champions of moral and religious reform while also strengthening their capacity to rule their territories. The result was an increasingly close link between national rulers and the national churches over which they ruled.

Having given away so many of their other revenues, the popes of the late fifteenth century became even more dependent on their own territories in central Italy than their predecessors had been. To build up the Papal States, however, the popes had to rule like other Italian princes: leading armies, jockeying for alliances with other princes, and undermining their oppponents by every possible means. Judged in secular terms, their efforts were by no means a failure. By 1520, the Papal States were one of the better-governed and wealthier principalities in Italy. But such methods did nothing to increase the popes' reputation for piety or to respond to the calls from both clergy and laity for a thorough-going reform of religious life. By 1500, disillusionment with the late medieval papacy as a force for spiritual and religious reform within the church was widespread. In the Protestant Reformation, that smoldering tinder would erupt into a European-wide conflagration.

The Pursuit of Holiness in Late Medieval Piety

Were late medieval people disillusioned with their church?

Despite the travails of the institutional church, religious devotion among the laity was more widespread and intense during the later Middle Ages than it had ever been before. The fundamental theme of high medieval preaching, that salvation lay open to any Christian who strove for it, bore fruit during the later Middle Ages in a rapidly multiplying variety of paths that promised to lead the individual believer to God. Some of these paths led their adherents in directions the church declared heretical. For the vast majority of late medieval Christians, however, heresy held no appeal. The church, and especially the sacraments performed by their local parish priests, was the center of their religious lives. To understand late medieval Christianity, we need therefore to start in the parishes.

SACRAMENT, RITUAL, AND SERMON

By 1300, nearly all of Europe was covered by a network of local parish churches within which priests administered the sacraments of the church to the laity. These sacraments—baptism, confirmation, the Mass, confession, marriage, ordination, and extreme unction —were rituals that conveyed the grace and power of God to individual Christian believers. Late medieval piety revolved around them. Baptism initiated the Christian into the life of the church. In the later Middle Ages, it was administered to infants as soon as possible after birth; without baptism, salvation was generally thought to be impossible. Confirmation "confirmed" the promises made on a child's behalf at baptism. Through the priest's ministrations during the Mass (which was celebrated every Sunday and on feast days as well), bread and wine were transubstantiated into the actual body and blood of Christ, which the Christian faithful honored and consumed. Confession of sins to a priest guaranteed their forgiveness by God; but if satisfactory penance for sins were not completed on earth, then it would have to be done after death in purgatory, a nether world between heaven and hell. Marriage was a relatively new sacrament, increasingly emphasized in the later Middle Ages; but still only a minority of Christians would have had their unions solemnized by the church. Ordination conveyed to a priest his special power to bring God's grace to earth through the sacraments, a power that could never be lost, even by a priest who led an immoral life. Extreme unction (or last rites) was administered to a dying person. It ensured the final confession of all sins and so was essential to a good death with the assurance of salvation to come. Like baptism, extreme unction could, in an emergency, be administered by any Christian believer. The other sacraments, however, could be administered only by a properly ordained priest—or, in the case of confirmation and ordination, by a bishop.

This sacramental system was the foundation on which the other practices of late medieval popular piety rested. Pilgrimages, for example, were a form of penance, which could lessen one's time in purgatory. Crusading was a kind of extreme pilgrimage that promised the complete fulfillment of all penances the crusader might owe for all the sins of his (or her) life. Many other pious acts—saying the prayers of the rosary, for example, or giving alms to the poor—could also serve as penance for one's sins as well as constituting good works that would help the believer in his or her journey toward salvation.

But there was more to late medieval piety than simply penance. Like all good works, prayer had other purposes also. The saints generally, and the Virgin Mary in particular, were regarded as powerful intercessors with God. In danger or ill health, believers would pray to such holy figures. Some saints were known for responding to particular ailments; if afflicted with hemorrhoids, for example, one might be well advised to pray to Saint Fiacre. Devotion to the saints might be increased by contact with the relics of a saint, typically pieces of bone or clothing that had belonged to the saint. No relic was more powerful, however, or more central to late medieval piety, than the bread and wine of the Mass, which became, through priestly consecration, the true body and blood of Christ. Believers sometimes attributed astonishing properties to the eucharistic bread of the Mass, feeding it to sick animals or rushing from church to church to see the consecrated bread as many times as possible in a day. Understandably, some of these beliefs and practices, and many alleged relics of the saints, were criticized by church reformers as superstitious. But by and large, these were not practices foisted on an ignorant and credulous laity by a group of clerical con men. They arose and continued because of the deep devotion of laypeople to them, frequently in opposition to the efforts of church reformers to shut them down.

RELIGION AND THE SOCIAL ORDER

Late medieval people understood their religion as a thoroughly integrated part of the social world in which they lived. The church stood literally at the center of their lives. Churchyards were communal meeting places; sometimes they were even the sites of markets. Church buildings were a refuge from attack and a gathering place for village business, whose upkeep and repair was a village responsibility. The church's holidays marked the passage of the year, and the church's bells marked the hours of the day. Understandably, therefore, the holiness of the church tended to be seen as an element in the larger holiness of the community, local or national, of which it was a part.

Not everyone found the conventional practices of late medieval piety spiritually satisfying. Although honored in death, many late medieval saints were distinctly controversial in life; and the lines between a saint and a witch could sometimes be very fine, as Joan of Arc's example reveals. As a child, Saint Catherine of Siena refused altogether to help with the housework and then took over one of the two rooms in her working-class family's house for her prayers, forcing her parents and her dozen siblings into the one remaining room. Julianna of Norwich withdrew from the world into a small cell built next to her local church, where she spent the rest of her life in prayer and contemplation; while Margery Kempe was so moved by the suffering of Jesus on the cross that she would cry hysterically for hours, completely disrupting the Mass and deeply alienating her fellow parishioners.

The extraordinary piety of such individuals could be awe inspiring, but it could also threaten the church's control over religious life and the links that bound individuals to their communities. It could, therefore, be dangerous. Some believers, for example, sought to achieve a mystical union with God through rigorous spiritual exercises; a few of these were ultimately condemned for heresy for declaring that, having succeeded in their mystical quest, they were no longer obliged to obey God's church on earth. And even less radical figures might find themselves treading on dangerous ground, especially if they wrote religious tracts in vernacular languages, so that the laity could more easily read them. Master Eckhart (c. 1260–1327), for example, a German Dominican, taught and wrote in both Latin and German that there was a power or "spark" deep within every human soul wherein God dwelt. By renouncing all sense of self, one could retreat into one's innermost recesses and there find divinity. Eckhart did not recommend ceasing attendance at church—he hardly could have because he preached in churches—but he made it clear that for those seeking to find God, even the sacraments were of lesser importance than the inward journey he described. He also gave the impression to his lay audiences that they might attain godliness largely on their own volition. Church authorities charged him with inciting "ignorant and undisciplined people to wild and dangerous excesses." Although Eckhart pleaded his own doctrinal orthodoxy, some of his teachings were ultimately condemned as heretical.

More safely orthodox was the practical mysticism preached to both monastic and lay audiences during the fifteenth century by such figures as Thomas à Kempis, whose *Imitation of Christ* (c. 1427) did not aim for full mystical union with God but rather for an ongoing sense of divine presence during the conduct of daily life. The *Imitation* taught its readers to be pious Christians while still living actively in the world, emphasizing the importance of the Mass but otherwise stressing inward rather than outward piety and urging believers to meditate on the Bible and to live a simple, moral life. Although written in Latin, the *Imitation* was quickly translated into the leading European vernacular languages. For almost six centuries, it has been more widely read than any other Christian religious work except the Bible.

LOLLARDS AND HUSSITES

For the most part, popular heretical movements were less widespread and less dangerous to the church during the later Middle Ages than they had been in the twelfth and thirteenth centuries. In England and Bohemia, however, heretical movements did pose serious challenges to the established authorities of both church and state. In England, the Lollard heresy began with John Wyclif (c. 1330–1384), an Oxford theologian whose extreme predestinarianism (see page 229) led him to conclude that the sacraments of a corrupt church could not save anyone. He urged the English Crown, therefore, to appropriate ecclesiastical wealth and to replace corrupt priests and bishops with men who would live according to apostolic standards of poverty and piety. Wyclif's followers went even further, presenting themselves as the only true church and dismissing the sacraments of the church as fraudulent attempts to squeeze money from parishioners. In place of the corrupt, official church, Lollard preachers traveled the countryside, bringing with them an English translation of the Bible (which Wyclif himself may have begun) and other vernacular religious literature, which they put directly into the hands of the laity.

Lollardy gained numerous adherents in the last two decades of the fourteenth century, including a group of noble supporters who may have helped fund the movement in its early days. But after the failure of a Lollard uprising in 1414, the movement lost its noble support and went underground. Lollards survived into the sixteenth century, in numbers sufficient to cause occasional alarm to church authorities. But Lollards were never more than a tiny minority movement, which stood in flat opposition to almost everything (including pilgrimages, the sacraments, and religious images) that their neighbors found most satisfying in late medieval religious life.

Wyclif's ideas struck much deeper roots in Bohemia, where they were adopted by Jan Hus (c. 1373–1415), a charismatic preacher at Charles University in Prague who had already been inveighing in well-attended sermons against "the world, the flesh, and the devil." In contrast to the Lollards, however, whose dismissal of the Eucharist cost them much support, Hus emphasized

Title page from the teachings of Jan Hus. An eloquent religous reformer, Jan Hus was burned at the stake in 1415 for heresy. He accused the Catholic church of being corrupt and demanded that the church reform the Eucharist.

the centrality of the Eucharist to Christian piety by demanding that the laity should receive not only the consecrated bread of the Mass but also the consecrated wine, which the late medieval church reserved solely for priests. This demand, known as Utraquism, gained broad popular support among the Bohemian laity and became a rallying symbol for the Hussite movement. Influential nobles also supported Hus, partly out of national pride but partly too in the hope that the reforms Hus demanded in the church might restore to them the revenues they had lost to the church over the previous century. Accordingly, most of Bohemia was behind him when Hus in 1415 agreed to travel to the Council of Constance to defend his views and try to convince the assembled prelates to undertake sweeping reforms of church life. The council had guaranteed Hus's safety, but this assurance was revoked as soon as he arrived there. Rather than being given a fair hearing, Hus was convicted of heresy and burned at the stake.

Hus's supporters in Bohemia quickly raised the banner of open revolt. Nobles took advantage of the situation to seize church lands, while priests, artisans, and peasants rallied together to pursue Hus's goals of religious reform and social justice. Between 1420 and 1424 armies of radical Hussites known as Taborites, lead by a brilliant blind general, Jan Zizka, resoundingly defeated several invading forces of crusading knights sent against them by the papacy. These victories increased the radicalism of the Taborites, inspiring them to heights of apocalyptic fervor. Finally, in 1434 more conservative, aristocratically dominated Hussites overcame the radicals and negotiated a settlement with the church that permitted Utraquism in the Bohemian church alongside Catholic orthodoxy. But Bohemia did not return fully to the Catholic fold until the seventeenth century.

Lollardy and Hussitism exhibit a number of striking similarities. Both began in the universities and then spread to the countryside. Both called for the clergy to live in simplicity and poverty, and both attracted noble support, especially in their early days. Both movements were also strongly nationalistic, employing their own vernacular languages (English and Czech) instead of Latin and identifying themselves with the English or Czech people in opposition to an international, and therefore foreign, official church. They also strongly emphasized the importance of vernacular preaching to the laity. In all these respects, they established patterns that would emerge again in the vastly larger currents of the Protestant Reformation.

Thought, Literature, and Art

What accounts for the remarkable creativity of late medieval cultural life?

The hardships of the later Middle Ages might have led intellectual and artistic life to stagnate, but in fact the period was an extremely creative one in thought, literature, and art. In this section we postpone treatment of certain developments most closely related to the early history of the Italian Renaissance but discuss some of the other important intellectual and artistic accomplishments of the fourteenth and fifteenth centuries.

THEOLOGY AND PHILOSPHY

During the twelfth and thirteenth centuries, scholastic thinkers like Saint Thomas Aquinas had constructed a picture of a rational, organized, and comprehensible natural world that was structured to lead the inquiring human mind to a knowledge of God and hence to salvation. After 1300, however, confidence in this picture began to ebb. Nominalist thinkers such as the English Franciscan William of Ockham (d. 1349) denied that human reason could prove fundamental theological truths such as the existence of God. Instead, they argued, human knowledge of God, and hence salvation, depended entirely on what God himself had chosen to reveal through scripture. Humans could investigate the natural world but only as a collection of individual entities and interactions. Categories (such as plants or chairs or rocks) were merely human inventions; strictly speaking, they did not exist. And any regularities that were observable in nature existed solely because an all-powerful God actively willed them to continue in this regular way. There was thus no necessary connection between the observable regularities of nature and the unknowable essence of divinity, and no hope of reasoning from the laws of nature to the nature of God. To argue otherwise—to suggest that God *had* to act in accordance with certain natural laws (such as gravity), and that these laws could therefore tell us something about God himself—was an affront to the absolute power and majesty of God.

Nominalism became enormously influential in late medieval universities and had an immense impact on European thought. Ockham's concern about what God might do led his followers to raise some of the seemingly absurd questions for which medieval theology has been mocked—for example, asking whether God can undo the past or whether an infinite number of pure spirits can simultaneously inhabit the same place (the nearest medieval thinkers actually came to asking how many angels can dance on the head of a pin). Nonetheless, the nominalists' insistence on God's omnipotence became one of the basic presuppositions of sixteenth-century Protestantism. The distinction they drew between the rational comprehensibility of the natural world and the incomprehensibility of God encouraged intellectuals to investigate the natural world without reference to supernatural explanations—one of the most important foundations of the modern scientific method. The nominalists' insistence that only individual entities, and not abstract categories, were real and could be studied also helped encourage empiricism: the belief, that is, that knowledge of the world should rest on sense experience rather than abstract reason. This too would be a fundamental building block in the emergence of a modern scientific worldview.

VERNACULAR LITERATURE

Like Ockham's philosophical work, the literature of the later Middle Ages was characterized by an intense concern to describe the world as it is. Such naturalism was not new. High medieval authors such as Wolfram von Eschenbach and Dante had already established the precedents on which their late medieval successors would build. But late medieval authors went much further, especially in describing the foibles and failings of everyday human life. They also pioneered the development of new literary forms for vernacular writing, sometimes in poetry but especially in prose. Most late medieval authors also continued to compose in Latin; but increasingly, the most innovative and ambitious literary work was being written in the vernacular languages of Europe. Behind this development lay three fundamental changes of the later Middle Ages: a growing identification between vernacular languages and nationalism, the continuing spread of lay education, and the emergence of a substantial reading public for vernacular literature. We can see these influences at work in three of the major vernacular authors of the later Middle Ages: Giovanni Boccaccio (1313–1375), Geoffrey Chaucer (c.1340–1400), and Christine de Pisan (c.1365–c.1435).

BOCCACCIO

Boccaccio (*bohk-KAHT-chee-oh*) would deserve an honored place in literary history even for his lesser works, which included courtly romances, pastoral lyrics, and learned treatises. His masterpiece, however, is the *Decameron*, a collection of 100 prose tales, mostly about love, sex, adventure, and trickery, told by a sophisticated party of seven young women and three men temporarily residing in a country villa outside Florence to escape the Black Death. Boccaccio borrowed the outlines of many of these tales from earlier sources, but he transformed them with his own characteristic exuberance and wit.

Boccaccio deliberately wrote in an unaffected, colloquial style, eschewing literary "elegance" to portray men and women exactly as they are. His women are not pallid playthings, distant goddesses, or steadfast virgins but flesh-and-blood creatures with minds and bodies, who interact with men more comfortably and naturally than any women in Western literature had ever done before. His clerics are all too human, much more like other men than they are like angels on earth. His treatment of sexual relations is often graphic, but never demeaning. For all these reasons the *Decameron* is a robust and delightful appreciation of what it means to be human.

CHAUCER

Similar in many ways to Boccaccio as a creator of naturalistic vernacular literature was the Englishman Geoffrey Chaucer (c. 1340–1400). Chaucer was the first major writer whose English can still be read today with relatively little effort. Remarkably, he was both a founder of England's mighty literary tradition and one of the four or five greatest contributors to it: most critics rank him just behind Shakespeare and in a class with Milton, Wordsworth, and Dickens.

Chaucer wrote several highly impressive works, but his masterpiece is unquestionably the *Canterbury Tales*. Like the *Decameron*, this is a collection of stories held together by a frame, in Chaucer's case the device of having a group of people tell stories while on a pilgrimage from London to Canterbury. But there are also differences between the *Decameron* and the *Canterbury Tales*. Chaucer's stories are told in sparkling verse instead of prose, and they are recounted by people of all different classes—from a chivalric knight to a dedicated university student to a thieving miller with a wart on his nose. Lively women also appear, most memorably the gap-toothed, oft-married Wife of Bath, who knows all "the remedies of love." Each character tells a story that is particularly illustrative of his or her own occupation and outlook on the world. By this device Chaucer was able to create a highly diverse human comedy. His range is greater than Boccaccio's; and although he is no less witty, frank, and lusty than the Italian, he is sometimes more profound.

CHRISTINE DE PISAN

The later Middle Ages saw the emergence of professional authors who made their living with their pens. Significantly, one of the first of these professional *litterati* was a woman, Christine de Pisan (c. 1364–c. 1431). Although born in Italy, Christine spent her adult life in France, where her husband was a member of the king's household. When he died, the widowed Christine turned to writing to support herself and her children. She wrote in a wide variety of literary genres, including treatises on chivalry and warfare that she dedicated to her patron, King Charles VI of France. But she also wrote for a larger and more popular audience. Her

Christine de Pisan. A leading writer of late medieval vernacular prose literature, Christine de Pisan (1365–c. 1430) was intent on upholding the dignity of women. She is shown here writing about a gigantic Amazon warrior who could defeat men effortlessly in armed combat.

imaginative tract *The City of Ladies* is an extended defense of the character, nature, and capacities of women against their male detractors, written in the form of an allegory. She also took part in a vigorous pamphlet literature that debated the misogynistic claims made against women in the *Romance of the Rose* (see Chapter Nine). This debate continued for several hundred years and became so famous that it was given a name: the *querelle des femmes*, "the debate over women." Christine was by no means the first female writer of the Middle Ages, but she was the first lay woman to earn a living by her writing.

SCULPTURE AND PAINTING

As naturalism was a dominant trait of late medieval literature, so it was of late medieval art. Already by the thirteenth century Gothic sculptors were paying far more attention than their Romanesque predecessors had to the way plants, animals, and human beings really looked. Whereas early medieval art had emphasized abstract design, the stress was now increasingly on realism: thirteenth-century carvings of leaves and flowers must have been made from direct observation and are clearly recognizable to modern botanists as distinct species. Statues of humans also gradually became more natural and realistic in their portrayals of facial expressions and bodily proportions. By around 1290 the concern for realism had become so great that a sculptor working on a tomb portrait of the German emperor Rudolf of Habsburg allegedly made a hurried return trip to view Rudolf in person, because he had heard that a new wrinkle had appeared on the emperor's face.

In the next two centuries the trend toward naturalism continued in sculpture and was extended to manuscript illumination and painting. The latter was in certain respects a new art. Wall paintings were common in the Middle Ages and long afterward, especially in the form of *frescoes*, paintings done on wet plaster. But in addition to frescoes, Italian artists in the thirteenth century also began painting pictures on pieces of wood or canvas. These were first done in tempera (pigments mixed with water and natural gums or egg whites), but around 1400 painting in oils was introduced in the European north. These new technical developments created new artistic opportunities. Artists were now

> Whereas early medieval art had emphasized abstract design, the stress was now increasingly on realism: thirteenth-century carvings of leaves and flowers must have been made from direct observation and are clearly recognizable to modern botanists as distinct species.

able to paint religious scenes on portable altarpieces. They also began painting strikingly sensitive and realistic portraits of their patrons on both wood and canvas.

The most innovative painter of the later Middle Ages was the Florentine Giotto (c. 1267–1337), who brought deep humanity to the religious images he painted on both walls and movable panels. Giotto was preeminently an imitator of nature. Not only do his human beings and animals look more lifelike than those of his predecessors but they seem to do more natural things. When Christ enters Jerusalem on Palm Sunday, boys climb trees to get a better view; when Saint Francis is laid out in death, one onlooker takes the opportunity to see whether the saint had really received Christ's wounds; and when the Virgin's parents, Joachim and Anna, meet after a long separation, they actually embrace and kiss—perhaps the first deeply tender kiss in Western art. Giotto was also the first to conceive of the painted space in fully three-dimensional terms: as one art historian has put it, Giotto's frescoes were the first to "knock a hole into the wall." After Giotto's death a reaction in Italian painting set in. Mid-fourteenth-century artists briefly moved away from naturalism and painted stern, forbidding religious figures who seemed to float in space. But by around 1400 artists came back down to earth and started to build on Giotto's influence in ways that led to the great Italian renaissance in painting.

In the north of Europe painting did not advance impressively beyond manuscript illumination until the early fifteenth century, but then it suddenly came very much into its own. The leading northern European painters were Flemish, first and foremost Jan van Eyck (c. 1380–1441), Roger van der Weyden (c. 1400–1464), and Hans Memling (c. 1430–1494). These three were the greatest early practitioners of painting in oil, a medium that allowed them to engage in brilliant coloring and sharp-focused realism. Van Eyck and van der Weyden excelled at communicating a sense of deep religious piety and portraying minute details of familiar everyday experience. These may at first seem incompatible, but it should be remembered that contemporary manuals of practical mysticism such as the *Imitation of Christ* also sought to link deep piety with everyday existence. Thus it was by no means blasphemous when a Flemish painter portrayed behind a tender Virgin and

The Meeting of Joachim and Anna, by Giotto. Notice how the haloes merge. This aged and infertile couple will soon miraculously have their only child: Mary, the mother of Jesus.

Child a vista of contemporary life with people going about their usual business and a man even urinating against a wall. This union of the sacred and the profane tended to fall apart in the work of Memling, who excelled in either straightforward religious pictures or secular portraits, but it would return in the work of the greatest painters of the Low Countries, Brueghel and Rembrandt.

Advances in Technology

> How did technological advances affect everyday life?

No account of enduring late medieval accomplishments would be complete without mention of certain epoch-making technological advances. Sadly, but probably not unexpectedly, treatment of this subject has to begin with reference to the invention of artillery and firearms. The prevalence of warfare stimulated the development of new weaponry. Gunpowder itself was a Chinese invention, but it was first put to devastating military uses in the late medieval West. Heavy cannons were first employed around 1330. The earliest cannons were so primitive that it often was more dangerous to stand behind than in front of them, but by the middle of the fifteenth century they were greatly improved and began to revolutionize the nature of warfare. In one year, 1453, heavy artillery played a leading role in determining the outcome of two crucial conflicts: the Ottoman Turks used German and Hungarian cannons to breach the defenses of Constantinople—hitherto the most impregnable in Europe—and the French used heavy artillery to take the city of Bordeaux, thereby ending the Hundred Years' War. Cannons thereafter made it difficult for rebellious aristocrats to hole up in their stone castles, and thus they aided in the consolidation of the national monarchies. Placed aboard ships, cannons also enabled European vessels to dominate foreign waters in the subsequent age of overseas expansion. Hand-held firearms, also invented in the fourteenth century, were gradually perfected. Shortly after 1500 the most effective new variety of gun, the musket, allowed foot soldiers to end

How did technological advances affect everyday life?

A Fifteenth-Century Siege with Cannon. By the mid fifteenth century, cannons were an essential element in siege warfare.

once and for all the earlier military dominance of heavily armored mounted knights. Once lance-bearing cavalries became outmoded and fighting could more easily be carried on by all, the monarchical states that could turn out the largest armies completely subdued internal resistance and dominated the battlefields of Europe.

Other late medieval technological developments were more life enhancing. Eyeglasses, first invented in the 1280s, were perfected in the fourteenth century. These allowed older people to keep on reading when farsightedness would otherwise have stopped them. The great fourteenth-century scholar Petrarch, who boasted excellent sight in his youth, wore spectacles after his sixtieth year and was thus able to complete some of his most important works. Around 1300 the use of the magnetic compass helped ships sail farther away from land and venture out into the Atlantic. One immediate result was the opening of direct sea commerce between Italy and the north. Subsequently, numerous improvements in shipbuilding, map making, and navigational devices enabled Europe to start expanding overseas. In the fourteenth century the Azores and Cape Verde Islands were reached; then, after a long pause caused by Europe's plagues and wars, the African Cape of Good Hope was rounded in 1488, the West Indies reached in 1492, India reached by the sea route in 1498, and Brazil sighted in 1500. Partly as a result of technology, the world was thus suddenly made much smaller.

Among the most familiar implements of our modern life that were invented by Europeans in the later Middle Ages were clocks and printed books. Mechanical clocks were invented shortly before 1300 and proliferated in the years immediately thereafter. The earliest clocks were too expensive for private purchase, but towns vied with each other to install the most elaborate clocks in their prominent public buildings. The new invention ultimately had two profound effects. One was the further stimulation of European interest in complex machinery of all sorts. This interest had already been awakened by the high medieval proliferation of mills, but clocks ultimately became even more omnipresent than mills because after about 1650 they became quite cheap and were brought into practically every European home. Household clocks served as models of marvelous machines. Equally if not more significant was the fact that clocks began to rationalize the course of European daily affairs.

> The earliest clocks were too expensive for private purchase, but towns vied with each other to install the most elaborate clocks in their prominent public buildings.

THE SPREAD OF PRINTING

Note how quickly the new technology of printing spread throughout Europe between 1470 and 1500. Where were printing presses most heavily concentrated? Why were there so relatively few printing presses in France, Spain, and England compared with the Low Countries, northern Italy, and Germany? Why were so many printing centers located in river ports?

CONCLUSION 413

Devil with Eyeglasses. As spectacles became more common in the later Middle Ages, they were even sported by devils in hell.

Until the advent of clocks in the later Middle Ages time was flexible. Men and women had only a rough idea of how late in the day it was and rose and retired more or less with the sun. In the fourteenth century, however, clocks first started relentlessly striking equal hours through the day and night. Thus they began to regulate work with new precision. People were expected to start and end work "on time" and many came to believe that "time is money." This emphasis on timekeeping brought new efficiencies but also new tensions: Lewis Carroll's white rabbit, who is always looking at his pocket watch and muttering "how late it's getting," is a telling caricature of time-obsessed Western humanity.

The invention of printing with movable type was equally momentous. The major stimulus for this invention was the replacement of parchment by paper as Europe's primary writing material between 1200 and 1400. Parchment, made from the skins of sheep or calves, was extremely expensive: since it was possible to get about only four good parchment leaves from one animal, it was necessary to slaughter between 200 and 300 sheep or calves to gain enough parchment for a Bible! Paper, made from rags turned into pulp by mills, brought prices down dramatically. Late medieval records show that paper sold at one sixth the price of parchment. Accordingly, it became cheaper to learn how to read and write. With literacy becoming ever more widespread, there was a growing market for still cheaper books, and the invention of printing with movable type around 1450, associated most famously with the Bible produced by Johann Gutenberg in 1454, fully met this demand. By greatly saving labor, the invention made printed books about one fifth as expensive as handwritten ones within about two decades.

As soon as books became easily accessible, literacy increased even more, and book culture became a basic part of the European way of life. After about 1500, Europeans could afford to read and buy books of all sorts—not just religious tracts but instructional manuals, light entertainment, and, by the eighteenth century, newspapers. Printing ensured that ideas would spread quickly and reliably; moreover, revolutionary ideas could no longer be easily extinguished once they were set down in hundreds of copies of books. Thus the greatest religious reformer of the sixteenth century, Martin Luther, gained an immediate following throughout Germany by employing the printing press to run off pamphlets: had printing not been available to him, Luther might have died as Hus did. The spread of books also helped stimulate the growth of cultural nationalism. Before printing, regional dialects in most European countries were often so diverse that people who supposedly spoke the same language often could barely understand each other. After the invention of printing, however, each European country began to develop its own linguistic standards, which were disseminated uniformly by books. The "king's English" was what was printed in London and carried to Yorkshire or Wales. Thus communications were enhanced and governments were able to operate ever more efficiently.

CONCLUSION

Despite economic dislocation and demographic collapse, the later Middle Ages were one of the most creative and inventive periods in the history of western Europe. Why this was so will always remain something of a mystery, until and unless future scholars should unlock the secrets of human creativity itself. What we can see behind the artistic, philosophical, literary, and

CHAPTER 10

THE LATER MIDDLE AGES, 1300–1500

technological developments of the period, however, is a consistent drive to understand, control, and replicate the workings of the natural world. This fact may offer some clues toward explaining the sources of these developments.

Perhaps most fundamentally, in the later Middle Ages intellectuals broke with the traditional, Neoplatonic vision of nature as a book in which one could read the mind of God. Instead, they came to see the natural world as operating according to its own laws, which were empirically verifiable but which could tell human beings nothing about the God who lay behind them. The resulting sense of the contingency and independence of the natural world was an essential step toward the emergence of a scientific worldview. It also encouraged Europeans to believe that nature itself could be manipulated and directed toward human ends.

Powerful economic and political factors also encouraged the technological inventiveness of the period. Despite the disruptive impact of plague and war, the market for goods was not destroyed. Instead, the resulting labor shortages encouraged European entrepreneurs to experiment with labor-saving technologies and new crops. Incessant warfare encouraged a remarkable burst of military inventiveness. It also enabled more powerful governments to extract a larger percentage of their subjects' wealth through taxation, which they proceeded to invest in ships, cannons, muskets, and

the standing armies that the new weaponry made possible. Increasing per capita wealth produced the capital necessary to invest in mills, factories, clocks, books, and compasses. It also made possible a remarkable increase in the educational level of the European population. Between 1300 and 1500 hundreds and perhaps thousands of new grammar schools were established, and scores of new universities emerged, because parents saw such schools as a reliable route to social advancement for their sons. Women were still excluded from the schools, but increasing numbers of girls were being taught at home, making women an extremely important (perhaps even the dominant) part of the reading public that was emerging in later medieval Europe.

Finally, it may be that dislocation itself promotes innovation, so long as it does not destroy people's confidence in the ultimate improvability of their lives. Europeans suffered enormously from war, plague, and economic crises during the later Middle Ages. But those who survived seized the opportunities their new world presented to them. The confidence they had developed in the High Middle Ages was not destroyed by the travails of the later Middle Ages. By 1500, most Europeans lived more secure lives than their ancestors had 200 years before; and they stood on the verge of an extraordinary new period of expansion and conquest that would take European armies, merchants, and settlers around the globe.

KEY TERMS

Black Death	Master Eckhart	Ivan the Great	William of Ockham
Jacquerie	Hundred Years' War	Boccaccio	
Richard II	Joan of Arc	*Canterbury Tales*	
Avignon	Wars of the Roses	Christine de Pisan	

SELECTED READINGS

Allmand, Christopher T. *The Hundred Years' War: England and France at War, c. 1300–c. 1450.* Cambridge and New York, 1988. Still the best analytic account of the war; after a short narrative, the book is organized topically.

Allmand, Christopher T., ed. *Society at War: The Experience of England and France During the Hundred Years' War.* Edinburgh, 1973. An outstanding collection of documents.

Boccaccio, Giovanni. *The Decameron.* Trans. Mark Musa and P. E. Bondanella. New York, 1977.

Chaucer, Geoffrey. *The Canterbury Tales.* Trans. Nevill Coghill. New York, 1951. A modern English verse translation, lightly annotated.

Cohn, Samuel K., Jr. *Lust for Liberty: The Politics of Social Revolt in Medieval Europe, 1200–1425. Italy, France, and Flanders.* Cambridge, Mass., 2006. An important new account.

Cole, Bruce. *Giotto and Florentine Painting, 1280–1375.* New York, 1976. A clear and stimulating introduction.

Crummey, Robert O. *The Formation of Muscovy, 1304–1613.* New York, 1987. The standard account.

Dobson, R. Barrie. *The Peasants' Revolt of 1381*, 2d ed. London, 1983. A comprehensive source collection, with excellent introductions to the documents and an illuminating discussion of the revolt.

Duffy, Eamon. *The Stripping of the Altars: Traditional Religion in England, 1400–1580*. New Haven, Conn., 1992. The fullest study anywhere of the patterns of fifteenth-century piety at the parish level.

Dyer, Christopher. *Standards of Living in the Later Middle Ages: Social Change in England, c. 1200–1520*. Cambridge and New York, 1989. Detailed but highly rewarding.

Froissart, Jean. *Chronicles*. Trans. Geoffrey Brereton. Baltimore, Md., 1968. A selection from the most famous contemporary account of the Hundred Years' War to about 1400.

Horrox, Rosemary, ed. *The Black Death*. New York, 1994. A fine collection of documents reflecting the impact of the Black Death, especially in England.

Huizinga, Johan. *The Waning of the Middle Ages: A Study of the Forms of Life, Thought, and Art in France and the Netherlands in the Dawn of the Renaissance*, New York, 1924. A classic picture of the "expiring" Middle Ages; a book from whose influence historians are still struggling to escape. Frequently republished, the most recent translation of this work is titled *The Autumn of the Middle Ages*. Trans. Rodney J. Payton and Ulrich Mammitzsch. Chicago, 1996.

John Hus at the Council of Constance. Trans. M. Spinka, New York, 1965. The translation of a Czech chronicle with an expert introduction and appended documents.

Jordan, William Chester. *The Great Famine: Northern Europe in the Early Fourteenth Century*. Princeton, N.J., 1996. An outstanding social and economic study of the disastrous famines that swept northern Europe between 1315 and 1322.

Keen, Maurice, ed. *Medieval Warfare: A History*. Oxford and New York, 1999. The most attractive introduction to this crucially important subject. Lively and well illustrated.

Kempe, Margery. *The Book of Margery Kempe*. Trans. Barry Windeatt. New York, 1985. A fascinating autobiography by an early fifteenth-century Englishwoman who hoped she might be a saint.

Lerner, Robert E. *The Heresy of the Free Spirit in the Later Middle Ages*, 2d ed. Notre Dame, Ind., 1991. A revealing study of a heretical movement that terrified contemporaries, yet hardly existed at all.

Lewis, Peter S. *Later Medieval France: The Polity*. London, 1968. Still fresh and suggestive after forty years. A masterwork.

Memoirs of a Renaissance Pope: The Commentaries of Pius II. Abridged ed. Trans. F. A. Gragg, New York, 1959. Remarkable insights into the mind of a particularly well-educated mid-fifteenth-century pope.

Nicholas, David. *The Transformation of Europe, 1300–1600*. Oxford and New York, 1999. The best textbook presently available.

Oakley, Francis C. *The Western Church in the Later Middle Ages*. Ithaca, N.Y., 1979. The best book by far on the history of conciliarism, the late medieval papacy, Hussitism, and the efforts at institutional reform during this period. On popular piety, see Swanson.

Pernoud, Régine, ed. *Joan of Arc, by Herself and Her Witnesses*. New York, 1966. A collection of contemporary writings about Joan, including the transcripts of her trial.

Shirley, Janet, trans. *A Parisian Journal, 1405–1449*. Oxford, 1968. A marvelous panorama of Parisian life recorded by an eyewitness.

Swanson, R. N. *Religion and Devotion in Europe, c. 1215–c. 1515*. Cambridge and New York, 1995. An excellent study of late medieval popular piety; an excellent complement to Oakley.

Sumption, Jonathan. *The Hundred Years' War*. Vol. 1: *Trial by Battle*. Vol. 2: *Trial by Fire*. Philadelphia, 1999. The first two volumes of a massive narrative history of the war take the story up to 1369.

Vaughan, Richard. *Valois Burgundy*. London, 1975. A summation of the author's four-volume study of the Burgundian dukes.

Ziegler, Philip. *The Black Death*. New York, 1969. A popular account, but reliable and engrossing.

Chapter Eleven

Chapter Contents

The Mongols 418

The Rise of the Ottoman Empire 422

Mediterranean Colonialism 427

Europe Encounters a New World 434

Conclusion 438

Commerce, Conquest, and Colonization, 1300–1600

BY 1300, THE GREAT EUROPEAN expansion of the High Middle Ages was coming to an end. In Iberia, there would be no further conquests of Muslim territory until 1492, when Granada fell to King Ferdinand and Queen Isabella. In the East, the Crusader kingdoms of Constantinople and Acre collapsed, in 1261 and 1291 respectively. Only the German drive into eastern Europe continued; but by the mid-fourteenth century, it too had been slowed by the rise of a new Baltic state in Lithuania. Internal expansion was also ending, as Europe reached the ecological limits of its resources. Thereafter, the pressure on resources was eased only by the dramatic population losses that resulted during the fourteenth century from the combined effects of famine, plague, and war.

But despite these checks, Europeans in the late Middle Ages did not turn inward. Although land-based conquests slowed, new sea-based empires emerged in the Mediterranean world during the fourteenth and fifteenth centuries, with colonies that extended from the Black Sea to the Canary Islands. New maritime trade routes were opened up through the Strait of Gibraltar, resulting in greater economic integration between the Mediterranean and Atlantic economies and increasing the demand in northwestern Europe for Asian spices and African gold. By the late fifteenth century, Mediterranean mariners and colonists had extended their domination out into the Atlantic, from the Azores in the north to the Canary Islands in the south. Portuguese navigators were also pushing down the west coast of Africa. In 1498 one such expedition would sail all the way around the Cape of Good Hope to India.

The fifteenth-century conquest of the "Atlantic Mediterranean" was the essential preliminary to the dramatic events that began in 1492 with Columbus's attempt to reach China by sailing westward across the Atlantic Ocean and that led, by 1600, to the Spanish and Portuguese conquests of the Americas. Because these events are so familiar, we can easily underestimate their importance. For the native peoples and empires of the Americas, the results of European contact were cataclysmic. By 1600, somewhere between 50 and 90 percent of the indigenous peoples of the

FOCUS QUESTIONS

- What impact did the Mongol conquests have on Europe?
- Why were slaves so important to Ottoman society?

- How were the Portuguese able to control Indian Ocean trade?
- What was the impact of New World silver on the European economy?

Americas had perished from disease, massacre, and enslavement. For Europeans, the results of their conquests were less lethal but no less far reaching. By 1300, Europe had eclipsed both Byzantium and the lands of Islam as a Mediterranean power, but outside the Mediterranean and the north Atlantic European power was negligible. By 1600, however, Europe had emerged as the first truly global power in world history, capable of pursuing its imperial ambitions and commercial interests wherever its ships could sail and its guns could reach. Europeans would not achieve full control over the interiors of the African, Asian, and American land masses until the end of the nineteenth century, and their control would last thereafter for less than a century. By 1600, however, European navies ruled the seas, and the world's resources were increasingly being channeled through European hands—patterns that have continued until the present day.

THE MONGOLS

What impact did the Mongol conquests have on Europe?

Trade between the Mediterranean world and the Far East dated back to antiquity, but it was not until the late thirteenth century that Europeans began to establish direct trading connections with India, China, and the Spice Islands of the Indonesian archipelago. For Europeans, these connections would prove profoundly important, although less for their economic significance than for their impact on the European imagination. For the peoples of Asia, however, the appearance of European traders on the Silk Road between Central Asia and China was merely a curiosity. The really consequential event was the rise of the Mongol Empire that made such connections possible.

THE RISE OF THE MONGOL EMPIRE

The Mongols were one of a number of nomadic peoples inhabiting the steppes of Central Asia. Although closely connected with various Turkish-speaking peoples with whom they frequently intermarried, the Mongols spoke their own distinctive language and had their own homeland to the north of the Gobi Desert in present-day Mongolia. Sheep provided them with shelter (in the form of wool tents), clothing, milk, and meat.

Like many nomadic peoples throughout history, the Mongols were highly accomplished cavalry soldiers who supplemented their own pastoralism and craft production by raiding the sedentary peoples to their south. (It was in part to control such raiding from Mongolia that, many centuries before, the Chinese had built the famous Great Wall.) Primarily, however, China defended itself by attempting to ensure that the Mongols remained internally divided and so turned their martial energies most often against each other.

In the late twelfth century, however, a Mongol chief named Temüjin began to unite the various Mongol tribes under his rule. By incorporating the army of each defeated tribe into his own army, Temüjin quickly built up a large military force. In 1206, his supremacy was formally acknowledged by all the Mongols, and he took the title Chingiz (Genghis) Khan—"the oceanic [possibly meaning "universal"] ruler." Chingiz now turned his enormous army against his non-Mongol neighbors. China at this time was divided into three hostile states. In 1209, Chingiz launched an attack on northwestern China; in 1211 he invaded the Chin Empire in north China. At first these attacks were probably looting expeditions rather than deliberate attempts at conquest, but by the 1230s a full-scale Mongol conquest of northern and western China was under way, culminating in 1234 with the fall of the Chin. In 1279, Chingiz's grandson Qubilai (Kublai) Khan completed the conquest of southern (Sung) China, thus reuniting China for the first time in centuries.

Meanwhile, Chingiz turned his forces westward, conquering much of Central Asia and incorporating the important commercial cities of Tashkent, Samarkand, and Bukhara into his expanding empire. When Chingiz died in 1227, he was succeeded by his third son Ögedei (*EHRG-uh-day*), who completed the conquest of the Chin, conquered the lands between the Oxus River and the Caspian Sea and then laid plans for a massive inva-

CHRONOLOGY

RISE OF THE MONGOL EMPIRE, 1206–1260

Temujin crowned as Chingiz Khan	1206
Mongols conquer northern China	1234
Mongols conquer southern Russia	1237–1240
Mongol forces withdraw from Europe	1241
Mamluk sultanate halts Mongol advance in Egypt	1260

What impact did the Mongol conquests have on Europe?

sion toward the west. Between 1237 and 1240, the Mongol horde (so called from the Turkish word *ordu*, meaning "tent" or "encampment") conquered southern Russia and then launched a two-pronged assault farther west. The smaller of the two Mongol armies swept through Poland toward eastern Germany; the larger army went southwest toward Hungary. In April 1241 the smaller Mongol force met a hastily assembled army of Germans and Poles at the battle of Liegnitz, where the two sides fought to a bloody standstill. Two days later, the larger Mongol army annihilated the Hungarian army at the River Sajo.

How much farther west the Mongol armies might have pushed will forever remain in doubt, for in December 1241 the Great Khan Ögedei died, and the Mongol forces withdrew from eastern Europe. It took five years before a new great khan could establish himself, and when he died in 1248, the resulting interregnum lasted

The Mongol Successor States

Consider the breakup of Chingiz Khan's empire after 1259 and the passing similarities its fracture might possess to the disintegration of Alexander's empire, also conquered swiftly and encompassing vast swaths of Europe and Asia. Why did Chingiz Khan's empire splinter? How did the Mongol onslaught against and occupation of major sections of the Arab Muslim world possibly aid the expansion of European civilization and trade into the Mediterranean? At the same time, how did it complicate the situation for the crusader efforts in the Holy Land?

The Head of Timur the Lame. A forensic reconstruction based on his exhumed skull.

for three more years. Mongol conquests continued in Persia, the Middle East, and China; but after 1241 the Mongols never resumed their attacks on Europe. By 1300, the period of Mongol expansion had come to an end.

But the Mongol threat did not suddenly disappear. Descendants of Chingiz Khan continued to rule this enormous land empire (the largest such empire in the history of the world) until the mid-fourteenth century. Later, under the leadership of Timur the Lame (known as Tamerlane to Europeans) it looked briefly as if the Mongol Empire might be reunited. But Timur died in 1405 on his way to invade China; thereafter the various parts of the Mongol Empire fell into the hands of local rulers, including (in Asia Minor) the Ottoman Turks. Mongol cultural influence continued, however, and can be seen in the enormously impressive artwork produced during the fifteenth and sixteenth centuries in Persia and in Mughal India.

The Mongols owed their success to the size, speed, and training of their mounted armies; to the intimidating savagery with which they butchered those who resisted them; and to their ability to adapt the administrative traditions of their subjects to their own purposes. Partly because the Mongols themselves put little store even in their own shamanistic religious traditions, they were also unusually tolerant of the religious beliefs of others—a distinct advantage in controlling an empire that comprised a dizzying array of Buddhist, Christian, and Muslim sects. However, little was distinctively "Mongol" about the way they governed their empire. Except in China, where the Mongol Yuan Dynasty inherited and maintained a complex administrative bureaucracy, the Mongols' rule was relatively unsophisticated, being chiefly directed at securing the steady payment of tribute from their subjects.

EUROPE, THE MONGOLS, AND THE FAR EAST

The Mongols had a keen eye for the commercial advantages their empire could offer them. They took steps to control the caravan routes that led from China through Central Asia to the Black Sea. They also encouraged commercial contacts with European traders, especially through the Iranian city of Tabriz, from which both land and sea routes led on to China. Until the Mongol conquests, the Silk Road to China had been closed to Western merchants and travelers. But almost as soon as the Mongol Empire was established, we find Europeans venturing on these routes. The first such travelers were Franciscan missionaries such as William de Rubruck, sent by King Louis IX of France in 1253 as his ambassador to the Mongol court. But Western merchants quickly followed. The most famous of these early merchants were three Venetians: Niccolo, Maffeo, and Marco Polo. Marco Polo's account of his twenty-year sojourn in China in the service of Qubilai Khan and of his journey home through the Spice Islands, India, and Iran, is one of the most famous travel accounts of all time. Its effect on the imagination of his contemporaries was enormous. For the next two centuries, most of what Europeans knew about the Far East they learned from Marco Polo's *Travels*. Christopher Columbus's copy of this book still survives.

European connections with the western end of the Silk Road would continue until the mid-fourteenth century. The Genoese were especially active in this trade, not least because their rivals, the Venetians, already dominated the Mediterranean trade with Alexandria

MARCO POLO'S DESCRIPTION OF JAVA

The Venetian merchants Niccolo and Maffeo Polo traveled overland from Constantinople to the court of Qubilai Khan between 1260 and 1269. When they returned a few years later, they brought with them Niccolo's son Marco. A gifted linguist, Marco would remain at the Mongol court until the early 1290s, when he returned to Europe after a journey through Southeast Asia, the Spice Islands, and the Indian Ocean. Marco's account of his travels would shape European images of the Far East for centuries.

Departing from Ziamba, and steering between south and south-east, fifteen hundred miles, you reach an island of very great size, named Java. According to the reports of some well-informed navigators, it is the greatest in the world, and has a compass above three thousand miles. It is under the dominion of one king only, nor do the inhabitants pay tribute to any other power. They are worshipers of idols.

The country abounds with rich commodities. Pepper, nutmegs, spikenard, galangal, cubebs, cloves and all the other valuable spices and drugs, are the produce of the island; which occasion it to be visited by many ships laden with merchandise, that yields to the owners considerable profit.

The quantity of gold collected there exceeds all calculation and belief. From thence it is that . . . merchants . . . have imported, and to this day import, that metal to a great amount, and from thence also is obtained the greatest part of the spices that are distributed throughout the world. That the Great Khan [Qubilai] has not brought the island under subjection to him, must be attributed to the length of the voyage and the dangers of the navigation.

The Travels of Marco Polo, rev. and ed. Manuel Komroff (New York, 1926), pp. 267–268.

QUESTIONS FOR ANALYSIS

1. What effect did Marco Polo's *Travels* have on European images of the Far East?
2. Why did Marco Polo refer to various spices as "rich commodities"? Why were spices so highly valued by Europeans?

and Beirut, through which the bulk of Europe's Far Eastern luxury goods continued to pass. But the Mongols of Iran become progressively more hostile to Westerners as the fourteenth century progressed. By 1344, the Genoese had abandoned Tabriz after attacks on Westerners had made their position there untenable. In 1346, the Mongols of the Golden Horde besieged the Genoese colony at Caffa on the Black Sea. Apart from crippling Genoese commerce in the Black Sea, this siege is memorable chiefly because during it the Black Death was passed from the Mongol army (which had inadvertently brought it from the Gobi Desert, where the disease was endemic) to the Genoese defenders, who returned with it to western Europe, where it proceeded to kill at least one third of the entire European population.

The window of opportunity that made Marco Polo's travels possible was thus relatively short. By the middle of the fourteenth century, hostilities between the various parts of the Mongol Empire were already making travel along the Silk Road perilous. After 1368, when the Mongol (Yuan) Dynasty was overthrown, Westerners were excluded from China altogether, and Mongols were restricted to cavalry service in the Ming imperial armies. The overland trade routes from China to the Black Sea continued to operate; Europeans, however, were no longer able to travel along them. But the new, more integrated commercial world the Mongols created had a lasting impact on Europe, despite the relatively short time during which Europeans themselves were able to participate directly in it. European memories of the Far East would be preserved, and the dream of reestablishing direct connections between Europe and China would survive to influence a new round of European commercial and imperial expansion from the late fifteenth century onward.

THE RISE OF THE OTTOMAN EMPIRE

Why were slaves so important to Ottoman society?

Like the Mongols, the Ottoman Turks were initially a nomadic people whose economy continued to depend on raiding even after they had conquered an extensive empire. The peoples who would become the Ottomans were already established in northwestern Anatolia when the Mongols arrived and were already at least nominally Muslims. But unlike the established Muslim powers in the region, whom the Mongols destroyed, the Ottoman Turks were among the principal beneficiaries of the Mongol conquest. By toppling the Seljuk sultanate and the Abbasid caliphate of Baghdad, the Mongols eliminated the two traditional authorities that had previously kept Turkish border chieftains like the Ottomans in check. Now the Ottomans were free to raid along their soft frontiers with Byzantium unhindered. At the same time, however, they remained far enough away from the centers of Mongol authority to avoid being destroyed themselves.

> By toppling the Seljuk sultanate and the Abbasid caliphate of Baghdad, the Mongols eliminated the two traditional authorities that had previously kept Turkish border chieftains like the Ottomans in check.

THE CONQUEST OF CONSTANTINOPLE

By the end of the thirteenth century, the Ottoman Dynasty had established itself as the leading family among the Anatolian border lords. By the mid-fourteenth century, it had solidified its preeminence by capturing a number of important cities. These successes brought the Ottomans to the attention of the Byzantine emperor, who in 1345 hired a contingent of Ottomans as mercenaries. Thus introduced into Europe, the Ottomans quickly made themselves at home. By 1370, they had extended their control all the way to the Danube. In 1389 Ottoman forces defeated the powerful Serbian Empire at the battle of Kosovo, enabling them to consolidate their control over Greece, Bulgaria, and the Balkans.

In 1396 the Ottomans attacked Constantinople, but withdrew to repel a Western crusading force that had been sent against them. In 1402, they attacked Constantinople again, but once more were forced to withdraw, this time to confront a Mongolian invasion of Anatolia. Led by Timur the Lame, the Mongol army captured the Ottoman sultan and destroyed his army; for the next decade it appeared that Ottoman hegemony over Anatolia might be gone forever. By 1413, however, Timur was dead, a new sultan had emerged, and the Ottomans were able to resume their conquests. Ottoman pressure on Constantinople continued during the 1420s and 1430s, producing a steady stream of Byzantine refugees who brought with them to Italy the surviving masterworks of classical Greek literature. But it was not until 1451 that a new sultan, Mehmet II, turned his full attention to the conquest of the imperial city. In 1453, after a brilliantly executed siege, Mehmet succeeded in breaching the city's walls. The Byzantine emperor was killed in the assault, the city itself was thoroughly plundered, and its population was sold into slavery. The Ottomans then settled down to rule their new capital in a style reminiscent of their Byzantine predecessors.

The Ottoman conquest of Constantinople was an enormous psychological shock to Christian Europe, but its economic impact on western Europe was minor. Ottoman control over the former Byzantine Empire did reduce European access to the Black Sea, but the bulk of the Far Eastern luxury trade with Europe had never passed through the Black Sea ports in the first place. Europeans got most of their spices and silks through Venice, which imported them from Alexandria and Beirut. These two cities did not fall to the Ottomans until the 1520s. In no sense, therefore, can the Ottomans be seen as the spur that propelled Portuguese efforts during the late fifteenth century to establish a direct sea route between Europe, India, and the Spice Islands. If anything, the opposite is the case. After the Portuguese established a direct sea route between Europe and India, it was their attempts to exclude Muslims from the Indian Ocean spice trade that helped spur the Ottoman conquests of Syria, Egypt, and Hungary during the 1520s and 1530s. To be sure, these Ottoman conquests had other motives also, including the desire to control the Egyptian grain trade. But by eliminating the merchants who had traditionally dominated the overland spice trade through Beirut and Alexandria, the Ottomans also hoped to redirect this trade through Constantinople, and then up the Danube into western Europe.

The effects of the Ottoman conquest of Constantinople on western Europe were modest. On the Ottomans themselves, however, their conquest was transformative. Vast new wealth poured into Ottoman society, which the Ottomans increased by carefully tending to the industrial and commercial interests of their new capital city. Trade routes were redirected to feed the capital, and the Ottomans became a naval power in the eastern Mediterranean and the Black Sea. As a result, Constantinople's population grew from less than 100,000 in 1453 to more than 500,000 in 1600, making it the largest city in the world outside China.

WAR, SLAVERY, AND SOCIAL ADVANCEMENT

Despite the Ottomans' careful attention to commerce, their empire rested on raiding and conquest. Until the end of the sixteenth century, the Ottoman Empire was therefore on an almost constant war footing. To continue its conquests, the size of the Ottoman army and administration grew exponentially. But this growth drew more and more manpower from the empire. Because the Ottoman army and administration were largely composed of slaves, the demand for more soldiers and administrators could best be met through further conquests that would capture yet more slaves. Further conquests, however, required a still larger army and an even more extensive bureaucracy; and so the cycle continued.

Sultan Mehmet II, "The Conqueror" (1451–1481), by Ottoman Artist Siblizade Ahmed. The sultan's pose and handkerchief are Central Asian conventions in portraiture, but the subdued color and three-quarter profile show the influence of Italian Renaissance portraits. The sultan wears the white turban of a scholar but also wears the thumb ring of an archer, neatly reflecting his combination of scholarly and military attainments.

CHRONOLOGY

RISE OF THE OTTOMAN EMPIRE, 1300–1571

Ottomans become leading Anatolian family	1300
Byzantine emperor hires Ottoman mercenaries	1345
Ottomans enter Europe	1350s
Ottomans defeat Serbian empire	1389
Ottomans conquer Constantinople	1453
Ottomans conquer Syria, Egypt, Hungary	1520s
Battle of Lepanto	1571

Slaves were the backbone of the Ottoman army and administration, as they had been in Mamluk Egypt. But slaves were also critical to the lives of the Ottoman upper class. One of the important measures of status in Ottoman society was the number of slaves in one's household. After 1453, new wealth permitted some Ottoman notables to maintain households in which thousands of slaves attended to their masters' whims. In the sixteenth century, the sultan's household alone numbered more than 20,000 slave attendants, not including his bodyguard and his elite infantry units, both of which were also composed of slaves.

The result was an almost insatiable demand for slaves, especially in Constantinople itself. Many of these slaves were captured in war. Many others were taken from Poland and Ukraine in raids by Crimean slave merchants, who then shipped their captives to the slave markets of Constantinople. But slaves were also recruited (some willingly, some by coercion) from rural areas of the Ottoman Empire itself. Because the vast majority of Ottoman slaves were household servants and administrators rather than laborers, some people willingly accepted enslavement, believing that they would be better off as slaves in Constantinople than as impoverished peasants in the countryside. In the Balkans especially, many people were enslaved as children, handed over by their families to pay the infamous child tax the Ottomans imposed on rural areas too poor to pay a monetary tribute. Although unquestionably a wrenching experience for families, this practice did open up opportunities for social advancement. Special academies were created at Constantinople to train the most able of these enslaved children to act as administrators and soldiers, and some rose to become powerful figures in the Ottoman Empire. Slavery therefore carried relatively little social stigma. Even the sultan himself was most often the son of an enslaved woman.

Because Muslims were not permitted to enslave other Muslims, the vast majority of Ottoman slaves were from Christian families (although many converted to Islam later in life). But because so many of the elite positions within Ottoman government were held by slaves, the paradoxical result of this reliance on slave administrators was that Muslims, including Turks, were effectively excluded from the main avenues of social and political advancement in Ottoman society. Nor was Ottoman society characterized by a powerful hereditary nobility of the sort that dominated contemporary European society. As a result, power in the fifteenth- and sixteenth-century Ottoman Empire was remarkably, perhaps even uniquely, open to men of ability and talent, provided that such men were slaves and therefore not Muslims by birth. Nor was this pattern of Muslim exclusion limited to government and the army. Commerce and business also remained largely in the hands of non-Muslims, most frequently Greeks, Syrians, and Jews. Jews in particular found in the Ottoman Empire a welcome refuge from the persecutions and expulsions that had characterized Jewish life in late medieval Europe. After their 1492 expulsion from Spain, more than 100,000 Spanish (Sephardic) Jews ultimately immigrated into the Ottoman Empire.

Ottoman Orthodoxy. This Ottoman genealogical chart shows the descent of Sultan Mehmet III (1595–1603) from the Prophet Muhammad (shown veiled).

OTTOMAN JANISSARIES

The following account is from a memoir written by a Christian Serb who was captured as a youth by Sultan Mehmet II the Conqueror, converted to Islam, and then served eight years in the Ottoman janissary corps. In 1463, however, the fortress he was defending for the Sultan was captured by the Hungarians, and the author thereupon returned to Christianity.

Whenever the Turks invade foreign lands and capture their people an imperial scribe follows immediately behind them, and whatever boys there are, he takes them all into the Janissaries and gives five gold pieces for each one and sends them across the sea [to Anatolia]. There are about two thousand of these boys. If, however, the number of them from enemy peoples does not suffice, then he takes from the Christians in every village in his land who have boys, having established what is the most every village can give so that the quota will always be full. And the boys whom he takes in his own land are called *cilik*. Each one of them can leave his property to whomever he wants after his death. And those whom he takes among the enemies are called *pendik*. These latter after their deaths can leave nothing; rather, it goes to the emperor, except that if someone comports himself well and is so deserving that he be freed, he may leave it to whomever he wants. And on the boys who are across the sea the emperor spends nothing; rather, those to whom they are entrusted must maintain them and send them where he orders. Then they take those who are suited for it on ships and there they study and train to skirmish in battle. There the emperor already provides for them and gives them a wage. From there he chooses for his own court those who are trained and then raises their wages.

Konstantin Mihailovic, *Memoirs of a Janissary* (Michigan Slavic Translations 3), trans. Benjamin Stolz (Ann Arbor, Mich., 1975), pp. 157–159.

QUESTIONS FOR ANALYSIS

1. What role did the janissary corps play in the Ottoman Empire?
2. Were the Ottoman incursions into the West a serious threat to the European balance of power?

Religious Conflicts

The Ottoman sultans were relentlessly orthodox Sunni Muslims, who lent staunch support to the religious and legal pronouncements of the Islamic scholarly schools. In 1516, the Ottomans captured the cities of Medina and Mecca, thus becoming the defenders of the holy sites. Soon after, they captured Jerusalem and Cairo, putting an end to the Mamluk sultanate of Egypt. In 1538 the Ottoman ruler formally adopted the title of caliph, thereby declaring himself to be the legitimate successor of the Prophet Muhammad.

In keeping with Sunni traditions, the Ottomans were also religiously tolerant toward non-Muslims, especially during the fifteenth and sixteenth centuries. They organized the major religious groups of their empire into legally recognized units known as *millets*, permitting them considerable rights of religious self-government. After

11 COMMERCE, CONQUEST, AND COLONIZATION, 1300–1600

1453, however, the Ottomans were particularly careful to protect and promote the authority of the Greek Orthodox patriarch of Constantinople over the Orthodox Christians of their empire. As a result, the Ottomans enjoyed staunch support from their Orthodox Christian subjects during their sixteenth-century wars with the Latin Christians of western Europe. Despite the religious diversity of their empire, the Ottomans' principal religious conflicts were therefore not with their own subjects, but with the Shi'ite Muslim Dynasty that ruled neighboring Persia. Time and again during the sixteenth century, Ottoman expeditions against western Europe had to be abandoned when hostilities erupted with the Persians.

THE OTTOMANS AND EUROPE

During the sixteenth century, the Habsburg rulers of Spain, Germany, and Austria were similarly distracted by their own conflicts with the Catholic kings of France (with whom the Ottomans made an alliance) and with the Protestant princes of Germany, the Netherlands, and England. As a result, the contest between the Ottoman Empire and the Western powers never really lived up to the rhetoric of holy war that both sides employed in their propaganda. In 1396, a Western crusader army was annihilated by the Ottomans at the battle of Nicopolis. In the sixteenth and seventeenth centuries, Ottoman armies several times

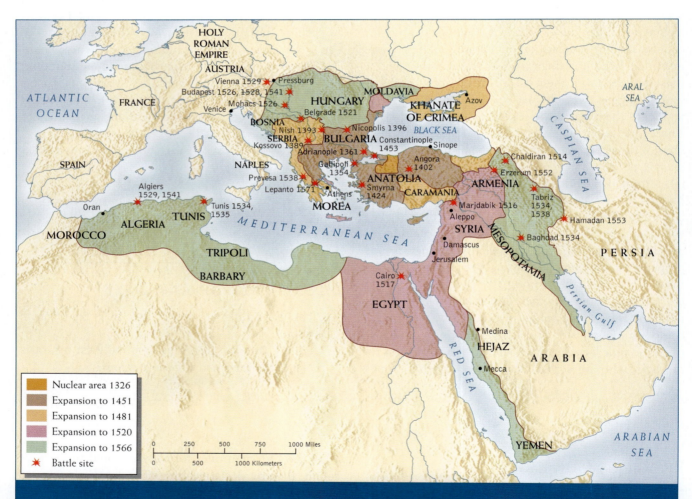

THE GROWTH OF THE OTTOMAN EMPIRE

Consider the patterns of Ottoman expansion revealed in this map. Did the 1453 capture of Constantinople lead to immediate further conquests? Why do you suppose this was? Compare the extent of the Ottoman Empire in 1566 with that of the Byzantine Empire under Justinian (see the map on page 237). How would you account for these similarities? Why didn't the Ottoman Empire continue its rapid expansion after 1566?

besieged Vienna. But despite these dramatic moments, conflicts between the Ottomans and the rulers of western Europe were fought out mainly through pirate raids and naval battles in the Mediterranean. The main result of this contest was thus a steady escalation in the scale and cost of navies. In 1571, when a combined Habsburg and Venetian force defeated the Ottoman fleet at Lepanto, more than 400 ships took part, with both sides deploying naval forces ten times larger than they had possessed half a century before.

Although undeniably a victory for the Habsburgs and their Venetian allies, the battle of Lepanto was far less decisive than is often suggested. The Ottoman navy was speedily rebuilt; by no means did Lepanto put an end to Ottoman influence over the eastern Mediterranean Sea. Nevertheless, after 1571 both Ottoman and Habsburg interests shifted away from their conflict with each other. The Ottomans embarked on a long and costly war with Persia, while the Spanish Habsburgs turned their attention toward their new empire in the Atlantic. By the mid-seventeenth century, when a new round of Ottoman-European conflicts began, the strength of the Ottoman Empire had been sapped by a series of indolent, pleasure-loving sultans and by the tensions that arose within the Ottoman Empire itself as it ceased to expand. The Ottoman Empire would last until 1918; but from the mid-seventeenth century on, it was no longer a serious rival to the global hegemony the European powers were beginning to achieve.

> Silver production in Europe fell markedly during the 1340s and remained at a low level thereafter, as Europeans reached the limits of their technological capacity to extract silver ore from deep mines.

MEDITERRANEAN COLONIALISM

> How were the Portuguese able to control Indian Ocean trade?

During the fifteenth century, Europeans focused their colonial and commercial ambitions more and more on the western Mediterranean and the Atlantic world. Although historians have sometimes argued the contrary, this reorientation was not a result of the rising power of the Ottoman Empire. Instead, this westward orien-

tation was the product of two related developments: the growing importance to late medieval Europe of the African gold trade; and the growth of European colonial empires in the western Mediterranean Sea.

SILVER SHORTAGES AND THE SEARCH FOR AFRICAN GOLD

Europeans had been trading for African gold for centuries, mainly through Muslim middlemen who transported this precious metal in caravans from the Niger River area where it was produced to the North African ports of Algiers and Tunis. From the thirteenth century on, Catalan and Genoese merchants maintained colonies in Tunis, where they traded woolen cloth for North African grain and sub-Saharan gold.

What accelerated the late medieval demand for gold, however, was a serious silver shortage that affected the entire European economy during the fourteenth and fifteenth centuries. Silver production in Europe fell markedly during the 1340s and remained at a low level thereafter, as Europeans reached the limits of their technological capacity to extract silver ore from deep mines. This shortfall in silver production was compounded during the fifteenth century by a serious balance-of-payments problem: more European silver was flowing east in the spice trade than could be replaced using existing mining techniques on known silver deposits. Gold currencies represented an obvious alternative for large transactions, and from the thirteenth century on European rulers with access to gold were minting gold coins. But Europe itself had few natural gold reserves. To maintain and expand these gold coinages, new and larger supplies of gold were needed. The most obvious source for this gold was Africa.

MEDITERRANEAN EMPIRES: CATALUNYA, VENICE, AND GENOA

The growing European interest in the African gold trade coincided with the creation of sea-based Mediterranean empires by the Catalans, the Venetians, and the Genoese. During the thirteenth century, the Catalans conquered and colonized a series of western Mediterranean islands, including Majorca, Ibiza, Minorca, Sicily, and Sardinia.

COMMERCE, CONQUEST, AND COLONIZATION, 1300–1600

Except in Sicily, the pattern of Catalan exploitation was largely the same on all these islands: expropriation or extermination of the native (usually Muslim) population; economic concessions to attract new settlers; and a heavy reliance on slave labor to produce foodstuffs and raw materials for export.

Unlike Catalan colonization efforts, which were mainly carried on by private individuals operating under a crown charter, Venetian colonization was directed by the city's rulers and was focused mainly on the eastern Mediterranean, where the Venetians dominated the trade in spices and silks. The Genoese, by contrast, had more extensive interests in the western Mediterranean world where they traded bulk goods such as cloth, hides, grain, timber, and sugar. Genoese colonies tended to be more informal and family based than Venetian or Catalan colonies, constituting more of a network than an extension of a sovereign empire. They were also more closely integrated into the native societies of North Africa, Spain, and the Black Sea than were the Venetian or the Catalan colonies. Genoese colonies pioneered the production of sugar and sweet Madeira wines in the western Mediterranean, first in Sicily and later in the Atlantic islands off the west coast of Africa. To transport such bulky goods, the Genoese moved away from the oared galleys favored by the Venetians toward larger, fuller-bodied sailing ships that could carry greater volumes of cargo. With further modifications to accommodate the rougher sailing conditions of the Atlantic Ocean, these were the ships that would carry sixteenth-century Europeans around the globe.

> Starting around 1270, however, Italian merchants began to sail through the Strait of Gibraltar and on to the wool-producing regions of England and the Netherlands. This was the essential first step in the extension of Mediterranean patterns of commerce and colonization into the Atlantic Ocean.

FROM THE MEDITERRANEAN TO THE ATLANTIC

Until the late thirteenth century, European maritime commerce had been divided between a Mediterranean and a north Atlantic world. Starting around 1270, however, Italian merchants began to sail through the Strait of Gibraltar and on to the wool-producing regions of England and the Netherlands. This was the essential first step in the extension of Mediterranean patterns of commerce and colonization into the Atlantic Ocean. The second step was the discovery (or possibly rediscovery), during the fourteenth century,

of the Atlantic island chains known as the Canaries and the Azores by Genoese sailors. Efforts to colonize the Canary Islands, and to convert and enslave their inhabitants, began almost immediately. But an effective conquest of the Canary Islands did not really begin until the fifteenth century, when it was undertaken by Portugal and completed by Castile. The Canaries, in turn, became the base from which further Portuguese voyages down the west coast of Africa proceeded. They were also the jumping-off point from which Christopher Columbus would sail westward across the Atlantic Ocean in hopes of reaching Asia.

THE TECHNOLOGY OF SHIPS AND NAVIGATION

The European empires of the fifteenth and sixteenth centuries rested on a mastery of the oceans. The Portuguese caravel—the workhorse ship of the fifteenth-century voyages to Africa—was based on ship and sail designs that had been in use among Portuguese fishermen since the thirteenth century. Starting in the 1440s, however, Portuguese shipwrights began building larger caravels of about 50 tons displacement with two masts, each carrying a triangular (lateen) sail. Such ships were capable of sailing against the wind much more effectively than were the older, square-rigged vessels. They also required much smaller crews than did the multi-oared galleys that were still commonly used in the Mediterranean. By the end of the fifteenth century, even larger caravels of around 200 tons were being constructed, with a third mast and a combination of square and lateen sails. Columbus's *Niña* was of this design, having been refitted with two square sails in the Canary Islands to enable it to sail more efficiently before the wind during the Atlantic crossing.

Europeans were also making significant advances in navigation during the fifteenth and sixteenth centuries. Quadrants, which calculated latitude in the Northern Hemisphere by the height of the North Star above the horizon, were in widespread use by the 1450s. As sailors approached the equator, however, the quadrant became less and less useful, and they were forced instead to make use of astrolabes, which reckoned latitude by the height of the sun. Like quadrants, astrolabes

HOW WERE THE PORTUGUESE ABLE TO CONTROL INDIAN OCEAN TRADE?

MEDITERRANEAN COLONIALISM   429

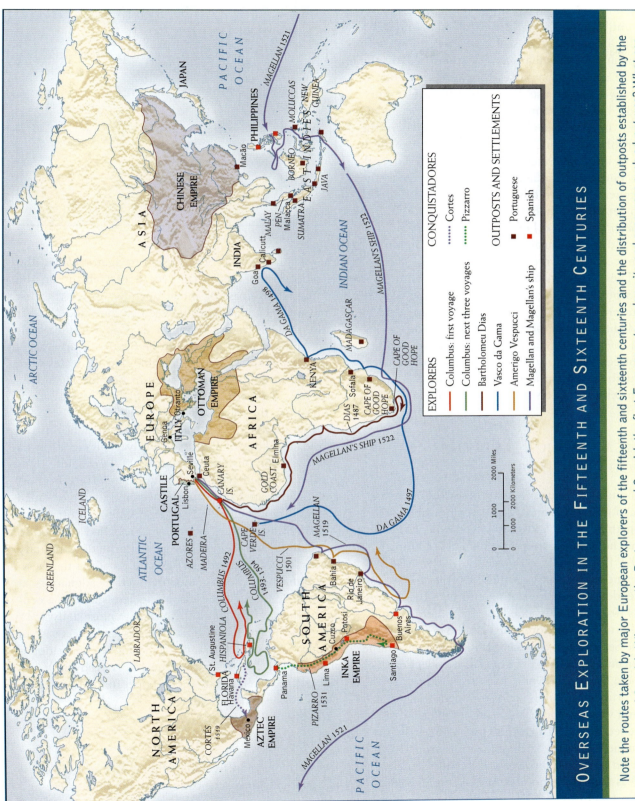

OVERSEAS EXPLORATION IN THE FIFTEENTH AND SIXTEENTH CENTURIES

Note the routes taken by major European explorers of the fifteenth and sixteenth centuries and the distribution of outposts established by the Portuguese and Spanish. Why were the Portuguese and Spanish the first Europeans to underwrite and encourage such adventures? What economic and cultural factors precipitated such efforts? What were the motives for such voyages? How did the establishment of economic outposts in Africa, America, and the East Indies radically alter the balance of power in the Old World, and why? Might the Americas have had to wait even longer for European "discovery" had da Gama found the route around Africa sooner?

CHAPTER 11

COMMERCE, CONQUEST, AND COLONIZATION, 1300–1600

had been known in western Europe for centuries. But it was not until the 1480s that the astrolabe became a really useful instrument for seaborne navigation, with the preparation of standard tables sponsored by the Portuguese crown. Compasses too were also coming into more widespread use during the fifteenth century. Longitude, however, remained impossible to calculate accurately until the eighteenth century, when the invention of the marine chronometer finally made it possible to keep accurate time at sea. In the sixteenth century, Europeans sailing east or west across the oceans generally had to rely on their skill at dead reckoning to determine where they were on the globe.

European sailors also benefited from a new interest in maps and navigational charts. Especially important to Atlantic sailors were books known as *rutters* or *routiers*. These contained detailed sailing instructions and descriptions of the coastal landmarks a pilot could expect to encounter on route to a variety of destinations. Mediterranean sailors had had similar books, known as *portolani*, since at least the fourteenth century. In the fifteenth century, however, this tradition was extended to the Atlantic Ocean; by the end of the sixteenth century, rutters spanned the globe.

PORTUGAL, AFRICA, AND THE SEA ROUTE TO INDIA

It was among the Portuguese that these dual interests—the African gold trade and Atlantic colonization—first came together. In 1415, a Portuguese expedition captured the north African port of Ceuta. During the 1420s the Portuguese colonized both the island of Madeira and the Canary Islands. During the 1430s, they extended these colonization efforts to the Azores. By the 1440s they had reached the Cape Verde Islands. In 1444 Portuguese explorers first landed in the area between the Senegal and the Gambia River mouths on the African mainland, where they began to collect cargoes of gold and slaves for export back to Portugal. By the 1470s, Portuguese sailors had rounded the African "bulge" and were exploring the Gulf of Guinea. In 1483 they reached the mouth of the Congo River. In 1488 the Portuguese captain Bartholomeu Dias rounded the southern tip of Africa. Blown around it accidentally by a gale, Dias named the point "Cape of Storms," but the king of Portugal took a more optimistic view of Dias's achievement. He renamed it the Cape of Good Hope and began planning a naval expedition to India. Finally in 1497–1498, Vasco da Gama rounded the cape, and

CHRONOLOGY

PORTUGUESE MARITIME EXPANSION, 1420s–1515

Colonization of Madeira and Canary Islands	1420s
Colonization of the Azores	1430s
Dias rounds the Cape of Good Hope	1488
Da Gama reaches India	1497–1498
Portuguese reach Malacca in Southeast Asia	1511
Portuguese reach Spice Islands	1515

then, with the help of a Muslim navigator named Ibn Majid, crossed the Indian Ocean to Calicutt on the southwestern coast of India, opening up for the first time a direct sea route between Europe and the Far Eastern spice trade. Although da Gama lost half his fleet and one third of his men on his two-year voyage, his cargo of spices was so valuable that his losses were deemed insignificant. His heroism became legendary, and his story became the basis for the Portuguese national epic, the *Lusiads*.

Now master of the quickest route to riches in the world, the king of Portugal swiftly capitalized on da Gama's accomplishment. After 1500, Portuguese trading fleets sailed regularly to India. In 1509, the Portuguese defeated an Ottoman fleet and then blockaded the mouth of the Red Sea, attempting to cut off one of the traditional routes by which spices had traveled to Alexandria and Beirut. By 1510 Portuguese military forces had established a series of forts along the western Indian coastline, including their headquarters at Goa. In 1511 Portuguese ships seized Malacca, a center of the spice trade on the Malay peninsula. By 1515 they had reached the Spice Islands and the coast of China. So completely did the Portuguese now dominate the spice trade that by the 1520s even the Venetians were forced to buy their pepper in the Portuguese capital of Lisbon.

ARTILLERY AND EMPIRE

Larger, more maneuverable ships and improved navigational aids made it possible for the Portuguese and other European mariners to reach Africa, Asia, and the Americas by sea. But fundamentally, these sixteenth-century European commercial empires were a military achievement. As such, they reflected what Europeans

How were the Portuguese able to control Indian Ocean trade?

had learned in their wars against each other during the fourteenth and fifteenth centuries. Perhaps the most critical military advance of the late Middle Ages was the increasing sophistication of artillery, a development made possible not only by gunpowder, but also by improved metallurgical techniques for casting cannon barrels. By the middle of the fifteenth century, the use of artillery pieces had rendered the stone walls of medieval castles and towns obsolete, a fact brought home in 1453 by the successful French siege of Bordeaux (which brought to an end the Hundred Years' War), and by the Ottoman siege of Constantinople (which brought to an end the Byzantine Empire).

One of the reasons the new ship designs (first caravels, and later the even larger galleons) were so important was that their larger size made it possible to mount more effective artillery pieces on them. Increasingly during the sixteenth century, European naval vessels were conceived as floating artillery platforms, with scores of guns mounted in fixed positions along their sides and swivel guns mounted fore and aft. These guns were vastly expensive, as were the ships that carried them; but for those rulers who could afford to possess them, such ships made it possible to project military power around the world. In 1498, Vasco da Gama became the first Portuguese captain to sail into the Indian Ocean; but the Portuguese did not gain control of that ocean until 1509, when they defeated a combined Ottoman and Indian naval force at the battle of Diu. Portuguese trading outposts in Africa and Asia were fortifications, built not only to guard against the attacks of native peoples but also to ward off assaults from other Europeans. Without this essential military component, the European maritime empires of the sixteenth century would not have existed.

Prince Henry the Navigator

Because we know that these fifteenth-century Portuguese expeditions down the African coast did ultimately open up a sea route to India and the Far East, it is tempting to presume that this was their goal from the beginning. It was not. The traditional narrative of these events, which presents exploration as their mission, India as their goal, and Prince Henry the Navigator as the guiding genius behind them, no longer commands the confidence of most historians. Only from the 1480s did India clearly become the goal toward which these voyages were directed. Before the 1480s, Portuguese involvement in Africa was driven instead by much more traditional goals: crusading ambitions against the Muslims of North Africa; the desire to establish direct links with the sources of African gold production south of the Sahara Desert; the desire to colonize the Atlantic islands; the burgeoning market for slaves in Europe and in the Ottoman Empire; and the hope that somewhere in Africa they might find the legendary Prester John, a mythical Christian king whom Europeans believed would be their ally against the Muslims if only they could locate him. In the twelfth and thirteenth centuries, they had sought him in Asia. But from the 1340s on, he was believed to reside in Ethiopia, an expansive term that to most Europeans seems to have meant "somewhere in Africa."

Nor does Prince Henry (whose title, "the Navigator," was not assigned to him until the seventeenth century) seem so central a figure in Portuguese exploration as he was once thought to be. In fact, he directed only eight of the thirty-five Portuguese voyages to Africa between 1419 and his death in 1460; and the stories about his gathering a

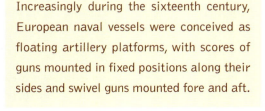
Increasingly during the sixteenth century, European naval vessels were conceived as floating artillery platforms, with scores of guns mounted in fixed positions along their sides and swivel guns mounted fore and aft.

A Turkish Brass Cannon of the Fifteenth Century. This eighteen-ton gun fired balls twenty-five inches in diameter.

THE LEGEND OF PRESTER JOHN

The Travels of Sir John Mandeville is an almost entirely fictional account of the wonders of the East, written by an English expatriate during the first half of the fourteenth century. Despite the fact that Mandeville (almost certainly a pseudonym) knew almost nothing about the lands he describes, his book became a primary source for European ideas about South and East Asia. Although Mandeville locates the legendary Prester John in Persia, India, or China (his geography is fuzzy, to say the least), by the fifteenth century Europeans were searching for Prester John in Africa.

This emperor Prester John has great lands and has many noble cities and good towns in his realm and many great, large islands. For all the country of India is separated into islands by the great floods that come from Paradise, that divide the land into many parts. And also in the sea he has many islands. . . .

This Prester John has under him many kings and many islands and many varied people of various conditions. And this land is full good and rich, but not so rich as is the land of the Great Khan. For the merchants do not come there so commonly to buy merchandise as they do in the land of the Great Khan, for it is too far to travel to. . . .

[Mandeville then goes on to describe the difficulties of reaching Prester John's lands by sea.]

This emperor Prester John always takes as his wife the daughter of the Great Khan, and the Great Khan in the same way takes to wife the daughter of Prester John. For these two are the greatest lords under the heavens.

In the land of Prester John there are many diverse things, and many precious stones so great and so large that men make them into vessels such as platters, dishes, and cups. And there are many other marvels there that it would be too cumbrous and too long to put into the writing of books. But of the principal islands and of his estate and of his law I shall tell you some part.

This emperor Prester John is Christian and a great part of his country is Christian also, although they do not hold to all the articles of our faith as we do. . . .

And he has under him 72 provinces, and in every province there is a king. And these kings have kings under them, and all are tributaries to Prester John.

And he has in his lordships many great marvels. For in his country is the sea that men call the Gravelly Sea, that is all gravel and sand without any drop of water. And it ebbs and flows in great waves as other seas do, and it is never still. . . . And a three-day journey from that sea there are great mountains out of which flows a great flood that comes out of Paradise. And it is full of precious stones without any drop of water. . . .

He dwells usually in the city of Susa [in Persia]. And there is his principal palace, which is so rich and so noble that no one will believe the report unless he has seen it. And above the chief tower of the palace there are two round pommels of gold and in each of them are two great, large rubies that shine full brightly upon the night. And the principal gates of his palace are of a precious stone that men call sardonyxes [a type of onyx], and the frames and the bars are made of ivory. And the windows of the halls and chambers are of crystal. And the tables upon which men eat, some are made of emeralds, some of amethyst, and some of gold full of precious stones. And the legs that hold up the tables are made of the same precious stones. . . .

Mandeville's Travels, ed. M. C. Seymour (Oxford, 1967), pp. 195–199 (language modernized from Middle English by R. C. Stacey).

QUESTIONS FOR ANALYSIS

1. How persuasive was the myth of Prester John? Would you consider such a myth important enough to serve as a primary motive for European exploration?

HOW WERE THE PORTUGUESE ABLE TO CONTROL INDIAN OCEAN TRADE?

Prince Henry the Navigator, by a Fifteenth-Century Portuguese Painter. This portrait is taken from a group portrait of the Portuguese royal family. Although thought to depict Henry, the identification is not certain.

school of navigators and cartographers on the Atlantic coast of Portugal, about his role in designing improved ships and navigational instruments, and about his encouragement of scientific learning generally have all been shown to be false. Henry did play an important role in organizing Portuguese colonization of Madeira, the Canary Islands, and the Azores; and he also pioneered the Portuguese slave trade, first on the Canaries (whose Stone Age population was almost entirely enslaved) and then along the Sene-Gambian coast of Africa. His main goal, however, was to outflank the cross-Saharan African gold trade by intercepting this trade at its source. To this end, he built a series of forts along the African coastline, most famously at Arguim, to which he hoped to divert the cross-Saharan gold caravans. This was also his reason for colonizing the Canary Islands, which he saw as a staging ground for expeditions into the African interior. There is no evidence that he ever dreamed of reaching India by sailing around Africa. Indeed, quite the opposite seems to

be the case. Portuguese progress toward the Cape of Good Hope proceeded much more rapidly in the years after Henry's death than it had during his lifetime. Henry himself was a crusader against Islam, a prince in search of a kingdom, a lord seeking resources to support his followers, and an aspiring merchant who hoped to make a killing in the gold trade but found his main profits in slaving. He was, in all these respects, a man of his time, which is to say, of the fifteenth century. He was not the architect, or even the visionary, of Portugal's sixteenth-century maritime empire.

ATLANTIC COLONIZATION AND THE GROWTH OF SLAVERY

The profits Prince Henry had hoped would come from the African gold trade did not materialize during his lifetime. He therefore had to make his expeditions pay by other means. One of those means was the slave trade. Although slavery in most of western Europe had effectively disappeared by the early twelfth century, slavery continued in Iberia (and to a lesser extent in Italy) throughout the high and late Middle Ages. Until the mid-fifteenth century, however, slavery on the Iberian mainland and in Italy remained very small in scale. The major Mediterranean slave markets of the fourteenth and early fifteenth centuries lay in Muslim lands, and especially in the Ottoman Empire. Relatively few of the slaves who passed through these markets were Africans. Most were European Christians, predominantly Poles, Ukrainians, Greeks, and Bulgarians. Thus the patterns of slavery were not racialized in the late medieval Mediterranean world, except insofar as "primitive" peoples such as the natives of the Canary Islands or of Sardinia were more likely to be regarded as targets for enslavement.

From the mid-fifteenth century on, however, Lisbon began to emerge as a significant market for enslaved Africans. Something on the order of 15,000 to 20,000 Africans were sold in Lisbon during Prince Henry's lifetime, most of them between 1440 and 1460. In the half century after his death, the numbers grew, amounting to perhaps 150,000 African slaves imported into Europe by 1505. For the most part, these slaves were regarded as status symbols—one reason they were so frequently depicted in paintings of the period. Even in the Atlantic colonies—Madeira, the Canaries, and the Azores—the land was worked mainly by European settlers and sharecroppers. Slave labor, if it was employed at all, was generally used only in sugar mills. This meant that on the Azores, which remained a wheat-producing colony, slavery found no real foothold. On Madeira and the Canaries, where sugar became the predominant cash crop during the last quarter of the fifteenth century, some slaves were introduced. But even sugar production did not lead to the widespread introduction of slavery on these islands.

A new style of slave-based sugar plantations began to emerge in Portugal's Atlantic colonies only in the 1460s, starting on the Cape Verde Islands and then extending southward into the Gulf of Guinea. These islands were not populated when the Portuguese began to settle them, and their climate was such as to discourage any large number of Europeans from settling there. They were ideally located, however, to purchase laborers from the slave traders along the nearby West African coast. No comparable system of large-scale, slave-based plantation production had been seen in Europe or Africa since the Roman period. But it was this model of sugar plantations staffed by enslaved Africans that would be exported to the Caribbean islands of the Americas by their Spanish conquerors, with incalculable consequences for Africa, the Americas, and Europe.

Europe Encounters A New World

What was the impact of New World silver on the European economy?

The decision by Spain's rulers to underwrite Columbus's famous voyage was an outgrowth of the progress of these Portuguese ventures. After 1488, when Dias successfully rounded the Cape of Good Hope, it was clear that Portugal would soon dominate the sea lanes leading eastward to Asia. The only alternative for Portugal's Spanish rivals was to finance someone bold enough to try to reach Asia by sailing west. The popular image of Christopher Columbus (1451–1506) as a visionary who struggled to convince hardened ignoramuses that the world was round does not bear up under scrutiny. In fact, the sphericity of the earth had been

widely known throughout European society since at least the twelfth century. What made Columbus's scheme seem plausible to King Ferdinand and Queen Isabella was, first, the discovery and colonization of the Canary Islands and the Azores, which had reinforced a view of the Atlantic as being dotted with islands all the way to Japan; and second, the Genoese mariner's own astonishing miscalculation of the actual size of the earth, which convinced him that he could reach Japan and China in about a month's clear sailing westward from the Canary Islands. America was actually rediscovered by Europeans at the end of the fifteenth century as the result of a colossal error in reckoning. Columbus himself never realized his mistake. When he reached the Bahamas and the island of Hispaniola in 1492 after only a month's sailing, he returned to Spain to report that he had indeed reached the outer islands of Asia.

The Discovery of a New World

Columbus was not the first European to set foot on the American continents. Viking sailors had reached and briefly settled present-day Newfoundland, Labrador, and perhaps New England around the year 1000. But knowledge of these Viking landings had been forgotten or ignored throughout Europe for hundreds of years. In the fifteenth century, even the Scandinavian settlements in Greenland had been abandoned. It would be perverse, therefore, to deny Columbus credit for his accomplishments. Although Columbus himself never accepted the reality of what he had discovered, those who followed him soon did and busily set out to exploit this new world.

Understandably, Columbus brought back no Asian spices from his voyages. He did, however, return with some small samples of gold and a few indigenous people, whose existence gave promise of entire tribes that might be "saved" (by conversion to Christianity) and enslaved by Europeans. This provided sufficient incentive for the Spanish monarchs to finance three more expeditions by Columbus and many more by others. Soon the mainland was discovered as well as further islands, and the conclusion quickly became inescapable that a new world had indeed been found. Awareness of this new world was most widely publicized by the Italian geographer Amerigo Vespucci. Though he may not have deserved this honor, the continents of the Western Hemisphere became known thereafter as "America" after Vespucci's first name.

WHAT WAS THE IMPACT OF NEW WORLD SILVER ON THE EUROPEAN ECONOMY?

The realization that this was indeed a new world was at first a disappointment to the Spanish, for with a major land mass lying between Europe and Asia, Spain could not hope to beat Portugal in the race for Asian spices. Any remaining doubt that not one, but two vast oceans separated Europe from Asia was completely removed in 1513, when Vasco Núñez de Balboa first viewed the Pacific Ocean from the Isthmus of Panama. Not entirely admitting defeat, Ferdinand and Isabella's grandson, the Holy Roman emperor Charles V, accepted Ferdinand Magellan's offer in 1519 to see whether a route to Asia could be found by sailing around South America. But Magellan's voyage demonstrated beyond question that the globe was simply too large for any such plan to be feasible. Of the five ships that left Spain under Magellan's command, only one returned three years later, having been forced to circumnavigate the globe. Out of a crew of 265 sailors, only eighteen survived. Most had died from scurvy or starvation; Magellan himself had been killed in a skirmish with native peoples in the Philippines. This fiasco brought to an end all hope of discovering an easy southwest passage to Asia. The dream of a northwest passage survived, however, and continued to motivate European explorers of North America until the nineteenth century.

THE SPANISH CONQUEST OF AMERICA

Although the discovery of this new continent was initially a disappointment to the Spanish, it quickly became clear that the New World had great wealth of its own. From the start, Columbus's gold samples, in themselves rather paltry, had nurtured hopes that somewhere in America gold might lie piled in ingots, ready to enrich whatever European adventurer discovered them. Rumor fed rumor, until a few freelance Spanish soldiers really did strike it rich beyond their most avaricious imaginings. Between 1519 and 1521, the *conquistador* (Spanish for "conqueror") Hernando Cortés, with a force of 600 Europeans but with the assistance of thousands of the Aztecs' unhappy subjects,

Spanish Conquistadors in Mexico. This sixteenth-century drawing of conquistadors massacring Mexican natives emphasizes the advantages that plate armor and steel swords gave to the Spanish soldiers.

COMMERCE, CONQUEST, AND COLONIZATION, 1300–1600

overthrew the Aztec Empire of Mexico and carried off its rulers' fabulous wealth. Then in 1533 another conquistador, Francisco Pizarro, this time with only 180 men, toppled the highly centralized South American empire of the Inkas and carried off its great stores of gold and silver. Cortés and Pizarro had the advantage of some cannons and a few horses (both unknown to the native peoples of the Americas), but they achieved their victories primarily by sheer audacity, courage, and treachery. They were aided also by the unwillingness of the indigenous peoples whom the Aztecs and the Inkas had subjected to fight on behalf of their oppressors. Little did the Spaniards' erstwhile allies know how much worse their new conquerors would soon prove to be.

THE PROFITS OF EMPIRE IN THE NEW WORLD

Cortés and Pizarro were plunderers who captured in one fell swoop hoards of gold and silver that had been accumulated for centuries by the native civilizations of Mexico and Peru. Already, however, a search had begun for the sources of these precious metals. The first gold deposits were discovered in Hispaniola, where surface mines were speedily established using native laborers who died in appalling numbers from disease, brutality, and overwork. Of the approximately 1 million native people who lived on Hispaniola in 1492, only 100,000 survived by 1510. By 1538, their numbers were down to 500.

With the loss of so many workers, the Hispaniola mines became uneconomical to operate, and the European colonists turned instead to cattle raising and sugar production. Modeling their sugarcane plantations on those of the Cape Verde Islands and St. Thomas in the Gulf of Guinea, colonists imported African slaves to labor in the new industry. Sugar production was by its nature a highly capital-intensive undertaking. The need to import slave labor added further to its costs, guaranteeing that control over the sugar industry would fall into the hands of a few extremely wealthy planters and financiers.

Despite the importance of sugar production on the Caribbean islands and of cattle ranching on the Mexican mainland, mining shaped the Spanish colonies of Central and South America most fundamentally. Gold was the lure that had initially drawn the Spanish conquerors to the New World, but silver became their most lucrative export. Between 1543 and 1548, vast silver deposits were discovered north of Mexico City and at Potosí in Bolivia. Even before the discovery of these deposits, the Spanish crown had taken steps to assume direct governmental control over its Central and South American colonies. It was therefore to the Spanish crown that the profits from these astonishingly productive mines accrued. Potosí quickly became the most important mining town in the world. By 1570, it numbered 120,000 inhabitants, despite being located at an altitude of 15,000 feet where the temperature never climbs above 59 degrees Fahrenheit. As in Hispaniola, enslaved native laborers died by the tens of thousands in these mines and in the disease-infested boom towns that surrounded them.

New mining techniques (in particular, the mercury-amalgamation process, introduced into Mexico in 1555 and Potosí in 1571) made it possible to produce even greater quantities of silver, at the cost of even greater mortality among the native laborers. Between 1571 and 1586, silver production at Potosí quadrupled, reaching a peak in the 1590s, when 10 million ounces of silver per year were arriving in Spain from the Americas. In the 1540s, the corresponding figure was only 1.5 million ounces. In the peak years of domestic European silver production, between 1525 and 1535, only about 3 million ounces of silver per year were being produced, and this figure dropped steadily from about 1550 on. Europe's silver shortage came triumphantly to an end during the sixteenth century, but the silver that now circulated there came almost entirely from the New World.

This massive infusion of silver into the European economy accelerated an inflation that had begun already in the later fifteenth century. Initially, this inflation was driven by the renewed growth of the European

CHRONOLOGY

ENCOUNTERING THE NEW WORLD, c. 1000–1545

Vikings settle Newfoundland	c. 1000
Columbus reaches Hispaniola	1492
Balboa reaches Pacific Ocean	1513
Magellan's fleet sails around the world	1519–1522
Cortés conquers the Aztecs	1521
Pizarro conquers the Inkas	1533
Potosí silver deposits discovered	1545

ENSLAVED NATIVE LABORERS AT POTOSÍ

Since the Spanish crown received one fifth of all the revenues from mines (as well as maintaining a monopoly over the mercury used to refine the silver ore into silver), it had an important stake in ensuring the productivity of the mines. To this end, the crown granted colonial mine owners the right to conscript native peoples to work in the mines. This account from about 1620 describes the conditions under which these forced native laborers worked. It is not surprising that mortality rates among such laborers were horrendous.

According to His Majesty's warrant, the mine owners on this massive range [at Potosí] have a right to the conscripted labor of 13,300 Indians in the working and exploitation of the mines, both those which have been discovered, those now discovered, and those which shall be discovered. It is the duty of the *Corregidor* (municipal governor) of Potosí to have them rounded up and to see that they come in from all the provinces between Cuzco . . . and as far as the frontiers of Tarija and Tomina. . . .

The conscripted Indians go up every Monday morning to the . . . foot of the range; the *Corregidor* arrives with all the provincial captains or chiefs who have charge of the Indians assigned him for his miner or smelter; that keeps him busy till 1 P.M., by which time the Indians are already turned over to these mine and smelter owners.

After each has eaten his ration, they climb up the hill, each to his mine, and go in, staying there from that hour until Saturday evening without coming out of the mine; their wives bring them food, but they stay constantly underground, excavating and carrying out the ore from which they get the silver. They all have tallow candles, lighted day and night; that is the light they work with, for as they are underground, they have need for it all the time. . . .

These Indians have different functions in the handling of the silver ore; some break it up with bar or pick, and dig down in, following the vein in the mine; others bring it up; others up above keep separating the good and the poor in piles; others are occupied in taking it down from the range to the mills on herds of llamas; every day they bring up more than 8,000 of these native beasts of burden for this task. These teamsters who carry the metal are not conscripted, but are hired.

Antonio Vázquez de Espinosa, *Compendium and Description of the West Indies*, trans. Charles Upson Clark (Washington, D.C., 1968), p. 62.

QUESTIONS FOR ANALYSIS

1. What was the human cost of the Potosí silver mine?

---

population, an expanding economy, and a relatively fixed supply of food. From the 1540s on, however, inflation was largely the product of the greatly increased supply of silver that was now entering the European economy. The result was what historians have termed "the Price Revolution." Although the effects of this inflation were felt throughout the European continent, Spain was affected with particular severity. Between

1500 and 1560, Spanish prices doubled; between 1560 and 1600, they doubled again. Such exceptionally high prices in turn undermined the competitiveness of Spanish industries. When the flow of New World silver to Spain slowed dramatically during the 1620s and 1630s, the Spanish economy collapsed.

After 1600, lessening quantities of New World silver entered the European economy, but prices continued to rise, albeit more slowly than before. By 1650, the price of grain within Europe had risen to five or six times its level in 1500, producing social dislocation and widespread misery for many of Europe's poorest inhabitants. In England, the period between about 1590 and 1610 was probably the most desperate the country had experienced for 300 years. As the population rose and wages fell, living standards dropped dramatically. If we compute living standards by dividing the price of an average basket of food by the average daily wage of a building laborer, then standards of living were lower in England in 1600 than they had been even in the terrible years of the early fourteenth century. It is no wonder, then, that so many Europeans found emigration to the Americas a tempting prospect. We may wonder, indeed, what might have happened in seventeenth-century Europe had the new world of the Americas not existed as an outlet for Europe's growing population.

Conclusion

By 1600, colonization and overseas conquest had profoundly changed both Europe and the wider world. The emergence during the sixteenth century of Portugal and Spain as Europe's leading long-distance traders permanently moved the center of gravity of European economic power away from Italy and the Mediterranean toward the Atlantic. Deprived of its role as the principal conduit for the spice trade, Venice gradually declined. The Genoese moved increasingly into the world of finance, backing the commercial ventures of others, particularly of Spain. By contrast, the Atlantic ports of Spain and Portugal bustled with vessels and shone with wealth. By the mid-seventeenth century, however, economic predominance was passing to the north Atlantic states of England, Holland, and France. Spain and Portugal would retain their American colonies until the nineteenth century. But from the seventeenth century on, it would be the Dutch, the French, and especially the English who would establish new European empires in North America, Asia, Africa, and Australia. By and large, these new empires would last until the World War II.

Key Terms

Chingiz Khan
Marco Polo
Timur the Lame
Ottoman Janissaries

gunpowder
Canary Islands
caravels
astrolabe

Prince Henry the Navigator
Christopher Columbus
conquistador

New World silver
Aztecs
Inkas

Selected Readings

Abu-Lughod, Janet L. *Before European Hegemony: The World System A.D. 1250–1350*. Oxford and New York, 1989. A study of the trading links among Europe, the Middle East, India, and China, with special attention to the role of the Mongol Empire; extensive bibliography.

Allsen, Thomas T. *Culture and Conquest in Mongol Eurasia*. Cambridge and New York, 2001. A synthesis of the author's earlier studies, emphasizing Mongol involvement in the cultural and commercial exchanges that linked China, Central Asia, and Europe.

Amitai-Preiss, Reuven, and David O. Morgan, eds. *The Mongol Empire and Its Legacy*. Leiden, 1999. A collection of essays that represents some of the new trends in Mongol studies.

The Book of Prophecies, Edited by Christopher Columbus. Trans. Blair Sullivan, ed. Roberto Rusconi. Berkeley and Los Angeles, 1996. After his third voyage, from which Columbus was returned to Spain in chains, he compiled a book of quotations from various sources, selected to emphasize the millenarian implications of his discoveries; a fascinating insight into the mind of the explorer.

Christian, David. *A History of Russia, Central Asia and Mongolia.* Volume 1: *Inner Eurasia from Prehistory to the Mongol Empire.* Oxford, 1998. The authoritative English-language work on the subject.

Coles, Paul. *The Ottoman Impact on Europe.* London, 1968. An excellent introductory text, still valuable despite its age.

Fernández-Armesto, Felipe. *Before Columbus: Exploration and Colonisation from the Mediterranean to the Atlantic, 1229–1492.* London, 1987. An indispensible study of the medieval background to the sixteenth-century European colonial empires.

Fernández-Armesto, Felipe. *Columbus.* Oxford and New York, 1991. An excellent biography that stresses the millenarian ideas that underlay Columbus's thinking. A good book to read after Phillips and Phillips.

Flint, Valerie I. J. *The Imaginative Landscape of Christopher Columbus.* Princeton, N.J., 1992. A short, suggestive analysis of the intellectual influences that shaped Columbus's geographical ideas.

The Four Voyages: Christopher Columbus. Trans. J. M. Cohen. New York, 1992. Columbus's own self-serving account of his four voyages to the Indies.

Goffman, Daniel. *The Ottoman Empire and Early Modern Europe.* Cambridge and New York, 2002. A revisionist account that presents the Ottoman Empire as a European state.

The History and the Life of Chinggis Khan: The Secret History of the Mongols. Trans. Urgunge Onon. Leiden, 1997. A newer version of *The Secret History*, now the standard English version of this important Mongol source.

Inalcik, Halil. *The Ottoman Empire: The Classical Age, 1300-1600.* London, 1973. The standard history by the dean of Turkish historians.

Inalcik, Halil, ed. *An Economic and Social History of the Ottoman Empire, 1300–1914.* Cambridge, 1994. An important collection of essays, spanning the full range of Ottoman history.

Jackson, Peter. *The Mongols and the West, 1221–1410.* Harlow, UK, 2005. A well-written survey that emphasizes the interactions among the Mongol, Latin Christian, and Muslim worlds.

Kafadar, Cemal. *Between Two Worlds: The Construction of the Ottoman State.* Berkeley, Calif., and Los Angeles, 1995. An important study of Ottoman origins in the border regions between Byzantium, the Seljuk Turks, and the Mongols.

Larner, John. *Marco Polo and the Discovery of the World.* New Haven, Conn., 1999. A study of the influence of Marco Polo's *Travels* on Europeans.

Morgan, David. *The Mongols*, 2d ed. Oxford, 2007. An accessible introduction to Mongol history and its sources, written by a noted expert on medieval Persia.

Parker, Geoffrey. *The Military Revolution: Military Innovation and the Rise of the West (1500–1800),* 2d ed. Cambridge and New York, 1996. A work of fundamental importance for understanding the global dominance achieved by early modern Europeans.

Phillips, J. R. S. *The Medieval Expansion of Europe,* 2d ed. Oxford, 1998. An outstanding study of the thirteenth- and fourteenth-century background to the fifteenth-century expansion of Europe. Important synthetic treatment of European relations with the Mongols, China, Africa, and North America. The second edition includes a new introduction and a bibliographical essay; the text is the same as in the first edition (1988).

Phillips, William D., Jr., and Carla R. Phillips. *The Worlds of Christopher Columbus.* Cambridge and New York, 1991. The first book to read on Columbus: accessible, engaging, and scholarly. Then read Fernández-Armesto's biography.

Ratchnevsky, Paul. *Genghis Khan: His Life and Legacy.* Trans. Thomas Nivison Haining. Oxford, 1991. An English translation and abridgment of a book first published in German in 1983. The author was one of the greatest Mongol historians of his generation.

Rossabi, M. *Khubilai Khan: His Life and Times.* Berkeley, Calif., 1988. The standard English biography.

Russell, Peter. *Prince Henry "The Navigator": A Life.* New Haven, Conn., 2000. A masterly biography by a great historian who has spent a lifetime on the subject. The only book one now needs to read on Prince Henry.

Saunders, J. J. *The History of the Mongol Conquests.* London, 1971. Still the standard English-language introduction; somewhat more positive about the Mongols' accomplishments than is Morgan.

Scammell, Geoffrey V. *The First Imperial Age: European Overseas Expansion, 1400–1715.* London, 1989. A useful introductory survey, with a particular focus on English and French colonization.

The Secret History of the Mongols. Trans. F. W. Cleaves. Cambridge, Mass., 1982.

The Secret History of the Mongols and Other Pieces. Trans. Arthur Waley. London, 1963. The later Chinese abridgment of the Mongol original.

The Travels of Marco Polo, trans. R. E. Latham. Baltimore, Md., 1958. The most accessible edition of this remarkably interesting work.

Chapter Twelve

Chapter Contents

The Renaissance and the Middle Ages 442

The Renaissance in Italy 443

The Italian Renaissance: Painting, Sculpture, and Architecture 451

The Waning of the Italian Renaissance 459

The Renaissance in the North 462

Conclusion 469

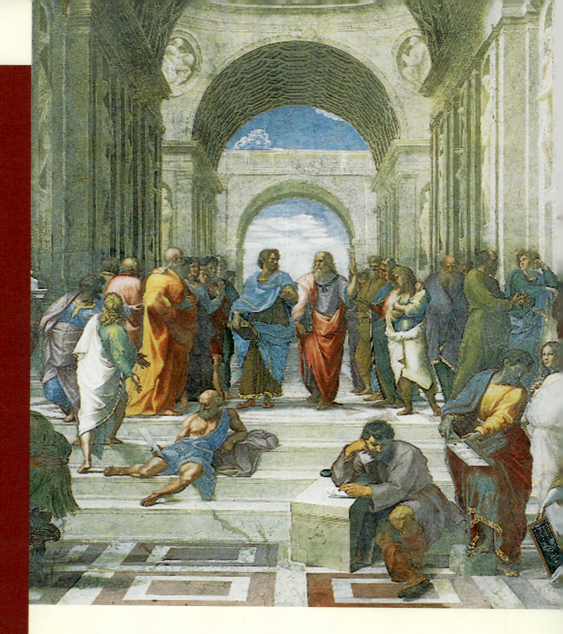

The Civilization of the Renaissance, c. 1350–1550

THE PREVALENT MODERN NOTION that a "Renaissance period" followed western Europe's Middle Ages was first expressed by numerous Italian writers who lived between 1350 and 1550. According to them, 1,000 years of unrelieved darkness had intervened between the Roman era and their own times. During these dark ages the muses of art and literature had fled Europe before the onslaught of barbarism and ignorance. Almost miraculously, however, in the fourteenth century the muses suddenly returned, and Italians happily collaborated with them to bring forth a glorious "renaissance of the arts."

Ever since this periodization was advanced, historians have taken for granted the existence of some sort of renaissance intervening between medieval and modern times. Indeed, from the late eighteenth to the early twentieth centuries many scholars went so far as to argue that the Renaissance was not just an epoch in the history of learning and culture but that a unique Renaissance spirit transformed all aspects of European life—political, economic, and religious as well as intellectual and artistic. Today, however, most experts no longer accept this characterization because they find it impossible to locate any truly distinctive "Renaissance" politics, economics, or religion. Instead, most scholars reserve the term *Renaissance* to describe certain trends in thought, literature, and the arts that emerged in Italy from roughly 1350 to 1550 and then spread to northern Europe during the sixteenth century. That is the approach that we follow here: accordingly, when we refer to a "Renaissance" period in this chapter, we mean to limit ourselves to an epoch in intellectual and cultural history.

FOCUS QUESTIONS

• How did the Italian Renaissance culture differ from the culture of the High Middle Ages?

• Why did the Renaissance occur in Italy?

• What were the principal characteristics of Italian Renaissance art?

• Why did the Renaissance decline around 1550?

• How did the northern and Italian Renaissances differ from one another?

CHAPTER 12

THE CIVILIZATION OF THE RENAISSANCE, C. 1350–1550

THE RENAISSANCE AND THE MIDDLE AGES

How did Italian Renaissance culture differ from the culture of the High Middle Ages?

Granted this restriction, some further qualifications are still necessary. Since the word *renaissance* literally means "rebirth," it is sometimes thought that after about 1350 certain Italians who were newly cognizant of Greek and Roman cultural accomplishments initiated a rebirth of classical culture after a long period during which that culture had been essentially dead. In fact, however, the High Middle Ages witnessed no "death" of classical learning. Saint Thomas Aquinas considered Aristotle to be "the Philosopher;" Dante revered Virgil. Similar examples could be cited almost without limit. It would be equally false to contrast an imaginary Renaissance paganism with a medieval age of faith because, however much most Renaissance personalities loved the classics, none saw classicism as superseding Christianity. And finally, all discussions of the Renaissance must be qualified by the fact that there was no single Renaissance position on anything. Renaissance thinkers and artists were enormously diverse in their attitudes, achievements, and approaches. As we assess their accomplishments, we need to beware not to force them into too narrow a mold.

> In the twelfth and thirteenth centuries Greek scientific and philosophical treatises became available to western Europeans in Latin translations through Islam, but none of the great Greek literary masterpieces and practically none of the major works of Plato were yet known.

RENAISSANCE CLASSICISM

Nonetheless, in the realms of thought, literature, and the arts, we can certainly find distinguishing traits that make the concept of a "Renaissance" meaningful for intellectual and cultural history. First, regarding knowledge of the classics, there was a significant quantitative difference between the learning of the Middle Ages and that of the Renaissance. Medieval scholars knew many Roman authors, such as Virgil, Ovid, and Cicero, but during the Renaissance the works of others such as Livy, Tacitus, and Lucretius were rediscovered and made familiar. Equally if not more important was the Renaissance recovery of the literature of classical Greece from Byzantium. In the twelfth and thirteenth

centuries Greek scientific and philosophical treatises became available to western Europeans in Latin translations through Islam, but none of the great Greek literary masterpieces and practically none of the major works of Plato were yet known. Nor could more than a handful of medieval Westerners read the Greek language. During the Renaissance, on the other hand, large numbers of Western scholars learned Greek and mastered almost the entire Greek literary heritage that is known today.

Second, Renaissance thinkers not only knew many more classical texts than their medieval counterparts but they used them in new ways. Whereas medieval writers presumed that their ancient sources would complement and confirm their own Christian assumptions, Renaissance writers were more aware of the conceptual and chronological gap that separated their own world from that of their classical sources. At the same time, however, the structural similarities between the ancient city-states and those of Renaissance Italy encouraged Italian thinkers in particular to find in these ancient sources models of thought and action directly applicable to their own day. This firm determination to learn from classical antiquity was even more pronounced in the realms of architecture and art, areas in which classical models contributed most strikingly to the creation of fully distinct Renaissance styles.

Third, although Renaissance culture was by no means pagan, it was more worldly and overtly materialistic in its orientation than was the culture of the twelfth and thirteenth centuries. The evolution of the Italian city-states created a supportive environment for attitudes that stressed the importance of the urban political arena and of living well in this world. Such ideals helped create a culture that was increasingly nonecclesiastical. The relative weakness of the church in Italy also contributed to the more secular culture that emerged there. Italian bishoprics were small and for the most part poorly endowed. Italian universities were also largely independent of ecclesiastical supervision and control. Even the papacy was severely limited in its ability to intervene in the cultural life of the Italian city-states, not least because the papacy's role as a political rival in central Italy compromised its moral authority as an arbiter of cultural and religious values. All these factors helped create a space within which the worldly, materialistic culture of the Renaissance could emerge effectively untrammeled by ecclesiastical opposition.

Renaissance Humanism

One word above all comes closest to summing up the most common and basic Renaissance intellectual ideals—namely *humanism*. Renaissance humanism was a program of studies that aimed to replace the thirteenth- and fourteenth-century scholastic emphasis on logic and metaphysics with the study of language, literature, rhetoric, history, and ethics. The humanists always preferred ancient literature; although some (notably Francesco Petrarch and Leon Batista Alberti) wrote in both Latin and the vernacular, most humanists regarded vernacular literature as at best a diversion for the uneducated. Serious scholarship and literature could be written only in Latin or Greek. That Latin, moreover, had to be the Latin of Cicero and Virgil. Renaissance humanists were self-conscious elitists who condemned the living Latin of their scholastic contemporaries as a barbarous departure from ancient (and therefore correct) standards of Latin style. Despite their belief that they were thereby reviving the study of the classics, the humanists' position was thus inherently ironic. By insisting on ancient standards of Latin grammar, syntax, and word choice, the humanists of the Renaissance succeeded ultimately in turning Latin into a fossilized language that thereafter ceased to evolve. They thus contributed, quite unwittingly, to the ultimate triumph of the European vernaculars as the primary languages of intellectual and cultural life.

> By insisting on ancient standards of Latin grammar, syntax, and word choice, the humanists of the Renaissance succeeded ultimately in turning Latin into a fossilized language that thereafter ceased to evolve.

Humanists were convinced that their own educational program—which placed the study of Latin language and literature at the core of the curriculum and then encouraged students to go on to Greek—was the best way to produce virtuous citizens and able public officials. Their elitism was to this extent intensely practical and directly connected to the political life of the city-states in which they lived. Because women were excluded from Italian political life, the education of women was therefore of little concern to most humanists, although some aristocratic women did acquire humanist training. As more and more fifteenth-century city-states fell into the hands of princes, however, the humanist educational curriculum lost its immediate connection to the republican ideals of Italian political life. Nevertheless, humanists never lost their conviction that the study of the "humanities" (as the humanist curriculum came to be known) was the best way to produce leaders for European society.

The Renaissance in Italy

Why did the Renaissance occur in Italy?

Although the Renaissance eventually became a Europe-wide intellectual and artistic movement, it developed first and most distinctively in fourteenth- and fifteenth-century Italy. Understanding why this was so is important not only to explaining the origins of this movement but also to understanding its fundamental characteristics.

The Origins of the Italian Renaissance

The Renaissance originated in Italy for several reasons. The most fundamental reason was that Italy in the later Middle Ages was the most advanced urban society in all of Europe. Unlike aristocrats north of the Alps, Italian aristocrats customarily lived in urban centers rather than in rural castles and consequently became fully involved in urban public affairs. Moreover, since the Italian aristocracy built its palaces in the cities, the aristocratic class was less sharply set off from the class of rich merchants than in the north. Hence, whereas in France or Germany most aristocrats lived on the income from their landed estates while rich town dwellers (*bourgeois*) gained their living from trade, in Italy so many town-dwelling aristocrats engaged in banking or mercantile enterprises and so many rich mercantile families imitated the manners of the aristocracy that by the fourteenth and fifteenth centuries the aristocracy and upper bourgeoisie were becoming virtually indistinguishable. The noted Florentine family of the Medici (*MEH-dih-chee*), for example, emerged as a family of physicians (as the name suggests), made its fortune in banking and commerce, and rose into the aristocracy in the fifteenth century. The results of these developments for the history of education are obvious: not only was there a great demand for education in the skills of reading and counting

THE HUMANISTS' EDUCATIONAL PROGRAM

These three selections illustrate the confidence of civic humanists such as Vergerius, Bruni, and Alberti that their elite educational program would be of supreme value to the state as well as to the individual students who pursued it. Not everyone agreed with the humanists' claims, however, and a good deal of self-promotion lies behind them.

VERGERIUS ON LIBERAL STUDIES

We call those studies *liberal* which are worthy of a free man; those studies by which we attain and practice virtue and wisdom; that education which calls forth, trains, and develops those highest gifts of body and of mind which ennoble men, and which are rightly judged to rank next in dignity to virtue only. . . . It is, then, of the highest importance that even from infancy this aim, this effort, should constantly be kept alive in growing minds. For . . . we shall not have attained wisdom in our later years unless in our earliest we have sincerely entered on its search. [P. P. Vergerius (1370–1444), *"Concerning Excellent Traits."*]

ALBERTI ON THE IMPORTANCE OF LITERATURE

Letters are indeed so important that without them one would be considered nothing but a rustic, no matter how much a gentlemen [he may be by birth]. I'd much rather see a young nobleman with a book than with a falcon in his hand. . . .

Be diligent, then, you young people, in your studies. Do all you can to learn about the events of the past that are worthy of memory. Try to understand all the useful things that have been passed on to you. Feed your minds on good maxims. Learn the delights of embellishing your souls with good morals. Strive to be kind and considerate [of others] when conducting civil business. Get to know those things human and divine that have been put at your disposal in books for good reason. Nowhere [else] will you find . . . the elegance of a verse of Homer, or Virgil, or of some other excellent poet. You will find no field so delightful or flowering as in one of the orations of Demosthenes, Cicero, Livy, Xenophon, and other such pleasant and perfect orators. No effort is more fully compensated . . . as the constant reading and rereading of good things. From such reading you will rise rich in good maxims and good arguments, strong in your ability to persuade others and get them to listen to you; among the citizens you will willingly be heard, admired, praised, and loved. [Leon Battista Alberti (1404–1472), *"On the Family."*]

BRUNI ON THE HUMANIST CURRICULUM

The foundations of all true learning must be laid in the sound and thorough knowledge of Latin: which implies study marked by a broad spirit, accurate scholarship, and careful attention to details. Unless this solid basis be secured it is useless to attempt to rear an enduring edifice. Without it the great monuments of literature are unintelligible, and the art of composition impossible. To attain this essential knowledge we must never relax our careful attention to the grammar of the language, but perpetually confirm and extend our acquaintance with it until it is thoroughly our own. . . .

But the wider question now confronts us, that of the subject matter of our studies, that which I have already called the realities of fact and principle, as distinct from literary form. . . . First among such studies I place History: a subject which must not on any account be neglected by one who aspires to true cultivation. . . . For the careful study of the past enlarges our foresight in contemporary affairs and affords to citizens and to monarchs lessons . . . in the ordering of public policy. From History, also, we draw our store of examples of moral precepts. . . .

The great Orators of antiquity must by all means be included. Nowhere do we find the virtues more warmly extolled, the vices so fiercely decried. From them we may learn, also, how to express consolation, encouragement, dissuasion or advice. . . .

Familiarity with the great poets of antiquity is essential to any claim to true education. For in their writings we find deep speculations upon Nature, and upon the Causes and Origins of things, which must carry weight with us both from their antiquity and from their authorship. . . .

Proficiency in literary form, not accompanied by broad acquaintance with facts and truths, is a barren attainment; whilst information, however vast, which lacks all grace of expression would seem to be put under a bushel or partly thrown away. . . . Where, however, this double capacity exists—breadth of learning and grace of style—we allow the highest title to distinction and to abiding fame. . . . [Leonardo Bruni (1369–1444), *"Concerning the Study of Literature."*]

Vergerius and Bruni: William Harrison Woodward, ed., *Vittorino da Feltre and Other Humanist Educators* (London:, 1897), pp. 96–110, 124–129, 132–133. Alberti: Eric Cochrane and Julius Kirshner, eds., *University of Chicago Readings in Western Civilization*, Vol. 5: *The Renaissance* (Chicago, 1986), pp. 81–82.

QUESTIONS FOR ANALYSIS

1. Why did the Italian Renaissance produce such a strong spirit of civic humanism?
2. Do you think that Socrates' and Cicero's perceptions of virtue were identical to those of Vergerius and Bruni? Were Renaissance virutes and classical virtues one and the same thing?
3. Why did humanists such as Leonardo Bruni consider the study of history essential to a full education?

---

necessary to become a successful merchant but the richest and most prominent families sought above all to find teachers who would impart to their sons the knowledge and skills necessary to argue well in the public arena. Consequently, Italy produced a large number of lay educators, many of whom not only taught students but also demonstrated their learning by producing political and ethical treatises and works of literature. Italian schools created the best-educated upper-class public in all of Europe, along with a considerable number of wealthy patrons who were ready to invest in the cultivation of new ideas and new forms of literary and artistic expression.

A second reason why late medieval Italy was the birthplace of an intellectual and artistic renaissance lay in the fact that it had a far greater sense of rapport with the classical past than any other territory in western Europe. Ancient Roman monuments were omnipresent throughout the peninsula, and classical Latin literature referred to cities and sites that Renaissance Italians recognized as their own. Italians were particularly intent on reappropriating their classical heritage in the fourteenth and fifteenth centuries because they were also seeking to establish an independent cultural identity in opposition to a scholasticism most closely associated with France. Not only did the removal of the papacy to Avignon for most of the fourteenth century and then the Great Schism from 1378 to 1417 heighten antagonisms between Italy and France but, during the fourteenth century, an intellectual reaction against scholasticism on all fronts encouraged Italians to prefer the intellectual alternatives offered by classical literary sources. As Roman literature and learning took root in Italy, so too did Roman art and architecture, for Roman models could help Italians create a splendid artistic alternative to French Gothicism just as Roman learning offered an intellectual alternative to French scholasticism.

Finally, the Italian Renaissance could not have occurred without the underpinning of Italian wealth. The Italian economy as a whole was probably more prosperous in the thirteenth century than it was in the fourteenth and fifteenth. But late medieval Italy was wealthier in comparison with the rest of Europe than it had been before, a fact that meant that Italian writers and artists were more likely to stay at home than to seek employment abroad. In late medieval Italy, intensive investment in culture arose both from an intensification of urban pride and the concentration of per capita wealth. During the fourteenth century, cities themselves were the primary patrons of art and learning. During the fifteenth century, however, when most Italian city-states succumbed to the hereditary rule of noble families, patronage was monopolized by the princely aristocracy. Among these great princes were

Pope Julius II, by Raphael. The acorns at the top of the throne posts are visual puns for the pope's family name, della Rovere ("of the oak").

the popes in Rome, who based their strength on temporal control of the Papal States. The most worldly of the Renaissance popes—Alexander VI (1492–1503); Julius II (1503–1513); and Leo X (1513–1521), son of the Florentine ruler Lorenzo de' Medici—employed the greatest artists of the day and for a few decades made Rome the artistic capital of Western Europe.

The Italian Renaissance: Literature and Thought

In surveying the accomplishments of Italian Renaissance scholars and writers it is natural to begin with the work of Petrarch (Francesco Petrarca, 1304–1374), the "father of Renaissance humanism." Petrarch was a deeply committed Catholic who believed that scholasticism was entirely misguided because it concentrated on abstract speculation rather than on teaching people how to live virtuously and attain salvation. Petrarch thought that the Christian writer must instead cultivate literary eloquence so that he could inspire people to do good. For him the best models of eloquence were to be found in the classical texts of Latin literature, which were doubly valuable because they were also filled with ethical wisdom. Petrarch dedicated himself, therefore, to rediscovering such texts and to writing his own poems and moral treatises in a Latin style modeled on classical authors. But Petrarch was also a remarkable vernacular poet. The Italian sonnets—later called Petrarchan sonnets—that he wrote for his beloved Laura in the chivalrous style of the troubadours were widely imitated and admired throughout the Renaissance period, and continue to be read today.

Because he was a very traditional Christian, Petrarch's ultimate ideal for human conduct was the solitary life of contemplation and asceticism. But from about 1400 to 1450, subsequent Italian thinkers and scholars, located mainly in Florence, developed a different vision customarily called civic humanism. Civic humanists such as the Florentines Leonardo Bruni (c. 1370–1444) and Leon Battista Alberti (1404–1472) agreed with Petrarch on the need for eloquence and the value of classical literature, but they also taught that man's nature equipped him for action, for usefulness to his family and society, and for serving the state—ideally a republican city-state after the classical or contemporary Florentine model. In their view ambition and the quest for glory were noble impulses that ought to be encouraged. They refused to condemn the striving for material possessions, for they argued that the history of human progress is inseparable from our success in mastering the earth and its resources.

Perhaps the most famous of the civic humanists' writings is Alberti's *On the Family* (1443), in which he argued that the nuclear family was instituted by nature for the well-being of humanity. Within this framework, however, Alberti consigned women to purely domestic roles, asserting that "man [is] by nature more energetic and industrious," and that woman was created "to increase and continue generations, and to nourish and preserve those already born." Although such dismissals of women's intellectual abilities were fiercely resisted by a few notable women humanists, for the most part Italian Renaissance humanism was characterized by a pervasive denigration of women—a denigration expressed also in the works of classical literature that the humanists so much admired.

The Emergence of Textual Scholarship

The civic humanists also went far beyond Petrarch in their knowledge of classical (and especially Greek) literature and philosophy. In this they were aided by a number of Byzantine scholars who had migrated to

SOME RENAISSANCE ATTITUDES TOWARD WOMEN

Italian society in the fourteenth and fifteenth centuries was characterized by marriage patterns in which men in their late twenties or thirties customarily married women in their mid- to late teens. This demographic fact probably contributed to the widely shared belief in this period that wives were essentially children, who could not be trusted with important matters and who were best trained by being beaten. Renaissance humanism did little to change such attitudes. In some cases, it even reinforced them.

After my wife had been settled in my house a few days, and after her first pangs of longing for her mother and family had begun to fade, I took her by the hand and showed her around the whole house. I explained that the loft was the place for grain and that the stores of wine and wood were kept in the cellar. I showed her where things needed for the table were kept, and so on, through the whole house. At the end there were no household goods of which my wife had not learned both the place and the purpose....

Only my books and records and those of my ancestors did I determine to keep well sealed.... These my wife not only could not read, she could not even lay hands on them. I kept my records at all times... locked up and arranged in order in my study, almost like sacred and religious objects. I never gave my wife permission to enter that place, with me or alone....

[Husbands] who take counsel with their wives... are madmen if they think true prudence or good counsel lies in the female brain.... For this very reason I have always tried carefully not to let any secret of mine be known to a woman. I did not doubt that my wife was most loving, and more discreet and modest in her ways than any, but I still considered it safer to have her unable, and not merely unwilling, to harm me.... Furthermore, I made it a rule never to speak with her of anything but household matters or questions of conduct, or of the children.

Leon Battista Alberti, "On the Family," in *The Family in Renaissance Florence*, trans. and ed. Renée N. Watkins. (Columbia, S.C., 1969), pp. 208–213, as abridged in Julie O'Faolain and Lauro Martines, eds., *Not in God's Image: Women in History from the Greeks to the Victorians* (New York, 1973), pp. 187–188.

QUESTIONS FOR ANALYSIS

1. For what reasons did Leon Battista Alberti argue that his wife should have no access to his books or records?
2. Would you expect Renaissance attitudes toward women to have been more liberal and more modern? Did Alberti's comments refer to Italian society as a whole or merely to a small segment of it?

Italy in the first half of the fifteenth century and gave instruction in the Greek language. Italian scholars also traveled to Constantinople and other Eastern cities in search of Greek masterpieces hitherto unknown in the West. In 1423 one Italian, Giovanni Aurispa, alone brought back 238 manuscript books, including works of Sophocles, Euripides, and Thucydides, which were quickly translated into Latin, not word for word, but sense for sense to preserve the literary force of the original. By 1500, most of the Greek classics, including the writings of Plato, the dramatists, and the historians, were available to western Europe.

Related in his textual interests to the civic humanists, but by no means a full adherent of their movement, was the atypical yet highly influential Renaissance thinker Lorenzo Valla (1407–1457). Born in Rome and active primarily as a secretary in the service of the king of Naples, Valla had no allegiance to the republican ideals of the Florentine civic humanists. Instead, he used his skills in grammar, rhetoric, and the painstaking analysis of Greek and Latin texts to show how the thorough study of language could discredit old verities. Most remarkable in this regard was Valla's brilliant demonstration that the Donation of Constantine was a medieval forgery. Whereas papal propagandists had argued that the papacy's rights to temporal rule in western Europe derived from this charter purportedly granted by the emperor Constantine in the fourth century, Valla proved that the charter was full of nonclassical Latin usages and anachronistic terms. Hence he concluded that the "Donation" was the work of a medieval forger whose "monstrous impudence" was exposed by the "stupidity of his language." This demonstration not only discredited a prize specimen of "medieval ignorance" but, more important, introduced the concept of anachronism into all subsequent textual study and historical thought. In his *Notes on the New Testament* he also applied his expert knowledge of Greek to elucidating the true meaning of Saint Paul's letters, which he believed had been obscured by Saint Jerome's Latin Vulgate translation. This work was to prove an important link between Italian Renaissance scholarship and the subsequent Christian humanism of the north.

Renaissance Neoplatonism

From about 1450 until about 1600 Italian thought was dominated by a school of Neoplatonists who sought to blend the ideas of Plato, Plotinus, and various strands of ancient mysticism with Christianity. Foremost among these were Marsilio Ficino (1433–1499) and Giovanni Pico della Mirandola (1463–1494), both of whom were members of the Platonic Academy founded by Cosimo de' Medici in Florence. The academy was a loosely organized society of scholars who met to hear readings and lectures. Their hero was Plato: sometimes they celebrated Plato's birthday by holding a banquet in his honor, after which everybody gave speeches as if they were characters in a Platonic dialogue. From the standpoint of posterity, Ficino's greatest achievement was his translation of Plato's works into Latin, which made them widely available to western Europeans for the first time. Ficino himself, however, regarded his *Hermetic Corpus*, a collection of passages drawn from a number of

Pico della Mirandola. When the young nobleman Pico arrived in Florence at age nineteen he was said to have been "of beauteous feature and shape." This contemporary portrait may have been done by the great Florentine painter Botticelli.

ancient mystical writings including the Hebrew Kabbalah, as his greatest contribution to learning.

It is debatable whether Ficino's own philosophy should be called humanist because he moved away from ethics to metaphysics and taught that the individual should look primarily to the hereafter. In Ficino's opinion, "the immortal soul is always miserable in its mortal body." The same issue arises with respect to Ficino's disciple Giovanni Pico della Mirandola. Pico was certainly not a civic humanist because he saw little worth in mundane public affairs. He also fully shared his teacher's penchant for extracting and combining snippets taken out of context from ancient mystical tracts. But he did also believe—and so argued in his famous *Oration on the Dignity of Man*—that there is "nothing more wonderful than man" because he believed that man is endowed with the capacity to achieve union with God if he so wills.

Machiavelli

Hardly any of the Italian thinkers between Petrarch and Pico were really original: their greatness lay mostly in their manner of expression, their scholarship, and their popularization of different themes of ancient thought. The same, however, cannot be said of Renaissance Italy's greatest political philosopher, the Florentine Niccolò Machiavelli (*mah-kee-uh-VEHL-ee*, 1469–1527). Machiavelli's writings reflect the unstable condition of Italy in his time. At the end of the fifteenth century Italy had become the cockpit of international struggles. Both France and Spain had invaded the peninsula and were competing for the allegiance of the Italian city-states, which in turn were torn by internal dissension. In 1498 Machiavelli became a prominent official in the government of the Florentine republic, set up four years earlier when the French invasion had led to the expulsion of the Medici. His duties largely involved diplomatic missions to other Italian city-states. While in Rome he became fascinated with the attempt of Cesare Borgia, son of Pope Alexander VI, to create his own principality in central Italy. He noted with approval Cesare's ruthlessness and shrewdness and his complete subordination of personal morality to political ends. In 1512 the Medici returned to overthrow the republic of Florence, and Machiavelli was deprived of his position. Disappointed and embittered, he spent the remainder of his life at his country estate, devoting his time to writing.

Machiavelli remains a controversial figure even today. Some modern scholars see him as an amoral theorist of realpolitik, disdainful of morality and Christian piety, caring nothing about the proper purposes of political life, but interested solely in the acquisition and exercise of power as an end in itself. Others see him as an Italian patriot, who viewed princely tyranny as the only way to liberate Italy from its foreign conquerors. Still others see him as a follower of Saint Augustine of Hippo, who understood that in a fallen world populated by sinful people, a ruler's good intentions do not guarantee that his policies will have good results. Instead, Machiavelli insisted that a prince's actions must be judged by their consequences and not by their intrinsic moral quality. Human beings, Machiavelli argued, "are ungrateful, fickle, and deceitful, eager to avoid dangers, and avid for gain." This being so, "the necessity of preserving the state will often compel a prince to take actions which are opposed to loyalty, charity, humanity, and religion. . . . So far as he is able, a prince should stick to the path of good but, if the necessity arises, he should know how to follow evil."

> In the political chaos of early sixteenth-century Italy, Machiavelli saw a ruthless prince such as Borgia as the only hope for revitalizing the spirit of independence among his contemporaries, and so making them fit, once again, for republican self-rule.

The puzzle is heightened by the fact that, on the surface, Machiavelli's two great works of political analysis appear to contradict each other. In his *Discourses on Livy* he praised the ancient Roman republic as a model for his own contemporaries, lauding constitutional government, equality among the citizens of a republic, political independence for city-states, and the subordination of religion to the service of the state. There is little doubt, therefore, that Machiavelli was a committed republican, who believed in the free city-state as the ideal form of human government. But Machiavelli also wrote *The Prince*, "a handbook for tyrants" in the eyes of his critics, and he dedicated this work to Lorenzo, son of Piero de' Medici, whose family had overthrown the Florentine republic that Machiavelli himself had served.

Because *The Prince* has been so much more widely read than the *Discourses*, interpretations of Machiavelli's political thought have often mistaken the admiration he expressed in *The Prince* for Cesare Borgia as an endorsement of princely tyranny for its own sake. Machiavelli's real position was quite different. In the political chaos of early sixteenth-century Italy, Machiavelli saw a ruthless prince such as Borgia as the only hope for revitalizing the spirit of independence among his contemporaries, and so making them fit, once again, for republican self-rule. However dark his vision of human nature, Machiavelli never ceased to hope that his Italian contemporaries would rise up, expel their French and Spanish conquerors, and restore their ancient traditions of republican liberty and equality. Princes such as Borgia were necessary steps toward that end, but for Machiavelli their rule was not the ideal form of government for humankind. In Italy's sunken political situation, however, a princely state was the best form of government toward which Machiavelli's downtrodden contemporaries could aspire.

THE IDEAL OF THE COURTIER

Far more congenial to contemporary tastes than the shocking political theories of Machiavelli were the guidelines for proper aristocratic conduct offered in *The Book of the Courtier* (1528) by the diplomat and count Baldassare Castiglione. This cleverly written forerunner of modern handbooks of etiquette stands in sharp contrast to the earlier civic humanist treatises of Bruni and Alberti. Whereas they taught the sober republican

MACHIAVELLI'S ITALIAN PATRIOTISM

These passages are from the concluding chapter to Machiavelli's treatise The Prince. *Like the book itself, they are addressed to Lorenzo, the son of Piero de' Medici.*

Reflecting on the matters set forth above and considering within myself whether the times were propitious in Italy at present to honor a new prince and whether there is at hand the matter suitable for a prudent and virtuous leader to mold in a new form, giving honor to himself and benefit to the citizens of the country, I have arrived at the opinion that all circumstances now favor such a prince, and I cannot think of a time more propitious for him than the present. If, as I said, it was necessary in order to make apparent the virtue of Moses, that the people of Israel should be enslaved in Egypt, and that the Persians should be oppressed by the Medes to provide an opportunity to illustrate the greatness and the spirit of Cyrus, and that the Athenians should be scattered in order to show the excellence of Theseus, thus at the present time, in order to reveal the valor of an Italian spirit it was essential that Italy should fall to her present low estate, more enslaved than the Hebrews, more servile than the Persians, more disunited than the Athenians, leaderless and lawless, beaten, despoiled, lacerated, overrun and crushed under every kind of misfortune.... So Italy now, left almost lifeless, awaits the coming of one who will heal her wounds, putting an end to the sacking and looting in Lombardy and the spoliation and extortions in the Realm of Naples and Tuscany, and cleanse her sores that have been so long festering. Behold how she prays God to send her some one to redeem her from the cruelty and insolence of the barbarians. See how she is ready and willing to follow any banner so long as there be some one to take it up. Nor has she at present any hope of finding her redeemer save only in your illustrious house [the Medici] which has been so highly exalted both by its own merits and by fortune and which has been favored by God and the church, of which it is now ruler....

This opportunity, therefore, should not be allowed to pass, and Italy, after such a long wait, must be allowed to behold her redeemer. I cannot describe the joy with which he will be received in all these provinces which have suffered so much from the foreign deluge, nor with what thirst for vengeance, nor with what firm devotion, what solemn delight, what tears! What gates could be closed to him, what people could deny him obedience, what envy could withstand him, what Italian could withhold allegiance from him? THIS BARBARIAN OCCUPATION STINKS IN THE NOSTRILS OF ALL OF US. Let your illustrious house then take up this cause with the spirit and the hope with which one undertakes a truly just enterprise....

Niccolò Machiavelli, *The Prince,* trans. and ed. Thomas G. Bergin (Arlington Heights, Ill:, 1947), pp. 75–76, 78.

QUESTIONS FOR ANALYSIS

1. Why did Machiavelli argue that Italy needed the type of prince he had outlined in his book *The Prince*?
2. According to Machiavelli, what was wrong with the Italy of his own day?
3. Did Machiavelli espouse the cause of Italian nationalism or the banner of a strong prince like Lorenzo de' Medici? Or were his visions of patriotism and leadership concurrent?

virtues of strenuous service in behalf of city-state and family, Castiglione, writing in an Italy dominated by magnificent princely courts, taught how to attain the elegant and seemingly effortless qualities necessary for acting like a true gentleman. More than anyone else, Castiglione popularized the ideal of the "Renaissance man": one who is accomplished in many different pursuits and is also brave; witty; and "courteous," meaning civilized and learned. Unlike Alberti, Castiglione said nothing about women's role in "hearth and home" but stressed instead the ways in which court ladies could be "gracious entertainers." Widely read throughout Europe for over a century after its publication, Castiglione's *Courtier* spread Italian ideals of civility to princely courts north of the Alps, resulting in the ever-greater patronage of art and literature by the European aristocracy.

Sixteenth-century Italians were also highly accomplished creators of imaginative prose and verse. Machiavelli himself wrote a delightful short story, "Belfagor," and an engagingly bawdy play, *Mandragola*; the great artist Michelangelo wrote many moving sonnets; and Ludovico Ariosto (1474–1533), the most eminent of sixteenth-century Italian epic poets, wrote a lengthy verse narrative called *Orlando Furioso* (The madness of Roland). Although based on the medieval Charlemagne cycle, this work differed radically from any of the medieval epics because it introduced elements of lyrical fantasy and, above all, because it was totally devoid of heroic idealism. Ariosto wrote to make readers laugh and to charm them with descriptions of the quiet splendor of nature and the passions of love. His work embodies the disillusionment of the late Renaissance, the loss of hope and faith, and the tendency to seek consolation in the pursuit of pleasure and aesthetic delight.

The Italian Renaissance: Painting, Sculpture, and Architecture

What were the principal characteristics of Italian Renaissance art?

Despite numerous intellectual and literary advances, the longest-lived achievements of the Italian Renaissance were made in the realm of art. Of all the arts, painting was undoubtedly supreme. We have already seen the artistic genius of Giotto around 1300, but it was not until the fifteenth century that Italian painting began to come fully of age. One reason for this was that in the early fifteenth century the laws of linear perspective were discovered and first employed to give the fullest sense of three dimensions. Fifteenth-century artists also experimented with effects of light and shade (*chiaroscuro*) and for the first time carefully studied the anatomy and proportions of the human body. By the fifteenth century, too, increasing private wealth and the growth of lay patronage had opened the domain of art to a variety of nonreligious themes and subjects. Even subject matter from biblical history was now frequently infused with nonreligious themes. Artists sought to paint portraits that revealed the hidden mysteries of the soul. Paintings intended to appeal primarily to the intellect were paralleled by others whose main purpose was to delight the eye with gorgeous color and beauty of form. The introduction

The Impact of Perspective. Masaccio's painting *The Trinity with the Virgin* illustrates the startling sense of depth made possible by the rules of perspective.

of painting in oil, probably from Flanders, also characterized fifteenth-century painting. The use of the new technique doubtless had much to do with the artistic advance of this period. Because oil does not dry as quickly as fresco pigment, the painter could now work more slowly, taking time with the more difficult parts of the picture and making corrections if necessary as he or she went along.

Renaissance Painting in Florence

The majority of the great painters of the fifteenth century were Florentines. First among them was the precocious Masaccio (1401–1428), known to his contemporaries as "Giotto reborn." Although he died at the age of twenty-seven, Masaccio inspired the work of Italian painters for a hundred years. Masaccio's greatness as a painter is based on his success in "imitating nature," which became a primary value in Renaissance painting. To achieve this effect he employed perspective, perhaps most dramatically in his fresco of the Trinity; he also used chiaroscuro with originality, leading to strikingly dramatic effects.

Masaccio's best-known successor was the Florentine Sandro Botticelli (1445–1510), who depicted both classical and Christian subjects. Botticelli's work excels in linear rhythms and sensuous depiction of natural detail. He is most famous for paintings that portray figures from classical mythology without any overtly Christian frame of reference. His *Allegory of Spring* and *Birth of Venus* employ a style greatly indebted to Roman depictions of gods, goddesses, zephyrs, and muses moving gracefully in natural settings. Consequently, these works were once understood as the expression of Renaissance paganism at its fullest, a celebration of earthly delights breaking sharply with Christian asceticism. More recently, however, scholars have preferred to view them as allegories fully compatible with Christian teachings. According to this interpretation, Botticelli was addressing himself to learned aristocratic viewers, well versed in the Neoplatonic theories of Ficino, which considered ancient gods and goddesses to represent various Christian virtues. Venus, for example, might have stood for a species of chaste love. Although Botticelli's great "classical" works remain cryptic, two points remain certain: any viewer is free to enjoy them on their naturalistic sensuous level,

Birth of Venus, **by Botticelli.** Botticelli was a mystic as well as a lover of beauty, and this painting is most often interpreted as a Neoplatonic allegory.

WHAT WERE THE PRINCIPAL CHARACTERISTICS OF ITALIAN RENAISSANCE ART?

THE ITALIAN RENAISSANCE: PAINTING, SCULPTURE, AND ARCHITECTURE   453

and Botticelli had surely not broken with Christianity, since he painted frescoes for the pope in Rome at just the same time.

LEONARDO DA VINCI

Perhaps the greatest of the Florentine artists was Leonardo da Vinci (1452–1519), one of the most versatile geniuses who ever lived. Leonardo personified the Renaissance man: he was a painter, architect, musician, mathematician, engineer, and inventor. The illegitimate son of a notary and a peasant woman, Leonardo set up an artist's shop in Florence by the time he was twenty-five and gained the patronage of the Medici ruler of the city, Lorenzo the Magnificent. But if Leonardo had any weakness, it was his slowness in working and difficulty in finishing anything. This naturally displeased Lorenzo and other Florentine patrons, who thought an artist was little more than an artisan, commissioned to produce a certain piece of work of a certain size for a certain price on a certain date. Leonardo, however, strongly objected to this view because he considered himself to be no menial craftsman

The Virgin of the Rocks, **by Leonardo da Vinci.** This painting reveals Leonardo's interest in the human face and in the atmosphere of natural settings.

The Last Supper, **by Leonardo da Vinci.**

but an inspired creator. Therefore in 1482 he left Florence for the Sforza court of Milan where he was given freer rein in structuring his time and work. He remained there until the French invaded Milan in 1499; after that he wandered about Italy, finally accepting the patronage of the French king, Francis I, under whose auspices Leonardo lived and worked in France until his death.

The paintings of Leonardo da Vinci began what is known as the High Renaissance in Italy. His approach to painting was that it should be the most accurate possible imitation of nature. Leonardo was like a naturalist, basing his work on his own detailed observations of a blade of grass, the wing of a bird, a waterfall. He obtained human corpses for dissection and reconstructed in drawing the minutest features of anatomy, which knowledge he carried over to his paintings. Leonardo worshiped nature and was convinced of the essential divinity in all living things. It is not surprising, therefore, that he was a vegetarian and that he went to the marketplace to buy caged birds, which he released to their native habitat.

It is generally agreed that Leonardo's masterpieces are *The Virgin of the Rocks* (which exists in two versions), *The Last Supper*, and his portraits of the Mona Lisa and Ginevra da Benci. *The Virgin of the Rocks* typifies not only his marvelous technical skill but also his passion for science and his belief in the universe as a well-ordered place. The figures are arranged geometrically, with every rock and plant depicted in accurate detail. *The Last Supper*, painted on the walls of the refectory of Santa Maria delle Grazie in Milan, is a study of psychological reactions. A serene Christ, resigned to his terrible fate, has just announced to his disciples that one of them will betray him. The artist succeeds in portraying the mingled emotions of surprise, horror, and guilt in the faces of the disciples as they gradually perceive the meaning of their master's statement. The third and fourth of Leonardo's major triumphs, the *Mona Lisa* and *Ginevra da Benci*, reflect a similar interest in the varied moods of the human soul.

THE VENETIAN SCHOOL

The beginning of the High Renaissance around 1490 also witnessed the rise of the so-called Venetian school, the major members of which were Giovanni Bellini (c. 1430–1516), Giorgione (1478–1510), and Titian (c. 1490–1576). The work of all these men reflected the luxurious, pleasure-loving life of the thriving commercial city of Venice. Most Venetian painters showed little of the Florentine school's concerns with philosophical and psychological issues. Their aim was to appeal to the senses by painting idyllic landscapes and sumptuous portraits of the rich and powerful. In the subordination of form and meaning to color and elegance they mirrored the sumptuous tastes of the wealthy merchants for whom they were created.

Doge Francesco Venier (1555), by Titian. Titian served as the official painter of the Venetian Republic for sixty years. This superb portrait of Venice's ruler shows Titian's mastery of light and color.

WHAT WERE THE PRINCIPAL CHARACTERISTICS OF ITALIAN RENAISSANCE ART?

PAINTING IN ROME

High Renaissance painting reached its peak in the first half of the sixteenth century. During this period, Rome became the major artistic center of the Italian peninsula, although the traditions of the Florentine school still exerted a potent influence.

RAPHAEL

Among the eminent painters of this period was Raphael (1483–1520), a native of Urbino, and perhaps the most beloved artist of the entire Renaissance. The lasting appeal of his style is due primarily to his ennobling portrayals of human beings as temperate, wise, and dignified creatures. Although Raphael was influenced by Leonardo, he cultivated a much more symbolical or allegorical approach to his painting. His *Disputà* illustrated the relationship between the church in heaven and the church on earth. In a worldly setting against a brilliant sky, theologians debate the meaning of the Eucharist, while in the clouds above, saints and the Trinity repose in the possession of a holy mystery. Raphael's *School of Athens* depicts the harmony between Platonism and Aristotelianism. Plato (painted as a portrait of Leonardo) is shown pointing upward to emphasize the spiritual basis of his world of Ideas, while Aristotle stretches a hand forward to exemplify his claim that the created world embodies these same principles in physical form. Raphael is noted also for his portraits and Madonnas. To the latter, especially, he gave a softness and warmth that seemed to endow them with a sweetness and piety quite different from Leonardo's enigmatic and somewhat distant Madonnas.

MICHELANGELO

The last towering figure of the High Renaissance was Michelangelo (1475–1564), a native of Florence. If Leonardo was a naturalist, Michelangelo was an idealist; where the former sought to recapture and interpret fleeting natural phenomena, Michelangelo, who

School of Athens, by Raphael.

THE CIVILIZATION OF THE RENAISSANCE, C. 1350–1550

The Creation of Adam, by Michelangelo (1475–1564). One of a series of frescoes on the ceiling of the Sistine Chapel in Rome. Inquiring into the nature of humanity, it represents Renaissance affirmativeness at its height.

embraced Neoplatonism as a philosophy, was more concerned with expressing enduring, abstract truths. Michelangelo was a painter, sculptor, architect, and poet—and he expressed himself in all these forms with a similar power and in a similar manner. At the center of all of his paintings is the male figure, which is always powerful, colossal, magnificent. If humanity, embodied in the male body, lay at the center of Italian Renaissance culture, then Michelangelo, who depicted the male figure without cease, is the supreme Renaissance artist.

Michelangelo's greatest achievements in painting appear in a single location—the Sistine Chapel in Rome—yet they are products of two different periods in the artist's life and consequently exemplify two different artistic styles and outlooks on the human condition. More famous are the sublime frescoes Michelangelo painted on the ceiling of the Sistine Chapel from 1508 to 1512, depicting scenes from the book of Genesis. All the panels in this series, including *God Dividing the Light from Darkness, The Creation of Adam,* and *The Flood,* exemplify the young artist's commitment to classical Greek aesthetic principles of harmony, solidity, and dignified restraint. Correspondingly, all exude a sense of sublime affirmation regarding the Creation and the heroic qualities of humankind. But a quarter of a century later, when Michelangelo returned to work in the Sistine Chapel, both his style and mood had changed dramatically. In the enormous *Last Judgment,* a fresco done for the Sistine Chapel's altar wall in 1536, Michelangelo repudiated classical restraint and substituted a style that emphasized tension and distortion to communicate the older man's pessimistic conception of a humanity wracked by fear and bowed by guilt.

SCULPTURE

In the realm of sculpture the Italian Renaissance took a great step forward by creating statues that were no longer carved as parts of columns or doorways on church buildings or as effigies on tombs. Instead, Italian sculptors for the first time since antiquity carved free-standing statues "in the round." By freeing sculpture from its bondage to architecture, the High Renaissance reestablished sculpture as a separate and potentially secular art form.

DONATELLO

The first great master of Renaissance sculpture was Donatello (c. 1386–1466). His bronze statue of David triumphant over the head of the slain Goliath, the first free-standing nude since antiquity, imitated classical sculpture not just in the depiction of a nude body but also in the subject's posture of resting his weight on one leg. Yet this David is clearly a lithe adolescent rather than a muscular Greek athlete. Later in his career, Donatello more consciously imitated ancient statuary in his commanding portrayal of the proud warrior Gattamelata—the first monumental equestrian statue in bronze executed in the West since the time of the Romans.

MICHELANGELO

Certainly the greatest sculptor of the Italian Renaissance—indeed, probably the greatest sculptor of all time—was Michelangelo. Believing with Leonardo that the artist was an inspired creator, Michelangelo regarded sculpture as the most exalted of the arts because it allowed the artist to imitate God most fully in re-creating human forms. Furthermore, in Michelangelo's view the most God-like sculptor disdained slavish naturalism, for anyone could make a plaster cast of a human figure, but only an inspired creative genius could endow his sculpted figures with a sense of life. Accordingly, Michelangelo subordinated naturalism to the force of his imagination and sought restlessly to express his ideals in ever more arresting forms.

Like his painting, Michelangelo's sculpture followed a course from classicism to mannerism—that is, from

David, **by Donatello (c. 1386–1466).** The first free-standing nude statue executed in the West since antiquity.

harmonious modeling to dramatic distortion. The sculptor's most distinguished early work, his *David,* executed in 1501, is surely his most perfect classical statue. Choosing, like Donatello, to depict a male nude, Michelangelo conceived of his own *David* as a public expression of Florentine civic ideals and hence as heroic rather than merely graceful. To this end he worked in marble—the "noblest" sculptural medium—and created a figure twice as large as life. By sculpting a serenely confident young man at the peak of physical fitness, Michelangelo celebrated the Florentine republic's own fortitude in resisting tyrants and upholding

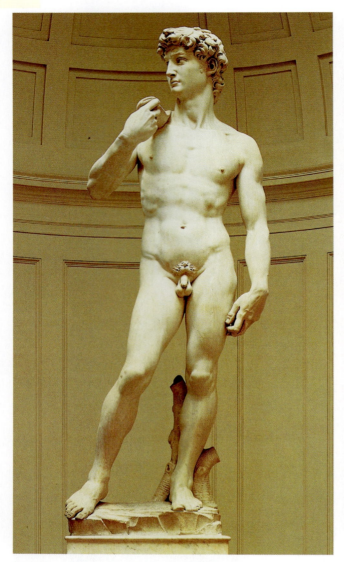

David, by Michelangelo. Over thirteen feet high, this serenely self-confident affirmation of the beauty of the human form was placed prominently by the Florentine government in front of Florence's city hall to proclaim the city's humanistic values.

The Descent from the Cross, by Michelangelo. This portrayal of tragedy was made by the sculptor for his own tomb. Note the distortion for effect exemplified by the elongated body and left arm of the figure of Christ. The figure in the rear is Nicodemus, but was probably intended to represent Michelangelo himself.

ideals of civic justice. The serenity seen in *David* was no longer prominent in the works of Michelangelo's middle period; rather, in a work such as his *Moses* of about 1515, the sculptor had begun to explore the use of anatomical distortion to create effects of emotional intensity—in this case, the biblical prophet's righteous rage. While such statues remained awesomely heroic, as Michelangelo's life drew to a close he experimented more and more with exaggerated stylistic mannerisms for the purpose of communicating moods of brooding pensiveness or outright pathos. The culmination of this trend in Michelangelo's statuary is his unfinished but intensely moving *Descent from the Cross*, a depiction of an old man resembling the sculptor himself grieving over the distorted, slumping body of the dead Christ.

ARCHITECTURE

To a much greater extent than either sculpture or painting, Renaissance architecture had its roots in the past. The new building style was a compound of elements derived from the Middle Ages and from antiquity. It was not the Gothic, however, a style that had never found a congenial soil in Italy, but the Italian Romanesque that

The Villa Rotonda, by Palladio. A highly influential Renaissance private dwelling near Vicenza.

provided the medieval basis for the architecture of the Italian Renaissance. The great architects of the Renaissance generally adopted their building plans from Romanesque churches, some of which they believed, mistakenly, to be Roman rather than medieval. They also copied their decorative devices from the ruins of ancient Rome. The result was an architecture based on the cruciform floor plan of transept and nave, but embodying the decorative features of the column and arch or the column and lintel, the colonnade, and frequently the dome. Renaissance architecture also emphasized geometrical proportion because Italian builders, under the influence of Neoplatonism, concluded that certain mathematical ratios reflect the harmony of the universe. A fine example of Renaissance architecture is St. Peter's Basilica in Rome, built under the patronage of popes Julius II and Leo X and designed by some of the most celebrated architects of the time, including Donato Bramante (c. 1444–1514) and Michelangelo. Equally impressive are the artfully proportioned aristocratic country houses designed by the northern Italian architect Andrea Palladio (1508–1580), who created secular miniatures of ancient temples such as the Roman Pantheon to glorify the aristocrats who dwelled within them.

CHRONOLOGY

LIVES OF ITALIAN RENAISSANCE SCHOLARS AND ARTISTS

Petrarch	1304–1374
Leon Battista Alberti	1404–1472
Giovanni Pico della Mirandola	1463–1494
Niccolò Machiavelli	1469–1527
Leonardo da Vinci	1452–1519
Titian	c. 1490–1576
Raphael	1483–1520
Michelangelo	1475–1564

The Waning of the Italian Renaissance

Why did the Renaissance decline around 1550?

Around 1550 the Renaissance in Italy began to decline. The causes of this decline were varied. The French invasion of 1494 and the incessant warfare that ensued was one of the major factors. The French king Charles VIII viewed Italy as an attractive target for his expansive dynastic ambitions. In 1494 he led an army of 30,000 well-trained troops across the Alps to press his claims to the Duchy of Milan and the Kingdom of Naples. Florence swiftly capitulated; within less than a year the French had promenaded down the peninsula and conquered Naples. By so doing, however, they aroused the suspicions of the rulers of Spain, who feared an attack on their own territory of Sicily. An alliance among Spain, the Papal States, the Holy Roman Empire, Milan, and Venice finally forced Charles to withdraw from Italy. But the respite was brief. Charles's successor, Louis XII, launched a second invasion, and from 1499 until 1529 warfare in Italy was virtually uninterrupted. Alliances and counteralliances followed each other in bewildering succession, but they managed only to prolong the hostilities. The French won a great victory at Marignano in 1515, but they were decisively defeated by the Spanish at Pavia in 1525. The worst disaster came in 1527 when rampaging troops under the command of the Spanish ruler and Holy Roman emperor Charles V sacked the city of Rome, causing enormous destruction. Only in 1529 did Charles V finally manage to gain control over most of the Italian peninsula, putting an end to the fighting for a time. Once triumphant, Charles retained two of the largest portions of Italy for Spain—the Duchy of Milan and the Kingdom of Naples—and installed favored princes as the rulers of almost all the other Italian political entities except for Venice and the Papal States. These protégés of the Spanish crown continued to preside over their own courts, to patronize the arts, and to adorn their cities with luxurious buildings; but they were puppets of a foreign power and unable to inspire their retinues with a sense of vigorous cultural independence.

To these political disasters was added a waning of Italian prosperity. Italy's virtual monopoly of trade with Asia in the fifteenth century had been one of the chief economic supports for Italian Renaissance culture, but the gradual shifting of trade routes from the Mediterranean to the Atlantic region, following the overseas discoveries of around 1500, slowly but surely cost Italy its supremacy as the center of European trade. Warfare also contributed to Italy's economic hardships, as did Spanish financial exactions in Milan and Naples. As Italian wealth diminished, there was less and less of a surplus to support artistic endeavors.

A final cause of the decline of the Italian Renaissance was the Counter-Reformation. During the sixteenth century the Roman church sought increasingly to exercise firm control over thought and art as part of a campaign to combat worldliness and the spread of Protestantism. In 1542 the Roman Inquisition was established; in 1564 the first Roman Index of Prohibited Books was published. Even Michelangelo's great *Last Judgment* in the Sistine Chapel was criticized for showing too many naked bodies. Therefore, Pope Paul IV ordered a second-rate artist to paint in clothing wherever possible. (The unfortunate artist was afterward known as the "underwear maker.") Although this incident may appear merely grotesquely humorous, the determination of ecclesiastical censors to enforce doctrinal uniformity could lead to death, as in the case of the unfortunate Neoplatonic philosopher Giordano Bruno, whose insistence that there may be more than one world (in contravention of the biblical book of Genesis) resulted in his being burned at the stake by the Roman Inquisition in 1600.

Galileo was not willing to die for his beliefs, but after he publicly retracted his view that the earth revolves around the sun he supposedly whispered, "despite everything, it still moves."

The most notorious example of inquisitorial censorship of intellectual speculation was the disciplining of the great scientist Galileo, whose achievements we will discuss in more detail in Chapter Sixteen. In 1616 the Holy Office in Rome condemned the new astronomical theory that the earth moves around the sun as "foolish, absurd, philosophically false, and formally heretical." When Galileo published a brilliant defense of the heliocentric system in 1632 the Inquisition ordered Galileo to recant his "errors" and sentenced him to house arrest for the duration of his life. Galileo was not willing to die for his beliefs, but after he publicly retracted his view that the earth revolves around the sun he supposedly whispered, "despite everything, it still moves." It is not surprising that the great astronomical discoveries of the next generation were made in northern Europe, not in Italy.

Cultural and artistic achievement was by no means extinguished in Italy after the middle of the sixteenth century. On the contrary, impressive new artistic styles were cultivated between about 1540 and 1600 by painters who drew on traits found in the later work of Raphael and Michelangelo. In the seventeenth cen-

WHY DID THE RENAISSANCE DECLINE AROUND 1550?

THE WANING OF THE ITALIAN RENAISSANCE

THE STATES OF ITALY DURING THE RENAISSANCE, C. 1494

Note the political divisions of Italy on the eve of the French invasion in 1494. Contemporary observers often described Italy as being divided among five great powers: Milan, Venice, Florence, the Papal States, and the Kingdom of Naples. Which of these powers were most interested in expanding their territory? Which neighboring territories would be most threatened by such attempts at expansion? Why did Florence and the Papal States so often find themselves in conflict with each other?

tury came the dazzling Baroque style, which was born in Rome under ecclesiastical auspices. Similarly, Italian music registered enormous accomplishments virtually without interruption from the sixteenth to the twentieth century. But as Renaissance culture spread from Italy to the rest of Europe, the cultural dominance of the Italians began to wane, and the focus of European high culture shifted toward the princely courts of Spain, France, England, Germany, and Poland.

12 THE CIVILIZATION OF THE RENAISSANCE, C. 1350–1550

THE RENAISSANCE IN THE NORTH

How did the northern and Italian Renaissances differ from one another?

Contacts between Italy and northern Europe continued throughout the fourteenth and fifteenth centuries. Italian merchants and financiers were familiar figures at northern courts; students from all over Europe studied at Italian universities such as Bologna or Padua; authors (including Chaucer) and their works traveled to and from Italy; and northern soldiers were frequent participants in Italian wars. Only at the end of the fifteenth century, however, did the new currents of Italian Renaissance learning begin to take firm hold in Spain and northern Europe.

A variety of explanations have been offered for this delay. Northern European intellectual life in the late Middle Ages was dominated by universities such as Paris, Oxford, and Charles University in Prague, whose curricula focused on the study of philosophical logic and Christian theology. This approach left little room for the study of classical literature. In Italy, by contrast, universities were more often professional schools for law and medicine, and universities themselves exercised much less influence over intellectual life. As a result, a more secular, urban-oriented educational tradition took shape in Italy, within which Renaissance humanism was able to develop. Even in the sixteenth century, northern scholars influenced by Italian Renaissance ideals usually worked outside the university system under the patronage of kings and princes.

Before the sixteenth century, northern rulers were also less interested in patronizing artists and intellectuals than were the city-states and princes of Italy. In Italy, such patronage was an important arena for competition between political rivals. In northern Europe, political units were larger and political rivals were fewer. It was therefore more difficult to use art for political purposes in a kingdom than it was in a city-state. In Florence, a statue erected in a central square would be seen by nearly all the city's residents. In Paris, such a statue would be seen only by a tiny minority of the French king's subjects. Only in the sixteenth century, as northern nobles began to spend more time in residence at the royal court, could kings be reasonably certain that their patronage of artists and intellectuals would be noticed by those whom they were trying to impress.

CHRISTIAN HUMANISM AND THE NORTHERN RENAISSANCE

The northern Renaissance was the product of the grafting of certain Italian Renaissance ideals onto pre-existing northern traditions. This can be seen very clearly in the case of the most prominent northern Renaissance intellectual movement, Christian humanism. Although they shared the Italian humanists' contempt for scholasticism, northern Christian humanists more often looked for ethical guidance from biblical and religious precepts rather than from Cicero or Virgil. Like their Italian counterparts, they sought wisdom from antiquity, but the antiquity they had in mind was Christian rather than classical—the antiquity, that is, of the New Testament and the early church fathers. Similarly, northern Renaissance artists were inspired by the accomplishments of Italian masters to learn classical techniques. But northern artists depicted classical subject matter far less frequently than did the Italians and almost never portrayed completely nude human figures.

> Although they shared the Italian humanists' contempt for scholasticism, northern Christian humanists more often looked for ethical guidance from biblical and religious precepts rather than from Cicero or Virgil.

DESIDERIUS ERASMUS

Any discussion of northern Renaissance accomplishments in the realm of thought and literary expression must begin with the career of Desiderius Erasmus (c. 1469–1536), the "prince of the Christian humanists." The illegitimate son of a priest, Erasmus was born near Rotterdam in Holland but later, as a result of his wide travels, became in effect a citizen of all northern Europe. Forced into a monastery against his will when he was a teenager, the young Erasmus found there little religion or formal instruction of any kind but plenty of freedom to read what he liked. He devoured all the classics he could get his hands on and the writings of many of the church fathers. When he was

HOW DID THE NORTHERN AND ITALIAN RENAISSANCES DIFFER FROM ONE ANOTHER?

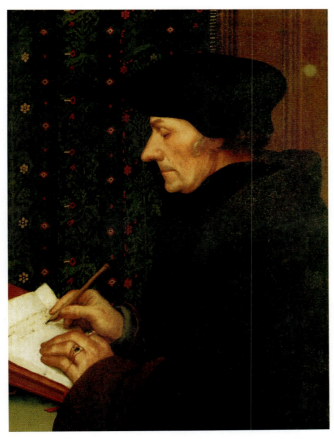

Erasmus, by Hans Holbein the Younger (1497–1543). This portrait is generally regarded as the most telling visual characterization of the prince of the Christian humanists.

about thirty years of age, he obtained permission to leave the monastery and enroll in the University of Paris, where he completed the requirements for the degree of bachelor of divinity. But Erasmus subsequently rebelled against what he considered the arid learning of Parisian scholasticism. Nor did he ever serve actively as a priest. Instead he made his living from teaching, writing, and the proceeds of various ecclesiastical offices that required no spiritual duties of him. Ever on the lookout for new patrons, he traveled often to England, stayed once for three years in Italy, and resided in several different cities in Germany and the Netherlands before settling finally toward the end of his life in Basel, Switzerland. By means of a voluminous correspondence that he kept up with learned friends he made wherever he went, Erasmus became the leader of a northern European humanist coterie. And through the popularity of his numerous publications, he became the arbiter of northern European cultural tastes during his lifetime.

Erasmus's many-sided intellectual activity may best be appraised from two different points of view: the literary and the doctrinal. As a Latin prose stylist, Erasmus was unequaled since the days of Cicero. Extraordinarily learned and witty, he reveled in tailoring his mode of discourse to fit his subject, creating dazzling verbal effects and coining puns that took on added meaning if the reader knew Greek as well as Latin. Above all, Erasmus excelled in the deft use of irony, poking fun at all and sundry, including himself. For example, in his *Colloquies* (from the Latin for "discussions") he had a fictional character lament the evil signs of the times thus: "kings make war, priests strive to line their pockets, theologians invent syllogisms, monks roam outside their cloisters, the commons riot, and Erasmus writes colloquies."

But although Erasmus's urbane Latin style and wit earned him a wide audience for purely literary reasons, he intended everything he wrote to promote what he called the "philosophy of Christ." Erasmus believed that the entire society of his day was caught up in corruption and immorality because people had lost sight of the simple teachings of the Gospels. Accordingly, he offered to his contemporaries three different categories of publication: clever satires meant to show people the error of their ways, serious moral treatises meant to offer guidance toward proper Christian behavior, and scholarly editions of basic Christian texts.

In the first category belong the works of Erasmus that are still most widely read today—*The Praise of Folly* (1509), in which he pilloried scholastic pedantry and dogmatism as well as the ignorance and superstitious credulity of the masses; and the *Colloquies* (1518), in which he held up contemporary religious practices for examination in a more serious but still pervasively ironic tone. In such works Erasmus let fictional characters do the talking; hence his own views can be determined only by inference. But in his second mode Erasmus did not hesitate to speak clearly in his own voice. The most prominent treatises in this genre are the quietly eloquent *Handbook of the Christian Knight* (1503), which urged the laity to pursue lives of serene inward piety, and the *Complaint of Peace* (1517), which pleaded movingly for Christian pacifism. Erasmus's pacifism was one of his most deeply held values, and he returned to it again and again in his published works.

Despite the success of his literary works, Erasmus considered his textual scholarship his greatest achievement. Revering the authority of the early Latin fathers Augustine, Jerome, and Ambrose, he brought out reliable editions of all their works. He also used his extraordinary command of Latin and Greek to produce a more accurate edition of the New Testament. After reading Lorenzo Valla's *Notes on the New Testament* in 1504, Erasmus became convinced that nothing was more imperative than divesting the New Testament of the myriad errors in transcription and translation that had piled up during the Middle Ages, for no one could be a good Christian without being certain of exactly what Christ's message really was. Hence he spent ten years studying and comparing all the best early Greek biblical manuscripts he could find in order to establish an authoritative text. When it finally appeared in 1516, Erasmus's Greek New Testament, published together with explanatory notes and his own new Latin translation, was one of the most important landmarks of biblical scholarship of all time. In the hands of Martin Luther, it would play a critical role in the early stages of the Protestant Reformation.

SIR THOMAS MORE

One of Erasmus's closest friends, and a close second to him in distinction among the ranks of the Christian humanists, was the Englishman Sir Thomas More (1478–1535). Following a successful career as a lawyer and as speaker of the House of Commons, in 1529 More was appointed lord chancellor of England. He was not long in this position, however, before he incurred the wrath of King Henry VIII. More, who was loyal to Catholic universalism, opposed the king's design to establish a national church under royal control. Finally, in 1534, when More refused to take an oath acknowledging Henry as head of the Church of England, he was thrown into the Tower of London, and a year later met his death on the scaffold as a Catholic martyr. Much earlier, however, in 1516, long before More had any inkling of how his life was to end, he published the one work for which he will ever be best remembered, *Utopia*. Purporting to describe an ideal community on an imaginary island, the book is really an Erasmian critique of the glaring abuses of the time—poverty undeserved and wealth unearned, drastic punishments, religious persecution, and the senseless slaughter of war. The inhabitants of Utopia hold all their goods in common, work only six hours a day so that all may have leisure for intellectual pursuits, and practice the natural virtues of wisdom, moderation, fortitude, and justice. Iron is the precious metal "because it is useful," war and monasticism do not exist, and toleration is granted to all who recognize the

Sir Thomas More, by Hans Holbein the Younger.

existence of God and the immortality of the soul. Although More advanced no explicit arguments in his *Utopia* in favor of Christianity, he clearly meant to imply that if the Utopians could manage their society so well without the benefit of Christian revelation, Europeans who knew the Gospels ought to be able to do even better.

ULRICH VON HUTTEN

Whereas Erasmus and More were basically conciliatory in their temperaments and preferred to express themselves by means of wry understatement, Erasmus's German disciple Ulrich von Hutten (1488–1523) was of a much more combative disposition. Dedicated to the cause of German cultural nationalism, von Hutten spoke up truculently to defend the "proud and free" German people against foreigners. But his chief claim to fame was his collaboration with another German humanist, Crotus Rubianus, in the authorship of the *Letters of Obscure Men* (1515), one of the most stinging satires in the history of literature. This was written as part of a propaganda war in favor of a scholar named Johann Reuchlin who wished to pursue his study of

Hebrew writings—above all, the Talmud. When scholastic theologians and the German inquisitor general tried to have all Hebrew books in Germany destroyed, Reuchlin and his party strongly opposed the move. After a while it became apparent that direct argument was accomplishing nothing, so Reuchlin's supporters resorted to ridicule. Von Hutten and Rubianus published a series of letters, written in intentionally bad Latin, purportedly by some of Reuchlin's scholastic opponents from the University of Cologne. These opponents, given such ridiculous names as Goatmilker, Baldpate, and Dungspreader, were shown to be learned fools who paraded absurd religious literalism or grotesque erudition. Heinrich Sheep's-mouth, for example, the supposed writer of one of the letters, professed to be worried that he had sinned grievously by eating on Friday an egg that contained the embryo of a chick. The author of another boasted of his "brilliant discovery" that Julius Caesar could not have written Latin histories because he was too busy with his military exploits ever to have learned Latin. Although immediately banned by the church, the letters circulated nonetheless and were widely read, giving ever more currency to the Erasmian proposition that scholastic theology and external religious observances had to be set aside in favor of the most earnest dedication to the simple teachings of the Gospels.

THE DECLINE OF CHRISTIAN HUMANISM

With Erasmus, More, and von Hutten the list of energetic and eloquent Christian humanists is by no means exhausted, for the Englishman John Colet (c. 1467–1519), the Frenchman Jacques Lefèvre d'Étaples (c. 1455–1536), and the Spaniards Cardinal Francisco Ximénez de Cisneros (1436–1517) and Juan Luís Víves (1492–1540) all made signal contributions to the collective enterprise of editing biblical and early Christian texts and expounding Gospel morality. But despite a host of achievements, the Christian humanist movement, which possessed such an extraordinary degree of international solidarity and vigor from about 1500 to 1525, was thrown into disarray by the rise of Protestantism and subsequently lost its momentum.

The irony here is obvious, for the Christian humanists' emphasis on the literal truth of the Gospels and their devastating criticisms of clerical corruption and religious ceremonialism certainly helped pave the way for the Protestant Reformation initiated by Martin Luther in 1517. But, as we will see in Chapter Thirteen, very few of the older generation of Christian humanists were willing to join Luther in rejecting the fundamental principles on which Catholicism was based, and the few who did became such ardent Protestants that they lost the sense of quiet irony that had been a hallmark of Christian humanist expression. Most Christian humanists tried to remain within the Catholic fold while still espousing their ideal of nonritualistic inward piety. But as time went on, the leaders of Catholicism grew less and less tolerant because lines were hardening in the war with Protestantism. Hence any internal criticism of Catholic religious practices seemed like giving covert aid to the enemy. Erasmus himself, who remained a Catholic, died early enough to escape opprobrium, but several of his less fortunate followers lived on to suffer as victims of the Inquisition.

> Most Christian humanists tried to remain within the Catholic fold while still espousing their ideal of nonritualistic inward piety. But as time went on, the leaders of Catholicism grew less and less tolerant because lines were hardening in the war with Protestantism.

LITERATURE, ART, AND MUSIC IN THE NORTHERN RENAISSANCE

Yet if Christian humanism faded rapidly after about 1525, the northern Renaissance continued to flourish throughout the sixteenth century in literature and art. In France, Pierre de Ronsard (c. 1524–1585) and Joachim du Bellay (c. 1522–1560) wrote elegant sonnets in the style of Petrarch, and in England the poets Sir Philip Sidney (1554–1586) and Edmund Spenser (c. 1552–1599) drew impressively on Italian literary innovations. Indeed, Spenser's *Faerie Queene*, a long chivalric romance written in the manner of Ariosto's *Orlando Furioso*, communicates as well as any Italian work the gorgeous sensuousness typical of Italian Renaissance culture.

RABELAIS

More original than any of the aforementioned poets was the French prose satirist François Rabelais (ra-beh-LAY, c. 1494–1553), probably the best loved of all the great European creative writers of the sixteenth century. Like Erasmus, whom he greatly admired, Rabelais began his career in the clergy, but soon after taking holy orders he left his cloister to study medicine. As a practicing physician Rabelais interspersed his professional activities with literary endeavors, composing almanacs, satires against quacks and astrologers, and burlesques of popular superstitions. But by far his most enduring work was his five volumes of "chronicles" published under the collective title *Gargantua and Pantagruel*.

Rabelais's account of the adventures of Gargantua and Pantagruel, originally the names of legendary medieval giants noted for their fabulous size and gross appetites, served as a vehicle for his lusty humor and his penchant for exuberant narrative as well as for the expression of his philosophy of naturalism. To some degree, Rabelais drew on the precedents of Christian humanism. Thus, like Erasmus, he satirized religious ceremonialism, ridiculed scholasticism, scoffed at superstitions, and pilloried every form of bigotry. But unlike Erasmus, who wrote in a highly cultivated classical Latin style comprehensible to only the most learned readers, Rabelais chose to address a far wider audience by writing in an extremely down-to-earth French loaded with the crudest vulgarities. Likewise, Rabelais wanted to avoid seeming in any way preachy and therefore eschewed all suggestions of moralism in favor of giving the impression that he wished merely to offer his readers some rollicking good fun. Yet, aside from the critical satire in *Gargantua and Pantagruel*, there runs through all five volumes a common theme of glorifying the human and the natural. For Rabelais, whose robust giants were really life-loving human beings writ very large, every instinct of humanity was healthy, provided it was not directed toward tyranny over others. Thus in his ideal community, the utopian "abbey of Thélème," there was no repressiveness whatsoever, but only a congenial environment for the pursuit of life-affirming, natural human attainments, guided by the single rule of "love and do what thou wouldst."

Architecture

Just as Rabelais recounted stories of medieval giants to affirm Renaissance values, so French architects who constructed such splendid Loire châteaux as Amboise,

Chambord. Built in the early sixteenth century by an Italian architect in the service of King Francis I of France, this magnificent Loire Valley château combines Gothic and Renaissance architectural traits.

Chenonceaux, and Chambord combined elements of the late medieval French flamboyant Gothic style with an up-to-date emphasis on classical horizontality to produce some of the most impressively distinctive architectural landmarks ever constructed in France. Yet much closer architectural imitation of Italian models occurred in France as well, for just as Ronsard and du Bellay modeled their poetic style very closely on Petrarch, so Pierre Lescot, the French architect who began work on the new royal palace of the Louvre in Paris in 1546, hewed closely to the classicism of Italian Renaissance masters in constructing a facade that emphasized classical pilasters and pediments.

Painting

Northern Renaissance painting is another realm in which we can discern links between thought and art. Certainly the most moving visual embodiments of the ideals of Christian humanism were conceived by the foremost of northern Renaissance artists, the German Albrecht Dürer (1471–1528). Dürer (*DOOR-er*) was the first northerner to master Italian Renaissance techniques of proportion, perspective, and modeling. Dürer also shared with contemporary Italians a fascination with reproducing the manifold works of nature down to the minutest details and a penchant for displaying the human nude in various postures. But whereas Michelangelo portrayed his *David* or *Adam* entirely without covering, Dürer's nudes are seldom lacking their fig leaves, in deference to more restrained northern traditions. Moreover, Dürer consistently refrained from abandoning himself to the pure classicism and sumptuousness of much Italian Renaissance art because he was inspired primarily by the more traditionally Christian ideals of Erasmus. Thus Dürer's serenely radiant engraving of Saint Jerome expresses the sense of accomplishment that Erasmus or any other contemporary Christian humanist may have had while working quietly in his study; and his *Four Apostles* intones a solemn hymn to the dignity and penetrating insight of Dürer's favorite New Testament authors, Saints Paul, John, Peter, and Mark.

Dürer would have loved nothing more than to have immortalized Erasmus in a major painted portrait, but circumstances prevented him from doing this because the paths of the two men crossed only once, and after Dürer started sketching his hero on that occasion his work was interrupted by Erasmus's press of business.

***Saint Jerome in His Study*, by Dürer.** Saint Jerome, a hero to both Dürer and Erasmus, represents inspired Christian scholarship. Note how the scene exudes contentment, even down to the sleeping lion, which seems rather like an overgrown tabby cat.

CHAPTER 12

THE CIVILIZATION OF THE RENAISSANCE, C. 1350–1550

Instead, the accomplishment of capturing Erasmus's pensive spirit in oils was left to another great northern Renaissance artist, the German Hans Holbein the Younger (1497–1543; see p. 463). As good fortune would have it, during a stay in England, Holbein also painted an extraordinarily acute portrait of Erasmus's friend and kindred spirit Sir Thomas More, which enables us to see clearly why a contemporary called More "a man of . . . sad gravity; a man for all seasons" (see p. 464). These two portraits in and of themselves point out a major difference between medieval and Renaissance culture. Whereas the Middle Ages produced no convincing naturalistic likenesses of any leading intellectual figures, Renaissance culture's greater commitment to capturing the essence of human individuality created the environment in which Holbein was able to make Erasmus and More come to life.

MUSIC

Music in western Europe in the fifteenth and sixteenth centuries reached such a high point of development that it constitutes, together with painting and sculpture, one of the most brilliant aspects of Renaissance endeavor. The musical theory of the Renaissance was driven largely by the humanist-inspired but largely fruitless effort to recover and imitate classical musical forms and modes. Musical practice, however, showed much more continuity with medieval musical traditions of number and proportion. At the same time, however, a new expressiveness emerges in Renaissance music, along with a new emphasis on coloration and emotional quality. New musical instruments were also developed, including the lute, the viol, the violin, and a variety of woodwind and keyboard instruments including the harpsichord. New musical forms also emerged: madrigals, motets, and, at the end of the sixteenth century, a new Italian form, the opera. As earlier, musical leadership came from men trained in the service of the church. But the distinction between sacred and profane music was becoming less sharp, and most composers did not restrict their activities to a single field. Music was no longer regarded merely as a diversion or an adjunct to worship but came into its own as a serious independent art.

> The madrigals, ballads, and other songs composed by the ars nova musicians testify to a rich fourteenth-century tradition of secular music, but the greatest achievement of the period was a highly complicated yet delicate contrapuntal style adapted for ecclesiastical motets.

During the fourteenth century, before or in the early Renaissance period, a musical movement called *ars nova* ("new art") flourished in Italy and France. Its outstanding composers were Francesco Landini (c. 1325–1397) and Guillaume de Machaut (c. 1300–1377). The madrigals, ballads, and other songs composed by the ars nova musicians testify to a rich fourteenth-century tradition of secular music, but the greatest achievement of the period was a highly complicated yet delicate contrapuntal style adapted for ecclesiastical motets. Machaut, moreover, was the first known composer to provide a polyphonic version of the major sections of the Mass.

The fifteenth century ushered in a synthesis of French, Flemish, and Italian elements in the ducal court of Burgundy. This music was melodious and gentle, but in the second half of the century it hardened a little as northern Flemish elements gained in importance. As the sixteenth century opened, Franco-Flemish composers appeared in every important court and cathedral all over Europe, gradually establishing regional-national schools, usually in attractive combinations of Flemish with German, Spanish, and Italian musical cultures. The various genres thus created show a close affinity with Renaissance art and poetry. In the second half of the sixteenth century the leaders of the nationalized Franco-Flemish style were the Fleming Roland de Lassus (1532–1594), the most versatile composer of the age, and the Italian Giovanni Pierluigi da Palestrina (c. 1525–1594), who specialized in highly intricate polyphonic choral music written for Catholic church services under the patronage of the popes in Rome. Music also flourished in sixteenth-century England, where the Tudor monarchs Henry VIII and Elizabeth I were active patrons of the arts. Not only did the Italian madrigal, imported toward the end of the sixteenth century, take on remarkable new life in England, but songs and instrumental music of an original cast anticipated future developments on the Continent. In William Byrd (1543–1623), English music produced a master fully the equal of the great Flemish and Italian composers of the Renaissance period. The general level of musical proficiency seems to have been higher in Queen Elizabeth's day than in ours: the singing of part-songs was a popular pastime in homes

CHRONOLOGY

LIVES OF NORTHERN RENAISSANCE SCHOLARS AND ARTISTS

Erasmus	c. 1469–1536
Thomas More	1478–1535
Ulrich von Hutten	1488–1523
Edmund Spenser	c. 1552–1599
François Rabelais	c. 1494–1553
Albrecht Dürer	1471–1528
Hans Holbein the Younger	1497–1543

and at informal social gatherings, and the ability to read a part at sight was expected of the educated elite.

Although accomplishments in counterpoint were already very advanced in the Renaissance period, our modern harmonic system was still in its infancy, and thus there remained much room for experimentation. At the same time we should realize that the music of the Renaissance constitutes not merely a stage in evolution but a magnificent achievement in itself, with masters who rank among the greatest of all time. The composers Lassus, Palestrina, and Byrd are as truly representative of the artistic triumph of the Renaissance as are the painters Leonardo, Raphael, and Michelangelo. Their heritage, long neglected, has within recent years begun to be appreciated, and is now gaining in popularity as interested groups of musicians devote themselves to its revival.

Conclusion

The contrasts between the Italian and the northern Renaissance are real, but they must not be exaggerated. The intellectuals of Renaissance Italy were formed in a more secular, more urban educational environment than were the northerners, but they were no less fervent in their Christianity. Petrarch's criticism of scholasticism was not that it was too Christian but, rather, that it was not Christian enough. Petrarch opposed the emotional aridity and stylistic inelegance of scholasticism because he believed they threatened the salvation of Christians. Much the same point might be made about Lorenzo Valla. His critique of the temporal claims of the papacy sprang not only from the conclusions of his textual scholarship but also from a firm Christian piety. The Platonic Academy might honor Plato as if he were a saint of the church, but these men approached Plato's works in the same spirit with which thirteenth-century scholastic theologians had approached the works of Aristotle. As committed Christians, they were convinced that the conclusions reached by the greatest philosophical minds of classical antiquity must be compatible with Christian truth. It was the task of Christian intellectuals to reveal this compatibility and, by so doing, to strengthen the one true faith.

In considering the contrasts between "civic" and "Christian" humanism, we must also keep in mind the enormous diversity of Renaissance thought. Machiavelli is no more typical an Italian Renaissance thinker than is Ficino, Alberti, or Bruno. In comparing Italian thinkers with northern thinkers, we must therefore be careful to compare like with like. Too often, scholars overdraw the contrasts between Renaissance thought in Italy and northern Europe by choosing Machiavelli, for example, to represent all of Italian humanism and Erasmus to represent northern humanism. Two more different figures can hardly be imagined; but their differences have much more to do with their contrasting presuppositions about human nature than with their allegiances to Italian or northern humanism. A very different picture emerges if we compare, for example, John Colet as a representative of northern humanism with Marsilio Ficino as a representative of Italian humanism or if we compare Petrarch with Sir Thomas More.

Nor should we overdraw the contrasts between the Renaissance and the High Middle Ages. Both Italian and northern humanists shared an optimistic view of human nature as improvable despite the consequences of Adam and Eve's disobedience; but none was more optimistic on this score than was Saint Thomas Aquinas. Both groups emphasized the importance of personal introspection and self-examination; but none took this injunction more seriously than did the Cistercian thinkers of the twelfth century. And finally, both groups shared a belief that the exhortations of intellectuals would lift everyone's morals and conduct them to new heights of virtue. In this regard, High Renaissance intellectual life has a kind of naive optimism that contrasts sharply with the darker, more psychologically complex world of the Middle Ages and with the Reformation era that was about to begin.

Key Terms

humanism
Medici
Petrarch
The Prince
Baldassare Castiglione
Leonardo da Vinci
Raphael
Michelangelo
Erasmus
Utopia
Rabelais

Selected Readings

Alberti, Leon Battista. *The Family in Renaissance Florence (Della Famiglia)*. Trans. Renée Neu Watkins. Columbia, S.C., 1969.

Baxandall, Michael. *Painting and Experience in Fifteenth Century Italy*. Oxford, 1972. A classic study of the perceptual world of the Renaissance.

Brucker, Gene. *Florence, the Golden Age, 1138–1737*. Berkeley and Los Angeles, 1998. The standard account by a master historian.

Bruni, Leonardo. *The Humanism of Leonardo Bruni: Selected Texts*. Trans. Gordon Griffiths, James Hankins, and David Thompson. Binghamton, N.Y., 1987. Excellent translations, with introductions, to the Latin works of a key Renaissance humanist.

Burke, Peter. *The Renaissance*. New York, 1997. A brief introduction by an influential modern historian.

Burkhardt, Jacob. *The Civilization of the Renaissance in Italy*. Many editions. The nineteenth-century work that first crystallized an image of the Italian Renaissance with which scholars have been wrestling ever since.

Cassirer, Ernst, et al., eds. *The Renaissance Philosophy of Man*. Chicago, 1948. Important original works by Petrarch, Ficino, and Pico della Mirandola, among others.

Castiglione, Baldassare. *The Book of the Courtier*. Many editions. The translations by C. S. Singleton (New York, 1959) and by George Bull (New York, 1967) are both excellent.

Cellini, Benvenuto. *Autobiography*. Trans. George Bull. Baltimore, 1956. This Florentine goldsmith (1500–1571) is the source for many of the most famous stories about the artists of the Florentine Renaissance.

Cochrane, Eric, and Julius Kirshner, eds. *The Renaissance*. Chicago, 1986. An outstanding collection, from the University of Chicago Readings in Western Civilization series.

Erasmus, Desiderius. *The Praise of Folly*. Trans. J. Wilson. Ann Arbor, Mich., 1958.

Fox, Alistair. *Thomas More: History and Providence*. Oxford, 1982. A balanced account of a man too easily idealized.

Grafton, Anthony, and Lisa Jardine. *From Humanism to the Humanities: Education and the Liberal Arts in Fifteenth- and Sixteenth-Century Europe*. London, 1986. An influential account that presents Renaissance humanism as the elitist cultural program of a self-interested group of pedagogues.

Grendler, Paul, ed. *Encyclopedia of the Renaissance*. New York, 1999. A valuable reference work.

Hale, John R. *The Civilization of Europe in the Renaissance*. New York, 1993. A synthetic volume summarizing the life's work of a major Renaissance historian.

Hankins, James. *Plato in the Italian Renaissance*. Leiden and New York, 1990. A definitive study of the reception and influence of Plato on Renaissance intellectuals.

Hankins, James, ed. *Renaissance Civic Humanism: Reappraisals and Reflections*. Cambridge and New York, 2000. An excellent collection of scholarly essays reassessing republicanism in the Renaissance.

Jardine, Lisa. *Worldly Goods*. London, 1996. A revisionist account that emphasizes the acquisitive materialism of Italian Renaissance society and culture.

Kanter, Laurence, Hilliard T. Goldfarb, and James Hankins. *Botticelli's Witness: Changing Style in a Changing Florence*. Boston, 1997. This catalog for an exhibit of Botticelli's works, at the Gardner Museum in Boston, offers an excellent introduction to the painter and his world.

King, Margaret L. *Women of the Renaissance*. Chicago, 1991. Deals with women in all walks of life and in a variety of roles.

Kristeller, Paul O. *Eight Philosophers of the Italian Renaissance*. Stanford, 1964. An admirably clear and accurate account that fully appreciates the connections between medieval and Renaissance thought.

Kristeller, Paul O. *Renaissance Thought: The Classic, Scholastic, and Humanistic Strains*. New York, 1961. Very helpful in defining the main trends of Renaissance thought.

Lane, Frederic C. *Venice: A Maritime Republic*. Baltimore, 1973. An authoritative account.

Machiavelli, Niccolò. *The Discourses* and *The Prince*. Many editions. These two books must be read together if one is to understand Machiavelli's political ideas properly.

Martines, Lauro. *Power and Imagination: City-States in Renaissance Italy*. New York, 1979. Insightful account of the connections among politics, society, culture, and art.

Selected Readings

More, Thomas. *Utopia.* Many editions.

Murray, Linda. *High Renaissance and Mannerism.* London, 1985. The place to start for fifteenth- and sixteenth-century Italian art.

Olson, Roberta, *Italian Renaissance Sculpture,* New York, 1992. The most accessible introduction to the subject.

Perkins, Leeman L. *Music in the Age of the Renaissance.* New York, 1999. A massive new study that nonetheless needs to be read in conjunction with Reese.

Rabelais, François. *Gargantua and Pantagruel.* Trans. J. M. Cohen. Baltimore, Md., 1955. A robust modern translation.

Reese, Gustave. *Music in the Renaissance,* rev. ed. New York, 1959. A great book; still authoritative, despite the more recent work by Perkins, which supplements but does not replace it.

Rice, Eugene F., Jr., and Anthony Grafton. *The Foundations of Early Modern Europe, 1460–1559,* 2d ed. New York, 1994. The best textbook account of its period.

Rowland, Ingrid D. *The Culture of the High Renaissance: Ancients and Moderns in Sixteenth-Century Rome.* Cambridge and New York, 2000. Beautifully written examination of the social, intellectual, and economic foundations of the Renaissance in Rome.

Chapter Thirteen

Chapter Contents

The Lutheran Upheaval 474

The Spread of Protestantism 482

The Domestication of the Reformation, 1525–1560 487

The English Reformation 490

Catholicism Transformed 495

Conclusion 499

Reformations of Religion

AFTER TWO CENTURIES of economic, social, and political turmoil, Europe in the year 1500 was well on the road to recovery. Population was increasing, the economy was expanding, cities were growing, and the national monarchs of France, England, Spain, Scotland, and Poland were all securely established on their thrones. Throughout Europe, governments at every level were extending and deepening their control over their subjects' lives. After a late-fourteenth-century hiatus, Europe had also resumed its commercial and colonial expansion. Even Catholic Christianity appeared to be going from strength to strength as the sixteenth century dawned. Although the papacy remained mired in territorial wars in Italy, the church itself had weathered the storms that had beset it during the fifteenth century. The Lollards had been suppressed and the Hussites reincorporated into the church. In the struggle over conciliarism, the papacy had successfully won the support of all the major European rulers, reducing the conciliarists to academic isolation at the University of Paris. Meanwhile, at the parish level, the devotion of ordinary Christians to their faith had probably never been higher. To be sure, there were also problems. Although the educational standards of the parish clergy were higher than they had ever been, reformers were quick to note that too many priests were still absent, ignorant, or neglectful of their spiritual duties. Monasticism, by and large, seemed to have lost its spiritual fire; among the populace, religious enthusiasm sometimes led the faithful into gross superstition and doctrinal error. But these were manageable problems. On the whole, the "prospect of Europe" had not looked brighter for several centuries.

No one in 1500 could have predicted that within fifty years Europe's religious unity would be irreparably shattered by a new and powerful Protestant reform movement—or that in the century thereafter an appallingly destructive series of religious wars would shake to their core the foundations of European political life. Yet remarkably, these extraordinary events began with a single German monk named Martin

FOCUS QUESTIONS

• What were the theological premises of Lutheranism?

• Why did Switzerland emerge as such an important center for sixteenth-century Protestantism?

• How did notions of family and marriage change during the Reformation?

• Why did England become a Protestant country?

• How did the Catholic Reformation differ from the Counter-Reformation?

13 REFORMATIONS OF RELIGION

Luther (1483–1546), whose personal quest for a more certain understanding of sin, grace, and Christian salvation set off a chain reaction throughout Europe, resulting in the secession of millions of Europeans from the Roman Catholic Church and affecting the religious practices of nearly every Christian in Europe, whether Catholic or Protestant. The religious movement that Luther touched off was much larger than Luther himself; nor should Martin Luther's own spiritual journey be seen as an epitome for all of Protestantism. But that said, there is no doubt that the Reformation movement began with Martin Luther—and so must we if we are to understand the extraordinary upheaval this new religious movement brought about.

The Lutheran Upheaval

What were the theological premises of Lutheranism?

To explain the success of the Lutheran revolt in Germany, we must answer three central questions: (1) Why did Luther's theological ideas lead him to break with Rome? (2) Why did large numbers of Germans rally to his cause? (3) Why did so many German princes and towns impose the new religion within their territories? As we shall see, those who followed Luther found his message appealing for different reasons. Many peasants hoped the new religion would free them from the exactions of their lords; towns and princes thought it would allow them to consolidate their political independence; nationalists thought it would liberate Germany from the demands of foreign popes bent on feathering their own nest in central Italy.

What Luther's followers shared, however, was a conviction that their new, Lutheran understanding of Christianity would lead them to heaven, whereas contemporary Catholicism would not. To this degree, *reformation* is a misleading label for the movement Luther initiated. Although Luther himself did begin as a reformer seeking to cleanse contemporary Christianity from its abuses, he quickly developed into an uncompromising opponent of the basic principles of Catholic belief and practice. Many of his followers became even more radical. The religious movement that began with Martin Luther was thus no mere "reformation." It was a frontal assault on the foundations of late medieval religious life.

Luther's Quest for Religious Certainty

Although Martin Luther became an inspiration to millions, he was at first a terrible disappointment to his father. The elder Luther was a Thuringian peasant who had prospered by leasing some mines. Eager to see his clever son rise still further, he sent young Luther to the University of Erfurt to study law. In 1505, however, Martin shattered his father's hopes by becoming a monk of the Augustinian order. In some sense, however, Luther always remained faithful to his father's humble roots. Throughout his life, Martin Luther always lived simply and expressed himself in the vigorous, earthy vernacular of the German peasantry.

Like many great figures in the history of religion, Luther arrived at his new understanding of religious truth by a dramatic conversion experience. As a monk, young Luther zealously pursued all the traditional means for achieving his own salvation. Not only did he fast and pray continuously but he confessed so often that his exhausted confessor would sometimes jokingly suggest that if he really wanted to have a rousing confession he should go out and do something dramatic like committing adultery. Yet, try as he might, Luther could find no spiritual peace because he feared that he

Martin Luther. A portrait by Lucas Cranach.

could never perform enough good deeds to deserve so great a gift as salvation. But in 1513 he hit on an insight that granted him relief and changed the course of his life.

Luther's guiding insight pertained to the problem of the justice of God. For years he had worried that it seemed unjust for God to issue commandments that he knew human beings could not observe and then punish them with eternal damnation for not observing them. But after becoming a professor of biblical theology at the University of Wittenberg (many members of his monastic order were expected to teach), Luther was led by his study of the Bible to a new understanding of the problem. Specifically, while meditating on the words in the Psalms "deliver me in thy justice," it suddenly struck him that God's justice had nothing to do with his power to punish but rather with his mercy in saving sinful mortals through faith. As Luther later wrote, "At last, by the mercy of God, I began to understand the justice of God as that by which God makes us just in his mercy and through faith . . . and at this I felt as though I had been born again, and had gone through open gates into paradise." Since this fateful revelation came to Luther in the tower room of his monastery, it is customarily called his "tower experience."

After that, everything seemed to fall into place. Lecturing at Wittenberg in the years immediately following 1513, Luther pondered a passage in Saint Paul's Letter to the Romans (1:17): "[T]he just shall live by faith" until he reached his central doctrine of "justification by faith alone." Luther concluded that God's justice does not demand endless good works and religious rituals for salvation, because humans can never be saved by their own efforts. Rather, humans are saved by God's grace alone, which God offers as an utterly undeserved gift to those whom he has predestined for salvation. Because this grace comes to humans through the gift of faith, from the human perspective men and women are "justified" (i.e., made worthy of salvation) by faith alone. Those whom God has justified through faith will manifest that fact by performing works of piety and charity, but such works are not what saves them. Piety and charity are merely visible signs of each believer's invisible spiritual state, which is known to God alone.

The essence of this doctrine was not original to Luther. It harked back to around the year 400 with the predestinarianism of Saint Augustine (see Chapter Six),

the patron saint of Luther's own monastic order. During the twelfth and thirteenth centuries, however, theologians such as Peter Lombard and Saint Thomas Aquinas had developed a very different understanding of salvation, emphasizing the role that both the church itself (through its sacraments) and the individual believer (through acts of piety and charity) could play in the process of salvation. None of these theologians claimed that a human being could earn his or her way to heaven by good works alone. But the late medieval church unwittingly encouraged such misunderstandings by presenting the process of salvation in increasingly quantitative terms, declaring, for example, that by performing a specific meritorious act (such as a pilgrimage or a pious donation), a believer could reduce the penance she or he owed to God by a specific number of days. From the fourteenth century on, popes claimed to dispense such special grace to the living from the "Treasury of Merits," a storehouse of surplus good works piled up by Christ and the saints in heaven. After 1476, popes also began to assign such excess grace to the dead, to speed their way through purgatory. Most commonly, grace was withdrawn from this treasury and reassigned to needy sinners through indulgences: special remissions of the penitential obligations imposed on Christians by their priests as part of the sacrament of penance. When indulgences began, in the eleventh and twelfth centuries, they could be earned only by demanding spiritual exercises, such as joining a crusade. By the end of the fifteenth century, however, indulgences were often being granted in return for monetary payments to favored papal causes. To many reformers, this looked like simony: the sin of selling grace in return for cash.

> By the end of the fifteenth century, indulgences were often being granted in return for monetary payments to favored papal causes. To many reformers, this looked like simony: the sin of selling grace in return for cash.

Abuses of this sort were widely criticized by early sixteenth-century church reformers such as Erasmus. But Luther's objections to indulgences and prayers for the dead had much more radical consequences, because they rested on a set of Augustinian theological presuppositions that, if taken to their logical conclusion, could result only in dismantling much of contemporary Catholic religious practice. Luther himself may not have realized this when he took the first steps that would lead to his breach with Rome. But as the implications of his ideas became clear, Luther did not withdraw from them. Instead, he pressed on, declaring to his opponents, "Here I stand; God help me, I can do no other."

THE REFORMATION BEGINS

Luther first developed his theological ideas as an academic lecturer, but in 1517 he was goaded into attacking some of the actual practices of the church by a provocation that was too much for him to bear. The story of the indulgence campaign of 1517 in Germany is colorful but unsavory. The worldly Albert of Hohenzollern, youngest brother of the elector of Brandenburg, had sunk himself into enormous debt for several discreditable reasons. In 1513 he had to pay large sums for papal permission to hold the bishoprics of Magdeburg and Halberstadt concurrently, and for assuming these offices, even though at twenty-three he was not old enough to be a bishop at all. Not satisfied, when the prestigious archbishopric of Mainz fell vacant in the next year, Albert gained election to that too, even though he knew this would mean even larger payments to Rome. Obtaining the necessary funds by loans from the German banking firm of the Fuggers, he then struck a bargain with Pope Leo X (1513–1521): Leo authorized the sale of indulgences in Albert's ecclesiastical territories on the understanding that half of the income raised would go to Rome for the building of St. Peter's Basilica, with the other half going to Albert so that he could repay the Fuggers.

Luther did not know the sordid details of Albert's bargain, but he did know that a Dominican friar named Tetzel was soon hawking indulgences throughout much of northern Germany, with Fugger banking agents in his train, and that Tetzel was deliberately giving people the impression that an indulgence was an automatic ticket to heaven for oneself or one's loved ones in purgatory. For Luther, this was doubly offensive: not only was Tetzel violating Luther's conviction that people are saved by faith, not works, he was also misleading people into thinking that if they purchased an indulgence, then they no longer needed to confess their sins to a priest. Tetzel was thus putting their very salvation at risk. So on October 31, 1517, Luther offered to his university colleagues a list of ninety-five theses objecting to Catholic indulgence doctrine, an act conventionally seen as the beginning of the Protestant Reformation.

Luther had not initially intended to publicize his criticisms of Tetzel. He wrote his objections in Latin, not German, and meant them only for academic discussion within the University of Wittenberg. But when some unknown person translated and published Luther's theses, the hitherto obscure monk suddenly gained widespread notoriety. Tetzel and his allies outside the university now demanded that Luther withdraw his theses or defend himself. Rather than backing down, however, Luther became even bolder in his attacks on the church hierarchy. In 1519, in a public disputation held before throngs in Leipzig, Luther defiantly maintained that the pope and all clerics were merely fallible men and that the highest authority for an individual's conscience was the truth of Scripture. Pope Leo X responded by charging Luther with heresy; after that Luther had no alternative but to break with the Catholic Church entirely.

Luther's year of greatest creative activity came in 1520 when, in the midst of the crisis caused by his defiance, he composed a series of pamphlets setting forth his three primary theological premises: justification by faith, the primacy of scripture, and "the priesthood of all believers." We have already examined the meaning of the first premise. By the second he simply meant that the literal meaning of scripture took precedence over church traditions and that beliefs (such as purgatory) or practices (such as prayers to the saints) not explicitly grounded in scripture could be rejected as human inventions. Luther also declared all Christian believers to be spiritually equal before God. Denying

Jacob Fugger "The Rich" (1459–1528). His loans to Albert of Hohenzollern helped to touch off the Protestant Reformation.

WHAT WERE THE THEOLOGICAL PREMISES OF LUTHERANISM?

THE LUTHERAN UPHEAVAL

Pope Leo X. Raphael's highly realistic portrait shows the pope with his nephews Giulio de' Medici, who would succeed him as pope, and Cardinal de Rossi.

that priests, monks, and nuns had any special spiritual qualities by virtue of their vocations, Luther argued instead for "the priesthood of all believers."

From these premises a host of practical consequences followed. Because works could not lead to salvation, Luther declared fasts, pilgrimages, and the veneration of relics to be spiritually valueless. He also called for the dissolution of all monasteries and convents. He also took steps to demystify the rites of the church, proposing the substitution of German for Latin in church services and reducing the number of sacraments from seven to two (baptism and the Eucharist; in 1520, he also included penance, but he later changed his mind on this). Although Luther continued to believe that Christ was really present in the consecrated bread and wine of the Lord's Supper, he denied that the Mass was a repetition of Christ's sacrifice on the cross and insisted that it was only through the faith of each individual believer that the sacrament could lead anyone to God. To further emphasize that those who presided in churches had no supernatural authority, he insisted on calling them ministers or pastors rather than priests. He also proposed to abolish the entire ecclesiastical hierarchy of popes, bishops, and archdeacons. Finally, firm in the belief that no spiritual distinction existed between clergy and laity, Luther argued that ministers could marry, and in 1525 he took a wife himself.

THE BREAK WITH ROME

Widely disseminated by means of the printing press, Luther's brilliant polemical pamphlets of 1520 electrified much of Germany, gaining him passionate popular support and touching off a national religious revolt against the papacy. In highly intemperate colloquial German, Luther declared that "if the pope's court were reduced ninety-nine percent it would still be large enough to give decisions on matters of faith"; that "the cardinals have sucked Italy dry and now turn to Germany"; and that, given Rome's corruption, "the reign of Antichrist could not be worse." As word of Luther's defiance spread, his pamphlets became a publishing sensation. Whereas the average press run of a printed book before 1520 had been 1,000 copies, the first run of *To the Christian Nobility* (1520) was 4,000 which sold out in a few days. Many more thousands of copies quickly followed. Even more popular were woodcut illustrations mocking the papacy and exalting Luther. These sold in the tens of thousands and could be readily understood even by the illiterate.

Luther's denunciations of the papacy reflected widespread public dissatisfaction with recent popes. Pope Alexander VI (1492–1503) had bribed the cardinals to gain the papacy, used the money raised from the jubilee of 1500 to support the military campaigns of his son Cesare, and was so morally corrupt that he was suspected of incest with his own daughter Lucrezia Borgia. Julius II (1503–1513) devoted his reign to enlarging the Papal States through war; a contemporary remarked of him that he would have gained the greatest glory if only he had been a secular prince. Leo X (1513–1521), Luther's opponent, was a member of the Medici family of Florence. Although not spectacularly corrupt or immoral, he was a self-indulgent aesthete who, in the words of a modern Catholic historian, "would not have been deemed fit to be a doorkeeper in the house of the Lord had he lived in the days of the apostles." Nor was criticism of the papacy limited to those who would ultimately become

> Denying that priests, monks, and nuns had any special spiritual qualities by virtue of their vocations, Luther argued instead for "the priesthood of all believers."

Pope Alexander VI: "Appearance and Reality." Even before Luther initiated the German Reformation, anonymous critics of the dissolute Alexander VI surreptitiously spread propaganda showing him to be a devil. By lifting a flap one can see Alexander transformed into a monster who proclaims, "I am the pope."

Protestants. In *The Praise of Folly*, first published in 1511 and frequently reprinted, Erasmus declared that if the popes of his day were ever forced to lead Christ-like lives they would be inconsolable. In *Julius Excluded*, published anonymously in Basel in 1517, Erasmus went even further, imagining a conversation at the gates of heaven between Saint Peter and Pope Julius II in which Peter absolutely refused to admit Julius to heaven because he could not believe that the armored, vainglorious figure who stood before him could possibly be the pope.

In Germany, however, resentment of the papacy ran especially high. Because fifteenth-century Germany was so politically fractured, there were no agreements (known as concordats) between pope and emperor limiting papal authority in Germany, as there were with the rulers of Spain, France, and England. As a result, by 1500 the German princes were complaining that papal taxes were so high they were draining the country of its coin. But despite paying such large sums of money to Rome, Germans had almost no influence over papal policy. Frenchmen, Spaniards, and Italians dominated the college of cardinals and the papal bureaucracy, and the popes themselves were invariably Italian (as they would continue to be until 1978). As a result, graduates from the rapidly growing German universities almost never found employment in Rome. Instead, many joined the throngs of Luther's supporters to become leaders of the new religious movement.

THE DIET OF WORMS

Luther's personal drama was now moving swiftly toward a crisis. Late in 1520, Luther responded to Pope Leo X's bull ordering him to recant by casting not only the bull but all of church law onto a roaring bonfire in front of a huge crowd. Since in the eyes of the church Luther was now a stubborn heretic, he was formally "released" for punishment to his lay overlord, the elector Frederick the Wise of Saxony. Frederick, however, was loath to silence the pope's antagonist. Rather than burning Luther at the stake for heresy, Frederick declared that Luther had not yet received a fair hearing. Early in 1521, he therefore brought him to the city of Worms to be examined by a formal assembly (a "diet") of the princes of the Holy Roman Empire.

At Worms the initiative lay with the presiding officer, the newly elected Holy Roman emperor, Charles V. Charles was not a German; indeed, it is doubtful if he had any national identity at all. As a member of the Habsburg family, he had been born and bred in his ancestral holding of the Netherlands. By 1521, however, through the unpredictable workings of dynastic inheri-

WHAT WERE THE THEOLOGICAL PREMISES OF LUTHERANISM?

THE LUTHERAN UPHEAVAL 479

tance, marriage, election, and luck, he had become not only the ruler of the Netherlands, but also king of Germany and Holy Roman emperor, duke of Austria, duke of Milan, and ruler of Franche-Comté. As the grandson of Ferdinand and Isabella on his mother's side, he was also king of Spain; king of Naples, Sicily, and Sardinia; and ruler of all the Spanish possessions in the New World.

Governing such an extraordinary combination of territories posed enormous challenges. Charles's empire

THE EMPIRE OF CHARLES V, c. 1550

Note the dispersed lands Charles V ruled directly through inheritance and marriage; as Holy Roman emperor, he was also the titular ruler of Germany. Which countries and rulers were most threatened by Charles's extraordinary combination of territories? Where might these threatened rulers and countries look for allies against Charles V? How did the threat posed by the Ottoman Empire complicate the political and religious struggles within Christian Europe?

CHAPTER 13 REFORMATIONS OF RELIGION

The Emperor Charles V. This view by the Venetian painter Titian depicts the emperor as a sage ruler.

had no capital and no centralized administrative institutions; it shared no common language, no common culture, and no geographically contiguous borders. It thus stood completely apart from the growing nationalism of late medieval political life. Charles recognized the diversity of his empire and tried wherever possible to rule it through local officials and institutions. But he could not tolerate threats to the two fundamental forces that held his empire together: the emperor himself and Catholicism. Beyond such political calculations, however, Charles was also a faithful and committed Catholic, who was deeply disturbed by the prospect of heresy within his empire. There was therefore little doubt that the Diet of Worms would condemn Martin Luther for heresy. But when Luther refused to back down, even before the emperor himself, Frederick the Wise once more intervened, this time by arranging a "kidnapping" whereby Luther was spirited off to the elector's castle of the Wartburg and kept out of harm's way for a year.

Thereafter Luther was never again to be in danger of his life. Although the Diet of Worms proclaimed him an outlaw, this edict was never enforced. Instead, Luther went into hiding, and Charles V left Germany to conduct a war with France. In 1522 Luther returned in triumph from the Wartburg to Wittenberg to find that the changes he had called for in ecclesiastical government and worship had already been put into practice by his university supporters. Then, in rapid succession, several German princes formally converted to Lutheranism, bringing their territories with them. By 1530, a considerable part of Germany had thus been brought over to the new faith.

THE GERMAN PRINCES AND THE LUTHERAN REFORMATION

At this point, then, the last of the three major questions regarding the early history of Lutheranism arises: Why did some German princes, secure in their own powers, nonetheless heed Luther's call by establishing Lutheran religious practices within their territories? This is a crucial question, because despite Luther's popular support, his cause surely would have failed had it not been embraced by a number of powerful German princes and free cities. In 1520, Luther was more or less equally popular throughout Germany, but it was only in those territories where rulers formally established Lutheranism (mostly in the German north) that the new religion prevailed. Elsewhere, Luther's sympathizers were forced to flee, face death, or conform to Catholicism.

The power of the princes to determine the religion of their territory reflected developments occuring throughout European society. Everywhere in Europe the major political trend in the years around 1500 was toward dominance by the state in all walks of life, religious as well as secular. Hence rulers sought to control appointments to church offices in their own realms, to restrict the flow of money to Rome, and to limit the independence of church courts. The most powerful rulers in western Europe—primarily the kings of France and Spain—took particular advantage of the continuing struggles between the papacy and the conciliarists (see Chapter Ten) to extract such concessions from the embattled popes. Thus in 1482 Sixtus IV conceded to the Spanish monarchs Ferdinand and Isabella the right to name candidates for all major church offices. In 1487

What were the theological premises of Lutheranism?

Innocent VIII consented to the establishment of a Spanish Inquisition controlled by the crown, giving the rulers extraordinary powers to dictate religious policies. And in 1516, by the Concordat of Bologna, Leo X granted the choice of bishops and abbots in France to the French king, Francis I, in return for Francis's support against the conciliarists who had gathered at the Fifth Lateran Council (1512–1517). In Germany, however, neither the emperor nor the princes were strong enough to gain such concessions. Hence what they could not achieve by concordats some princes decided to wrest by force.

In this determination they were fully abetted by Luther. As early as 1520 the fiery reformer had recognized that he could never hope to institute new religious practices without the strong arm of the princes behind him, so he implicitly encouraged them to confiscate the wealth of the Catholic Church as an incentive for creating a new order. At first the princes bided their time, but when they realized that Luther had enormous public support and that Charles V would not act swiftly to defend the Catholic faith, several moved to introduce Lutheranism into their territories. Personal piety surely played a role in individual cases, but political and economic considerations were more generally decisive. By instituting Lutheranism within their territories, Protestant princes could consolidate their authority by naming pastors, cutting off fees to Rome, and curtailing the jurisdiction of church courts. They could also guarantee that the political and religious boundaries of their territories would now coincide. No longer, therefore, would a rival ecclesiastical prince (such as a bishop or archbishop) be able to use his spiritual position to undermine a neighboring secular prince's sovereignty over his territory.

Similar considerations also moved a number of free cities (so called because they were not ruled by territorial princes) to adopt Lutheranism. By adopting the new religion, town councils and guild masters could establish themselves (rather than local aristocrats or bishops) as the supreme governing authority within their towns. Given the added fact that under Lutheranism monasteries and convents could be shut down and their lands appropriated by the newly sovereign secular authorities,

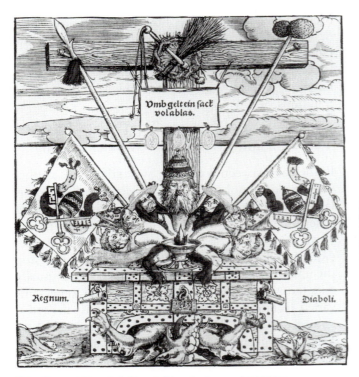

The Seven-Headed Papal Beast. Around 1530 a Lutheran cartoon was circulated in Germany that turned the papacy into the seven-headed beast of the Book of Revelation. The papacy's seven heads consist of pope, cardinals, bishops, and priests; the sign on the cross reads "For money, a sack full of indulgences."

The Seven-Headed Martin Luther. In response, a German Catholic propagandist showed Luther as Revelation's beast. In this cartoon Luther's seven heads show him by turn to be a hypocrite, a fanatic, and Barabbas—the thief who should have been crucified instead of Jesus.

CHAPTER 13

REFORMATIONS OF RELIGION

the practical advantages of the new faith were overwhelming, quite apart from any considerations of religious zeal.

Once safely ensconced in Wittenberg under princely protection, Luther began to express ever more vehemently his own profound conservatism in political and social matters. In a treatise of 1523, *On Temporal Authority*, he insisted that "godly" rulers must be obeyed in all things and that even ungodly ones should never be actively resisted since tyranny "is not to be resisted but endured." Then, in 1525, when peasants throughout Germany rebelled against their landlords—in some places encouraged by the religious radical Thomas Müntzer (c. 1490–1525), who urged the use of fire and sword against "ungodly" powers—Luther responded with intense hostility. In his vituperative pamphlet of 1525, *Against the Thievish, Murderous Hordes of Peasants*, he urged all who could to hunt the rebels down like mad dogs, to "strike, strangle, stab secretly or in public, and remember that nothing can be more poisonous than a man in rebellion." After the ruthless suppression of the Peasants' Revolt (which may have cost as many as 100,000 lives), the firm alliance of Lutheranism with state power helped preserve and sanction the existing social order. Never again would there be a mass lower-class uprising in Germany.

As for Luther himself, he concentrated in his last years on debating with younger, more radical religious reformers and on offering spiritual counsel to all who sought it. Never tiring in his amazingly prolific literary activity, he wrote an average of one treatise every two weeks for twenty-five years. To the end Luther was unswerving in his new faith: on his deathbed in 1546

he responded to the question "Will you stand firm in Christ and the doctrine which you have preached?" with a resolute yes.

THE SPREAD OF PROTESTANTISM

> Why did Switzerland emerge as such an important center for sixteenth-century Protestantism?

Originating as a term applied to Lutherans who "protested" an action of the German Imperial Diet of 1529, the word *Protestant* was soon applied to a much wider range of European Christians in rebellion against Rome. Lutheranism itself struck lasting roots only in northern Germany and Scandinavia, where it became the state religion of Denmark, Norway, and Sweden during the 1520s. Early Lutheran successes in southern Germany, Poland, and Hungary were eventually rolled back. Elsewhere in Europe, however, competing forms of Protestantism soon emerged from the seeds that Luther had sown. By the 1550s, Protestantism had become a truly international movement; in so doing, however, it also split into a number of competing traditions.

THE REFORMATION IN SWITZERLAND

In the early sixteenth century Switzerland was neither ruled by kings nor dominated by all-powerful territorial princes; instead, prosperous Swiss cities were either independent or on the verge of becoming so. Hence when the leading citizens of a Swiss municipality decided to adopt Protestant reforms no one could stop them, and Protestantism in Switzerland could usually take its own course. Although religious arrangements varied from city to city, three main forms of Protestantism emerged in Switzerland between 1520 to 1550: Zwinglianism, Anabaptism, and Calvinism.

ULRICH ZWINGLI

Zwinglianism, founded by Ulrich Zwingli (*ZWIHNG-lee*, 1484–1531) in Zürich, was the most theologically moderate form of the three. Although Zwingli began his career as a somewhat indifferent Catholic priest,

---

CHRONOLOGY

ORIGINS OF THE REFORMATION, 1450–1529

Christian humanists call for reforms	1400s–1500s
Growth of German universities	1450–1517
Luther posts the Ninety-five Theses	1517
Luther charged with heresy	1519
Publication of Lutheran theological premises	1520
Diet of Worms declares Luther an outlaw	1521
Peasants' Revolt defeated	1525
Luther's break with Zwingli	1529

around 1516 his humanist-inspired study of the Bible convinced him that Catholic theology and practice conflicted with the Gospels. His biblical studies eventually led him also to condemn religious images and hierarchical authority within the church. But he did not speak out publicly until Luther set the precedent. In 1522, however, Zwingli began attacking the authority of the Catholic Church in Zürich. Soon all Zürich and much of northern Switzerland had accepted his religious leadership. Zwingli's reforms closely resembled those of the Lutherans in Germany. Zwingli differed from Luther, however, concerning the theology of the Eucharist: whereas Luther believed in the real presence of Christ's body in the sacrament, for Zwingli the Eucharist conferred no grace at all; it was simply a reminder and communal celebration of Christ's historical sacrifice on the cross. This fundamental disagreement prevented Lutherans and Zwinglians from uniting in a common Protestant front. Fighting independently, Zwingli fell in battle against Catholic forces in 1531. Soon thereafter, his movement was absorbed by the more systematic Protestantism of John Calvin.

Anabaptism

Before Calvinism prevailed, however, an even more radical form of Protestantism arose in Switzerland and Germany. The first Anabaptists were members of Zwingli's circle in Zürich, but they broke with him around 1525 on the issue of infant baptism. Because Anabaptists were convinced that the sacrament of baptism was only effective if administered to willing adults who understood its significance, they rejected infant baptism altogether and required followers who had been baptized as infants to be baptized again as adults (the term *Anabaptism* means "rebaptism"). This doctrine reflected the Anabaptists' fundamental belief that the true church was a small community of believers gathered out of the world (in sociological terms, a sect), whose members had to make a deliberate, inspired decision to join it. No other Protestant groups were prepared to go so far in rejecting the medieval Christian view of the church as a single body to which all members of society belonged from birth. In an age when almost everyone assumed that church and state were inextricably connected, Anabaptism was bound to be anathema to the established powers, both Protestant and Catholic. Yet in its first few years the movement did gain numerous adherents in Switzerland and Germany, above all because it appealed to sincere religious piety in calling for extreme simplicity of worship, pacifism, and strict personal morality.

Disastrously, however, an unrepresentative group of Anabaptist extremists managed to gain control of the

The Anabaptists' Cages, Then and Now. After the three Anabaptist leaders who had reigned in Münster for a year were executed in 1535, their corpses were prominently displayed in cages hung from a tower of the marketplace church. As can be seen from the photo on the right, the bones are now gone but the iron cages remain as a grisly reminder of the horrors of sixteenth-century religious strife.

German city of Münster in 1534. These zealots combined sectarianism with millenarianism, or the belief that God wished to institute a completely new order of justice and spirituality throughout the world before the end of time. Determined to help God bring about this goal, the extremists attempted to turn Münster into a new Jerusalem. A former tailor named John of Leyden assumed the title of "King of the New Temple" and proclaimed himself the successor of the Hebrew king David. Under his leadership Anabaptist religious practices were made obligatory, private property was abolished, the sharing of goods was introduced, and even polygamy was permitted on the grounds of Old Testament precedents. Such practices were deeply shocking to both Protestants and Catholics alike. Münster was besieged and captured by Catholic forces little more than a year after the Anabaptist takeover; and the new David, together with two of his lieutenants, was put to death by excruciating tortures. Thereafter, Anabaptists throughout Europe were ruthlessly persecuted from all sides. Among the few who survived were some who banded together in the Mennonite sect, named for its founder, the Dutchman Menno Simons (c. 1496–1561). This sect, dedicated to pacifism and the simple "religion of the heart" of original Anabaptism, has continued to exist to the present day.

John Calvin's Reformed Theology

A year after events in Münster sealed the fate of Anabaptism, a twenty-six-year-old French Protestant named John Calvin (1509–1564), who had fled to the Swiss city of Basel to escape religious persecution, published the first version of his *Institutes of the Christian Religion*, the most influential systematic formulation of Protestant theology ever written. Born in Noyon in northern France, Calvin originally had been trained for the law and around 1533 was studying the Greek and Latin classics while living off the income from a church benefice. But then, as he later wrote, while he was "obstinately devoted to the superstitions of Popery," a stroke of light made him feel that God was extricating him from "an abyss of filth." He thereupon became a Protestant theologian and propagandist.

Although some of these details resemble the early career of Luther, the two men were very different figures. Luther was an emotionally volatile personality and a controversialist. He responded to theological problems as they arose or as the impulse struck him, but he never attempted to write systematic theology. Calvin, however, was a coolly analytical legalist, who resolved in

John Calvin. A recently discovered anonymous portrait.

his *Institutes* to set forth all the principles of Protestantism comprehensively, logically, and systematically. As a result, after several revisions and enlargements (the definitive edition appeared in 1559), Calvin's *Institutes* became the most theologically authoritative statement of Protestant beliefs and the nearest Protestant equivalent to Saint Thomas Aquinas's *Summa Theologica*.

Calvin's austere theology started with the omnipotence of God and worked downward. For Calvin the entire universe depends utterly on the will of the Almighty, who created all things for his greater glory. Because of the original fall from grace, all human beings are sinners by nature, bound hand and foot to an evil inheritance they cannot escape. Nevertheless, the Lord for reasons of his own has predestined some for eternal salvation and damned all the rest to the torments of hell. Nothing that human beings may do can alter their fate; their souls are stamped with God's blessing or curse before they are born. Nevertheless, Christians cannot be indifferent to their conduct on earth. If they are among the elect, God will implant in them the desire to live according to his laws. Upright conduct is thus a sign, though not an infallible one, that an individual has been chosen to sit at the throne of glory. Membership in the reformed church (as Calvinist churches are more properly known) is another presumptive sign of election to salvation. But most of all, Calvin urged Christians to conceive of themselves as chosen instruments of God, charged to work actively to fulfill God's purposes on earth. Because sin offends God, Christians should do all they can to prevent it, not because their actions will lead to anyone's salvation (they will not), but simply because God's glory is diminished if sin is allowed to flourish unchecked by the efforts of those whom he has chosen for salvation.

Calvin always acknowledged a great theological debt to Luther, but his religious teachings differed from those of the Wittenberg reformer in several essentials. First of all, Luther's attitude toward proper Christian conduct in the world was much more passive than Calvin's. For Luther, a Christian should endure the trials of this life in suffering, whereas for Calvin the world was to be mastered in unceasing labor for God's sake. Calvin's religion was also more legalistic than Luther's. Luther, for example, insisted that his followers attend church on Sunday, but he did not demand that during the remainder of the day they refrain from all pleasure or work. Calvin, on the other hand, issued stern strictures against worldliness of any sort on the Sabbath day of rest and forbade all sorts of minor self-indulgences even on non-Sabbath days.

The two men also differed on fundamental matters of church government and worship. Although Luther broke with the Catholic system of hierarchical church governance, Lutheran district superintendents continued to exercise some of the powers of bishops, including supervision of the parish clergy. Luther also retained many features of traditional worship, including altars, music, ritual, and vestments (special clothing for the clergy). Calvin, however, rejected everything that smacked to him of popery. Thus he argued for the elimination of all traces of nonelective governance within the church. Instead, each congregation should elect its own ministers, and assemblies of ministers and "elders" (laymen responsible for maintaining proper religious conduct among the faithful) were to govern the reformed church as a whole. Calvin also insisted on the utmost simplicity in worship, prohibiting (among much else) vestments, processions, instrumental music, and religious images of any sort, including stained-glass windows. He also dispensed with all remaining vestiges of Catholic sacramental theology by making the sermon, rather than the Eucharist, the centerpiece of reformed worship. When these teachings were put into practice, Calvinist services became little more than "four bare walls and a sermon."

CALVINISM IN GENEVA

Consistent with his theological convictions, Calvin was intent on putting his religious teachings into practice. Sensing an opportunity in the French-speaking Swiss city of Geneva, then in the throes of political and religious upheaval, he moved there late in 1536 and began preaching and organizing immediately. In 1538 his activities caused him to be expelled, but in 1541 he returned and the city soon came completely under his sway. Under Calvin's guidance Geneva's government became a theocracy. Supreme authority was vested in a "Consistory" composed of twelve lay elders and between ten and twenty pastors, whose weekly meetings Calvin dominated. Aside from passing legislation

> Calvin also insisted on the utmost simplicity in worship, prohibiting (among much else) vestments, processions, instrumental music, and religious images of any sort, including stained-glass windows.

Calvin as Seen by His Enemies. A Catholic caricature in which Calvin's face is a composite made from a fish, a toad, and a chicken.

13 | REFORMATIONS OF RELIGION

RELIGIOUS SITUATION IN EUROPE, c. 1560

The religious boundaries of Europe around 1560, roughly thirty years after Martin Luther's movement began, were quite complicated. To what extent did the religious divisions of Europe follow its political boundaries? How would you account for the dispersed areas in which Calvinists predominated? Why did Lutheranism spread north into Scandinavia but not south into Bavaria or west across the Rhine?

proposed to it by a congregation of ministers, the Consistory's main function was to supervise morality, both public and private. To this end, Geneva was divided into districts, and a committee of the Consistory visited every household without warning to check on the behavior of its members. Dancing, card playing, attending the theater, and working or playing on the Sabbath—all were outlawed as works of the devil. Innkeepers were forbidden to allow anyone to consume food or drink without first saying grace or to permit any patron to stay up after nine o'clock. Murder, treason, adultery, witchcraft, blasphemy, and heresy were all capital crimes. Even penalties for lesser crimes were severe. During the first four years after Calvin gained control in Geneva, there were no fewer than fifty-eight executions out of a total population of only 16,000.

As objectionable as such interference in the private sphere may seem today, in the mid-sixteenth century Calvin's Geneva was a beacon of light to thousands of Protestants throughout Europe. Calvin's disciple John Knox, who brought reformed religion to Scotland, declared Geneva under Calvin "the most perfect school of Christ that ever was on earth since the days of the Apostles." Converts such as Knox flocked to Geneva for refuge or instruction and then returned home to become ardent proselytizers for the new religion. Geneva thus became the center of an international movement dedicated to spreading reformed religion to France and the rest of Europe through organized missionary activity and propaganda.

These missionary efforts were remarkably successful. By the end of the sixteenth century, Calvinists were a majority in Scotland (where they were known as Presbyterians), Holland (where they founded the Dutch Reformed Church), and England (where the Church of England adopted reformed theology but not reformed worship; Calvinists who sought further reforms in worship were known as Puritans). There were also substantial Calvinist minorities in France (where they were called Huguenots), Germany, Hungary, Lithuania, and Poland. God's kingdom on earth had not yet been fully realized; on his deathbed in 1564, Calvin pronounced the Genevans to be still "a perverse and unhappy nation." But an extraordinary revolution had taken place nonetheless in the religious life and practice of Europe.

THE DOMESTICATION OF THE REFORMATION, 1525–1560

How did notions of family and marriage change during the Reformation?

Protestantism had begun as a revolutionary doctrine whose radical claims for the spiritual equality of all true Christian believers had the potential to undermine the social, religious, political, and even gender hierarchies on which European society rested. Luther himself seems not to have anticipated that his ideas might have such implications, and he was genuinely shocked when the rebellious German peasants and the religious millenarianists at Münster interpreted his teachings in this way. But Luther was by no means solely responsible for the increasing conservatism of Protestant social ideology after 1525. Outside the ranks of the Anabaptists, none of the early Protestant leaders was a social or political radical. To spread their reform message, moreover, Protestant reformers depended on the support of existing social and political leaders: the princes, of course, but no less important, the ruling elites of the German and Swiss towns. As a result, the Reformation movement was speedily "domesticated" in two senses. Not only was the revolutionary potential of Protestantism curbed (Luther rarely spoke about the priesthood of all believers after 1525) but there was also an increasing emphasis within all branches of the burgeoning Protestant movement on the patriarchal family as the central institution of reformed life.

REFORM AND DISCIPLINE

As we saw in Chapter Eleven, efforts to constrain the common people of Europe to lead more strictly disciplined and godly lives had been a frequent feature of the fifteenth-century religious reform movements. Many of these reform efforts were actively embraced and promoted by princes and town councils, most famously perhaps in Florence, where, from 1494 to 1498, the Dominican preacher Girolamo Savonarola led the city on an extraordinary but short-lived campaign of puritanism and moral reform. But there were many other examples of rulers legislating against sin, both before and after Savonarola. When, in 1518, Desiderius Erasmus called on secular rulers to think of themselves as abbots and of their territories as giant monasteries, he was thus sounding for a new century an already-famliar theme.

Protestant rulers, however, took the need to enforce godly discipline on their people with particular seriousness, because the depravity of human nature was a fundamental tenet of their Protestant beliefs. Like Saint Augustine at the end of the fourth century, Protestants believed that people would inevitably turn out badly unless they were compelled to be good. It was, therefore, the responsibility of pastors and magistrates to discipline and control the behavior of their people—not because their good deeds would lead them to heaven but because their evil deeds would anger God and destroy human society.

Protestant godly discipline began with the education of children. Luther himself wrote two catechisms (statements of belief) to teach children the tenets of their faith and the obligations—toward parents, masters, and rulers—that God imposed on them. Luther also insisted that all children, boys and girls alike, should be taught to read the Bible in their own vernacular language. Schooling thus became a characteristically Protestant preoccupation. Even the Protestant family was conceived of as a "school of godliness," in which fathers were expected to instruct and discipline their wives, their children, and their household servants.

But family life in the early sixteenth century still left much to be desired in the eyes of Protestant reformers. Drunkenness, domestic violence, illicit sexual relations, lascivious dancing, and the blasphemous swearing of oaths were commonplace, even among the religiously reformed. Various methods were tried by Protestant congregations to discipline their unruly members, including private counseling, public confessions of wrongdoing, public penances and shamings, exclusion from church services, and even imprisonment. All these efforts met with varying, but generally modest, success. To create godly Protestant families, and to enforce godly discipline on entire communities, was going to require the active cooperation of godly authorities in both church and state.

PROTESTANTISM, GOVERNMENT, AND THE FAMILY

The domestication of the Reformation in this sense took place principally in the free towns of Germany and Switzerland. Here, Protestant attacks on monasticism and clerical celibacy found a receptive audience among townsmen who resented the immunity of monastic houses from taxation, and regarded clerical celibacy as a subterfuge for the seduction of their wives and daughters. Protestant emphasis on the depravity of the human will and the consequent need for that will to be disciplined by godly authority also resonated powerfully with guilds and town governments, which were anxious to maintain and increase the control exercised by town elites (mainly merchants and master craftsmen) over the apprentices and journeymen who made up the majority of the town's male population. By eliminating the competing jurisdictional authority of the Catholic Church, Protestantism also allowed town governments to consolidate all authority within the city into their own hands.

Protestantism reinforced the control of individual craftsmen over their own households by bringing a new emphasis on the family as a "school of godliness," in which an all-powerful father figure was expected to assume responsibility for instructing and disciplining his household according to the precepts of reformed religion. At the same time, Protestantism also introduced a new religious ideal for women. No longer was the celibate nun the exemplar of female holiness; in her place now stood the married and obedient Protestant "goodwife." As one Lutheran prince wrote in 1527: "Those who bear children please God better than all the monks and nuns singing and praying." To this extent, Protestantism resolved the tensions between piety and sexuality that had characterized late medieval Catholicism by declaring firmly in favor of the holiness of marital sexuality.

This did not reflect a newly elevated view of women's spiritual potential, however—quite the contrary. Luther, like his medieval predecessors, continued to regard women as more sexually driven than men and less capable of controlling their sexual desires (although, to be fair, Luther had only a slightly higher view of men's capacity for celibacy). His opposition to convents rested on his belief that, except in extraordinary circumstances, it was impossible for women to remain celibate, so convents simply made illicit sexual behavior inevitable. To control women and prevent sin, it was therefore necessary that all women should be married, preferably at a young age, and so placed under the governance of a godly husband.

For the most part, Protestant town governments were happy to cooperate in shutting down convents. The convent's property went to the town, and most of the nuns were from aristocratic families anyway. But conflicts did arise between Protestant reformers and town fathers over marriage and sexuality, especially over the reformers' insistence that both men and women should marry young as a check on sin. Many German towns were like Augsburg, where men were expected to delay marriage until they had achieved the status of a master craftsman—a requirement that had become increasingly difficult to enforce as guilds sought to restrict the number of journeymen permitted to become masters. In theory, however, apprentices and journeymen were not supposed to marry. Instead, they were expected to frequent the brothels and taverns, a legally recognized world of nonmarital sexuality that town fathers saw as necessary to protect their own wives and daughters from seduction or rape, but that Protestant reformers found morally abhorrent and demanded be abolished.

Towns responded in a variety of ways to these opposing pressures. Some instituted special committees

MARRIAGE AND CELIBACY: TWO VIEWS

These two selections illustrate the strongly contrasting views on the spiritual value of marriage versus celibacy that came to be embraced by Protestant and Catholic religious authorities. The first selection is part of Martin Luther's more general attack on monasticism but emphasizes his view that marriage is the natural and divinely intended state for all human beings. The second selection, from the decrees of the Council of Trent (1545–1563), restates traditional Catholic teaching on the holiness of marriage but also emphasizes the spiritual superiority of virginity to marriage and the necessity of clerical celibacy.

Listen! In all my days I have not heard the confession of a nun, but in the light of Scripture I shall hit upon how matters fare with her and know I shall not be lying. If a girl is not sustained by great and exceptional grace, she can live without a man as little as she can without eating, drinking, sleeping, and other natural necessities. Nor, on the other hand, can a man dispense with a wife. The reason for this is that procreating children is an urge planted as deeply in human nature as eating and drinking. That is why God has given and put into the body the organs, arteries, fluxes, and everything that serves it. Therefore what is he doing who would check this process and keep nature from running its desired and intended course? He is attempting to keep nature from being nature, fire from burning, water from wetting, and a man from eating, drinking, and sleeping.

E. M. Plass, ed., *What Luther Says*, vol. 2 (St. Louis, 1959), pp. 888–889.

CANONS ON THE SACRAMENT OF MATRIMONY (1563)

Canon 1. If anyone says that matrimony is not truly and properly one of the seven sacraments . . . instituted by Christ the Lord, but has been devised by men in the Church and does not confer grace, let him be anathema [cursed].

Canon 9. If anyone says that clerics constituted in sacred orders or regulars who have made solemn profession of chastity can contract marriage . . . and that all who feel that they have not the gift of chastity, even though they have made such a vow, can contract marriage, let him be anathema, since God does not refuse that gift to those who ask for it rightly, neither does *he suffer us to be tempted above that which we are able.*

Canon 10: If anyone says that the married state excels the state of virginity or celibacy, and that it is better and happier to be united in matrimony than to remain in virginity or celibacy, let him be anathema.

H. J. Schroeder, *Canons and Decrees of the Council of Trent* (St. Louis and London, 1941), pp. 181–182.

QUESTIONS FOR ANALYSIS

1. Why did Luther believe that the monastic demands for celibacy were impossible to meet? How important an issue was celibacy in the context of sixteenth-century religious conflicts?

REFORMATIONS OF RELIGION

to police public morals, of the sort we have seen already in Calvin's Geneva. Some abandoned Protestantism altogether. Others, like Augsburg, flip-flopped back and forth between Protestantism and Catholicism for several decades before finally settling on one religion or the other. But regardless of a town's final choice of religious allegiance, by the end of the sixteenth century a revolution had taken place with respect to town governments' attitudes toward public morality. In their competition with each other, neither Catholics nor Protestants wished to be seen as soft on sin. The result, by 1600, was the abolition of publicly recognized brothels throughout Europe, the illegalization of prostitution, and far stricter governmental supervision of many other aspects of private life in both Catholic and Protestant urban communities.

PROTESTANTISM AND CONTROL OVER MARRIAGE

Protestantism also increased parents' control over their children's choice of marital partners. The medieval Catholic Church defined marriage as a sacrament that did not require the involvement of a priest. The mutual free consent of the two parties, even if given without witnesses or parental approval, was enough to constitute a legally valid marriage in the eyes of the church; at the same time, however, the church would annul a marriage if either of the parties could prove that they had not freely consented to it. Opposition to this doctrine came from many quarters, but especially from parents and other relatives. Because marriage involved rights of inheritance to property, most families regarded it as far too important a matter to be left to the free choice of their children. Instead, parents wanted the power to prevent unsuitable matches and, ideally, to force their children to accept the marriage arrangements their families might negotiate on their behalf. Protestantism offered an opportunity to achieve such control. Luther had declared marriage to be a purely secular matter, not a sacrament at all, that could be regulated however the governing authorities thought best. Calvin largely followed suit, although Calvinist theocracy drew less of a distinction than did Lutheranism between the powers of church and state. Even Catholicism was eventually forced to give way. Although it never entirely abandoned its insistence that both members of the couple must freely consent to their marriage, by the end of the sixteenth century the Catholic

---

CHRONOLOGY

SPREAD OF PROTESTANTISM, 1520–1560

Lutheranism becomes state religion in Denmark, Norway, and Sweden	1520s
England breaks with Rome	1534
Geneva adopts theocratic government based on Calvinism	1541
Calvinism spreads to Scotland, England, the Netherlands, and France	1540–1560s
Elizabethan settlement	1559

Church required formal public notice of intent to marry and insisted on the presence of a priest at the actual wedding ceremony. Both were efforts to prevent elopements, allowing families time to intervene before an unsuitable marriage was concluded. Individual Catholic countries sometimes went even further in trying to reassert parental control over their children's choice of marital partners. In France, for example, although couples might still marry without parental consent, those who did so now forfeited all of their rights to inherit their families' property. In somewhat different ways, both Protestantism and Catholicism thus moved to strengthen the control that parents could exercise over their children—and, in the case of Protestantism, that husbands could exercise over their wives.

THE ENGLISH REFORMATION

Why did England become a Protestant country?

In England, the Reformation took a rather different course than it did in continental Europe. Although a tradition of popular Lollardy survived into the sixteenth century, the number of Lollards was too small and their influence too limited for Lollardy to have played a significant role in paving the way for the ultimate triumph of Protestantism in England. Nor was England particularly oppressed by the papal exactions and abuses that roiled Germany. English monarchs already exercised close control over church appointments within their kingdom when the sixteenth century began; they also received the lion's share of the papal taxation collected from England. Nor did the church courts inspire any particular resentments. On the contrary, church courts would continue to function in Protestant England until the eighteenth century. Why, then, did sixteenth-century England become a Protestant country at all?

Henry VIII and the Break with Rome

As is often the case in English history, an answer to this question must begin with the Crown. By 1527 the imperious King Henry VIII had been married for eighteen years to Ferdinand and Isabella's daughter Catherine of Aragon, yet all the offspring of this union had died in infancy, save only Princess Mary. Because Henry needed a male heir to preserve the succession of his Tudor Dynasty and because Catherine was now past childbearing age, Henry had good reasons of state to break his marriage bonds. He also had more personal motives, having become infatuated with a dark-eyed lady-in-waiting named Anne Boleyn. To marry Anne, Henry appealed to Rome to annul his marriage to Catherine, arguing that because Queen Catherine had previously been married to Henry's older brother Arthur (who had died shortly after the ceremony was performed), Henry's marriage to Catherine had been invalid from the beginning. As Henry's representatives pointed out, the Bible pronounced it "an unclean thing" for a man to take his brother's wife and cursed such a marriage with childlessness (Leviticus 20:31). Even a papal dispensation (which Henry and Catherine had obtained for their marriage) could not dispose of such a clear prohibition, as the marriage's childlessness proved.

Henry's suit put Pope Clement VII (1523–1534) in a quandary. Henry was firmly convinced that this scriptural curse had blighted his chances of perpetuating his dynasty; and both Henry and Clement knew that popes in the past had granted annulments to reigning monarchs on far weaker grounds than the ones Henry was alleging. If, however, the pope granted Henry's annulment he would cast doubt on the validity of all papal dispensations. More seriously, however, he would also provoke the wrath of the emperor Charles V, Catherine of Aragon's nephew, whose armies were in firm command of Rome and who at that moment held the pope himself in captivity. Clement was trapped; all he could do was procrastinate and hope for better days. For two years, he allowed the suit to proceed in England without ever reaching a verdict. Then, suddenly, he transferred the case to Rome, where the legal process began all over again.

Exasperated by these delays, Henry began to increase the pressure on the pope. In 1531 he compelled an assembly of English clergy to declare him "protector and only supreme head" of the church in England. In 1532 he encouraged Parliament to produce an inflammatory list of grievances against the clergy, and used this threat to force the clergy to concede his right as king to approve or disapprove of all church legislation. In January 1533, Henry married Anne Boleyn (already pregnant) even though his marriage to Queen Catherine had still not been annulled. (The new archbishop of Canterbury, Thomas Cranmer, provided the required annulment in May.) In September, Princess Elizabeth was born; her father, disappointed again in his hopes for a son, refused to attend her christening. Nevertheless, Parliament settled the succession to the throne on the children of Henry and Anne, redirected all papal revenues from England into the king's hands,

Henry VIII, by Hans Holbein the Younger.

THE SIX ARTICLES

Although Henry VIII withdrew the Church of England from obedience to the papacy, he continued to lean more toward Catholic than Protestant theology. Some of his advisers, most notably Thomas Cromwell, were committed Protestants; and the king allowed his son and heir, Edward VI, to be raised as a Protestant. But after several years of rapid (and mostly Protestant) change in the English church, in 1539 the king reasserted a set of traditional Catholic doctrines in the Six Articles. These would remain binding on the Church of England until the king's death in 1547.

First, that in the most blessed sacrament of the altar, by the strength and efficacy of Christ's mighty word, it being spoken by the priest, is present really, under the form of bread and wine, the natural body and blood of our Savior Jesus Christ, conceived of the Virgin Mary, and that after the consecration there remains no substance of bread or wine, nor any other substance but the substance of Christ, God and man;

Secondly, that communion in both kinds is not necessary for salvation, by the law of God, to all persons, and that it is to be believed and not doubted . . . that in the flesh, under the form of bread, is the very blood, and with the blood, under the form of wine, is the very flesh, as well apart as though they were both together;

Thirdly, that priests, after the order of priesthood received as afore, may not marry by the law of God;

Fourthly, that vows of chastity or widowhood by man or woman made to God advisedly ought to be observed by the law of God. . . .

Fifthly, that it is right and necessary that private masses be continued and admitted in this the king's English Church and congregation . . . whereby good Christian people . . . do receive both godly and goodly consolations and benefits; and it is agreeable also to God's law;

Sixthly, that oral, private confession is expedient and necessary to be retained and continued, used and frequented in the church of God.

Statutes of the Realm, vol. 3 (London, 1810–1828), p. 739 (modernized).

QUESTIONS FOR ANALYSIS

1. If he leaned more toward Catholicism, then why did Henry VIII allow his son to be raised a Protestant? What does this tell us about the Reformation in England?

---

prohibited appeals to the papal court, and formally declared "the King's highness to be Supreme Head of the Church of England [having] the authority to redress all errors, heresies, and abuses." In 1536, Henry executed Sir Thomas More for his refusal to endorse this declaration of supremacy and took the first steps toward dissolving England's monasteries. By the end of 1539, the monasteries and convents were gone and their lands

and wealth confiscated by the king, who distributed them to his supporters.

These measures broke the bonds that linked the English church to Rome, but they did not make England a Protestant country. Although certain traditional practices (such as pilgrimages and relics) were prohibited, the English church remained overwhelmingly Catholic in organization, doctrine, ritual, and language. The Six Articles promulgated by Parliament in 1539 at Henry VIII's behest left no room for doubt as to official orthodoxy: oral confession to priests, masses for the dead, and clerical celibacy were all confirmed; the Latin Mass continued; and Catholic eucharistic doctrine was not only confirmed but its denial made punishable by death. To most English people, only the disappearance of the monasteries and the king's own continuing matrimonial adventures (he married six wives in all) gave certain evidence that their church was no longer part of the Roman obedience.

EDWARD VI

For truly committed Protestants, and especially those who had visited Calvin's Geneva, the changes Henry VIII enforced on the English church did not go nearly far enough. In 1547, the accession of the nine-year-old king Edward VI (Henry's son with his third wife, Jane Seymour) gave them their opportunity to finish the task of reformation. Encouraged by the clear Protestant sympathies of the young king himself, Edward's government moved quickly to reform the creeds and ceremonies of the English church. Priests were permitted to marry; English services replaced Latin ones; the veneration of images was abolished, and the images themselves defaced or destroyed; prayers for the dead were abolished, and endowments for such prayers were confiscated; and new articles of belief were drawn up, repudiating all sacraments except baptism and communion and affirming the Protestant doctrine of justification by faith alone. Most important, a new prayer book was published to define precisely how the new, English-language services of the church were to be conducted. Much remained unsettled with respect to both doctrine and worship; but by 1553, when the youthful Edward died, the English church appeared to have become a distinctly Protestant institution.

> Encouraged by the clear Protestant sympathies of the young king himself, Edward's government moved quickly to reform the creeds and ceremonies of the English church.

MARY TUDOR AND THE RESTORATION OF CATHOLICISM

Edward's successor, however, was his pious and deeply Catholic sister Mary (1553–1558), Henry VIII's daughter with Catherine of Aragon. Mary speedily reversed her brother's religious policies, restoring the Latin Mass and requiring married priests to give up their wives. She even prevailed on Parliament to vote a return to papal allegiance. Hundreds of Protestants leaders fled abroad, many to Geneva; others, including Archbishop Thomas Cranmer, were burned at the stake for refusing to abjure their Protestantism. News of the martyrdoms spread like wildfire through Protestant Europe. In England, however, Mary's policies sparked relatively little outright resistance at the local level. After two decades of religious upheaval, most English men and women were probably hoping that Mary's reign would bring some stability to their religious lives.

This, however, Mary could not do. The executions she ordered were insufficient to wipe out religious resistance—instead, Protestant propaganda about "Bloody Mary" and the "fires of Smithfield" caused widespread disaffection, even among those who welcomed the return of traditional religious forms. Nor could she do anything to restore monasticism: too many leading families had profited from Henry VIII's dissolution of the monasteries for this to be reversed. Mary's marriage to her cousin Philip, Charles V's son and heir to the Spanish throne, was another miscalculation. Although the marriage treaty stipulated that in the event of Mary's death Philip could not succeed her, her English subjects never trusted him. When the queen allowed herself to be drawn by Philip into a war with France on Spain's behalf in which England lost Calais, its last foothold on the European continent, many English people became highly disaffected. Ultimately, however, what doomed Mary's religious counter-revolution was simply the accidents of biology. Mary was unable to conceive an heir, and when she died after only six years of rule, her throne passed to her Protestant sister, Elizabeth.

THE ELIZABETHAN RELIGIOUS SETTLEMENT

The daughter of Henry VIII and Anne Boleyn, and one of the most capable and popular monarchs ever to sit on the English throne, Queen Elizabeth I (1558–1603) was predisposed in favor of Protestantism by the circumstances of her parents' marriage as well as by her upbringing. But Elizabeth was no zealot and wisely recognized that supporting radical Protestantism in England might provoke bitter sectarian strife. Accordingly, she presided over what is customarily known as

Queen Mary and Queen Elizabeth. These two daughters of Henry VIII had strikingly different fates as rulers: the pious Catholic Mary sparked religious division in England and died after only six years on the throne, whereas Elizabeth angled toward the Protestant cause but managed to mediate between the two faiths and become one of England's most popular monarchs.

"the Elizabethan settlement." By a new Act of Supremacy (1559), Elizabeth repealed Mary's Catholic legislation, prohibiting foreign religious powers (i.e., the pope) from exercising any authority within England and declaring herself "supreme governor" of the English church—a more Protestant title than Henry VIII's "supreme head" insofar as most Protestants believed that Christ alone was the head of the church. She also adopted many of the Protestant liturgical reforms instituted by her brother, Edward, including a revised version of the Edwardian prayer book. But she also retained vestiges of Catholic practice, including bishops, church courts, and vestments for the clergy. On most doctrinal matters, including predestination and free will, Elizabeth's Thirty-Nine Articles of Faith (approved in 1562) struck a decidedly Protestant, even Calvinist, tone. But the prayer book was more moderate, and on the critical issue of the Eucharist was deliberately ambiguous. By combining Catholic and Protestant interpretations ("this is my body.... Do this in remembrance of me") into a single declaration, the prayer book permitted an enormous latitude for competing interpretations of the service by priests and parishioners alike.

Despite such "latitudinarianism," religious tensions persisted in Elizabethan England, not only between Protestants and Catholics but also between moderate and more extreme Protestants. The queen's artful fudging of these differences was by no means a recipe guaranteed to succeed. Rather, what preserved the Elizabethan religious settlement, and ultimately made England a Protestant country, was the extraordinary length of Queen Elizabeth's reign combined with the fact that for much of that time Protestant England was at war with Catholic Spain. Under Elizabeth, Protestantism and English nationalism gradually fused together into a potent conviction that God himself had chosen England for greatness. After 1588, when English naval forces won an improbable victory over the "invincible" Spanish Armada, Protestantism and Englishness became nearly indistinguishable to most of Queen Elizabeth's subjects. Laws against Catholic recusants became increasingly severe, and although an

English Catholic tradition did survive, its adherents were a persecuted minority. Much more alarming was the situation in Ireland, where the vast majority of the population remained Catholic despite the government's efforts to impose Protestantism on them. By 1603, Irishness was as firmly identified with Catholicism as was Englishness with Protestantism; but it was the Protestants who were in the ascendant in both countries.

CATHOLICISM TRANSFORMED

How did the Catholic Reformation differ from the Counter-Reformation?

The historical novelty of Protestantism inevitably casts the spotlight on such religious reformers as Luther and Calvin; but there was also a powerful internal reform movement within the Catholic Church during the sixteenth century. Historians differ about whether to call this movement the "Catholic Reformation" or the "Counter-Reformation." Some prefer the former term because it emphasizes that significant efforts to reform the Catholic Church began before Luther posted his theses and continued long after. Others, however, insist that from the mid-sixteenth century on, most Catholic reformers were inspired primarily by the urgent need to resist the Protestant schism. We will use both terms to refer to two complementary phases of Catholic reform: a Catholic Reformation that came before Luther, and a Counter-Reformation that came after him.

In northern Europe, Christian humanists such as Erasmus and Thomas More also played a role in this Catholic reform movement, not only by criticizing abuses and editing sacred texts, but also by encouraging the laity to lead lives of simple but sincere religious piety.

THE CATHOLIC REFORMATION

The Catholic Reformation began around 1490, and was primarily a movement for moral and institutional reform within the religious orders. Although these efforts received strong support from several secular rulers, the papacy showed little interest in them. As a result, the Catholic Reformation never became a truly international movement. In Spain, reform activities directed by Cardinal Francisco Ximenes de Cisneros (1436–1517) and supported by the monarchy led to the imposition of strict rules of behavior on Franciscan friars and the elimination of abuses prevalent among the diocesan clergy. Ximenes also helped regenerate the spiritual life of the Spanish church. In Italy, earnest clerics labored to make the Italian church more worthy of its calling. Reforming the existing monastic orders was a difficult task, not least because the papal court set such a poor example; but Italian reformers did manage to establish several new religious orders dedicated to high ideals of piety and social service. In northern Europe, Christian humanists such as Erasmus and Thomas More also played a role in this Catholic reform movement, not only by criticizing abuses and editing sacred texts but also by encouraging the laity to lead lives of simple but sincere religious piety.

As a response to the challenges posed by Protestantism, however, the Catholic Reformation proved entirely inadequate. Starting in the 1530s, therefore, a second, more aggressive phase of reform under a new style of vigorous papal leadership began to gather momentum. The leading Counter-Reformation popes—Paul III (1534–1549), Paul IV (1555–1559), Saint Pius V (1566–1572), and Sixtus V (1585–1590)—were collectively the most zealous reforming popes since the High Middle Ages. All led upright personal lives. Some, indeed, were so grimly ascetic that contemporaries wondered whether they were not too holy: as a Spanish councilor wrote of Pius V in 1567, "We should like it even better if the present Holy Father were no longer with us, however great, inexpressible, unparalleled, and extraordinary His Holiness may be." In confronting Protestantism, however, an excessively holy pope was vastly preferable to a self-indulgent one. But these Counter-Reformation popes were not merely holy men. They were also accomplished administrators who reorganized papal finances and filled ecclesiastical offices with bishops and abbots no less renowned for austerity and holiness than were the popes themselves.

These papal reform efforts intensified at the Council of Trent, a general council of the entire church convoked by Paul III in 1545 and which met at intervals thereafter until 1563. The decisions taken at Trent provided the foundations on which a new, Counter-Reformation Catholic Church would be erected. Although the council began by debating

CHAPTER 13 REFORMATIONS OF RELIGION

The Council of Trent. This fresco depicts the general council of the entire Catholic Church that met from 1545 and 1563 and produced the foundation for the new Counter-Reformation church.

some form of compromise with Protestantism, Trent ended by reaffirming all of the Catholic doctrinal tenets challenged by Protestant critics. Good works were declared necessary for salvation, and all seven sacraments were declared indispensable means of grace, without which salvation was impossible. Transubstantiation, purgatory, the invocation of saints, and the rule of celibacy for the clergy were all confirmed as essential elements in the Catholic system. The Bible and the traditions of apostolic teaching were held to be of equal authority as sources of Christian truth. Papal supremacy over every bishop and priest was expressly maintained, and the supremacy of the pope over any church council was taken for granted. The Council of Trent even reaffirmed the doctrine of indulgences that had touched off the Lutheran revolt, although it did condemn the worst abuses connected with their sale.

The legislation of Trent was not confined to matters of doctrine. To improve pastoral care of the laity, bishops and priests were forbidden to hold more than one spiritual office. To address the problem of an ignorant priesthood, a theological seminary was to be established in every diocese. The council also suppressed a variety of local religious practices and saints' cults, replacing them with new cults authorized and approved by Rome. To prevent heretical ideas from corrupting the faithful, the council also decided to censor or suppress dangerous books. In 1564, a specially appointed commission published the first Index of Prohibited Books, an official list of writings that ought not to be read by faithful Catholics. All of Erasmus's works were immediately placed on the index, even though he had been a chosen Catholic champion against Martin Luther only forty years before. A permanent agency known as the Congregation of the Index was later set up to revise the list, which was revised more than forty times until it was abolished in 1966. The majority of the books condemned have been theological treatises, and probably the effect in retarding the progress of learning has been slight. Nonetheless, the index is a chilling sign of the doctrinal intolerance that characterized sixteenth-century Christianity, both in its Catholic and Protestant varieties.

SAINT IGNATIUS LOYOLA AND THE SOCIETY OF JESUS

In addition to the independent activities of popes and the legislation of the Council of Trent, a third main force propelling the Counter-Reformation was the foundation of the Society of Jesus, commonly known as the Jesuit order, by Saint Ignatius Loyola (1491–1556). In the midst of a youthful career as a worldly soldier, the Spanish nobleman Loyola was wounded in battle in 1521 (the same year in which Luther defied Charles V at Worms). While recuperating, he decided to change his ways and become a spiritual soldier of Christ. For ten months he lived as a hermit in a cave near the Spanish town of Manresa, during which time he experienced ecstatic visions and worked out the principles of his subsequent meditational guide, the *Spiritual Exercises*. This manual, completed in 1535 and first published in 1541, offered practical advice on how to master one's will and serve God through a systematic program of meditations on sin and the life of Christ. Soon made a basic handbook for all Jesuits and widely studied by numerous Catholic laypeople as well, Loyola's *Spiritual Exercises* has had an influence second only to Calvin's *Institutes* among all the religious writings of the sixteenth century.

Nonetheless, Loyola's founding of the Jesuit order itself was certainly his greatest single accomplishment.

Originating as a small group of six disciples who gathered around Loyola in Paris in 1534 to serve God in poverty, chastity, and missionary work, the Society of Jesus was formally constituted as an order of the church by Pope Paul III in 1540; by the time of Loyola's death it already numbered 1,500 members. The Society of Jesus was by far the most militant of the religious orders fostered by the Catholic reform movements of the sixteenth century. It was not merely a monastic society but a company of soldiers sworn to defend the faith. Their weapons were not to be bullets and spears but eloquence, persuasion, and instruction in correct doctrines; but the society quickly became accomplished in more worldly methods of exerting influence also. Its organization was patterned after that of a military company, with a general as commander in chief and iron discipline enforced on all members. Individuality was suppressed, and a soldierlike obedience to the general was required from the rank and file. The Jesuit general, sometimes known as the "black pope" (from the color of the order's habit), was elected for life and was not bound to take advice offered by any other member. His sole superior was the pope, to whom all senior Jesuits took a special vow of strict obedience. As a result of this vow, all Jesuits were held to be at the pope's disposal at all times.

The activities of the Jesuits consisted primarily of proselytizing Christians and non-Christians and establishing schools. Originally founded to engage in missionary work abroad, the early Jesuits preached to non-Christians in India, China, and Spanish America. For example, one of Loyola's closest early associates, Saint Francis Xavier (1506–1552), baptized thousands of native people and covered thousands of miles missionizing in South and East Asia. Yet, although Loyola had not at first conceived of his society as comprising shock troops against Protestantism, that is what it primarily became as the Counter-Reformation mounted in intensity. Through preaching and diplomacy—sometimes at the risk of their lives—Jesuits in the second half of the sixteenth century fanned out across Europe in direct confrontation with Calvinists. In many places the Jesuits succeeded in keeping rulers and their subjects loyal to Catholicism, in others they met martyrdom, and in some others—notably Poland and parts of Germany and France—they succeeded in regaining territory previously lost to Protestantism. Wherever they were allowed to settle, the Jesuits set up schools and colleges, for they firmly believed that a vigorous Catholicism depended on widespread literacy and education. Their schools were so well regarded that, after the fires of religious hatred began to subside, upper-class Protestants sometimes sent their children to receive a Jesuit education.

The Inspiration of Saint Jerome, by Guido Reni. In 1546 the Council of Trent declared Saint Jerome's Latin translation of the Bible, known as the Vulgate, to be the official version of the Catholic church; then, in 1592, Pope Clement VIII chose one edition of the Vulgate to be authoritative above all others. Since biblical scholars had known since the early sixteenth century that Saint Jerome's translation contained numerous mistakes, Counter-Reformation defenders of the Vulgate insisted that even his mistakes had been divinely inspired. The point is made visually in Guido Reni's painting of 1635.

COUNTER-REFORMATION CHRISTIANITY

From the foregoing it should be evident that there is a Counter-Reformation heritage every bit as much as there is a Protestant one. The greatest achievement of these sixteenth-century Catholic reform movements was to

OBEDIENCE AS A JESUIT HALLMARK

The necessity of obedience in the spiritual formation of monks and nuns had been a central theme in Catholic religious thought since the Rule of Saint Benedict. By focusing its demands for obedience specifically on the papacy, however, the Society of Jesus brought a new militancy to this old ideal.

Rules for Thinking with the Church

1. Always to be ready to obey with mind and heart, setting aside all judgment of one's own, the true spouse of Jesus Christ, our holy mother, our infallible and orthodox mistress, the Catholic Church, whose authority is exercised over us by the hierarchy.
2. To commend the confession of sins to a priest as it is practised in the Church; the reception of the Holy Eucharist once a year, or better still every week, or at least every month, with the necessary preparation....
4. To have a great esteem for the religious orders, and to give the preference to celibacy or virginity over the married state....
6. To praise relics, the veneration and invocation of Saints: also the stations, and pious pilgrimages, indulgences, jubilees, the custom of lighting candles in the churches, and other such aids to piety and devotion....
9. To uphold especially all the precepts of the Church, and not censure them in any manner; but, on the contrary, to defend them promptly, with reasons drawn from all sources, against those who criticize them.
10. To be eager to commend the decrees, mandates, traditions, rites and customs of the Fathers in the Faith or our superiors....
13. That we may be altogether of the same mind and in conformity with the Church herself, if she shall have defined anything to be black which to our eyes appears to be white, we ought in like manner to pronounce it to be black. For we must undoubtingly believe, that the Spirit of our Lord Jesus Christ, and the Spirit of the Orthodox church His Spouse, by which Spirit we are governed and directed to salvation, is the same....

From the Constitutions of the Jesuit Order

Let us with the utmost pains strain every nerve of our strength to exhibit this virtue of obedience, firstly to the Highest Pontiff, then to the Superiors of the Society; so that in all things ... we may be most ready to obey his voice, just as if it issued from Christ our Lord ... leaving any work, even a letter, that we have begun and have not yet finished; by directing to this goal all our strength and intention in the Lord, that holy obedience may be made perfect in us in every respect, in performance, in will, in intellect; by submitting to whatever may be enjoined on us with great readiness, with spiritual joy and perseverance; by persuading ourselves that all things [commanded] are just; by rejecting with a kind of blind obedience all opposing opinion or judgment of our own....

Henry Bettenson, ed., *Documents of the Christian Church*, 2d ed. (Oxford, 1967), pp. 259–261.

QUESTIONS FOR ANALYSIS

1. Did total obedience to the church contradict the aspirations of Renaissance humanism?
2. What role did the Jesuits play in the Catholic Reformation? Did the establishment of the Jesuit order somehow serve as a general indictment of the church itself?

CHRONOLOGY

THE COUNTER-REFORMATION, 1534–1590

Counter-Reformation popes	1534–1590
Saint Ignatius Loyola founds the Jesuits	1534
Council of Trent convenes	1545–1563
Index of Prohibited Books	1564

defend and revitalize the faith. Had it not been for the determined efforts of these reformers, Catholicism would not have swept over the globe during the seventeenth and eighteenth centuries or reemerged in Europe as the vigorous spiritual force it remains today. But other results stemmed from the Counter-Reformation as well. One was the spread of literacy in Catholic countries due to the educational activities of the Jesuits. Another was the growth of intense concern for acts of charity. Because Counter-Reformation Catholicism continued to emphasize good works as well as faith, charitable activities took on an extremely important role in the revitalized religion. Counter-Reformation spiritual leaders such as Saint Francis de Sales (1567–1622) and Saint Vincent de Paul (1581–1660) urged almsgiving in their sermons and writings, and a wave of founding of orphanages and houses for the poor swept over Catholic Europe.

The Counter-Reformation also brought a new emphasis on the importance of religious women. Counter-Reformation Catholicism did not exalt marriage as a route to holiness for women to the same degree as did Protestantism, but it did foster a distinctive role for a female religious elite—countenancing the mysticism of Saint Teresa of Avila (1515–1582) and establishing new orders of nuns such as the Ursulines and the Sisters of Charity, which had no parallel under Protestantism. Both Protestants and Catholics continued to exclude women from the priesthood or ministry, but Catholic celibate women could pursue religious lives with at least some degree of independence.

The Counter-Reformation did not, however, perpetuate the tolerant Christianity of Erasmus. Instead, Christian humanists lost favor with Counter-Reformation popes, and even natural scientists such as Galileo were sometimes regarded with suspicion (see Chapter Sixteen). But sixteenth-century Protestantism was just as theologically intolerant as sixteenth-century Catholicism, and even more hostile to the cause of rationalism.

Saint Theresa of Avila. She was one of a number of religious women who were honored by Counter-Reformation Catholicism.

Indeed, because Counter-Reformation theologians returned for guidance to the scholasticism of Saint Thomas Aquinas, they tended to be much more committed to the dignity of human reason than were their Protestant counterparts, who emphasized pure scriptural authority and unquestioning faith. It is not entirely coincidental, therefore, that René Descartes, one of the pioneers of seventeenth-century rationalism (and who coined the famous phrase "I think, therefore I am"), was trained as a youth by the Jesuits.

CONCLUSION

Protestantism emerged after the height of the Italian Renaissance and before the scientific revolution and the Enlightenment. It may be tempting, therefore, to think of historical events advancing in an inevitably cumulative way, from the Renaissance to the Reformation to the Enlightenment to the "Triumph of the Modern World." But history is seldom as neat as that. Although scholars continue to disagree on points of detail, most agree that the Protestant Reformation drew relatively little from the civilization of the Renaissance. Indeed, in certain basic respects Protestant principles were completely at odds with the major assumptions of most Renaissance humanists.

Certainly the Renaissance contributed something to the origins of the Protestant Reformation. Criticisms of religious abuses by Christian humanists helped prepare Germany for the Lutheran revolt. Close textual study of the Bible led to the publication of new, more reliable biblical editions used by the Protestant reformers. In this regard a direct line ran from the Italian humanist Lorenzo Valla to Erasmus to Luther: Valla's *Notes on the New Testament* inspired Erasmus to produce his own Greek edition and Latin translation of the New Testament in 1516; Erasmus's New Testament in turn enabled Luther in 1518 to reach some crucial conclusions concerning the literal biblical meaning of penance and became the foundation for Luther's own 1522 translation of the Bible into German. For these and related reasons, Luther addressed Erasmus in 1519 as "our ornament and our hope."

But, in fact, Erasmus quickly showed that he had no sympathy whatsoever with Lutheran principles. Most other Christian humanists followed suit, shunning Protestantism as soon as it became clear to them what Luther and other Protestant reformers were actually teaching. The reasons for this split are clear enough. Most humanists believed in free will, whereas Protestants believed in predestination; humanists tended to think of human nature as basically good, whereas Protestants found it unspeakably corrupt; and most humanists favored urbanity and tolerance, whereas the followers of Luther and Calvin emphasized obedience and conformity.

The Protestant Reformation was not the natural outgrowth of the civilization of the Renaissance. It did, however, contribute to certain traits characteristic of modern European historical development. Foremost among these was the increasing power of Europe's sovereign states. As we have seen, those German princes who converted to Protestantism were moved to do so primarily by the search for sovereignty. The kings of Denmark, Sweden, and England followed suit for much the same reasons. Since Protestant leaders—Calvin as well as Luther—preached absolute obedience to godly rulers, and since the state in Protestant countries assumed direct control of the church, the spread of Protestantism definitely resulted in the growth of state power. But we must not make any simple equation between state power and Protestantism. The power of the state was growing already by 1500, especially in such countries as France and Spain, where Catholic kings already exercised most of the same rights over the church that were forcibly seized by

Lutheran German princes and Henry VIII in the course of their own reformations.

Nationalism too was already a part of this world, as we can see from the way Luther played on it in his appeals during the 1520s. But Luther also did much to foster German cultural nationalism, not least by translating the Bible into vigorous, colloquial German. Until the sixteenth century, Germans from different regions spoke such different dialects of German that they often could not understand each other. Luther's Bible, however, gained such currency that it eventually became the linguistic standard for the entire nation. Protestantism did not unite the German nation politically; instead, Germany soon divided into Protestant and Catholic camps. But elsewhere, as in Holland or parts of central Europe, where Protestants fought successfully against a foreign, Catholic overlord, Protestantism enhanced a sense of national identity. Perhaps the most familiar case of all is that of England, where a sense of nationhood existed long before the advent of Protestantism, but where the new faith lent to that nationalism a new confidence that England was indeed a nation peculiarly favored by God.

Finally, we come to the subject of Protestantism's effects on relationships between the sexes. No consensus among historians exists on this subject. What does seem clear, however, is that Protestant men as individuals could be just as ambivalent about women as their medieval Catholic predecessors had been. John Knox, for example, inveighed against the Catholic regent of Scotland, Mary Stuart, in a treatise called *The First Blast of the Trumpet against the Monstrous Regiment of Women*, yet maintained deeply respectful relationships with women of his own faith. When Queen Mary Tudor required formerly Protestant English priests to give up their wives, many did so with disheartening alacrity. But if one asks how Protestantism as a belief system affected women's social roles, the answer appears to be that it enabled women to become just a shade more equal to men within a framework of continuing subjection. Because Protestantism called on women as well as men to undertake serious study of the Bible, it encouraged primary schooling for both sexes. But Protestant male leaders still insisted that women were naturally inferior to men and should defer to men both within the family and in the larger society. As Calvin himself said, "[L]et the woman be satisfied with her state of subjection and not take it ill that she is made inferior to the more distinguished sex." Both Luther and Calvin appear to have been happily married, but that clearly meant being happily married on their own terms.

Key Terms

Martin Luther	Diet of Worms	John Calvin	Elizabeth I
Lutheranism	Ulrich Zwingli	Henry VIII	Council of Trent
Erasmus	Anabaptists	Mary Tudor	Society of Jesus

Selected Readings

Bainton, Roland. *Erasmus of Christendom*. New York, 1969. Still the best biography in English of the Dutch reformer and intellectual.

Bainton, Roland. *Here I Stand: A Life of Martin Luther*. Nashville, Tenn., 1950. Although old and obviously biased in Luther's favor, this remains an absorbing and dramatic introduction to Luther's life and thought.

Benedict, Philip. *Christ's Churches Purely Reformed: A Social History of Calvinism*. New Haven, Conn., 2002. A wide-ranging recent survey of Calvinism in both western and eastern Europe.

Bossy, John. *Christianity in the West, 1400–1700*. Oxford and New York, 1985. A brilliant, challenging picture of the changes that took place in Christian piety and practice as a result of the sixteenth-century reformations.

Bouwsma, William J. *John Calvin: A Sixteenth-Century Portrait*. Oxford and New York, 1988. The best biography of the magisterial reformer.

Collinson, Patrick. *The Religion of Protestants: The Church in English Society, 1559–1625*. Oxford, 1982. A great book by the best contemporary historian of early English Protestantism.

Dillenberger, John. *John Calvin: Selections from His Writings*, Garden City, N.Y., 1971. A judicious selection, drawn mainly from Calvin's *Institutes*.

Dillenberger, John, ed. *Martin Luther: Selections from His Writings*. Garden City, N.Y., 1961. The standard selection, especially good on Luther's theological ideas.

Dixon, C. Scott, ed. *The German Reformation: The Essential Readings*. Oxford, 1999. A collection of important recent articles.

Duffy, Eamon. *The Stripping of the Altars: Traditional Religion in England, c. 1400–c. 1550*. The best study of the hesitant way in which England eventually became a Protestant country.

Hillerbrand, Hans J., ed. *The Protestant Reformation*. New York, 1967. Source selections are particularly good for illuminating the political consequences of Reformation theological ideas.

Loyola, Ignatius. *Personal Writings*. Trans. by Joseph A. Munitiz and Philip Endean. London and New York, 1996. An excellent collection that includes Loyola's autobiography, his spiritual diary, and some of his letters, as well as his *Spiritual Exercises*.

Luebke, David, ed. *The Counter-Reformation: The Essential Readings*. Oxford, 1999. A collection of nine important recent essays.

MacCulloch, Diarmaid. *Reformation: Europe's House Divided, 1490–1700*. London and New York, 2003. A definitive new survey; the best single-volume history of its subject in a generation.

McGrath, Alister E. *Reformation Thought: An Introduction*. Oxford, 1993. A useful explanation, accessible to non-Christians, of the theological ideas of the major Protestant reformers.

Mullett, Michael A. *The Catholic Reformation*. London, 2000. A sympathetic survey of Catholicism from the mid-sixteenth to the eighteenth century that presents the mid-sixteenth-century Council of Trent not as a response to Protestantism but as a continuation of reform efforts dating from the fifteenth century.

Oberman, Heiko A. *Luther: Man between God and the Devil*. Trans. by Eileen Walliser-Schwarzbart. New Haven, Conn., 1989. The best recent biography of Luther, stressing his preoccupations with sin, death, and the devil.

O'Malley, John W. *The First Jesuits*. Cambridge, Mass., 1993. A scholarly account of the origins and early years of the Society of Jesus.

O'Malley, John W. *Trent and All That: Renaming Catholicism in the Early Modern Era*. Cambridge, Mass., 2000. Short, lively, up to date, and with a full bibliography.

Pettegree, Andrew, ed. *The Reformation World*. New York, 2000. An exhaustive multiauthor work representing the most recent thinking about the Reformation.

Pelikan, Jaroslav. *Reformation of Church and Dogma, 1300–1700*. Volume 4: *A History of Christian Dogma*. Chicago, 1984. A masterful synthesis of Reformation theology in its late medieval context.

Roper, Lyndal. *The Holy Household: Women and Morals in Reformation Augsburg*. Oxford, 1989. A pathbreaking study of how Protestantism was adopted and adapted by the town councilors of Augsburg, with special attention to its impact on attitudes toward women, the family, and marriage.

Shagan, Ethan H. *Popular Politics and the English Reformation*. Cambridge, 2002. Argues that the English Reformation reflects an ongoing process of negotiation, resistance, and response between government and people.

Tracy, James D. *Europe's Reformations, 1450–1650*. 2d ed. Lanham, Md., 2006. An outstanding survey, especially strong on Dutch and Swiss developments, but excellent throughout.

Williams, George H. *The Radical Reformation*. 3d ed. Kirksville, Mo., 1992. Originally published in 1962, this is still the best book on Anabaptism and its offshoots.

Chapter Fourteen

Chapter Contents

Economic, Religious, and Political Tests 504

A Century of Religious Wars 506

Divergent Paths: Spain, France, and England, 1600–1660 513

The Problem of Doubt and the Quest for Certainty 522

Literature and the Arts 526

Conclusion 532

Religious Wars and State Building, 1540–1660

STRANGE AS IT MAY SEEM in retrospect, Martin Luther never intended to fracture the religious unity of Europe. He sincerely believed that once the Bible was available to everyone in an accurate, vernacular translation, then everyone who read the Bible would interpret it in exactly the same way as did he himself. The result, of course, was quite different, as Luther quickly discovered in his bitter disputes with Zwingli and Calvin. Nor did Catholicism crumble in the face of reformed teachings as Luther had believed that it would. Instead, Europe's religious divisions multiplied, speedily crystallizing along political lines. By Luther's death in 1546, a clear pattern had already emerged. With only rare exceptions, Protestantism triumphed in those areas where political authorities supported the reformers. Where rulers remained Catholic, so too did their territories.

This was not the result Martin Luther had intended, but it did faithfully reflect the most basic presumptions of sixteenth-century European life. Anabaptists apart, neither Protestant nor Catholic reformers set out to challenge the standard medieval beliefs about the mutual interdependence of religion and politics—quite the contrary. Sixteenth-century Europeans continued to believe that the proper role of the state was to enforce true religion on its subjects, and sixteenth-century rulers remained convinced that religious pluralism would bring disunion and disloyalty to any state that embraced it. Ultimately, both Catholics and Protestants believed that western Europe had to return to a single religious faith enforced by properly constituted political authorities. What they could not agree on was which faith and which authorities.

The result was a brutal series of religious wars between 1540 and 1660 whose reverberations would continue to be felt until the eighteenth century. Vastly expensive and enormously destructive, these wars affected everyone in Europe, from peasants to princes. They did not arise solely from conflicts over religion. Regionalism, dynasticism, and nationalism were also potent contributors to the chaos into which Europe now plunged. Together, however, these forces of division and disorder brought into question the very survival of the European political order that had emerged since the thirteenth century. Faced with the prospect of political collapse,

FOCUS QUESTIONS

• Why was the period 1540–1660 one of the most turbulent in European history?

• Why did religious conflicts become so deeply entwined with political conflicts during this period?

• What caused the decline of Spain in the seventeenth century?

• Why was this period such a fertile one for political philosophy?

• What was the relationship between the Baroque school and the Counter-Reformation?

Europeans by 1660 were forced to embrace, gradually and grudgingly, a notion that in 1540 had seemed impossible to conceive: that religious toleration, however limited in scope, might be the only way to preserve the political, social, and economic order of the European world.

ECONOMIC, RELIGIOUS, AND POLITICAL TESTS

Why was the period 1540–1660 one of the most turbulent in European history?

The troubles that engulfed Europe during the traumatic century between 1540 and 1660 caught contemporaries unaware. From the mid-fifteenth century on, most of Europe had enjoyed steady economic growth, and the discovery of the New World seemed the basis of greater prosperity to come. Political trends too seemed auspicious, because most western European governments were becoming ever more efficient and providing more internal peace for their subjects. By the middle of the sixteenth century, however, thunderclouds were gathering that would soon burst into terrible storms.

THE PRICE REVOLUTION

Although the causes of these storms were interrelated, we can examine each separately, starting with the great price inflation. Nothing like the upward price trend that affected western Europe in the second half of the sixteenth century had ever happened before. In Flanders the cost of wheat tripled between 1550 and 1600, grain prices in Paris quadrupled, and the overall cost of living in England more than doubled. The twentieth century would see much more dizzying inflations than this, but since the skyrocketing of prices in the later sixteenth century was a novelty, most historians agree on calling it a "price revolution."

Two developments in particular underlay the soaring prices. The first was demographic. Starting in the later fifteenth century, Europe's population began to grow again after the plague-induced falloff: roughly estimated, Europe had about 50 million people around 1450 and 90 million around 1600. Because Europe's food supply remained more or less constant, owing to the lack of any noteworthy breakthroughs in agricultural technology, food prices were driven sharply higher by greater demand. At the same time, wages stagnated or even declined. As a result, workers around 1600 were paying a higher percentage of their wages to buy food than ever before, even though their basic nutritional levels were declining.

Population trends explain much, but since Europe's population did not increase nearly so rapidly in the second half of the sixteenth century as did prices, other explanations for the great inflation are necessary. Foremost among these is the enormous influx of bullion from Spanish America. From 1556 to 1560 roughly 10 million ducats worth of silver passed through the Spanish entry port of Seville. Between 1576 and 1580 that figure doubled, and between 1591 and 1595 it more than quadrupled. Most of this silver was used by the Spanish crown to pay its foreign creditors and its armies abroad; as a result, this bullion quickly circulated throughout Europe, where much of it was minted into coins. This dramatic increase in the volume of money in circulation fueled the spiral of rising prices. "I learned a proverb here," said a French traveler in Spain in 1603, "everything costs much here except silver."

Aggressive entrepreneurs and large-scale farmers profited most from the changed economic circumstances, while the masses of laboring people were hurt the worst. Landlords benefited from the rising prices of agricultural produce and merchants from the increasing demand for luxury goods. But laborers were caught in a squeeze because wages rose far more slowly than prices, owing to the presence of a more than adequate labor supply. Moreover, because the cost of food staples rose at a sharper rate than the cost of most other items of consumption, poor people had to spend an ever greater percentage of their paltry incomes on necessities. When disasters such as wars or poor harvests drove grain prices out of reach, some of the poor literally starved to death. The picture that emerges is one of the rich getting richer and the poor getting poorer—splendid feasts enjoyed amid the most appalling suffering.

The price revolution also placed new pressures on the sovereign states of Europe. Since the inflation depressed the real value of money, fixed incomes from taxes and tolls yielded less and less. Thus merely to keep their incomes constant governments would have been forced to raise taxes. But to compound this problem, most states needed much more real income than previously because they were undertaking more wars;

and warfare, as always, was becoming increasingly expensive. The only recourse, then, was to raise taxes precipitously, but such draconian measures aroused great resentment. Hence governments faced continuous threats of defiance and potential armed resistance.

After 1600 prices rose less rapidly, as population growth slowed and the flood of silver from America began to abate. On the whole, however, the period from 1600 to 1660 was one of economic stagnation rather than growth, even though a few areas—notably Holland—bucked the trend. The rich were usually able to hold their own, but the poor as a group made no advances, because the relationship of prices to wages remained fixed to their disadvantage. Indeed, if anything, the lot of the poor in many places deteriorated because the mid-seventeenth century saw some particularly expensive and destructive wars in which helpless civilians were plundered by rapacious tax collectors or looting soldiers, or sometimes both. The Black Death also returned, wreaking havoc in London and elsewhere during the 1660s.

> On the whole, the period from 1600 to 1660 was one of economic stagnation rather than growth, even though a few areas—notably Holland—bucked the trend.

RELIGIOUS CONFLICTS

It goes without saying that most people would have been far better off had there been fewer wars during this difficult century, but given prevalent attitudes, newly arisen religious rivalries made wars inevitable. Simply stated, until religious passions began to cool toward the end of the period, most Catholics and Protestants viewed each other as minions of Satan who could not be allowed to live. Worse, sovereign states attempted to enforce religious uniformity on the grounds that "crown and altar" offered each other mutual support and in the belief that governments would totter where diversity of faith prevailed. Rulers on both sides felt certain that religious minorities, if allowed to survive in their realms, would inevitably engage in sedition; nor were they far wrong, since militant Calvinists and Jesuits were indeed dedicated to subverting constituted powers in areas where their parties had not yet triumphed. Thus states tried to extirpate all potential religious resistance but, in the process, sometimes provoked civil wars in which each side tended to assume there could be no victory until the other was exterminated. And of course civil wars might become international in scope if foreign powers chose to aid their embattled religious allies elsewhere.

Peasants Harvesting Wheat, Sixteenth Century. The inflation that swept through Europe in the late 1500s most affected the poor workers, as the abundant labor supply dampened wages while the cost of food rose with poor harvests.

POLITICAL INSTABILITY

Compounding the foregoing problems were the inherent weaknesses of the major European kingdoms. Most of the major states of early modern Europe had grown during the later Middle Ages by absorbing smaller, traditionally autonomous territories, sometimes by conquest, but more often through marriage alliances or inheritance arrangements between their respective ruling families (a policy known as "dynasticism"). At first some degree of provincial autonomy was usually preserved in these newly absorbed territories. But between 1540 and 1660, when governments were making ever greater financial claims on all their subjects or trying to enforce religious uniformity, rulers often rode roughshod over the rights of these traditionally autonomous provinces. The result, once again, was civil war, in which regionalism, economic grievances, and religious animosities were compounded into a volatile and destructive mixture. Nor was that all, since most governments seeking money and/or religious uniformity tried to rule with a firmer hand than before and thus sometimes provoked armed resistance from subjects seeking to preserve their traditional constitutional liberties. Given this bewildering variety of motives for revolt, it is not surprising that the long century between 1540 and 1660 was one of the most turbulent in all of European history.

A Century of Religious Wars

Why did religious conflicts become so deeply entwined with political conflicts during this period?

The greatest single cause of warfare during this period was religious conflict. The wars themselves divide into four phases: a series of German wars from the 1540s to 1555; the French wars of religion from 1562 until 1598; the Dutch wars with Spain between 1566 and 1609; and the Thirty Years' War in Germany between 1618 and 1648.

The German Wars of Religion to 1555

Wars between Catholics and Protestants in Germany began in the 1540s when the Holy Roman emperor Charles V, a devout Catholic, tried to reestablish Catholic unity in Germany by launching a military campaign against several German princes who had instituted Lutheran worship in their territories. Despite several notable victories, Charles's efforts to defeat the Protestant princes failed. Partly this was because he was simultaneously involved in wars against France and so could not devote his entire attention to German affairs. Primarily, however, Charles failed because the Catholic princes of Germany feared that if Charles succeeded in defeating the Protestant princes, he might then suppress their own independence also. As a result, the Catholic princes' support for the foreign-born Charles was only lukewarm; at times, they even joined with the Protestant princes in battle against the

The Emperor Charles V at Muehlberg by Titian. Charles V's attempts to re-create a united Catholic Germany by military means failed. In 1555, he was forced to accept the Peace of Augsburg, which recognized the existence of Protestant and Catholic territories.

emperor. Accordingly, religious warfare sputtered on and off until a compromise settlement was reached in the Peace of Augsburg (1555). This rested on the principle of *cuius regio, eius religio* ("as the ruler, so the religion"), which meant that in those principalities where Lutheran princes ruled, Lutheranism would be the sole state religion; where Catholic princes ruled, their territories would be Catholic also. Although the Peace of Augsburg was a historical milestone inasmuch as Catholic rulers for the first time acknowledged the legality of Protestantism, it boded ill for the future in assuming that no sovereign state larger than a free city (for which it made exceptions) could tolerate religious diversity. Moreover, in excluding Calvinism entirely, it ensured that the German Calvinists would become aggressive opponents of the status quo.

The French Wars of Religion

From the 1560s on, Europe's religious wars became far more brutal, partly because the combatants had become more intransigent (Calvinists and Jesuits customarily took the lead on their respective sides) and partly because the later religious wars were aggravated by regional, political, and dynastic hostilities. Because Geneva bordered on France and because Calvin himself was a Frenchman who longed to convert his mother country, the next act in the tragedy of Europe's confessional warfare was played out on French soil. Calvinist missionaries made considerable headway in France between 1541 (when Calvin took power in Geneva) and the outbreak of religious warfare in 1562. By 1562, Calvinists made up between 10 and 20 percent of France's population, with their numbers swelling daily. Greatly assisting the Calvinist (Huguenot; HYOO-guh-noh) cause in France was the conversion of many aristocratic Frenchwomen to Calvinism. Such women often won over their husbands, who in turn maintained large private armies. The foremost example is that of Jeanne d'Albret, queen of the tiny Pyrenean kingdom of Navarre, who brought over to Calvinism her husband, the prominent French aristocrat Antoine de Bourbon, and her brother-in-law, the prince de Condé. Condé took command of the French Huguenot party when civil war broke out in 1562 and was later succeeded in this capacity by Jeanne's son, Henry of Navarre, who came to rule all of France at the end of the century as King Henry IV. But Calvinism in France was also nourished by long-standing regional hosilities within the French kingdom, especially in southern France, where the animosities aroused by the thirteenth-century Albigensian crusade continued to fester.

Until 1562, an uneasy peace continued between the Catholic and the Calvinist forces in France. In 1562, however, the French king died unexpectedly, leaving a young child as his heir. A struggle immediately broke out between the Huguenot Condé and the ultra-Catholic duke of Guise for control of the regency government. And since both Catholics and Protestants assumed that France could have only a single *roi, foi,* and *loi* ("king," "faith," and "law"), this political struggle immediately took on a religious aspect. Soon all France was aflame. Rampaging mobs, often incited by members of the clergy, ransacked churches and settled local scores. Although the Huguenots were not strong or numerous enough to gain victory, they were too strong to be defeated, especially in their southern French territorial stronghold. Hence, despite intermittent truces, warfare dragged on at great cost of life until 1572, when a truce was arranged by which the Protestant leader, Henry of Navarre, was to marry the Catholic sister of the reigning French king. At this point, however, the cultivated queen mother, Catherine de' Medici, normally a woman who favored compromise, panicked. Instead of honoring the truce, she plotted with members of the Catholic Guise faction to kill all the Huguenot leaders while they were assembled in Paris for her daugher's wedding to Henry of Navarre. In the early morning of St. Bartholomew's Day (August 24) most of the Huguenot chiefs were murdered in bed, and 2,000 to 3,000 other Protestants were slaughtered in the streets or drowned in the Seine by Catholic mobs. When word of the Parisian massacre spread to the provinces, some 10,000 more Huguenots were killed in a frenzy of blood lust that swept through France. Henry of Navarre escaped, along with his new bride; but after 1572, the conflict entered a new and even more bitter phase.

Only when the politically astute Henry of Navarre succeeded to the French throne as Henry IV (1589–1610), initiating the Bourbon Dynasty that would rule until 1792, did the civil war finally come to an end.

Henry IV. The rule of Henry of Navarre initiated the Bourbon Dynasty in France and ended the bitter civil war.

In 1593 Henry abjured his Protestantism to placate France's Catholic majority, declaring as he did so that "Paris is worth a mass." In 1598, however, he offered limited religious freedom to the Huguenots by the Edict of Nantes. Although the edict recognized Catholicism as the official religion of the kingdom, guaranteeing Catholics the right to practice their religion everywhere in France, Huguenot nobles were now allowed to hold Protestant services privately in their castles; other Huguenots were allowed to worship at specified places (excluding Paris and all cities where bishops and archbishops resided); and the Huguenot party was permitted to fortify some towns, especially in the south and west, for their own military defense. Huguenots were also guaranteed the right to serve in all public offices and to enter the universities and hospitals without hindrance.

Although the Edict of Nantes did not countenance absolute freedom of worship, it nevertheless took a major stride in the direction of toleration. But despite its efforts to create one kingdom with two faiths, the effect of the edict was to divide the French kingdom into separate religious enclaves. In southern and western France, Huguenots came to have their own law courts, staffed by their own judges. They also received substantial powers of self-government, because it was presumed on all sides that the members of one religious group could not be ruled equitably by the adherents of a competing religion. Because of its regional character, Nantes also represented a concession to the long-standing traditions of provincial autonomy within the kingdom of France. In some ways, indeed, the Huguenot areas became a state within a state, thus raising again the perpetual fear in Paris that the kingdom of which it was the capital might once again fly apart into its constituent parts, as had happened during the Hundred Years' War. On its own terms, however, the Edict of Nantes was a success. With religious peace established, France quickly began to recover from decades of devastation, even though Henry IV himself was cut down by the dagger of a Catholic fanatic in 1610.

THE REVOLT OF THE NETHERLANDS

Bitter warfare also broke out between Catholics and Protestants in the Netherlands, where national resentments exacerbated the predictable religious hatreds. For almost a century the Netherlands (or Low Countries), comprising modern-day Holland in the north and Belgium in the south, had been ruled by the Habsburg family of Holy Roman emperors. The southern Netherlands in particular had prospered greatly from trade and manufacture: southern Netherlanders had the greatest per capita wealth of all Europe, and their metropolis of Antwerp was northern Europe's leading commercial and financial center. Moreover, the half-century-long rule of the Habsburg emperor Charles V (1506–1556) had been popular because Charles, who had been born in the Belgian city of Ghent, felt a sense of rapport with his subjects and allowed them a large degree of local self-government.

But around 1560 the good fortune of the Netherlands began to ebb. When Charles V retired to a monastery in 1556 (dying two years later) he ceded all his vast territories outside of the Holy Roman Empire and Hungary—not only the Netherlands, but Spain, Spanish America, and half of Italy—to his son Philip II

MAP OF THE NETHERLANDS

Why were the southern provinces of the Netherlands more wealthy than the northern ones? How did William the Silent use the geography of the northern Netherlands to his advantage when fighting the Spanish? Why did the north become Calvinist while the south remained Catholic?

WHY DID RELIGIOUS AND POLITICAL CONFLICTS BECOME ENTWINED DURING THIS PERIOD?

Protestants Ransacking a Catholic Church in the Netherlands. The Protestant fury of 1566 was responsible for the large-scale destruction of religious art and statuary in the Low Countries, provoking the stern repression of Phillip II.

(1556–1598). Unlike Charles, Philip had been born in Spain and, thinking of himself as a Spaniard, made Spain his residence and the focus of his policy. He viewed the Netherlands primarily as a source of income necessary for pursuing Spanish affairs. The better to exploit the region's wealth, Philip tried to tighten his own control over the government of the Netherlands. This aroused the resentment of the local magnates who had dominated the government under Charles V. A religious storm was also brewing. After 1559, when a long war between France and Spain ended, French Calvinists began to stream over the border into the southern Netherlands, making converts wherever they went. Soon there were more Calvinists in Antwerp than in Geneva. To Philip, an ardent supporter of Counter-Reformation Catholicism, this was intolerable. As he declared to the pope on the eve of conflict, "rather than suffer the slightest harm to the true religion and service of God, I would lose all my states and even my life a hundred times over because I am not and will not be the ruler of heretics."

Worried by the growing tensions, a group of local Catholic noblemen led by William of Orange (known as "William the Silent" because he was so successful at hiding his religious and political leanings; in fact he was quite talkative!) appealed to Philip to allow toleration for Calvinists. But before Philip could respond, radical Protestant mobs suddenly began ransacking Catholic churches throughout the country, desecrating hosts, smashing statuary, and shattering stained-glass windows. Local troops soon brought the situation under control, but Philip II nonetheless decided to dispatch an army of 10,000 Spanish troops, led by the duke of Alva, to wipe out Protestantism in the Netherlands. Alva's rule quickly became a reign of terror. Operating under martial law, his "Council of Blood" examined some 12,000 people on charges of heresy or sedition, of whom 9,000 were convicted and 2,000 to 3,000 executed. William the Silent fled the country, and all hope for a free Netherlands seemed lost.

But the tide turned quickly for two related reasons. First, instead of giving up, William the Silent converted to Protestantism; sought help from Protestants in France, Germany, and England; and organized bands of sea rovers to harass Spanish shipping on the Netherlandish coast. And second, Alva's tyranny helped William's cause, especially when the hated Spanish governor attempted to levy a 10 percent sales tax. With internal disaffection growing, in 1572 William, for tactical military reasons, was able to seize the northern Netherlands even though the north until then had been predominantly Catholic. Thereafter geography played a major role in determining the outcome of the conflict. Spanish armies repeatedly attempted to win back the north, but they were stopped by a combination of impassable rivers and dikes that could be opened to flood out the invaders. Although William the Silent was assassinated by a Catholic in 1584, his son continued to lead the resistance until the Spanish crown finally agreed to a truce in 1609 that implicitly recognized the independence of the northern

CHRONOLOGY

RELIGIOUS WARS, 1540s–1648

German wars	1540s–1555
French wars of religion	1562–1598
Dutch wars with Spain	1566–1609
Thirty Years' War	1618–1648

Dutch Republic. Meanwhile, the pressures of war and persecution had made the whole north Calvinist, whereas the south—which remained under Spanish control—returned to uniform Catholicism.

ENGLAND AND THE DEFEAT OF THE SPANISH ARMADA

Religious strife could spark civil war, as in France, or political rebellions, as in the Netherlands. But it could also provoke warfare between sovereign states, as in the late-sixteenth-century struggle between England and Spain. After persecution by the Catholic queen Mary and her Spanish husband Philip II, English Protestants rejoiced in the rule of Queen Elizabeth I (1558–1603) and naturally harbored great antipathy toward Philip II and the Counter-Reformation. Furthermore, English economic interests were directly opposed to those of the Spanish. A seafaring and trading people, the English in the later sixteenth century were steadily making inroads into Spanish naval and commercial domination and were also determined to resist any Spanish attempt to block England's lucrative trade with the Low Countries. But the greatest source of antagonism lay in the Atlantic, where English privateers, with the tacit consent of Queen Elizabeth, began attacking Spanish treasure ships. Taking as an excuse the Spanish oppression of Protestants in the Netherlands, English admirals or pirates (the terms were really interchangeable) such as Sir Francis Drake and Sir John Hawkins plundered Spanish vessels on the high seas. In a particularly dramatic sailing exploit lasting from 1577 to 1580, prevailing winds and lust for treasure propelled Drake all the way around the world, to return with stolen Spanish treasure worth twice as much as Queen Elizabeth's annual revenue.

All this would have been sufficient provocation for Philip II to retaliate against England, but because he had his hands full in the Netherlands he resolved to invade the island only after the English openly allied with the Dutch rebels in 1585. Even then, Philip moved slowly and made careful plans. Finally, in 1588 he dispatched an enormous fleet, confidently called the "Invincible Armada," to invade insolent Britannia. After an initial standoff in the English Channel, however, the smaller, longer-gunned English warships outmaneuvered the Spanish fleet, while English fireships set some Spanish galleons ablaze and forced the rest to break formation. "Protestant gales" did the rest. After a disastrous circum-

navigation of the British Isles and Ireland, the shattered Spanish flotilla limped home with almost half its ships lost.

The defeat of the Spanish Armada was one of the decisive battles of Western history. Had Spain conquered England, the Spanish might have gone on to crush Holland and perhaps even to destroy Protestantism elsewhere in Europe. But as it was, the Protestant day was saved; and not long afterward Spanish power began to decline, as English and Dutch ships seized command of the seas. In England, patriotic Protestant fervor became especially intense. Popular even before then, "Good Queen Bess" was virtually revered by her subjects until her death in 1603, and England embarked on its golden Elizabethan Age of literary endeavor. War with Spain dragged on inconclusively until 1604, but the fighting never brought England any serious harm and was just lively enough to keep the English people deeply committed to their queen, their country, and the Protestant religion.

> The defeat of the Spanish Armada was one of the decisive battles of Western history.

THE THIRTY YEARS' WAR

With the promulgation of the Edict of Nantes in 1598, the peace between England and Spain of 1604, and the truce between Spain and Holland of 1609, religious warfare in northwestern Europe came briefly to an end. But in 1618 a major new war broke out, this time in Germany. Because this struggle raged more or less unceasingly until 1648 it is known as the Thirty Years' War. Spain and France quickly became engaged in the conflict in Germany and eventually in war with one another. Meanwhile, domestic resentments in Spain, France, and England flared up during the 1640s into concurrent outbreaks of civil war. As an English preacher said in 1643, "these are days of shaking, and this shaking is universal."

The Thirty Years' War began in a welter of religious passions as a war between Catholics and Protestants but ended as an international struggle in which the initial religious dimension was almost entirely forgotten. Between the Peace of Augsburg in 1555 and the outbreak of war in 1618, Calvinists had replaced Lutherans in a few German territories, but the overall balance between Protestants and Catholics within the Holy Roman Empire had remained undisturbed. In 1618, however, war broke out after Ferdinand, the Catholic Habsburg prince of Poland, Austria, and Hungary, was elected king of the Protestant territory of Bohemia. The staunchly Protestant Bohemian nobility had

THE DESTRUCTIVENESS OF THE THIRTY YEARS' WAR

Hans Jakob Christoph von Grimmelshausen (1621–1676) lived through the horrors of the Thirty Years' War. His parents were killed, probably when he was thirteen years of age, and he himself was kidnapped the following year. By age fifteen, he was a soldier. His comic masterpiece, Simplicissimus, *from which this extract is taken, drew heavily on these wartime experiences. Although technically fiction, it portrays with brutal accuracy the cruelty and destructiveness of this war, especially for its peasant victims.*

Although it was not my intention to take the peace-loving reader with these troopers to my dad's house and farm, seeing that matters will go ill therein, yet the course of my history demands that I should leave to kind posterity an account of what manner of cruelties were now and again practised in this our German war: yes, and moreover testify by my own example that such evils must often have been sent to us by the goodness of Almighty God for our profit. For, gentle reader, who would ever have taught me that there was a God in Heaven if these soldiers had not destroyed my dad's house, and by such a deed driven me out among folk who gave me all fitting instruction thereupon? . . .

The first thing these troopers did was, that they stabled their horses: thereafter each fell to his appointed task: which task was neither more nor less than ruin and destruction. For though some began to slaughter and to boil and to roast so that it looked as if there should be a merry banquet forward, yet others there were who did but storm through the house above and below stairs. Others stowed together great parcels of cloth and apparel and all manner of household stuff, as if they would set up a frippery market. All that they had no mind to take with them they cut in pieces. Some thrust their swords through the hay and straw as if they had not enough sheep and swine to slaughter: and some shook the feathers out of the beds and in their stead stuffed in bacon and other dried meat and provisions as if such were better and softer to sleep upon. Others broke the stove and the windows as if they had a never-ending summer to promise. Houseware of copper and tin they beat flat, and packed such vessels, all bent and spoiled, in with the rest. Bedsteads, tables, chairs, and benches they burned, though there lay many cords of dry wood in the yard. Pots and pipkins must all go to pieces, either because they would eat none but roast flesh, or because their purpose was to make there but a single meal.

Our maid was so handled in the stable that she could not come out; which is a shame to tell of. Our man they laid bound upon the ground, thrust a gag into his mouth, and poured a pailful of filthy water into his body: and by this, which they called a Swedish draught, they forced him to lead a party of them to another place where they captured men and beasts, and brought them back to our farm, in which company were my dad, my mother, and our Ursula.

And now they began: first to take the flints out of their pistols and in place of them to jam the peasants' thumbs in and so to torture the poor rogues as if they had been about the burning of witches: for one of them they had taken they thrust into the baking oven and there lit a fire under him, although he had as yet confessed no crime: as for another, they put a cord round his head and so twisted it tight with a piece of wood that the blood gushed from his mouth and nose and ears. In a word each had his own device to torture the peasants, and each peasant his several tortures.

Hans Jakob Christoph von Grimmelshausen, *Simplicissimus*, Trans. S. Goodrich (New York, 1995), pp. 1–3, 8–10, 32–35.

QUESTIONS FOR ANALYSIS

1. Defend the statement that the Thirty Years' War was the first modern war and the Peace of Westphalia was the first modern peace.

EUROPE AT THE END OF THE THIRTY YEARS' WAR

What was at issue in the Thirty Years' War? Why did Catholic France ally with Lutheran Sweden against German and Austrian Catholics? Why did this war, which began as a religious conflict within the Holy Roman Empire, turn into an international struggle? Which European powers stayed out of the war? Why did they do so?

opposed Ferdinand's election, and when Ferdinand began to suppress Protestantism in Bohemia, they rebelled. German Catholic forces ruthlessly counterattacked, first in Bohemia and then in Germany proper, led by Ferdinand, who in 1619 also became Holy Roman emperor. Within a decade, a German Catholic league seemed close to extirpating Protestantism throughout Germany.

Ferdinand's success raised once again the prospect that an overly powerful Holy Roman emperor might threaten the political autonomy of the German princes, Catholic and Protestant alike. Thus when the Lutheran king of Sweden, Gustavus Adolphus, the "Lion of the North," marched into Germany in 1630 to champion the Protestant cause, he was welcomed by several German Catholic princes who preferred to see the former religious balance restored rather than risk surrendering their sovereignty to Ferdinand II. To make matters still more ironic, Gustavus's Protestant army was secretly subsidized by Catholic France, whose policy was then dictated by a cardinal of the church, Cardinal Richelieu. This was because Habsburg Spain had been fighting in Germany on the side of Habsburg Austria, and Richelieu was determined to prevent France from being surrounded by a strong Habsburg alliance on the north, east, and south. In any event, the military genius Gustavus Adolphus started routing the Habsburgs; but when he fell in battle in 1632, Cardinal Richelieu had little choice but to send ever greater support to the remaining Swedish troops in Germany, until in 1635 French armies entered the war directly on Sweden's side. From then until 1648 the struggle was really one of France and Sweden against Austria and Spain, with Germany a helpless battleground.

Germany suffered more from warfare in the terrible years between 1618 and 1648 than it ever did before or after until the twentieth century. Several German cities were besieged and sacked nine or ten times over, and soldiers from all nations, who often had to sustain themselves by plunder, gave no quarter to defenseless civilians. With plague and disease adding to the toll of outright butchery, some parts of Germany lost more than half their populations, although others went relatively unscathed. Most horrifying was the loss of life in the final four years of the war, when the carnage continued unabated even while peace negotiators had already arrived at broad areas of agreement and were dickering over subsidiary clauses.

Nor did the Peace of Westphalia, which finally ended the Thirty Years' War in 1648, do much to vindicate anyone's death, even though it did establish some abiding landmarks in European history. Above all, from the international perspective, the Peace of Westphalia marked the emergence of France as the predominant power on the continental European scene, replacing Spain. France would hold this position for the next two centuries. The greatest losers in the conflict (aside, of course, from the German people themselves) were the Austrian Habsburgs, who were forced to surrender all the territory they had gained in Germany and to abandon their hopes of using the office of Holy Roman emperor to dominate central Europe. Otherwise, something very close to the German status quo of 1618 was reestablished, with Protestant principalities in the north balancing Catholic ones in the south and Germany so hopelessly divided that it could play no united role in European history until the nineteenth century.

> Above all, from the international perspective, the Peace of Westphalia marked the emergence of France as the predominant power on the continental European scene, replacing Spain.

DIVERGENT PATHS: SPAIN, FRANCE, AND ENGLAND, 1600–1660

What caused the decline of Spain in the seventeenth century?

The long century of war between 1540 and 1660 decisively altered the balance of power among the major kingdoms of western Europe. Germany emerged from the Thirty Years' War a devastated and exhausted land. But after 1600, Spain too was crippled by its unremitting military commitments and exertions. The French monarchy, by contrast, steadily increased its authority over France. By 1660 France had become the most powerful country on the European mainland, decisively eclipsing Spain. In England, meanwhile, a bloody civil war broke out between the king and his critics in Parliament; but after a short-lived experiment in republican rule, England in 1660 returned to its constitutional status as a "mixed" monarchy in which power was shared between king and Parliament.

THE DECLINE OF SPAIN

The story of seventeeth-century Spain's fall from grandeur is almost like a Greek tragedy in its relentless unfolding. Despite the defeat of the Invincible Armada in 1588, in 1600 the Spanish Empire—comprising all of the Iberian Peninsula (including Portugal, which had been annexed by Phillip II in 1580), half of Italy, half of the Netherlands, all of Central and South America, and the Philippine Islands in the Pacific Ocean—was still the mightiest power not just in Europe but in the world. Yet a bare half century later this empire on which the sun never set was beginning to fall apart.

Spain's greatest underlying weakness was economic. At first this may seem odd considering that in 1600, as in the three or four previous decades, huge amounts of American silver were being unloaded on the docks of Seville. Yet as contemporaries themselves recognized, "the new world that Spain had conquered was conquering Spain in turn." Lacking either rich agricultural or mineral resources, Spain desperately needed to develop industries and a balanced trading pattern as its Atlantic rivals were doing. But the Spanish nobility had prized ideals of chivalry over practical business ever since the days when they were reconquering Christian territory from the Muslims. Thus the Spanish governing class was only too glad to use American silver to buy manufactured goods from other parts of Europe to live in splendor and dedicate itself to military exploits. As a result, few new industries were established; and when the influx of silver began to decline, the Spanish economy was left with nothing except increasing debts.

Nonetheless, the crown, dedicated to supporting the Counter-Reformation and maintaining Spain's international dominance, could not cease fighting abroad. Even in the relatively peaceful year of 1608, about 4 million ducats, out of a total revenue of 7 million, were spent on military expenditures. Thus when Spain became engaged in fighting France during the Thirty Years' War it overextended itself. In 1643 French troops inflicted a stunning defeat on the famed Spanish infantry at Rocroi, the first time that a Spanish army had been overcome in battle since the reign of

The Battle of Rocroi, 1643. Spain's defeat at Rocroi by the French was the first time the Spanish army had lost in battle since the reign of Ferdinand and Isabella, yet another contributing factor to the decline of Spanish power during the Thirty Years' War.

Ferdinand and Isabella. Worse still was the fact that by then two territories belonging to Spain's European empire were in open revolt.

To understand the causes of these revolts, we must recognize that in the seventeenth century the governing power of Spain lay entirely in Castile. After the marriage of Isabella of Castile and Ferdinand of Aragon in 1469, Castile had emerged as the dominant partner in the Spanish union, becoming even more dominant when it took over Portugal in 1580. In the absence of any great financial hardships, semi-autonomous Catalunya (the most fiercely independent part of Aragon) endured Castilian hegemony. But in 1640, when the strains of warfare induced Castile to limit Catalan liberties to raise more money and men for combat, Catalunya revolted and drove out its Castilian governors. When the Portuguese learned of the Catalan uprising, they revolted as well, followed by southern Italians who rose up against Castilian viceroys in Naples and Sicily in 1647. Only the momentary inability of Spain's greatest external enemies, France and England, to take advantage of its plight saved the Spanish Empire from utter collapse. This gave the Castilian government time to put down the Italian revolts; by 1652 it had also brought Catalunya to heel. But Portugal retained its independence; and by the Peace of the Pyrenees, signed with France in 1659, Spain in effect abandoned its ambition of dominating Europe.

THE GROWING POWER OF FRANCE

A comparison of the fortunes of Spain and France in the first half of the seventeenth century shows some striking similarities between the two countries, but in the end their differences turned out to be most decisive. Spain and France were of almost identical territorial extent, and both countries had been created by the same process of accretion. Just as the Castilian crown had gained Aragon, Catalunya, Granada, and then Portugal, so the kingdom of France had grown by adding such diverse territories as Languedoc, Dauphiné, Provence, Burgundy, and Brittany. Since the inhabitants of all these territories cherished traditions of local independence as much as the Catalans or Portuguese and since the rulers of France, like those of Spain, were determined to govern their provinces ever more firmly—

especially when costs of the Thirty Years' War made ruthless tax collecting urgently necessary—a direct confrontation between the central government and the provinces in France became inevitable, just as in Spain. But France weathered the storm whereas Spain did not, a result largely attributable to France's greater wealth and the greater prestige of the French crown.

In good times most French people, including those from the outlying provinces, tended to revere their king. Certainly they had excellent reason to do so during the reign of Henry IV. Having established religious peace in 1598 by the Edict of Nantes, the affable Henry, who declared that there should be a chicken in every French family's pot each Sunday, set out to restore the prosperity of a country devastated by four decades of civil war. Fortunately, France had enormous economic resiliency, owing primarily to its extremely rich and varied agricultural resources. Unlike Spain, which had to import food, France normally was able to feed itself; and Henry's finance minister, the duke of Sully, quickly saw to it that France could feed itself once more. Among other things, Sully distributed throughout the country free copies of a guide to recommended farming techniques and financed the rebuilding or new construction of roads, bridges, and canals to facilitate the flow of goods. Henry IV also ordered the construction of royal factories to manufacture luxury goods such as crystal, glass, and tapestries and supported the growth of silk, linen, and woolen cloth industries in many different parts of the country. Henry's patronage also allowed the explorer Samuel de Champlain to claim parts of Canada as France's first foothold in the New World. Thus Henry IV's reign certainly must be counted as one of the most benevolent in all French history.

> Having established religious peace in 1598 by the Edict of Nantes, the affable Henry, who declared that there should be a chicken in every French family's pot each Sunday, set out to restore the prosperity of a country devastated by four decades of civil war.

CARDINAL RICHELIEU

Far less benevolent was Henry's de facto successor as ruler of France, Cardinal Richelieu (*RIH-shub-loo*, 1585–1642). The cardinal, of course, was never the real king of France—the actual title was held from 1610 to 1643 by Henry IV's ineffectual son Louis XIII. But as first minister from 1624 to his death in 1642 Richelieu governed as he wished, enhancing centralized royal power at home and expanding French influence in Europe.

CARDINAL RICHELIEU ON THE COMMON PEOPLE OF FRANCE

Armand Jean du Plessis, duke of Richelieu and cardinal of the Roman Catholic church, was the effective ruler of France from 1624 until his death in 1642. His Political Testament *was assembled after his death from historical sketches and memoranda of advice he prepared for King Louis XIII, the ineffectual monarch whom he served. Although the book itself was not published until 1688, there is now little doubt that the writings it contains are indeed Richelieu's own thoughts.*

All students of politics agree that when the common people are too well off it is impossible to keep them peaceable. The explanation for this is that they are less well informed than the members of the other orders in the state, who are much more cultivated and enlightened, and so if not preoccupied with the search for the necessities of existence, find it difficult to remain within the limits imposed by both common sense and the law.

It would not be sound to relieve them of all taxation and similar charges, since in such a case they would lose the mark of their subjection and consequently the awareness of their station. Thus being free from paying tribute, they would consider themselves exempted from obedience. One should compare them with mules, which being accustomed to work, suffer more when long idle than when kept busy. But just as this work should be reasonable, with the burdens placed upon these animals proportionate to their strength, so it is likewise with the burdens placed upon the people. If they are not moderate, even when put to good public use, they are certainly unjust. I realize that when a king undertakes a program of public works it is correct to say that what the people gain from it is returned by paying the *taille* [the most important tax paid to the crown by the French peasantry]. In the same fashion it can be maintained that what a king takes from the people returns to them, and that they advance it to him only to draw upon it for the enjoyment of their leisure and their investments, which would be impossible if they did not contribute to the support of the state.

The Political Testament of Cardinal Richelieu, trans. Henry Bertram Hill (Madison, Wisc., 1961), pp. 31–32.

QUESTIONS FOR ANALYSIS

1. According to Cardinal Richelieu, what does the state need to fear from an educated populace?
2. What theory of the state can be adduced from Richelieu's *Political Testament*?

Accordingly, when Huguenots rebelled against restrictions placed on them by the Edict of Nantes, Richelieu put them down with an iron fist and amended the edict in 1629 by depriving them of their political and military rights. Because his armed campaigns against the Huguenots had been very costly, the cardinal then moved to gain more income for the crown by abolishing the semi-autonomy of Burgundy, Dauphiné, and Provence so that he could introduce direct royal taxation in all three areas. Later, to make sure taxes were efficiently collected, Richelieu instituted a new system of local government by royal officials known as intendants, who were expressly commissioned to ride roughshod over any provincial resistance. By these and other methods Richelieu made French government more centralized than ever and managed to double the crown's income during his rule. But since he also engaged in an ambitious foreign policy directed against the Habsburgs of Austria and Spain, resulting in France's costly involvement in the Thirty Years' War, internal pressures mounted in the years after Richelieu's death.

THE FRONDE

A reaction against French governmental centralization manifested itself in a series of revolts between 1648 and 1653 collectively known as "the slingshot tumults," or in French, the *Fronde*. By this time Louis XIII had been succeeded by his son Louis XIV; but because the latter was still a boy, France was governed by a regency consisting of Louis's mother, Anne of Austria, and her paramour Cardinal Mazarin. Both were foreigners (Anne was a Habsburg and Mazarin originally an Italian adventurer named Giulio Mazarini), and many of their subjects, including some extremely powerful nobles, hated them. Popular resentments were greater still because the costs of war, combined with several consecutive years of bad harvests, had brought France temporarily into a grave economic plight. Thus when cliques of nobles expressed their disgust with Mazarin for primarily self-interested reasons, they found much support throughout the country, and uncoordinated revolts against the regency government flared on and off for several years.

France, however, did not come close to falling apart. Above all, the French crown itself, which retained great reservoirs of prestige, owing to a well-established national tradition and the undoubted achievements of Henry IV and Richelieu, was by no means under attack. On the contrary; neither the aristocratic leaders of the Fronde nor the commoners who joined them in revolt claimed to be resisting the young king but only the alleged corruption and mismanagement of Mazarin. Some of the rebels, it is true, insisted that part of Mazarin's fault lay in his pursuit of Richelieu's centralizing, antiprovincial policy. But because most of the aristocrats who led the Fronde were merely "outs" who wanted to be "in," they often squabbled among themselves—sometimes even arranging agreements of convenience with the regency or striking alliances with France's enemy, Spain—and proved completely unable to rally any unified support behind a common program. Thus when Louis XIV began to rule in his own name in 1651 and pretexts for revolt against corrupt ministers

no longer existed, the opposition was soon silenced. As so often happens, the idealists and poor people paid the greatest price for revolt: in 1653 a defeated leader of popular resistance in Bordeaux was broken on the wheel, and not long afterward a massive new round of taxation was proclaimed. Remembering the turbulence of the Fronde for the rest of his life, Louis XIV resolved never to let his aristocracy or his provinces get out of hand again and ruled as the most effective royal absolutist in all of French history.

THE ENGLISH CIVIL WAR

Of all the revolts that shook mid-seventeenth-century Europe, the most radical in its consequences was the English civil war. The causes of this conflict were similar to those that sparked rebellions in Spain and France: constitutional hostilities between the component parts of a composite kingdom; religious animosities between Catholics and Protestants and within the ruling (Protestant) camp itself; struggles for power among competing factions of aristocrats at court; and a fiscal system that could not keep pace even with the increasing costs of government, much less of war. Only in England, however, did these conflicts lead to the deposition and execution of the king (1649), an eleven-year "interregnum" during which England was officially a republic (1649–1660), and ultimately to the restoration of the monarchy under conditions designed to safeguard Parliament's place in government and to guarantee a limited degree of religious toleration for all Protestants.

THE ORIGINS OF THE ENGLISH CIVIL WAR

The chain of events that led to war between king and Parliament in 1642 began in the last decades of Queen Elizabeth's reign (1559–1603). During the 1590s, the expenses of war with Spain together with a rebellion in Ireland, widespread crop failures, and the inadequacies of the antiquated English taxation system drove the queen's government deeply into debt. Factional disputes around the court also became more bitter as courtiers, anticipating the aging queen's death, jockeyed for position under her presumed successor, the Scottish king James Stuart. Only on her deathbed, however, did the queen finally confirm that her throne should go to her Scottish cousin. As a result, neither James nor his new English subjects knew very much about one another when he took the throne at the end of 1603.

The relationship did not begin well. James's English subjects looked down on the Scots whom he brought with him to London. Although English courtiers were pleased to accept their new king's generosity to themselves, they resented the grants he made to his Scottish supporters, whom they blamed, quite unreasonably, for the Crown's indebtedness. James, meanwhile, saw clearly that to resolve his debts he had to have more revenue. But rather than bargain with parliamentary representatives for increased taxation he chose to lecture them on the prerogatives of kingship, comparing kings to gods on earth and declaring: "As it is atheism and blasphemy to dispute what God can do, so it is presumption and high contempt in a subject to dispute what a king can do." When this approach failed to produce the taxation he needed, James made peace with Spain and then took steps to raise revenues without parliamentary approval, imposing new tolls on trade and selling trading monopolies to favored courtiers. These measures aroused further resentments against the king and so made voluntary grants of taxation from Parliament even less likely to be approved. As a result, the king's financial situation steadily worsened.

James I. "The wisest fool in Christendom."

James was more adept with respect to religious policy. Scotland had been a firmly Calvinist country since the 1560s. In England, however, the Elizabethan religious settlement had produced much less theological definition. By 1603 England was clearly a Protestant country, but a significant number of English Protestants continued to hope for a second, or further, reformation that would bring their church more firmly into line with Calvinist principles. Other Protestants resisted such efforts, and labeled those who supported them "Puritans." As king, James was compelled to mediate these conflicts. By and large, he did so successfully. In Scotland, he convinced the reformed church to retain its bishops, and in England, he encouraged Calvinist doctrine while resisting any alterations in the prayer book or the Thirty-Nine Articles of the Faith. Only in Ireland, which remained overwhelmingly Catholic, did James store up future trouble. By encouraging the "plantation" of more than 8,000 Scottish Calvinists in the northern province of Ulster, he undermined the property rights of Irish Catholics and created religious animosities that have lasted until the present day.

The delicate religious balance preserved by James I was shattered in 1625 by the accession of his only surviving son, Charles I. Throwing his father's habitual caution to the winds, Charles immediately launched a new war with Spain, exacerbating his financial problems and alarming his Protestant subjects by proposing to raise Irish Catholic troops for military service in Germany. Protestant alarm was further increased when Charles married Henrietta Maria, the Catholic daughter of King Louis XIII of France. The situation became truly dangerous, however, when Charles, aided by his newly appointed archbishop of Canterbury, William Laud, openly began to favor the most anti-Calvinist elements in the English church and then attempted to impose this religious policy (including a full-fledged system of church government by bishops and a new prayer book) on the forthrightly Calvinist church in Scotland. The Scots rebelled, and in 1640 a Scottish army marched south into England to demand the withdrawal of Charles's Catholicizing religious reforms.

To meet the Scottish threat, Charles was forced to summon the English Parliament for the first time in eleven years. Relations between the king and his parliament had broken down in the late 1620s, when Charles responded to Parliament's refusal to grant him additional funds by demanding forced loans from his subjects and then punishing those who refused to comply by quartering soldiers in their homes or throwing

Charles I. This portrait by Anthony Van Dyck vividly captures the ill-fated monarch's arrogance.

them into prison without trial. In response, in 1628 Parliament forced the king to accept the Petition of Right, which declared all taxes not voted by Parliament illegal, condemned the quartering of soldiers in private houses, and prohibited arbitrary imprisonment and martial law in time of peace. Angered rather than chastened by the Petition of Right, Charles resolved to rule without Parliament entirely, funding his government during the 1630s with a variety of levies and fines imposed without parliamentary consent.

It was only the Scottish invasion that forced Charles to summon a new Parliament. Once summoned, however, the parliamentarians were determined to impose a series of radical reforms on the king's government before they would even consider granting him funds to raise an army against the Scots. Charles initially cooperated with these reforms, even allowing Parliament to execute his chief minister. But it soon became clear that the parliamentary leaders had no intention of fighting the Scots. Instead, a de facto alliance emerged between them, which was reinforced by their common, Calvinist, religious outlook.

> Angered rather than chastened by the Petition of Right, Charles resolved to rule without Parliament entirely, funding his government during the 1630s with a variety of levies and fines imposed without parliamentary consent.

By 1642, Charles had had enough. Marching his guards into the House of Commons, he tried (but failed) to arrest five of its leaders. Charles then withdrew from London to raise his own army. Parliament responded by summoning its own force and voting the taxation to pay for it. By the end of 1642, open warfare had erupted between king and Parliament.

CIVIL WAR AND COMMONWEALTH

Arrayed on the king's side were most of England's aristocrats and largest landowners, who were almost all loyal to the established Church of England, despite their opposition to some of Charles's own religious innovations. The parliamentary forces were made up of smaller landholders, tradesmen, and artisans, most of whom were Puritans. The king's supporters were commonly known by the aristocratic name of Cavaliers. Their opponents, who cut their hair short in contempt for the fashionable custom of wearing curls, were derisively called Roundheads. At first the royalists, having obvious advantages of military experience, won most of the victories. In 1644, however, the parliamentary army was reorganized, and soon afterward the fortunes of battle shifted. The Cavalier forces were badly beaten, and in 1646 the king was compelled to surrender. Soon thereafter, the episcopate was abolished and a Calvinist-style church was established throughout England.

The struggle might now have ended had not a quarrel developed within the parliamentary party. The majority of its members were ready to restore Charles to the throne as a limited monarch under an arrangement whereby a uniformly Calvinist faith would be imposed on both Scotland and England as the state religion. But a radical minority of Puritans, commonly known as Independents, distrusted Charles and insisted on religious toleration for themselves and all other Protestants. Their leader was Oliver Cromwell (1599–1658), who had risen to command the Roundhead army.

Taking advantage of the dissension within the ranks of his opponents, Charles renewed the war in 1648 but, after a brief campaign, was forced to surrender. Cromwell now resolved to end the life of "that man of blood" and, ejecting all the moderate Protestants from Parliament by force of arms, obliged the "Rump"

DEMOCRACY AND THE ENGLISH CIVIL WAR

The English civil war raised fundamental issues about the political rights and responsibilities of Englishmen. Many of these issues were addressed in a lengthy debate held within the General Council of Cromwell's New Model Army at Putney in October 1647. It is interesting that none of the participants in these debates seems to have recognized the implications their arguments might have for the political rights of women. Only King Charles, speaking moments before his execution in 1649, saw the radical implications of the constitutional experiment on which the parliamentary forces had embarked— but, ironically, it was his own radical assertions of monarchical authority that prompted the rebellion that overthrew him.

THE ARMY DEBATES, 1647

Colonel Rainsborough: Really, I think that the poorest man that is in England has a life to live as the greatest man; and therefore truly, sir, I think it's clear, that every man that is to live under a government ought first by his own consent to put himself under that government; and I do think that the poorest man in England is not at all bound in a strict sense to that government that he has not had a voice to put himself under . . . insomuch that I should doubt whether I was an Englishman or not, that should doubt of these things.

General Ireton: Give me leave to tell you, that if you make this the rule, I think you must fly for refuge to an absolute natural right, and you must deny all civil right; and I am sure it will come to that in the consequence. . . . For my part, I think it is no right at all. I think that no person has a right to an interest or share in the disposing of the affairs of the kingdom, and in determining or choosing those that shall determine what laws we shall be ruled by here, no person has a right to this that has not a permanent fixed interest in this kingdom, and those persons together are properly the represented of this kingdom who, taken together, and consequently are to make up the representers of this kingdom. . . .

We talk of birthright. Truly, birthright there is. . . . [M]en may justly have by birthright, by their very being born in England, that we should not seclude them out of England. That we should not refuse to give them air and place and ground, and the freedom of the highways and other things, to live amongst us, not any man that is born here, though he in birth or by his birth there come nothing at all that is part of the permanent interest of this kingdom to him. That I think is due to a man by birth. But that by a man's being born here he shall have a share in that power that shall dispose of the lands here, and of all things here, I do not think it is a sufficient ground.

Divine Right and Democracy: An Anthology of Political Writing in Stuart England, ed. David Wootton (New York, 1986), pp. 286–287 (language modernized).

CHARLES I ON THE SCAFFOLD, 1649

I think it is my duty, to God first, and to my country, for to clear myself both as an honest man, a good king, and a good Christian.

I shall begin first with my innocence. In truth I think it not very needful for me to insist long upon this, for all the world knows that I never did begin a war with the two Houses of Parliament; and I call God to witness, to whom I must shortly make an account, that I never did intend to incroach upon their privileges. . . .

As for the people—truly I desire their liberty and freedom as much as anybody whatsoever. But I must tell you that their liberty and freedom consists in having of government those laws by which their lives and goods may be most their own. It is not for having share in government. That is nothing pertaining to them. A subject and a sovereign are clean different things, and therefore, until they do that—I mean that you do put the people in that liberty as I say—certainly they will never enjoy themselves.

Sirs, it was for this that now I am come here. If I would have given way to an arbitrary way, for to have all laws changed according to the power of the sword,

I needed not to have come here. And therefore I tell you (and I pray God it be not laid to your charge) that I am the martyr of the people.

Brian Tierney, Donald Kagan, and L. Pearce Williams, eds., *Great Issues in Western Civilization* (New York, 1967), pp. 46–47.

QUESTIONS FOR ANALYSIS

1. What issues did the English civil war raise regarding the rights of freeborn Englishmen? What are the natural rights of man? What are civil rights?
2. For what reasons was Charles I brought to trial and ultimately beheaded? Was Charles truly the "martyr of the people"?

Parliament that remained to vote an end to the monarchy. On January 30, 1649 Charles I was beheaded; a short time later the hereditary House of Lords was abolished, and England became a republic.

But founding a republic was far easier than maintaining one. Officially called a Commonwealth, the new form of government did not last long. Technically the Rump Parliament continued as the legislative body; but Cromwell, with the army at his command, possessed the real power and soon became exasperated by the legislators' attempts to enrich themselves by confiscating their opponents' property. Accordingly, in 1653 he marched a detachment of troops into the Rump Parliament. Declaring "Come, I will put an end to your prating," he ordered the members to disperse. The Commonwealth thus ceased to exist and was soon replaced by the "Protectorate," a thinly disguised

autocracy established under a constitution drafted by officers of the army. Called the Instrument of Government, this text was the nearest approximation to a written constitution England has ever had. Extensive powers were given to Cromwell as lord protector for life, and his office was made hereditary. At first a new Parliament exercised limited authority to make laws and levy taxes, but in 1655 Cromwell abruptly dismissed its members also. Thereafter the government became a virtual dictatorship, with Cromwell wielding a sovereignty more absolute than any Stuart monarch ever dreamed of claiming.

THE RESTORATION OF THE MONARCHY

Given the choice between a Puritan military dictatorship and the old royalist regime, when the occasion arose England unhesitatingly opted for the latter. Years of unpopular Calvinist austerities such as the prohibition of any public recreation on Sundays had discredited the Puritans, making most people long for the milder style of the Elizabethan church. Thus not long after Cromwell's death in 1658, one of his generals seized power and called for elections to a new Parliament, which met in the spring of 1660 and proclaimed as king Charles I's exiled son, Charles II, after Charles first gave the traditional promises of good government and then promised a limited religious toleration for all Protestants.

Charles II (1660–1685) restored bishops to the Church of England, but he did not return to the provocative religious policies of his father. Declaring

CHRONOLOGY

ORIGINS OF THE ENGLISH CIVIL WAR, 1603–1660

Reign of the Stuarts begins	1603
Reign of Charles I	1625–1649
Rule without Parliament	1629–1640
English civil war	1642–1649
Charles I beheaded	1649
Commonwealth	1649–1653
Protectorate	1653–1658
Restoration of the monarchy	1660

CHAPTER 14

RELIGIOUS WARS AND STATE BUILDING, 1540–1660

with characteristic good humor that he did not wish to "resume his travels," Charles agreed to respect Parliament and observe the Petition of Right. He also accepted all the legislation passed by Parliament immediately before the outbreak of civil war in 1642, including the requirement that Parliament be summoned at least once every three years. After one further test in the late seventeenth century, England thus emerged from its civil war as a limited monarchy, in which power was exercised by "the king in parliament."

THE PROBLEM OF DOUBT AND THE QUEST FOR CERTAINTY

Why was this period such a fertile one for political philosophy?

Between 1540 and 1660, Europeans were forced to confront a world in which all that they had once taken for granted was suddenly cast into doubt. An entirely new world had been discovered in the Americas, populated by millions of people whose very existence compelled Europeans to rethink some of their most basic ideas about humanity and human nature. Equally disorienting, the religious uniformity of Europe, although never absolute, had been shattered to an unprecedented extent by the Reformation and the religious wars that arose from it. In 1540, it was still possible to imagine that these religious divisions might be temporary. By 1660, it was clear they would be permanent. No longer, therefore, could Europeans regard revealed religious faith as an adequate foundation for universal philosophical conclusions, for even Christians now disagreed about the fundamental truths of the faith. Political allegiances were similarly under threat, as intellectuals and common people alike began to assert a right to resist princes with whom they disagreed on matters of religion. Even morality and custom were beginning to seem arbitrary and detached from the natural ordering of the world.

Europeans responded to this pervasive climate of doubt in a variety of ways, ranging from radical skepti-

> Europeans responded to this pervasive climate of doubt in a variety of ways, ranging from radical skepticism to authoritarian assertions of religious fideism and political absolutism.

cism to authoritarian assertions of religious fideism and political absolutism. What united their responses, however, was a sometimes desperate search for new foundations on which to reconstruct some measure of certainty in the face of Europe's new intellectual, religious, and political challenges.

WITCHCRAFT ACCUSATIONS AND THE POWER OF THE STATE

Adding to the fears of Europeans was their conviction that witchcraft was a mortal and increasing threat to their world. Although most people in the Middle Ages believed that certain individuals, usually women, could heal or harm through the practice of magic, it was not until the fifteenth century that learned authorities began to insist that such powers could derive only from some kind of pact made by the witch with the devil. Once this belief became accepted, judicial officers became much more active in seeking out suspected witches for prosecution. In 1484 Pope Innocent VIII ordered papal inquisitors to use all the means at their disposal to detect and eliminate witchcraft, including torture of suspected witches. Predictably, torture increased the number of accused witches who confessed to their alleged crimes; and as more accused witches confessed, more and more witches were "discovered," accused, and executed—even in areas (such as England) where torture was not employed and where the Inquisition did not operate.

In considering the rash of witchcraft persecution that swept early modern Europe, we need to keep two facts in mind. First of all, the witchcraft trials were by no means limited to Catholic countries. Protestant reformers believed in the insidious powers of Satan just as much as Catholics did. Both Luther and Calvin urged that people accused as witches be tried more peremptorily and sentenced with less leniency than ordinary criminals, a recommendation their followers were only too happy to heed. Second, it was only when the efforts of religious authorities to detect witchcraft were backed up by the coercive powers of secular governments to execute them that the fear of witches became truly murderous. Between 1580 and about 1660, however, enthusiasm for catching and killing witches became something like a mania across much of Europe, claiming tens of thou-

Supposed Witches Worshiping the Devil in the Form of a Billy Goat. In the background other witches ride bareback on flying demons. This is one of the earliest visual conceptions of witchcraft, dating from around 1460.

sands of victims, of whom at least three quarters were women. The final death toll will never be known, but in the 1620s there was an average of 100 burnings a year in the German cities of Würzburg and Bamberg; around the same time it was said that the town square of Wolfenbüttel "looked like a little forest, so crowded were the stakes." After 1660, accusations of witchcraft gradually diminished; but isolated incidents, such as the one at Salem, Massachusetts, continued to crop up for another half century.

This witch mania reflects the fears that early modern Europeans held not only about the devil but also about the adequacy of traditional remedies (such as prayers, amulets, and holy water) to combat the evils of their world. But it also reflects their growing conviction that only the state, and not the church, had the power to protect them. One of the most striking features of the mania for hunting down witches is the extent to which these prosecutions, in both Catholic and Protestant countries, were state-sponsored affairs, carried out by secular authorities claiming to act as the protectors of society against the spiritual and temporal evils that assailed it. Even in Catholic countries, where witchcraft prosecutions were sometimes begun in church courts, these cases would be transferred to the state's courts for final judgment and punishment, because church courts were forbidden to impose capital penalties. In Protestant countries, where church courts had been abolished (only England retained church courts), the entire process of detecting, prosecuting, and punishing suspected witches was carried out under the supervision of the state. In both Catholic and Protestant countries, the result of these witchcraft trials was thus a considerable increase in the scope of the state's powers and responsibilities to regulate the lives of its subjects.

THE SEARCH FOR AUTHORITY

The crisis of Europe's iron century (as even contemporaries sometimes called it) was fundamentally a crisis of authority. Attempts to reestablish some foundation for agreed authority took many forms. For the French nobleman Michel de Montaigne (1533–1592), who wrote during the height of the French wars of religion, the result was a searching skepticism about the possibilities of any certain knowledge whatsoever. The son of a Catholic father and a Huguenot mother of Jewish ancestry, the well-to-do Montaigne retired from a legal career at the age of thirty-eight to devote himself to a life of leisured reflection. The *Essays* that resulted were a new literary form originally conceived as "experiments" in writing (the French *essai* simply means "trial"). Because they are extraordinarily well written as well as searchingly reflective, Montaigne's *Essays* are among the most enduring classics of French literature and thought.

Although the range of subjects of the *Essays* is wide, two main themes are dominant. One is a pervasive skepticism. Making his motto *Que sais-je?* ("What do I know?"), Montaigne decided that he knew very little for certain. According to him, "it is folly to measure truth and error by our own capacities" because our capacities are severely limited. Thus, as he maintained in one of his most famous essays, "On Cannibals," what may seem indisputably true and proper to one nation may seem absolutely false to another because "everyone gives the title of barbarism to everything that is not of his usage." From this Montaigne's second main principle followed—the need for moderation. Because all people think they know the perfect religion and the perfect government, yet few agree on what that perfection might be, Montaigne concluded that no religion or government is really perfect and consequently no belief is worth fighting for to the

MONTAIGNE ON SKEPTICISM AND FAITH

Michel de Montaigne's Essays *reflect the curious contradictions of his thought, which in turn mirror the tortured combination of uncertainty and faith that characterized the century in which he lived. Although he begins here by asserting the limits on human knowledge, he ends by concluding that these limits impose on human beings an obligation to accept completely every aspect of the church's religious teachings.*

Perhaps it is not without reason that we attribute facility in belief and conviction to simplicity and ignorance; for . . . the more a mind is empty and without counterpoise, the more easily it gives beneath the weight of the first persuasive argument. That is why children, common people, women, and sick people are most subject to being led by the ears. But then, on the other hand, it is foolish presumption to go around disdaining and condemning as false whatever does not seem likely to us; which is an ordinary vice in those who think they have more than common ability. I used to do so once. . . . But reason has taught me that to condemn a thing thus, dogmatically, as false and impossible, is to assume the advantage of knowing the bounds and limits of God's will and of the power of our mother Nature; and that there is no more notable folly in the world than to reduce these things to the measure of our capacity and competence. . . .

It is a dangerous and fateful presumption, besides the absurd temerity that it implies, to disdain what we do not comprehend. For after you have established, according to your fine understanding, the limits of truth and falsehood, and it turns out that you must necessarily believe things even stranger than those you deny,

you are obliged from then on to abandon these limits. Now what seems to me to bring as much disorder into our consciences as anything, in these religious troubles that we are in, is this partial surrender of their beliefs by Catholics. It seems to them that they are being very moderate and understanding when they yield to their opponents some of the articles in dispute. But, besides the fact that they do not see what an advantage it is to a man charging you for you to begin to give ground and withdraw, and how much that encourages him to pursue his point, those articles which they select as the most trivial are sometimes very important. We must either submit completely to the authority of our ecclesiastical government, or do without it completely. It is not for us to decide what portion of obedience we owe it.

Montaigne: Selections from the Essays, trans. and ed. Donald M. Frame (Arlington Heights, Ill., 1971), pp. 34–38.

QUESTIONS FOR ANALYSIS

1. How does Montaigne reconcile the seemingly contradictory nature of skepticism and faith? How can one be skeptical and maintain faith?

death. Instead, people should accept the teachings of religion on faith, and obey the governments constituted to rule over them, without resorting to fanaticism in either sphere.

Although Montaigne can sound surprisingly modern, he was very much a man of the sixteenth century, believing that "reason does nothing but go astray in everything" and that intellectual curiosity "which prompts us to thrust our noses into everything" is a "scourge of the soul." Montaigne was also a fatalist who thought that in a world governed by unpredictable fortune the best human strategy was to face the good and the bad with steadfastness and dignity. Nonetheless, despite his unheroic and highly personal tone, the wide circulation of Montaigne's *Essays* did help combat fanaticism and religious intolerance in his own and subsequent ages.

Montaigne sought refuge from the trials of his age in skepticism, distance, and resigned dignity. His contemporary the French lawyer Jean Bodin (1530–1596), looked instead to resolve the disorders of the day by reestablishing the powers of the state on new and more secure foundations. Like Montaigne, Bodin was particularly troubled by the upheavals caused by the religious wars in France—he had even witnessed the frightful St. Bartholomew's Day Massacre of 1572 in Paris. But instead of shrugging his shoulders about the bloodshed, he resolved to offer a political plan to make sure turbulence would cease. This he did in his monumental *Six Books of the Commonwealth* (1576), the earliest fully developed statement of absolute governmental sovereignty in Western political thought. According to Bodin, the state arises from the needs of collections of families, but once constituted should brook no opposition, because maintaining order is its paramount duty. For Bodin, sovereignty was "the most high, absolute, and perpetual power over all subjects," consisting principally in the power "to give laws to subjects without their consent." Although Bodin acknowledged the theoretical possibility of government by aristocracy or democracy, he assumed that the nation-states of his day would be ruled by monarchs and insisted that such monarchs could in no way be limited, either by legislative or judicial bodies or even by laws made by their predecessors or themselves. Bodin maintained that every subject must trust in the ruler's "mere and frank good will." Even if the ruler proved a tyrant, Bodin insisted that the subject had no warrant to resist, for any resistance would open the door "to a licentious anarchy which is worse than the harshest tyranny in the world."

Like Bodin, who was moved by the events of St. Bartholomew's Day to formulate a doctrine of political absolutism, Thomas Hobbes (1588–1679) was moved by the turmoil of the English civil war to do the same in his classic of political theory, *Leviathan* (1651). Yet Hobbes differed from Bodin in several respects. For one, whereas Bodin assumed that the absolute sovereign power would be a royal monarch, Hobbes made no such assumption. Any form of government capable of protecting its subjects' lives and property might act as a sovereign (and hence all-powerful) Leviathan. Then too, whereas Bodin defined his state as "the lawful government of families" and hence did not believe that the state could abridge private property rights because families could not exist without property, Hobbes's state existed to rule over atomistic individuals and thus was licensed to trample over both liberty and property if the government's own survival was at stake.

But the most fundamental difference between Bodin and Hobbes lay in the latter's uncompromisingly pessimistic view of human nature. Hobbes posited that the "state of nature" that existed before civil government came into being was a condition of "war of all against all." Because man naturally behaves as "a wolf" toward other men, human life without government is necessarily "solitary, poor, nasty, brutish, and short." To escape such consequences, people therefore surrendered their liberties to a sovereign ruler in exchange for his agreement to keep the peace. Having granted away their liberties, subjects have no right whatsoever to seek them back, and the sovereign could therefore tyrannize as he likes—free to oppress his charges in any way other than to kill them, an act that would negate the very purpose of his rule, which is to preserve his subjects' lives.

Perhaps the most moving attempt to respond to the problem of doubt in seventeenth-century culture was offered by the French moral and religious philosopher Blaise Pascal (1623–1662). Pascal began his career as a mathematician and scientific rationalist. But at age thirty Pascal abandoned science as the result of a conversion experience and became a firm adherent of Jansenism, a puritanical faction within French Catholicism. From then until his death he worked on a highly ambitious philosophical-religious project meant to persuade doubters of the truth of Christianity by appealing simultaneously to their intellects and their emotions. Because of his premature death all that

CHRONOLOGY

THE SEARCH FOR AUTHORITY, 1572–1670

Montaigne's *Essays*	1572–1580
Bodin's *Six Books of the Commonwealth*	1576
Hobbes's *Leviathan*	1651
Pascal's *Pensées*	1670

came of this effort was his *Pensées* (Thoughts), a collection of fragments and short informal pieces about religion written with great literary power. In these he argued that faith alone could show the way to salvation and that "the heart has its reasons of which reason itself knows nothing." Pascal's *Pensées* expresses the author's own terror, anguish, and awe in the face of evil and eternity but presents that awe itself as evidence for the existence of God. Pascal's hope was that on this foundation, some measure of hopefulness about humanity and its capacity for self-knowledge could be re-erected that would avoid both the dogmatism and the extreme skepticism that were so prominent in seventeenth-century society.

LITERATURE AND THE ARTS

What was the relationship between the Baroque school and the Counter-Reformation?

Doubt and the uncertainty of human knowledge were also primary themes in the profusion of literature and art produced during western Europe's iron century. Of course not every poem, play, or painting of the era expressed the same message. During 120 years of extraordinary literary and artistic creativity, works of all genres and sentiments were produced, ranging from the frothiest farces to the darkest tragedies, from the serenest still lifes to the most violent scenes of religious martyrdom. The greatest writers and painters of the period all were moved by a realization of the ambiguities and ironies of human existence not unlike that expressed in different ways by Montaigne and Pascal. They all were fully aware of the horrors of war and human suffering so rampant in their day, but they also sought some measure of redemption for human beings caught up in a world that treated them so cruelly. Out of this tragic balance came some of the greatest works in the entire history of European literature and art.

MIGUEL DE CERVANTES (1547–1616)

Cervantes's masterpiece, the satirical romance *Don Quixote*, recounts the adventures of a Spanish gentleman, Don Quixote of La Mancha, who becomes slightly unbalanced by his constant reading of chivalric epics. His mind filled with all kinds of fantastic

adventures, he sets out at the age of fifty on the slippery road of knight-errantry, imagining windmills to be glowering giants and flocks of sheep to be armies of infidels whom it is his duty to rout with his spear. In his distorted fancy he mistakes inns for castles and serving girls for courtly ladies on fire with love. Set off in contrast to the knight-errant is the figure of his faithful squire, Sancho Panza. The latter represents the ideal of the practical man, with his feet on the ground and content with the modest but substantial pleasures of eating, drinking, and sleeping. Yet Cervantes clearly does not wish to say that the realism of a Sancho Panza is categorically preferable to the "quixotic" idealism of his master. Rather, the two men represent different facets of human nature. Without any doubt, *Don Quixote* is a devastating satire on the anachronistic chivalric mentality that was already hastening Spain's decline. But for all that, the reader's sympathies remain with the protagonist, the man from La Mancha who dares to "dream the impossible dream."

ELIZABETHAN AND JACOBEAN DRAMA

Writing after England's victory over the Spanish Armada, when national pride was at a peak, the dramatists of the so-called English Renaissance exhibited great exuberance without descending into a facile optimism. In fact a strain of reflective seriousness pervades all their best works; and a few, such as the tragedian John Webster (c. 1580–c. 1625), who "saw the skull beneath the skin," were if anything morbid pessimists. Among a bevy of great Elizabethan and Jacobean playwrights, however, the most outstanding were Christopher Marlowe (1564–1593), Ben Jonson (c. 1572–1637), and William Shakespeare (1564–1616). Of the three, the fiery Marlowe, whose life was cut short in a tavern brawl before he reached the age of thirty, was the most popular in his own day. In plays such as *Tamburlaine* and *Doctor Faustus* Marlowe created larger-than-life heroes who seek and come close to conquering everything in their path and feeling every possible sensation. But they meet unhappy ends because, for Marlowe, there are limits on human striving, and wretchedness as well as greatness lies in the human lot. Thus although Faustus asks a reincarnated Helen of Troy, conjured up by Satan, to make him "immortal with a kiss," he dies and is damned in the end because immortality is not awarded by the devil or to be found in earthly kisses.

In contrast to the heroic tragedies of Marlowe, Ben Jonson wrote corrosive comedies that expose human vices and foibles. In the particularly bleak *Volpone* Jonson shows people behaving like deceitful and lustful animals, but in the later *Alchemist* he balances an attack on quackery and gullibility with admiration for resourceful lower-class characters who cleverly take advantage of their supposed betters.

The greatest of the Elizabethan dramatists, William Shakespeare, was born into the family of a tradesman in the provincial town of Stratford-on-Avon. Little is known about his early life. He left his native village, having gained a modest education, when he was about twenty, and went to London where he found employment in the theater. How he eventually became an actor and still later a writer of plays is uncertain, but by the age of twenty-eight he had definitely acquired a reputation as an author sufficient to excite the jealousy of his rivals. Before he retired to his native Stratford about 1610 to spend the rest of his days in ease, he had written or collaborated in writing nearly forty plays, over and above 150 sonnets, and two long narrative poems.

Since their author's death, Shakespeare's plays have become a kind of secular Bible wherever the English language is spoken. The reasons lie in the author's unrivaled gift of expression, in his scintillating wit, and most of all in his profound analysis of human character seized by passion and tried by fate. Shakespeare's dramas fall thematically into three groups. Those written during the playwright's early years are characterized by a sense of confidence that, despite human foolishness, the world is fundamentally orderly and just. These include a number of the history plays, which recount England's struggles and glories leading up to the triumph of the Tudor Dynasty; the lyrical romantic tragedy *Romeo and Juliet*; and a number of comedies, including the magical *Midsummer Night's Dream, Twelfth Night, As You Like It,* and *Much Ado about Nothing.* Despite the last-named title, few even of the plays of Shakespeare's early, lightest period are much ado about nothing. Rather, most explore fundamental problems of psychological identity, honor and ambition, love and friendship. Occasionally, they also contain touches of deep seriousness, as in *As You Like It,* when Shakespeare has a character pause to reflect that "all the world's a stage, and all the men and women merely players" who pass through seven "acts" or stages of life.

The plays from Shakespeare's second period are far darker in mood, being characterized by bitterness, pathos, and a troubled searching into the mysteries and meaning of human existence. The series begins with the tragedy of indecisive idealism represented by *Hamlet,* goes on to the cynicism of *Measure for Measure* and *All's Well That Ends Well,* and culminates in the searing tragedies of *Macbeth* and *King Lear,* wherein characters assert that "life's but a walking shadow . . . a tale told by an idiot, full of sound and fury signifying nothing," and that "as flies to wanton boys are we to the gods; they kill us for their sport." Despite their gloom, however, the plays of Shakespeare's second period contain some of the dramatist's greatest flights of poetic grandeur.

Shakespeare ended his dramatic career, however, with a third period characterized by a profound spirit of reconciliation and peace. Of the three plays (all idyllic romances) written during this final period, the last, *The Tempest,* is the widest ranging in its reflections on human nature and the power of art. Ancient animosities are buried and wrongs are righted by a combination of natural and supernatural means, and a wide-eyed, youthful heroine rejoices on first seeing men with the words "O brave new world, that has such people in it!" Here, then, Shakespeare seems to be saying that despite humanity's trials, life is not so bitter after all, and the divine plan of the universe is ultimately benevolent and just.

> Since their author's death, Shakespeare's plays have become a kind of secular Bible wherever the English language is spoken.

Though less versatile than Shakespeare, not far behind him in eloquent grandeur stands the Puritan poet John Milton (1608–1674). The leading publicist of Oliver Cromwell's regime, Milton wrote the official defense of the beheading of Charles I as well as a number of treatises justifying Puritan positions in contemporary affairs. But he also loved the Greek and Latin classics at least as much as the Bible and wrote a perfect pastoral elegy, *Lycidas,* mourning in purely classical terms the loss of a dear friend. Later, when forced into retirement by the accession of Charles II, Milton, though now blind, embarked on writing a classical epic, *Paradise Lost,* out of material found in Genesis concerning the creation of the world and the fall of humanity. Setting out to "justify the ways of God to man," Milton in *Paradise Lost* first plays "devil's advocate" by creating the compelling character of Satan, who defies God with boldness and subtlety. But Satan is more than counterbalanced in the end by the real "epic hero" of *Paradise Lost,* Adam, who learns to accept the human lot of moral responsibility and suffering, and is last seen leaving Paradise with Eve, the world "all before them."

MANNERISM

The ironies and tensions inherent in human existence were also portrayed with eloquence and profundity by several immortal masters of the visual arts who flourished during this tumultuous century. The dominant goal in Italian and Spanish painting during the first half of this period, the years between about 1540 and 1600, was to fascinate the viewer with special effects. This goal, however, was achieved by means of two entirely different styles. (Confusingly, both styles are sometimes referred to as "Mannerism.") The first was based on the style of the Renaissance master Raphael but moved from that painter's gracefulness to a highly self-conscious elegance bordering on the bizarre and surreal. Representatives of this approach were the Florentines Pontormo (1494–1557) and Bronzino (1503–1572). Their sharp-focused portraits are flat and cold, yet strangely riveting.

The other extreme was theatrical in a more conventional sense—highly dramatic and emotionally compelling. Painters who followed this approach were indebted to Michelangelo but went much farther than he did in emphasizing shadowy contrasts, restlessness, and distortion. Of this second group, the two most outstanding were the Venetian Tintoretto (1518–1594) and the Spaniard El Greco (c. 1541–1614). Combining aspects of Michelangelo's style with the traditionally Venetian taste for rich color, Tintoretto produced an enormous number of monumentally large canvases devoted to religious subjects that still inspire awe with their broodingly shimmering light and gripping drama. More emotional still is the work of Tintoretto's disciple, El Greco. Born Domenikos Theotokopoulos on the Greek island of Crete, this extraordinary artist absorbed some of the stylized elongation characteristic of Greco-Byzantine icon painting before traveling to Italy to learn color and drama from Tintoretto. Finally he settled in Spain, where he was called "El Greco"—"the Greek." El Greco's paintings were too strange to be greatly appreciated in his own age, and even now they appear so unbalanced as to seem the work of one almost deranged. Yet such a view slights El Greco's deeply mystical Catholic fervor as well as his technical achievements. Best known today is his transfigured landscape, the *View of Toledo,* with its somber but awesome light breaking where no sun shines. But equally inspiring are his swirling religious scenes and several of his stunning portraits in which gaunt, dignified Spaniards radiate a rare blend of austerity and spiritual insight.

BAROQUE ART AND ARCHITECTURE

The dominant artistic school of southern Europe from about 1600 until the early 1700s was that of the Baroque, a school not only of painting but of sculpture and architecture. The Baroque style retained aspects of the dramatic and the irregular, but it avoided seeming bizarre or overheated and aimed above all to instill a sense of the affirmative. Originating in Rome as an expression of the ideals of the Counter-Reformation papacy and the Jesuit order, Baroque architecture in particular aimed to promote a specifically Catholic worldview. Similarly, Baroque painting often was done in the service of the Counter-Reformation church, which at its high tide around 1620 seemed everywhere to be on the offensive. When Baroque painters were not celebrating Counter-Reformation ideals,

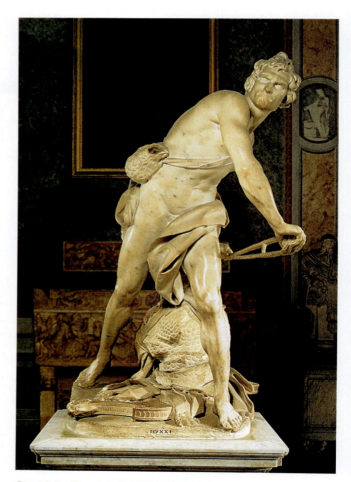

David, **by Bernini (1598–1680).** Whereas the earlier conceptions of David by the Renaissance sculptors Donatello and Michelangelo were reposeful (see pages 457 and 458), the Baroque sculptor Bernini chose to portray his young hero at the peak of physical exertion.

most of them worked in the service of monarchs who sought their own glorification.

The most imaginative and influential figure of the Roman Baroque was the architect and sculptor Gianlorenzo Bernini (1598–1680), a frequent employee of the papacy who created a magnificent celebration of papal grandeur in the sweeping colonnades leading up to St. Peter's Basilica. Breaking with the serene Renaissance classicism of Palladio, Bernini's architecture retained such classical elements as columns and domes but combined them in ways meant to express both aggressive restlessness and great power. Bernini was also one of the first to experiment with church facades built "in depth"—building frontages not conceived as continuous surfaces but that jutted out at odd angles and seemed to invade the open space in front of them. If the purpose of these innovations was to draw the viewer emotionally into the work of art, the same may be said for Bernini's aims in sculpture. Harking back to the restless motion of Hellenistic statuary—particularly the Laocoön group—and building on tendencies already present in the later sculpture of Michelangelo, Bernini's statuary emphasizes drama and incites the viewer to respond to it rather than serenely to observe.

The Maids of Honor, by **Diego Velázquez.** The artist himself is at work on a double portrait of the king and queen of Spain (who can be seen in the rear mirror), but reality is more obvious in the foreground in the persons of the delicately impish princess, her two maids, and a misshapen dwarf. The twentieth-century Spanish artist Picasso gained great inspiration from this work.

Because most Italian Baroque painters lacked Bernini's artistic genius, to view the very greatest masterpieces of southern European Baroque painting one must look to Spain and the work of Diego Velázquez (1599–1660). Unlike Bernini, Velázquez, a court painter in Madrid just when Spain hung on the brink of ruin, was not an entirely typical exponent of the Baroque style. Certainly many of his canvases display a characteristically Baroque delight in motion, drama, and power; but Velázquez's best work is characterized by a more restrained thoughtfulness than is usually found in the Baroque. Thus his famous *Surrender of Breda* shows muscular horses and splendid Spanish grandees on the one hand but un-Baroque sympathy for defeated, disarrayed troops on the other. Velázquez's single greatest painting, *The Maids of Honor,* done around 1656 after Spain's collapse, is one of the most thoughtful and probing artistic examinations of illusion and reality ever executed.

Dutch Painting in the Golden Age

Southern Europe's main northern rival for artistic laurels was the Netherlands, where three extremely dissimilar painters all explored the theme of the greatness and wretchedness of man to the fullest. The earliest, Peter Brueghel (c. 1525–1569), worked in a vein related to earlier Netherlandish realism. But unlike his

Chapter 14: Religious Wars and State Building, 1540–1660

The Massacre of the Innocents, **by Brueghel (c. 1525–1569).** This painting shows how effectively art can be used as a means of social commentary. Many art historians believe that Brueghel was tacitly depicting the suffering of the Netherlands at the hands of the Spanish in his own day.

The Horrors of War, **by Rubens (1577–1640).** The war god Mars here casts aside his mistress, Venus, and threatens humanity with death and destruction. In his old age Rubens took a far more critical view of war than he did for most of his earlier career.

What was the relationship between the Baroque school and the Counter-Reformation?

predecessors, who favored quiet urban scenes, Brueghel exulted in portraying the busy, elemental life of the peasantry. Most famous in this respect are his rollicking *Peasant Wedding* and *Peasant Wedding Dance* and his spacious *Harvesters,* in which guzzling and snoring field hands are taking a well-deserved break from their heavy labors under the noon sun. Such vistas give the impression of uninterrupted rhythms of life, but late in his career Brueghel became appalled by the intolerance and bloodshed he witnessed during the Calvinist riots and the Spanish repression in the Netherlands and expressed his criticism in an understated yet searing manner. In *The Blind Leading the Blind,* for example, we see what happens when ignorant fanatics start showing the way to each other. More powerful still is Brueghel's *Massacre of the Innocents,* which from a distance looks like a snug scene of a Flemish village buried in snow. In fact, however, heartless soldiers are methodically breaking into homes and slaughtering babies, the simple peasant folk are fully at their mercy, and the artist—alluding to a Gospel forgotten by warring Catholics and Protestants alike—seems to be saying "as it happened in the time of Christ, so it happens now."

Vastly different from Brueghel was the Netherlandish Baroque painter Peter Paul Rubens (1577–1640). Since the Baroque was an international movement closely linked to the spread of the Counter-Reformation, it should offer no surprise that Baroque style was extremely well represented in just that part of the Netherlands which, after long warfare, had been retained by Spain. In fact, Rubens of Antwerp was a far more typical Baroque artist than Velázquez of Madrid, painting literally thousands of robust canvases that glorified resurgent Catholicism or exalted second-rate aristocrats by portraying them as epic heroes dressed in bearskins. Even when Rubens's intent was not overtly propagandistic he customarily reveled in the sumptuous extravagance of the Baroque manner, being perhaps most famous today for the pink and rounded flesh of his well-nourished nudes. But unlike a host of lesser Baroque artists, Rubens was not lacking in subtlety and was a man of many moods. His gentle portrait of his son Nicholas catches unaffected childhood in a moment of repose; and though throughout most of his career Rubens had celebrated martial valor, his late *Horrors of War* movingly portrays what he himself called "the grief

Self-Portraits. Self-portraits became common during the sixteenth and seventeenth centuries, reflecting the intense introspection of the period. Left: Rembrandt painted more than sixty self-portraits; this one, dating from around 1660, captures the artist's creativity, theatricality (note the costume), and the honesty of his self-examination. Right: Judith Leyster (1609–1660) was a Dutch contemporary of Rembrandt who pursued a successful career as an artist during her early twenties, before she married. Respected in her own day, she was all but forgotten for centuries thereafter.

of unfortunate Europe, which, for so many years now, has suffered plunder, outrage, and misery."

In some ways a blend of Brueghel and Rubens, the greatest of all Netherlandish painters, Rembrandt van Rijn (1606–1669), defies all attempts at easy characterization. Living across the border from the Spanish Netherlands in staunchly Calvinistic Holland, Rembrandt belonged to a society that was too austere to tolerate the unbuckled realism of a Brueghel or the fleshy Baroque pomposity of a Rubens. Yet Rembrandt managed to put both realistic and Baroque traits to new uses. In his early career he gained fame and fortune as a painter of biblical scenes that lacked the Baroque's fleshiness but retained its grandeur in their swirling forms and stunning experiments with light. Rembrandt was also active as a portrait painter who knew how to flatter his subjects by emphasizing their Calvinistic steadfastness, to the great advantage of his purse. But gradually his prosperity faded, apparently in part because he grew tired of flattering and definitely because he made some bad investments. As personal tragedies mounted in the painter's middle and declining years, his art became more pensive and somber, but it gained in dignity, subtle lyricism, and awesome mystery. Thus his later portraits, including several self-portraits, are imbued with introspective qualities and a suggestion that only half the story is being told. Equally moving are explicitly philosophical paintings such as *Aristotle Contemplating the Bust of Homer*, in which the philosopher seems spellbound by the radiance of the epic poet, and *The Polish Rider*, in which realistic and Baroque elements merge into a higher synthesis portraying a pensive young man setting out fearlessly into a perilous world. Like Shakespeare, Rembrandt knew that life's journey is full of perils, but his most mature paintings suggest that these can be mastered with a courageous awareness of one's human shortcomings.

Conclusion

Between 1540 and 1660, Europe was racked by a combination of religious war, political rebellions, and economic crises that undermined confidence in traditional structures of social, religious, and political authority. The result was fear, skepticism, and a search for new, more certain foundations on which to rebuild the social, political, and religious order of Europe. For artists and intellectuals, the period proved to be one of the most creative epochs in the history of Europe. But for common people, the century was one of extraordinary suffering.

After a hundred years of destructive efforts to restore the religious unity of Europe through war, a de facto religious toleration between states was beginning to emerge by 1660 as the only way to preserve the European political order. Within states, toleration was still very limited when this terrible century ended. But in territories where religious rivalries ran too deep to be overcome, rulers were beginning to discover that loyalty to the state was a value that could override even the religious divisions among their subjects. The end result of this century of crises was thus to strengthen Europeans' confidence in the powers of the state to heal their wounds and right their wrongs, with religion relegated more and more to the private sphere of individual conscience. In the following centuries, this new confidence in the state as an autonomous moral agent that acts in accordance with its own "reasons of state," and for its own purposes, would prove a powerful challenge to the traditions of limited consensual government that had emerged out of the Middle Ages.

Key Terms

Religious Peace of Augsburg
Henry of Navarre
Spanish Armada
Thirty Years' War
Cardinal Richelieu
James I
Oliver Cromwell
Michel de Montaigne
Leviathan
Don Quixote
Baroque
William Shakespeare
Rembrandt Van Rijn

Selected Readings

Bonney, Richard. *The European Dynastic States, 1494–1660*. Oxford and New York, 1991. An excellent survey of continental Europe during the "long" sixteenth century.

Briggs, Robin. *Early Modern France, 1560–1715*, 2d ed. Oxford and New York, 1997. Updated and authoritative, with new bibliographies.

Briggs, Robin. *Witches and Neighbors: The Social and Cultural Context of European Witchcraft*. New York, 1996. An influential recent account of continental witchcraft.

Cervantes, Miguel de. *Don Quixote*. Trans. Edith Grossman. New York, 2003. A splendid new translation.

Clarke, Stuart. *Thinking with Demons: The Idea of Witchcraft in Early Modern Europe*. Oxford and New York, 1999. By placing demonology into the context of sixteenth- and seventeenth-century intellectual history, Clarke makes sense of it in new and exciting ways.

Cochrane, Eric, Charles M. Gray, and Mark A. Kishlansky. *Early Modern Europe: Crisis of Authority*. Chicago, 1987. An outstanding source collection from the University of Chicago Readings in Western Civilization series.

Held, Julius S., and Donald Posner. *Seventeenth- and Eighteenth-Century Art: Baroque Painting, Sculpture, Architecture*. New York, 1971. The most complete and best-organized introductory review of the subject in English.

Hibbard, Howard. *Bernini*. Baltimore, Md., 1965. The basic study in English of this central figure of Baroque artistic activity.

Hirst, Derek. *England in Conflict, 1603–1660: Kingdom, Community, Commonwealth*. Oxford and New York, 1999. A complete revision of the author's *Authority and Conflict* (1986), this is an up-to-date and balanced account of a period that has been a historical battleground over the past twenty years.

Hobbes, Thomas. *Leviathan*. Ed. Richard Tuck. 2d ed. Cambridge and New York, 1996. The most recent edition, containing the entirety of *Leviathan*, not just the first two parts.

Holt, Mack P. *The French Wars of Religion, 1562–1629*. Cambridge and New York, 1995. A clear account of a confusing time.

Kors, Alan Charles, and Edward Peters. *Witchcraft in Europe, 400–1700: A Documentary History*, 2d ed. Philadelphia, 2000. A superb collection of documents, significantly expanded in the second edition, with up-to-date commentary.

Kingdon, Robert. *Myths about the St. Bartholomew's Day Massacres, 1572–1576*. Cambridge, Mass., 1988. A detailed account of this pivotal moment in the history of France.

Levack, Brian P. *The Witch-Hunt in Early Modern Europe*, 2d ed. London and New York, 1995. The best account of the persecution of suspected witches; coverage extends from Europe in 1450 to America in 1750.

Levin, Carole. *The Heart and Stomach of a King: Elizabeth I and the Politics of Sex and Power*. Philadelphia, 1994. A provocative argument for the importance of Elizabeth's gender for understanding her reign.

Limm, Peter, ed. *The Thirty Years' War*. London, 1984. An outstanding short survey, followed by a selection of primary-source documents.

Lynch, John. *Spain, 1516–1598: From Nation-State to World Empire*. Oxford and Cambridge, Mass., 1991. The best book in English on Spain at the pinnacle of its sixteenth-century power.

MacCaffrey, Wallace. *Elizabeth I*. New York, 1993. An outstanding traditional biography by an excellent scholar.

Martin, Colin, and Geoffrey Parker. *The Spanish Armada*. London, 1988. Incorporates recent discoveries from undersea archaeology with more traditional historical sources.

Martin, John Rupert. *Baroque*. New York, 1977. A thought-provoking, thematic treatment, less a survey than an essay on the painting, sculpture, and architecture of the period.

Mattingly, Garrett. *The Armada*. Boston, 1959. A great narrative history that reads like a novel; for more recent work, however, see Martin and Parker.

Parker, Geoffrey. *The Dutch Revolt*, 2d ed. Ithaca, N.Y., 1989. The standard survey in English on the revolt of the Netherlands.

Parker, Geoffrey. *Philip II*. Boston, 1978. A fine biography by an expert in both the Spanish and the Dutch sources.

Parker, Geoffrey, ed. *The Thirty Years' War*, rev. ed. London and New York, 1987. A wide-ranging collection of essays by scholarly experts.

Pascal, Blaise. *Pensées* (French-English edition). Ed. H. F. Stewart. London, 1950.

Quint, David. *Montaigne and the Quality of Mercy: Ethical and Political Themes in the "Essais."* Princeton, N.J., 1999. A fine treatment that presents Montaigne's thought as a response to the French wars of religion.

Roberts, Michael. *Gustavus Adolphus and the Rise of Sweden*. London, 1973. Still the authoritative English-language account.

Russell, Conrad. *The Causes of the English Civil War*. Oxford, 1990. A penetrating and provocative analysis by one of the leading "revisionist" historians of the period.

Tracy, James D. *Holland under Habsburg Rule, 1506–1566: The Formation of a Body Politic*. Berkeley, Calif., and Los Angeles, 1990. A political history and analysis of the formative years of the Dutch state.

Van Gelderen, Martin. *Political Theory of the Dutch Revolt*. Cambridge, 1995. A fine book on a subject whose importance is too easily overlooked.

EARLY MODERN EUROPE

SEVENTEENTH- AND EIGHTEENTH-CENTURY European life was shaped by the combined effects of commerce, war, and a steadily growing population. A commercial revolution spurred the development of overseas colonies and trade while opening up new markets for European industry. Agricultural productivity increased, making it possible for Europe to feed a population that had now reached unprecedented levels. Population growth in turn enabled European governments to wage more frequent wars and to employ larger and larger armies.

Although monarchs continued to meet with opposition from the various estates within their realms, they increasingly asserted their power as absolute rulers. Warfare remained the chief instrument of European foreign policy; but slowly the notion of a diplomatic and military balance of power began to displace the pursuit of unrestrained aggrandizement as the primary goal of European state relations.

Profound changes were also occurring in European intellectual life during these centuries. Using new instruments and applying new mathematical techniques, astronomers proved beyond question that the earth was not the center of the universe. Biologists and physicians pioneered a more sophisticated understanding of the nature and processes by which life was created and sustained, and physicists such as Sir Isaac Newton established for the first time a true science of mechanics. During the eighteenth century, these discoveries gave rise to a new confidence in the capacity of human reason alone to understand nature and so to improve human life—a confidence those who held to it declared to be a sign of Enlightenment.

EARLY MODERN EUROPE

POLITICS	SOCIETY AND CULTURE	ECONOMY	INTERNATIONAL RELATIONS
	Copernicus's *On the Revolutions of the Heavenly Spheres* (1543) Claudio Monteverdi, father of opera (1567–1643) Johannes Kepler (1571–1630) William Harvey (1578–1657)	Enclosure movement (1500–1700s) Demand for sugar escalates in Europe (late 1500s)	Sir Francis Drake leads attack on Spanish fleet at Cadíz (1587)
	Literacy increases across Europe (1600–1800) Increased urbanization (1600–1750) Smoking spreads in Europe (early 1600s) Over 80,000 leave England for the New World (1607–1650) Galileo's *Starry Messenger* (1610)	Widespread crop failure in France (1597–1694) Mechanically powered saws and calico printing from the Far East (1600s) Dutch East India Company founded (1602)	A total of 11 million Africans forci[...] shipped across the middle passag[...] (1500–1800) English colonists establish Jamestown (1607)
Jean Baptiste Colbert, French finance minister (1619–1683)	Bacon's *New Instruments* (1620) Galileo charged with heresy (1632) John Locke (1632–1704) Descartes's *Discourse on Method* (1637)		*Mayflower* lands in the New World (1620)
Reign of Louis XIV, the Sun King (1643–1715) England promulgates Navigation Acts (1651, 1660) Restoration and return of Charles II (1660)	(1637) Plague outbreaks (1649–1665) Edmond Halley (1656–1742) Founding of the Royal Society of London and the French Academy of Sciences (1660) Daniel Defoe, author of *Robinson Crusoe* (1660–1731)	French government introduces head tax (c. 1645) Coffee consumption escalates in Europe (1650s) Bank of Sweden founded (1657)	
Louis XIV revokes the Edict of Nantes (1685)	The Great Fire in London (1666) Johann Sebastian Bach (1685–1750) George Frideric Handel (1685–1759) Newton's *Principia Mathematica* (1687)		Dutch surrender New Amsterdam to England (1667) Austrian Habsburgs repulse Turks' assault on Vienna (1683) Peace of Augsburg (1686) Portugal regains independence from Spain (1688) William of Orange rules England and Holland (1688) War of the League of Augsburg (1688–1697)
Glorious Revolution in England (1688–1689) Reign of Peter the Great of Russia (1689–1725)	Locke's *Treatise of Civil Government* and *Essay Concerning Human Understanding* (1690)	Bank of England founded (1694)	Battle of the Boyne, English solidif[...] control of Ireland (1690)
	Maize and the potato are introduced in Europe (1700s) Proliferation of salons and coffee-houses (1700s) First daily newspaper in England (1702)	Fly shuttle for weaving loom invented (early 1700s) Physiocrats promote concept of laissez-faire (1700s)	
Reign of Charles VI, emperor of Holy Roman Empire (1711–1740) Treaty of Utrecht (1713) Reign of George I, first of Hanoverian dynasty in England (1714–1727) Louis XV (1715–1774) Robert Walpole serves as England's first prime minister (1720–1742)	Rousseau's *Social Contract* (1762)		War of Spanish Succession (1702–1713) England and Scotland unite to form Great Britain (1707)

EARLY MODERN EUROPE

POLITICS	SOCIETY AND CULTURE	ECONOMY	INTERNATIONAL RELATIONS
		German imperial law prohibits journeyman associations (1731)	
	Voltaire's *The Philosophical Letters* (1734)	France establishes the Road and Bridge Corps of Engineering (1747)	
Reign of Frederick the Great, the "enlightened despot" (1740–1786)	Montesquieu's *Spirit of Laws* (1748)		
	Steady increase in population begins (1750)		War of Austrian Succession (1740–1748)
	Encyclopedia published by Diderot and d'Alembert (1751–1772)		
	Wolfgang Amadeus Mozart (1756–1791)	Antislavery movements emerge in Europe (1760s)	Seven Years' War/French and Indian War (1756–1763)
Reign of George III of England (1760–1820)	Beccaria's *On Crimes and Punishment* (1764)		
Reign of Catherine the Great of Russia (1762–1796)		James Cook explores Pacific (1768–1779)	Treaty of Paris: France concedes Canada and India to England (1763)
Maria Theresa and Joseph II of Austria rule jointly (1765–1780)		Abbe Raynal's *Philosophical History of Europeans in the Two Indies* (1770)	French East India Company dissolves (1769)
			Russo-Turkish War (1769–1792)
			American Revolution (1775–1783)
Reign of Louis XVI of France (1774–1792)	Kant's "What Is Enlightenment?" (1784)	Smith's *Inquiry into the Nature and Causes of the Wealth of Nations* (1776)	
French Revolution breaks out (1789)			
	Wollstonecraft's *Vindication of the Rights of Woman* (1792)		Russia, Austria, and Prussia fully partition Poland (1795)
	Austen's *Pride and Prejudice* (1813–1817)		

Chapter Fifteen

Chapter Contents

- The Appeal and Justification of Absolutism 540
- Alternatives to Absolutism 542
- The Absolutism of Louis XIV 546
- The Remaking of Central and Eastern Europe 553
- Autocracy in Russia 557
- Commerce and Consumption 561
- Colonization and Trade in the Seventeenth Century 564
- Colonialism and Empire 570
- Conclusion 575

Absolutism and Empire, 1660–1789

THE PERIOD FROM AROUND 1660 (when the English monarchy was restored and Louis XIV of France began his personal rule) to 1789 (when the French Revolution erupted) is traditionally known as the age of absolutism. *Absolutism* was a political theory that encouraged rulers to claim complete sovereignty within their territories. To seventeenth- and eighteenth-century absolutists, complete sovereignty meant that a ruler could make law, dispense justice, create and direct a bureaucracy, declare war, and levy taxation according to his or her own will, without needing the formal approval of any other governing authorities. Frequently, assertions of absolute authority were buttressed by claims that rulers governed their territories by the same divine right that established a father's absolute authority over his household. After the chaos of Europe's "iron century," many Europeans had come to believe that it was only by exalting the sovereignty of such absolute, "patriarchal" rulers that order could be restored to European life.

The age of absolutism was also an age of empire. By 1660, the French, Spanish, Portuguese, English, and Dutch had all established important colonies in the Americas and in Asia. Rivalry among these competing colonial powers was intense and fraught with consequence. In the late seventeenth century, European wars almost always had a colonial aspect. By the middle of the eighteenth century, however, Europe's wars were being driven by colonial considerations and imperial conflicts, as worldwide trade assumed a larger and larger role in the European economy.

Absolutism was not the only political theory according to which European governments sought to rule during this period. England, Scotland, the Dutch Republic, Switzerland, Venice, Sweden, and Poland-Lithuania were all either limited monarchies or republics; in Russia, an extreme autocracy was emerging that ascribed to the tsar

FOCUS QUESTIONS

- What were the aims of absolutist rulers?
- Did John Locke's political principles lie behind the Glorious Revolution in England?
- How did Louis XIV strengthen his control over France?
- What changes lay behind the growing power of Prussia?
- In what ways did Russian absolutism differ from its western European counterparts?

- What factors facilitated the commercial revolution?
- How did the patterns of European colonial settlement in the Americas differ from each other?
- In what ways did eighteenth-century European colonialism differ from seventeenth-century European colonialism?

CHAPTER 15

ABSOLUTISM AND EMPIRE, 1660–1789

a degree of control over his subjects' lives and property far beyond anything imagined by western European absolutists. Even in Russia, however, absolutism was never so unlimited in practice as it was in theory. Even the most absolute monarchs of seventeenth- and eighteenth-century Europe could rule effectively only so long as their subjects (and particularly their nobility) were prepared to consent, at least tacitly, to their policies. When serious opposition erupted, even absolutists were forced to back down. And when, in 1789, an outright political revolution occurred, the entire structure of absolutism came crashing to the ground.

THE APPEAL AND JUSTIFICATION OF ABSOLUTISM

What were the aims of absolutist rulers?

Absolutism's promise of stability, prosperity, and order was an appealing alternative to the disorder of the "iron century" that preceded it. This was especially the case for the quintessential absolutist monarch, Louis XIV (1643–1715) of France. The political disturbances of his minority made a lasting impression on the young king. When marauding Parisians entered his bedchamber one night in 1651, Louis saw the intrusion as a horrid affront not only to his own person but to the majesty of the French state he personified. Squabbles among the nobility and criticisms of royal policy by the Paris parlement during his minority convinced him that he must rule assertively and without limitation if France was to survive as a great European state.

Absolutist monarchs sought to gather into their own hands command of the state's armed forces, control over its legal system, and the right to collect and spend the state's financial resources at will. To achieve these goals, they also needed to create an efficient, centralized bureaucracy that owed its allegiance directly to the monarch himself. Creating and sustaining such a bureaucracy was expensive but essential to the larger absolutist goal of weakening the privileged special in-

terests that had hindered the free exercise of royal power in the past. The legally privileged estates of nobility and clergy; the political authority of semi-autonomous regions; and the pretensions of independent-minded representative assemblies such as parliaments, diets, or estates general were all obstacles—in the eyes of absolutists—to strong, centralized monarchical government. The history of absolutism is, as much as anything, a history of attempts by aspiring absolutists to bring such institutions to heel.

In most Protestant countries, the independent power of the church had already been subordinated to the interests of the state when the age of absolutism began. In France, Spain, and Austria, however, where Roman Catholicism had remained the state religion, absolutist monarchs now devoted concerted attention to nationalizing the church and its clergy within their territories. These efforts built on the concordats the French and Spanish monarchies had extracted from the papacy during the fifteenth and sixteenth centuries, but they went much further in consolidating authority over the church into the hands of the monarchy. Even Charles III, the devout Spanish king who ruled from 1759 to 1788, pressed successfully for a papal concordat granting him control over ecclesiastical appointments and the right to nullify any papal bull affecting Spain of which he did not approve.

The most important potential opponents of royal absolutism were not churchmen, however, but nobles. Monarchs dealt with their threat in various ways. Louis XIV deprived the French nobility of political power in the provinces while increasing their social prestige by requiring them to reside at his own lavish court at Versailles. Peter the Great of Russia (1689–1725) forced all his nobles into lifelong government service. Later in the century, Catherine II of Russia (1762–1796) struck a bargain whereby in return for vast estates and a variety of social and economic privileges (including exemption from taxation) the Russian nobility virtually surrendered the administrative and political power of the state into the empress's hands. In Prussia the army was staffed by nobles, as was generally the case in Spain, France, and England also. But in eighteenth-century Austria, the emperor Joseph II (1765–1790) adopted a policy of confrontation rather than accommodation, denying the nobility exemption

> Even the most absolute monarchs of seventeenth- and eighteenth-century Europe could rule effectively only so long as their subjects (and particularly their nobility) were prepared to consent, at least tacitly, to their policies.

ABSOLUTISM AND PATRIARCHY

These selections show how two political theorists justified royal absolutism by deriving it from the absolute authority of a father over his household. Bishop Jacques-Benigne Bossuet (1627–1704) was a famous French preacher who served as tutor to the son of King Louis XIV of France before becoming bishop of Meaux. Sir Robert Filmer (1588–1653) was an English political theorist. Filmer's works attracted particular attention in the 1680s, when John Locke directed the first of his Two Treatises of Government to refuting Filmer's views on the patriarchal nature of royal authority.

BOSSUET ON THE NATURE OF MONARCHICAL AUTHORITY

There are four characteristics or qualities essential to royal authority. First, royal authority is sacred; Secondly, it is paternal; Thirdly, it is absolute; Fourthly, it is subject to reason. . . . All power comes from God. . . . Thus princes act as ministers of God, and his lieutenants on earth. It is through them that he exercises his empire. . . . In this way . . . the royal throne is not the throne of a man, but the throne of God himself. . . .

We have seen that kings hold the place of God, who is the true Father of the human race. We have also seen that the first idea of power that there was among men, is that of paternal power; and that kings were fashioned on the model of fathers. Moreover, all the world agrees that obedience, which is due to public power, is only found . . . in the precept which obliges one to honor his parents. From all this it appears that the name "king" is a father's name, and that goodness is the most natural quality in kings. . . .

Royal authority is absolute. In order to make this term odious and insupportable, many pretend to confuse absolute government and arbitrary government. But nothing is more distinct, as we shall make clear when we speak of justice. . . . The prince need account to no one for what he ordains. . . . Without this absolute authority, he can neither do good nor suppress evil: his power must be such that no one can hope to escape him. . . . [T]he sole defense of individuals against the public power must be their innocence. . . .

One must, then, obey princes as if they were justice itself, without which there is neither order nor justice in affairs. They are gods, and share in some way in divine independence. . . . It follows from this that he who does not want to obey the prince . . . is condemned irremissibly to death as an enemy of public peace and of human society. . . . The prince can correct himself when he knows that he has done badly; but against his authority there can be no remedy. . . .

Jacques-Benigne Bossuet, *Politics Drawn from the Very Words of Holy Scripture*, trans. Patrick Riley (Cambridge, 1990), pp. 46–69 and 81–83.

FILMER ON THE PATRIARCHAL ORIGINS OF ROYAL AUTHORITY

The first government in the world was monarchical, in the father of all flesh, Adam being commanded to multiply, and people the earth, and to subdue it, and having dominion given him over all creatures, was thereby the monarch of the whole world; none of his posterity had any right to possess anything, but by his grant or permission, or by succession from him. . . . Adam was the father, king and lord over his family: a son, a subject, and a servant or a slave were one and the same thing at first. . . .

I cannot find any one place or text in the Bible where any power . . . is given to a people either to govern themselves, or to choose themselves governors, or to alter the manner of government at their pleasure. The power of government is settled and fixed by the commandment of "honour thy father"; if there were a higher power than the fatherly, then this commandment could not stand and be observed. . . .

All power on earth is either derived or usurped from the fatherly power, there being no other original to be found of any power whatsoever. For if there should be granted two sorts of power without any subordination of one to the other, they would be in perpetual strife which should be the supreme, for two supremes cannot agree. If the fatherly power be supreme, then the power of the people must be subordinate and depend on it. If the power of the people be supreme, then the fatherly power must submit to it, and cannot be exercised without the licence of the people, which must quite destroy the frame and course of nature. Even the power which God himself exercises over mankind is by right of fatherhood: he is both the king and father of us all. As God has exalted the dignity of earthly kings . . . by saying they are gods, so . . . he has been pleased . . . [t]o humble himself by assuming the title of a king to express his power, and not the title of any popular government.

Robert Filmer, "Observations upon Aristotle's Politiques" (1652), in *Divine Right and Democracy: An Anthology of Political Writing in Stuart England*, ed. David Wootton (Harmondsworth, UK, 1986), pp. 110–118.

QUESTIONS FOR ANALYSIS

1. Why did some political theorists argue the necessity of absolutism based on the model of the father? Was there an alternative to this model?
2. What would John Locke find so objectionable about the political theory of Robert Filmer? How would Filmer have answered Locke?

---

from taxation and deliberately blurring the distinctions between nobles and commoners.

Struggles between monarchs and nobles frequently affected relations between local and central government also. In France, the monarch sought to undermine the autonomy of noble-led provincial institutions by requiring the upper nobility to live at his palace. In Spain the monarchy, based in Castile, battled the independent-minded nobles of Aragon and Catalunya. Prussian rulers intruded themselves into the governance of formerly "free" cities by claiming the right to police and tax their inhabitants. The Habsburg emperors tried, unsuccessfully, to suppress the largely autonomous nobility of Hungary. Rarely, however, was the path of confrontation between crown and nobility successful in the long run. The most effective absolutist monarchies of the eighteenth century established a *modus vivendi* with their nobility, in which nobles came to see their own interests as tied to those of the crown. For this reason, cooperation more often characterized the relations between kings and nobles during the eighteenth-century "old regime" (*ancien régime*) than did conflict.

 ALTERNATIVES TO ABSOLUTISM

> Did John Locke's political principles lie behind the Glorious Revolution in England?

Although absolutism was the dominant model for seventeenth- and eighteenth-century European monarchs, it was by no means the only system by which Europeans governed themselves. In Venice, a republican oligarchy continued to rule the city. In the Netherlands, the territories that had won their independence from Spain during the early seventeenth century combined to form the United Provinces, the only truly new country to take shape in Europe during the early modern era. The Spanish wars created a deep distrust among the Dutch toward monarchs of any stripe. As a result, although Holland dominated the United Provinces, its House of Orange, which had led the wars for independence, never attempted to transform the new country from a republic into a monarchy. Even after 1688, when William of Orange also became King William III of England, the United Provinces remained a republic.

LIMITED MONARCHY: THE CASE OF ENGLAND

At a time when the powers of representative assemblies were being undermined across much of Europe, the English Parliament was the longest-surviving and most highly developed such body in Europe. English political theorists had for centuries seen their government as a mixed monarchy, composed of monarchical, noble, and nonnoble elements. During the seventeenth century, however, these traditions had come under threat, first through Charles I's attempts to rule without Parliament and then during Oliver Cromwell's dictatorial Protectorate. The restoration of the monarchy in 1660 resolved the question of whether England would in future be a republic or a monarchy; but the sort of monarchy England would become remained an open question as the reign of Charles II began.

THE REIGN OF CHARLES II

Despite the fact that he was the son of the beheaded and much-hated Charles I, Charles II (1660–1685) was initially welcomed by most English men and women. On his accession, he declared limited religious toleration for Protestant "dissenters" (Protestants who were not members of the official Church of England). He also promised to observe Magna Carta and the Petition of Right, declaring, with characteristic good humor, that he did not wish to "resume his travels." The unbuttoned moral atmosphere of his court, with its risqué plays, dancing, and sexual licentiousness, reflected a public desire to forget the restraints of the Puritan past. Some critics suggested that Charles, "that known enemy to virginity and chastity," took his role as the father of his country rather too seriously; but in fact he produced no legitimate heir and only a single illegitimate son to vie for the throne.

Having grown up an exile in France, Charles was an admirer of all things French. During the 1670s, however, he began openly to model his kingship on the absolutism of Louis XIV. As a result, the great men of England soon came to be publically divided between Charles's supporters (called by their opponents "Tories," a popular nickname for Irish Catholic bandits) and his opponents (called by their opponents "Whigs," a nickname for Scottish Presbyterian rebels). Both sides feared absolutism, just as both sides feared a return to the bad old days of the 1640s, when resistance to the Crown had led to civil war and ultimately to republicanism. What they could not agree on was which possibility frightened them more.

Religion also remained a divisive issue. Charles was sympathetic to Roman Catholicism, even to the point of a deathbed conversion in 1685. During the 1670s, he briefly suspended civil penalties against Catholics and Protestant dissenters by asserting his right as king to ignore Parliamentary legislation. The resulting public outcry compelled him to retreat; but this controversy, together with rising opposition to Charles's ardently Catholic brother James as the heir to the throne, led to a series of Whig electoral victories between 1679 and 1681. When a group of radical Whigs attempted to exclude James by law from succeeding his brother on the throne, however, Charles stared the opposition down in the so-called Exclusion Crisis. Thereafter, Charles found that his rising revenues from customs duties, combined with a secret subsidy from Louis XIV, enabled him to govern without relying on Parliament for money. Charles further alarmed Whig politicans by executing several of them on charges of treason and by remodeling local government to make

Charles II.

it more amenable to royal control. Charles died in 1685 with his power enhanced, but he left behind a political and religious legacy that was to be the undoing of his less able and adroit successor.

THE REIGN OF JAMES II

James II was the very opposite of his worldly brother. A zealous Catholic convert, he alienated his Tory supporters, almost all of whom were members of the established Church of England, by suspending the laws preventing Catholics and Protestant dissenters from holding political office. James also flaunted his own Roman Catholicism, openly declaring his wish that all his subjects might be converted and publicly parading papal legates through the streets of London. When, in June 1688, he ordered all Church of England clergymen to read his decree of religious toleration from their pulpits, seven bishops refused and were promptly thrown in prison on charges of seditious libel. At their trial, however, they were declared not guilty, to the enormous satisfaction of the Protestant English populace.

Mary Stuart. Queen Mary and her husband William of Orange became Protestant joint rulers of England in a bloodless coup, taking power from her father, the Catholic James II.

The trial of the bishops was one event that brought matters to a head. The other was the unexpected birth of a son in 1688 to James and his second wife, Mary of Modena. This child, who was to be raised a Catholic, replaced James's much older Protestant daughter Mary Stuart as heir to the thrones of Scotland and England. So unexpected was this birth that there were widespread rumors that the child was not in fact James's son at all but had been smuggled into the royal bedchamber in a warming pan.

With the birth of the "warming-pan baby," events moved swiftly toward a climax. A delegation of Whigs and Tories crossed the channel to Holland to invite Mary Stuart and her Protestant husband, William of Orange, to cross to England with an invading army to preserve Protestantism and English liberties by summoning a new Parliament. As the leader of a continental coalition then at war with France, William also welcomed the opportunity to make England an ally against Louis XIV's expansionist foreign policy.

THE GLORIOUS REVOLUTION

William and Mary's invasion became a bloodless coup (although James is reputed to have suffered a nosebleed at the moment of crisis). Because James fled the country, Parliament was able to declare the throne vacant, clearing the way for William and Mary to accede as joint sovereigns by right of succession. The Bill of Rights, passed by Parliament and accepted by the new king and queen in 1689, reaffirmed English civil liberties such as trial by jury, habeas corpus (a guarantee that no one could be imprisoned unless charged with a crime), and the right to petition the monarch through Parliament for redress of grievances. The Bill of Rights also declared that the monarchy was subject to the law of the land. The Act of Toleration, also passed in 1689, granted Protestant dissenters the right to worship freely, though not to hold political office. And in 1701, the Act of Succession ordained that every future English monarch must be a member of the Church of England. With the childless Queen Mary now dead, this meant that the throne would pass, after King William's death, first to Mary's Protestant sister Anne (1702–1714) and then, if Anne died childless, to George, elector of the German principality of Hanover and the Protestant great-grandson of James I. In 1707, the formal Act of Union between Scotland and England ensured that the Catholic heirs of King James II would in future have no more right to the throne of Scotland than they did to the throne of England.

Did John Locke's political principles lie behind the Glorious Revolution in England?

The English soon referred to the events of 1688 and 1689 as the "Glorious Revolution": glorious because it occurred without bloodshed and also because it firmly established England as a mixed monarchy governed by the "King in Parliament." Although William and Mary and their successors continued to exercise a large measure of executive power, after 1688 no English monarch attempted to govern without Parliament, which has met annually from that time on. Parliament, and especially the House of Commons, also strengthened its control over taxation and expenditure. Protestants in particular celebrated the Glorious Revolution as another sign of God's special favor to England, noting the favorable (Protestant) winds that blew William and Mary so speedily to England and kept King James's fleet from mounting an effective resistance.

Yet 1688 was not all glory. It was a revolution that consolidated the position of large property holders, whose control over local government had been threatened by Charles II and James II. It thus restored the status quo on behalf of a wealthy class of magnates that would soon become even wealthier from government patronage and the profits of war. It also brought misery to the Catholic minority in Scotland and to the Catholic majority in Ireland. After 1690, when King William won a decisive victory over James II's forces at the battle of the Boyne, power in Ireland would lie firmly in the hands of a "Protestant Ascendancy," whose dominance over Irish society would last until modern times.

John Locke and the Contract Theory of Government

The Glorious Revolution was the product of unique political circumstances, but it also reflected anti-absolutist theories of politics that were taking shape in the late seventeenth century in response to the ideas of writers such as Bodin, Hobbes, Filmer, and Bossuet. Chief among these opponents of absolutism was the Englishman John Locke (1632–1704), whose *Two Treatises of Government* were written before the revolution but published for the first time in 1690.

Locke maintained that humans had originally lived in a state of nature characterized by absolute freedom and equality, in which there was no government of any kind. The only law was the law of nature (which Locke equated with the law of reason), by which individuals enforced for themselves their natural rights to life, liberty, and property. Soon, however, humans began to perceive that the inconveniences of the state of nature outweighed its advantages. Accordingly, they agreed first to establish a civil society based on absolute equality and then to set up a government to arbitrate the disputes that might arise within this civil society. But they did not make government's powers absolute. Government was simply the combined power of all members of the society; as such, its authority could "be no more than those persons had in a state of nature before they entered into society, and gave it up to the community." All powers not expressly surrendered to the government were reserved to the people themselves; as a result, governmental authority was both contractual and conditional. If a government exceeded or abused the authority granted to it, society had the right to dissolve it and create another.

Locke condemned absolutism in every form. He denounced absolute monarchy, but he was no less critical of claims for the sovereignty of parliaments. Government, he argued, had been instituted to protect life, liberty, and property; no political authority could infringe an individual's natural rights to preserve these inviolate. The law of nature, which embodied these

> Locke maintained that humans had originally lived in a state of nature characterized by absolute freedom and equality, in which there was no government of any kind.

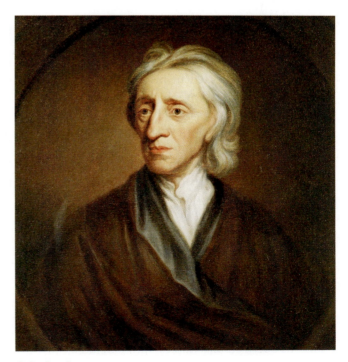

John Locke.

rights, was therefore an automatic and absolute limitation on every branch of government, whether legislative, executive, or judicial.

In the late eighteenth century, Locke's ideas would become an important element in the intellectual background of both the American and French revolutions. Between 1690 and 1720, however, they served a far less radical purpose. The landed magnates who replaced James II with William and Mary read Locke as a defense of their conservative revolution. Rather than protecting their liberty and property, James II had threatened both; hence the magnates were entitled to overthrow the tyranny he had established and replace it with a government that would defend their interests by preserving these natural rights. English government after 1689 would be dominated by Parliament; Parliament in turn was controlled by a landed aristocracy whose common interests far outweighed their incessant competition for office or their occasional disagreements over principle.

royalty. The main facade of the palace was a third of a mile in length. Inside, tapestries and paintings celebrated French military victories and royal triumphs; mirrors reflected shimmering light throughout the building. In the vast gardens outside, statues of the Greek god Apollo, god of the sun, recalled Louis's claim to be the "Sun King" of France. Noblemen vied to attend him when he arose from bed, ate his meals (usually stone cold after having traveled the distance of several city blocks from kitchen to table), strolled in his gardens (even the way the king walked was choreographed by the royal dancing master), or rode to the hunt. As the home of the Sun King, Louis's court was the epicenter of his gleaming royal resplendence. France's leading nobles were required to reside with him at Versailles for a portion of the year; the splendor of Louis's court was deliberately calculated to blind them to the possibility of disobedience while raising their prestige by associating them with himself. Instead of plotting some minor treason on his estate, a

The Absolutism of Louis XIV

> How did Louis XIV strengthen his control over France?

In Louix XIV's state portrait, it is all but impossible to discern the human being behind the facade of the absolute monarch, dressed in his coronation robes and surrounded by the symbols of his authority. That facade was carefully and artfully constructed by Louis, who recognized, perhaps more fully than any other early modern ruler, the importance of theater to effective kingship. Louis and his successors deliberately staged theatrical demonstrations of their sovereignty to enhance their position as rulers endowed with godlike powers far removed from common humanity.

Performing Royalty at Versailles

Louis's most elaborate exhibitions of his sovereignty took place at his palace at Versailles (*vuhr-SY*), the town outside of Paris to which he moved his court. The palace and its grounds became a stage on which Louis mesmerized his nobles into obedience by his performance of the daily rituals and demonstrations of

Louis XIV's State Portrait. This portrait by Hyacinthe Rigaud illustrates the degree to which absolute monarchy was defined in terms of studied performance.

How did Louis XIV strengthen his control over France?

The Château of Versailles. Dramatically expanded by Louis XIV in the 1660s from a hunting lodge to the principal royal residence and the seat of government, the château became a monument to the international power and prestige of the grand monarch.

marquis could instead enjoy the pleasure of knowing that on the morrow he would be privileged to engage the king in two or three minutes of conversation as the royal party made its stately progress through the vast palace halls. At the same time, however, the elaborate and almost impossibly detailed rules of etiquette around the court left these privileged nobles in constant suspense, forever fearful of offending the king by committing some trivial violation of proper manners.

Louis understood such theatricality as part of his duty as sovereign, a duty that he took with utmost seriousness. Though far from brilliant, he was hard-working and conscientious. Whether or not he actually remarked *"L'état, c'est moi"* ("I am the state"), he clearly saw himself as serving the interests of the state. As such, he considered himself personally responsible for the well-being of his subjects. "The deference and the respect that we receive from our subjects," he wrote in a memoir he prepared for his son on the art of ruling, "are not a free gift from them but payment for the justice and the protection that they expect from us. Just as they must honor us, we must protect and defend them."

Administration and Centralization

Louis defined his responsibilities in absolutist terms: to concentrate royal power so as to produce domestic tranquillity. While coopting the nobility into his own theater of royalty, he conciliated the upper bourgeoisie by enlisting them as royal administrators and especially as intendants, responsible for administering the thirty-six *generalités* into which France was divided. Intendants usually served outside the region where they were born and were thus unconnected with the local elites over whom they exercised authority. They held office at the king's pleasure and were clearly his men. Other administrators, often from families newly ennobled as a reward for their service, assisted in directing affairs of state from Versailles. These men were not actors in the theater of Louis the Sun King; rather, they were the hardworking assistants of Louis the royal custodian of his country's welfare.

Louis's administrators devoted much of their time and energy to collecting the taxes necessary to finance the large standing army on which his aggressive and highly personal foreign policy depended. These personal elements of early modern absolutism are important to remark. Despite its pretensions to be a political theory, absolutism was fundamentally an approach to government by which ambitious monarchs could increase their own power through conquest and display. As such, it was enormously expensive. In addition to the *taille*, or land tax, which increased throughout the seventeenth century and on which a surtax was levied as well, Louis's government introduced a *capitation* (a head tax) and pressed successfully for the collection of indirect taxes on salt (the *gabelle*), wine, tobacco, and other goods. Because the nobility was exempt from the *taille*, its burden fell most heavily on the peasantry, whose local revolts Louis easily crushed.

Regional opposition was curtailed, but by no means eliminated, during Louis's reign. By removing the provincial nobility to Versailles, Louis cut them off from their local sources of power and influence. To put an end to the obstructive powers of regional parlements, Louis also decreed that members of any parlement that refused to approve and enforce his laws would be summarily exiled. He also crippled the authority of the provincial estates of Brittany, Languedoc, and Franche-Comté. The Estates-General, the national French representative assembly last summoned in 1614, did not meet at all during Louis's reign. It would not meet again until 1789.

> Despite its pretensions to be a political theory, absolutism was fundamentally an approach to government by which ambitious monarchs could increase their own power through conquest and display.

LOUIS XIV'S RELIGIOUS POLICIES

Both for reasons of state and of personal conscience, Louis was determined to impose religious unity on France, regardless of the economic and social costs this entailed. Louis believed firmly that God would favor him in return for such fidelity.

Although the vast majority of the French population was Roman Catholic, French Catholics were divided between Quietists, Jansenists, Jesuits, and Gallicans. Quietists preached retreat into personal mysticism, emphasizing a direct relationship between God and the individual human heart. Such doctrine, dispensing as it did with the intermediary services of the church, was suspect in the eyes of absolutists wedded to the doctrine of *un roi, une loi, une foi* ("one king, one law, one

faith"). Jansenism—a movement named for its founder Cornelius Jansen, a seventeenth-century bishop of Ypres—held to an Augustinian doctrine of predestination that could sound and look surprisingly like a kind of Catholic Calvinism. Louis vigorously persecuted Quietists and Jansenists, offering them the choice of recanting or of prison and exile. Instead, he supported the Jesuits in their efforts to create a Counter-Reformation Catholic Church in France. Louis's support for the Jesuits upset the traditional Gallican Catholics of France, however, who desired a French church independent of papal, Jesuit, and Spanish influence (which they tended to equate). As a result of this dissension among Catholics, the religious aura of Louis's kingship diminished during the course of his reign.

Against the Protestant Huguenots, however, Louis waged unrelenting war. Protestant churches and schools were destroyed, and Protestants were banned from many professions, including medicine and printing. In 1685, Louis revoked the Edict of Nantes, the legal foundation of the toleration Huguenots had enjoyed since 1598. Protestant clerics were exiled, laymen were sent to the galleys as slaves, and their children were forcibly baptized as Catholics. Many families converted, but 200,000 Protestant refugees fled to England, Holland, Germany, and America, bringing with them their professional and artisanal skills. This was an enormous loss to France. Among many other examples, the silk industries of Berlin and London were established by Huguenots fleeing Louis XIV's persecution.

COLBERT AND ROYAL FINANCE

Louis's drive to unify and centralize France depended on a vast increase in royal revenues engineered by Jean Baptiste Colbert, the king's finance minister from 1664 until his death in 1683. Colbert tightened the process of tax collection and eliminated wherever possible the practice of tax farming (which permitted collection agents to retain for themselves a percentage of the taxes they gathered for the king). When Colbert assumed office, only about 25 percent of the taxes collected throughout the kingdom reached the treasury. By the time he died, that figure had risen to 80 percent. Under Colbert's direction, the state sold public

MERCANTILISM AND WAR

Jean-Baptiste Colbert (1619–1683) served as Louis XIV's finance minister from 1664 until his death. He worked assiduously to promote commerce, build up French industry, and increase exports. However much Colbert himself may have seen his economic policies as ends in themselves, to Louis they were always means to the end of waging war. Ultimately, Louis's wars undermined the prosperity that Colbert tried so hard to create. This memorandum, written to Louis in 1670, illustrates clearly the mercantilist presumptions of self-sufficiency on which Colbert operated: every item needed to build up the French navy must ultimately be produced in France, even if it could be acquired at less cost from elsewhere.

And since Your Majesty has wanted to work diligently at reestablishing his naval forces, and since afore that it has been necessary to make very great expenditures, since all merchandise, munitions and manufactured items formerly came from Holland and the countries of the North, it has been absolutely necessary to be especially concerned with finding within the realm, or with establishing in it, everything which might be necessary for this great plan.

To this end, the manufacture of tar was established in Médoc, Auvergne, Dauphiné, and Provence; iron cannons, in Burgundy, Nivernois, Saintonge and Périgord; large anchors in Dauphiné, Nivernois, Brittany, and Rochefort; sailcloth for the Levant, in Dauphiné; coarse muslin, in Auvergne; all the implements for pilots and others, at Dieppe and La Rochelle; the cutting of wood suitable for vessels, in Burgundy, Dauphiné, Brittany, Normandy, Poitou, Saintonge, Provence, Guyenne, and the Pyrenees; masts, of a sort once unknown in this realm, have been found in Provence, Languedoc, Auvergne, Dauphiné, and in the Pyrenees. Iron, which was obtained from Sweden and Biscay, is currently manufactured in the realm. Fine hemp for ropes, which came from Prussia and from Piedmont, is currently obtained in Burgundy, Mâconnais, Bresse, Dauphiné; and markets for it have since been established in Berry and in Auvergne, which always provides money in these provinces and keeps it within the realm.

In a word, everything serving for the construction of vessels is currently established in the realm, so that Your Majesty can get along without foreigners for the navy and will even, in a short time, be able to supply them and gain their money in this fashion. And it is with this same objective of having everything necessary to provide abundantly for his navy and that of his subjects that he is working at the general reform of all the forests in his realm, which, being as carefully preserved as they are at present, will abundantly produce all the wood necessary for this.

Charles W. Cole, *Colbert and a Century of French Mercantilism*, 2 vols (New York, 1939), p. 320.

QUESTIONS FOR ANALYSIS

1. Could Colbert's economic policies have been used more wisely by Louis XIV? Can mercantilist policies be implemented without resorting to warfare? Is war a necessary component of mercantilism?

offices, including judgeships and mayoralities, and guilds purchased the right to enforce trade regulations. Colbert also tried to increase the nation's income by controlling and regulating its foreign trade. As a confirmed mercantilist (see "Mercantilism and War" on the previous page), Colbert believed that France's wealth would increase if its imports were reduced and its exports increased. He therefore imposed tariffs on foreign goods imported into France while using state money to promote the domestic manufacture of such formerly imported goods as silk, lace, tapestries, and glass. He was especially anxious to create domestic industries capable of producing all the goods France would need for war. To encourage domestic trade, he also improved France's roads, bridges, and waterways.

Despite Colbert's efforts to increase crown revenues, his policies ultimately foundered on the insatiable demands of Louis XIV's wars. Colbert himself foresaw this result when he lectured the king in 1680: "Trade is the source of public finance and public finance is the vital nerve of war. . . . I beg your Majesty to permit me only to say to him that in war as in peace he has never consulted the amount of money available in determining his expenditures." Louis, however, paid him no heed. As a result, by the end of Louis's reign, his aggressive foreign policy lay in ruins and his country's finances had been shattered by the unsustainable costs of war.

THE WARS OF LOUIS XIV TO 1697

Absolutism was never an end in itself for Louis. It was, rather, a means to an end: glory at home achieved through military victories abroad. From 1661, when Louis began his personal rule, until his death in 1715, Louis kept France on an almost constant war footing. His wars had two main objectives: to lessen the threat posed to France by the Habsburg powers that surrounded it in Spain, the Spanish Netherlands, and the Holy Roman Empire; and to promote the dynastic interests of his own family. Happily for Louis, these two objectives frequently coincided. In 1667–1668 he attacked the Spanish Netherlands, which he claimed on behalf of his wife, capturing the territory of Lille. In 1672, offended by the Dutch role in thwarting his earlier attacks on the Spanish Netherlands and by Dutch propaganda belittling him, Louis attacked Holland and its new leader William of Orange (1672–1702). The great-grandson of the sixteenth-century Protestant champion William the Silent, William of Orange would become the leading figure in Europe resisting Louis's wars of conquest.

The Dutch war ended in 1678–1679 with the Treaty of Nijmegen. Although Louis made little headway in the Low Countries, he did succeed in conquering and holding the eastern territory of Franche-Comté. Thus encouraged, he now turned his attentions eastward, capturing the free city of Strasbourg (1681), Luxembourg (1684), and Cologne (1688). He then pushed across the Rhine to pillage and burn the middle Rhineland, which he claimed on behalf of his unhappy sister-in-law, the daughter of the territory's ruler, the Elector Palatine.

In response to these new aggressions, William of Orange organized the League of Augsburg, which eventually united Holland, England, Spain, Sweden, Bavaria, Saxony, the Rhine Palatinate, and the Austrian Habsburgs against Louis. The resulting Nine Years' War (1689–1697) was extraordinarily destructive. Most of its campaigns were fought in the Low Countries, but the conflict extended from Ireland to India to North America (where it was known as King William's War). Finally, in 1697, the Peace of Ryswick compelled Louis to return most of France's recent gains, except for Strasbourg and its surrounding territory of Alsace. This treaty also recognized William of Orange as the new king of England, thus legitimizing the Glorious Revolution of 1688 that had replaced the Catholic King James II with the Protestant monarchs William and Mary.

THE WAR OF THE SPANISH SUCCESSION

The League of Augsburg reflected the emergence of a new diplomatic goal in western and central Europe: the preservation of a balance of power designed to prevent any single country, such as France, from becoming so powerful as to threaten the position of the other major powers within the European state system. This goal

CHRONOLOGY

THE SPANISH SUCCESSION

Philip IV	1621–1665
Charles II	1665–1700
Philip V (Philip of Anjou)	1700–1746
Louis XV (of France)	1715–1774

would animate European diplomacy for the next 200 years, until the entire balance-of-power system collapsed in 1914 with the outbreak of World War I. The main proponents of balance-of-power diplomacy were England, the United Provinces, Prussia, and Austria. A balance of power was not, however, a goal to which Louis XIV subscribed. Louis made peace in 1697 with the League of Augsburg because his country was exhausted by war and famine (almost a million people had died in the great French famine of 1693–1694, approximately 5 percent of the entire population). But he was also looking ahead to the real prize: a French claim to succeed to the throne of Spain and so to control the Spanish Empire in the New World, Italy, the Netherlands, and the Philippines.

Louis had married, as his first wife, the elder daughter of King Philip IV of Spain (1621–1665). Philip's younger daughter had married the Holy Roman emperor, Leopold I of Austria (1658–1705). Neither daughter was expected to inherit the Spanish throne. But Philip's only son, King Charles II of Spain (1665–1700), was a mental and physical invalid throughout his life. As it became clear during the 1690s that he would not live much longer, all the major European powers began to concern themselves with the succession to the Spanish throne. The stakes were high. If one of Leopold's sons succeeded, then France would be surrounded on all sides by a united Habsburg power. If Louis XIV's son or grandson succeeded, however, then France would become the preponderant power in Europe and the Americas.

Several schemes to resolve the crisis were floated during the 1690s. One would have given the Spanish succession to the six-year-old prince of Bavaria, a grandnephew of Charles II, but the boy died before the scheme could come to fruition. Another proposal was to give Spain's Italian possessions to Louis XIV and the rest of the Spanish Empire to Leopold; but Leopold blocked this, arguing that the Italian territories should belong to him anyway as Holy Roman emperor and acknowledging, at least tacitly, that Austria lacked the naval capacity to rule Spain's colonial territories in Asia and America.

King Charles II's advisers were not consulted on any of these plans. Their interests were to avoid partition altogether by passing the entire Spanish Empire to a single heir. To achieve this, they arranged for King Charles, in his will, to leave all his possessions to Louis XIV's younger grandson, Philip of Anjou, on two conditions: that Philip renounce his claim to the French throne in favor of his elder brother Louis (who had the first claim by inheritance anyway) and that he keep the Spanish Empire intact. The terms of this will were kept secret but were arranged in consultation with Louis XIV. As soon as Charles II died, Philip V (1700–1746) was therefore proclaimed the new king of Spain, and Louis XIV rushed French troops into the Spanish Netherlands. Louis also sent French merchants into Spanish America and withdrew recognition from William of Orange as king of England.

The resulting war pitted England, the United Provinces, Austria, and Prussia against France, Bavaria, and Spain. William of Orange died in 1702, just as the war began. His role as first general of the coalition passed to two brilliant strategists: the Englishman John Churchill, Duke of Marlborough, and Prince Eugene of Savoy, an upper-class Austrian soldier of fortune. Under their command the allied forces fought a series of fierce battles in the Low Countries and Germany, including an extraordinary march deep into Bavaria, where they inflicted a devastating defeat on the French and their Bavarian allies at Blenheim (1704), killing or capturing 30,000 of the 50,000 troops arrayed against them. Soon thereafter, the English navy captured Gibraltar and the island of Minorca, thus establishing a strategic and commercial foothold in the Mediterranean and opening a new military theater in Spain itself.

By 1709, France was on the verge of defeat. But the allies overreached themselves by demanding that Louis join their war against his own grandson in Spain. The war therefore continued, at enormous cost to both sides. At the battle of Malplaquet (1709), 80,000 French soldiers faced 110,000 allied troops. Marlborough and Eugene forced the French to retreat but suffered 24,000 casualties, twice those of the French. Louis's general wrote to him after the battle, "if God gives us the grace to lose another such battle, Your Majesty may count on his enemies being destroyed."

Queen Anne of England (Mary's sister and William's successor) gradually grew disillusioned with the war and dismissed Marlborough, her most competent general. English and Dutch merchants were also complaining loudly about the damage the war was doing to trade and commerce. A new Tory government in England

> The main proponents of balance-of-power diplomacy were England, the United Provinces, Prussia, and Austria. A balance of power was not, however, a goal to which Louis XIV subscribed.

CHAPTER 15 ABSOLUTISM AND EMPIRE, 1660–1789

replaced the Whigs and began sending out peace feelers to France. Meanwhile, the diplomatic situation in Europe was also changing. Leopold I of Austria had died in 1705. When his elder son and successor Joseph I died in 1711, the Austrian monarchy fell to Leopold's younger son, the archduke Charles, who had been the allies' candidate for the throne of Spain. With Charles VI (1711–1740) now the Austrian ruler and the Holy Roman emperor, the prospect of his accession to the Spanish throne threatened to upset the balance of power in Europe all over again.

THE TREATY OF UTRECHT

In 1713 the war finally came to an end with the Treaty of Utrecht. Its terms were reasonably fair to all sides. Philip V, Louis XIV's grandson, remained on the throne of Spain and retained Spain's colonial empire intact; but in return, Louis agreed that France and Spain would never be united under the same ruler. Austria gained territories in the Spanish Netherlands and Italy, including Milan and Naples. The Dutch were guaranteed protection of their borders against

EUROPE AFTER THE TREATY OF UTRECHT (1713)

To what extent did the balance of power within Europe change as a result of the Treaty of Utrecht? Given their geographic location and the extent after 1713, would you expect the Habsburg lands to dominate eighteenth-century Europe? Why or why not?

WHAT CHANGES LAY BEHIND THE GROWING POWER OF PRUSSIA?

THE REMAKING OF CENTRAL AND EASTERN EUROPE   553

The Treaty of Utrecht reshaped the balance of power in western Europe in fundamental ways. Spain's collapse was already precipitous; by 1713 it was complete. Spain would remain the "sick man of Europe" for the next two centuries. Holland's decline was more gradual, but by 1713 its greatest days were also over. The Dutch would continue to control the Spice Islands, but in the Atlantic world Britain and France were now the dominant powers. They would continue to duel for another half century for control over North America; but at Utrecht the balance of colonial power shifted decisively in Britain's favor. Within Europe, the myth of French military supremacy had been shattered. Britain's navy, not France's army, would rule the new imperial and commercial world of the eighteenth century.

THE REMAKING OF CENTRAL AND EASTERN EUROPE

> What changes lay behind the growing power of Prussia?

The decades between 1680 and 1720 were equally decisive in reshaping the balance of power in central and eastern Europe. As Ottoman power waned, the Austro-Hungarian Empire of the Habsburgs emerged as the dominant power in central and southeastern Europe. To the north, Brandenburg-Prussia was also a rising power. The most dramatic changes, however, were occurring in Russia, which would emerge from a long war with Sweden as the dominant power in the Baltic Sea and would soon become a mortal threat to the combined kingdom of Poland-Lithuania.

THE HABSBURG EMPIRE

In 1683, the Ottoman Turks launched their last assault on Vienna. Only the arrival of 70,000 Polish troops saved the Austrian capital from capture. Thereafter, however, Ottoman power in southeastern Europe declined rapidly. By 1699, Austria had reconquered most of Hungary from the Ottomans; by 1718, it controlled all of Hungary and also Transylvania and Serbia. In 1722, Austria acquired the territory of Silesia from Poland. With Hungary now a buffer state between Austria and the Ottomans, Vienna emerged as one of the great cultural and political capitals of eighteenth-century Europe, and

The Treaty of Utrecht, 1713. This illustration from a French royal almanac depicts the treaty that ended the war of Spanish Succession and reshaped the balance of power in western Europe in favor of Britain and France.

future invasions by France, but the French retained both Lille and Strasbourg. The biggest winner by far was Great Britain (as the combined kingdoms of England and Scotland were known after 1707), which kept Gibraltar and Minorca and also acquired large chunks of French territory in the New World, including Newfoundland, mainland Nova Scotia, the Hudson Bay, and the Caribbean island of St. Kitts. Even more valuable, however, Britain also extracted from Spain the right to transport and sell African slaves in Spanish America. As a result, the British were now poised to become the principal slave merchants and the dominant colonial and commercial power of the eighteenth-century world.

Austria became one of the arbiters of the European balance of power.

Although the Austrian Habsburgs retained their title as Holy Roman emperors and after 1713 also held lands in the Netherlands and Italy, their real power lay in Austria, Bohemia, Moravia, Galicia, and Hungary. These territories were geographically contiguous, but they were deeply divided by ethnicity, religion, and language. Despite the centralizing efforts of a series of Habsburg rulers, their empire would remain a rather loose confederation of highly disparate territories and possessions.

In Bohemia and Moravia, the Habsburgs encouraged landlords to produce crops for export by forcing peasants to provide three days of unpaid work service per week to their lords. In return, the landed elites of these territories permitted the emperors to reduce the political independence of their traditional legislative Estates. In Hungary, however, the powerful and independent nobility resisted such blandishments. Habsburg efforts to administer Hungary through the army and to impose Catholic religious uniformity also met with stiff resistance. As a result, Hungary would remain a semi-autonomous region within the empire whose support the Austrians could never take for granted.

After 1740, the empress Maria Theresa (1740–1780) and her son Joseph II (1765–1790; from 1765 until 1780 the two were co-rulers) pioneered a new style of "enlightened absolutism" within their empire: centralizing the administration in Vienna, increasing taxation, creating a professional standing army, and tightening their control over the church while creating a statewide system of primary education, relaxing censorship, and instituting a new, more liberal criminal code. But in practice, Habsburg absolutism, whether enlightened or not, was always limited by the diversity of its imperial territories and by the weakness of its local governmental institutions.

THE RISE OF BRANDENBURG-PRUSSIA

After the Ottoman collapse, the main threat to Austria came from the rising power of Brandenburg-Prussia. Like Austria, Prussia was a composite state made up of several geographically divided territories acquired

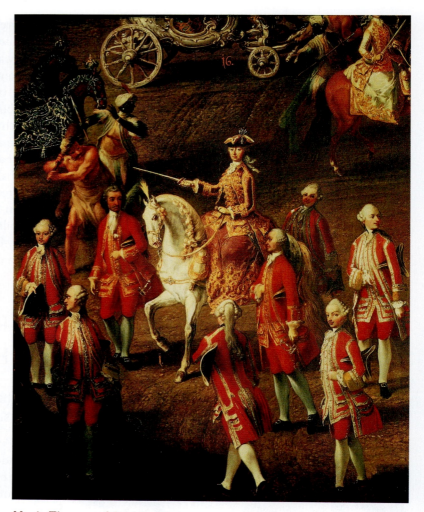

Maria Theresa of Austria. The empress was a formidable monarch and a match for Frederick the Great.

through inheritance by the Hohenzollern family. Their two main holdings, however, were Brandenburg, centered on its capital city, Berlin, and the duchy of East Prussia. Between these two territories lay Pomerania (claimed by Sweden) and an important part of the kingdom of Poland, including the port of Gdansk (Danzig). The Hohenzollerns' aim was to unite their state by acquiring these intervening territories. Over the course of more than a century of steady state building, they finally succeeded in doing so. In the process, Brandenburg-Prussia became the dominant military power of central Europe and a key player in the balance-of-power diplomacy of the mid-eighteenth century.

The foundations of Prussian greatness were laid by Frederick William, the "Great Elector" (1640–1688). By siding with Poland in a war against Sweden in the late 1650s, he obtained the Polish king's surrender of nominal overlordship of East Prussia. By some crafty diplomatic shuffling during the 1670s, he also protected his western provinces from French attack by returning Pomerania, captured in a recent war, to France's Swedish ally. Behind these diplomatic triumphs, however, lay the Elector's success in building an army and mobilizing the resources to pay for it. By granting to the powerful nobles of his territories (known as *Junkers*) the right to enserf their peasants, by relying on them to staff the officer corps of his army, and by guaranteeing their immunity from taxation, Frederick William gained their support for the effective and highly autocratic taxation system he imposed on the rest of the country. Secure in their control over their own estates and increasingly wealthy from the profits of their grain trade with western Europe, the Junkers were content to surrender management of the Prussian state to a centralized bureaucracy whose most important duty was to increase the size and strength of the Prussian army. In turn, the army became the Great Elector's most important instrument in tightening his own control over the far-flung territories he ruled.

By supporting Austria in the War of the Spanish Succession, the Great Elector's son, Frederick I (1688–1713), received the right to style himself king of Prussia. (As Holy Roman emperor, the Austrian monarch had the right to create kings.) And by joining the Great Northern War on the side of Russia against Sweden (discussed later in this chapter), Frederick paved the way for Prussia to recover and extend its control over Pomerania. As king, however, his main attention was devoted to developing the cultural life of his new royal capital, Berlin, along the lines laid down by Louis XIV of France.

Frederick William I (1713–1740) returned to the policies of his grandfather. His overriding concern was to build a first-rate army; so single-mindedly did he pursue this goal that he came to be called "the sergeant king." During his reign, the Prussian army grew from 30,000 to 83,000 men, the fourth largest army in Europe after those of France, Russia, and Austria. He also increased the size of the Prussian army in another way by creating a private regiment, the Potsdam Giants, composed exclusively of soldiers over six feet in height. To support his army, Frederick William I increased taxes and streamlined their collection, while shunning the expensive luxuries of court life. So reluctant was he

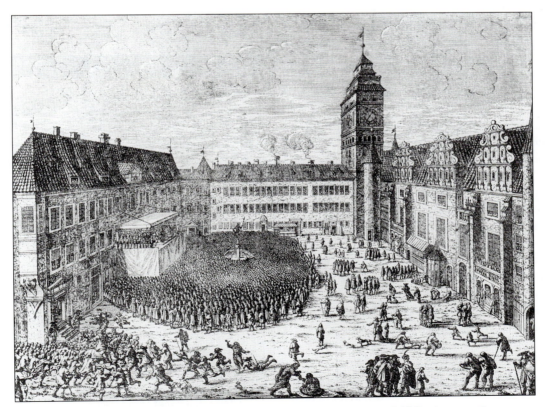

Prussians Swearing Allegiance to the Great Elector at Königsberg, 1663. The occasion on which the Prussian estates first acknowledged the overlordship of their ruler. This ceremony marked the beginning of the centralization of the Prussian state.

ABSOLUTISM AND EMPIRE, 1660–1789

to waste state resources on personal indulgences that it was said he had to invite himself to a nobleman's table to enjoy a good meal. For him, the theater of absolutism was not the palace but the office, where he personally supervised his beloved army and the offices of state that sustained it.

A hard, unimaginative man, Frederick William I had little use for his son Frederick, whose passion was not the army but the flute and who admired French culture as much as his father disdained it. It is not surprising that young Frederick rebelled; in 1730, when he was eighteen, he ran away from court with a friend. Apprehended, the companions were returned to the king, who executed his son's friend before Frederick's eyes. The grisly lesson took. Although Frederick never gave up his love of music and literature, he thereafter bound himself to his royal duties, living in accordance with his own image of himself as "first servant of the state" and earning history's title of Frederick the Great.

> Although Frederick never gave up his love of music and literature, he thereafter bound himself to his royal duties, living in accordance with his own image of himself as "first servant of the state" and earning history's title of Frederick the Great.

Frederick William I had made Prussia a strong state. Frederick the Great (1740–1786) raised his country to the status of a major power. As soon as he became king in 1740, Frederick mobilized the army his father had never taken into battle and occupied the Austrian province of Silesia. Prussia had no conceivable claim to Silesia, but the territory was both rich and poorly defended, and so Frederick seized it with the support of France. The new Habsburg empress Maria Theresa counterattacked; but despite the support of both Britain and Hungary, she was unable to recover Silesia. Emboldened by this early success, Frederick spent the rest of his reign consolidating his gains in Silesia and extending his control over the Polish territories that lay between Prussia and Brandenburg. Through relentless diplomacy and frequent war, Frederick succeeded by 1786 in transforming Prussia into a powerful, contiguous territorial kingdom.

To ensure a united domestic front against Prussia's enemies, Frederick was careful to guarantee the support of the Junkers for his policies. His father had recruited civil servants according to merit rather than birth, but Frederick relied on the nobility to staff the army and his expanding administration. Remarkably, Frederick's strategy worked. His nobility remained loyal, while Frederick fashioned the most highly professional and efficient bureaucracy in Europe.

Frederick showed the same concern for Junker sensibilities in his domestic policies. Like his contemporary Joseph II of Austria, Frederick was an enlightened absolutist who supervised a series of social reforms, prohibited the judicial torture of accused criminals and the bribing of judges, and established a system of elementary schools. Although strongly anti-Semitic, he encouraged religious toleration toward Christians and even declared that he would happily build a mosque in Berlin if he could find enough Muslims to fill it. On his own royal estates he abolished capital punishment, curtailed the forced labor services of his peasantry, and granted them long leases on the land they worked. He also fostered scientific forestry and the cultivation of new crops. He cleared new lands in Silesia and brought in thousands of immigrants to cultivate them. When wars ruined their farms, he supplied his peasants with new livestock and tools. But he never attempted to extend these reforms to the estates of the nobility. To have done so would have alienated the very group on whom Frederick's rule depended.

CHRONOLOGY

ABSOLUTIST RULERS IN CENTRAL EUROPE

France	
Louis XIV	1643–1715
Louis XV	1715–1774
Louis XVI	1774–1792
Brandenburg-Prussia	
Frederick William, The Great Elector	1640–1688
Frederick I	1688–1713
Frederick William I	1713–1740
Frederick the Great	1740–1786
Austria	
Leopold I	1658–1705
Charles VI	1711–1740
Maria Theresa	1740–1780
Joseph II	1765–1790
Russia	
Peter the Great	1689–1725
Catherine the Great	1762–1796

Autocracy in Russia

> In what ways did Russian absolutism differ from its western European counterparts?

An even more dramatic transformation took place in Russia under the dynamic rule of Tsar Peter I (1672–1725). Peter's accomplishments alone would have earned him his title of "Great." But his imposing height—he was six feet eight inches tall—as well as his mercurial personality—jesting one moment, raging the next—certainly added to the outsize impression he made on his contemporaries. Peter was not the first tsar to bring his country into contact with western Europe, but his policies were decisive in making Russia a great European power.

The Early Years of Peter's Reign

Since 1613 Russia had been ruled by members of the Romanov Dynasty, who had attempted with some success to restore political stability after the chaotic "time of troubles" that followed the death of the bloodthirsty, half-mad tsar Ivan the Terrible in 1584. But the Romanovs faced a severe threat to their rule between 1667 and 1671, when a Cossack leader (the Russian Cossacks were semi-autonomous bands of peasant cavalrymen) named Stenka Razin led a rebellion in southeastern Russia. This uprising found widespread support, not only from oppressed serfs but also from non-Russian tribes in the lower Volga region who longed to cast off the domination of Moscow. But ultimately Tsar Alexis I (1654–1676) and the Russian nobility were able to defeat Razin's zealous but disorganized bands of rebels, slaughtering more than 100,000 of them in the process.

Like Louis XIV of France, Peter came to the throne as a young boy, and his minority was marked by political dissension and court intrigue. In 1689, however, at the age of seventeen, he overthrew the regency of his half-sister Sophia and assumed personal control of the state. Determined to make Russia into a great military power, the young tsar traveled to Holland and England during the 1690s to study shipbuilding and to recruit skilled foreign workers to help him build a navy. While he was abroad, however, his elite palace guard (the *streltsy*) rebelled, attempting to restore Sophia to the throne. Peter quickly returned home from Vienna and crushed the rebellion with striking savagery. About 1,200 suspected conspirators were summarily executed, many of them gibbeted outside the walls of the Kremlin, where their bodies rotted for months as a graphic reminder of the fate awaiting those who dared challenge the tsar's authority.

The Transformation of the Tsarist State

Peter is most famous as the tsar who attempted to westernize Russia by imposing a series of social and cultural reforms on the traditional Russian nobility: ordering noblemen to cut off their long beards and flowing sleeves; publishing a book of manners that forbade spitting on the floor and eating with one's fingers; encouraging polite conversation between the sexes; and requiring noblewomen to appear, together with men, in Western garb at weddings, banquets, and other public occasions. The children of Russian nobles were sent to western European courts for their education. Thousands of western European experts were brought to Russia to staff the new schools and academies Peter

Peter the Great. As tsar, Peter I westernized Russia with social and cultural reforms, among them the mandate that traditional nobles cut off their long beards.

ABSOLUTISM AND EMPIRE, 1660–1789

built; to design the new buildings he constructed; and to serve in the tsar's army, navy, and administration.

These measures were important, but it is misleading to see them as driven by the tsar's desire to modernize or westernize Russia. Peter's policies transformed Russian life in fundamental ways, but his real goal was to make Russia a great military power, not to remake Russian society. His new taxation system (1724), for example, which assessed taxes on individuals rather than on households, rendered many of the traditional divisions of Russian peasant society obsolete. It was created, however, to raise more money for war. His Table of Ranks, imposed in 1722, had a similar impact on the nobility. By insisting that all nobles must work their way up from the (lower) landlord class to the (higher) administrative class and to the (highest) military class, Peter reversed the traditional hierarchy of Russian noble society, which had valued landlords by birth above administrators and soldiers who had risen by merit. But he also created a powerful new incentive to lure his nobility into administrative and military service to the tsar.

As autocrat of all the Russias, Peter the Great was the absolute master of his empire to a degree unmatched elsewhere in Europe. After 1649, Russian peasants were legally the property of their landlords; by 1750, half were serfs and the other half were state peasants who lived on lands owned by the tsar himself. State peasants could be conscripted to serve as soldiers in the tsar's army, workers in his factories (whose productive capacity increased enormously during Peter's reign), or as forced laborers in his building projects. But serfs too could be taxed by the tsar and summoned for military service, as could their lords. All Russians, of whatever rank, were thus expected to serve the tsar, and all Russia was considered in some sense to belong to him.

To further consolidate his power, Peter replaced the Duma—the nation's rudimentary national assembly—with a hand-picked senate, a group of nine administrators who supervised military and civilian affairs. In religious matters, he took direct control over the Russian Orthodox church by appointing an imperial official to manage its affairs. To cope with the demands of war, he also fashioned a new, larger, and more efficient administration, for which he recruited both nobles and nonnobles. But rank in the new bureaucracy did not depend on birth. One of his principal advisers, Alexander Menshikov, began his career as a cook and finished as a prince. This degree of social mobility would have been impossible in any contemporary western European country. Instead, noble status depended on governmental service, with all nobles expected to participate in Peter's army or administration. Peter was not entirely successful in enforcing this requirement, but the administrative machinery he devised furnished Russia with its ruling class for the next 200 years.

> By insisting that all nobles must work their way up from the (lower) landlord class to the (higher) administrative class and to the (highest) military class, Peter reversed the traditional hierarchy of Russian noble society, which had valued landlords by birth above administrators and soldiers who had risen by merit.

PETER'S FOREIGN POLICY

The goal of Peter's foreign policy was to secure year-round ports for Russia on the Black Sea and the Baltic Sea. In the Black Sea, his enemy was the Ottomans. Here, however, he had little success; although he captured the port of Azov in 1696, he was forced to return it in 1711. Russia would not secure its position in the Black Sea until the end of the eighteenth century. In the north, however, Peter achieved much more. In 1700, he began what would become a twenty-one-year war with Sweden, hitherto the dominant power in the Baltic Sea. By 1703, Peter had secured a foothold on the Gulf of Finland and immediately began to build a new capital city there, which he named St. Petersburg. After 1709, when Russian armies, supported by Prussia, decisively defeated the Swedes at the battle of Poltava, work on Peter's new capital city accelerated. An army of serfs was now conscripted to build the new city, whose centerpiece was a royal palace designed to imitate and rival Louis XIV's Versailles.

The Great Northern War with Sweden ended in 1721 with the Peace of Nystad. This treaty marks a realignment of power in eastern Europe comparable to that effected by the Treaty of Utrecht in the west. Sweden lost its North Sea territories to Hanover and its Baltic German territories to Prussia. Its eastern territories, including the entire Gulf of Finland, Livonia, and Estonia, passed to Russia. Sweden was now a second-rank power in the northern European world. Poland-Lithuania survived but faced the expanding power of Prussia in the west and the expanding power of Russia in the east. It too was a declining power; by

IN WHAT WAYS DID RUSSIAN ABSOLUTISM DIFFER FROM ITS WESTERN EUROPEAN COUNTERPARTS?

AUTOCRACY IN RUSSIA 559

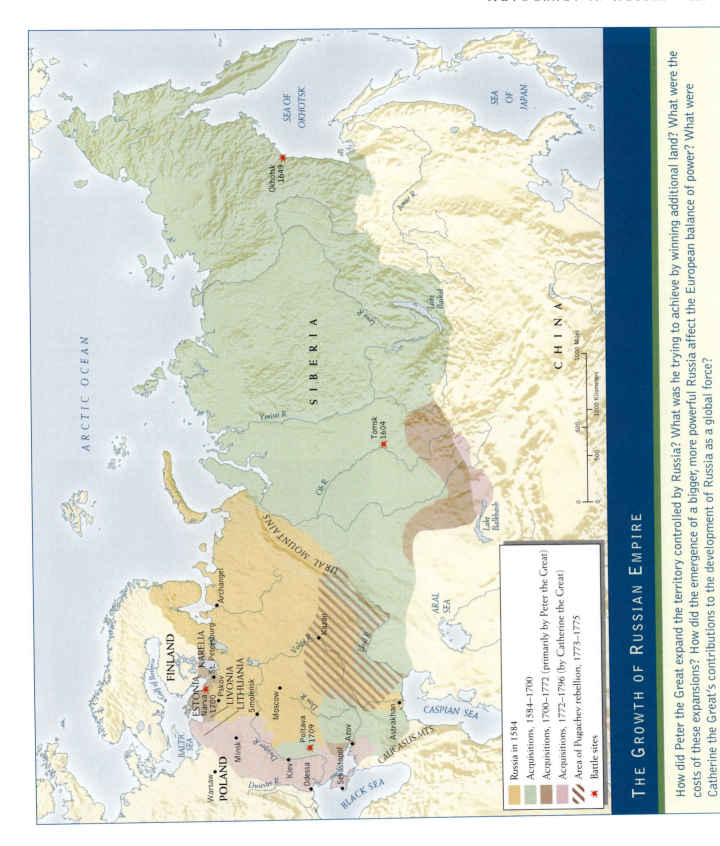

The Growth of Russian Empire

How did Peter the Great expand the territory controlled by Russia? What was he trying to achieve by winning additional land? What were the costs of these expansions? How did the emergence of a bigger, more powerful Russia affect the European balance of power? What were Catherine the Great's contributions to the development of Russia as a global force?

the end of the eighteenth century, the kingdom would disappear altogether, its territories swallowed up by its more powerful neighbors. The victors at Nystad were the Prussians and the Russians, both of whom secured their position along the Baltic coast and so positioned themselves to take advantage of the lucrative eastern European grain trade with western Europe.

Peter's victory had come at enormous cost. Direct taxation increased 500 percent during his reign, and his army in the 1720s numbered more than 300,000 men. Peter had made Russia a force to be reckoned with on the European scene; but in so doing, he had also aroused great resentment, especially among his nobility. Peter's only son and heir, Alexis, became the focus for conspiracies against the tsar, until finally Peter had him arrested and executed in 1718. As a result, when Peter died in 1725, he left no son to succeed him. A series of ineffective tsars followed, mostly creatures of the palace guard, under whom the resentful nobles reversed many of Peter the Great's reforms. In 1762, however, the crown passed to Catherine the Great, a ruler whose ambitions and determination were equal to those of her great predecessor.

Catherine the Great and the Partition of Poland

Catherine was a German who came to the throne in 1762 on the death of her husband, the weak (and possibly mad) Tsar Peter III, who was deposed and executed in a palace coup that Catherine herself may have helped arrange. Although she cultivated an image of herself as an enlightened ruler (she corresponded with French philosophers, wrote plays, and began to compose a history of Russia), Catherine was determined not to lose the support of the nobility who had placed her on the throne. As a result, her efforts at social reform did not extend much beyond the founding of hospitals and orphanages and the creation of an elementary school system for the children of the provincial nobility. Like her contemporary enlightened absolutists Joseph of Austria and Frederick the Great of Prussia, she too summoned a commission, in 1767, to codify and revise Russian law. But few of its radical proposals (which included the abolition of capital punishment, an end to judicial torture, and prohibitions on the selling of serfs) were ever implemented. Any possibility such measures might have been enforced ended in 1773–1775, when a massive peasant revolt led by a Cossack named Emelyan Pugachev briefly threatened Moscow itself. Catherine responded to the uprising by further centralizing her own government and by tightening aristocratic control over the peasantry.

Catherine's greatest achievements were gained through war and diplomacy. In 1769, she renewed Peter the Great's push to secure a warm-water port on the Black Sea. In the resulting war with the Ottoman Turks (which ended in 1774), Russia won control over the northern coast of the Black Sea, secured the independence of Crimea (which Russia would annex in 1783), and obtained safe passage for Russian ships through the Bosporus and into the Mediterranean Sea. In the course of this campaign, Russia also won control over several Ottoman provinces along the Danube River.

Russia's gains in the Balkans alarmed Austria, however, which now found itself with the powerful Russian Empire on its southern doorstep. Prussia too was threatening to become involved in the war as an ally of the Ottomans. Frederick the Great's real interests, however, lay much closer to home. To preserve the peace among Russia, Prussia, and Austria, he proposed instead a partition of Poland. Russia would abandon its Danubian conquests and, in return, would acquire the grain fields of eastern Poland, along with a population of 1 to

Catherine the Great.

Dividing the Royal Spoils. A contemporary cartoon showing the monarchs of Europe at work carving up a hapless Poland.

2 million Poles. Austria would take Galicia, acquiring 2.5 million Poles. Prussia, meanwhile, would take the coastal regions of Poland, including the port of Gdansk (Danzig), that separated Brandenburg and Pomerania from East Prussia. As a result of this agreement, finalized in 1772, Poland lost about 30 percent of its territory and about half of its population.

Poland was now paying the price for its political conservatism. Alone among the major central European powers, the Polish nobility had successfully opposed any move toward monarchical centralization as a threat to its liberties, among which was the right of every individual noble to veto any measure proposed in the Polish representative assembly, the Diet. To make matters worse, Polish aristocrats were also quite prepared to accept bribes from foreign powers in return for their vote in elections for the Polish king. In 1764, Catherine the Great had intervened in this way to secure the election of one of her former lovers, Stanislaus Poniatowski, as the new king of Poland. In 1772, King Stanislaus reluctantly accepted the partition of his country because he was too weak to resist it.

In 1788, however, he took advantage of a new Russo-Turkish war to try to strengthen his control over what remained of his kingdom. In May 1791 a new constitution was adopted that established a much stronger monarchy than had previously existed. But it was too late. In January 1792 the Russo-Turkish war ended, and Catherine the Great pounced. Together the Russians and Prussians took two more enormous bites out of Poland in 1793, destroying the new constitution in the process. A final swallow by Russia, Austria, and Prussia in 1795 left nothing of Poland or Lithuania at all.

Commerce and Consumption

> What factors facilitated the commercial revolution?

Despite the increased military power of Russia, Prussia, and Austria, the balance of power within Europe was shifting steadily toward the west during the eighteenth century. The North Atlantic economies in particular were growing more rapidly than those anywhere else in Europe. As a result, France and Britain were becoming preponderant powers both in Europe and the wider world.

Economic Growth in Eighteenth-Century Europe

The reasons for this rapid economic and demographic growth in northwestern Europe are complex and continue to be disputed by historians. In Britain and Holland, new, more intensive agricultural systems were producing more food per acre than ever before. Combined with improved transportation systems, the new farming methods resulted in fewer famines and a better-nourished population. New crops, especially maize and potatoes (both introduced to Europe from the Americas), also helped increase the supply of food available to feed Europe's growing population. But although famines became less common and less widespread, infectious disease continued to kill half of all Europeans before they reached the age of twenty. Even here, however, some progress was being made. Plague in particular was ceasing to be a major killer, as a

ABSOLUTISM AND EMPIRE, 1660–1789

degree of immunity (perhaps the result of a genetic mutation) began to emerge within the European population. Together with a better diet, improved sanitation may also have played some role in reducing the infection rates from such killers as typhoid, cholera, smallpox, and measles.

Northwestern Europe was also becoming increasingly urbanized. Across Europe as a whole the total number of urban dwellers did not change markedly between 1600 and 1800. At both dates, approximately 200 cities in Europe had a population of over 10,000. What did change was, first, the fact that these cities were increasingly concentrated in northern and western Europe and, second, the extraordinary growth of the very largest cities. Patterns of trade and commerce had much to do with these shifts. Cities such as Hamburg in Germany, Liverpool in England, Toulon in France, and Cadíz in Spain grew by about 250 percent between 1600 and 1750. Amsterdam, the hub of early modern international commerce, increased from 30,000 in 1530 to 115,000 in 1630 and 200,000 by 1800. Naples, the busy Mediterranean port, went from a population of 300,000 in 1600 to nearly half a million by the late eighteenth century. But even more spectacular population growth occurred in the administrative capitals of Europe. London grew from 674,000 in 1700 to 860,000 a century later. Paris went from 180,000 people in 1600 to more than 500,000 in 1800. Berlin grew from a population of 6,500 in 1661 to 60,000 in 1721 to 140,000 in 1783, of whom approximately 65,000 were state employees or members of their families.

Increased food supplies were needed to feed these burgeoning cities; but to the rising prosperity of northwestern Europe as a whole, developments in trade and manufacturing contributed even more than did agriculture. Spurred by improvements in transportation—better roads and bridges, and new canals—entrepreneurs began to promote the production of textiles in the countryside by distributing ("putting out") wool and flax to rural workers who would card, spin, and weave it into cloth on a piece-rate basis. The entrepreneur would then collect and sell the finished cloth in a market that now extended from local towns to international exporters. For country dwellers, this system (sometimes called *protoindustrialization*) provided welcome employment during otherwise slack seasons of the agricultural year. For the merchant-entrepreneurs

> Increased food supplies were needed to feed these burgeoning cities, but to the rising prosperity of northwestern Europe as a whole, developments in trade and manufacuring contributed even more than did agriculture.

who administered it, the system allowed them to avoid expensive guild restrictions in the towns and to reduce their levels of capital investment, thus reducing their overall costs of production. Urban cloth workers suffered, but the system led nonetheless to markedly increased employment and to much higher levels of industrial production, not only for textiles but also for iron, metalworking, and even toy and clock making.

Despite rural protoindustrialization, the role of cities as manufacturing centers continued to grow during the eighteenth century. In northern France, many of the million or so men and women employed in the textile trade lived and worked in cities such as Amiens, Lille, and Rheims. The rulers of Prussia made it their policy to develop Berlin as a manufacturing center, taking advantage of an influx of French Protestants to establishing a silk-weaving industry there and constructing canals to link the city with Breslau and Hamburg. Most urban manufacturing continued to be carried out in small shops employing anywhere from five to twenty journeymen working under the supervision of a master. But the scale of such enterprise was growing and also becoming more specialized, as workshops began to group together to form a single manufacturing district in which several thousand workers might be employed to produce the same product.

Techniques in some crafts remained much as they had been for centuries. In others, however, inventions changed the pattern of work as well as the nature of the product. Knitting frames, simple devices to speed the manufacture of textile goods, made their appearance in Britain and Holland. Wire-drawing machines and slitting mills, the latter enabling nail makers to convert iron bars into rods, spread from Germany into Britain. Techniques for printing colored designs directly on calico cloth were imported from Asia. New and more efficient printing presses appeared, first in Holland and then elsewhere. The Dutch even invented a machine called a "camel," with which the hulls of ships could be raised in the water so that they could be more easily repaired.

Workers did not readily accept innovations of this kind. Labor-saving machines threw people out of work. Artisans, especially those organized into guilds, were by nature conservative, anxious to protect not only their rights but also their "mysteries," the secrets of their trade. Often, therefore, governments would

WHAT FACTORS FACILITATED THE COMMERCIAL REVOLUTION?

COMMERCE AND CONSUMPTION

POPULATION GROWTH C. 1600

Why did the population of northwestern Europe grow more rapidly? What was the impact of urbanization? How did it affect patterns of life and trade? Why were the largest gains in population on the coasts? How did the expansion of trade and innovations in transportation affect ordinary people in these new urban centers?

intervene to block the widespread use of machines if they threatened to increase unemployment or in some other way to create unrest. The Dutch and some German states, for example, prohibited the use of what was described as a "devilish invention," a ribbon loom capable of weaving sixteen or more ribbons at the same time. But states might also intervene to protect the interests of their powerful commercial and financial backers. On behalf of domestic textile manufacturers and importers of Indian goods, both Britain and France outlawed calico printing for a time. Mercantilist doctrines could also impede innovation. In both Paris and Lyons, for example, the use of indigo dyes was banned because they were manufactured abroad. But

Topsy-Turvy World, **by Jan Steen.** This Dutch painting depicts a household in the throes of the exploding consumer economy that hit Europe in the eighteenth century. Consumer goods ranging from silver and china to clothing and furniture cluttered the houses of ordinary people as never before.

the pressures for economic innovation were irresistable, because behind them lay an insatiable eighteenth-century appetite for goods.

A World of Goods

In the eighteenth century, for the first time, a mass market for consumer goods emerged in Europe, and especially in northwestern Europe. Houses became larger, particularly in towns; but even more strikingly, the houses of relatively ordinary people were starting to be crammed with hitherto uncommon luxuries such as sugar, tobacco, tea, coffee, chocolate, newspapers, books, pictures, clocks, toys, china, glassware, pewter, silver plate, soap, razors, furniture (including beds with mattresses, chairs, and chests of drawers), shoes, cotton cloth, and spare clothing. Demand for such products consistently outstripped the supply, causing prices for these items to rise faster than the price of foodstuffs throughout the century. But the demand for them continued unabated. Such goods were indulgences, of course, but they were also repositories of value in which families could invest their surplus cash, knowing that they could pawn them in hard times if cash were needed.

The exploding consumer economy of the eighteenth century spurred demand for manufactured goods of all sorts. But it also encouraged the provision of services. In eighteenth-century Britain, the service sector was the fastest-growing part of the economy, outstripping both agriculture and manufacturing. Almost everywhere in urban Europe, the eighteenth century was the golden age of the small shopkeeper. People bought more prepared foods and more ready-made (as opposed to personally tailored) clothing. Advertising became an important part of doing business, helping create demand for new products and shaping popular taste for changing fashions. Even political allegiances could be expressed through consumption when people purchased plates and glasses commemorating favorite rulers or causes.

The result of all these developments was a European economy vastly more complex, more specialized, more integrated, more commercialized, and more productive than anything the world had seen before.

Colonization and Trade in the Seventeenth Century

> How did the patterns of European colonial settlement in the Americas differ from each other?

Many of the new consumer goods that propelled the economy of eighteenth-century Europe, including such staples as sugar, tobacco, tea, coffee, chocolate, china, and cotton cloth, were the products of Europe's colonial empires in Asia, Africa, and the Americas. Europe's growing wealth was not simply the result of its colonial possessions, but it is impossible to imagine this prosperity without them. We need, therefore, to examine these European empires and the developing role they played in the economy of the eighteenth-century world. To do so, however, we need to begin by looking at the patterns of seventeenth-century European colonialism.

SPANISH COLONIALISM

After the exploits of the conquistadors, the Spanish established colonial governments in Peru and in Mexico, which they controlled from Madrid. In keeping with the doctrines of mercantilism, the Spanish government allowed only Spanish merchants to trade with their American colonies, requiring all colonial exports and imports to pass through a single Spanish port (first Seville, then later the more navigable port of Cadíz), where they were registered at the government-operated customs house. During the sixteenth century, this system worked reasonably well. The Spanish colonial economy was dominated by mining; the lucrative market for silver in East Asia even made it profitable to establish an outpost in Manila, where Spanish merchants exchanged Asian silk for South American bullion. But Spain also took steps to promote farming and ranching in Central and South America and established settlements in Florida and California.

The wealth of Spain's colonial trade tempted the merchants of other countries to win a share of the treasure for themselves. Probably the boldest challengers were the English, whose leading buccaneer was the sea dog Sir Francis Drake. Three times Drake raided the east and west coasts of Spanish America. In 1587 he attacked the Spanish fleet at its anchorage in Cadíz harbor; and in 1588 he played a key role in defeating the Spanish Armada. His career illustrates the mixture of piracy and patriotism that characterized England's early efforts to break into the colonial trade. Until the 1650s, however, the English could only dent the lucrative Spanish trade in bullion, hides, silks, and slaves.

ENGLISH COLONIALISM

England's own American colonies had no significant mineral wealth. As a result, English colonists sought profits by establishing agricultural settlements in North America and the Caribbean basin. Their first permanent, though ultimately unsuccessful, colony was founded in 1607 at Jamestown, Virginia. Over the next forty years, 80,000 English emigrants would sail to more than twenty autonomous settlements in the New World. Many of these early settlers were driven by religious motives. The Pilgrims who landed at Plymouth, Massachusetts, in 1620 were one of many dissident groups, both Protestant and Catholic, that sought to escape the English government's attempt to impose religious conformity by emigrating to North America. Strikingly, however, English colonists showed little interest in trying to convert Native American peoples to Christianity. Missionizing played a much larger role in Spanish efforts to colonize Central and South America and French efforts to penetrate the North American hinterlands.

Most of these early English settlements were privately organized. As they began to prosper, however, the governments of both Oliver Cromwell and Charles II began to intervene in their management. Mercantilist-inspired navigation acts, passed in 1651 and 1660 and rigorously enforced thereafter, decreed that all exports from English colonies to the mother country be carried in English ships and forbade the direct exporting of certain "enumerated" products directly from the colonies to continental ports.

The most valuable of those colonial products were sugar and tobacco. Sugar, virtually unknown in Christian Europe during the Middle Ages, became a popular luxury item in the late fifteenth century, when Europeans began to produce it in their Mediterranean and African colonies. Only in the New World, however, did sugar production reach such volumes as to create a mass market for the product. By the middle of the seventeenth century, European demand for sugar had already reached enormous proportions. In the eighteenth century, the sugar England imported from its tiny West Indian colonies of Barbados and Jamaica was worth more than all of its imports from China and India combined.

Sugar, however, could be grown in only a fairly limited geographical and climatic area. Tobacco was much more adaptable. Although tobacco was first imported into Europe by the Spaniards in the mid-sixteenth century, another half century passed before Europeans took up the habit of smoking. At first the plant was believed to possess miraculous healing powers and was referred to as "divine tobacco" and "our holy herb nicotian." (The word *nicotine* derives from the name of the French ambassador to Portugal, Jean Nicot, who brought the tobacco plant to France.) The practice of smoking was first popularized by English explorers, especially by Sir Walter Raleigh, who had learned to smoke while living among the Indians of Virginia. Thereafter, it spread rapidly through all classes of European society. Governments at first joined the

> The Spanish colonial economy was dominated by mining; the lucrative market for silver in East Asia even made it profitable to establish an outpost in Manila, where Spanish merchants exchanged Asian silk for South American bullion.

15 ABSOLUTISM AND EMPIRE, 1660–1789

THE ATLANTIC WORLD

Why were European governments so concerned with closely controlling the means by which certain products traveled from the colonies to European ports? How and why did the financial institutions of the late medieval period thrive on and encourage the economic policies of colonial powers? Why are the trade routes carrying slaves so prominently marked on this map? What does this suggest about the importance of unfree labor to the economic achievements of Europeans in the New World?

church in condemning the use of tobacco, but by the end of the seventeenth century, having realized the profits to be made from it, they were actively encouraging its production and consumption.

FRENCH COLONIALISM

French colonial policy matured during the administration of Louis XIV's mercantilist finance minister, Jean Baptiste Colbert, who regarded overseas expansion as an integral part of state economic policy. To compete with the English, he encouraged the development of sugar-producing colonies in the West Indies, the largest of which was St. Domingue (present-day Haiti). France also dominated the interior of the North American continent, where French traders bought furs and missionaries preached Christianity to the Indians in a vast territory that stretched from Acadia to Quebec to Louisiana. Yet the financial returns from these lands were never commensurate with their size. Furs, fish, and tobacco were exported to European markets in large quantities but never matched the profits from the Caribbean sugar colonies or from the trading outposts the French maintained in India.

The Dutch East India Company Warehouse and Timber Wharf at Amsterdam. The substantial warehouse, the stockpiles of lumber, and the company ship under construction in the foreground illustrate the degree to which overseas commerce could stimulate the economy of the mother country.

DUTCH COLONIALISM

Until the 1670s, the Dutch controlled the most prosperous commercial empire of the seventeenth century. Although some Dutch settlements were established, including one at the Cape of Good Hope in modern-day South Africa, Dutch colonialism generally followed the "fort and factory" model established by the Portuguese in Asia. In Southeast Asia, the Dutch East India Company, founded in 1602, seized control of Sumatra, Borneo, and the Moluccas (Spice Islands), driving Portuguese traders from an area they had previously dominated and establishing a Dutch monopoly within Europe over pepper, cinnamon, nutmeg, mace, and cloves. The Dutch also secured an exclusive right to trade with Japan and maintained military and trading outposts in China and India as well. In the Western Hemisphere, however, their achievements were less spectacular. After a series of trade wars with England, in 1667 they formally surrendered their colony of New Amsterdam (subsequently renamed New York), retaining only Surinam (off the northern coast of South America) and Curaçao and Tobago (in the West Indies). Although they dominated the seventeenth-century slave trade with Africa, after 1713 the Dutch would lose this position also to the British.

As the primary financiers of seventeenth-century Europe, the Dutch also pioneered new mechanisms for investing in colonial enterprises. One of the most important of these was the joint-stock company, of which the Dutch East India Company was among the first. Such companies raised cash by selling shares in their enterprise to investors. Even though the investors might not take any role in managing the company, they were joint owners of the business and

> As the primary financiers of seventeenth-century Europe, the Dutch also pioneered new mechanisms for investing in colonial enterprises. One of the most important of these was the joint-stock company, of which the Dutch East India Company was among the first.

ABSOLUTISM AND EMPIRE, 1660–1789

therefore entitled to a share in its profits in proportion with the amount they had invested. Initially, the Dutch East India Company had intended to pay off its investors ten years after its founding, but the directors soon recognized the impossibility of this plan. By 1612, the company's assets—ships, wharves, warehouses, and cargoes—were scattered around the globe. Moreover, its commercial prospects were continuing to improve. The directors therefore urged investors anxious to realize their profits to sell their shares on the Amsterdam stock exchange to other investors, thereby ensuring the continued operation of their enterprise and, in the process, establishing a method of continuous business financing that would soon spread elsewhere in Europe.

CONTRASTING PATTERNS OF COLONIAL SETTLEMENT

Differences in the commercial relationships European countries established with their New World colonies reflected important differences in settlement patterns among these colonies. In Central and South America, a relatively small number of Spaniards had conquered complex, highly populous Native American societies. To rule these new territories, the Spanish quickly replaced native elites with Spanish administrators and churchmen. But by and large they did not attempt to uproot or eliminate existing native cultures. Instead, Spain focused its efforts on controlling and exploiting native labor, so as to extract the maximum possible profit for the crown from the colonies' mineral resources. The native peoples of Spanish America already lived, for the most part, in large, well-organized villages and towns. Spanish colonial policy was to collect tribute from such communities and to convert them to Catholicism but to do so without fundamentally disrupting their existing patterns of life.

The result was widespread cultural assimilation between the Spanish colonizers and the native populace, combined with a relatively high degree of intermarriage between them. Out of this reality emerged a complex and distinctive system of racial and social castes, with pure-blooded Spaniards at the top, peoples of mixed descent in the middle (native, Spanish, and African, in various combinations), and nontribal Indians at the bottom. In theory, these racial categories corresponded with class distinctions; but in practice race and class did not always coincide, and race itself was often a social fiction. Mixed-race individuals who prospered economically often found ways to establish

their "pure" Spanish ancestry by adopting the social practices that characterized elite (i.e., Spanish) status. Spaniards, however, always remained at the top of the social hierarchy, even when they fell into poverty.

Like the Spanish colonies, the French colonies were established and administered as direct crown enterprises. French colonial settlements were conceived mainly as military outposts and trading centers; as a result, they were overwhelmingly populated by men. The elite members of French colonial society were the military officers and administrators sent out from Paris. But below their ranks there was a broad community of interest between the fishermen, fur traders, small farmers, and common soldiers who constituted the bulk of the French settlers of North America. Except in the Caribbean, French colonies depended largely on the fur trade and on fishing; both enterprises relied in turn on cooperative relationships with native peoples. A mutual economic interdependence therefore grew up between these French colonies and the peoples of the surrounding region. Intermarriage, especially between French fur traders and native women, was common. But most French colonies in North America remained dependent on the wages and supplies sent to them from the mother country. Only rarely did they become truly self-sustaining economic enterprises.

The English colonies along the Atlantic seaboard followed a different model. English colonies did not begin as Crown enterprises. Instead they were established either by joint-stock companies (as in Virginia and the Massachusetts Bay colony) or as private, proprietary colonies (such as Maryland and Pennsylvania). Building on their experience in Ireland, English colonists established planned settlements known as plantations, in which they attempted to replicate as many features of English life as possible. Geography also contributed to the resulting concentration of English settlement patterns. The rivers and bays of eastern North America provided the first footholds for English colonists in the New World, and the Atlantic Ocean helped tie these separated settlements together. But aside from the Hudson, there were no great rivers to lead colonists very far inland. Instead, the English colonies clung to the seacoast, and so to each other.

Like the French colonies, the early English colonies relied on fishing and the fur trade for their exports. But primarily, English colonies were agricultural communities, populated by small- and medium-scale landholders for whom control over land was the key to wealth. Partly this was a reflection of the kinds of people whom these privately sponsored colonial enterprises could persuade to immigrate to the New World. But

How did the patterns of European colonial settlement in the Americas differ from each other?

Colonization and Trade in the Seventeenth Century

Illinois Indians Trading with French Settlers. This engraving from Nicholas De Fer's 1705 map of the Western Hemisphere illustrates the economic interdependence that developed between early French colonies and the native people of the surrounding region.

this focus on agriculture was also the result of the demographic catastrophe that had struck the native populations of the Atlantic seaboard during the last half of the sixteenth century. European diseases—brought by Spanish armies and by the French, English, and Portuguese fishermen who frequented the rich fishing banks off the New England coast—had already decimated the native peoples of eastern North America even before the first European colonists set foot there. By the early seventeenth century, a great deal of rich agricultural land had been abandoned simply because there were no longer enough native farmers to till it—one reason that many native groups initially welcomed the new arrivals.

Unlike the Spanish, English colonists along the Atlantic seaboard therefore had neither the need nor the opportunity to control a large native labor force. What they wanted, rather, was complete and exclusive control over native lands. To this end, the English colonists soon set out to eliminate, through expulsion and massacre, the indigenous peoples of their colonies. To be sure, there were exceptions. In the Quaker colony of Pennsylvania, colonists and Native Americans maintained friendly relations for more than half a century. In the Carolinas, by contrast, there was widespread enslavement of native people, either for sale to the West Indies or, from the 1690s, to work on the rice plantations along the coast. Elsewhere, however, attempts to enslave the native peoples of North America failed. When English planters looked for bond laborers, they therefore either recruited indentured servants from England (most of whom would be freed after a specified period of service) or else they purchased African captives (who would usually be enslaved for life).

Social relations between the English colonists and native peoples also differed from the patterns we find elsewhere in the New World. In contrast to the Spanish and French colonies, intermarriage between English colonists and natives was rare. Instead, a rigid racial division emerged that distinguished all Europeans, regardless of class, from all Native Americans and Africans. Intermarriage between natives and Africans was relatively common, but between the English and the indigenous peoples of their colonies an unbridgeable gulf soon developed.

> In contrast to the Spanish and French colonies, intermarriage between English colonists and natives was rare. Instead, a rigid racial division emerged that distinguished all Europeans, regardless of class, from all Native Americans and Africans.

COLONIAL RIVALRIES

The fortunes of these colonial empires changed dramatically in the course of the seventeenth and early eighteenth centuries. Spain, mired in persistent economic stagnation and embroiled in a series of expensive wars and domestic rebellions, proved unable to defend its monopoly over colonial trade. In a war with Spain in the 1650s, England captured not only the island of Jamaica but treasure ships lying off the Spanish harbor of Cadíz. Further profit was obtained by bribing Spanish customs officials on a grand scale. During the second half of the century, two thirds of the imported goods sold in Spanish colonies were smuggled in by Dutch, English, and French traders. By 1700, although Spain still possessed a colonial empire, that empire lay at the mercy of its more dynamic rivals. A brief revival of fortunes under more enlightened leadership in the mid-eighteenth century did nothing to prevent its ultimate eclipse.

Portugal, too, found it impossible to prevent foreign penetration of its colonial empire. England in particular worked diligently to win commercial advantages there. In 1703, the English signed a treaty with Portugal allowing English merchants to export woolens duty free into Portugal and allowing Portugal to ship its wines duty free into England. Increasing English trade with Portugal also led to English trade with the Portuguese colony of Brazil, an important sugar producer and the largest of all the New World markets for African slaves. In the eighteenth century, English merchants would dominate these Brazilian trade routes.

COLONIALISM AND EMPIRE

> In what ways did eighteenth-century European colonialism differ from seventeenth-century European colonialism?

The 1713 Treaty of Utrecht opened a new era in these colonial rivalries. As we have seen, the biggest losers in these negotiations were the Dutch, who gained only a guarantee of security for their own borders, and the Spanish, who were forced to concede to Britain the right to market slaves in the Spanish colonies. The winners were the British (who acquired large chunks of French territory in North America) and, to a lesser extent, the French, who retained Cape Breton Island, Quebec, the interior portions of North America, and their foothold in India. The eighteenth century would witness a continuing struggle between Britain and France for control over the expanding commerce that now bound the European economy to the Americas and to Asia.

The Defense of Cadíz against the English, by Francisco Zurbaran. The rivalry between European powers that played out over the new colonial possessions further proved the decline of Spain, which lost the island of Jamaica and ships in the harbor of Cadíz to the English in the 1650s.

THE TRIANGULAR TRADE IN SUGAR AND SLAVES

During the eighteenth century, European colonial trade came to be dominated by trans-Atlantic routes that developed in response to the lucrative West Indian sugar industry and to the demand for slaves from Africa to work those Caribbean plantations. In this "triangular" trade, naval superiority gave Britain a decisive

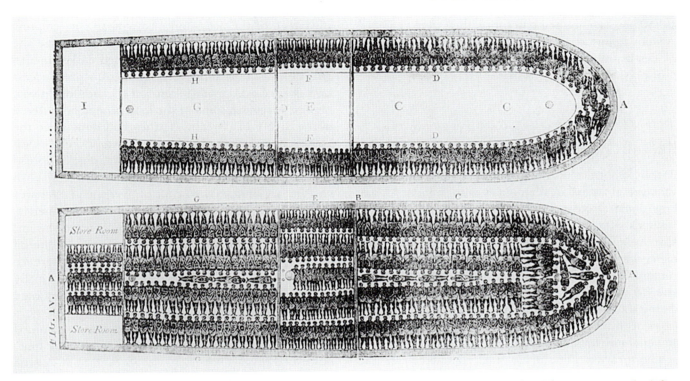

How Slaves Were Stowed aboard Ship during the Middle Passage. Men were "housed" on the right; women on the left; children in the middle. The human cargo was jammed onto platforms six feet wide without sufficient headroom to permit an adult to sit up. This diagram is from evidence gathered by English abolitionists and depicts conditions on the Liverpool slave ship *Brookes*.

advantage over its French, Spanish, Portuguese, and Dutch rivals. Typically, a British ship might begin its voyage from New England with a consignment of rum and sail to Africa, where the rum would be exchanged for a cargo of slaves. From the west coast of Africa the ship would then cross the South Atlantic to the sugar colonies of Jamaica or Barbados, where slaves would be traded for molasses. It would then make the final leg of the journey back to New England, where the molasses would be made into rum. A variant triangle might see cheap manufactured goods move from England to Africa, where they would be traded for slaves. Those slaves would then be shipped to Virginia and exchanged for tobacco, which would be shipped to England and processed there for sale throughout Europe.

The cultivation of New World sugar and tobacco depended on slave labor. As European demand for these products increased, so too did the traffic in enslaved Africans. At the height of the Atlantic slave trade in the eighteenth century, 75,000 to 90,000 Africans were shipped across the Atlantic yearly: at least 6 million in the eighteenth century, out of a total of over 11 million for the entire history of the trade. About 35 percent went to English and French Caribbean plantations; 5 percent (roughly 500,000) to North America; and the rest to the Portuguese colony of Brazil and to the Spanish colonies in Central and South America. By the 1780s, there were more than 500,000 slaves on the largest French plantation island, St. Domingue, and at least 200,000 on its English counterpart, Jamaica.

Although run as a monopoly by various governments in the sixteenth and early seventeenth centuries, the slave trade in the eighteenth century was open to private entrepreneurs who operated ports on the West African coast. These traders exchanged Indian cloth, metal goods, rum, and firearms with African slave merchants in return for their human cargo, who would then be packed by the hundreds into the holds of slave ships for the gruesome Middle Passage across the Atlantic (so called to distinguish it from the slave ship's voyage from Europe to Africa, and then from the colonies back to Europe). Shackled belowdecks without sanitary facilities, the captive men, women, and children suffered horribly. The mortality rate, however, remained at about 10 or 11 percent, not much higher than the rate for a normal sea voyage of 100 days or more. Since traders had to invest as much

CHAPTER 15

ABSOLUTISM AND EMPIRE, 1660–1789

as £10 per slave in their enterprise, they were generally anxious to ensure that their consignment would reach its destination in good enough shape to be sold for a profit.

THE COMMERCIAL RIVALRY BETWEEN BRITAIN AND FRANCE

British dominance of the slave trade gave it decisive advantages in its colonial struggles with France. As one Englishman wrote in 1749, the slave trade had provided "an unexhastible fund of wealth to this nation." But even apart from the slave trade, the value of colonial commerce was increasing dramatically during the eighteenth century. French colonial trade, valued at 25 million livres in 1716, rose to 263 million livres in 1789. In England, during roughly the same period, foreign trade increased in value from £10 million to £40 million, the latter amount more than twice that for France.

The growing value of colonial commerce tied the interests of governments and transoceanic merchants together in an increasingly tight embrace. Merchants engaged in the colonial trade depended on their governments to protect and defend their overseas investments; but governments depended in turn on merchants and their financial backers to build the ships and sustain the trade on which national power depended. In the eighteenth century, even the ability to wage war rested largely (and increasingly) on a government's ability to borrow the necessary funds from wealthy investors and then to pay back those debts, with interest, over time. As it did in commerce, so too in finance, Britain came to enjoy a decisive advantage in this respect over France. The Bank of England, founded in the 1690s, managed the English national debt with great success, providing the funds required for war by selling shares to investors, then repaying those investors at moderate rates of interest. In contrast, chronic governmental indebtedness forced the French crown to borrow at ruinously high rates of interest, provoking a series of fiscal crises that in 1789 finally led to the collapse of the French monarchy.

WAR AND EMPIRE IN THE EIGHTEENTH-CENTURY WORLD

After 1713, western Europe remained largely at peace for a generation. In 1740, however, that peace was shattered when Frederick the Great of Prussia took advantage of the accession of a woman, the empress Maria Theresa, to the throne of Austria to seize the Austrian province of Silesia (discussed earlier in this chapter). In the resulting War of the Austrian Succession, France and Spain fought on the side of Prussia, hoping to reverse some of the losses they had suffered in the Treaty of Utrecht. As they had done since the 1690s, Britain and the Dutch Republic sided with Austria. Like those earlier wars, this war quickly spread beyond the frontiers of Europe. In India, the English East India Company lost control over the coastal area of Madras to its French rival; but in North America, British colonists from New England captured the important French fortress of Louisbourg on Cape Breton Island, hoping to put a stop to French interference with their fishing and shipping. When the war finally ended in 1748, Britain recovered Madras and returned Louisbourg to France.

Eight years later, these colonial conflicts reignited when Prussia once again attacked Austria. This time, however, Prussia allied itself with Great Britain. Austria found support from both France and Russia. In Europe, the Seven Years' War (1756–1763) ended in stalemate. In India and North America, however, the war had decisive consequences. In India, mercenary troops employed by the British East India Company joined with native allies to elimate their French competitors. In North America (where the conflict was known as the French and Indian War), British troops captured both Louisbourg and Quebec and also drove French forces from the Ohio River Valley and the Great Lakes. By the Treaty of Paris in 1763, which brought the Seven Years' War to an end, France formally surrendered both Canada and India to the British. Six years later, the French East India Company was dissolved.

THE AMERICAN REVOLUTION

Along the Atlantic seaboard, however, the rapidly growing British colonies were beginning to chafe at rule from London. To recover some of the costs of the Seven Years' War and to pay for the continuing costs of protecting its colonial subjects, the British Parliament imposed a series of new taxes on its American colonies. These taxes were immediately unpopular. Colonists complained that because they had no representatives in Parliament, they were being taxed without their consent—a fundamental violation of their rights as British subjects. They also complained that British restrictions on colonial trade, particularly the requirement that certain goods pass first through British ports

HOW DID EIGHTEENTH- AND SEVENTEENTH-CENTURY COLONIALISM DIFFER?

COLONIALISM AND EMPIRE 573

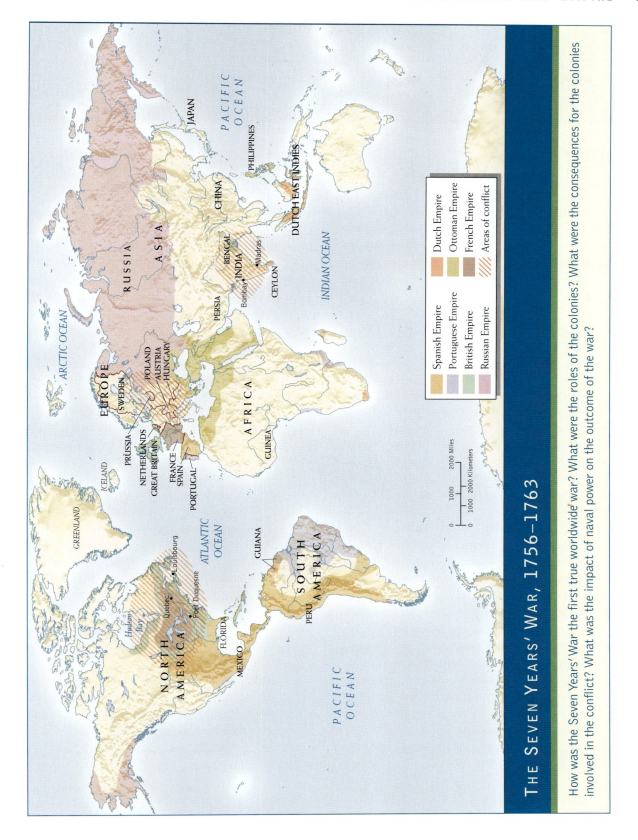

THE SEVEN YEARS' WAR, 1756–1763

How was the Seven Years' War the first true worldwide war? What were the roles of the colonies? What were the consequences for the colonies involved in the conflict? What was the impact of naval power on the outcome of the war?

THE AMERICAN DECLARATION OF INDEPENDENCE

The Declaration of Independence, issued from Philadelphia on July 4, 1776, is perhaps the most famous single document of American history. But its familiarity does not lesssen its interest as a piece of political philosophy. The indebtedness of the document's authors to the ideas of John Locke will be obvious from the selections here. But Locke, in turn, drew many of his ideas about the contractual and conditional nature of human government from the conciliarist thinkers of the fifteenth and early sixteenth centuries. The appeal of absolutism notwithstanding, the Declaration shows how vigorous the medieval tradition of contractual, limited government remained at the end of the eighteenth century.

When in the course of human events, it becomes necessary for one people to dissolve the political bonds which have connected them with another, and to assume among the powers of the earth the separate and equal station to which the Laws of Nature and of Nature's God entitle them, a decent respect to the opinions of mankind requires that they should declare the causes which impel them to the separation. . . . We hold these truths to be self-evident, that all men are created equal, that they are endowed by their Creator with certain unalienable rights, that among these are Life, Liberty and the pursuit of Happiness. . . . That to secure these rights, Governments are instituted among men, deriving their just powers from the consent of the governed. . . . That whenever any form of Government becomes destructive of these ends, it is the Right of the People to alter or to abolish it, and to institute new Government, laying its foundation upon such principles and organizing its power in such form, as to them shall seem most likely to effect their Safety and Happiness. Prudence, indeed, will dictate that Governments long established should not be changed for light and transient causes;

and accordingly all experience has shown, that mankind are more disposed to suffer, while evils are sufferable, than to right themselves by abolishing the forms to which they are accustomed. But when a long train of abuses and usurpations, pursuing invariably the same Object, evinces a design to reduce them under absolute despotism, it is their right, it is their duty, to throw off such Government, and to provide new Guards for their future security. . . . Such has been the patient sufferance of these Colonies; and such is now the necessity which constrains them to alter their former Systems of Government. . . .

QUESTIONS FOR ANALYSIS

1. In what way was the Declaration of Independence a document that could have been drafted by John Locke? Could the Declaration have been written in the seventeenth rather than the eighteenth century?
2. What is meant by the expression, "life, liberty, and the pursuit of happiness"?

before being transshipped to the Continent, were strangling American livelihoods and so making it impossible to pay even the king's legitimate taxes.

The British government, led since 1760 by the young and inexperienced King George III, responded to these complaints with a badly calculated mixture of vacillation and force. Various taxes were imposed and then withdrawn in the face of colonial resistance. In 1773, however, when East India Company tea was dumped in Boston Harbor by rebellious colonials objecting to the customs duties that had been imposed on it, the British government closed the port of Boston and curtailed the colony's representative institutions. These "Coercive Acts" galvanized the support of the other American colonies for Massachusetts. In 1774, representatives from all the American colonies met at Philadelphia to form the Continental Congress to negotiate with the Crown over their grievances. In April 1775, however, local militiamen at Lexington and Concord clashed with regular British troops sent to disarm them. Soon thereafter, the Continental Congress began raising an army, and an outright rebellion erupted against the British government.

On July 4, 1776, the thirteen colonies formally declared their independence from Great Britain. During the first two years of the war, it seemed unlikely that such independence would ever become a reality. In 1778, however, France, anxious to undermine the colonial hegemony Great Britain had established since 1713, joined the war on the side of the Americans. Spain entered the war in support of France, hoping to recover Gibraltar and Florida (the latter lost in 1763 to Britain). In 1780, Britain also declared war on the Dutch Republic for continuing to trade with the rebellious colonies. Now facing a coalition of its colonial rivals, Great Britain saw the war turn against it. In 1781, combined land and sea operations by French and American troops forced the surrender of the main British army at Yorktown in Virginia. As the defeated British soldiers surrendered their weapons, their band played a song titled "The World Turned Upside Down."

Negotiations for peace began soon after the defeat at Yorktown but were not concluded until September 1783. The Treaty of Paris left Great Britain in control of Canada and Gibraltar. Spain retained its possessions west of the Mississippi River and recovered Florida.

CHRONOLOGY

SEVENTEENTH- AND EIGHTEENTH-CENTURY WARS

Glorious Revolution	1688–1689
War of the League of Augsburg	1689–1697
War of the Spanish Succession	1702–1713
Seven Years' War	1756–1763
American Revolution	1775–1783
The Russo-Turkish War	1787–1792

The United States gained its independence; its western border was fixed on the Mississippi River, and it secured valuable fishing rights off the eastern coast of Canada. France gained only the satisfaction of defeating its colonial rival; but even that satisfaction was short lived. Six years later, the massive debts France had incurred in supporting the American Revolution helped bring about another, very different kind of revolution in France that would permanently alter the history of Europe.

CONCLUSION

Seen in this light, the American War of Independence was the final military conflict in a century-long struggle between Great Britain and France for colonial dominance. But the consequences of Britain's defeat in 1783 were far less significant than might have been expected. Even after American independence, Great Britain would remain the most important trading partner for its former American colonies, while elsewhere around the globe, the commercial dominance Britain had already established would continue to grow. The profits of slavery certainly helped fuel the eighteenth-century British economy; by the end of the century, however, British trade and manufacturing had reached such high levels of productivity that even the abolition of the slave trade (in 1808) and of slavery itself (in 1833) did not impede its continuing growth.

The economic prosperity of late-eighteenth-century Britain was mirrored to some degree throughout northwestern Europe. Improved transportation systems, more reliable food supplies, and growing quantities of consumer goods brought improved standards of living to large numbers of Europeans, even as the overall population of Europe was rising faster after 1750 than it had ever done before. Population growth was especially rapid in the cities, where a new urban middle class was emerging whose tastes drove the market for goods and whose opinions were reshaping the world of ideas.

But the prosperity of late-eighteenth-century Europe remained very unevenly distributed. In the cities, rich and poor lived separate lives in separate neighborhoods. In the countryside, regions bypassed by the developing commercial economy of the period continued to suffer from hunger and famine, just as they had done in the sixteenth and seventeenth centuries. In eastern Europe the contrasts between rich and poor were even more extreme, as many peasants fell into a new style of serfdom that would last until the end of the nineteenth century. War too remained a fact of European life, bringing death and destruction to hundreds of thousands of people across the continent and around the world—yet another consequence of the worldwide reach of these European colonial empires.

Political change was more gradual. Throughout Europe, the powers of governments steadily increased. Administrators became more numerous, more efficient, and more demanding, partly to meet the mounting costs of war but also because governments were starting to take on a much wider range of responsibilities for the welfare of their subjects. Despite the increasing scope of government, however, the structure and principles of government changed relatively little. Apart from Great Britain and the Dutch Republic, the great powers of eighteenth-century Europe were still governed by rulers who styled themselves as absolutist monarchs in the mold of Louis XIV. By 1789, however, the European world was a vastly different place than it had been a century before, when the Sun King had dominated European politics. The full extent of those differences was about to be revealed.

Key Terms

balance of power	*Two Treatises on*	Versailles	Catherine the Great
Louis XIV	*Government*	Frederick the Great	Triangular trade
William and Mary	Treaty of Utrecht	Peter the Great	

Selected Readings

Berlin, Ira. *Many Thousands Gone: The First Two Centuries of Slavery in North America.* Cambridge, Mass., 1998. An outstanding synthesis that tells the story from the perspective of the enslaved.

Blanning, T. C. W., ed. *The Eighteenth Century: Europe 1688–1815.* Oxford and New York, 2000. Chapters on political, economic, cultural, and religious developments written by leading experts.

Brewer, John S. *The Sinews of Power: War, Money, and the English State, 1688–1783.* London, 1988; New York, 1989. An extremely influential study of the impact of war on eighteenth-century British government and finance.

Cameron, Euan, ed. *Early Modern Europe: An Oxford History.* Oxford and New York, 1999. A wide-ranging, stimulating, multiauthor survey, topically arranged, that spans the entire period from the Renaissance to the French Revolution.

Campbell, Peter R. *Louis XIV, 1661–1715.* London, 1993. A reliable recent biography; short, with primary source material and a good bibliography.

Collins, James B. *The State in Early Modern France.* Cambridge and New York, 1995. A challenging account of French government and finance between 1620 and 1789.

Doyle, William. *The Old European Order, 1660-1800.* Oxford and New York, 1992. An excellent account of European society during the *ancien régime*, with chapters on population, trade, the social order, and public affairs.

Hufton, Olwen. *The Prospect before Her: A History of Women in Western Europe, 1500–1800.* New York, 1996. A great book by a great social historian.

Hughes, Lindsey. *Russia in the Age of Peter the Great.* New Haven, Conn., 1998. A detailed, scholarly account by the leading British authority on Peter's reign.

Ingrao, Charles. *The Habsburg Monarchy, 1618–1815.* 2d ed. Cambridge and New York, 2000. A recently revised and updated edition of this standard work.

Israel, Jonathan I. *The Dutch Republic: Its Rise, Greatness, and Fall, 1477–1806.* Oxford and New York, 1995. The standard work, especially good on economic developments.

Kishlansky, Mark A. *A Monarchy Transformed: Britain, 1603–1714.* London, 1996. An excellent survey that takes seriously its claims to be a "British" rather than merely an "English" history.

Klein, Herbert S. *The Atlantic Slave Trade.* Cambridge and New York, 1999. An accessible survey by a leading quantitative historian.

Koch, H. W. *A History of Prussia.* London, 1978. Still the best account of its subject.

Lewis, William Roger, gen. ed. *The Oxford History of the British Empire.* Vol. I: *The Origins of Empire: British Overseas Enterprise to the Close of the Seventeenth Century,* ed. Nicholas Canny. Vol. II: *The Eighteenth Century,* ed. Peter J. Marshall. Oxford and New York, 1998. A definitive, multiauthor account.

Locke, John. *Two Treatises of Government.* Ed. Peter Laslett. Rev. ed. Cambridge and New York, 1963. Laslett has revolutionized our understanding of the historical and ideological context of Locke's political writings.

Miller, John, ed. *Absolutism in Seventeenth-Century Europe.* London, 1990. An excellent, multiauthor survey, organized by country.

Monod, Paul K. *The Power of Kings: Monarchy and Religion in Europe, 1589–1715.* New Haven, Conn. 1999. A study of the seventeenth century's declining confidence in the divinity of kings.

Quataert, Donald. *The Ottoman Empire, 1700–1822.* Cambridge and New York, 2000. Well balanced, up to date, and intended to be read by students.

Riasanovsky, Nicholas V., and Steinberg, Mark D. *A History of Russia.* 7th ed. Oxford and New York, 2005. Far and away the best single-volume textbook on Russian history: balanced, comprehensive, intelligent, and with full bibliographies.

Saint-Simon, Louis. *Historical Memoirs.* Many editions. The classic source for life at Louis XIV's Versailles.

Thomas, Hugh. *The Slave Trade: The History of the Atlantic Slave Trade, 1440–1870.* London and New York, 1997. A survey notable for its breadth and depth of coverage and for its attractive prose style.

Tracy, James D. *The Rise of Merchant Empires: Long-Distance Trade in the Early Modern World, 1350–1750.* Cambridge and New York, 1990. Important collection of essays by leading authorities.

White, Richard. *It's Your Misfortune and None of My Own: A History of the American West.* Norman, Okla., 1991. An outstanding textbook with excellent introductory chapters on European colonialism in the Americas.

Chapter Sixteen

Chapter Contents

- The Intellectual Origins of the Scientific Revolution 580
- The Copernican Revolution 582
- Tycho's Observations and Kepler's Laws 583
- New Heavens, New Earth, and Worldly Politics: Galileo 585
- Methods for a New Philosophy: Bacon and Descartes 589
- "And All Was Light": Isaac Newton 594
- Conclusion 600

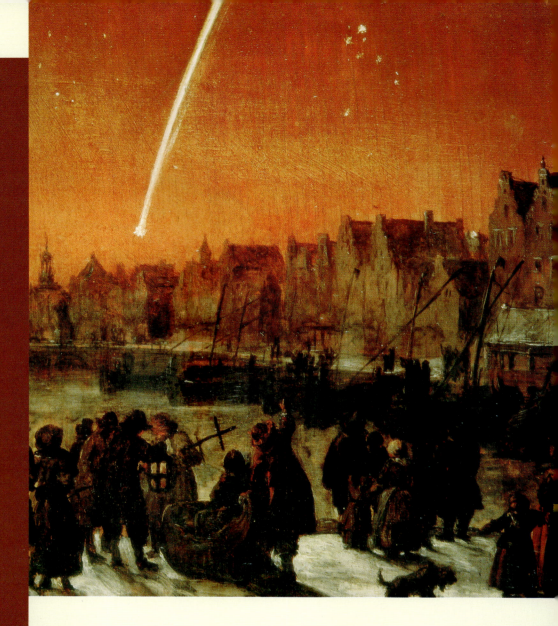

The New Science of the Seventeenth Century

Doubt thou the stars are fire,
Doubt that the sun doth move,
Doubt truth to be a liar,
But never doubt I love.

SHAKESPEARE, *HAMLET*, II.2

"Doubt thou that the stars are fire" and "that the sun doth move." Was Shakespeare alluding to new ideas that might unsettle the ancient understanding of the cosmos? *Hamlet* (c. 1600) was written more than fifty years after Copernicus had suggested, in his treatise *On the Revolutions of the Heavenly Spheres* (1543), that the sun did not move and that the earth did, revolving around the sun. Shakespeare probably knew of such theories, although they circulated only among small groups of learned Europeans, and, as Hamlet's love-torn speech to Ophelia makes clear, they were considered conjecture—or strange mathematical hypotheses. These theories flatly contradicted traditional learning and, just as important, they defied common sense and observation. Learned philosophers, young lovers, shepherds, and sailors alike could watch the sun and the stars move from one horizon to the other each day and night, or so they thought.

Still, a small handful of thinkers did doubt. Shakespeare was born in 1564, the same year as Galileo. By the time the English playwright and the Italian natural philosopher were working, the long process of revising knowledge about the universe, and discovering a new set of rules that explained how the universe worked was under way. By the end of the seventeenth century 100 years later, the building blocks of the new view had been put in place. This intellectual transformation brought sweeping changes to European philosophy and to Western views of the natural world and of humans' place in it.

FOCUS QUESTIONS

- What developments paved the way for the scientific revolution and how?
- How did Copernicus propose to correct the weaknesses in the inherited model of the cosmos?
- To what extent did breakthroughs depend on new observations? To what extent on new theories?

- Was Galileo a success? Why?
- What thinkers and institutions were important in the development of science as a practice?
- What problems did Newton solve?

CHAPTER 16

THE NEW SCIENCE OF THE SEVENTEENTH CENTURY

"Science" entails at least three things: a body of knowledge, a method or system of inquiry, and a community of practitioners and the institutions that support them and their work. The "scientific revolution" of the seventeenth century (usually understood to have begun in the mid-sixteenth century and culminated in 1687 with Newton's *Principia*) involved each of these three realms. As far as the content of knowledge is concerned, the scientific revolution saw the emergence and confirmation of a heliocentric (sun-centered) view of the planetary system, which displaced the earth—and humans—from the center of the universe. Even more fundamental, it brought a new mathematical physics that described and confirmed such a view. Second, the scientific revolution established a method of inquiry for understanding the natural world: a method that emphasized the role of observation, experiment, and the testing of hypotheses. Third, "science" emerged as a distinctive branch of knowledge. During the period covered in this chapter, people referred to the study of matter, motion, optics, or the circulation of blood as natural philosophy (the more theoretical term), experimental philosophy, medicine, and—increasingly—science. The growth of societies and institutions dedicated to what we now commonly call scientific research was central to the changes at issue here. Science required not only brilliant thinkers but patrons, states, and communities of researchers; the scientific revolution was thus embedded in other social, religious, and cultural transformations.

The scientific revolution was not an organized effort. Brilliant theories sometimes led to dead ends, discoveries were often accidental, and artisans grinding lenses for telescopes played a role in the advance of knowledge just as surely as did great abstract thinkers. Old and new worldviews often overlapped as individual thinkers struggled to reconcile their discoveries with their faith or to make their theories (about the earth's movements, for instance) fit with received wisdom. Science was slow to work its way into popular understanding. It did not necessarily undermine religion, and it certainly did not intend to; figures like Isaac Newton thought their work confirmed and deepened their religious beliefs. In short, change came slowly and fitfully. But as the new scientific method began to produce radical new insights into the workings of nature, it eventually came to be accepted well beyond the small circles of experimenters, theologians, and philosophers with whom it began.

> "Printing, firearms, and the compass," wrote Francis Bacon, "no empire, sect or star appears to have exercised a greater power and influence on human affairs than these three mechanical discoveries."

THE INTELLECTUAL ORIGINS OF THE SCIENTIFIC REVOLUTION

> What developments paved the way for the scientific revolution and how?

The scientific revolution marks one of the decisive breaks between the Middle Ages and the modern world. For all its novelty, however, it was rooted in earlier developments. Medieval artists and intellectuals had been observing and illustrating the natural world with great precision since at least the twelfth century. Medieval sculptors carved plants and vines with extraordinary accuracy, and fifteenth-century painters and sculptors devoted the same careful attention to the human face and form. Nor was the link between observation, experiment, and invention new to the sixteenth century. The magnetic compass had been known in Europe since the thirteenth century; gunpowder since the early fourteenth; printing, which permeated the intellectual life of the period and opened new possibilities—disseminating ideas quickly, collaborating more easily, buying books, and building libraries—since the middle of the fifteenth. "Printing, firearms, and the compass," wrote Francis Bacon, "no empire, sect or star appears to have exercised a greater power and influence on human affairs than these three mechanical discoveries." A fascination with light, which was a powerful symbol of divine illumination for medieval thinkers, encouraged the study of optics and, in turn, new techniques for grinding lenses. Lens grinders laid the groundwork for the seventeenth-century inventions of the telescope and microscope, creating reading glasses along the way. Astrologers were also active in the later Middle Ages, charting the heavens in the firm belief that the stars controlled the fates of human beings.

Behind these efforts to understand the natural world lay a nearly universal conviction that the natural world had been created by God. Religious belief spurred scientific study. One school of thinkers (the Neoplatonists) argued that nature was a book written by its creator to reveal the ways of God to humanity. Convinced that God's perfection must be reflected in

THE INTELLECTUAL ORIGINS OF THE SCIENTIFIC REVOLUTION

nature, Neoplatonists searched for the ideal and perfect structures they believed must lie behind the "shadows" of the everyday world. Mathematics, particularly geometry, were important tools in this quest. Johannes Kepler, for example, was deeply influenced by Neoplatonism.

Renaissance humanism also helped prepare the grounds for the scientific revolution. The humanists' educational program placed a low value on natural philosophy, directing attention instead toward the recovery and study of classical antiquity, and humanists revered the authority of the ancients. Yet the energies the humanists poured into recovering, translating, and understanding classical texts (the source of conceptions of the natural world) made many of those important works available for the first time, and to a wider audience. Previously, Arabic sources had provided Europeans with the main route to ancient Greek learning; Greek classics were translated into Arabic and then picked up by late medieval scholars in Spain and Sicily. The humanists' return to the texts themselves—and the fact that the new texts could be more easily printed and circulated—encouraged new study and debate. Islamic scholars knew Ptolemy better than did Europeans until the humanist scholar and printer Johannes Regiomontanus recovered and prepared a new summary of Ptolemy's work. The humanist rediscovery of works by Archimedes—the great Greek mathematician who had proposed that the natural world operated on the basis of mechanical forces, like

> The humanists' return to the texts themselves—and the fact that the new texts could be more easily printed and circulated—encouraged new study and debate.

a great machine, and that these forces could be described mathematically—profoundly impressed important late-sixteenth- and seventeenth-century thinkers, including the Italian scientist Galileo, and shaped mechanical philosophy in the seventeenth century.

The Renaissance also encouraged collaboration between artisans and intellectuals. Twelfth- and thirteenth-century thinkers had observed the natural world, but they rarely tinkered with machines and they had little contact with the artisans who developed expertise in constructing machines for practical use. During the fifteenth century, however, these two worlds began to come together. Renaissance artists such as Leonardo da Vinci were accomplished craftsmen; they investigated the laws of perspective and optics, they worked out geometric methods for supporting the weight of enormous architectural domes, they studied the human body, and they devised new and more effective weapons for war. The Renaissance brought a vogue for alchemy and astrology; wealthy amateurs built observatories and measured the courses of the stars. These social and intellectual developments laid the groundwork for the scientific revolution.

What of the voyages of discovery? Sixteenth-century observers often linked the exploration of the globe to new knowledge of the cosmos. An admirer wrote to Galileo that he had kept the spirit of exploration alive: "The memory of Columbus and Vespucci will be renewed through you, and with even greater nobility, as the sky is more worthy than the earth." The parallel does not work quite so neatly. Columbus had not been driven by an interest in science. Moreover, it took centuries for European thinkers to process the New World's implications for different fields of study, and the links between the voyages of discovery and breakthroughs in science were largely indirect. The discoveries made the most immediate impact in the field of natural history, which was vastly enriched by travelers' detailed accounts of the flora and fauna of the Americas. Finding new lands and cultures in Africa and Asia and the revelation of the Americas, a world unknown to the ancients and unmentioned in the Bible, also laid bare gaps in Europeans' inherited body of knowledge. In this sense, the exploration of the New World dealt a blow to the authority of the ancients.

In sum, the late medieval recovery of ancient texts long thought to have been lost, the expansion of print culture and reading, the turmoil in the church and the

CHRONOLOGY

THE SCIENTIFIC REVOLUTION, 1543–1687

Publication of Copernicus's *On the Revolutions of the Heavenly Spheres*	1543
Tycho Brahe sets up Uranibourg observatory	1576
Kepler sets out his laws in his *Astronomia Nova*	1609
Galileo publishes *The Starry Messenger*	1610
Bacon publishes *Novum Organum*	1620
Galileo publishes *Dialogue Concerning the Two Chief World Systems*	1632
Descartes publishes *Discourse on Method*	1637
Newton publishes *Principia*	1687

fierce wars and political maneuvering that followed the Reformation, and the discovery of a new world across the oceans to explore and exploit, all shook the authority of older ways of thinking. What we call the scientific revolution was part of the intellectual excitement that surrounded these challenges, and, in retrospect, the scientific revolution enhanced and confirmed the importance of these other developments.

The Copernican Revolution

How did Copernicus propose to correct the weaknesses in the inherited model of the cosmos?

Medieval cosmology (the medieval model of the universe) rested on ancient texts, particularly the work of Aristotle (384–322 B.C.E.), refined and systematized by Ptolemy of Alexandria (100–178 C.E.). Ptolemy himself built on the ideas of earlier Greek astronomers (see Chapter Four). According to this inherited cosmology, the heavens orbited the earth in a carefully organized hierarchy of spheres. Earth and the heavens were fundamentally different, made of different matter and subject to different laws of motion. The sun, moon, stars, and planets were formed of an unchanging (and perfect) quintessence or ether. The earth, by contrast, was composed of four elements (earth, water, fire, and air), and each of these elements had its natural place: the heavy elements (earth and water) toward the center and the lighter ones farther out. The heavens—first the planets, then the stars—traced perfect circular paths around the stationary earth. The motion of these celestial bodies was produced by a prime mover, whom Christians identified as God. The view fit Aristotelian physics, according to which objects could move only if acted on by an external force, and it fit with a belief that each fundamental element of the universe had a natural place. Moreover, the view both followed from and confirmed belief in the purposefulness of God's universe.

By the late Middle Ages astronomers knew that this cosmology, called the "Ptolemaic system," did not correspond exactly to what many had observed. Orbits did not conform to the Aristotelian ideal of perfect circles. Planets, Mars in particular, sometimes appeared to loop backward before continuing on their paths. Ptolemy had managed to account for these orbital irregularities, but with complicated mathematics. By the early fifteenth century, the efforts to make the observed motions of the planets fit into the model of perfect circles in a geocentric (earth-centered) cosmos had produced astronomical charts that were mazes of complexity. Finally, the Ptolemaic system proved unable to solve serious difficulties with the calendar. That practical crisis precipitated Nicholas Copernicus's intellectual leap forward.

By the early sixteenth century the old Roman calendar was significantly out of alignment with the movement of the heavenly bodies. The major saints' days, Easter, and the other holy days were sometimes weeks off where they should have been according to the stars. Catholic authorities tried to correct this problem, consulting mathematicians and astronomers all over

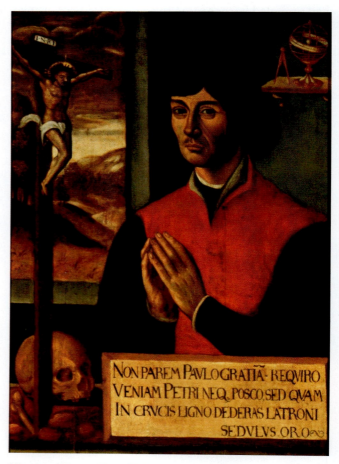

Nicolaus Copernicus. This anonymous portrait of Copernicus characteristically blends his devotion and his scientific achievements. His scholarly work (behind him in the form of an early planetarium) is driven by his faith (as he turns toward the image of Christ triumphant over death).

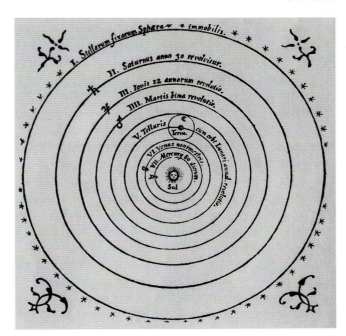

The Copernican Planetary System, 1617. A diagram from a seventeenth-century Dutch treatise depicting the heliocentric structure of the Copernican planetary system.

Europe. One of these was a Polish church official and astronomer, Nicholas Copernicus (1473–1543). Educated in Poland and northern Italy, he was a man of diverse talents. He was trained in astronomy, canon law, and medicine. He read Greek. He was well versed in ancient philosophy. He was also a careful mathematician and a devout Catholic, who did not believe that God's universe could be as messy as the one in Ptolemy's model. His proposed solution, based on mathematical calculations, was simple and radical: Ptolemy was mistaken; the earth was neither stationary nor at the center of the planetary system; the earth rotated on its axis and orbited with the other planets around the sun. Reordering the Ptolemaic system simplified the geometry of astronomy and made the orbits of the planets comprehensible.

Copernicus was in many ways a conservative thinker. He did not consider his work to be a break with either the church or with the authority of ancient texts. He believed, rather, that he had restored a pure understanding of God's design, one that had been lost over the centuries. Still, the implications of his theory troubled him. His ideas contradicted centuries of astronomical thought, and they were hard to reconcile with the observed behavior of objects on earth. If the earth moved, why was that movement imperceptible? Copernicus calculated the distance from the Earth to the Sun to be at least 6 million miles. Even by Copernicus's very low estimate, the Earth was hurtling around the Sun at the dizzying rate of many thousands of miles an hour. How did people and objects remain standing? (The earth is actually about 93 million miles from the sun, moving through space at 67,000 miles an hour and spinning on its axis at about 1,000 miles an hour!)

Copernicus was not a physicist. He tried to refine, rather than overturn, traditional Aristotelian physics, but his effort to reconcile that physics with his new model of a sun-centered universe created new problems and inconsistencies that he could not resolve. These frustrations and complications dogged Copernicus's later years, and he hesitated to publish his findings. Just before his death, he consented to the release of his major treatise, *On the Revolutions of the Heavenly Spheres* (*De Revolutionibus*), in 1543. To fend off scandal, the Lutheran scholar who saw his manuscript through the press added an introduction to the book declaring that Copernicus's system should be understood as an abstraction, a set of mathematical tools for doing astronomy and not a dangerous claim about the nature of heaven and earth. For decades after 1543, Copernicus's ideas were taken in just that sense—as useful but not realistic mathematical hypotheses. In the long run, however, as historian Steven Shapin puts it, Copernicanism represented the first "serious and systematic" challenge to the Ptolemaic conception of the universe.

Tycho's Observations and Kepler's Laws

> To what extent did breakthroughs depend on new observations? To what extent on new theories?

Within fifty years, Copernicus's cosmology was revived and modified by two astronomers also critical of the Ptolemaic model of the universe: Tycho Brahe (*TI-koh BRAH-hee*, 1546–1601) and Johannes Kepler (1571–1630). Each was considered the greatest astronomer of his day. Tycho was born into the Danish nobility but he abandoned his family's military and political legacy to pursue his passion for astronomy. He was hot headed as well as talented; at twenty he lost part of his nose in a duel. Like Copernicus he sought to correct the contradictions in traditional astronomy.

Chapter 16: The New Science of the Seventeenth Century

Tycho Brahe, 1662. This seventeenth-century tribute shows the master astronomer in his observatory.

Unlike Copernicus, who was a theoretician, Tycho championed observation and believed careful study of the heavens would unlock the secrets of the universe. He first made a name for himself by observing a completely new star, a "nova," that flared into sight in 1572. The Danish king Friedrich II, impressed by Tycho's work, granted him the use of a small island, where he built a castle specially designed to house an observatory. For over twenty years, Tycho meticulously charted the movements of each significant object in the night sky, compiling the finest set of astronomical data in Europe.

Tycho was not a Copernican. He suggested that the planets orbited the sun and the whole system then orbited a stationary earth. This picture of cosmic order, though clumsy, seemed to fit the observed evidence better than the Ptolemaic system, and it avoided the upsetting physical and theological implications of the Copernican model. In the late 1590s, Tycho moved his work and his huge collection of data to Prague, where he became court astronomer to the Holy Roman emperor Rudolph II. In Prague he was assisted by a young mathematician from a troubled family, Johannes Kepler. Kepler was more impressed with the Copernican model than was Tycho, and Kepler combined study of Copernicus's work with his own interest in mysticism, astrology, and the religious power of mathematics.

Kepler believed that everything in creation, from human souls to the orbits of the planets, had been created according to mathematical laws. Understanding those laws would thus allow humans to share God's wisdom and penetrate the inner secrets of the universe. Mathematics was God's language. Kepler's search for the pattern of mathematical perfection took him through musical harmonies, nested geometric shapes inside the planets' orbits, and numerical formulas. After Tycho's death, Kepler inherited Tycho's position in Prague, as well as his trove of observations and calculations. That data demonstrated to Kepler that two of Copernicus's assumptions abut planetary motion simply

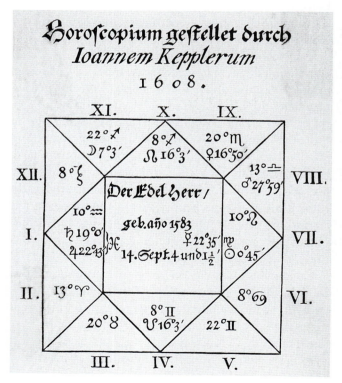

Kepler's Horoscope for von Wallenstein. Kepler, famous for his contribution to modern astronomy, also believed in astrology. He made this horoscope for Eusebius von Wallenstein, who was a general for the Holy Roman Emperor during the Thirty Years' War.

NEW HEAVENS, NEW EARTH, AND WORLDLY POLITICS: GALILEO

did not match observations. Copernicus, in keeping with Aristotelian notions of perfection, had believed that planetary orbits were circular. Kepler calculated that the planets traveled in elliptical orbits around the sun; this finding became his First Law. Copernicus held that planetary motion was uniform; Kepler's Second Law stated that the speed of the planets varied with their distance from the sun. Kepler also argued that magnetic forces between the sun and the planets kept the planets in orbital motion, an insight that paved the way for Newton's law of universal gravitation formulated nearly eighty years later, at the end of the seventeenth century.

Each of Kepler's works, beginning with *Cosmographic Mystery* in 1596 and continuing with *New Astronomy or Celestial Physics* in 1609 and *The Harmonies of the World* in 1619, revised and augmented Copernicus's theory. His version of Copernicanism fit with remarkable accuracy the best observations of the time (which were Tycho's). Kepler's search for rules of motion that could account for the earth's movements in its new position was also significant. More than Copernicus, Kepler broke down the distinction between the heavens and the earth that had been at the heart of Aristotelian physics.

NEW HEAVENS, NEW EARTH, AND WORLDLY POLITICS: GALILEO

Was Galileo a success? Why?

Kepler had a friend deliver a copy of *Cosmographic Mystery* to the "mathematician named Galileus Galileus," then teaching mathematics and astronomy at Padua, near Venice. Galileo thanked Kepler in a letter that nicely illustrates the Italian's views at the time (1597).

> So far I have only perused the preface of your work, but from this I gained some notion of its intent, and I indeed congratulate myself of having an associate in the study of Truth who is a friend of Truth. . . . I adopted the teaching of Copernicus many years ago, and his point of view enables me to explain many phenomena of nature which certainly remain

inexplicable according to the more current hypotheses. I have written many arguments in support of him and in refutation of the opposite view—which, however, so far I have not dared to bring into the public light. . . . I would certainly dare to publish my reflections at once if more people like you existed; as they don't, I shall refrain from doing so.

Kepler replied, urging Galileo to "come forward!" Galileo did not answer.

At Padua, Galileo couldn't teach what he believed; Ptolemic astronomy and Aristotelian cosmology were the established curriculum. As other opportunities opened up, the ambitious natural philosopher would become less cagey about his views. By the end of his career, Galileo had provided powerful evidence in support of the Copernican model and laid the foundation for a new physics. What was more, he was a witty and persuasive writer, who wrote in the vernacular (Italian) as well as in Latin. Kepler may have been a "friend of Truth," but his work was abstruse and bafflingly mathematical. (So was Copernicus's.) By contrast, Galileo's writings were widely translated and widely read, raising awareness of changes in natural philosophy across Europe. Galileo was a popularizer, and what he popularized was a non-Aristotelian approach to science, with Copernicanism as its centerpiece.

Galileo (1564–1642) was self-assured and contentious—known, as one of his biographers puts it, for his opinions as well as his discoveries. He was impatient with those who opposed him, and his temperament got him into serious and ultimately stifling controversies. He made the case for a new relationship between religion and science, challenging in the process some of the most powerful churchmen of his day. His discoveries made him the most famous scientific figure of his time, but his confidence in his convictions and his penchant for controversy put him on a collision course with Aristotelian philosophy and the authority of the Catholic Church.

Galileo became famous by way of discoveries with the telescope. In 1609 he heard reports from Holland of a lens grinder who had made a spyglass that could magnify very distant objects. Excited, Galileo quickly devised his own telescope; trained it first on earthly objects to demonstrate that it worked; and then, momentously, pointed it at the night sky. The results

> By the end of his career, Galileo had provided powerful evidence in support of the Copernican model and laid the foundation for a new physics.

THE NEW SCIENCE OF THE SEVENTEENTH CENTURY

made his career. Galileo studied the moon, finding on it mountains, plains, and other features of an earth-like landscape. His observations suggested that celestial bodies resembled the earth, a view at odds with the conception of the heavens as an unchanging sphere of heavenly perfection, inherently and necessarily different from the earth. He saw moons orbiting Jupiter, evidence that earth was not at the center of all orbits. He saw spots on the sun. Galileo published the results of his observations, first in *The Starry Messenger* (1610) and then in *Letters on Sunspots* in 1613. *The Starry Messenger*, with its amazing reports of Jupiter's moons, was short, aimed to be read by many, and bold. Its frontispiece declared that its pages revealed "great, unusual, and remarkable spectacles, opening these to the consideration of every man, especially of philosophers and astronomers." *The Starry Messenger*, however, only hinted at Galileo's Copernicanism. The *Letters on Sunspots* declared it openly.

A seventeenth-century scientist needed powerful and wealthy patrons. As a professor of mathematics at Padua, Galileo (as he wrote to Kepler) chafed at the power of university authorities. Princely courts offered an inviting alternative. Centers of power and wealth and dispensers of patronage, they were also less subject to church control than the universities. The Medici family of Tuscany, like others, burnished its reputation and bolstered its power by surrounding itself with intellectuals as well as artists. (In the fifteenth century, the Medicis had been patrons of Michelangelo.) Persuaded he would be freer at its court than in Padua, Galileo took a position as tutor to the Medicis and flattered and successfully cultivated the family. He addressed *The Starry Messenger* to them. He named the newly discovered moons of Jupiter "the Medicean stars." He was rewarded with the title of chief mathematician and philosopher to Cosimo de' Medici, the grand duke of Tuscany. Now well positioned in Italy's networks of power and patronage, Galileo was able to pursue his work on astronomy and his conviction that Copernicus's heliocentric (sun-centered) model of the planetary system was correct.

This pursuit, however, was a high-wire act, for he could not afford to antagonize the Catholic Church. Not all churchmen opposed Galileo's work. The great Jesuit astronomers of the day, in fact, accepted his telescopic discoveries. They argued, however, that those discoveries fit perfectly well with Tycho's system and did not require displacing the earth from its position at the center of the universe. Yet politics, intellectual rivalries, Galileo's enthusiastic Copernican friends, and

his own zest for controversy made it hard for Galileo to avoid trouble. In 1614, an ambitious and outspoken Dominican monk denounced Galileo's ideas as dangerous deviations from biblical teachings. Other philosophers and churchmen began to ask Galileo's patrons, the Medicis, whether their court mathematician was teaching heresy.

Disturbed by the murmurings against Copernicanism, Galileo penned a series of letters to defend himself, letters that addressed the relationship between natural philosophy and religion. The best known of these was written in 1615 to the Grand Duchess Christina, mother of Galileo's patron, Cosimo (see next page). Galileo argued that one could be a sincere Copernican and a sincere Catholic. The church, Galileo said, did the sacred work of teaching scripture and saving souls. Accounting for the workings of the physical world was a task better left to natural philosophy, grounded in observation and mathematics. The Bible was a notoriously difficult book, and it was the role of the church's theologians to reconcile its complexity with the new conclusions of natural philosophy. For the church to take a side in controversies over natural science, however, was both needless and risky; to do so might compromise the church's spiritual authority and credibility. Galileo envisioned natural philosophers and theologians as partners in a search for truth, but with very different roles. In a brilliant rhetorical moment, he quoted Cardinal Baronius in suppport of his own argument: the purpose of the Bible was to "teach us how to go to heaven, not how heaven goes."

In spite of Galileo's arguments, the church moved against Copernicanism and against him. In 1616 the Inquisition ruled the propositions that the earth moves and the sun does not "foolish and absurd in philosophy and formally heretical." A decree placed Copernicus's *De Revolutionibus* on the Index of Prohibited Books, and Galileo was warned not to teach Copernicanism.

For a while, he did as he was asked. But when his Florentine friend and admirer Maffeo Barberini was elected pope as Urban VIII in 1623, Galileo believed the door to Copernicanism was (at least half) open. He drafted one of his most famous works, *A Dialogue Concerning the Two Chief World Systems* published in 1632. The *Dialogue* was a hypothetical debate between supporters of the old Ptolemaic system, represented by a character he named Simplicio (simpleton) on the one hand and proponents of the new astronomy on the other. Throughout, Galileo gave the best lines to the Copernicans. At the very end, however, to satisfy the letter

GALILEO ON NATURE, SCRIPTURE, AND TRUTH

One of the clearest statements of Galileo's convictions about religion and science comes from his 1615 letter to the grand duchess Christina, mother of Galileo's patron, Cosimo de' Medici and a powerful figure in her own right. Galileo knew that others objected to his work. The church had warned him that Copernicanism was inaccurate and impious; it could be disproved scientifically, and it contradicted the authority of those who interpreted the Bible. Thoroughly dependent on the Medicis for support, he wrote to the grand duchess to explain his position. In this section of the letter, Galileo sets out his understanding of the parallel but distinct roles of the church and natural philosophers. He walks a fine line between acknowledging the authority of the church and standing firm in his convictions.

Possibly because they are disturbed by the known truth of other propositions of mine which differ from those commonly held, and therefore mistrusting their defense so long as they confine themselves to the field of philosophy, these men have resolved to fabricate a shield for their fallacies out of the mantle of pretended religion and the authority of the Bible....

Copernicus never discusses matters of religion or faith, nor does he use arguments that depend in any way upon the authority of sacred writings which he might have interpreted erroneously. He stands always upon physical conclusions pertaining to the celestial motions, and deals with them by astronomical and geometrical demonstrations, founded primarily upon sense experiences and very exact observations. He did not ignore the Bible, but he knew very well that if his doctrine were proved, then it could not contradict the Scriptures when they were rightly understood....

I think that in discussions of physical problems we ought to begin not from the authority of scriptural passages, but from sense-experiences and necessary demonstrations; for the holy Bible and the phenomena of nature proceed alike from the divine Word, the former as the dictate of the Holy Ghost and the latter as the observant executrix of God's commands. It is necessary for the Bible, in order to be accommodated to the understanding of every man, to speak many things which appear to differ from the absolute truth so far as the bare meaning of the words is concerned. But Nature, on the other hand, is inexorable and immutable; she never transgresses the laws imposed upon her, or cares a whit whether her abstruse reasons and methods of operation are understandable to men. For that reason it appears that nothing physical which sense-experience sets before our eyes, or which necessary demonstrations prove to us, ought to be called in question (much less condemned) upon the testimony of biblical passages which may have some different meaning beneath their words. For the Bible is not chained in every expression to conditions as strict as those which govern all physical effects; nor is God any less excellently revealed in Nature's actions than in the sacred statements of the Bible....

Galileo, "Letter to the Grand Duchess Christina," in *The Discoveries and Opinions of Galileo Galilei*, ed. Stillman Drake (Garden City, N.Y., 1957), pp. 177–183.

QUESTIONS FOR ANALYSIS

1. Why did Galileo need to defend his views in a letter to Christina de' Medici?
2. For Galileo, what is the relationship among God, man, and nature?

of the Inquisition's decree, he had them capitulate to Simplicio.

The Inquisition banned the *Dialogue* and ordered Galileo to stand trial in 1633. Pope Urban, provoked by Galileo's scorn and needing support from church conservatives during a difficult stretch of the Thirty Years' War, refused to protect his former friend. The verdict of the secret trial shocked Europe. Galileo was the most famous scientific figure of his day and the pride of one of the great intellectual centers of Europe. Yet the Inquisition forced Galileo to repent his Copernican position, banned him from working on or even discussing Copernican ideas, and placed him under house arrest for life. According to a story that began to circulate shortly afterward, as he left the court for house arrest he stamped his foot and muttered defiantly, looking down at the earth: "Still, it moves."

The Inquisition could not put Galileo off his life's work. He refined the theories of motion he had begun to develop early in his career. He proposed an early version of the theory of inertia, which held that an object's motion stays the same until an outside force changed it. He calculated that objects of different weights fall at almost the same speed and with a uniform acceleration. He argued that the motion of objects follows regular mathematical laws. The same laws that govern the motions of objects on earth (which could be observed in experiments) could also be observed in the heavens—again a direct contradiction of Aristotelian principles and an important step toward a coherent physics based on a sun-centered model of the universe. Compiled under the title *Two New Sciences* (1638), this work was smuggled out of Italy and published in Protestant Holland.

Galileo provided powerful, though not conclusive, evidence for Copernican cosmology. He also combined discovery, observation, experiment, and mathematics to suggest universal laws of motion. Among his legacies, however, was exactly the rift between religion and science that he had hoped to avoid. Galileo believed that Copernicanism and natural philosophy in general need not subvert theological truths, religious belief, or

Galileo Galilei before the Inquisition by Francois Richard Fleury. This nineteenth-century painting of Galileo before the Holy Office dramatizes the conflict between science and religion and depicts the Italian natural philosopher as defiant. In fact, Galileo submitted, but continued his work under house arrest and published, secretly, in the Netherlands.

Methods for a New Philosophy: Bacon and Descartes

What thinkers and institutions were important in the development of science as a practice?

As the practice of the new sciences became concentrated in Protestant northwest Europe, new thinkers began to spell out standards of practice and evidence. Sir Francis Bacon and René Descartes (*deb-KAHRT*) loomed especially large in this development: setting out methods or the rules that should govern modern science. Bacon (1561–1626) lived at roughly the same time as Kepler and Galileo—and Shakespeare; Descartes (1596–1650) was slightly younger. Both Bacon and Descartes came to believe that theirs was an age of profound change, open to the possibility of astonishing discovery. Both were persuaded that knowledge could take the European moderns beyond the ancient authorities. Both set out to formulate a philosophy to encompass the learning of their age.

"Knowledge is power." The phrase is Bacon's and captures the changing perspective of the seventeenth century and its new confidence in the potential of human thinking. Bacon trained as a lawyer, served in Parliament and, briefly, as lord chancellor to James I of England. His abiding concern was with the assumptions, methods, and practices that he believed should guide natural philosophers and the progress of knowledge. The authority of the ancients should not constrain the ambition of modern thinkers. Deferring to accepted doctrines could block innovation or obstruct understanding. "There is but one course left . . . to try the whole thing anew upon a better plan, and to com-

> "Knowledge is power." The phrase is Bacon's and captures the changing perspective of the seventeenth century and its new confidence in the potential of human thinking.

mence a total reconstruction of sciences, arts, and all human knowledge, raised upon the proper foundations." To pursue knowledge did not mean to think abstractly and leap to conclusions; it meant observing, experimenting, confirming ideas, or demonstrating points. If thinkers will be "content to begin with doubts," Bacon wrote, "they shall end with certainties." We thus associate Bacon with the gradual separation of scientific investigation from philosophical argument.

Bacon advocated an *inductive* approach to knowledge: amassing evidence from specific observations to draw general conclusions. In Bacon's view, many philosophical errors arose from beginning with assumed first principles. The traditional view of the cosmos, for instance, rested on the principles of a prime mover and the perfection of circular motion. The inductive method required accumulating data (as Tycho had done, for example) and then, after careful review and experiment, drawing appropriate conclusions. Bacon argued that knowledge was best tested through the cooperative efforts of researchers performing experiments that could be repeated and verified. The knowledge thus gained would be predictable and useful to philosophers and artisans alike, contributing to a wide range of endeavors from astronomy to shipbuilding.

Bacon's vision of science and progress is vividly illustrated by two images. The first, more familiar, is the title page of Bacon's *Great Instauration* (*Instauratio Magna*, 1620) with its bold ships sailing out beyond the Strait of Gibraltar, formerly the limits of the west, into the open sea, in pursuit of unknown but great things to come. The second is Bacon's description of an imagined factory of discovery, "Solomon's house," at end of his utopian *New Atlantis* (1626). Inside the factory, "sifters" would examine and conduct experiments, passing on findings to senior researchers who would draw conclusions and develop practical applications.

Descartes was French, though he lived all over Europe. He was intellectually restless as well; he worked in geometry, cosmology, optics, and physiology—for a while dissecting cow carcasses daily. He was writing a (Copernican) book on physics when he heard of Galileo's condemnation in 1633, a judgement that impressed on him the dangers of "expressing judgements on this world." Descartes's *The Discourse on Method* (1637), for which he is best known, began simply as an preface to three essays on optics, geometry, and

TWO REACTIONS TO THE "NEW PHILOSOPHY"

In his poem "An Anatomie of the World" (1611), the English poet John Donne (1572–1631) summed up the sense of loss and confusion created by the new discoveries in science. "The element of fire" refers to Aristotle's physics. The second selection here is an excerpt from Francis Bacon's Novum Organum *(1620), or "The New Instrument." (The Organon was the name given in the Middle Ages to Aristotle's writings on logic, which became the basic texts of a university education.) Bacon boldly summed up the new learning and new forms of reasoning. Bacon, like Donne, was English. His view of the world, of human knowledge, and of human possibility, however, was very different.*

AN ANATOMIE OF THE WORLD

And new Philosophy calls all in doubt,
The element of Fire is quite put out;
The Sun is lost, and th' Earth, and no man's wit
Can well direct him where to looke for it.
And freely men confesse that this world's spent,
When in the Planets, and the Firmament,
They seeke so many new; they see that this
Is crumbled out againe to his Atomis.
'Tis all in pieces, all cohaerence gone,
All just supply, and all Relation:
Prince, Subject, Father, Sonne, are things forgot,
For every man alone thinkes he hath got
To be a Phoenix, and that then can be
None of that kinde, of which he is, but he.
This is the worlds condition now. . . .

APHORISMS FROM *NOVUM ORGANUM*

XXXI

It is idle to expect any great advancement in science from the superinducing and engrafting of new things upon old. We must begin anew from the very foundations, unless we would revolve forever in a circle with mean and contemptible progress. . . .

XXXVI

One method of delivery alone remains to us which is simply this: we must lead men to the particulars themselves, and their series and order; while men on their side must force themselves for a while to lay their notions by and begin to familiarize themselves with facts. . . .

XLV

The human understanding of its own nature is prone to suppose the existence of more order and regularity in the world than it finds. And though there be many things in nature which are singular and unmatched, yet it devises for them parallels and conjugates and relatives which do not exist. Hence the fiction that all celestial bodies move in perfect circles. . . . Hence too the element of fire with its orb is brought in, to make up the square with the other three which the sense perceives. . . . And so on of other dreams. And these fancies affect not dogmas only, but simple notions also. . . .

XCV

Those who have handled sciences have been either men of experiment or men of dogmas. The men of experiment are like the ant, they only collect and use; the reasoners resemble spiders, who make cobwebs out of their own substance. But the bee takes a middle course: it gathers its material from the flowers of the garden and of the field, but transforms and digests it by a power of its own. Not unlike this is the true business of philosophy; for it neither relies solely or chiefly on the powers of the mind, nor does it take the matter which it gathers from natural history and mechanical experiments and lay it up in the memory whole . . . but lays it up in the understanding altered and digested. Therefore, from a closer and purer league between these two faculties, the experimental and the rational (such as has never yet been made), much may be hoped. . . .

Michael R. Matthews, ed., *The Scientific Background to Modern Philosophy: Selected Readings* (Indianapolis and Cambridge, 1989), pp. 47–48, 50–52.

QUESTIONS FOR ANALYSIS

1. How does Bacon see the relationship between human understanding and science?

---

meteorology. It is personal, recounting Descartes's dismay at the "strange and unbelievable" theories he encountered in his traditional education. His first response, as he described it, was to systematically doubt everything he had ever known or been taught. Better to clear the slate, he believed, than to build an edifice of knowledge on received assumptions. His first rule was "never to receive anything as a truth which [he] did not clearly know to be such." He took the human ability to think as his point of departure, summed up in his famous and enigmatic, *Je pense, donc je suis,* later translated into Latin as *cogito ergo sum* and in English as "I think, therefore I am." As the phrase suggests, Descartes's doubting led (quickly, by our standards) to self-assurance and truth: the thinking individual existed, reason existed, God existed. For Descartes, then, doubt was a ploy, or a piece that he used in an intellectual chess game to defeat skepticism. Certainty, not doubt, was the centerpiece of the philosophy he bequeathed to his followers.

Descartes, like Bacon, sought a "fresh start for knowledge" or the rules for understanding of the world as it was. Unlike Bacon, Descartes emphasized *deductive* reasoning, proceeding logically from one certainty to another. "So long as we avoid accepting as true what is not so," he wrote in *Discourse on Method,* "and always preserve the right order of deduction of one thing from another, there can be nothing too remote to be reached in the end, or too well hidden to be discovered." For

Descartes, author of *Discourse on Method* (1637), explaining his theories to Queen Kristina of Sweden.

Descartes, mathematical thought expressed the highest standards of reason, and his work contributed greatly to the authority of mathematics as a model for scientific reasoning.

Descartes made a particularly forceful statement for *mechanism*, a view of the world shared by Bacon and Galileo and one that came to dominate seventeenth-century scientific thought. As the name suggested, mechanical philosophy proposed to consider nature as a machine. It rejected the traditional Aristotelian distinction between the works of humans and those of nature and the view that nature, as God's creation, necessarily belonged to a different—and higher—order. In the new picture of the universe that was emerging from the discoveries and writings of the early seventeenth century, it seemed that all matter was composed of the same material and all motion obeyed the same laws. Descartes sought to explain everything, including the human body, mechanically. As he put it firmly, "There is no difference between the machines built by artisans and the diverse bodies that nature alone composes." Nature operated according to regular and predictable laws and was thus accessible to human reason. The belief guided, indeed inspired, much of the scientific experiment and argument of the seventeenth century.

THE POWER OF METHOD AND THE FORCE OF CURIOSITY: SEVENTEENTH-CENTURY EXPERIMENTERS

For nearly a century after Bacon and Descartes, most of England's natural philosophers were Baconian, and most of their colleagues in France, Holland, and elsewhere in northern Europe were Cartesians (followers of Descartes). The English Baconians concentrated on performing experiments in many different fields, producing results that could then be debated and discussed. The Cartesians turned instead toward mathematics and logic. Descartes himself pioneered analytical geometry. Blaise Pascal (1623–1662) worked on probability theory and invented a calculating machine before applying his intellectual skills to theology. The Cartesian thinker Christian Huygens (1629–1695) from Holland combined mathematics with experiments to understand problems of impact and orbital motion. The Dutch Cartesian Baruch Spinoza (1632–1677) applied geometry to ethics and believed he had gone beyond Descartes by proving that the universe was composed of a single substance that was both God and nature.

English experimenters pursued a different course. They began with practical research, putting the alchemist's tool, the laboratory, to new uses. They also sought a different kind of conclusion: empirical laws or provisional generalizations based on evidence rather than absolute statements of deductive truth. Among the many English laboratory scientists of the era were the physician William Harvey (1578–1657), the chemist Robert Boyle (1627–1691), and the inventor and experimenter Robert Hooke (1635–1703).

Harvey's contribution was enormous: he observed and explained that blood circulated through the arteries, heart, and veins. To do this he was willing to dissect living animals (vivisection) and experiment on himself. Boyle performed experiments and established a law (known as Boyle's law) showing that at a constant temperature the volume of a gas decreases in proportion to the pressure placed on it. Hooke introduced the microscope to the experimenter's tool kit. The compound microscope had been invented in Holland early in the seventeenth century. But it was not until the 1660s that Hooke and others demonstrated its potential by using it to study the cellular structure of plants. Like the telescope before it, the microscope revealed an unexpected dimension of material phenom-

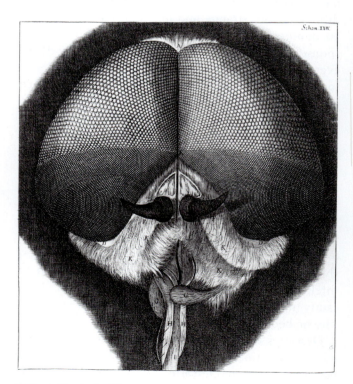

Robert Hooke's *Micrographia*. Hooke's diagram of a fly's eye as seen through a microscope seemed to reveal just the sort of intricate universe the mechanists predicted.

CHRONOLOGY

MAJOR FIGURES OF THE SCIENTIFIC REVOLUTION

Nicholas Copernicus	1473–1543
Tycho Brahe	1546–1601
Francis Bacon	1561–1626
Galileo Galilei	1564–1642
Johannes Kepler	1571–1630
William Harvey	1578–1657
René Descartes	1596–1650
Blaise Pascal	1623–1662
Robert Boyle	1627–1691
Christian Huygens	1629–1695
Baruch Spinoza	1632–1677
Robert Hooke	1635–1703
Isaac Newton	1642–1727

ena. Examining even the most ordinary objects revealed detailed structures of perfectly connected smaller parts and persuaded many that with improved instruments they would uncover even more of the world's intricacies.

The microscope also provided what many regarded as new evidence of God's existence. The way each minute structure of a living organism, when viewed under a microscope, corresponded to its purpose testified not only to God's existence but to God's wisdom as well. The mechanical philosophy did not exclude God but in fact could be used to confirm his presence. If the universe was a clock, after all, there must be a clockmaker. Hooke himself declared that only imbeciles would believe that what they saw under the microscope was "the production of chance" rather than of God's creation.

SCIENCE, SOCIETY, AND THE STATE

Seventeenth-century state building (see Chapter Fourteen) helped secure the rise of science. In 1660, England's monarchy was restored after two decades of revolution and civil war. The newly crowned King Charles II granted a group of natural philosophers and mathematicians a royal charter (1662) to establish the Royal Society of London, for the "improvement of natural knowledge" and committed to experimentation and collaborative work among natural philosophers. The founders of the Royal Society, in particular Boyle, believed it could serve a political as well as an intellectual purpose. The Royal Society would pursue Bacon's goal of collective research in which members would conduct formal experiments, record the results, and share them with other members. These members would in turn study the methods, reproduce the experiment, and assess the outcome. The enterprise would give England's natural philosophers a common sense of purpose and a system to reach reasoned, gentlemanly agreement on "matters of fact." But by separating systematic scientific research from the dangerous language of politics and religion that had marked the civil war, the Royal Society could also help restore a sense of order and consensus to English intellectual life.

The society's journal, *Philosophical Transactions*, reached out to professional scholars and experimenters throughout Europe. Similar societies began to appear elsewhere. The French Academy of Sciences was founded in 1666 and was also tied to seventeenth-century state building, in this case Bourbon absolutism (see Chapter Fifteen). Royal societies, devoted to natural philosophy as a collective enterprise, provided a state (or princely) sponsored framework for science and an alternative to the important but uncertain patronage of smaller nobles or to the religious (and largely conservative, Aristotelian) universities. Scientific societies reached rough agreement about what constituted legitimate research. They established the modern scientific custom of crediting discoveries to those who were first to publish results. They enabled information and theories to be exchanged more easily across national boundaries, although philosophical differences among Cartesians, Baconians, and traditional Aristotelians remained very difficult to bridge. Science began to take shape as a discipline.

Natural philosophy was, officially, a gentlemanly pursuit. Neither the Royal Society of England nor its French counterpart admitted women. Although women had almost no access to formal education, some could educate themselves by associating with learned men. The aristocratic Margaret Cavendish (1623–1673), for instance, gleaned the information necessary to get her started largely from her family. That observatories were built in private residences

> The French Academy of Sciences was founded in 1666 and was also tied to seventeenth-century state building, in this case Bourbon absolutism.

enabled some women living in such homes to work their way into the growing field of astronomy. In fact, 14 percent of German astronomers between 1650 and 1710 were women, the most famous of whom was Maria Winkelmann (1670–1720). Winkelmann discovered a comet and prepared calendars for the Berlin Academy of Science but was barred from entering the academy. Gottfried Leibniz, the academy's president explained that, "Already during her husband's lifetime the society was burdened with ridicule because its calendar was prepared by a woman. If she were now to be kept on in such capacity, mouths would gape even wider." Maria Sibylla Merian (1647–1717) also made a career based on observation, in the field of entomology. Merian supported herself and her two daughters by selling exotic insects she collected in the Dutch colony of Surinam. She fought the colony's sweltering climate and malaria to publish her most important scientific work, the *Metamorphosis of the Insects of Surinam,* which details the life cycles of Surinam's insects in sixty ornate illustrations. Merian's *Metamorphosis* was well received in her time; in fact, Peter I of Russia proudly displayed Merian's portrait and books in his study.

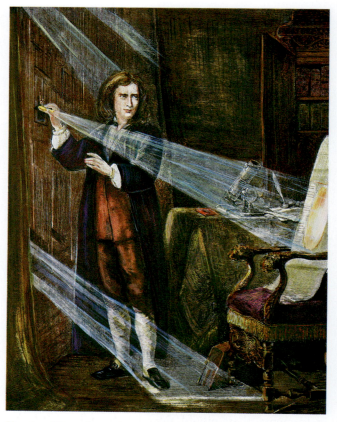

Newton Experimenting with Light. Newton showed that what seemed to be a single ray of light could be broken down into many different ones.

"And All Was Light": Isaac Newton

What problems did Newton solve?

Sir Isaac Newton's work marks the culmination of the scientific revolution. Galileo, peering through his telescope in the early 1600s, had come to believe that the Earth and the heavens were made of the same material. Galileo's experiments with pendulums aimed to discover the laws of motion (and he proposed theories of inertia). It was Newton who articulated those laws and presented a coherent, unified vision of how the universe worked. All bodies in the universe, Newton said, whether on Earth or in the heavens, obeyed the same basic laws. One set of forces and one pattern, which could be expressed mathematically, explained why planets orbited in ellipses and why (and at what speed) apples fell from trees. An Italian mathematician later commented that Newton was the "greatest and most fortunate of mortals"—because there was only one universe, and he had discovered its laws.

> The man who came to represent the personification of modern science was reclusive, secretive about his findings, and obsessive.

Isaac Newton (1642–1727) was born on Christmas Day to a family of small landowners. His father died before his birth, and it fell to a succession of relatives, family friends, and schoolmasters to spot, then encourage, his genius. In 1661 he entered Trinity College in Cambridge University, where he would remain for the next thirty-five years, first as a student, then as the Lucasian Professor of Mathematics. The man who came to represent the personification of modern science was reclusive, secretive about his findings, and obsessive. During his early work with optics he experimented with his own eyes, pressing them to see how different shapes would change the effects of light and then, intrigued by what he found, inserting a very thick needle "betwixt my eye and the bone as neare to the backside of my eye as I could" to actually curve his eyeball. (Please do not try this at home.)

Newton's first great burst of creativity came at Cambridge, in the years from 1664 to 1666, "the prime of my age for invention." During these years Newton broke new ground in three areas. The first was optics. Descartes believed that color was a secondary quality produced by the speed of particulate rotation but that light itself was white. Newton, using prisms he had purchased at a local fair, showed that white light was composed of different-colored rays. The second area in which Newton produced innovative work during these years was in mathematics. In a series of brilliant insights, he invented both integral calculus and differential calculus, providing mathematical tools to model motion in space. The third area of his creative genius involved his early works on gravity. Newton later told different versions of the same story: the idea about gravity had come to him when he was in a "contemplative mood" and was "occasioned by the fall of an apple." Why did the apple "not go sideways or upwards, but constantly to the earth's center?" "Assuredly the reason is, that the earth draws it. There must be a drawing power in matter." Voltaire, the eighteenth-century French essayist, retold the story to dramatize Newton's simple brilliance. But the theory of gravity rested on mathematical formulations, it was far from simple, and it would not be fully worked out until *Principia*, more than twenty years later.

Newton's work on the composite nature of white light led him to make a reflecting telescope, which used a curved mirror rather than lenses. The telescope earned him election to the Royal Society (in 1672) and drew him out of his sheltered obscurity at Cambridge. Encouraged by the Royal Society's support, he wrote a paper describing his theory of optics and allowed it to be published in *Philosophical Transactions*. Astronomers and scientists across Europe applauded the work. Robert Hooke, the Royal Society's curator of experiments, did not. Hooke was unpersuaded by Newton's mode of argument; he found Newton's claims that science had to be mathematical both dogmatic and high-handed; and he objected—in a series of sharp exchanges with the reclusive genius—that Newton had not provided any physical explanation for his results. Stung by the conflict with Hooke and persuaded

that few natural philosophers could understand his theories, Newton withdrew to Cambridge and long refused to share his work. Only the patient effort of friends and fellow scientists like the astronomer Edmond Halley (1656–1742), already well known for his astronomical observations in the Southern Hemisphere and the person for whom Halley's Comet is named, convinced Newton to publish again.

Newton's *Principia Mathematica* (Mathematical Principles of Natural Philosophy) was published in 1687. It was prompted by a visit from Halley, in which the astronomer asked Newton for his ideas on a question being discussed at the Royal Society: was there a mathematical basis for the elliptical orbits of the planets? Halley's question inspired Newton to expand calculations he had made earlier into an all-encompassing theory of celestial—and terrestrial—dynamics. Halley not only encouraged Newton's work but supervised and financed its publication (though he had less money than Newton); and on several occasions he had to persuade Newton, enraged again by reports of criticism from Hooke and others, to continue with the project and to commit his findings to print.

> Newton built on Galileo's work on inertia, Kepler's findings concerning the elliptical orbits of planets, the work of Boyle and Descartes, and even his rival Hooke's work on gravity.

Principia was long and difficult—purposefully so, for Newton said he did not want to be "baited by little smatterers in mathematics". Its central proposition was that gravitation was a universal force and one that could be expressed mathematically. Newton built on Galileo's work on inertia, Kepler's findings concerning the elliptical orbits of planets, the work of Boyle and Descartes, and even his rival Hooke's work on gravity. He once said, "If I have seen further, it is by standing on the shoulders of giants." But Newton's universal theory of gravity, although it drew on work of others before him, formulated something entirely new. His synthesis offered a single, descriptive account of mass and motion. "All bodies whatsoever are endowed with a principle of mutual gravitation." The law of gravitation was stated in a mathematical formula; supported by observation and experience; and, literally, universal.

The scientific elite of Newton's time was not uniformly persuaded. Many mechanical philosophers, particularly Cartesians, objected to the prominence in Newton's theory of forces acting across empty space. Such attractions smacked of mysticism (or the occult); they seemed to lack any driving mechanism. Newton

NEWTON ON THE PURPOSES OF EXPERIMENTAL PHILOSOPHY

When Newton added his General Scholium *to the second edition of* Principia *in 1713, he was seventy-one, president of the Royal Society, and widely revered. Responding to continental critics, he set out his general views on science and its methods, arguing against purely deductive reasoning and reliance on hypotheses about ultimate causes.*

Hitherto we have explained the phenomena of the heavens and of our sea by the power of gravity, but have not yet assigned the cause of this power. This is certain, that it must proceed from a cause that penetrates to the very centres of the sun and planets, without suffering the least diminution of its force; that operates not according to the quantity of the surfaces of the particles on which it acts (as mechanical causes used to do), but according to the quantity of the solid matter which they contain, and propagates its virtue on all sides to immense distances, decreasing always as the inverse square of the distances. . . . [H]itherto I have not been able to discover the cause of those properties of gravity from phenomena, and I frame no hypothesis; for whatever is not deduced from the phenomena is to be called an hypothesis; and hypotheses, whether metaphysical or physical, whether of occult qualities or mechanical, have no place in experimental philosophy. In this philosophy particular propositions are inferred from the phenomena, and afterwards rendered general by induction. . . . And to us it is enough that gravity does really exist, and acts according to the laws which we have explained, and abundantly serves to account for all the motions of the celestial bodies, and of our sea.

Michael R. Matthews, ed., *The Scientific Background to Modern Philosophy: Selected Readings* (Indianapolis and Cambridge, 1989), p. 152.

QUESTIONS FOR ANALYSIS

1. Why did Isaac Newton declare that "hypotheses, whether metaphysical or physical, whether of occult qualities or mechanical, have no place in experimental philosophy"?

responded to these criticisms in a note added to the next edition of the *Principia* (*General Scholium*, 1713). He did not know what *caused* gravity, he said, and he did not "feign hypotheses." "For whatever is not deduced from the phenomena must be called hypothesis," he wrote, and has "no place in the experimental philosophy." For Newton, certainty and objectivity lay in the precise mathematical characterization of phenomena —"the mathematization of the universe," as one historian puts it. Science could not, and need not, always uncover causes. It did describe natural phenomena and accurately predict the behavior of objects as confirmed by experimentation.

Other natural philosophers immediately acclaimed Newton's work for solving long-standing puzzles. Thinkers persuaded that the Copernican version of the universe was right had been unable to piece together the physics of a revolving earth. Newton made it possible to do so. Halley provided a poem to accompany the first edition of *Principia*. "No closer to the gods can

Newton and Satire. The English artist and satirist William Hogarth mocking both philosophy and "Newton worship" in 1763. The philosophers' heads are being weighed on a scale that runs from "absolute gravity" to "absolute levity" or "stark fool."

any mortal rise," he wrote, of the man with whom he had worked so patiently. Halley did have a financial as well as an intellectual interest in the book, and he also arranged for it to be publicized and reviewed in influential journals. John Locke (whose own *Essay Concerning Human Understanding* was written at virtually the same time, in 1690) read *Principia* twice and summarized it in French for readers across the Channel. By 1713 pirated editions of *Principia* were being published in Amsterdam for distribution throughout Europe. By the time Newton died, in 1727, he had become an English national hero and was given a funeral at Westminster Abbey. The poet Alexander Pope expressed the awe that Newton inspired in some of his contemporaries in a famous couplet

> Nature and nature's law lay hid in night;
> God said, "Let Newton be!" and all was light.

Voltaire, the French champion of the Enlightenment (discussed in the next chapter), was largely responsible for Newton's reputation in France. In this he was helped by a woman who was a brilliant mathematician in her own right, Emilie du Châtelet. Du Châtelet co-authored a book with Voltaire introducing Newton to a French audience; and she translated *Principia*, a daunting scientific and mathematical task and one well beyond Voltaire's mathematical abilities. Newton's French admirers and publicists disseminated Newton's findings. In their eyes Newton also represented a cultural transformation, a turning point in the history of knowledge.

SCIENCE AND CULTURAL CHANGE

From the seventeenth century on, science stood at the heart of what it meant to be "modern." It also grew increasingly central to the self-understanding of Western culture; indeed, scientific and technological power became one of the justifications for the expansion of Western empires and the subjugation of other peoples. For all these reasons, the revolution in understanding the universe was and often still is presented as a thorough-going break with the past, a moment that recast the architecture of Western culture. But as one historian has written "no house is ever built of entirely virgin materials, according to a plan bearing no resemblance to old patterns, and no body of culture is able to wholly reject its past. Historical change is not like that, and most 'revolutions' effect less sweeping changes than they advertise or than are advertised for them."

To begin with, the transformation we have canvassed in this chapter involved elite knowledge. Ordinary people inhabited a very different cultural world. Second, natural philosophers' discoveries—Tycho's mathematics and Galileo's observations, for instance—did not undo the authority of the ancients in one blow. They did not seek to do so. Third, science did not subvert religion. Even when traditional concepts collapsed in the face of new discoveries, natural philosophers seldom gave up on the project of restoring a picture of a divinely ordered universe. Mechanists argued that the intricate universe revealed by the discoveries of Copernicus, Kepler, Galileo, Newton, and others was evidence of God's guiding presence. Robert Boyle's will provided the funds for a lecture series on the "confutation of atheism" by scientific means. Isaac Newton was happy to have his work contribute to that project. "Nothing," he wrote to one of the lecturers in 1692, "can rejoice me more than to find [*Principia*] usefull for

CHAPTER 16: THE NEW SCIENCE OF THE SEVENTEENTH CENTURY

Establishment of the Academy of Sciences and Foundation of the Observatory, **1667.** The 1666 founding of the Academy of Sciences was a measure of the new prestige of science and the potential value of research. Louis XIV sits at the center, surrounded by the religious and scholarly figures who offer the fruits of their knowledge to the French state.

that purpose." The creation of "the Sun and Fixt stars," "the motion which the Planets now have could not spring from any naturall cause alone but were imprest with a divine Agent." Science was thoroughly compatible with belief in God's providential design, at least through the seventeenth century.

The greatest scientific minds were deeply committed to beliefs that do not fit our notion of "modern." Newton, again, is the most striking case in point. The great twentieth-century economist John Maynard Keynes was one of the first to read through Newton's private manuscripts. On the 300th anniversary of Newton's birth (the celebration of which was delayed because of World War II), Keynes offered the following reappraisal of the great scientist:

> I believe that Newton was different from the conventional picture of him. . . .
> In the eighteenth century and since, Newton came to be thought of as the first and greatest of the modern age of scientists, a rationalist, one who taught us to think on the lines of cold and untinctured reason.
> I do not see him in this light. I do not think that any one who has pored over the contents of that box which he packed up when he finally left Cambridge in 1696 and which, though partly dispersed, have come down to us, can see him like that. Newton was not the first of the age of reason. He was the last of the magicians, the last of the Babylonians and Sumerians, the last great mind which looked out on the visible and intellectual world with the same eyes as those who began to build our intellectual inheritance rather less than 10,000 years ago.

> The greatest scientific minds were deeply committed to beliefs that do not fit our notion of "modern."

Those eyes saw the world as a text, God's message to humanity. Close reading and study would unlock its mysteries. The same impulse led Newton to read about magic, to practice alchemy, and to immerse himself in the writings of the church fathers and in the Bible, which he knew in intimate detail. Newton then, was the last representative of an older tradition, and also, quite unintentionally, the first of a new one.

WHAT PROBLEMS DID NEWTON SOLVE?

What, then, did the scientific revolution change? Seventeenth-century natural philosophers had produced new answers to fundamental questions about the physical world. Age-old questions about astronomy and physics had been recast and, to some extent (although it was not yet clear to what extent), answered. In the process there had developed a new approach to amassing, deciphering, and integrating information in a systematic way, an approach that helped yield more insights into the workings of nature as time went on. In this period, too, the most innovative scientific work moved out of the restrictive environment of the church and the universities. Natural philosophers began talking to and working with each other in lay organizations that developed standards of research. England's Royal Society spawned imitators in Florence and Berlin and later in Russia. The French Royal Academy of Sciences had a particularly direct relationship with the monarchy and the French state. France's statesmen exerted control over the academy and sought to share in the rewards of any discoveries its members made.

New, too, were beliefs about the purpose and methods of science. The practice of breaking a complex problem down into parts made it possible to tackle more and different questions in the physical sciences. Mathematics assumed a more central role in the new science. Finally, rather than simply confirming established truths, the new methods were designed to explore the unknown and provide means to discover new truths. As Kepler wrote to Galileo, "How great a difference there is between theoretical speculation and visual experience, between Ptolemy's discussion of the Antipodes and Columbus's discovery of the New World." Knowledge itself was reconceived. In the

Ramelli, *Le diverse et artificiose* machine (1558). A model of humanist learning, this "book wheel" from the mid-sixteenth century allowed readers to consult several books at a time, cross-referencing, comparing, and immersing themselves in a body of book knowledge.

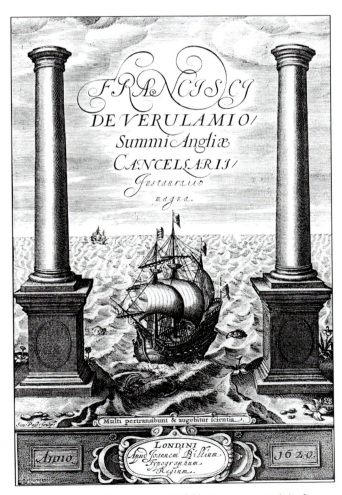

Bacon, *Instauratio magna* (1620). The new model of learning as discovery. The quotation below reads: "Many shall venture forth and science shall be increased."

older model, to learn was to read: to reason logically, to argue, to compare classical texts, and to absorb a finite body of knowledge. In the newer one, to learn was to discover, and what could be discovered was boundless.

Conclusion

The pioneering natural philosophers remained circumspect about their abilities. Some sought to lay bare the workings of the universe; others believed humans could only catalog and describe the regularities observed in nature. By unspoken but seemingly mutual agreement, the question of first causes was left aside. The new science did not say *why*, but *how*. Newton, for one, worked toward explanations that would reveal the logic of creation laid out in mathematics. Yet in the end, he settled for theories explaining motions and relationships that could be observed and tested.

The eighteenth-century heirs to Newton were much more daring. Laboratory science and the work of the scientific societies largely stayed true to the experimenters' rules and limitations. But as we will see in the next chapter, the natural philosophers who began investigating the human sciences cast aside some of their predecessors' caution. Society, technology, government, religion, even the individual human mind seemed to be mechanisms or parts of a larger nature waiting for study. The scientific revolution overturned the natural world as it had been understood for a millennium; it also inspired thinkers more interested in revolutions in society.

Key Terms

heliocentric
Aristotelian
Nicholas Copernicus

Galileo Galilei
Discourse on Method
scientific societies

Francis Bacon

Selected Readings

Biagioli, Mario. *Galileo, Courtier.* Chicago, 1993. Emphasizes the importance of patronage and court politics in Galileo's science and career.

Cohen, I. B. *The Birth of a New Physics.* New York, 1985. Emphasizes the mathematical nature of the revolution; unmatched at making the mathematics understandable.

Dear, Peter. *Revolutionizing the Sciences: European Knowledge and Its Ambitions, 1500–1700.* Princeton, N.J., 2001. Among the best short histories.

Drake, Stillman. *Discoveries and Opinions of Galileo.* Garden City, N.Y., 1957. The classic translation of Galileo's most important papers by his most admiring modern biographer.

Feingold, Mardechai, *The Newtonian Moment: Isaac Newton and the Making of Modern Culture.* New York, 2004. An engaging essay on the dissemination of Newton's thought, with excellent visual material.

Gaukroger, Stephen. *Descartes: An Intellectual Biography.* Oxford, 1995. Detailed and sympathetic study of the philosopher.

Gleick, James. *Isaac Newton.* New York, 2003. A vivid and well-documented brief biography.

Grafton, Anthony. *New Worlds, Ancient Texts: The Power of Tradition and the Shock of Discovery.* Cambridge, Mass., 1992. Accessible essay by one of the leading scholars of early modern European thought.

Hall, A. R. *The Revolution in Science, 1500–1750.* New York, 1983. Revised version of a 1954 classic.

Jones, Richard Foster. *Ancients and Moderns: A Study of the Rise of the Scientific Movement in Early Modern England.* Berkeley, Calif., 1961. Still a persuasive study of the scientific revolutionaries' attempts to situate their work in relation to that of the Greeks.

Koestler, Arthur. *The Sleepwalkers: A History of Man's Changing Vision of the Universe.* London, 1958. A readable classic.

Kuhn, Thomas. *The Structure of Scientific Revolutions.* Chicago, 1962. A classic and much-debated study of how scientific thought changes.

Pagden, Anthony, *European Encounters with the New World.* New Haven, Conn., and London, 1993. Subtle and detailed on how European intellectuals thought about the lands they saw for the first time.

Scheibinger, Londa. *The Mind Has No Sex? Women in the Origins of Modern Science.* Cambridge, Mass., 1989. A lively and important recovery of the lost role played by women mathematicians and experimenters.

Shapin, Steven. *The Scientific Revolution.* Chicago, 1996. Engaging, accessible, and brief—organized thematically.

Shapin, Steven, and Simon Schaffer. *Leviathan and the Air Pump.* Princeton, N.J., 1985. A modern classic, on one of the most famous philosophical conflicts in seventeenth-century science.

Stephenson, Bruce. *The Music of the Heavens: Kepler's Harmonic Astronomy.* Princeton, N.J., 1994. An engaging and important explanation of Kepler's otherworldly perspective.

Thoren, Victor. *The Lord of Uraniburg: A Biography of Tycho Brahe.* Cambridge, 1990. A vivid reconstruction of the scientific revolution's most flamboyant astronomer.

Westfall, Richard. *The Construction of Modern Science.* Cambridge, 1977.

Westfall, Richard. *Never at Rest: A Biography of Isaac Newton.* Cambridge, 1980. The standard work.

Wilson, Catherine. *The Invisible World: Early Modern Philosophy and the Invention of the Microscope.* Princeton, N.J., 1995. An important study of how the "microcosmic" world revealed by technology reshaped scientific philosophy and practice.

Zinsser, Judith P. *La Dame d'Esprit: A Biography of the Marquise Du Châtelet.* New York, 2006. An excellent cultural history. To be issued in paper as *Emilie du Châtelet: Daring Genius of the Enlightenment* (2007).

Chapter Seventeen

Chapter Contents

The Foundations of the Enlightenment 604

The World of the *Philosophes* 606

Internationalization of Enlightenment Themes 609

Empire and Enlightenment 612

The Radical Enlightenment 617

The Enlightenment and Eighteenth-Century Culture 621

Conclusion 630

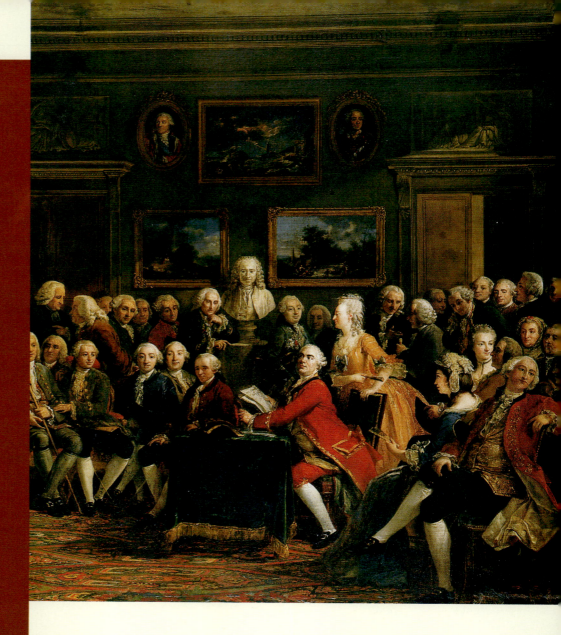

The Enlightenment

IN 1762, THE *PARLEMENT* (law court) of Toulouse, in France, convicted Jean Calas of murdering his son. Calas was Protestant, and Catholic–Protestant tensions ran high in the region. Witnesses called before the court claimed that the young Calas had wanted to break with his family and convert to Catholicism, and they convinced the magistrates that Calas had killed his son rather than let him fall from the Protestant faith. French law stipulated the punishment. Calas was tortured twice: first in an attempt to get him to confess and, next, as a formal part of certain death sentences, to force him to name his alleged accomplices. His arms and legs were slowly pulled apart, gallons of water were poured down his throat, and his body was publicly broken on the wheel, which meant that each of his limbs was smashed with an iron bar. Then the executioner cut off his head. Throughout the trial, torture, and execution, Calas maintained his innocence. Two years later, the *Parlement* reversed its verdict, declared Calas not guilty, and offered the family a payment in compensation.

François Marie Arouet, also known as Voltaire, was one of those appalled by the verdict and punishment. At the time of the case, Voltaire was the most famous Enlightenment thinker in Europe. Well connected and a prolific writer, Voltaire took up his pen to clear Calas' name; he contacted friends, hired lawyers for the family, and wrote briefs, letters, and essays to bring the case to the public eye. Calas's case exemplified nearly everything Voltaire opposed in his culture. Intolerance, ignorance, and what Voltaire throughout his life called religious "fanaticism" and "infamy" had made a travesty of justice. "Shout everywhere, I beg you, for Calas and against fanaticism, for it is *l'infame* that has caused their misery," he wrote to his friend Jean Le Rond d'Alembert, a fellow Enlightenment thinker. Using torture to uncover truth demonstrated the power of unquestioned and centuries-old practices. Legal procedures that included secret interrogations, trials behind closed doors, summary judgment (Calas was executed the day after being convicted, with no review by a higher court), and barbaric punishments defied reason, morality, and human dignity. Any criminal,

FOCUS QUESTIONS

- What were the common themes and aims of the Enlightenment writings?
- How did the French *philosophes* challenge the established order?
- What issues mattered to Enlightenment thinkers and why?

- Why were colonies and imperial policy important to Enlightenment thinkers?
- Was the Enlightenment revolutionary?
- How did social and cultural change shape the Enlightenment?

however wretched, "is a man," wrote Voltaire, "and you are accountable for his blood."

Voltaire's comments on the Calas case illustrate the classic concerns of the Enlightenment: the dangers of arbitrary and unchecked authority, the value of religious toleration, and the overriding importance of law, reason, and human dignity in all affairs. He borrowed most of his arguments from others—from his predecessor the baron de Montesquieu and from the Italian writer Cesare Beccaria, whose *On Crimes and Punishments* appeared in 1764. Voltaire's reputation did not rest on his originality as a philosopher. It came from his effectiveness as a writer and advocate, his desire and ability to reach a wide audience. In this, too, he was representative of the Enlightenment project.

THE FOUNDATIONS OF THE ENLIGHTENMENT

What were the common themes and aims of the Enlightenment writings?

The Enlightenment was an eighteenth-century phenomenon, lasting for close to the entire century. Not every important thinker who lived and worked in the eighteenth century rallied to the Enlightenment banner. Some, such as the Italian philosopher of history G. B. Vico (1668–1744), opposed almost everything the Enlightenment stood for; and others, most notably Jean-Jacques Rousseau, accepted certain Enlightenment values but sharply rejected others. Patterns of Enlightenment thought varied from country to country, and they changed in each country over the course of the century. Many eighteenth-century thinkers nonetheless shared the sense of living in an exciting new intellectual environment in which the "party of humanity" would prevail over customary practices and traditional thought.

Enlightenment writings shared several basic characteristics. They were marked, first, by a confidence in the powers of human reason. This self-assurance stemmed from the accomplishments of the scientific revolution. Even when the details of Newton's physics were poorly understood, his methods provided a model for scientific inquiry into other phenomena. Nature operated according to laws that could be grasped by study, observation, and thought. The work of the extraordinary Scottish writer David Hume (*A Treatise of Human Nature*, 1739–1740, and the *Enquiries Concerning Human Understanding*, 1748) provided the most direct bridge from science to the Enlightenment. Newton had refused hypotheses, or speculation about ultimate causes, arguing for the precise description of natural phenomena (see Chapter Sixteen). Hume took this same rigor and skepticism to the study of morality, the mind, and government, often using Newtonian language or drawing analogies to scientific laws. Hume criticized the "passion for hypotheses and systems" that dominated much philisophical thinking. Experience and careful observation, he argued, usually did not support the premises on which those systems rested. Among Hume's many examples was Thomas Hobbes's theory of human nature, which underpinned the latter's views on government (see Chapter Fourteen).

Human understanding and the exercise of human reason also entailed certain political conditions. "Dare to know!" the German philosopher Immanuel Kant challenged his contemporaries in his classic 1784 essay "What Is Enlightenment?" For Kant, the Enlightenment represented a declaration of intellectual independence. (He also called it an awakening and credited Hume with rousing him from his "dogmatic slumber.") Kant likened the intellectual history of humanity to the growth of a child. Enlightenment, in this view, was an escape from humanity's "self-imposed immaturity" and a long overdue break with humanity's self-imposed parental figure—namely, the Catholic Church. Coming of age meant the "determination and courage to think without the guidance of someone else," as an individual. Reason required autonomy, or freedom from tradition and well-established authorities.

Despite their declarations of independence from the past, Enlightenment thinkers recognized a great debt to their immediate predecessors. Voltaire called Bacon, Newton, and John Locke his "Holy Trinity." Indeed, much of the eighteenth-century Enlightenment consisted of translating, republishing, and thinking through the implications of the great works of the seventeenth century. Enlightenment thinkers drew heavily on Locke's studies of human knowledge, especially his *Essay Concerning Human Understanding* (1690), which was even more influential than his political philosophy. Locke's theories of how humans acquire knowledge gave education and environment a critical role in shaping human character. All knowledge, he argued, originates from sense perception. The human mind at birth is a "blank tablet" (in Latin, *tabula rasa*).

WHAT WERE THE COMMON THEMES AND AIMS OF THE ENLIGHTENMENT WRITINGS?

THE FOUNDATIONS OF THE ENLIGHTENMENT   605

Only when an infant begins to experience things, to perceive the external world with its senses, does anything register in its mind. Locke's starting point, which became a central premise for those who followed, was the goodness and perfectibility of humanity. Building on Locke, eighteenth-century thinkers made education central to their project, because education promised individual moral improvement and social progress. It is worth noting that Locke's theories had potentially more radical implications: education might be able to level hierarchies of status, sex, or race. As we will see, only a few Enlightenment thinkers made such egalitarian arguments. Still, optimism and a belief in universal human progress constituted a second defining feature of nearly all Enlightenment thinking.

Third, Enlightenment thinkers were extraordinarily ambitious and wide ranging. They sought nothing less than the organization of all knowledge. The *scientific*

> Historians have called the Enlightenment a "cultural project," emphasizing Enlightenment thinkers' interest in practical, applied knowledge and their determination to spread knowledge and to promote free public discussion.

method, by which they meant the empirical observation of particular phenomena to arrive at general laws, offered a way to pursue research in all areas—to study human affairs as well as natural ones. Thus they collected evidence to learn the laws governing the rise and fall of nations, and they compared governmental constitutions to arrive at an ideal and universally applicable political system. As the English poet Alexander Pope stated in his *Essay on Man* (1733), "the science of human nature [may be] like all other sciences reduced to a few clear points," and Enlightenment thinkers became determined to learn exactly what those few clear points were. They took up a strikingly wide array of subjects in this systematic manner: knowledge and the mind, natural history, economics, government, religious beliefs, customs of indigenous peoples in the New World, human nature, and sexual (or what we would call gender) and racial differences.

Historians have called the Enlightenment a "cultural project," emphasizing Enlightenment thinkers' interest in practical, applied knowledge and their determination to spread knowledge and to promote free public discussion. They intended, as Denis Diderot (*deed-ROH*) wrote, "to change the common way of thinking" and to advance the cause of "enlightenment" and humanity. Although they shared many of their predecessors' theoretical concerns, they wrote in a very different style and for a much larger audience. Hobbes and Locke had published treatises for small groups of learned seventeenth-century readers. Voltaire, in contrast, wrote plays, essays, and letters; Rousseau composed music, published his *Confessions*, and wrote novels that moved his readers to tears; Hume wrote history for a wide audience. A British aristocrat or a governor in the North American colonies would have read Locke. But a middle-class woman might have read Rousseau's fiction, and shopkeepers and artisans could become familiar with popular Enlightenment-inspired pamphlets. Among the elite, newly formed "academies" sponsored prize essay contests, and well-to-do women and men discussed affairs of state in salons. In other words, the intellectual achievements and goals of the Enlightenment followed from cultural developments in the eighteenth century. Those developments included the expansion of literacy and growing markets for books, new networks of

Voltaire. A brilliant and popular writer, his criticisms of the regime helped establish the international reputation of the *philosophes*.

readers, new forms of intellectual exchange, and the emergence of what some historians call the first "public sphere."

In sum, Enlightenment thinkers confronted their culture, exposing time-worn practices, beliefs, and authority to the shining light of reason. That often meant criticism and satire. They combined an irreverence for custom and tradition with a belief in human perfectibility and progress. They were confident in their ability to understand the world and passionately interested in the relationship between nature and culture, or environment, history, and human character and society. Their program of reform had immediate political implications; in a remarkably short time it changed the premises of government and society throughout the Atlantic world.

The World of the Philosophes

> How did the French *philosophes* challenge the established order?

Enlightenment thought was European in a broad sense, including southern and eastern Europe as well as Europe's colonies in the New World. British thinkers played a—perhaps *the*—key role. France, however, provided the stage for some of the most widely read Enlightenment books and the most closely watched battles. For this reason, Enlightenment thinkers, regardless of where they lived, are often called by the French word *philosophes*. Yet hardly any of the *philosophes*, with the exceptions of David Hume and Immanuel Kant, were philosophers in the sense of being highly original abstract thinkers. Especially in France, Enlightenment thinkers shunned forms of expression that might seem incomprehensible, priding themselves instead on their clarity and style. *Philosophe*, in French, simply meant "a free thinker," a person whose reflections were unhampered by the constraints of religion or dogma in any form.

Voltaire

At the time, the best known of the *philosophes* was Voltaire, born François Marie Arouet (1694–1778). As Erasmus two centuries earlier had embodied Christian humanism, Voltaire virtually personified the Enlightenment, commenting on an enormous range of subjects in a wide variety of literary forms. Educated by the Jesuits, he emerged quite young as a gifted and sharp-tongued writer. His gusto for provocation landed him in the Bastille (a notorious prison in Paris) for libel and soon afterward in temporary exile in England. In his three years there, Voltaire became an admirer of British political institutions, British culture, and British science; above all, he became an extremely persuasive convert to the ideas of Newton, Bacon, and Locke. His single greatest accomplishment may have been popularizing Newton's work in France and more generally championing the cause of British empiricism and the scientific method against the more Cartesian French.

Voltaire's *Philosophical Letters* (*Letters on the English Nation*), published after his return in 1734, made an immediate sensation. Voltaire's themes were religious and political liberty, and his weapons were comparisons.

Voltaire and Franklin, 1778. Voltaire blesses the grandson of Benjamin Franklin, who stands in the background. The two Enlightenment thinkers met in Paris shortly before Voltaire's death.

His admiration for British culture and politics became a stinging critique of France—and other absolutist countries on the Continent. He praised British open-mindedness and empiricism: the country's respect for scientists and its support for research. He considered the relative weakness of the British aristocracy a sign of Britain's political health. Unlike the French, the British respected commerce and people who engage in it, Voltaire wrote. The British tax system was rational, free of the complicated exemptions for the privileged that were ruining French finances. The British House of Commons represented the middle classes and, in contrast with French absolutism, brought balance to British government and checked arbitrary power. In one of the book's more incendiary passages, he argued that in Britain, violent revolution had actually produced political moderation and stability: "[T]he idol of arbitrary power was drowned in seas of blood. . . . The English nation is the only nation in the world that has succeeded in moderating the power of its kings by resisting them." Of all Britain's reputed virtues, religious toleration loomed largest of all. Britain, Voltaire argued, brought together citizens of different religions in a harmonious and productive culture. In this and other instances, Voltaire oversimplified: British Catholics, Dissenters, and Jews did not have equal civil rights. Yet the British policy of "toleration" did contrast with Louis XIV's intolerance of Protestants. Revoking the Edict of Nantes (1685) had stripped French Protestants of civil rights and had helped create the atmosphere in which Jean Calas—and others—were persecuted.

Voltaire's famous battle cry, "*Écrasez l'infâme*," translates as "crush infamy," and by *infamy* he meant all forms of repression, fanaticism, and bigotry. He wrote the following to an opponent, and it is a statement often cited as the first principle of civil liberty: "I do not agree with a word you say, but I will defend to the death your right to say it." Of all forms of intolerance Voltaire opposed religious bigotry most, and with real passion he denounced religious fraud, faith in miracles, and superstition. "The less superstition, the less fanaticism; and the less fanaticism, the less misery." He did not oppose religion per se; rather he sought to rescue morality, which he believed to come from God, from dogma—elaborate ritual, dietary laws, formulaic prayers—and from a powerful church bureaucracy. He argued for common sense and simplicity, persuaded that these would bring out the goodness in humanity and establish stable authority. "The simpler the laws are, the more the magistrates are respected; the simpler the religion will be, the more one will revere its ministers. Religion can be simple. When enlightened people will announce a single God, rewarder and avenger, no one will laugh, everyone will obey."

Voltaire relished his position as a critic, and it never stopped him from being successful. He was regularly exiled from France and other countries, his books banned and burned. As long as his plays attracted large audiences, however, the French king felt he had to tolerate their author. Voltaire had an attentive international public, including Frederick of Prussia, who invited him to his court at Berlin, and Catherine of Russia, with whom he corresponded about reforms she might introduce in Russia. Voltaire described himself as "contraband," but that seemed only to enhance his value. When he died in 1778, a few months after a triumphant return to Paris, he was possibly the best-known writer in Europe.

> Voltaire's famous battle cry, "*Écrasez l'infâme*," translates as "crush infamy," and by *infamy* he meant all forms of repression, fanaticism, and bigotry.

MONTESQUIEU

The Baron de Montesquieu (*mahn-tuhs-KYOO*, 1689–1755) was a very different kind of Enlightenment figure. Montesquieu was born to a noble family. He inherited both an estate and, since state offices were property that passed from father to son, a position as magistrate in the *Parlement*, or law court, of Bordeaux. He was not a stylist or a provocateur like Voltaire but a relatively cautious jurist. He did write a satirical novel, *The Persian Letters* (1721), published anonymously (to protect his reputation) in Amsterdam. The novel was composed as letters from two Persian visitors to France. The visitors detailed the odd religious superstitions they witnessed, compared manners at the French court with those in Turkish harems, and likened French absolutism to their own brands of *despotism*, or the abuse of government authority.

Montesquieu's serious treatise *The Spirit of Laws* (1748) may have been the most influential work of the Enlightenment. It was a groundbreaking study in what we would call comparative historical sociology and very Newtonian in its careful, empirical approach. Montesquieu asked about the structures that shaped law. How had different environments, histories, and religious traditions combined to create such a variety of governmental institutions? What were the different forms of government: what spirit characterized each, and what were their respective virtues and shortcomings? Montesquieu proposed a threefold classification of states. A republic was governed by the many—in his view either an elite aristocracy or the people. In the second type, monarchy, a single authority ruled in accordance with the law. Despotism, Montesquieu's most important negative example, allowed a single ruler to govern unchecked by law or other powers, sowing corruption and capriciousness. The soul or spirit of a republic was virtue; of monarchy, honor; of despotism, where no citizen could feel secure and punishment took the place of education, fear. Lest this seem abstract, Montesquieu devoted two chapters to the French monarchy, in which he spelled out what he saw as a dangerous drift toward despotism in his own land. Like other Enlightenment thinkers, Montesquieu admired the British system and its separate and balanced powers—executive, legislative, and judicial—which guaranteed liberty in the sense of freedom from the absolute power of any single governing individual or group. His idealization of "checks and balances" had formative influence on Enlightenment political theorists and members of the governing elites, particularly those who wrote the United States Constitution in 1787.

Montesquieu. The French baron's *Spirit of the Laws* (1748) was probably the most influential single text of the high Enlightenment.

DIDEROT AND THE *ENCYCLOPEDIA*

Voltaire's and Montesquieu's writings represent the themes and style of the French Enlightenment. But the most remarkable French publication of the century was a collective venture: the *Encyclopedia*. The *Encyclopedia* intended to summarize and disseminate all the most advanced contemporary philosophical, scientific, and technical knowledge. In terms of sheer scope, this was the grandest statement of the *philosophes'* goals. It demonstrated how scientific analysis could be applied in nearly all realms of thought. It aimed to reconsider an enormous range of traditions and institutions and to put reason to the task of bringing happiness and progress to humanity. The guiding spirit behind the venture was Denis Diderot. Diderot was helped by the Newtonian mathematician Jean Le Rond d'Alembert (1717–1783) and other leading men of letters, including Voltaire and Montesquieu. The *Encyclopedia* was published, in installments, between 1751 and 1772; by the time it was completed, it ran to seventeen large volumes of text and eleven more of illustrations. A collaborative project, it helped create the *philosophes'* image as the "party of humanity."

The *Encyclopedia* sought to "change the general way of thinking." Diderot commissioned articles that explained recent achievements in science and technology, showing how machines worked and illustrating new industrial processes. The point was to demonstrate how the everyday applications of science could promote progress and alleviate all forms of human misery. Diderot turned the same methods to matters of religion, politics, and the foundations of the social order, including articles on economics, taxes, and the slave trade. Censorship made it difficult to write openly antireligious articles. Diderot, therefore, thumbed his nose at religion in oblique ways; at the entry on the Eucharist, the reader found a terse cross-reference: "See *cannibalism*." Gibes like this aroused storms of controversy when the early volumes of the *Encyclopedia* appeared. The French government revoked permission for the *Encyclopedia* to be published, declaring in 1759 that the encyclopedists were trying to "propagate materialism," which meant atheism, "to destroy Religion, to inspire a spirit of independence, and to nourish the corruption of morals." The volumes sold remarkably well despite such bans and their hefty price. Purchasers belonged to the elite: aristocrats, government officials, prosperous merchants, and a scattering of members of the higher clergy. That elite, though, stretched across Europe, including its overseas colonies.

Technology and Industry. This engraving, from the mining section, is characteristic of Diderot's *Encyclopedia*. The project aimed to detail technological changes, manufacturing processes, and forms of labor—all in the name of advancing human knowledge.

Although the French *philosophes* sparred with the state and the church, they sought political stability and reform. Montesquieu, not surprising in light of his birth and position, hoped that an enlightened aristocracy would press for reforms and defend liberty against a despotic king. Voltaire, persuaded that aristocrats would represent only their particular narrow interests, looked to an enlightened monarch for leadership. Neither was a democrat, and neither conceived of reform from below. Still, their widely read writings were subversive. Their satires of absolutism and, more broadly, arbitrary power, stung. By the 1760s the French critique of despotism provided the language in which many people across Europe articulated their opposition to existing regimes.

INTERNATIONALIZATION OF ENLIGHTENMENT THEMES

What issues mattered to Enlightenment thinkers and why?

The party of humanity was international. French became the lingua franca of much Enlightenment discussion, but "French" books were often published in Switzerland, Germany, and Russia. As we have seen, Enlightenment thinkers admired British institutions and British scholarship, and they used both as points of reference. Great Britain also produced among the most important Enlightenment thinkers: the historian Edward Gibbon and the Scottish philosophers David Hume and Adam Smith. The *philosophes* considered Thomas Jefferson and Benjamin Franklin part of their group. Despite stiffer resistance from religious authorities, stricter state censors, and smaller networks of educated elites to discuss and support progressive thought, the Enlightenment flourished across central and southern Europe. Frederick II of Prussia housed Voltaire during one of his exiles from France, though the *philosophe* quickly wore out his welcome. Frederick also patronized a small but unusually productive group of Enlightenment thinkers. Northern Italy was an important center of Enlightenment thought. Enlightenment thinkers across Europe raised similar themes: humanitarianism, or the dignity and worth of all individuals; religious toleration; and liberty.

ENLIGHTENMENT THEMES: HUMANITARIANISM AND TOLERATION

Among the most influential writers of the entire Enlightenment was the Italian (Milanese) jurist Cesare Beccaria (1738–1794). Beccaria's *On Crimes and Punishments* (1764) sounded the same general themes as did the French *philosophes*—arbitrary power, reason, and human dignity—and it provided Voltaire with most of his arguments in the Calas case. Beccaria also proposed concrete legal reforms. He attacked the prevalent view that punishments should represent society's vengeance on the criminal. The only legitimate rationale for punishment was to maintain social order and to prevent other crimes. Beccaria argued for the greatest possible leniency compatible with deterrence; respect for individual dignity and humanity dictated that humans should punish other humans no more than is absolutely necessary. Above all, Beccaria's book eloquently opposed torture and the death penalty. The spectacle of public execution, which sought to dramatize the power of the state and the horrors of hell, instead dehumanized the victim, judge, and spectators. In 1766, a few years after the Calas case, another French trial provided an example of what horrified Beccaria and the *philosophes*. A nineteen-year-old French nobleman, convicted of blasphemy, had his tongue cut out and his hand cut off before he was burned at the stake. Since the court discovered the blasphemer had read Voltaire, it ordered the *Philosophical Dictionary* burned along with the body. Sensational cases such as this one helped publicize Beccaria's work, and *On Crimes and Punishments* was quickly translated into a dozen languages. Owing primarily to its influence, most European countries by around 1800 abolished torture, branding, whipping, and various forms of mutilation and reserved the death penalty for capital crimes.

Humanitarianism and reason also counseled religious toleration. Enlightenment thinkers spoke almost as one on the need to end religious warfare and the persecution of heretics and religious minorities. It is important, though, to differentiate between the church as an institution and dogma, against which many Enlightenment thinkers rebelled, and as religious belief, which most accepted. Only the smallest number of Enlightenment thinkers, notably Paul Henri d'Holbach (1723–1789), were atheists, and very few were even avowed agnostics. Many (Voltaire, for instance) were deists, holding a religious outlook that saw God as a "divine clockmaker" who, at the beginning of time, constructed a perfect timepiece and then left it to run with predictable regularity. Enlightenment inquiry proved compatible with very different stances on religion.

Toleration was limited. Most Christians saw Jews as heretics and Christ killers. And although Enlightenment thinkers deplored persecution, they commonly viewed Judaism and Islam as backward religions mired in superstition and obscurantist ritual. One of the few Enlightenment figures to treat Jews sympa-

> Enlightenment thinkers spoke almost as one on the need to end religious warfare and the persecution of heretics and religious minorities.

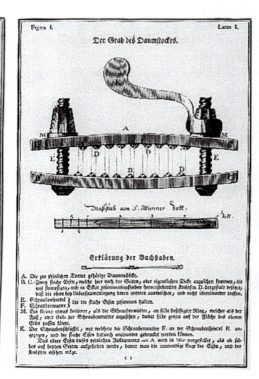

Instruments of Torture. A man being stretched on the rack (left) and a thumbscrew (right), both from an official Austrian government handbook. By 1800, Beccaria's influence had helped phase out the use of such instruments.

thetically was the German *philosophe* Gotthold Lessing (1729–1781). Lessing's extraordinary play *Nathan the Wise* (1779) takes place in Jerusalem during the Fourth Crusade and begins with a pogrom—or violent, orchestrated attack—in which the wife and children of Nathan, a Jewish merchant, are murdered. Nathan survives to become a sympathetic and wise father figure. He adopts a Christian-born daughter and raises her with three religions: Christianity, Islam, and Judaism. At several points, authorities ask him to choose the single true religion. Nathan shows none exists. The three great monotheistic religions are three versions of the truth. Religion is authentic, or true, only insofar as it makes the believer virtuous.

Lessing modeled his hero on his friend Moses Mendelssohn (1729–1786), a self-educated rabbi and bookkeeper (and the grandfather of the composer Felix Mendelssohn). Moses Mendelssohn moved—though with some difficulty—between the Enlightenment circles of Frederick II and the Jewish community of Berlin. Mendelssohn unsuccessfully tried to avoid religion as a subject. Repeatedly attacked and invited to convert to Christianity, he finally took up the question of Jewish identity. In a series of writings, the best-known of which is *On the Religious Authority of Judaism* (1783), he defended Jewish communities against anti-Semitic policies and Jewish religion against Enlightenment criticism. At the same time, he also promoted reform within the Jewish community, arguing that his community had special reason to embrace the broad Enlightenment project: religious faith should be voluntary, states should promote tolerance, humanitarianism would bring progress to all.

ECONOMICS, GOVERNMENT, AND ADMINISTRATION

Enlightenment ideas had a very real currency in affairs of state. The *philosophes* defended reason and knowledge for humanitarian reasons. But they also promised to make nations stronger, more efficient, and more prosperous. Beccaria's proposed legal reforms were a good case in point; he sought to make laws not simply more just but also more effective. In other words, the Enlightenment spoke to individuals but also to states. The *philosophes* addressed issues of liberty and rights but also took up matters of administration, tax collection, and economic policy.

The rising fiscal demands of eighteenth-century states and empires made these issues newly urgent. Which economic resources were most valuable to states? How could governments tap them? Enlightenment economic thinkers such as the physiocrats argued that long-standing mercantilist policies were misguided. By the eighteenth century, *mercantilism* had become a term for a very wide range of policies that shared a belief in government regulation of trade in manufactured goods and precious metals. The physiocrats, most of them French, held that real wealth came from the land and agricultural production. More important, they advocated simplifying the tax system and following a policy of laissez-faire, which comes from the French expression *laissez faire la nature* ("let nature take its course"), letting wealth and goods circulate without government interference.

The now-classic expression of laissez-faire economics, however, came from the Scottish economist Adam Smith (1723–1790), and especially from Smith's landmark treatise *Inquiry into the Nature and Causes of the Wealth of Nations* (1776). Smith disagreed with the physiocrats on the value of agriculture, but he shared their opposition to mercantilism. For Smith, the central issues were the productivity of labor and how labor was used in different sectors of the economy. Mercantile restrictions—such as

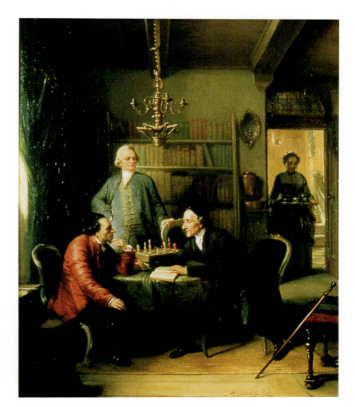

Lessing and Mendelssohn. The German philosopher Gotthold Lessing visits his friend Moses Mendelssohn, one of the major Jewish figures of the Enlightenment.

high taxes on imported goods, which was one of the grievances of the colonists throughout the American empires—did not encourage the productive deployment of labor and thus did not create real economic health. For Smith, general prosperity could best be obtained by allowing the famous "invisible hand" to guide economic activity. Individuals, in other words, should pursue their own interests without competition from state-chartered monopolies or legal restraints. As Smith wrote in his earlier *Theory of Moral Sentiments* (1759), self-interested individuals could be "led by an invisible hand . . . without knowing it, without intending it, [to] advance the interest of the society."

The *Wealth of Nations* spelled out, in more technical and historical detail, the different stages of economic development, how the invisible hand actually worked, and the beneficial aspects of competition. Its perspective owed much to Newton and to the Enlightenment's idealization of both nature and human nature. Smith wanted to follow what he called, in classic Enlightenment terms, the "obvious and simple system of natural liberty." Smith thought of himself as the champion of justice against state-sponsored economic privilege and monopolies. He was a theorist of human feelings as well as of market forces. Smith emerged as the most influential of the new eighteenth-century economic thinkers. In the following century, ironically, his work and his followers became the target of reformers and critics of the new economic world.

Empire and Enlightenment

Why were colonies and imperial policy important to Enlightenment thinkers?

Smith's *Wealth of Nations* formed part of a debate about the economics of empire: *philosophes* and statesmen alike asked how the colonies could be profitable, and to whom. The colonial world loomed large in Enlightenment thinking in several other ways. The new world across the Atlantic offered a foil to the old civilization of Europe, in other words, an often idealized portrait of natural humanity and simplicity, by comparison with which Europe looked decadent or corrupt. Second, Europeans' colonial activities—especially, by the eighteenth century, the slave trade—could not help

but raise pressing issues about humanitarianism, individual rights, and natural law. The effects of colonialism on Europe were a central Enlightenment theme.

Smith wrote in *The Wealth of Nations* that the "discovery of America, and that of a passage to the East Indies by the cape of Good Hope are the two greatest and most important events recorded in the history of mankind. What benefits, or what misfortunes to mankind may herafter result form those great events," he continued, "no human wisdom can foresee." Smith's language was nearly identical to that of a Frenchman, the Abbé Guillaume Thomas François Raynal. Raynal's massive *Philosophical History . . . of Europeans in the Two Indies* (1770), a co-authored work like the *Encyclopedia*, was one of the most widely read works of the Enlightenment, going through twenty printings and at least forty pirated editions. Raynal drew his inspiration from the *Encyclopedia* and aimed at nothing less than a total history of colonization: customs and civilizations of indigenous peoples, natural history, exploration, and commerce in the Atlantic world and India. He also tried to draw up a balance sheet, asking as did Smith, whether colonization had made humanity happier, more peaceful, or better. The question was fully in the spirit of the Enlightenment. So was the answer. Raynal believed that industry and trade brought improvement and progress. Like other Enlightenment writers, however, he and his co-authors considered natural simplicity an antidote to the corruptions of their culture. They sought out and idealized what they considered examples of "natural" humanity, many of them in the New World. For example, they wrote that what Europeans considered savage life might be "a hundred times preferable to that of societies corrupted by despotism" and lamented the loss of humanity's "natural liberty." They condemned the tactics of the Spanish in Mexico and Peru, of the Portuguese in Brazil, and of the British in North America. They echoed Montesquieu's theme that good government required checks and balances against arbitrary authority. In the New World, they argued, Europeans found themselves with virtually unlimited power, which encouraged them to be arrogant, cruel, and despotic. In a later edition, after the outbreak of the American Revolution, the book went even further, drawing parallels between exploitation in the colonial world and inequality at home: "We are mad in the way we act with our colonies, and inhuman and mad in our conduct toward our peasants," asserted one author. Eighteenth-century radicals repeatedly warned that overextended empires sowed seeds of decadence and corruption at home.

THE IMPACT OF THE NEW WORLD ON ENLIGHTENMENT THINKERS

The Abbé Guillaume Thomas François Raynal (1713–1796) was a clergyman and intellectual who moved in the inner circles of the Enlightenment. As a senior cleric he had access to the royal court; as a writer and intellectual he worked with the encyclopedists and other authors who criticized France's institutions, including the Catholic Church of which Raynal himself was a part. Here he tries to offer a perspective on the profound effects of discovering the Americas and ends by asking whether particular historical developments and institutions lead to the betterment of society.

There has never been any event which has had more impact on the human race in general and for Europeans in particular, as that of the discovery of the New World, and the passage to the Indies around the Cape of Good Hope. It was then that a commercial revolution began, a revolution in the balance of power, and in the customs, the industries and the government of every nation. It was through this event that men in the most distant lands were linked by new relationships and new needs. The produce of equatorial regions were consumed in polar climes. The industrial products of the north were transported to the south; the textiles of the Orient became the luxuries of Westerners; and everywhere men mutually exchanged their opinions, their laws, their customs, their illnesses, and their medicines, their virtues and their vices. Everything changed, and will go on changing. But will the changes of the past and those that are to come be useful to humanity? Will they give man one day more peace, more happiness, or more pleasure? Will his condition be better, or will it be simply one of constant change?

Abbé Guillaume Thomas François Raynal, *Philosophical and Political History of European Establishments and Commerce in the Two Indies* (1770), as cited in Dourinda Outram, *The Enlightenment* (Cambridge, 1995), p. 73.

QUESTIONS FOR ANALYSIS

1. Why was the discovery of America of such profound significance for eighteenth-century Europe?
2. Why was Raynal so concerned with people's conduct and happiness?
3. Why does Raynal ask whether historical developments lead to the betterment of society? What is his answer?

SLAVERY AND THE ATLANTIC WORLD

Discussing Europe's colonies and economies inevitably raised the issue of slavery. The sugar islands of the Caribbean were among the most valued possessions of the colonial world and the sugar trade one of the leading sectors of the Western economy. The Atlantic slave trade reached its peak in the eighteenth century. European slave traders sent at least 1 million Africans into New World slavery in the late seventeenth century, and at least 6 million in the eighteenth century. On this topic, however, even thinkers as radical as Raynal and Diderot hesitated, and their hesitations are revealing about the tensions in Enlightenment thought. Enlightenment thinking began with the premise that individuals could reason and govern themselves. Individual moral freedom lay at the heart of what the Enlightenment considered to be a just, stable, and harmonious society.

CHAPTER 17 — THE ENLIGHTENMENT

Slavery defied natural law and natural freedom. Montesquieu, for instance, wrote that civil law created chains, but natural law would always break them. Nearly all Enlightenment thinkers condemned slavery in the metaphorical sense. That the "mind should break free of its chains" and that "despotism enslaved the king's subjects" were phrases that echoed through much eighteenth-century writing. It was common for the central characters of eighteenth-century fiction, such as Voltaire's hero Candide, to meet enslaved people, learning compassion as part of their moral education. Writers dealt more gingerly, however, with the actual enslavement and slave labor of Africans.

Some Enlightenment thinkers skirted the issue of slavery. Others reconciled principle and practice in different ways. Smith condemned slavery as uneconomical. Voltaire, quick to expose his contemporaries' hypocrisy, wondered whether Europeans would look away if Europeans—rather than Africans—were enslaved. Voltaire, however, did not question his belief that Africans were inferior peoples. Montesquieu (who came from Bordeaux, one of the central ports for the Atlantic trade) believed that slavery debased master and slave alike. But he also argued that all societies balanced their systems of labor in accordance with their different needs, and slave labor was one such system. Finally, like many Enlightenment thinkers, Montesquieu defended property rights, including those of slaveholders.

The *Encyclopedia*'s article on the slave trade did condemn the slave trade in the clearest possible terms, as a violation of self-government. Humanitarian antislavery movements, which emerged in the 1760s, advanced similar arguments. From deploring slavery to imagining freedom for slaves, however, proved a very long step, and one that few were willing to take. In the end, the Enlightenment's environmental determinism—the belief that environment shaped character—provided a common way of postponing the entire issue. Slavery corrupted its victims, destroyed their natural virtue, and crushed their natural love of liberty. Enslaved people, by this logic, were not ready for freedom. It was characteristic for Warville de Brissot's Society of the Friends of Blacks to call for abolition of the slave trade and to invite Thomas Jefferson, a slaveholder, to join the organization. Only a very few advocated abolishing slavery, and they insisted that emancipation be

> Nearly all Enlightenment thinkers condemned slavery in the metaphorical sense. That the "mind should break free of its chains" and that "despotism enslaved the king's subjects" were phrases that echoed through much eighteenth-century writing.

gradual. Slavery proved one of several realms in which different currents in Enlightenment thought ran toward very different conclusions.

EXPLORATION AND THE PACIFIC WORLD

The Pacific world also figured prominently in Enlightenment thinking. Systematically mapping new sections of the Pacific was among the crucial developments of the age, and one with a tremendous impact on the public imagination. These explorations were also scientific missions, sponsored as part of the Enlightenment project of expanding scientific knowledge. In 1767 the French government sent Louis-Anne de Bougainville (1729–1811) to the South Pacific in search of a new route to China, new lands suitable for colonization, and new spices for the ever lucrative trade. They sent along scientists and artists to record his findings. Like many other explorers, Bougainville found none of what he sought, but his travel accounts—above all his fabulously lush descriptions of the earthly paradise of Nouvelle-Cythère, or Tahiti—captured the attention and imaginations of many at home. The British captain James Cook (1728–1779), who followed Bougainville, made two trips into the South Pacific (1768–1771 and 1772–1775), with impressive results. He charted the coasts of New Zealand and New Holland and added the New Hebrides and Hawaii to European maps. He explored the outer limits of the Antarctic continent, the shores of the Bering Sea, and the Arctic Ocean. The artists and scientists who accompanied Cook and Bougainville vastly expanded the boundaries of European botany, zoology, and geology. Their drawings—such as Sydney Parkinson's extraordinary portraits of the Maori—appealed to a wide public. So did the accounts of dangers overcome and peoples encountered. A misguided attempt to communicate with South Pacific islanders, perhaps with the intention of conveying them to Europe, ended in the grisly deaths of Cook and four royal marines on Hawaii in late January 1779, which surely added to European readers' fascination with his travels. Large numbers of people in Europe avidly read travel accounts of these voyages. When Cook and Bougainville brought Pacific islanders to the metropolis they at-

SLAVERY AND THE ENLIGHTENMENT

The encyclopedists made an exhaustive and deliberate effort to comment on every institution, trade, and custom in Western culture. The project was conceived as an effort to catalog, analyze, and improve each facet of society. Writing in an age of burgeoning maritime trade and expanding overseas empires, they could not, and did not wish to, avoid the subject of slavery. These were their thoughts on plantation slavery, the African slaves who bore its brunt, and broader questions of law and liberty posed by the whole system.

Thus there is not a single one of these hapless souls—who, we maintain, are but slaves—who does not have the right to be declared free, since he has never lost his freedom; since it was impossible for him to lose it; and since neither his ruler nor his father nor anyone else had the right to dispose of his freedom; consequently, the sale of his person is null and void in and of itself: this Negro does not divest himself, indeed cannot under any condition divest himself of his natural rights; he carries them everywhere with him, and he has the right to demand that others allow him to enjoy those rights. Therefore, it is a clear case of inhumanity on the part of the judges in those free countries to which the slave is shipped, not to free the slave instantly by legal declaration, since he is their brother, having a soul like theirs.

From *Encyclopédie*, Vol. 16 (1765), as cited in David Brion Davis, *The Problem of Slavery in Western Culture* (Ithaca, N.Y., 1966), p. 416.

QUESTIONS FOR ANALYSIS

1. What arguments against slavery does the *Encyclopedia* article present? Do you agree with the claim that slavery is legally impossible because no one can sell his or her natural rights? What are natural rights?
2. The enslavement of conquered peoples was historically an ancient and well-established custom, approved by civil and religious authorities. Even some Enlightenment figures, such as Thomas Jefferson, were slave owners. How did some Enlightenment *philosophes* use universal ideas of freedom to argue against custom in regard to slavery and other questions?

---

tracted large crowds. Joshua Reynolds painted portraits of the islanders.

THE IMPACT OF THE SCIENTIFIC MISSIONS

Back in Europe, Enlightenment thinkers drew freely on reports of scientific missions. Since they were already committed to understanding human nature and the origins of society and to studying the effects of the environment on character and culture, stories of new peoples and cultures were immediately fascinating. In 1772 Diderot, one of many eager readers of Bougainville's accounts, published his own reflections on the cultural significance of those accounts, the *Supplément au Voyage de Bougainville*. For Diderot, the Tahitians were the original human beings and, unlike the inhabitants of the New World, were virtually free of European influence. They represented humanity in its natural state, Diderot believed, uninhibited about sexuality and free of religious dogma. Their simplicity exposed the hypocrisy and rigidity of overcivilized Europeans. Others considered the indigenous peoples of the

Chapter 17 THE ENLIGHTENMENT

Maoris in a War Canoe near Lookout Point. This engraving copies an illustration by Sidney Parkinson from James Cook's explorations. Depictions of the exotic Pacific world captured the public's imagination during the Enlightenment.

Pacific akin to the classical civilizations of Greeks and Romans, associating Tahitian women, for instance, with Venus, the Roman goddess of love. All these views said more about Europe and European utopias than about indigenous cultures in the Pacific. Enlightenment thinkers found it impossible to see other peoples as anything other than primitive versions of Europeans. Even these views, however, marked a change from former times. In earlier periods Europeans had understood the world as divided between Christendom and heathen others. In sum, during the eighteenth century a religious understanding of Western identity was giving way to more secular conceptions.

One of the most important scientific explorers of the period was the German scientist Alexander von Humboldt. Humboldt spent five years in Spanish America, aiming to do nothing less than assess the civilization and natural resources of the continent. He went equipped with the most advanced scientific instruments Europe could provide. Between 1814 and 1819, Humboldt produced an impressive multivolume *Personal Narratives of Travels* much like the lavishly illustrated reports by Cook and Bougainville. The expense bankrupted him, sending him to the Prussian court in search of financial support. Humboldt's investigations provide an important link between the Enlightenment and nineteenth-century science. Humboldt, in good Enlightenment fashion, attempted to demonstrate that climate and physical environment determined which forms of life would survive in any given region. These investigations would continue in nineteenth-century discussions of evolutionary change. Charles Darwin referred to Humboldt as "the greatest scientific traveler who ever lived," and the German scientist's writing inspired Darwin's voyage to the Galapagos Islands off the coast of Ecuador.

Thus Europeans who looked outward did so for a variety of reasons and reached very different conclusions. For some Enlightenment thinkers and rulers, scientific reports from overseas fitted into a broad inquiry about civilization and human nature. That inquiry sometimes encouraged self-criticism and at others simply shored up Europeans' sense of their superiority. The late-eighteenth-century revolutions brought this Enlightenment discussion to a close. Yet these themes reemerged during the nineteenth century, when new empires were built and the West's place in the world was reassessed.

THE RADICAL ENLIGHTENMENT

Was the Enlightenment revolutionary?

How revolutionary was the Enlightenment? Enlightenment thought did undermine central tenets of eighteenth-century culture and politics. It did have a wide resonance, well beyond a small group of intellectuals. Yet Enlightenment thinkers did not hold to any single political position. Even the most radical among them disagreed on the implications of their thought. Jean-Jacques Rousseau and Mary Wollstonecraft provide good examples of such radical thinkers.

THE WORLD OF ROUSSEAU

Jean-Jacques Rousseau (roo-SOH, 1712–1778) was an "outsider" who quarreled with the other *philosophes* and contradicted many of their assumptions. He shared the *philosophes*' search for intellectual and political freedom, attacked inherited privilege, and believed in the good of humanity and the possibility of creating a just society. Yet he introduced other strains into Enlightenment thought, especially morality and what was then called "sensibility," or the cult of feeling. He was also considerably more radical than his counterparts, one of the first to talk about popular sovereignty and democracy. He was surely the most utopian, which made his work popular at the time and has opened it to different interpretations since. In the late eighteenth century he was the most influential and most often cited of the *philosophes*, the thinker who brought the Enlightenment to a larger audience.

Rousseau's milestone and difficult treatise on politics, *The Social Contract*, began with a now famous paradox: "Man was born free, and everywhere he is in chains." How had humans freely forged these chains? To ask this was to reformulate the key questions of seventeenth- and eighteenth-century thought. What were the origins of government? Was government's authority legitimate? If not, Rousseau asked, how could it become so? Rousseau argued that in the state of nature, all men had been equal. (On women, men, and nature, see later in this section.) Social inequality, anchored in private property, profoundly corrupted "the social contract," or the formation of government. Under conditions of inequality, governments and laws represented only the rich and privileged. They became instruments of repression and enslavement. Legitimate governments could be formed, Rousseau argued. "The problem is to find a form of association . . . in which each, while uniting himself with all, may still obey himself alone, and remain as free as before." Freedom did not mean the absence of restraint, it meant that equal citizens obeyed laws they had made themselves. Rousseau hardly imagined any social leveling, and by *equality* he meant only that no one would be "rich enough to buy another, nor poor enough to have to sell oneself."

Rousseau believed that legitimate authority arose from the people alone. His argument has three parts. First, sovereignty should not be divided among different branches of government (as suggested by Montesquieu), and it emphatically could not be usurped by a king. In the late seventeenth century, Locke had spelled out the people's right to rebel against a tyrannical king. Rousseau argued that a king never became sovereign to begin with. Instead, the people themselves acted together as legislators, executives, and judges. Second, exercising sovereignty transformed the nation. Rousseau argued that when individual citizens formed a "body politic," that body became more than just the sum of its parts. He offered what was to many an appealing image of a regenerated and more powerful nation, in which citizens were bound by mutual obligation rather than coercive laws and united in equality rather than divided and weakened by privilege. Third, the national

> Rousseau's milestone and difficult treatise on politics, *The Social Contract*, began with a now famous paradox: "Man was born free, and everywhere he is in chains."

ROUSSEAU'S *SOCIAL CONTRACT* (1762)

Jean-Jacques Rousseau (1712–1778) was one of the most radical Enlightenment thinkers. In his works he suggested that humans needed not only a clearer understanding of natural laws but also a much closer relationship with nature itself and a thorough reorganization of society. He believed that a sovereign society, formed by free association of equal citizens without patrons or factions, was the clearest expression of natural law. This society would make laws and order itself by the genuinely collective wisdom of its citizens. Rousseau sets out the definition of his sovereign society and its authority in the passages reprinted here.

Book I, Chapter 6

"To find a form of association that defends and protects the person and possessions of each associate with all the common strength, and by means of which each person, joining forces with all, nevertheless obeys only himself, and remains as free as before." Such is the fundamental problem to which the social contract furnishes the solution.

Book II, Chapter 4

What in fact is an act of sovereignty? It is not an agreement between a superior and an inferior, but an agreement between the body and each of its members, a legitimate agreement, because it is based upon the social contract; equitable, because it is common to all; useful, because it can have no other purpose than the general good; and reliable, because it is guaranteed by the public force and the supreme power. As long as the subjects are only bound by agreements of this sort, they obey no one but their own will, and to ask how far the respective rights of the sovereign and citizens extend is to ask to what point the latter can commit themselves to each other, one towards all and all towards one.

Jean-Jacques Rousseau, *Rousseau's Political Writings*, trans. Julia Conaway Bondanella, ed. Allan Ritter and Julia Conaway Bondanella (New York, 1988), pp. 92. 103.

QUESTIONS FOR ANALYSIS

1. How can one join a political association and yet remain free?
2. If sovereignty is a contract, how long does it last? Can anyone refuse to accept it? Or ignore it?

community would be united by what Rousseau called the "general will." This term is notoriously difficult. Rousseau proposed it as a way to understand the common interest, which rose above particular individual demands. The general will favored equality; that made it general, and in principle at least equality guaranteed that citizens' common interests would be represented in the whole.

Rousseau's lack of concern for balancing private interests against the general will leads some political theorists to consider him authoritarian, coercive, or moralistic. Others interpret the general will as one expression of his utopianism. In the eighteenth century, *The Social Contract* was the least understood of Rousseau's works. Yet it provided influential radical arguments and, more important, extraordinarily powerful images and phrases, which were widely cited during the French Revolution.

Rousseau was better known for his writing on education and moral virtue. His widely read novel *Emile* (1762) tells the story of a young man who learns virtue and moral autonomy in the school of nature rather than in the academy. Rousseau disagreed with other *philosophes'* emphasis on reason, insisting instead that "the first impulses of nature are always right." Children should not be forced to reason early in life. Books, which "teach us only to talk about things we do not know," should not be central to learning until adolescence. Emile's tutor thus walked him through the woods, studying nature and its simple precepts, cultivating his conscience and, above all, his sense of independence. "Nourished in the most absolute liberty, the greatest evil he can imagine is servitude."

Such an education aimed to give men moral autonomy and make them good citizens. Rousseau argued that women should have very different educations. "All education of women must be relative to men, pleasing them, being useful to them, raising them when they are young and caring for them when they are old, advising them, consoling them, making their lives pleasant and agreeable, these have been the duties of women since time began." Women were to be useful socially as mothers and wives. In *Emile*, Rousseau laid out just such an education for Emile's wife-to-be, Sophie. At times, Rousseau seemed convinced that women "naturally" sought out such a role: "Dependence is a natural state for women, girls feel themselves made to obey." At other moments he insisted that girls needed to be disciplined and weaned from their "natural" vices.

Rousseau's conflicting views on female nature provide a good example of the shifting meaning of *nature*, a concept central to Enlightenment thought. Enlightenment thinkers used nature as a yardstick against which to measure society's shortcomings. "Natural" was better, simpler, uncorrupted. What, though, was nature? It could refer to the physical world. It could refer to primitive societies. Often, it was a useful invention.

Rousseau's novels sold exceptionally well, especially among women. *Julie* (subtitled *La nouvelle Héloïse*), published just after *Emile*, went through seventy editions in three decades. *Julie* tells the story of a young woman who falls in love with one man but dutifully obeys her father's order to marry another. At the end, after many travails and twists of the plot, she dies of exposure after rescuing her children from a cold lake—a perfect example of domestic and maternal virtue. One of Rousseau's fellow *philosophes* deemed the tale "hysterical and obscene." What appealed to the public, however, was the love story, the tragedy, and Rousseau's

Enlightenment Education as Illustrated in *Emile*. These colored engravings from Rousseau's influential novel depict Emile's studies in the great outdoors as opposed to the classroom.

conviction that humans were ruled by their hearts as much as their heads, that passion was more important than reason. Rousseau's novels became part of a larger cult of *sensibilité* ("feeling") in middle-class and aristocratic circles, an emphasis on spontaneous expressions of feeling, and a belief that sentiment was an expression of authentic humanity. Thematically, this aspect of Rousseau's work contradicted much of the Enlightenment's cult of reason. It is more closely related to the concerns of nineteenth-century romanticism.

How did Rousseau's ideas fit into Enlightenment views on gender? As we have seen, Enlightenment thinkers considered education key to human progress. Many lamented the poor education of women, especially because, as mothers, governesses, and teachers, many women were charged with raising and teaching children. What kind of education, however, should girls receive? Here, again, Enlightenment thinkers sought to follow the guidance of nature, and they produced scores of essays and books in philosophy, history, literature, and medicine, discussing the nature or character of the sexes. Were men and women different? Were those differences natural, or had they been created by custom and tradition? Humboldt and Diderot wrote essays on the nature of the sexes; scientific travel literature reported on the family structures of indigenous peoples in the Americas, the South Pacific, and China. Histories of civilization by Smith among many others commented on family and gender roles at different stages of history. Montesquieu's *Spirit of the Laws* included an analysis of how the different stages of government affected women. To speculate on the subject, as Rousseau did, was a common Enlightenment exercise.

Some disagreed with his conclusions. Diderot, Voltaire, and the German thinker Theodor Von Hippel, among many others, deplored legal restrictions on women. Rousseau's prescriptions for women's education drew especially sharp criticism. The English writer and historian Catherine Macaulay set out to refute his points. The Marquis de Condorcet argued on the eve of the French Revolution that the Enlightenment promise of progress could not be fulfilled unless women were educated—and Condorcet was virtually alone in asserting that women should be granted political rights.

The World of Wollstonecraft

Rousseau's sharpest critic was the British writer Mary Wollstonecraft (1759–1797). Wollstonecraft published her best known work, *A Vindication of the Rights of Woman*, in 1792, during the French Revolution. Her argument, however, was anchored in Enlightenment debates and needs to be understood here. Wollstonecraft shared Rousseau's political views and admired his writing and influence. Like Rousseau and her countryman Thomas Paine, a writer who supported the American and French revolutionaries, Wollstonecraft was a republican. She called monarchy "the pestiferous purple which renders the progress of civilization a curse, and warps the understanding." She spoke even more forcefully than Rousseau against inequality and the artificial distinctions of rank, birth, or wealth. Believing that equality laid the basis for virtue, she contended, in classic Enlightenment language, that the society should seek "the perfection of our nature and capability of happiness." She argued more forcefully than any other Enlightenment thinker that (1) women had the same innate capacity for reason and self-government as men, (2) *virtue* should mean the same thing for men and women, and (3) relations between the sexes should be based on equality.

Wollstonecraft did what few of her contemporaries even imagined. She applied the radical Enlightenment critique of monarchy and inequality to the family. The legal inequalities of marriage law, which among other things deprived married women of property rights,

Mary Wollstonecraft. The British writer and radical was one of several Enlightenment thinkers to take up the "woman question."

gave husbands "despotic" power over their wives. Just as kings cultivated their subjects' deference, so culture, she argued, cultivated women's weakness. "Civilized women are . . . so weakened by false refinement, that, respecting morals, their condition is much below what it would be were they left in a state nearer to nature." Middle-class girls learned manners, grace, and seductiveness to win a husband; they were trained to be dependent creatures. "My own sex, I hope, will excuse me, if I treat them like rational creatures instead of flattering their *fascinating* graces, and viewing them as if they were in a state of perpetual childhood, unable to stand alone. I earnestly wish to point out in what true dignity and human happiness consists—I wish to persuade women to endeavor to acquire strength, both of mind and body." A culture that encouraged feminine weakness produced women who were childish, cunning, cruel—and vulnerable. Here Wollstonecraft echoed common eighteenth-century themes. The scheming aristocratic women in Choderlos de Laclos's *Dangerous Liaisons*, written in the 1780s, were meant to illustrate the same points. To Rousseau's specific prescriptions for female education, which included teaching women timidity, chasteness, and modesty, Wollstonecraft replied that Rousseau wanted women to use their reason to "burnish their chains rather than to snap them." Instead, education for women had to promote liberty and self-reliance.

Wollstonecraft was a woman of her time. She argued for the common humanity of men and women but believed that they had different duties and that women's foremost responsibility was mothering and educating children. Like many of her fellow Enlightenment thinkers, Wollstonecraft believed that a natural division of labor existed and that it would ensure social harmony. "Let there be no coercion *established* in society, and the common law of gravity prevailing, the sexes will fall into their proper places." Like others, she wrote about middle-class women, for whom education and property were issues. She was considered scandalously radical for merely hinting that women might have political rights.

The Enlightenment as a whole left a mixed legacy on gender, one that closely paralleled that on slavery. Enlightenment writers developed and popularized arguments about natural rights. They also elevated natural differences to a higher plane by suggesting that nature should dictate different, and quite possibly unequal, social roles. Mary Wollstonecraft and Jean-Jacques Rousseau shared a radical opposition to despotism and slavery, a moralist's vision of a corrupt society, and a concern with virtue and community. Their divergence on gender is characteristic of Enlightenment disagreements about nature and its imperatives and a good example of different directions in which the logic of Enlightenment thinking could lead.

THE ENLIGHTENMENT AND EIGHTEENTH-CENTURY CULTURE

> How did social and cultural change shape the Enlightenment?

THE BOOK TRADE

What about the social structures that produced these debates and received these ideas? To begin with, the Enlightenment was bound up in a much larger expansion of printing and print culture. From the early eighteenth century on, book publishing and selling flourished, especially in Britain, France, the Netherlands, and Switzerland. National borders, though, mattered very little. Much of the book trade was both international and clandestine. Readers bought books from stores, by subscription, and by special mail order

---

CHRONOLOGY

MAJOR PUBLICATIONS OF THE ENLIGHTENMENT, 1734–1792

Voltaire, *Philosophical Letters*	1734
Montesquieu, *The Spirit of Laws*	1748
The *Encyclopedia*	1751–1772
Rousseau, *The Social Contract*	1762
Rousseau, *Emile*	1762
Beccaria, *On Crime and Punishments*	1764
Smith, *Inquiry into Nature and Causes of the Wealth of Nations*	1776
Raynal, *Philosophical History*	1770
Wollstonecraft, *A Vindication of the Rights of Woman*	1792

ROUSSEAU AND HIS READERS

Jean-Jacques Rousseau's writings provoked very different responses from eighteenth-century readers—women as well as men. Many women readers loved his fiction and found his views about women's character and prescriptions for their education inspiring. Other women disagreed vehemently with his conclusions. In the first excerpt here, from Rousseau's novel Emile *(1762), the author sets out his views on a woman's education. He argues that her education should fit with what he considers her intellectual capacity and her social role. It should also complement the education and role of a man. The second selection is an admiring response to* Emile *from Anne-Louise-Germaine Necker, or Madame de Staël (1766–1817), a well-known French writer and literary critic. While she acknowledged that Rousseau sought to keep women from participating in political discussion, she also thought that he had granted women a new role in matters of emotion and domesticity. The third excerpt is from Mary Wollstonecraft, who shared many of Rousseau's philosophical principles but sharply disagreed with his assertion that women and men should have different virtues and values. She believed that women like Madame de Staël were misguided in embracing Rousseau's ideas.*

ROUSSEAU'S *EMILE*

Researches into abstract and speculative truths, the principles and axioms of sciences—in short, everything which tends to generalize our ideas—is not the proper province of women; their studies should be relative to points of practice; it belongs to them to apply those principles which men have discovered.... All the ideas of women, which have not the immediate tendency to points of duty, should be directed to the study of men, and to the attainment of those agreeable accomplishments which have taste for their object; for as to works of genius, they are beyond their capacity; neither have they sufficient precision or power of attention to succeed in sciences which require accuracy; and as to physical knowledge, it belongs to those only who are most active, most inquisitive, who comprehend the greatest variety of objects....

She must have the skill to incline us to do everything which her sex will not enable her to do herself, and which is necessary or agreeable to her; therefore she ought to study the mind of man thoroughly, not the mind of man in general, abstractedly, but the dispositions of those men to whom she is subject either by the laws of her country or by the force of opinion.

She should learn to penetrate into the real sentiments from their conversation, their actions, their looks and gestures. She should also have the art, by her own conversation, actions, looks, and gestures, to communicate those sentiments which are agreeable to them without seeming to intend it. Men will argue more philosophically about the human heart; but women will read the heart of men better than they.... Women have most wit, men have most genius; women observe, men reason. From the concurrence of both we derive the clearest light and the most perfect knowledge which the human mind is of itself capable of attaining.

Jean-Jacques Rousseau, *Emile* (1762), as cited in Mary Wollstonecraft, *A Vindication of the Rights of Woman* (New York and London, 1992), pp. 124–125.

MADAME DE STAËL

Though Rousseau has endeavoured to prevent women from interfering in public affairs, and acting a brilliant part in the theatre of politics; yet in speaking of them, how much has he done it to their satisfaction! If he wished to deprive them of some rights foreign to their sex, how has he for ever restored to them all those to which it has a claim! And in attempting to diminish their influence over the deliberations of men, how sacredly has he established the empire they have over

their happiness! In aiding them to descend from an usurped throne, he has firmly seated them upon that to which they were destined by nature; and though he be full of indignation against them when they endeavour to resemble men, yet when they come before him with all the *charms, weaknesses, virtues,* and *errors* of their sex, his respect for their *persons* amounts almost to adoration.

Cited in Mary Wollstonecraft, *A Vindication of the Rights of Woman* (New York and London, 1992), pp. 203–204.

MARY WOLLSTONECRAFT

Rousseau declares that a woman should never, for a moment, feel herself independent, that she should be governed by fear to exercise her *natural* cunning, and made a coquettish slave in order to render her a more alluring object of desire, a *sweeter* companion to man, whenever he chooses to relax himself. He carries the arguments, which he pretends to draw from the indications of nature, still further, and insinuates that truth and fortitude, the corner stones of all human virtue, should be cultivated with certain restrictions, because, with respect to the female character, obedience is the grand lesson which ought to be impressed with unrelenting rigour.

What nonsense! When will a great man arise with sufficient strength of mind to puff away the fumes which pride and sensuality have thus spread over the subject! If women are by nature inferior to men, their virtues must be the same in quality, if not in degree, or virtue is

a relative idea; consequently, their conduct should be founded on the same principles, and have the same aim.

Cited in Susan Bell and Karen Offen, eds., *Women, the Family, and Freedom: The Debate in Documents,* Vol. 1, *1750–1880* (Stanford, Calif., 1983), p. 58.

QUESTIONS FOR ANALYSIS

1. How could Rousseau assert that women were unsuited to study the sciences? What evidence did he produce? What arguments might persuade his contemporary readers?
2. According to Rousseau, what would women gain from the "study of men, and the attainment of agreeable accomplishments"?
3. Mary Wollstonecraft thought Rousseau's views on women were nonsense. Why?
4. Why did the two women read Rousseau so differently? Were they misreading?

---

from book distributors abroad. Cheaper printing and better distribution also helped multiply the numbers of journals, some specializing in literary or scientific topics and others quite general. They helped bring daily newspapers, which first appeared in London in 1702, to Moscow, Rome, and cities and towns throughout Europe. By 1780, Britons could read 150 different magazines, and 37 English towns had local newspapers. These changes have been called a "revolution in communication," and they form a crucial part of the larger picture of the Enlightenment.

Governments did little to check this revolutionary transformation. In Britain, the press encountered few restrictions, although the government did use a stamp tax on printed goods to raise the price of newspapers or

books and discourage buyers. Elsewhere, laws required publishers to apply in advance for the license or privilege (in the sense of "private right") to print and sell any given work. Some regimes granted more permissions than others. The French government, for instance, alternately banned and tolerated different volumes of the *Encyclopedia,* depending on the subjects covered in the volume, the political climate in the capital, and economic considerations. In practice, publishers frequently printed books without advance permission, hoping that the regime would not notice, but bracing themselves for fines, having their books banned, and finding their privileges temporarily revoked. Russian, Prussian, and Austrian censors tolerated much less dissent; but those governments also

THE ENLIGHTENMENT

sought to stimulate publishing and, to a certain degree, permitted public discussion. Vienna housed an important publishing empire during the reigns of Joseph and Maria Theresa. Catherine of Russia encouraged the development of a small publishing enterprise which, by 1790, was issuing 350 titles a year. In the smaller states of Germany and Italy, governed by many local princes, it was easier to find progressive local patrons, and English and French works also circulated widely through those regions. That governments were patrons as well as censors of new scholarship illustrates the complex relationship between the age of absolutism and the Enlightenment.

As one historian puts it, censorship only made banned books expensive, keeping them out of the hands of the poor. Clandestine booksellers, most near the French border in Switzerland and the Rhineland, smuggled thousands of books across the border to bookstores, distributors, and private customers. What did readers want, and what does this tell us about the reception of the Enlightenment? Many clandestine dealers specialized in what they called "philosophical books," which meant subversive literature of all kinds: stories of languishing in prison, gossipy memoirs of life at the court, pornographic fantasies (often about religious and political figures), and tales of crime and criminals. A book smuggler would have carried several copies of *The Private Lives of Louis XIV* or *The Black Gazette;* Voltaire's comments on *Encyclopedia;* and, less frequently, Rousseau's *Social Contract.* Much of this flourishing eighteenth-century "literary underground," as the historian Robert Darnton calls it, echoed the radical Enlightenment's themes, especially the corruption of the aristocracy and the monarchy's degeneration into despotism. Less explicitly political writings, however,

such as Raynal's *History,* Rousseau's novels, travel accounts, biographies, and futuristic fantasies such as Louis Sebastien Mercier's *The Year 2440* proved equally popular. Even expensive volumes like the *Encyclopedia* sold remarkably well, testifying to a keen public interest. It is worth underscoring that Enlightenment work circulated in popular form, and that Rousseau's novels sold as well as his political theory.

HIGH CULTURE, NEW ELITES, AND THE PUBLIC SPHERE

The Enlightenment was not simply embodied in books; it was produced in networks of readers and new forms of sociability and discussion. Eighteenth-century elite or "high" culture was small in scale but cosmopolitan and very literate, and it took discussion seriously. A new elite joined together members of the nobility and wealthy people from the middle classes. Among the institutions that produced this new elite were learned societies: the American Philosophical Society of Philadelphia, British literary and philosophical societies, and the Select Society of Edinburgh. Such groups organized intellectual life outside of the universities, and they provided libraries, meeting places for discussion, and journals that published members' papers or organized debates on issues from literature and history to economics and ethics. Elites also met in "academies," financed by governments to advance knowledge, whether through research into the natural sciences (the Royal Society of London, and the French Academy of Science, both founded in 1660), promoting the national language (the Académie Française, or French Academy of Literature), or safeguarding traditions in the arts (the various academies of painting). The Berlin Royal Academy, for instance, was founded in 1701 to demonstrate the Prussian state's commitment to learning. Members included scholars in residence, corresponding members in other countries, and honorary associates, so the academy's reach was quite broad; and the Prussian government made a point of bringing in scholars from other countries. Particularly under Frederick II, who was eager to sponsor new research, the Berlin Academy flourished as a center of Enlightenment thinking. The academy's journal published members' papers every year, in French, for a European audience. In France, provincial academies played much the same role. Works such as Rousseau's *Discourse on the Origins of Inequality* were entered in academy-sponsored essay contests. Academy members included government and

CHRONOLOGY

LIVES OF ENLIGHTENMENT THINKERS

Baron de Montesquieu	1689–1755
Voltaire	1694–1778
David Hume	1711–1776
Jean-Jacques Rousseau	1712–1778
Guillaume Thomas François Raynal	1713–1796
Denis Diderot	1717–1783
Adam Smith	1723–1790
Mary Wollstonecraft	1759–1797

military officials, wealthy merchants, doctors, noble landowners, and scholars. Learned societies and academies both brought together different social groups (most from the elite); and in so doing, they fostered a sense of common purpose and seriousness.

SALONS

Salons did the same but operated informally. Usually they were organized by well-connected and learned aristocratic women. The prominent role of women distinguished the salons from the academies and universities. Salons brought together men and women of letters with members of the aristocracy for conversation, debate, drink, and food. Rousseau loathed this kind of ritual and viewed salons as a sign of superficiality and vacuity in a privileged and overcivilized world. Thomas Jefferson thought the influence of women in salons had put France in a "desperate state." Some of the salons reveled in parlor games. Others, such as the one organized in Paris by Madame Necker, wife of the future French reform minister, lay quite close to the halls of power and served as testing ground for new policy ideas. Madame Marie-Thérèse Geoffrin, another celebrated French *salonière*, became an important patron of the *Encyclopedia* and exercised influence in placing scholars in academies. Moses Mendelssohn held an open house for intellectuals in Berlin. Salons in London, Vienna, Rome, and Berlin worked the same way; and like academies, they promoted among their participants a sense of belonging to an active, learned elite.

Scores of similar societies emerged in the eighteenth century. Masonic lodges, organizations with elaborate secret rituals whose members pledged themselves to the regeneration of society, attracted a remarkable array of aristocrats and middle-class men. Mozart, Frederick II, and Montesquieu were Masons. Behind their closed doors, the lodges were egalitarian. They pledged themselves to a common project of rational thought and benevolent action, and to banishing religion and social distinction—at least from their ranks.

Other networks of sociability were less exclusive. Coffeehouses multiplied with the colonial trade in sugar, coffee, and tea, and they occupied a central spot in the circulation of ideas. A group of merchants gathering to discuss trade, for instance, could turn to politics; and the many newspapers lying about the café tables provided a ready-to-hand link between their smaller discussions and news and debates elsewhere. The philosopher Immanuel Kant remarked that a sharper public consciousness seemed one of the hall-

marks of his time. "If we attend to the course of conversation in mixed companies consisting not merely of scholars and subtle reasoners but also of business people or women, we notice that besides storytelling or jesting they have another entertainment, namely, arguing." The ability to think critically and speak freely, without deferring to religion or tradition, was a point of pride, and not simply for intellectuals. Eighteenth-century cultural changes—the expanding networks of sociability, the flourishing book trade, the new genres of literature, and the circulation of Enlightenment ideas—widened the circles of reading and discussion, expanding what some historians and political theorists call the *public sphere*. That, in turn, began to change politics. Informal deliberations, debates about how to regenerate the nation, discussions of civic virtue, and efforts to forge a consensus played a crucial role in moving politics beyond the confines of the court.

The eighteenth century gave birth to the very idea of public opinion. A French observer described the changes this way: "In the last thirty years alone, a great and important revolution has occurred in our ideas. Today, public opinion has a preponderant force in Europe that cannot be resisted." Few thought the "public" involved more than the elite. Yet by the late eighteenth century, European governments recognized the existence of a civic-minded group that stretched from salons to coffeehouses, academies, and circles of government and to which they needed, in some measure, to respond.

MIDDLE-CLASS CULTURE AND READING

Enlightenment fare constituted only part of the new cultural interests of the eighteenth-century middle classes. Lower down on the social scale, shopkeepers, small merchants, lawyers, and professionals read more and more different kinds of books. Instead of owning one well-thumbed Bible to read aloud, a middle-class family would buy and borrow books to read casually, pass on, and discuss. This literature consisted of science, history, biography, travel literature, and fiction. A great deal of it was aimed at middle-class women, among the fastest-growing groups of readers in the eighteenth century. Etiquette books sold very well; so did how-to manuals for the household. Scores of books about the manners, morals, and education of daughters, popular versions of Enlightenment treatises on education and the mind, illustrate close parallels between the intellectual life of the high Enlightenment and everyday middle-class reading matter.

The rise of a middle-class reading public, much of it female, helps account for the soaring popularity and production of novels, especially in Britain. Novels were the single most popular new form of literature in the eighteenth century. A survey of library borrowing in late-eighteenth-century Britain, Germany, and North America showed that 70 percent of books taken out were novels. For centuries, Europeans had read romances such as tales of the knights of the Round Table. Novels, though, did not treat quasimythical subjects, the writing was less ornate, and the setting and situations were literally closer to home. The novel's more recognizable, nonaristocratic characters seemed more relevant to common middle-class experience. Moreover, examining emotion and inner feeling also linked novel writing with a larger eighteenth-century concern with personhood and humanity. As we have seen, classic Enlightenment writers like Voltaire, Goethe, and Rousseau wrote very successful novels; and those should be understood alongside the *Pamela* or *Clarissa* of Samuel Richardson (1689–1761), the *Moll Flanders* or *Robinson Crusoe* of Daniel Defoe (1660–1731), and the *Tom Jones* of Henry Fielding (1707–1754).

Many historians have noted that women figured prominently among fiction writers. In seventeenth-century France the most widely read authors of romances had been Madeleine de Scudéry and the countess de La Fayette. Later, in England, Fanny Burney (1752–1840), Ann Radcliffe (1764–1823), and Maria Edgeworth (1767–1849) all wrote extremely popular novels. The works of Jane Austen (1775–1817), especially *Pride and Prejudice* and *Emma*, are to many readers the height of a novelist's craft. Women writers, however, were not the only ones to write novels, nor were they alone in paying close attention to the domestic or private sphere. Their work took up central eighteenth-century themes of human nature, morality, virtue, and reputation. Their novels, like much of the nonfiction of the period, explored those themes in domestic as in public settings.

POPULAR CULTURE: URBAN AND RURAL

How much did books and print culture touch the lives of the common people? Literacy rates varied dramatically by gender, social class, and region, but were generally higher in northern than in southern and eastern Europe. It is not surprising that literacy ran highest in cities and towns—higher, in fact, than we might expect. In early eighteenth-century Paris, 85 percent of men and 60 percent of women could read. Well over half the residents of poorer Parisian neighborhoods, especially

A Coffeehouse in London, 1798. Coffeehouses served as centers of social networks and hubs of opinion, contributing to a public consciousness that was new to the Enlightenment. This coffeehouse scene illustrates a mixing of classes, lively debate, and the bourgeoning reading culture.

small shopkeepers, domestic servants and valets, and artisans, could read and sign their names. Even the illiterate, however, lived in a culture of print. They saw one-page newspapers and broadsides or flysheets posted on streets and tavern walls and regularly heard them read aloud. Moreover, visual material—inexpensive woodcuts especially, but also prints, drawings, satirical cartoons—figured as prominently as text in much popular reading material. By many measures, then, the circles of reading and discussion were even larger than literacy rates might suggest, especially in cities.

To be sure, poorer households had few books on their shelves, and those tended to be religious texts: an abridged Bible, *The Pilgrim's Progress*, or an illustrated prayer book bought or given on some special occasion and read aloud repeatedly. But popular reading was boosted by the increasing availability of new materials. From the late seventeenth century on, a French firm published a series of inexpensive small paperbacks, the so-called blue books, which itinerant peddlers carried from cities to villages in the countryside for a growing popular market. The blue library included traditional popular literature. That meant short catechisms, quasi-religious tales of miracles, and stories of the lives of the saints, which the church hoped would provide religious instruction. It also included almanacs, books on astrology, and manuals of medical cures for people or farm animals. In the eighteenth century, book peddlers began to carry abridged and simple novels and to sell books on themes popular in the middle classes, such as travel and history. Books provided an incentive to read.

Neither England nor France required any primary schooling, leaving education to haphazard local initiatives. In central Europe, some regimes made efforts to develop state-sponsored education. Catherine of Russia summoned an Austrian consultant to set up a system of primary schools, but by the end of the eighteenth century only 22,000 of a population of 40 million had attended any kind of schools. In the absence of primary schooling, most Europeans were self-taught. The varied texts in the peddler's cart—whether religious, political propaganda, or entertainment—attest to a widespread and rapidly growing popular interest in books and reading.

Like its middle-class counterpart, popular culture rested on networks of sociability. Guild organizations offered discussion and companionship. Street theater

> In early eighteenth-century Paris, 85 percent of men and 60 percent of women could read. Well over half the residents of poorer Parisian neighborhoods, especially small shopkeepers, domestic servants and valets, and artisans, could read and sign their names.

and singers mocking local political figures offered culture to people from different social classes. The difficulties of deciphering popular culture are considerable. Most testimony comes to us from outsiders who regarded the common people as hopelessly superstitious and ignorant. Still, historical research has begun to reveal new insights. It has shown, first, that popular culture did not exist in isolation. Particularly in the countryside, market days and village festivals brought social classes together, and popular entertainments reached a wide social audience. Folktales and traditional songs resist pigeonholing as either elite, middle-class, or popular culture, for they passed from one cultural world to another, being revised and reinterpreted in the process. Second, oral and literate culture overlapped. In other words, even people who could not read often had a great deal of "book knowledge": they argued seriously about points from books and believed that books conferred authority. A group of villagers, for instance, wrote this eulogy to a deceased friend: "he read his life long, and died without ever knowing how to read." The logic and worldview of popular culture needs to be understood on its own terms.

It remains true that the countryside, especially in less economically developed regions, was desperately poor. Life there was far more isolated than in towns. A yawning chasm separated peasants from the world of the high Enlightenment. The *philosophes*, well established in the summits of European society, looked at popular culture with distrust and ignorance. They saw the common people of Europe much as they did indigenous peoples of other continents. They were humanitarians, critical thinkers, and reformers; they were not democrats. The Enlightenment, while well entrenched in eighteenth-century elite culture, nonetheless involved changes that reached well beyond elite society.

EIGHTEENTH-CENTURY MUSIC

European elites sustained other forms of high culture. English gentlemen who read scientific papers aloud in clubs also commissioned architects to design classical revival country houses for the weekends. Royal courts underwrote the academies of painting, which upheld aristocratic taste and aesthetics; Austrian salons that hosted discussions of Voltaire also staged performances of Mozart. We have already noted that the

CHAPTER 17
THE ENLIGHTENMENT

philosophes' work crossed genres, from political theory to fiction. Rousseau not only wrote discourses and novels but composed music and wrote an opera. A flourishing musical culture was one of the most important features of the eighteenth century.

BACH AND HANDEL

The early eighteenth century brought the last phase of Baroque music and two of the greatest composers of all time: Johann Sebastian Bach (1685–1750) and George Frideric Handel (1685–1759). Bach was an intensely pious man who remained in the backwaters of provincial Germany all his life. As a church musician in Leipzig for most of his adult career, Bach had to supply music for nearly all Sunday and holiday services, and he combined imagination and brilliance with steely self-discipline and an ability to produce music on demand. He was an ardent Protestant, entirely unaffected by the secularism of the Enlightenment: each one of his church pieces is full of such fervor that the salvation of the world appears to hang on every note. He was also prolific, writing across the entire gamut of contemporary forms (excluding opera), from unaccompanied instrumental pieces to large-scale works for vocal soloists, chorus, and orchestra. Much of his work consists of religious cantatas (over 200 surviving), motets, and Passions, but he also wrote concertos and suites for orchestra, and composed the purest of "pure" music—subtle and complex fugues for keyboard.

> As a church musician in Leipzig for most of his adult career, Bach had to supply music for nearly all Sunday and holiday services, and he combined imagination and brilliance with steely self-discipline and an ability to produce music on demand.

Handel, by contrast, was a public-pleasing cosmopolitan, who sought out large, secular audiences. After spending his early years mastering Baroque compositional techniques in Italy, Handel established himself in London. He tried to make a living by composing Italian operas, but after initial success, opera sounded foreign and flowery to British ears. Handel eventually found a more marketable genre, the oratorio: a musical drama to be performed in concert, in English, without staging. Handel's oratorios were usually set to biblical stories but featured very worldly music, replete with ornate instrumentation and frequent flourishes of drums and trumpets. These heroic works succeeded in packing London's halls full of prosperous Britons, who interpreted the victories of the ancient Hebrews in such oratorios as *Israel in Egypt* and *Judas Maccabaeus* as implicit celebrations of Britain's own burgeoning national greatness. Handel's greatest oratorio, *Messiah,* is still sung widely throughout the English-speaking world every Christmas; its stirring "Hallelujah" chorus remains the most popular single choral piece in the entire classical repertoire.

HAYDN AND MOZART

Bach and Handel were among the last and certainly the greatest composers of Baroque music; the Austrians Joseph Haydn (1732–1809) and Wolfgang Amadeus Mozart (1756–1791) were the leading representatives of the Classical style, which swept Europe in the second half of the eighteenth century. Classicism here had nothing to do with imitating music written in classical antiquity. It sought to imitate classical principles of order, clarity, and symmetry—in other words, to sound as a Greek temple looked. The Classical era brought the string quartet and, most impressive, the symphony, sometimes called the novel of music, which has proved to be the most versatile and popular of all Classical musical forms. Composers of the Classical school created music that adhered rigorously to certain structural principles. For example, nearly all Classical symphonies have four movements, and nearly all symphonies open with a first movement in sonata form, characterized by the successive presentation of themes, development, and recapitulation.

Mozart's last three symphonies (out of his total of forty-one) are unequaled in their grace, variety, and technical perfection. But Mozart's short and famously difficult life captures the problems that even prodigiously talented eighteenth-century artists faced. Wolfgang began composing at four, became known as a keyboard virtuoso at six, and wrote his first symphony at nine. Wolfgang's father promoted his son, touring him as a child prodigy (with his very gifted sister) through the courts of Europe: "My boy as an eight-year-old knows as much as what one expects from a man of forty. In short: whoever does not see or hear it cannot believe it." These were the 1760s, the height of the Enlightenment, and Mozart senior grumbled about the climate of skepticism and disbelief. "Nowadays, people ridicule everything that is called a miracle," he wrote. "It was a great pleasure and a great victory for me to hear a Voltairian say to me, 'Now for once in my life I have seen a miracle; this is the first.'" Wolfgang gathered awards and honors from the pope and the Austrian empress Maria Theresa, attracted attention across

How did social and cultural change shape the Enlightenment?

THE ENLIGHTENMENT AND EIGHTEENTH-CENTURY CULTURE

Mozart's Last Portrait, 1789. Like the composer's famous *Requiem,* this portrait, painted by Mozart's brother-in-law Joseph Lange, was left unfinished at Mozart's death.

Europe, and became a moneymaker for his family. But once he was no longer a child prodigy, like nearly all eighteenth-century artists and writers he had to rely on patronage. Mozart, a difficult person himself, suffered in the service of the cantankerous Archbishop of Salzburg, a town he hated. He tried to support himself as a freelance composer and keyboard performer in Vienna. Despite his immense productivity and well-known genius, he could barely make ends meet. He lived hand to mouth, borrowing money from his fellow Masons in the Lodge of Beneficence. He was only thirty-five when he died of rheumatic fever. In keeping with eighteenth-century medical practice, his physicians bled him frequently in the last month of his life and may have hastened his death, possibly poisoning his blood with their unsterilized instruments. It is not true that he was buried, unrecognized, in a pauper's grave. His funeral was simple and cheap, in keeping with his poverty, but also with his Masonic principles and Enlightenment opposition to Catholic ritual. His fellow composer Joseph Haydn rued that "we have lost the greatest among us."

The career of Joseph Haydn (1732–1809) provides a revealing contrast. Knowing much better how to take care of himself, he spent most of his life employed by an extremely wealthy Austro-Hungarian aristocratic family that maintained its own private orchestra. But this security entailed the indignity of wearing the Esterházy uniform, like any common butler. Only toward the end of his life, in 1791, did Haydn, then famous, strike out on his own by traveling to London, where for five years (excluding a brief interval) he supported himself handsomely by writing for a paying public rather than for private patrons. Eighteenth-century London was one of the rare places with a commercial market for culture. In this regard London was the wave of the future, for in the nineteenth century serious music would leave the aristocratic salon for urban concert halls all over Europe. In deeply aristocratic Austria, Haydn had been obliged to wear servants' livery; in London he was greeted as a creative genius, one of the earliest composers to be regarded as such. Haydn's "Miracle" symphony, written for performance in a London concert hall, is called that because during one performance a chandelier came crashing down, narrowly missing the crowd gathered to see the genius conduct. Although not the first writer of symphonies, Haydn is often termed the "father of the symphony." In over 100 works in the symphonic form—especially his last 12 symphonies, which he composed in London—Haydn formulated the most enduring techniques of symphonic composition and demonstrated the symphony's enormous creative potential.

OPERA

Finally, opera flourished in the eighteenth century. Opera was a seventeenth-century creation, developed most significantly by the Italian Baroque composer Claudio Monteverdi (1567–1643), who combined music with theater for greater dramatic intensity. Monteverdi's new form of opera appealed immediately: within one generation operas were performed in all the leading cities of Italy, and by the eighteenth century they had captured attention across Europe. Staged within magnificent settings and calling on the talents of singers, musicians, dramatists, and stage designers, opera expressed as clearly as any art form Baroque artists' dedication to grandeur, drama, and display. In the Classical period, opera's popularity was boosted by Christoph Willibald von Gluck (1714–1787). Gluck, who came to Paris from Austria as the musical tutor of the young Marie Antoinette, insisted that the texts be as important as the music. He simplified arias, emphasized dramatic action, and produced high-end entertainment for the French court. Mozart, however, was the greatest operatic composer of the Classical era. *The Marriage of Figaro, Don Giovanni,* and *The Magic Flute* remain among the best-loved operas of all time.

Eighteenth-century musicians, like eighteenth-century writers, found their careers and art shaped by changing structures of culture. Despite a trend toward secularism, the church continued to provide support for much everyday music. In a very few cases—Haydn's in London is one—composers could be supported by the market. Aristocratic and court patronage, however, remained the pillars of support for musicians. And musicians, like Enlightenment writers, had an ambivalent relationship with their patrons and culture. Rousseau, in his role as a composer, railed at the way in which the aristocracy set the tone of opera productions in his time. He deplored pretentious staging and emotional inauthenticity. In his own opera he tried to bring different themes—nature, simplicity, and virtue—to the stage. The British writer Samuel Johnson called patrons "insolent wretches." Mozart relied on the overbearing Archbishop of Salzburg to commission work and, just as important, ensure that it would be performed; but he resented his position: "I did not know that I was a valet." One of Mozart's most popular operas—*The Marriage of Figaro,* based on a French play—circled around just these themes: relations between masters and servants, the abuses of privilege, and the presumptuousness of the European nobility.

The Marriage of Figaro, indeed, followed a classic eighteenth-century path to popularity. The author of the play was born Pierre Caron, the son of a watchmaker. Caron rose to become watchmaker to the king, bought a noble office, married well, took the name Pierre Augustin de Beaumarchais, and wrote several comedies in an Enlightenment tone satirizing the French nobility. *Figaro* ran into trouble with French censors, but like so many other banned works, the play sold well. It was translated into Italian, was set to music by Mozart (who was a Mason), and played to appreciative elite audiences from Paris to Prague. Satire, self-criticism, the criticism of hierarchy, optimism and social mobility, and a cosmopolitan outlook supported by what was in many ways a traditional society—all of these are key to understanding eighteenth-century culture as well as the Enlightenment.

Conclusion

The Enlightenment arose from the scientific revolution, from the new sense of power and possibility that science created, and from the rush of enthusiasm for new forms of inquiry. Together, the Enlightenment and the scientific revolution created science as a form of knowledge. Eighteenth-century thinkers scrutinized a remarkably wide range of topics: human nature, reason and the processes of understanding, religion, belief, law, the origins of government authority, economics, and social practices. Whether well-known *philosophes* or underground journalists, they raised problems that made regimes, their contemporaries, and even themselves uncomfortable. Ideas circulated in popular forms from plays and operas to journalism. Intellectual changes went hand in hand with social and cultural ones: government efforts to put their states on a new footing, the emergence of a new elite, and the expansion of the public sphere.

The Atlantic revolutions (the American Revolution of 1776, the French Revolution of 1789, and the Latin American upheavals of the 1830s) were steeped in the language of the Enlightenment. The constitutions of the new nations formed by these revolutions followed the basic ideas of Enlightenment liberalism: neither religion nor the state could impede individual freedom of conscience; government authority could not be arbitrary; equality and freedom were natural; humans sought happiness, prosperity, and the expansion of their potential. These arguments had been made, tentatively, earlier. But when the North American colonists declared their independence from Britain in 1776, they called these ideas "self-evident truths." That bold declaration marked both the distance traveled since the late seventeenth century and the self-confidence that was the Enlightenment's hallmark.

The Magic Flute, 1793. Mozart's opera opened in 1791, just before the extraordinary young composer died.

Key Terms

reason
Voltaire
The *Encyclopedia*

humanitarianism
Adam Smith
Jean-Jacques Rousseau

salons
Wolfgang Amadeus Mozart

Selected Readings

Baker, Keith. *Condorcet: From Natural Philosophy to Social Mathematics.* Chicago, 1975. An important reinterpretation of Condorcet as a social scientist.

Bell, Susan, and Karen Offen, eds. *Women, the Family, and Freedom: The Debate in Documents.* Vol. 1, *1750–1880.* Stanford, Calif., 1983. An excellent introduction to Enlightenment debates about gender and women.

Blum, Carol. *Rousseau and the Republic of Virtue: The Language of Politics in the French Revolution.* Ithaca and London, 1986. Fascinating account of how eighteenth-century readers interpreted Rousseau.

Buchan, James. *The Authentic Adam Smith: His Life and Ideas.* New York, 2006.

Calhoun, Craig, ed. *Habermas and the Public Sphere.* Cambridge, Mass., 1992. Calhoun's introduction is a good starting point for Habermas's argument.

Cassirer, E. *The Philosophy of the Enlightenment.* Princeton, N.J., 1951.

Chartier, Roger. *The Cultural Origins of the French Revolution.* Durham, N.C., 1991. Looks at topics from religion to violence in everyday life and culture.

Darnton, Robert. *The Business of Enlightenment: A Publishing History of the* Encyclopédie, *1775–1800.* Cambridge, Mass., 1979. Darnton's work on the Enlightenment offers a fascinating blend of intellectual, social, and economic history. See his other books as well: *The Literary Underground of the Old Regime* (Cambridge, Mass., 1982); *The Great Cat Massacre and Other Episodes in French Cultural History* (New York, 1984); and *The Forbidden Best Sellers of Revolutionary France* (New York and London, 1996).

Davis, David Brion. *The Problem of Slavery in Western Culture.* New York, 1988. A Pulitzer Prize–winning examination of a central issue as well as a brilliant analysis of different strands of Enlightenment thought.

Gay, Peter. *The Enlightenment: An Interpretation.* Vol. 1, *The Rise of Modern Paganism.* Vol. 2, *The Science of Freedom.* New York, 1966–1969. Combines an overview with an interpretation. Emphasizes the *philosophes'* sense of identification with the classical world and takes a generally positive view of their accomplishments. Includes extensive annotated bibliographies.

Gray, Peter. *Mozart.* New York, 1999. Brilliant short study.

Goodman, Dena. *The Republic of Letters: A Cultural History of the French Enlightenment.* Ithaca, N.Y., 1994. Important in its attention to the role of literary women.

Hazard, Paul. *The European Mind: The Critical Years (1680–1715).* New Haven, Conn., 1953. A basic and indispensable account of the changing climate of opinion that preceded the Enlightenment.

Hildesheimer, Wolfgang. *Mozart.* New York, 1982. An exceptionally literate and thought-provoking biography.

Israel, Jonathan Irvine. *Radical Enlightenment: Philosophy and the Making of Modernity, 1650–1750.* New York, 2001. Massive and erudite, a fresh look at the international movement of ideas.

Israel, Jonathan Irvine. *Enlightenment Contested: Philosophy, Modernity, and the Emancipation of Man, 1670–1752.* New York, 2006. Massive and erudite, a fresh look at the international movement of ideas.

Munck, Thomas. *The Enlightenment: A Comparative Social History 1721–1794.* London, 2000. An excellent recent survey, especially good on social history.

Outram, Dorinda. *The Enlightenment.* Cambridge, 1995. An excellent short introduction and a good example of new historical approaches.

Porter, Roy *The Creation of the Modern World: The Untold Story of the British Enlightenment.* New York, 2000.

Rendall, Jane. *The Origins of Modern Feminism: Women in Britain, France and the United States, 1780–1860.* New York, 1984. A very basic survey.

Sapiro, Virginia. *A Vindication of Political Virtue: The Political Theory of Mary Wollstonecraft.* Chicago, 1992. A subtle and intelligent analysis for more advanced readers.

Shklar, Judith. *Men and Citizens: A Study of Rousseau's Social Theory.* London, 1969.

Shklar, Judith. *Montesquieu.* Oxford, 1987. Shklar's studies are brilliant and accessible.

Taylor, Barbara. *Mary Wollstonecraft and the Feminist Imagination.* Cambridge and New York, 2003. Fascinating study that sets Wollstonecraft in the radical circles of eighteenth century England.

Venturi, Franco. *The End of the Old Regime in Europe, 1768–1776: The First Crisis.* Trans. R. Burr Litchfield. Princeton, N.J., 1989.

Venturi, Franco. *The End of the Old Regime in Europe, 1776–1789.* Princeton, N.J. 1991. Both detailed and wide-ranging, particularly important on international developments.

Watt, Ian P. *The Rise of the Novel.* London, 1957. The basic work on the innovative qualities of the novel in eighteenth-century England.

Part VI
THE AGE OF REVOLUTION

IN THE CENTURIES AFTER 1492, the West took on a new form, as Europe built empires extending out over the Atlantic. These Atlantic empires had enormous ramifications. They had made Europe a global power. They had become a source of wealth, trade, and economic development. They spurred thought, pushing Europeans to reflect on issues ranging from cosmology, physics, and navigation to history and how Europeans fit into the history of humanity. The Atlantic empires offered a new arena of conflict between European powers: imperial rivalry and colonial concerns increasingly assumed center stage in European wars. Finally, in the late eighteenth century, they became the staging ground for revolution.

What historians call the "age of revolution" lasted from the 1770s through at least half of the nineteenth century. It opened in the North American colonies, with a revolt against the British Empire. It became a crisis that shook eighteenth-century Europe and the Atlantic world, bringing revolutionary movements to the British Empire, France and her empire in the Caribbean, Belgium, and the Netherlands and then to the Spanish and Portugese empires in Central and South America. Repressed, or contained, by Europe's powerful states, revolutions nonetheless broke out again across Europe in 1848, reaching into the Austrian and Prussian empires in central Europe.

At the same time, a longer and slower but no less dramatic revolution in industry restructured the economies of the West. The Industrial Revolution took place in approximately the same period of time and affected many of the same people—though in different ways and to varying degrees. The major developments of the nineteenth and early twentieth centuries—the decline of landed aristocracies and the rise of new social groups, the emergence of dramatically new forms of politics, changes in political and social thought, industrial expansion, and the reorientation of European empires—all had their roots in these two revolutions. Together the revolutions toppled absolutism, mercantilism, and what was left of feudalism. They produced the theory and practice of economic individualism and political liberalism. The wrenching changes they wrought polarized Europe for several generations.

THE AGE OF REVOLUTION

	POLITICS	SOCIETY AND CULTURE	ECONOMY	INTERNATIONAL RELATIONS
1750		Johann Wolfgang von Goethe (1749–1852) William Blake (1757–1827)	British export production increases 80 percent (1750–1770) British Parliament increases enclosures (1750–1860) Spinning jenny, water frame, and spinning mule invented (1764–1799) James Watt patents improved steam engine (1769) Industrial Revolution (1780–1880)	
	Reign of Catherine the Great of Russia (1762–1796) American Revolution (1774–1782)	William Wordsworth (1770–1850) Goethe's *Faust* (1790)		Poland partitioned by Russia, Austria, and Prussia (1772, 1793, 1795)
	Louis XVI calls Assembly of Notables (1788) The French Revolution breaks out (1789) Great Fear in the French countryside (1789) Declaration of the Rights of Man and of the Citizen (1789) French National Assembly abolishes feudal rights and privileges (1789)	Jeremy Bentham's *Introduction to the Principles of Morals and Legislation* (1789)		
1790	Slave revolt in St. Domingue (1791)	Edmund Burke's *Reflections on the Revolution in France* (1790) Thomas Paine's *Rights of Man* (1791)		Slave rebellion in St. Domingue sparks British and Spanish invasion (1791)
	Louis XVI of France overthrown and French Republic declared (1792) Reign of Terror (1793–1794) French Convention abolishes slavery and primogeniture (1793–1794) Maximilien Robespierre executed (1794)		Eli Whitney invents cotton gin (1793)	France declares war on Austria and Prussia (1792) England enters war against France (1793) Revolutionary France occupies Low Countries, Rhineland, and parts of Spain and Italy (1794–1796)
		Heinrich Heine, German poet (1797–1856) Wordsworth's and Coleridge's *Lyrical Ballads* (1798) Thomas Malthus's *Essay on the Principle of Population* (1798) Eugène Delacroix, French painter (1799–1837) Honoré de Balzac, French novelist (1799–1850)		
1800	Napoleon Bonaparte is declared temporary consul (1799) President Thomas Jefferson (1800–1808) Bonaparte's Concordat with the pope (1801) Bonaparte elected Consul for Life by plebiscite (1802) Bonaparte crowns himself Emperor Napoleon I (1804)	Emergence of Romanticism (early 1800s) Continental population doubles (1800–1850) Napoleonic Code (1804) George Sand, novelist (1804–1876)	Women make up 50 percent of British textile workforce (c. 1800)	Peace of Amiens temporarily halts war between Britain and France (1801) Napoleon unsuccessfully tries to restore slavery in St. Domingue (1801–1803) Louisiana Purchase (1803) Independent state of Haiti (formerly St. Domingue) (1804) Nelson's victory at Trafalgar breaks French naval power (1805) Napoleon defeats Austria and Russia at battle of Austerlitz (1805)
			Napoleon's Continental System imposed (1806) Serfdom abolished in Prussia (1807)	
1808	Prussian reform era begins (1808)	Johann Gottlieb Fichte's *Addresses to the German Nation* (1808)		Napoleon invades Spain (1808)

THE AGE OF REVOLUTION

POLITICS	SOCIETY AND CULTURE	ECONOMY	INTERNATIONAL RELATIONS	
			Napoleon marries Mary Louise of the Habsburgs (1809)	1809
	Grimm's Fairy Tales by the Brothers Grimm (1813)		Napoleon's Russian campaign (1812) Napoleon exiled to Elba (1814) Congress of Vienna (1814–1815)	
Bourbon monarchy restored in France (1815)			Napoleon defeated at Waterloo (1815) German Confederation created by Congress of Vienna (1815)	
	Gustav Courbet, French painter (1819–1877)	Prussian Zollverein (customs union) founded (1818)	Quintuple Alliance formed (1818) Greek war of independence (1821–1827) Monroe Doctrine (1823)	
Decembrist Revolt in Russia (1825)			Serbia emerges from within Ottoman Empire (1828)	
Revolution in France, Belgium (1830) Mazzini founds Young Italy society (1831) Electoral Reform Act in England (1832)		First railway to carry passengers (1830)		
Poor Laws Reform in England (1834) Reign of Queen Victoria (1837–1901) British Chartist movement (1838–1848)	Alexis de Tocqueville's Democracy in America (1835–1840) The Economist is founded (1838) Emergence of Realism in art and literature (1840s) Great Famine in Ireland (1845–1849)	Rail transport spreads across Continent (1840s) Zollverein expands to include nearly all German states (1840s) Poor harvests contribute to economic crisis across Europe (1845)		
Repression of revolutionary movements in central and eastern Europe (1848–1850)	Seneca Falls Convention (1848)	Great Irish Famine (1845–1849)	Treaty of Guadalupe Hidalgo ends war between United States and Mexico (1848)	
	Florence Nightingale's medical reforms (1850s)	California gold rush (1849) Serfdom abolished in southern and eastern Europe (1850)	United States buys western territory, including California, for $15 million (1848)	1850
Louis-Napoleon Bonaparte overthrows Second Republic (1851)	Great Exhibit of the Works of Industry in All Nations, London (1851)	Great Exhibition of the Works of Industry in All Nations, London (1851) Britain exports half of world's iron (1852) Cotton accounts for 40 percent of domestic exports from Britain (1852)		
	Charles Darwin's On the Origin of Species (1859) John Stuart Mill's On Liberty (1859)	Agricultural laborers still largest workforce in Britain (1860) Britain and France sign free-trade agreement (1860)	Crimean War (1854–1856) Sardinia takes Lombardy, Papal States, and various duchies (1859)	
Reign of Kaiser Wilhelm I (1861–1888) Civil War in the United States (1861–1865) Otto von Bismarck appointed prime minister of Germany (1862)	Victor Hugo's Les Misérables (1862)	Emancipation of serfs in Russia (1861)	Victor Emmanuel II claims title of king of Italy (1861–1878)	
Reform Bill of 1867 in England (1867)	Fyodor Dostoyevsky's Crime and Punishment (1866) Mill's Subjection of Women (1869)	Slavery abolished in United States (1865) Railroad connects Mississippi Valley with Pacific coast (1869)	Seven Weeks' War; Prussia takes Schleswig-Holstein (1866) Canada gains independence (1867)	
			Franco-Prussian War (1870–1871) Italians take Rome from Napoleon III's protection (1870) German Empire proclaimed (1871)	1870

Chapter Eighteen

Chapter Contents

The French Revolution: An Overview 638

The Coming of the Revolution 639

The Destruction of the Old Regime 642

A New Stage: Popular Revolution 650

From the Terror to Bonaparte: The Directory 658

Napoleon and Imperial France 658

The Return to War and Napoleon's Defeat: 1806–1815 663

Conclusion 670

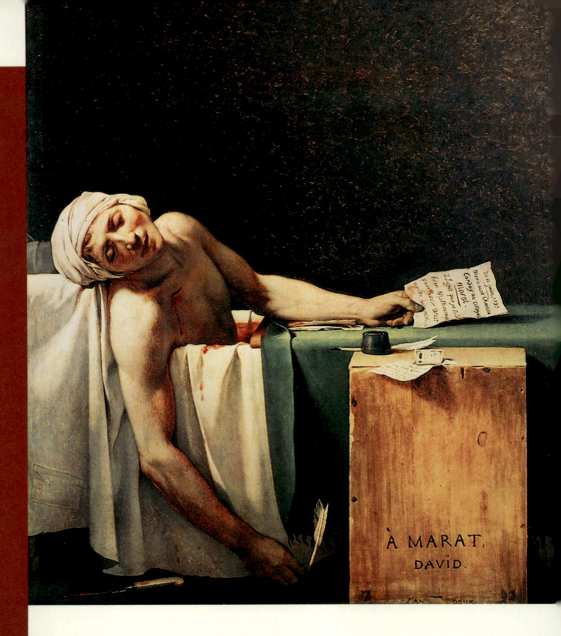

The French Revolution

IN 1789, ONE EUROPEAN out of every five lived in France. Many Europeans considered France the center of European culture. It followed that a revolution in France would immediately command the attention of Europe and assume international significance. Yet the French Revolution attracted and disturbed men and women for much more important reasons. Both its philosophical ideals and its political realities mirrored attitudes, concerns, and conflicts that had occupied the minds of educated Europeans for decades.

The revolutionaries raised issues that resonated across Europe. Absolutism was increasingly the bane of a wide spectrum of thoughtful opinion. Aristocrats across Europe and the colonies resented monarchical inroads on their ancient freedoms. Members of the middle class, many of whom were very successful, chafed under a system of official privilege that they increasingly considered outmoded. Peasants fiercely resented what seemed to them the never-ceasing demands of central government on their limited resources. Nor were resentments focused exclusively on absolutist monarchs. Tensions existed as well between country and city dwellers, between rich and poor, overprivileged and underprivileged, slave and free. The French Revolution of 1789 was the most dramatic, most tumultuous expression of all these conflicts.

The age of revolution opened in the North American colonies. The American Revolution of 1776 had been a crisis of the British Empire. It had been one of the last in a series of conflicts between England and France over colonial control of the New World. It became one of the first crises of the old regime in France. "The New World was where the fears and aspirations . . . were first dramatized, where extralegal associations of common citizens defied acts of a sovereign power, where

FOCUS QUESTIONS

- How were the French and American Revolutions different?
- What were the causes of the French Revolution?
- How did a fiscal crisis become a political crisis?

- Why did the French Revolution become more radical?
- How did Bonaparte come to power?
- How did Napoleon centralize his authority?
- What led to Napoleon's downfall?

Chapter 18 THE FRENCH REVOLUTION

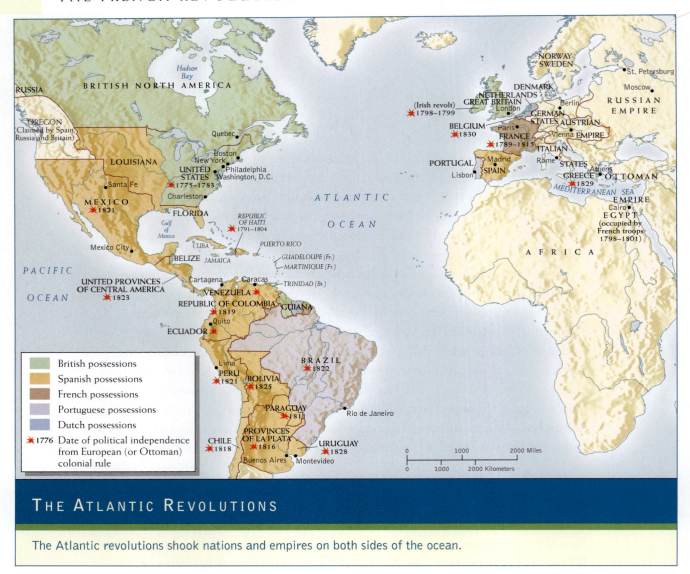

THE ATLANTIC REVOLUTIONS

The Atlantic revolutions shook nations and empires on both sides of the ocean.

abstract ideals of political philosophy were substantiated in the actions of ordinary men," as one historian says. Among "enlightened" Europeans, the success with which citizens of the new nation had thrown off British rule and formed a republic based on Enlightenment principles was the source of tremendous optimism. Change would come, many believed. Reform was possible. The costs would be modest.

If the American Revolution first dramatized Europeans' aspirations, the French Revolution deepened their fears. The French Revolution proved a more radical project, though it did not necessarily begin that way. It became immeasurably more costly—protracted, complex, and violent. It aroused much greater hopes and consequently, in many cases, bitter disillusionment. It raised issues that would not be settled for half a century.

THE FRENCH REVOLUTION: AN OVERVIEW

How were the French and American revolutions different?

In Charles Dickens's *Tale of Two Cities* (1859), the source of many popular images of revolution, the French upheaval blurs into a frightening picture of bloodthirsty crowds watching a guillotine. The picture is memorable but misleading. The term *French Revolution* is a shorthand for a complex series of events between 1789 and 1799. (Napoleon ruled from 1799 to 1814–1815.)

To simplify, those events can be divided into four stages. In the first stage, running from 1788 to 1792, the struggle was constitutional and relatively peaceful. An increasingly bold elite articulated its grievances against the king. Like the American revolutionaries, French elites refused taxation without representation; attacked despotism, or arbitrary authority; and offered an Enlightenment-inspired program to rejuvenate the nation. Reforms, many of them breathtakingly wide ranging, were instituted—some accepted or even offered by the king, and others passed over his objections. The peaceful, constitutional phase did not last. Unlike the American Revolution, the French Revolution did not stabilize around one constitution or one set of political leaders, for many reasons.

Reforms met with resistance, dividing the country. The threat of dramatic change within one of the most powerful countries in Europe created international tensions. In 1792, these tensions exploded into war; and the crises of war, in turn, spelled the end of the Bourbon monarchy and the beginning of the republic. The second stage of the revolution, which lasted from 1792 to 1794, was one of acute crisis, consolidation, and repression. A ruthlessly centralized government mobilized all the country's resources to fight the foreign enemy as well as counterrevolutionaries at home, to destroy traitors and the vestiges of the Old Regime.

The Terror, as this policy was called, did save the republic, but it exhausted itself in factions and recriminations and collapsed in 1794. In the third phase, from 1794 to 1799, the government drifted. France remained a republic. It continued to fight with Europe. Undermined by corruption and division, the state fell prey to the ambitions of a military leader, in this case Napoleon Bonaparte. Napoleon's rule, punctuated by astonishing victories and catastrophes, stretched from

1799 to 1815. It began as a republic, became an empire, and ended—after a last hurrah—in the muddy fields outside the Belgian village of Waterloo. After Napoleon's final defeat, the other European monarchs restored the Bourbons to the throne. That Restoration, however, would be short lived, and the cycle of revolution and reaction continued into the nineteenth century.

The Coming of the Revolution

> What were the causes of the French Revolution?

What were the long-term causes of the revolution in France? Historians long ago argued that the causes and outcomes should be understood in terms of class conflict. According to this interpretation, a rising bourgeoisie, or middle class, inspired by Enlightenment ideas and by its own self-interest, overthrew what was left of the aristocratic order. This interpretation drew on the writings of the nineteenth-century philosopher Karl Marx and on much twentieth-century sociology.

Historians have substantially modified this bold thesis. To be sure, the origins of the revolution lie in eighteenth-century French society. Yet that society was not simply divided between a bourgeois class and the aristocracy. Instead, it was increasingly dominated by a new elite or social group that brought together aristocrats, officeholders, professionals, and—to a lesser degree—merchants and businessmen. To understand the revolution, we need to understand this new social group and its conflicts with the government of Louis XVI.

French society was divided into Three Estates. (An individual's *estate* marked his standing, or status, and it determined legal rights, taxes, and so on.) The First Estate comprised all the clergy; the Second Estate, the nobility. The Third Estate, by far the largest, included everyone else, from wealthy lawyers and businessmen to urban laborers and poor peasants. Within the political and social elite of the country, a small but powerful group, these legal distinctions often seemed artificial. To begin with, in the upper reaches of society, the social boundaries between nobles and wealthy commoners were ill-defined. Noble title was accessible

---

CHRONOLOGY

Periods of the French Revolution Era, 1789–1815

1. The First French Revolution	July 1789–August 1792
2. The Second French Revolution	August 1792–July 1794
3. The Directory	1794–1799
4. The Napoleonic era	1799–1815

to those who could afford to buy an ennobling office. For example, close to 50,000 new nobles were created between 1700 and 1789. The nobility depended for its vigor on a constant infusion of talent and economic power from the wealthy social groups of the Third Estate.

The case of the family of the revolutionary figure Honoré Gabriel Riqueti, the comte de Mirabeau (*mihr-ah-BOH*), illustrates the changes. Mirabeau's sixteenth-century ancestors had been merchants. In 1570, however, one of them had purchased the seigneury (land that conferred noble title) of Mirabeau. In the following century another bought himself the title of marquis. Mirabeau, a lawyer, also held a commission in the cavalry that his grandfather once commanded. Aristocrats spoke of a distinction between the nobility of the sword and of the robe, the former supposedly of a more ancient and distinguished lineage derived from military service, the latter aristocrats because they had purchased administrative or judicial office (hence the robe). As the example of the Mirabeau family shows, even that distinction could be illusory.

Wealth did not take predictable forms. Most noble wealth was proprietary—that is, tied to land, urban properties, purchased offices, and the like. Yet noble families did not disdain trade or commerce, as historians long thought. In fact, noblemen financed most industry, and they also invested heavily in banking and such enterprises as ship owning, the slave trade, mining, and metallurgy. Moreover, the very wealthy members of the Third Estate also preferred to invest in secure, proprietary holdings. Thus, throughout the century, much bourgeois wealth was transformed into noble wealth, and a significant number of rich bourgeois became noblemen. Wealthy members of the bourgeoisie themselves did not see themselves as a separate class. They thought of themselves as different from—and often opposed to—the common people, who worked with their hands. But they identified with the values of a nobility to which they frequently aspired.

There were, nonetheless, important social tensions. Less prosperous lawyers—and there were an increasing number of them—were jealous of the privileged position of a favored few in their profession. Over the course of the century the price of offices rose, making it more difficult to buy one's way into the nobility, and creating tensions between middling members of the Third Estate and the very rich in trade and commerce who, by and large, were the only group able to afford to climb the social ladder. Less wealthy nobles resented the success of rich, upstart commoners whose income allowed them the luxury of life in the grand style that they could not have themselves. In sum, several fault lines ran through the elite and the middle classes. All these social groups could nonetheless join in attacking a government and an economy that were not serving their interests.

Prerevolutionary Propaganda, 1788–1789. These prints illustrate the popular view that the Third Estate (commoners) were carrying the burden of national taxation on its shoulders while doing the productive work of the nation.

The Enlightenment had changed public debate (see Chapter Seventeen). Although ideas did not cause the revolution, they played a critical role in articulating grievances. The political theories of Locke, Voltaire, and Montesquieu could appeal to both discontented nobles and members of the middle class. Voltaire was popular because of his attacks on noble privileges; Locke and Montesquieu gained widespread followings because of their defense of private property and limited sovereignty. Montesquieu's ideas appealed to the noble lawyers and officeholders who dominated France's powerful law courts, the *parlements*. They read his doctrine of checks and balances as a defense of parlements as the governmental bodies that would provide a check to the despotism of the king's government. When conflicts arose, noble leaders presented themselves as defenders of a national political community threatened by the king and his ministers.

The campaign for change was also fueled by economic reformers. The "physiocrats," as they were called in France, urged the government to simplify the tax system and free the economy from mercantilist regulations. They urged the government to lift its controls on the price of grain, for example, which had been imposed to keep the cost of bread low but, they argued, had interfered with the natural workings of the market.

In the countryside, peasants were caught in a web of obligations to landlords, church and state: a tithe, or levy, on farm produce owed to the church; fees for the use of a landlord's mill or wine press; fees to the land-

> Evidence indicates that between 1787 and 1789 the unemployment rate in many parts of urban France was as high as 50 percent.

lord; and fees when land changed hands. In addition, peasants paid a disproportionate share of both direct and indirect taxes—the most onerous of which was the salt tax—levied by the government. (For some time the production of salt had been a state monopoly; every individual was required to buy at least seven pounds a year from the government works. The result was a commodity whose cost was often as much as fifty or sixty times its actual value.) Further grievances stemmed from the requirement to maintain public roads (the corvée) and from the hunting privileges that nobles for centuries had regarded as the distinctive badge of their order.

Social and economic conditions deteriorated on the eye of the revolution. A general price increase during much of the eighteenth century, which permitted the French economy to expand by providing capital for investment, created hardship for the peasantry and for urban tradesmen and laborers. Their plight deteriorated further at the end of the 1780s, when poor harvests sent bread prices sharply higher. In 1788 families found themselves spending more than 50 percent of their income on bread, which made up the bulk of their diet. The following year the figure rose to as much as 80 percent. Poor harvests reduced demand for manufactured goods, and contracting markets in turn created unemployment. Many peasants left the countryside for the cities, hoping to find work there—only to discover that urban unemployment was far worse than that in rural areas. Evidence indicates that between 1787 and 1789 the unemployment rate in many parts of urban France was as high as 50 percent.

FAILURE AND REFORM

An inefficient tax system further weakened the country's financial position. Not only was taxation tied to differing social standings but it varied as well from region to region—some areas, for example, were subject to a much higher rate than others. Special circumstances and exemptions made the task of collectors more difficult. The financial system, already burdened by debts incurred under Louis XIV, all but broke down completely under the increased expenses brought on by French participation in the American Revolution. The cost of servicing the national debt of approximately 4 billion livres in the 1780s consumed 50 percent of the nation's budget.

CHRONOLOGY

ORIGINS OF THE FRENCH REVOLUTION, 1788–1789

Failure of fiscal reform	1787–1788
Louis XVI summons the Estates General	May 1788
Bread riots across France	Spring 1789
Estates General convenes in Paris	May 1789
Third Estate declares itself the National Assembly	May 1789
Oath of the Tennis Court	June 1789
Fall of the Bastille	July 14, 1789

Louis XVI. Louis inherited both absolutism and challenges to it.

Problems with the economy reflected weaknesses in France's administrative structure, ultimately the responsibility of the country's absolutist monarch, Louis XVI (1774–1792). Anxious to serve his people in "enlightened" ways, Louis wished to improve the lot of the poor, to abolish torture, and to shift the burden of taxation onto the richer classes. Yet he lacked the ability to put these reforms into effect. His well-intentioned attempts at reform ultimately undermined his own authority. He appointed such reformers as Anne-Robert-Jacques Turgot, a philosopher, physiocrat, and former provincial intendant, and Jacques Necker, a Swiss Protestant banker, as finance ministers, only to arouse opposition among traditionalist factions within the court. He allowed his wife, the young but strong-willed Marie Antoinette—daughter of Austria's Maria Theresa—a free hand to dispense patronage among her friends. The result was constant intrigue and frequently reshuffled alliances at Versailles.

Wrangling between the central government and the provincial parlements also slowed reform. As we have noted, the parlements had reasserted their independence during the early years of the reign of Louis XV. Throughout the century they had grown increasingly insistent on what they began to call their "constitutional" rights, or privileges. When Louis XVI pressed for new taxes to be paid by the nobility as well as the rest of the community after the expensive Seven Years' War, the parlements successfully defended the nobility's right to be exempt from major national taxes. In the mid-1770s this episode was reenacted when Turgot, Louis XVI's principal financial minister, proposed reducing the debt by curtailing court expenses, replacing the labor requirements with a small tax on landowners, and abolishing certain guild restrictions to stimulate manufacturing. The Paris parlement steadfastly opposed such innovations, claiming that Turgot was trampling on ancient prerogatives and privileges—and he was.

In the end, however, the plan failed because the king withdrew his support of Turgot. Although the parlements were jealous of their prerogatives, they could not indefinitely inhibit the reforms of a determined monarch. Louis XVI, however, was not determined. By 1788, a weak monarch, together with a chaotic financial situation and severe social tensions, brought absolutist France to the edge of political disaster.

The Destruction of the Old Regime

How did a fiscal crisis become a political crisis?

The fiscal crisis precipitated the revolution. In 1787 and 1788 the king's principal ministers, Charles de Calonne and Loménie de Brienne, attempted to institute a series of reforms to stave off bankruptcy. To meet the mounting deficit, they proposed new taxes, notably a stamp duty and a direct tax on the annual produce of the land.

Hoping to persuade the nobility to agree to these reforms, the king summoned an Assembly of Notables from among the aristocracy. This group used the financial emergency to attempt major constitutional reforms. Most important, they insisted that any new tax scheme must be approved by the Estates General, the

WHAT IS THE THIRD ESTATE? (1789)

The Abbé Emmanuel-Joseph Sieyès (1748–1836) was, by virtue of his office, a member of the First Estate of the Estates General. Nevertheless, his political savvy led him to be elected as a representative of the Third Estate from the district of Chartres. Sieyès was a formidable politician as well as a writer. His career during the Revolution, which he ended by assisting Napoleon's seizure of power, began with one of the most important radical pamphlets of 1789. In What Is the Third Estate?, *Sieyès posed fundamental questions about the rights of the estate, which represented the great majority of the population and helped provoke its secession from the Estates General.*

The plan of this book is fairly simple. We must ask ourselves three questions.

1. What is the Third Estate? *Everything.*
2. What has it been until now in the political order? *Nothing.*
3. What does it want to be? *Something.*

It suffices to have made the point that the so-called usefulness of a privileged order to the public service is a fallacy; that without help from this order, all the arduous tasks in the service are performed by the Third Estate; that without this order the higher posts could be infinitely better filled; that they ought to be the natural prize and reward of recognized ability and service; and that if the privileged have succeeded in usurping all well-paid and honorific posts, this is both a hateful iniquity towards the generality of citizens and an act of treason to the commonwealth.

Who is bold enough to maintain that the Third Estate does not contain within itself everything needful to constitute a complete nation? It is like a strong and robust man with one arm still in chains. If the privileged order were removed, the nation would not be something less but something more. What then is the Third Estate? All; but an "all" that is fettered and oppressed. What would it be without the privileged order? It would be all; but free and flourishing. Nothing will go well without the Third Estate; everything would go considerably better without the two others.

Emmanuel-Joseph Sieyès, *What is the Third Estate?* trans. M. Blondel, ed. S. E. Finer (London, 1964), pp. 53–63.

QUESTIONS FOR ANALYSIS

1. How might such a pamphlet change a political debate?
2. What images or arguments would have been persuasive?

---

representative body of the Three Estates of the realm, and that the king had no legal authority to arrest and imprison arbitrarily. In this, they echoed the English aristocrats of 1688 and the American revolutionaries of 1776.

Faced with economic hardship and financial chaos, Louis XVI summoned the Estates General (which had not met since 1614) to meet in 1789. His action appeared to many as the only solution to France's deepening problems. Long-term grievances and short-term hardships had produced bread riots across the country in the spring of 1789. Looting in Brittany, Flanders, Provence, and elsewhere was accompanied by demands that the king take measures to make bread affordable. Fear that the forces of law and order were collapsing and that the common people might take matters into their own hands spurred the Estates General. Each of the three orders elected its own

CHAPTER 18 THE FRENCH REVOLUTION

The Tennis Court Oath, by Jacques Louis David (1748–1825). In June 1789, in the hall where royalty played a game known as *jeu de paume* (similar to tennis), leaders of the revolution swore to draft a constitution. In the center of this painting, standing on the table, is Jean Bailly, president of the National Assembly. Seated at the table below him is the Abbé Sieyès. Mirabeau stands in the right foreground with a hat in his left hand.

deputies—the Third Estate indirectly through local assemblies. These assemblies were charged as well with the responsibility of drawing up lists of grievances (*cahiers des doléances*) further heightening expectations for fundamental reform.

The delegates of the Third Estate, though elected by assemblies chosen in turn by artisans and peasants, represented the outlook of the elite. Only 13 percent were men of business. About 25 percent were lawyers; 43 percent were government officeholders of some sort.

By tradition, each estate met and voted as a body. In the past, this had generally meant that the First Estate (the clergy) had combined with the Second (the nobility) to defeat the Third. Now the Third Estate made it clear it would not tolerate such an arrangement. The Third's interests were articulated most memorably by the Abbé Emmanuel Sieyès, a radical member of the clergy. "What Is the Third Estate?" asked Sieyès, in his famous pamphlet of January 1789. Everything, he answered, and pointed to eighteenth-century social changes to bolster his point. In early 1789, Sieyès's views were still unusually radical. But the leaders of the Third Estate agreed that the three orders should sit together and vote as individuals. More important, they insisted that the Third Estate should have twice as many members as the First and Second.

The king first opposed "doubling the Third" and then changed his position. His unwillingness to take a strong stand on voting procedures cost him support he might otherwise have obtained from the Third Estate. Shortly after the Estates General opened at Versailles in May 1789, the Third Estate, angered by the king's attitude, took the revolutionary step of leaving the body and declaring itself the National Assembly. Locked out of the Estates General meeting hall on June 20, the Third Estate and a handful of sympathetic nobles and clergymen moved to a nearby indoor tennis court.

Here, under the leadership of the volatile, maverick aristocrat Mirabeau and the radical clergyman Sieyès, they bound themselves by a solemn oath not to separate until they had drafted a constitution for France. This Oath of the Tennis Court, sworn on June 20,

1789, can be seen as the beginning of the French Revolution. By claiming the authority to remake the government in the name of the people, the National Assembly was not merely protesting against the rule of Louis XVI but asserting its right to act as the highest sovereign power in the nation. On June 27 the king virtually conceded this right by ordering all the delegates to join the National Assembly.

FIRST STAGES OF THE FRENCH REVOLUTION

The first stage of the French Revolution extended from June 1789 to August 1792. In the main, this stage was moderate, its actions dominated by the leadership of liberal nobles and men of the Third Estate. Yet three events in the summer and fall of 1789 furnished evidence that their leadership would be challenged.

POPULAR REVOLTS

From the beginning of the political crisis, public attention was high. It was roused not merely by interest in political reform but also by the economic crisis that, as we have seen, brought the price of bread to astronomical heights. Many believed that the aristocracy and the king were conspiring to punish the Third Estate by encouraging scarcity and high prices. Rumors circulated in Paris during the latter days of June 1789 that the king's troops were mobilizing to march on the city. The electors of Paris (those who had voted for the Third Estate—workshop masters, artisans, and shopkeepers) feared not only the king but also the Parisian poor, who had been parading through the streets and threatening violence. The common people would soon be referred to as *sans-culottes* (sahn koo-LAWTS). The term, which translates to "without breeches," was an antiaristocratic badge of pride: a man of the people wore full-length trousers rather than aristocratic breeches with stockings and gold-buckled shoes. Led by the electors, the people formed a provisional municipal government and organized a militia of volunteers to maintain order. Determined to obtain arms, they made their way on July 14 to the Bastille, an ancient fortress where guns and ammunition were stored. Built in the Middle Ages, the Bastille had served as a prison for many years but was no longer much used. Nevertheless, it symbolized hated royal authority. When crowds demanded arms from its governor, he procrastinated and then, fearing a frontal assault, opened fire, killing ninety-eight of the attackers. The crowd took revenge, capturing the fortress (which held only seven prisoners—five common criminals and

Women of Paris Leaving for Versailles, October 1789. A crowd of women, accompanied by Lafayette and the National Guard, marched to Versailles to confront the king about shortages and rising prices in Paris.

THE FRENCH REVOLUTION

two people confined for mental incapacity) and decapitating the governor. Similar groups took control in other cities across France. The fall of the Bastille was the first instance of the people's role in revolutionary change.

The second popular revolt occurred in the countryside. Peasants, too, expected and feared a monarchical and aristocratic counterrevolution. Rumors flew that the king's armies were on their way, that Austrians, Prussians, or "brigands" were invading. Frightened and uncertain, peasants and villagers organized militias; others attacked and burned manor houses, sometimes to look for grain but usually to find and destroy records of manorial dues. This "Great Fear," as historians have labeled it, compounded the confusion in rural areas. The news, when it reached Paris, convinced deputies at Versailles that the administration of rural France had simply collapsed.

The third instance of popular uprising, the "October Days of 1789," was brought on by economic crisis. This time Parisian women from the market district, angered by the soaring price of bread and fired by rumors of the king's continuing unwillingness to cooperate with the assembly, marched to Versailles on October 5 and demanded to be heard. Not satisfied with its reception by the assembly, the crowd broke through the gates to the palace, calling for the king to return to Paris from Versailles. On the afternoon of the following day the king yielded. The National Guard, sympathetic to the agitators, led the crowd back to Paris, the procession headed by a soldier holding aloft a loaf of bread on his bayonet.

Each of these popular uprisings shaped the political events unfolding at Versailles. The storming of the Bastille persuaded the king and nobles to agree to the creation of the National Assembly. The Great Fear compelled the most sweeping changes of the entire revolutionary period. In an effort to quell rural disorder, on the night of August 4 the assembly took a giant step toward abolishing all forms of privilege. It eliminated the church tithe (tax on the harvest), the labor requirement known as the corvée, the nobility's hunting privileges, and a wide variety of tax exemptions and monopolies. In effect, these reforms obliterated the remnants of feudalism. One week later, the assembly abolished the sale of offices, thereby sweeping away one of the fundamental institutions of the Old Regime. The king's return to Paris during the October Days of 1789 undercut his ability to resist further changes.

THE NATIONAL ASSEMBLY AND THE RIGHTS OF MAN

The assembly issued its charter of liberties, the Declaration of the Rights of Man and of the Citizen, in September 1789. It declared property to be a natural right, along with liberty, security, and "resistance to oppression." It declared freedom of speech, religious toleration, and liberty of the press inviolable. All citizens were to be treated equally before the law. No one was to be imprisoned or punished without due process of law. Sovereignty resided in the people, who could depose officers of the government if they abused their powers. These were not new ideas; they represented the outcome of Enlightenment discussions and revolutionary debates and deliberations. The Declaration became the preamble to the new constitution, which the assembly finished in 1791.

> The assembly issued its charter of liberties, the Declaration of the Rights of Man and of the Citizen, in September 1789. It declared property to be a natural right, along with liberty, security, and "resistance to oppression." It declared freedom of speech, religious toleration, and liberty of the press inviolable.

Whom did the Declaration mean by "man and the citizen"? The revolutionaries distinguished between "passive" citizens, guaranteed rights under law, and "active" citizens, who paid a certain amount in taxes and could thus vote and hold office. About half the adult males in France qualified as active citizens. Even their power was curtailed, because they could vote only for "electors," men whose property ownership qualified them to hold office. Later in the revolution, the more radical republic abolished the distinction between active and passive, and the conservative regimes reinstated it. Which men could be trusted to participate in politics and on what terms was a hotly contested issue.

So, to a certain extent, were the rights of religious minorities. The revolution gave full civil rights to Protestants, though in areas long divided by religious conflict those rights were challenged by Catholics. The revolution did, hesitantly, give civil rights to Jews, a measure that sparked protest in areas of eastern France. Religious toleration, a central theme of the Enlightenment, meant ending persecution; it did not mean that the regime was prepared to accommodate

DECLARATION OF THE RIGHTS OF MAN AND OF THE CITIZEN

One of the first important pronouncements of the National Assembly after the Tennis Court Oath was the Declaration of the Rights of Man and of the Citizen. The authors drew inspiration from the American Declaration of Independence, but the language is even more heavily influenced by the ideals of French Enlightenment philosophers, particularly Rousseau. Following are the Declaration's preamble and some of its most important principles.

The representatives of the French people, constituted as the National Assembly, considering that ignorance, disregard, or contempt for the rights of man are the sole causes of public misfortunes and the corruption of governments, have resolved to set forth, in a solemn declaration, the natural, inalienable, and sacred rights of man, so that the constant presence of this declaration may ceaselessly remind all members of the social body of their rights and duties; so that the acts of legislative power and those of the executive power may be more respected . . . and so that the demands of the citizens, grounded henceforth on simple and incontestable principles, may always be directed to the maintenance of the constitution and to the welfare of all. . . .

Article 1. Men are born and remain free and equal in rights. Social distinctions can be based only on public utility.

Article 2. The aim of every political association is the preservation of the natural and imprescriptible rights of man. These rights are liberty, property, security, and resistance to oppression.

Article 3. The source of all sovereignty resides essentially in the nation. No body, no individual can exercise authority that does not explicitly proceed from it.

Article 4. Liberty consists in being able to do anything that does not injure another; thus the only limits upon each man's exercise of his natural laws are those that guarantee enjoyment of these same rights to the other members of society.

Article 5. The law has the right to forbid only actions harmful to society. No action may be prevented that is not forbidden by law, and no one may be constrained to do what the law does not order.

Article 6. The law is the expression of the general will. All citizens have the right to participate personally, or through representatives, in its formation. It must be the same for all, whether it protects or punishes. All citizens, being equal in its eyes, are equally admissable to all public dignities, positions, and employments, according to their ability, and on the basis of no other distinction than that of their virtues and talents. . . .

Article 16. A society in which the guarantee of rights is not secured, or the separation of powers is not clearly established, has no constitution.

Declaration of the Rights of Man and of the Citizen, as cited in K. M. Baker, ed., *The Old Regime and the French Revolution* (Chicago; 1987), pp. 238–239.

QUESTIONS FOR ANALYSIS

1. How could a group of deputies elected to advise Louis XVI on constitutional reforms proclaim themselves a National Assembly? Why was the creation of the National Assembly a truly revolutionary act?
2. In what ways was the Declaration of the Rights of Man a moral document? What is it about the style or tone of the Declaration that identifies it as a peculiarly eighteenth-century document?

religious difference. The assembly abolished serfdom and banned slavery in continental France. It remained silent on colonial slavery; and although delegations pressed the assembly on political rights for free people of color, the assembly exempted the colonies from the constitution's provisions. Events in the Caribbean, as we will see, later forced the issue.

The rights and roles of women became the focus of sharp debate: not politics but working women's guilds or trade organizations, marriage and divorce, poor relief, and education. The Englishwoman Mary Wollstonecraft's milestone book *A Vindication of the Rights of Woman* (see Chapter Seventeen) was penned during the revolutionary debate over national education. Should girls be educated? To what end? Wollstonecraft, as we have seen, argued strongly that reforming education required forging a new concept of independent and equal womanhood. Even Wollstonecraft, however, only hinted at political representation, aware that such an idea would "excite laughter."

Only a handful of thinkers broached the subject of women in politics: the aristocratic Enlightenment thinker the Marquis de Condorcet and, from another shore, Marie Gouze, the self-educated daughter of a butcher. Gouze became an intellectual and playwright and renamed herself Olympe de Gouges. Like many "ordinary" people, she found in the explosion of revolutionary activity the opportunity to address the public by writing speeches, pamphlets, or newspapers. She composed her own manifesto, the *Declaration of the Rights of Woman and the Citizen* (1791). Beginning with the proposition that "social distinctions can only be based on the common utility," she declared that women had the same rights as men, including resistance to authority, participation in government, and naming the fathers of illegitimate children, and that last demand offers a glimpse of the shame, isolation, and hardship faced by a unmarried woman.

De Gouges's demand for equal rights was very unusual. Still, women fully participated in the everyday activities of the revolution, joining clubs, demonstrations, and debates; women artisans' organizations had a well-established role in municipal life and argued, forcefully, for their rights to produce and sell goods; market women were familiar public figures, often central to the circulation of news and spontaneous popular demonstrations (the October Days are a good example). The regime celebrated the support of women "citizens," and female figures were favorite allegories for liberty, prudence, and the bounty of nature. Those were abstractions. Real women were increasingly expected to contribute to the revolution as supportive mothers, educators, and tenders of the private sphere, not to be involved in public. When the revolution radicalized, the regime prohibited women's clubs entirely.

THE NATIONAL ASSEMBLY AND THE CHURCH

One of the central issues to confront the assembly involved religion, especially the organization of the church. In November 1789 the National Assembly resolved to confiscate the lands of the church and to use them as collateral for the issue of assignats, interest-bearing notes that eventually circulated as paper money. The assembly hoped—vainly, as it turned out—that this device would resolve the country's inflationary crisis. In July of the following year it enacted the Civil Constitution of the Clergy, which provided that all bishops and priests should be subject to the authority of the state. Their salaries were to be paid out of the public treasury, and they were required to swear allegiance to the new state, making it clear they served France rather than Rome. The assembly's aim was to make the Catholic Church of France a truly national and civil institution.

Reforming the church turned into a bitterly divisive matter; it polarized large sections of France. The church's privileged position during the Old Regime, including its vast monastic land holdings, had earned it the resentment of many. On the other hand, the practice of centuries had made the parish church an institution of enormous importance in the small towns and villages of France. In rural areas, the local priest not only baptized, married, and buried people but helped

C H R O N O L O G Y	
THE FIRST FRENCH REVOLUTION, 1789–1792	
Fall of the Bastille	July 14, 1789
The Great Fear	summer 1789
Declaration of the Rights of Man and of the Citizen	August 1789
The October Days	1789
National Assembly enacts the Civil Constitution of the Clergy	July 1790
Royal family tries to escape Paris	June 1791
National Assembly declares war on Austria and Prussia	April 1792

SOCIAL GRIEVANCES ON THE EVE OF THE REVOLUTION (1789)

During the elections to the Estates General, communities drew up "notebooks of grievances" to be presented the government. The following comes from a rural community, Lignère la Doucelle.

For a long time now, the inhabitants have been crushed beneath the excessive burden of the multiplicity of taxes that they have been obliged to pay. Their parish is large and spread out, but it is a hard land with many uncultivated areas, almost all of it divided into small parcels. There is not one single farm of appreciable size, and these small properties are occupied either by the poor or by people who are doing so poorly that they go without bread every other day. They buy bread or grain nine months of the year. No industries operate in this parish, and from the time they began complaining, no one has ever listened. The cry of anguish echoed all the way to the ministry after having fruitlessly worn out their intendants. They have always seen their legitimate claims being continuously denied, so may the fortunate moment of equality revive them.

* * *

That all lords, country gentlemen, and others of the privileged class who, either directly or through their proxies, desire to make a profit on their wealth, regardless of the nature of that wealth, pay the same taxes as the common people.

* * *

That the seigneur's mills not be obligatory, allowing everyone to choose where he would like to mill his grain.

* * *

That the children of common people living on a par with nobles be admitted for military service, as the nobility is.

That the king not bestow noble titles upon someone and their family line, but that titles be bestowed only upon those deserving it.

That nobility not be available for purchase or by any fashion other than by the bearing of arms or other service rendered to the State.

* * *

That church members be only able to take advantage of one position. That those who are enjoying more than one be made to choose within a fixed time period.

That future abbeys all be placed into the hands of the king, that His Majesty benefit from their revenue as the head abbots have been able to.

That in towns where there are several convents belonging to the same order, there be only one, and the goods and revenue of those that are to be abolished go to the profit of the crown.

That the convents where there are not normally twelve residents be abolished.

That no tenth of black wheat be paid to parish priests, priors or other beneficiaries, since this grain is only used to prepare the soil for the sowing of rye.

That they also not be paid any tenths of hemp, wool, or lamb. That in the countryside they be required to conduct burials and funerals free of charge. That the ten sous for audit books, insinuations, and the 100 [sous] collected for the parish be abolished.

* * *

That grain be taxed in the realm at a fixed price, or rather that its exportation abroad be forbidden except in the case where it would be sold at a low price.

Armand Bellée, ed., Cahiers de plaintes & doléances des paroisses de la province du Maine pour les Etats-généraux de 1789, vol. 2 (Le Mans, 1881–1892), pp. 578–582.

QUESTIONS FOR ANALYSIS

1. What, according to the petition, are the most significant problems the community faces? How are these problems explained?
2. What measures do the people expect the king to enact?
3. In what ways did the revolutionaries deal with these grievances?

with any written documents. The church provided poor relief and other services. In many areas peasants relied on and respected the local clergy. The dramatic changes enacted by the Civil Constitution of the Clergy thus sparked fierce resistance in some parts of rural France—resistance fueled by a combination of religious feeling and desire for local autonomy. When the pope threatened to excommunicate priests who signed the Civil Constitution, he raised the stakes: signing an oath of allegiance to the new French state now meant damnation later. When the government insisted, it drove many people, especially peasants in the deeply Catholic areas of western France into open counterrevolt, the rebel priests among them.

The National Assembly made a series of economic and governmental changes with lasting effects. To raise money, it sold off church lands, although few of the genuinely needy could afford to buy them. To encourage the growth of economic enterprise, it abolished guilds. To rid the country of local aristocratic power, it reorganized local governments, dividing France into eighty-three equal departments. These measures aimed to defend individual liberty and freedom from customary privilege. Their principal beneficiaries were, for the most part, members of the elite, people on their way up under the previous regime who were able to take advantage of the opportunities, such as buying land or being elected to office, that the new one offered. In this realm as elsewhere, the social changes of the revolution endorsed changes already under way in the eighteenth century.

> Though the constitution of 1791 declared France a monarchy, after Varennes, Louis was little more than a prisoner of the assembly.

A NEW STAGE: POPULAR REVOLUTION

Why did the French Revolution become more radical?

In the summer of 1792, the revolution entered a second stage. The moderate leaders were toppled and replaced by republicans, who repudiated the monarchy and claimed to rule on behalf of a sovereign people. Why this abrupt and drastic change? Was the revolution blown off course? These are among the most difficult questions about the French Revolution. Answers need to begin by taking account of (at least) three factors: changes in popular politics, a crisis of leadership, and international polarization.

First, the revolution politicized the common people, especially in cities. Newspapers filled with political and social commentary multiplied, freed from restrictions on printing. From 1789 forward, a wide variety of political clubs became part of daily political life. Some were formal, almost like political parties, gathering members of the elite to debate issues facing the country and influence decisions in the assembly. Other clubs opened their doors to those excluded from formal politics, and they read aloud from newspapers and discussed the options facing the country, from the provisions of the constitution to the trustworthiness of the king and his ministers. This political awareness was heightened by nearly constant shortages and fluctuating prices. Prices particularly exasperated the working people of Paris who had demanded changes in 1789 and had eagerly awaited change since then. Urban demonstrations, often led by women, demanded cheaper bread; political leaders in clubs and newspapers called for the government to control rising inflation. Club leaders spoke for men and women who felt cheated by the constitution.

A second major reason for the change of course was a lack of effective national leadership. Louis XVI remained a weak, vacillating monarch. He was forced to support measures personally distasteful to him, in particular the Civil Constitution of the Clergy. He was thus sympathetic to the plottings of the queen, who was in contact with her brother Leopold II of Austria. Urged on by Marie Antoinette, Louis agreed to attempt an escape from France in June 1791, hoping to rally foreign support for counterrevolution. The members of the royal family managed to slip past their palace guards in Paris, but they were apprehended near the border at Varennes and brought back to the capital. Though the constitution of 1791 declared France a monarchy, after Varennes, Louis was little more than a prisoner of the assembly.

THE COUNTERREVOLUTION

The third major reason for the dramatic turn of affairs was war. From the outset of the revolution, men and women across Europe had been compelled, by the very intensity of events in France, to take sides in the conflict. In the years immediately after 1789, the revolution in France won the enthusiastic support of a wide range of thinkers. The British poet William Wordsworth, who later became disillusioned, recalled his initial mood: "Bliss was it in that dawn to be alive." His sentiments were echoed across the Continent by poets and philosophers, including the German Johann Gottfried von Herder, who declared the revolution the most important historical moment since the Reformation. Political societies in Britain proclaimed their allegiance to the principles of the new revolution, often quite incorrectly, seeing it as nothing more than a French version of the events of 1688. In the Low Countries, western Germany, and Italy, "patriots" organized.

Others opposed the course of the revolution from the start. Exiled nobles, who had fled France for sympathetic royal courts in Germany and elsewhere, did all they could to stir up counterrevolutionary sentiment. In Britain the conservative cause was strengthened by the publication in 1790 of Edmund Burke's *Reflections on the Revolution* in France. A Whig politician who had sympathized with the American revolutionaries, Burke deemed the revolution in France a monstrous crime against the social order (see page 652).

Burke's famous book aroused some sympathy for the counterrevolutionary cause. That sympathy only slowly turned to active opposition. The first European states to express public concern about events in revolutionary France were Austria and Prussia, declaring in 1791 that order and the rights of the monarch of France were matters of "common interest to all sovereigns of Europe." The leaders of the French assembly pronounced the declaration an affront to national sovereignty. Nobles who had fled France played into their hands with plots and pronouncements against the government. Oddly, perhaps, almost all of the political factions in France believed war would serve their cause. The assembly's leaders expected an aggressive policy to shore up the people's loyalty and bring freedom to the rest of Europe. Counterrevolutionaries hoped the intervention of Austria and Prussia would undo all that had happened since 1789. Radicals, suspicious of aristocratic leaders and the king, believed that war would expose traitors with misgivings about the revolution and flush out those who sympathized with the king and European tyrants. On April 20, 1792, the assembly declared war against Austria and Prussia. Thus began the war that would keep the Continent in arms for a generation.

As the radicals expected, the French forces met serious reverses. By August 1792 the allied armies of Austria and Prussia had crossed the frontier and were threatening to capture Paris. Many, including soldiers, believed that the military disasters were evidence of

Playing Cards from the French Revolution. Revolutionaries tried to create entirely new images of politics and virtue; these were the cultural accompaniment to political transformation. The cards depict, from left to right, a Sans Culotte (note the long trousers), Jean-Jacques Rousseau, and Justice.

DEBATING THE FRENCH REVOLUTION: EDMUND BURKE AND THOMAS PAINE

The best-known debate on the French Revolution set the Irish-born conservative Edmund Burke against the British radical Thomas Paine. Burke opposed the French Revolution from the beginning. His Reflections on the Revolution in France *was published early, in 1790, when the French king was still securely on the throne. Burke disagreed with the premises of the revolution. Rights, he argued, were not abstract and "natural" but the results of specific historical traditions. Remodeling the French government without reference to the past and failing to pay proper respect to tradition and custom had, in his eyes, destroyed the fabric of French civilization.*

Thomas Paine was one of many to respond to Burke. The Rights of Man *(1791–1792) defended the revolution and, more generally, conceptions of human rights. In the polarized atmosphere of the revolutionary wars, simply possessing Paine's pamphlet was cause for imprisonment in Britain.*

Edmund Burke

You will observe, that from the Magna Charta to the Declaration of Rights, it has been the uniform policy of our constitution to claim and assert our liberties, as an entailed inheritance derived to us from our forefathers. . . . We have an inheritable crown; an inheritable peerage; and a house of commons and a people inheriting privileges, franchises, and liberties, from a long line of ancestors. . . .

You had all these advantages in your ancient states, but you chose to act as if you had never been moulded into civil society, and had every thing to begin anew. You began ill, because you began by despising every thing that belonged to you. . . . If the last generations of your country appeared without much luster in your eyes, you might have passed them by, and derived your claims from a more early race of ancestors. . . . Respecting your forefathers, you would have been taught to respect yourselves. You would not have chosen to consider the French as a people of yesterday, as a nation of low-born servile wretches until the emancipating year of 1789. . . . [Y]ou would not have been content to be represented as a gang of Maroon slaves, suddenly broke loose from the house of bondage, and therefore to be pardoned for your abuse of liberty to which you were not accustomed and ill fitted. . . .

. . . The fresh ruins of France, which shock our feelings wherever we can turn our eyes, are not the devastation of civil war; they are the sad but instructive monuments of rash and ignorant councel in time of profound peace. They are the display of inconsiderate and presumptuous, because unresisted and irresistible authority. . . .

Nothing is more certain, than that of our manners, our civilization, and all the good things which are connected with manners, and with civilization, have, in this European world of ours, depended upon two principles; and were indeed the result of both combined; I mean the spirit of a gentleman, and the spirit of religion. The nobility and the clergy, the one by profession, the other by patronage, kept learning in existance, even in the midst of arms and confusions. . . . Learning paid back what it received to nobility and priesthood. . . . Happy if they had all continued to know their indissoluble union, and their proper place. Happy if learning, not debauched by ambition, had been satisfied to continue the instructor, and not aspired to be the master! Along with its natural protectors and guardians, learning will be cast into the mire, and trodden down under the hoofs of a swinish multitude.

Edmund Burke, *Reflections on the Revolution in France* (1790) (New York, 1973), pp. 45, 48, 49, 52, 92.

THOMAS PAINE

Mr. Burke, with his usual outrage, abuses the *Declaration of the Rights of Man*. . . . Does Mr. Burke mean to deny that man has any rights? If he does, then he must mean that there are no such things as rights any where, and that he has none himself; for who is there in the world but man? But if Mr. Burke means to admit that man has rights, the question will then be, what are those rights, and how came man by them originally?

The error of those who reason by precedents drawn from antiquity, respecting the rights of man, is that they do not go far enough into antiquity. They stop in some of the intermediate stages of an hundred or a thousand years, and produce what was then a rule for the present day. This is no authority at all. . . .

To possess ourselves of a clear idea of what government is, or ought to be, we must trace its origin. In doing this, we shall easily discover that governments must have arisen either *out* of the people, or *over* the people. Mr. Burke has made no distinction. . . .

What were formerly called revolutions, were little more than a change of persons, or an alteration of local circumstances. They rose and fell like things of course, and had nothing in their existence or their fate that could influence beyond the spot that produced them. But what we now see in the world, from the revolutions of America and France, is a renovation of the natural order of things, a system of principles as universal as truth and the existence of man, and combining moral with political happiness and national prosperity.

Thomas Paine, *The Rights of Man* (New York, 1973), pp. 302, 308, 383.

QUESTIONS FOR ANALYSIS

1. What are the most significant points of disagreement between the two men?
2. What does each of them think has happened in France?
3. What images and language does each use to make his case? Why?

---

the king's treason. On August 10, Parisian crowds, organized by their radical leaders, attacked the royal palace. The king was imprisoned and a second and far more radical revolution began.

THE FRENCH REPUBLIC

From this point, the country's leadership passed into the hands of the more egalitarian leaders of the Third Estate. These new leaders were known as Jacobins, the name of the political club to which they belonged. Although their headquarters were in Paris, their membership extended throughout France. Their members included large numbers of professionals, government officeholders, and lawyers; but they proclaimed themselves spokesmen for the people and the nation. An increasing number of artisans joined Jacobin clubs as the movement grew, and other, more democratic clubs expanded as well.

The National Convention, elected by free white men, became the effective governing body of the country for the next three years. It was elected in September 1792, at a time when enemy troops were advancing, spreading panic. Rumors flew that prisoners in Paris were plotting to aid the enemy. They were hauled from their cells, dragged before hastily convened tribunals, and killed.

The "September Massacres" killed more than 1,000 "enemies of the Revolution" in less than a week. Similar riots engulfed Lyons, Orléans, and other French cities.

The newly elected convention was far more radical than its predecessor, and its leadership was determined to end the monarchy. On September 21, the convention declared France a republic. In December it placed the king on trial, and in January 1793 he was condemned to death by a narrow margin. The heir to the grand tradition of French absolutism met his end bravely as "citizen Louis Capet," beheaded by the guillotine. Introduced as a swifter and more humane form of execution, the frightful mechanical headsman came to symbolize revolutionary fervor.

The convention took other radical measures. It confiscated the property of enemies of the revolution, breaking up some large estates and selling them on easier terms to less-wealthy citizens. It abruptly canceled the policy of compensating nobles for their lost privileges. It repealed primogeniture, so that property would not be inherited exclusively by the oldest son but would be divided in substantially equal portions among all immediate heirs. It abolished slavery in French colonies (discussed later). It set maximum prices for grain and other necessities. In an astonishing effort to root out Christianity from everyday life, the convention adopted a new calendar. The calendar year began with the birth of the republic (September 22, 1792) and divided months in such a way as to eliminate the Catholic Sunday.

Most of this program was a hastily improvised response to crisis and political pressure from the common people in the cities and their leaders, by now a popular movement. In the three years after 1790, prices had risen staggeringly: wheat by 27 percent, beef by 136 percent, potatoes by 700 percent. While the government imposed its maximums in Paris, small vigilante militias, representing the sans-culottes, attacked those they considered hoarders and profiteers.

The convention also reorganized its armies, with astonishing success. By February 1793, Britain, Holland, Spain, and Austria were in the field against the French. Britain came into the war for strategic and economic reasons. The British feared French penetration into the Low Countries directly across the Channel and, more generally, France's threat to Britain's growing global power. The allied coalition, though united only in its desire to contain France, was nevertheless a formidable force. To counter it, the revolutionary government mustered all men capable of bearing arms. The revolution flung fourteen hastily drafted armies into battle under the leadership of newly promoted, young, and inexperienced officers. What they lacked in training and discipline they made up for in organization, mobility, flexibility, courage, and morale. (In the navy, however, where skill was of paramount importance, the revolutionary French never succeeded in matching the performance of the British.) In 1793–1794, the French armies preserved their homeland. In 1794–1795, they occupied the Low Countries; the Rhineland; and parts of Spain, Switzerland, and Savoy. In 1796, they invaded and occupied key parts of Italy and broke the coalition that had arrayed itself against them.

THE REIGN OF TERROR

In 1793, however, those victories lay in a hard-to-imagine future. France was in crisis. In 1793, the convention drafted a new democratic constitution based on male suffrage. That constitution never took effect—suspended indefinitely by wartime emergency. Instead, the convention prolonged its own life year after year

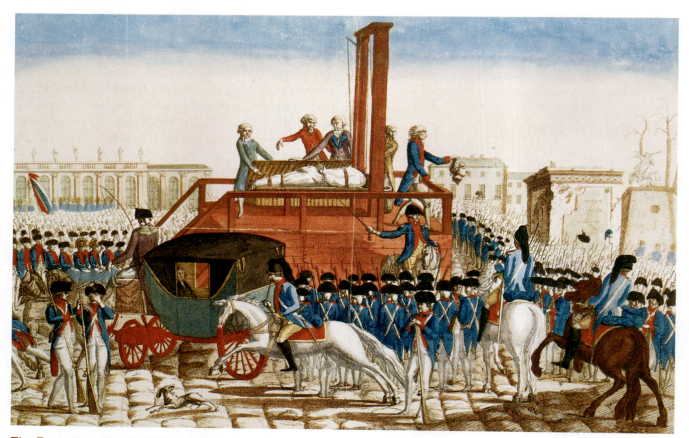

The Execution of Louis XVI. A revolutionary displays the king's head moments after his execution in January 1793.

and increasingly delegated its responsibilities to a group of twelve leaders, or the Committee of Public Safety. The committee's ruthlessness had two purposes: to seize control of the revolution and to prosecute all the revolution's enemies—"to make terror the order of the day." The Terror lasted less than two years but left a bloody and authoritarian legacy.

Perhaps the three best-known leaders of the radical revolution were Jean Paul Marat, Georges Jacques Danton, and Maximilien Robespierre, the latter two members of the Committee of Public Safety. Marat was educated as a physician and by 1789 had already earned enough distinction in that profession to be awarded an honorary degree by St. Andrews University in Scotland. Marat opposed nearly all of his moderate colleagues' assumptions, including their admiration for Great Britain, which Marat considered corrupt and despotic. Soon made a victim of persecution and forced to take refuge in unsanitary sewers and dungeons, he persevered as the editor of the popular news sheet *The Friend of the People*. Exposure to infection left him with a chronic and painful skin disease, from which baths provided the only relief. In the summer of 1793, at the height of the crisis of the revolution, he was stabbed in his bath by Charlotte Corday, a young royalist, and thus became a revolutionary martyr.

Danton, like Marat, was a popular political leader, well known in the more plebian clubs of Paris. Elected a member of the Committee of Public Safety in 1793, he had much to do with organizing the Terror. As time went on, however, he wearied of ruthlessness and displayed a tendency to compromise, which gave his opponents in the convention their opportunity. In April 1794, Danton was sent to the guillotine. On mounting the scaffold he is reported to have said, "Show my head to the people; they do not see the like every day."

The most famous of the radical leaders was Maximilien Robespierre. Born of a family reputed to be of Irish descent, Robespierre trained in law and quickly became a modestly successful lawyer. His eloquence and his consistent, or ruthless, insistence that leaders respect the "will of the people" eventually won him a following in the Jacobin club. Later, he became president of the National Convention and a member of the Committee of Public Safety. Though he had little to

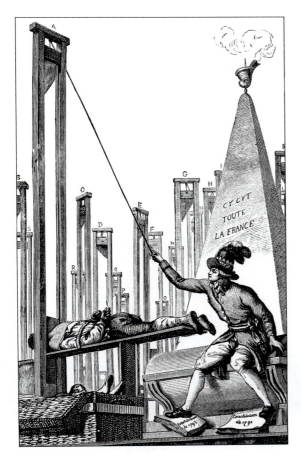

Robespierre Guillotining the Executioner. The original caption for this 1783 engraving read, "Robespierre guillotines the executioner after having had all the French guillotined." This caricature cost the engraver his life.

The Death of Robespierre. Robespierre being guillotined himself after his fall from power.

Chapter 18 The French Revolution

The Death of Marat. This painting by the French artist David immortalized Marat. The note in the slain leader's hand is from Charlotte Corday, his assassin.

defeated the counterrevolutionaries, and launched murderous campaigns of pacification—torching villages, farms, and fields and killing all who dared oppose them and many who did not.

During the period of the Terror, from September 1793 to July 1794, the most reliable estimates place the number of executions as high as 25,000 to 30,000 in France as a whole, fewer than 20,000 of whom were condemned by the courts. Approximately 500,000 were incarcerated between March 1793 and August 1794. These numbers, however, do not include the

FRANCE AND ITS SISTER REPUBLICS

The French revolutionaries, fighting against the conservative monarchs of Europe, conquered and annexed large sections of Italy, the Austrian Netherlands, and Switzerland. Napoleon did not begin these wars, though he continued and greatly expanded them.

do with starting the Terror, he was nevertheless responsible for enlarging its scope. "The Incorruptible," he came to represent ruthlessness justified as virtue and necessary to revolutionary progress.

The two years of the Terror brought dictatorship, centralization, suspension of any liberties, and war. The committee faced foreign enemies and opposition from both the political right and left at home. In June 1793, responding to an escalating crisis, leaders of the "Mountain," a party of radicals allied with Parisian artisans, purged moderates from the convention. Rebellions broke out in the provincial cities of Lyons, Bordeaux, and Marseilles, mercilessly repressed by the committee and its local representatives. The government also faced counterrevolution in the west, where movements enlisted peasants and artisans, who believed their local areas were being invaded and who fought for their local priest or against the summons from the revolutionaries' conscription boards. By the summer, the forces in the west posed a serious threat to the convention. Determined to stabilize France, whatever the cost, the committee redeployed its forces, pacification of the west and rebellious cities in the Rhone Valley, which took more than 100,000 lives. Few victims of the Terror were aristocrats. Many more were peasants or laborers accused of hoarding, treason, or counterrevolutionary activity. Anyone who appeared to threaten the republic, no matter what his or her social or economic position, was at risk. When some time later the Abbé Sieyès was asked what he had done to distinguish himself during the Terror, he responded dryly, "I lived."

THE LEGACY OF THE SECOND FRENCH REVOLUTION

Several points need to be made concerning this "second" French Revolution. First, for a time, revolutionary enthusiasm affected the everyday life of French men, women, and children in a remarkably direct way. Workers' trousers replaced the breeches that had been a sartorial badge of the middle classes and the nobility. A red cap, said to symbolize freedom from slavery, became popular headgear, wigs vanished. Men and women addressed each other as "citizen" or "citizeness." Public life was marked by ceremonies designed to dramatize the break with the Old Regime and celebrate new forms of fraternity. In the early stages of the revolution, these festivals seem to have captured genuine popular enthusiasm for new ways of living and thinking. Under the Committee of Public Safety, they became didactic and hollow.

Patriotic Women's Club. The members of this patriotic club wear constitutional bonnets to show their support for the revolution and the reforms of the convention.

CHRONOLOGY

THE SECOND FRENCH REVOLUTION, 1792–1794

First Republic established	summer 1792
National Convention elected	September 1792
Execution of the king	January 1793
War between Britain, Holland, Spain, and France	February 1793
Reign of Terror	September 1793–July 1794
Purge of the Jacobins	July 27, 1794
Execution of Robespierre	July 28, 1794

Second, the radical revolution of 1792–1793 dramatically reversed the trend toward decentralization and democracy. The assembly replaced local officials, some of them still royalist in sympathy, with "deputies on mission," whose task was to conscript troops and generate patriotic fervor. When these deputies appeared too eager to act independently, they were replaced by "national agents," with instructions to report directly to the committee. In another effort to stabilize authority, the assembly closed down all the women's political clubs, decreeing them a political and social danger. Ironically, those who claimed to govern in the name of the people found the popular movement threatening.

Third, the revolution eroded the strength of those traditional institutions—church, guild, parish—that had for centuries given people a common bond. In their place now stood patriotic organizations and a culture that insisted on loyalty to one national cause. Those organizations had first emerged with the election campaigns, meetings, and pamphlet wars of 1788 and the interest they heightened. They included the political clubs and local assemblies, which at the height of the revolution (1792–1793) met every day of the week and offered an apprenticeship in politics. The army of the republic become the premier national institution.

It is true that the revolution divided France, mobilizing counterrevolutionaries as well as revolutionaries. At the same time, the revolution, war, and culture of citizenly sacrifice forged new bonds. The sense that the rest of Europe, carrying what the verses of the *Marseillaise*, the most famous anthem of the revolution, called the "blood-stained flag of tyranny," would crush the new nation and its citizens unquestionably strengthened French national identity.

CHAPTER 18

THE FRENCH REVOLUTION

FROM THE TERROR TO BONAPARTE: THE DIRECTORY

How did Bonaparte come to power?

The Committee of Public Safety might have saved France from enemy armies but could not save itself. Inflation became catastrophic. The long string of military victories convinced growing numbers that the committee's demands for continuing self-sacrifice and Terror were no longer justified. By July 1794, the committee was virtually without allies. On July 27 (9 Thermidor, according to the new calendar), Robespierre was shouted down while attempting to speak on the floor of the convention. The following day, along with twenty-one other conspirators, he met his death by guillotine.

Ending the Terror did not immediately bring moderation. Vigilante groups of royalists hunted down Jacobins. The repeal of the maximum, or price controls, combined with the worst winter in a century caused widespread misery. Other measures that had constituted the Terror were gradually repealed. In 1795 the National Convention adopted a new and more conservative constitution. It granted suffrage to all adult male citizens who could read and write. Yet it set up indirect elections: citizens voted for electors, who in turn chose the legislative body. Wealthy citizens thus held authority. Eager to avoid personal dictatorship, it vested executive authority in a board of five men known as the Directory, chosen by the legislative body. The new constitution included not only a bill of rights but also a declaration of the duties of the citizen.

The Directory lasted longer than its revolutionary predecessors. It still faced discontent on both the radical left and the conservative right. On the left, the Directory repressed radical movements to abolish private property and parliamentary-style government, including one led by the radical "Gracchus Babeuf." Dispatching threats from the right proved more challenging. In 1797 the first free elections held in France as a republic returned a large number of monarchists to the councils of government, alarming politicians who had voted to execute Louis XVI. Backed by the army, the Directory annulled most of the election results. After two years of more uprisings and purges, and

On November 9, 1799 (18 Brumaire), Bonaparte was declared a "temporary consul." He was the answer to the prayers of the Directory: a strong, popular leader who was not a king.

with the country still plagued by severe inflation, the Directors grew desperate. This time they called the brilliant young general Napoleon Bonaparte to their assistance.

Bonaparte's first military victory had come in 1793, with the recapture of Toulon from royalist and British forces, and had earned him promotion from captain to brigadier general at the age of twenty-four. He had also been a supremely political general and was briefly arrested for his Jacobin associations. But he won the Directory's gratitude. In October 1795, he delivered what he called a "whiff of grapeshot," which saved the convention from attack by opponents of the new constitution. He won a string of victories in Italy, forcing Austria to withdrawal (temporarily) from the war. He attempted to defeat Britain by attacking British forces in Egypt and the Near East, a campaign that went well on land but ran into trouble at sea, where the French fleet was defeated by Admiral Horatio Nelson (Abukir Bay, 1798). Bonaparte found himself trapped in Egypt by the British and unable to win a decisive victory.

It was at this point that the call came from the Directory. Bonaparte slipped away from Egypt and appeared in Paris, already having agreed to participate in a coup d'état with the leading Director, that former revolutionary champion of the Third Estate, the Abbé Sieyès. On November 9, 1799 (18 Brumaire), Bonaparte was declared a "temporary consul." He was the answer to the Directory's prayers: a strong, popular leader who was not a king. Sieyès declared that Bonaparte would provide "Confidence from below, authority from above." With those words Sieyès pronounced the end of the revolutionary period.

NAPOLEON AND IMPERIAL FRANCE

How did Napoleon centralize his authority?

Few figures in Western history have compelled the attention of the world as Napoleon Bonaparte did during the fifteen years of his rule in France. Few men lived on with such persistence as myth, not just in their own countries, but across the West. Why? For the great majority of ordinary Europeans, memories of the French

Revolution were dominated by those of the Napoleonic wars, which devastated Europe, convulsed its politics, and traumatized its peoples for a generation. What began as political revolution and popular revolt continued in war and ended in an effort to create a new kind of European empire. To many observers, that entire drama seemed embodied in the career of one man. From the onset of war in 1792, France's revolutionaries had turned to France's armies for defense and survival. It seemed all too natural that the future of the revolution should be bound up with the successes of its greatest general, Napoleon Bonaparte.

Bonaparte's relationship to the revolution was not simple. His regime consolidated some of the revolution's political and social changes but sharply repudiated others. He presented himself as the son of the revolution, but he also borrowed freely from very different regimes, fashioning himself as the heir to Charlemagne, or to the Roman Empire. His regime remade revolutionary politics and the French state; offered stunning examples of the new kinds of warfare; and left a legacy of conflict and legends of French glory that lingered in the dreams, or nightmares, of Europe's statesmen and citizens for more than a century.

CONSOLIDATING AUTHORITY: 1799–1804

Bonaparte's early career reinforced the claim that the revolution rewarded the efforts of able men. The son of a provincial Corsican nobleman, he attended the École Militaire in Paris. In prerevolutionary France he would have been unable to rise beyond the rank of major, which required buying a regimental command. The revolution, however, had abolished the purchase of military office, and Bonaparte quickly became a general. Here, then, was a man who had risen from obscurity because of his own gifts, which he lent happily to the service of France's revolution. His character seemed to suit the age of Enlightenment as well, and his early admirers noted his wide range of talents and intellectual interests, including history, law, and mathematics. He took ideas seriously. He read—and wrote—constantly, even when on his military campaigns. His strengths as a leader were remarkable. He created financial, legal, and military plans and mastered their every detail. He worked endlessly and slept little. He inspired others, even those initially opposed to him. And he believed he was the destined savior of France. That last conviction made him a charismatic leader—and eventually led to his undoing.

In the first five years of his reign, Bonaparte quickly consolidated personal power. After he overthrew the government in 1799, he assumed the title of "first consul" and governed in the name of the republic. A new constitution established universal white male suffrage and set up two legislative bodies. Elections, however, were indirect, and the power of the legislative bodies sharply curbed. "The government?" said one observer. "There is Bonaparte." Bonaparte instituted what has since become a common authoritarian device, the plebiscite, which put a question directly to popular vote. This allows the head of state to bypass politicians or legislative bodies who might disagree with him—as well as permitting local officials to tamper with ballot boxes. In 1802, flush with victory abroad, he asked the legislature to proclaim him consul for life. When the senate refused to do so, Bonaparte's Council of State stepped in, offered him the title, and had it ratified by plebiscite. Throughout, his regime retained the appearance of consulting with the people, but its most important feature was the centralization of authority.

That authority came from reorganizing the state, and on this score Bonaparte's accomplishments were extraordinary and lasting. Bonaparte's regime confirmed the abolition of privilege, thereby promising "careers open to talent." Centralizing administrative departments, he accomplished what no recent French regime had yet achieved: an orderly and generally fair system of taxation. More efficient tax collection and fiscal management also helped halt the inflationary spiral that had crippled the revolutionary governments, although Bonaparte's regime relied heavily on resources from areas he had conquered to fund his military ventures. As we have seen, earlier revolutionary regimes began to reorganize France's administration—abolishing the ancient fiefdoms with their separate governments, legal codes, privileges, and customs—setting up a uniform system of departments. Bonaparte continued that work, pressing it further and putting an accent on centralization. He replaced elected officials and local self-government with centrally appointed prefects and subprefects, who answered directly to the Council of State in Paris. The prefects wielded considerable power, much more than any elected representative: they were in charge of everything from collecting statistics and reporting on the economy and the population to education, roads, and public works. Fifty years later, under the Second Empire of Napoleon's nephew, the prefect of Paris would mastermind a massive rebuilding of the French capital, which bears a Napoleonic stamp to this day. The state recruited civil servants according to talent, not title (though the elite remained dominant). With more integrated administration, in which the different branches were coordinated (and supervised from above), a more professional bureaucracy, and more rational and efficient taxation (though the demands of war strained the system), Napoleon's state marked the transition from Bourbon absolutism to the modern state.

LAW, EDUCATION, AND A NEW ELITE

Napoleon's most significant contribution to modern state building, and one exported to the areas he conquered, was the promulgation of a new legal code in 1804. Each revolutionary regime had taken up the daunting task of modernizing the laws; each had run out of time. Napoleon tolerated no delays, and threw himself into the project, pressing his own ideas and supervising half the meetings. The Napoleonic Code, as the civil code came to be called, bore the imprint of his philosophy and ambitions. The code pivoted on two principles that had remained significant through all the constitutional changes since 1789: uniformity and individualism. It cleared through the thicket of different and contradictory legal traditions that governed the ancient provinces of France, creating one uniform law. It confirmed the abolition of feudal privileges of all kinds: not only noble and clerical privileges but the special rights of craft guilds, municipalities, and so on. It set the conditions for exercising property rights: the drafting of contracts, leases, and stock companies. The code's provisions on the family, which Napoleon developed personally, insisted on the importance of paternal authority and the subordination of women and children. In 1793, during the most radical period of the revolution, men and women had been declared "equal in marriage"; now Napoleon's code affirmed the "natural supremacy" of the husband. Married women could not sell property, run a business, or have a profession without their husbands' permission. Fathers had the sole right to control their children's financial affairs, consent to their marriages, and (under the ancient right to correction) to imprison them for up to six months without showing cause. Divorce remained legal, but under unequal conditions; a man could sue for divorce on the grounds of adultery, but a woman could do so only if her husband moved his "concubine" into the family's house. Most important to the common people, the code prohibited paternity suits for illegitimate children.

In all, Napoleon developed seven legal codes covering commercial law, civil law and procedures, crime, and punishment. Like the civil code, the new criminal code consolidated some of the gains of the revolution, treating citizens as equals before the law and outlawing arbitrary arrest and imprisonment. Yet it, too, reinstated brutal measures that the revolutionaries had abolished, such as branding and cutting off the hands of parricides. The Napoleonic legal regime was more egalitarian than law under the Old Regime but no less concerned with authority.

Napoleon also rationalized the educational system. He ordered the establishment of *lycées* (high schools) in every major town to train civil servants and army officers and a school in Paris to train teachers. To supplement these changes, Napoleon brought the military and technical schools under state control and founded a national university to supervise the entire system. It is not surprising that he built up a new military academy. He reorganized and established solid financing for the premier schools of higher education: the polytechnic (for engineers) and the normal (for teachers), to which students would be admitted based on examinations and from which would issue the technical, educational, and political elites of the country. Like almost all his reforms, this one reinforced reforms introduced during the revolution, and it intended to abolish privilege and create "careers open to talent." Napoleon also embraced the burgeoning social and physical sciences of the Enlightenment. He sponsored the Institute of France, divided into four sections, or academies: fine arts, sciences, humanities, and language (the famous Academie Française). These academies dated back to the age of absolutism—now they were coordinated and put on a new footing. They acquired under Napoleon the character that they have preserved to this day: centralized, meritocratic, and geared to serving the state.

Who benefited from these changes? Like Bonaparte's other new institutions, the new schools helped confirm the power of a new elite. The new elite included businessmen, bankers, and merchants but was still composed primarily of powerful landowners. What was more, at least half of the fellowships to the high schools went to the sons of military officers and high civil servants. Finally, like most of Bonaparte's reforms, changes in education aimed to strengthen the empire: "My object in establishing a teaching corps is to have a means of directing political and moral opinion," Napoleon said bluntly.

Bonaparte's early measures were ambitious. To win support for them, he made allies without regard for their past political affiliations. He admitted back into the country exiles of all political stripes. His two fellow consuls were a regicide of the Terror and a bureaucrat of the Old Regime. His minister of police had been an extreme radical republican; his minister of foreign affairs was the aristocrat and opportunist Charles Talleyrand. The most remarkable act of political reconciliation came in 1801, with Bonaparte's concordat with the pope, an agreement that put an end to more than a decade of hostility between the French state and the Catholic Church. Although it shocked anticlerical revolutionaries, Napoleon, ever the pragmatist, believed that reconciliation would create domestic harmony and international solidarity. The agreement gave the pope the right to depose French bishops and to discipline the French clergy. In return, the Vatican agreed to forgo any claims to church lands expropriated by the revolution. That property would remain in the hands of its new middle-class rural and urban proprietors. The concordat did not revoke the principle of religious freedom established by the revolution, but it did win Napoleon the support of conservatives who had feared for France's future as a godless state.

Such political balancing acts increased Bonparte's general popularity. Combined with early military successes (peace with Austria in 1801 and with Britain in 1802), they muffled any opposition to his personal ambitions. He had married Josephine de Beauharnais, a Creole from Martinique and an influential mistress of the revolutionary period. Josephine had given the Corsican soldier-politician legitimacy and access among the revolutionary elite early in his career. Neither Bonaparte nor his ambitious wife were content to be first among equals, however; and in December of 1804, he finally cast aside any traces of republicanism. In a ceremony that evoked the splendor of medieval kingship and Bourbon absolutism, he crowned himself Emperor Napoleon I in the Cathedral of Notre Dame in Paris. Napoleon did much to create the modern state, but he did not hesitate to proclaim his links to the past.

IN EUROPE AS IN FRANCE: NAPOLEON'S EMPIRE

The nations of Europe had looked on—some in admiration, others in horror, all in astonishment—at the phenomenon that was Napoleon. A coalition of European powers led by Austria, Prussia, and Britain had fought France from 1792 until 1795, in hopes of maintaining European stability. This first coalition collapsed in disarray, defeated by the French armies and by financial exhaustion. The coalition was revived in 1798, at Britain's behest, but in the end it fared no better than the first effort. Despite Napoleon's debacle in Egypt, French victories in Europe split the alliance. Russia and Austria withdrew from the fray in 1801, and even the intransigent British were forced to make peace the following year.

That peace lasted a year; and by 1805 the Russians, Prussians, Austrians, and Swedes had joined the British in an attempt to contain France. Their efforts were to no avail. Napoleon's military superiority led to defeats, in turn, of all three continental allies. Napoleon was a master of well-timed, well-directed shock attacks on the battlefield: movement, regrouping, and pressing his advantage. He led an army that had transformed European warfare; first raised as a revolutionary militia, it was now a trained conscript army, loyal, well supplied by a nation whose economy was committed to serving the war effort, and led by generals promoted largely on the basis of talent. This new kind of army, directed with Napoleon's lethal flair, inflicted crushing defeats on his enemies. The battle of Austerlitz, in December 1805, was a triumph for the French against the combined forces of Austria and Russia and became a symbol of the emperor's apparent invincibility. His subsequent victory against the Russians at Friedland in 1807 only added to his reputation.

Out of these victories Napoleon created his new empire and affiliated states. To the southeast, the empire included Rome and the pope's dominions, Tuscany, and the Dalmatian territories of Austria (now the coastline of Croatia). To the east Napoleon's rule extended over a federation of German states known as the Confederation of the Rhine and a section of Poland. These new states were presented as France's gift of independence to patriots elsewhere in Europe, but in practice they served as a military buffer against renewed expansion by Austria. The empire itself was ringed by the allied kingdoms of Italy, Naples, Spain, and Holland, whose thrones were occupied by Napoleon's brothers, brothers-in-law, and trusted generals. "If only Father could see us now!" one of the siblings is supposed to have exclaimed.

The empire brought the French Revolution's practical consequences—a powerful, centralizing state and an end to old systems of privilege—to Europe's doorstep, applying to the empire principles that had already transformed France. Administrative modernization, which meant overhauling the procedures, codes, and practices of the state, was the most powerful feature of changes introduced. The empire changed the terms of government service (careers open to talent), handing out new titles and recruiting new men for the civil service and the judiciary. It ended the nobility's monopoly on the officer corps. The new branches of government hired engineers, mapmakers, surveyors, and legal consultants. Public works and education were reorganized.

Prefects in the outer reaches of the empire, as in France, built roads, bridges, dikes (in Holland), hospitals, and prisons; they reorganized universities and built observatories. In the empire and some of the satellite kingdoms tariffs were eliminated, feudal dues abolished, new tax districts formed, and plentiful new taxes collected to support the new state.

In the realm of liberty and law, Napoleon's rule eliminated feudal and church courts and created a single legal system. The Napoleonic Code was often introduced, but not always or entirely. (In southern Italy measures against the Catholic Church were deemed too controversial.) Reforms eliminated many inequalities and legal privileges. The Duchy of Warsaw in Poland ended serfdom but offered no land reform, so former serfs became impoverished tenants. In most areas, the empire gave civil rights to Protestants and Jews. In Rome, the conquering French opened the gates of the Jewish ghetto—and made Jews subject to conscription. In some areas, Catholic monasteries, convents, and other landholdings were broken up and sold, almost always to wealthy buyers. In the empire as in France, and under Napoleon as during the revolution, those who benefited were the elite: people and groups already on their way up and with the resources to take advantage of opportunities.

In government, the regime sought a combination of legal equality (for men) and stronger state authority. The French and local authorities created new electoral districts, expanded the suffrage, and wrote constitutions, but newly elected representative bodies were dismissed if they failed to cooperate, few constitutions were ever fully applied, and political freedoms were often fleeting. Napoleon's regime referred to revolutionary principles to anchor its legitimacy, but authority remained its guiding light. All governmental direction emanated from Paris and therefore from Napoleon.

Finally, in the empire as in France, Napoleon displayed his signature passions. The first of these was an Enlightenment zeal for accumulating useful knowledge. The empire gathered statistics as never before, for it was important to know the resources—including population—that a state had at its disposal. That spirit had been evident already in Bonaparte's extraordinary 1798 excursion into Egypt. He took hundreds of scholars and artists along with the army, founded the Egyptian institute in Cairo, and sent researchers off to make a systematic inventory of the country (its geology, rivers, minerals, antiquities, animal life) and to conduct archaeological expeditions to Upper Egypt, where they sketched the pyramids and excavated what would turn out to be the Rosetta stone (see Chapter Twenty). Napoleon's second passion was cultivating his relationship to imperial glories of the past. He poured time and energy into (literally) cementing his image for posterity. The Arc de Triomphe in Paris, designed to imitate the Arc of Constantine in Rome, is the best example; but Napoleon also ordered work to be undertaken to restore ruins in Rome, to make the Prado Palace in Madrid a museum, and to renovate and preserve the Alhambra in Granada.

Such were Napoleon's visions of his legacy and himself. How did others see him? Europe offered no single reaction. Some countries and social groups collaborated enthusiastically, some negotiated, some resisted. Napoleon's image as a military hero genuinely inspired young men from the elite, raised in a culture that prized military honor. By contrast, Catholic peasants in Spain fought him from the beginning. In many small principalities previously ruled by princes—the patchwork states of Germany, for example, and the repressive kingdom of Naples—reforms that provided for more efficient, less corrupt administration, a workable tax structure, and an end to customary privilege were welcomed by most of the local population. Yet the

Napoleon on Horseback at the St. Bernard Pass, by Jacques Louis David, 1801. David painted many episodes of the revolution: the Tennis Court Oath, the death of Marat, and the rise and rule of Napoleon. Here, Napoleon heroically leads his troops over the Alps into Italy to attack Austrian troops.

Napoleonic presence proved a mixed blessing. Vassal states contributed heavily to the maintenance of the emperor's military power. The French levied taxes, drafted men, and required states to support occupying armies. In Italy, the policy was called "liberty and requisitions"; and the Italians, Germans, and Dutch paid an especially high price for reforms—in terms of economic cost and numbers of men recruited. From the point of view of the common people, the local lord and priest had been replaced by the French tax collector and army recruiting board.

The demands of war and empire slowly but irretrievably cost Napoleon the support of revolutionaries, former Enlightenment thinkers, and liberals across the Continent. The German composer Ludwig van Beethoven originally planned to dedicate his Third Symphony, the *Eroica*, to Napoleon. Like so many European idealists, Beethoven at first hoped that Bonaparte would bring liberty to the whole continent. But Napoleon's empire building and his self-coronation in 1804 forced a swift and bitter change of judgment. Beethoven revoked the dedication to Bonaparte, declaring, "Now he, too, will trample on all the rights of man and indulge only his ambition."

Beethoven's words, however, were not the last verdict. It is telling that even Napoleon's enemies came to believe that the upstart emperor represented the wave of the future, particularly in regard to the reorganization of the state. Though they fought Napoleon, Prussian and Austrian administrators set about instituting reforms that resembled his: changing rules of promotion and recruitment, remodeling bureaucracies, redrawing districts, eliminating some privileges, and so on. Many who came of age under Napoleon's empire believed that, for better or worse, his empire was modern.

The Return to War and Napoleon's Defeat: 1806–1815

What led to Napoleon's downfall?

Napoleon's boldest attempt at consolidation, a policy banning British goods from the Continent, was a dangerous failure. Britain had bitterly opposed each of France's revolutionary regimes since the death of Louis XVI; now it tried to rally Europe against Napoleon with promises of generous financial loans and trade. The Continental System, established in 1806, sought to starve Britain's trade and force its surrender. The system failed for several reasons. Throughout the war Britain retained control of the seas. The British naval blockade of the Continent, begun in 1807, effectively countered Napoleon's system. While the French Empire strained to transport goods and raw materials overland to avoid the British blockade, the British successfully developed a lively trade with South America. A second reason for the failure of the system was its internal tariffs. Europe divided into economic camps, at odds with each other as they tried to subsist on what the Continent alone could produce and manufacture. Finally, the system hurt the Continent more than Britain. Stagnant trade in Europe's ports and unemployment in its manufacturing centers eroded public faith in Napoleon's dream of a working European empire.

The Continental System was Napoleon's first serious mistake. This ambition to create a European empire, modeled on Rome and ruled from Paris, was to become a second cause of his decline. The symbols of his empire—reflected in painting, architecture, and the design of furniture and clothing—were deliberately Roman in origin. This was not a novelty; the early revolutionaries, Jacobins in particular, harked back to the Roman republic as their model for political virtue, drawing on its imagery in art and political rhetoric. But the triumphal columns and arches Napoleon had erected to commemorate his victories recalled the ostentatious monuments of the Roman emperors. He made his brothers and sisters the monarchs of his newly created kingdoms. In 1809 he divorced the empress Josephine and ensured himself a successor of royal blood by marrying a Habsburg princess, Marie Louise—the great-niece of Marie-Antionette. As we have seen, the overextended empire could change quickly from a strength to a vulnerability.

Over time, the bitter tonic of defeat began to have an effect on Napoleon's enemies, who changed their own approach to waging war. After the Prussian army was humiliated at Jena in 1806 and forced out of the war, a whole generation of younger Prussian officers reformed their military and their state by demanding rigorous practical training for commanders and a genuinely national army made up of patriotic Prussian citizens rather than well-drilled mercenaries.

The myth of Napoleon's invincibility worked against him as well, as he took ever greater risks with France's military and national fortunes. Russian numbers and Austrian artillery inflicted horrendous losses on the French at Wagram in 1809, although these difficulties were forgotten in the glow of victory. Napoleon's allies and supporters shrugged off the British admiral Horatio Nelson's victory at Trafalgar in 1805 as no more than a temporary check to the emperor's ambitions. But Trafalgar broke French naval power in the Mediterranean and led to a rift with Spain, which had been France's equal partner in the battle and suffered equally in the defeat. In the Caribbean, too, Napoleon was forced to cut growing losses (see page 669).

A crucial moment in Napoleon's undoing came with his invasion of Spain in 1808. The invasion aimed, eventually, toward the conquest of Portugal, which had remained a stalwart ally of the British. Napoleon overthrew the Spanish king, installed his own brother on the throne, and then imposed a series of reforms similar to those he had instituted elsewhere in Europe. Napoleon's blow against the Spanish monarchy weakened its hold on its colonies across the Atlantic, and the Spanish crown never fully regained its grip (see Chapter Twenty). But in Spain itself, Napoleon reckoned without two factors that led to the ultimate failure of his mission: the presence of British forces under Sir Arthur Wellesley (later the Duke of Wellington) and the determined resistance of the Spanish people. They particularly detested Napoleon's interference in the affairs of the church. The peninsular wars, as the Spanish conflicts were called, were long and bitter. The smaller British force learned how to concentrate a devastating volume of gunfire on the French pinpoint attacks on the open battlefield and laid siege to French garrison towns. The Spanish quickly began to wear down French numbers, supplies, and morale through guerrilla warfare. Terrible atrocities were committed by both sides; the French military's torture and execution of Spanish guerrillas and civilians was immortalized by the Spanish artist Francisco Goya (1746–1828) with sickening accuracy in his prints and paintings. Though at one point Napoleon himself took charge of his army, he could not achieve anything more than temporary victory. The Spanish campaign was the first indication that Napoleon could be beaten, and it encouraged resistance elsewhere.

Napoleon on the Battlefield of Eylau. Amid bitter cold and snow, Napoleon engaged with the Russian army in February 1807. Although technically a victory for the French, it was only barely that, with the French losing at least 10,000 men and the Russians twice as many. This painting, characteristic of Bonaparte propaganda, emphasizes not the losses but the emperor's saintlike clemency—even enemy soldiers reach up toward him.

WHAT LED TO NAPOLEON'S DOWNFALL?

THE RETURN TO WAR AND NAPOLEON'S DEFEAT: 1806–1815

The second, and most dramatic stage in Napoleon's downfall began with the disruption of his alliance with Russia. As an agricultural country, Russia had suffered a severe economic crisis when it was no longer able to trade its surplus grain for British manufactures. The consequence was that Tsar Alexander I began to wink at trade with Britain and to ignore or evade the protests from Paris. By 1811 Napoleon decided that he could no longer endure this flouting of their agreement. He collected an army of 600,000 and set out for Russia in the spring of 1812. Only a third of the soldiers in this "Grande Armée" were French; nearly as many were Polish or German, joined by soldiers and adventurers from the rest of France's client states. It was the grandest of Napoleon's imperial expeditions, an army raised from across Europe and sent to punish the autocratic tsar. The invasion ended in disaster. The Russians refused to make a stand, drawing the French farther and farther into the heart of their country. Just before Napoleon reached the ancient Russian capital of Moscow, the Russian army drew the French forces into a bloody, seemingly pointless battle in the narrow streets of a town called Borodino, where both sides suffered terrible losses of men and supplies, harder on the French who were now so far from home. After the battle, the Russians permitted Napoleon to occupy Moscow. But on the night of his entry, Russian partisans put the city to the torch, leaving little but the blackened walls of the Kremlin palaces to shelter the French troops.

Hoping that the tsar would eventually surrender, Napoleon lingered amid the ruins for more than a month. On October 19 he finally ordered the homeward march. The delay was a fatal blunder. Long before he had reached the border, the terrible Russian winter was on his troops. Frozen streams, mountainous drifts of snow, and bottomless mud slowed the retreat almost to a halt. To add to the miseries of frostbite, disease, and starvation, mounted Cossacks rode out of the blizzard to harry the exhausted army. Each morning the miserable remnant that pushed on left behind circles of corpses around the campfires of the night before. Temperatures dropped to −27°F. On December 13 a few thousand broken soldiers crossed the frontier into Germany—a fragment of the once proud Grande Armée. Nearly 300,000 of its soldiers and untold thousands of Russians lost their lives in Napoleon's Russian adventure.

After the retreat from Russia, the anti-Napoleonic forces took renewed hope. United by a belief that they might finally succeed in defeating the emperor, Prussia, Russia, Austria, Sweden, and Britain renewed their attack. Citizens of many German states in particular saw this as a war of liberation, and indeed most of the fighting took place in Germany. The climax of the

***The 3rd of May, 1808,* by Francisco Goya.** This painting of the execution of Spanish rebels by Napoleon's army as it marched through Spain is one of the most memorable depictions of a nation's martyrdom.

campaign occurred in October 1813 when, at what was thereafter known as the Battle of the Nations, fought near Leipzig, the allies dealt the French a resounding defeat. Meanwhile, allied armies won significant victories in the Low Countries and Spain. By the beginning of 1814, they had crossed the Rhine into France. Left with an army of inexperienced youths, Napoleon retreated to Paris, urging the French people to resist despite constant setbacks at the hands of the larger invading armies. On March 31, Tsar Alexander I of Russia and King Frederick William III of Prussia made their triumphant entry into Paris. Napoleon was forced to abdicate unconditionally and was sent into exile on the island of Elba, off the Italian coast.

Napoleon was back on French soil in less than a year. In the interim the allies had restored the Bourbon dynasty to the throne, in the person of Louis XVIII, brother of Louis XVI. Despite his administrative abilities, Louis could not fill the void left by Napoleon's abdication. It was no surprise that, when the former emperor staged his escape from Elba, his fellow countrymen once more rallied to his side. By the time Napoleon reached Paris, he had generated enough support to cause Louis to flee the country. The allies, meeting in Vienna to conclude peace treaties with the French, were stunned by the news of Napoleon's return. They dispatched a hastily organized army to meet the emperor's typically bold offensive push into

NAPOLEON'S EUROPEAN EMPIRE AT ITS HEIGHT

What did Napoleon want from the rest of Europe? Where was he successful; where did he fail, and why? Where did his rule leave the most lasting impact? Could he have maintained his empire?

TWO LETTERS FROM NAPOLEON

Napoleon placed his brothers on the thrones of different vassal states in conquered territories throughout Europe. The first excerpt here is from a letter to his brother Eugène, head of one of the new Italian states, in which Napoleon explains how Italy's lucrative silk trade was to be diverted to damage English commercial interests and bolster the French Empire. It provides a revealing glimpse of Napoleon's vision of a united Europe, with the other countries' futures tied to France's.

On March 1, 1815, Napoleon landed in the south of France, having escaped from his exile on the island of Elba. The restored Bourbon king abdicated, and Napoleon ruled for 100 more days, until his defeat at the battle of Waterloo in June. The second selection is excerpted from a proclamation, addressed to the sovereigns of Europe, explaining the emperor's return. It is an excellent illustration of Napoleon's self-image, his rhetoric, and his belief that he represented the force of history itself.

Letter to Prince Eugène, August 23, 1810

I have received your letter of August 14. All the raw silk from the Kingdom of Italy goes to England, for there are no silk factories in Germany. It is therefore quite natural that I should wish to divert it from this route to the advantage of my French manufacturers: otherwise my silk factories, one of the chief supports of French commerce, would suffer substantial losses. I cannot agree with your observations. My principle is *France first.* You must never lose sight of the fact that, if English commerce is supreme on the high seas, it is due to her sea power: it is therefore to be expected that, as France is the strongest land power, she should claim commercial supremacy on the continent: it is indeed our only hope. And isn't it better for Italy to come to the help of France, in such an important matter as this, than to be covered with Customs Houses? For it would be short-sighted not to recognise that Italy owes her independence to France; that it was won by French blood and French victories; that it must not be misused; and that nothing could be more unreasonable than to start calculating what commercial advantages France gets out of it.

Piedmont and Parma produce silk too; and there also I have prohibited its export to any country except France. It is no use for Italy to make plans that leave French prosperity out of account; she must face the fact that the interests of the two countries hang together. Above all, she must be careful not to give France any reason for annexing her; for if it paid France to do this, who could stop her? So make this your motto too—*France first.*

Circular Letter to the Sovereigns of Europe, April 4, 1815

Monsieur, My Brother,

You will have learnt, during the course of last month, of my landing again in France, of my entry into Paris, and of the departure of the Bourbon family. Your Majesty must by now be aware of the real nature of these events. They are the work of an irresistible power, of the unanimous will of a great nation conscious of its duties and of its rights. A dynasty forcibly reimposed upon the French people was no longer suitable for it: the Bourbons refused to associate themselves with the natural feelings or the national customs; and France was forced to abandon them. The popular voice called for a liberator. The expectation which had decided me to make the supreme sacrifice was in vain. I returned; and from the place where my foot first touched the shore I was carried by the affection of my subjects into the bosom of my capital.

My first and heartfelt anxiety is to repay so much affection by the maintenance of an honourable peace. The re-establishment of the Imperial throne was necessary for the happiness of Frenchmen: my dearest hope is that it may also secure repose for the whole of Europe. Each national flag in turn has had its gleam of glory: often enough, by some turn of fortune, great victories have been followed by great defeats. . . . I have provided the world in the past with a programme of great contests; it will please me better in future to acknowledge no rivalry but that of the advocates of peace, and no combat but a crusade for the felicity of mankind. It is France's pleasure to make a frank avowal of this

noble ideal. Jealous of her independence, she will always base her policy upon an unqualified respect for the independence of other peoples. . . .

> *Monsieur* my Brother,
> Your good Brother,
>   Napoleon

K. M. Baker, ed., *The Old Regime and the French Revolution* (Chicago, 1987), pp. 419–420, 426–427.

QUESTIONS FOR ANALYSIS

1. How does Napoleon see his empire?
2. Can the different views be reconciled?
3. Do you think Napoleon was sincere?

---

the Low Countries. At the battle of Waterloo, fought over three bloody days from June 15 to 18, 1815, Napoleon was stopped by the forces of his two most persistent enemies, Britain and Prussia, and suffered his final defeat. This time the allies took no chances and shipped their prisoner off to the bleak island of St. Helena in the South Atlantic. The once-mighty emperor, now the exile Bonaparte, lived out a dreary existence writing self-serving memoirs until his death in 1821.

LIBERTY, POLITICS, AND SLAVERY: THE HAITIAN REVOLUTION

In the French colonies across the Atlantic, the revolution took a different course, with wide-ranging ramifications. The Caribbean islands of Guadeloupe, Martinique, and St. Domingue occupied a central role in the eighteenth-century French economy because of the sugar trade. Their planter elites had powerful influence in Paris. The French National Assembly (like its American counterpart) declined to discuss the matter of slavery in the colonies, unwilling to encroach on the property rights of slave owners and fearful of losing the lucrative sugar islands to their British or Spanish rivals should discontented slave owners talk of independence from France. (Competition between the European powers for the islands of the Caribbean was intense; that islands would change hands was a real possibility.) French men in the National Assembly also had to consider the question of rights for free men of color, a group that included a significant number of wealthy owners of property (and slaves).

St. Domingue had about 40,000 whites of different social classes, 30,000 free people of color, and 500,000 slaves, most of them recently enslaved in West Africa. In 1790, free people of color from St. Domingue sent a delegation to Paris, asking to be seated by the assembly, underscoring that they were men of property and, in many cases, of European ancestry. The assembly refused. Their refusal sparked a rebellion among free people of color in St. Domingue. The French colonial authorities repressed the movement quickly—and brutally. They captured Vincent Ogé, a member of the delegation to Paris and one of the leaders of the rebellion, and publicly executed him and his allies by breaking on the wheel and decapitation. Radical deputies, in Paris, including Robespierre, expressed outrage but could do little to change the assembly's policy.

In August 1791 the largest slave rebellion in history broke out in St. Domingue. How much that rebellion owed to revolutionary propaganda is unclear; like many rebellions during the period, it had its own roots. The British and the Spanish invaded, confident they could crush the rebellion and take the island. In the spring of 1792, the French government, on the verge of collapse and war with Europe, scrambled to win allies in St. Domingue by making free men of color citizens. A few months later (after the revolution of August 1792), the new French Republic dispatched commissioners to St. Domingue with troops and instructions to hold the island. There they faced a combination of different forces: Spanish and British troops, defiant St. Domingue planters, and slaves in rebellion. In this context, the local French commissioners reconsidered their commitment to slavery; in 1793 they promised freedom to slaves who would join the French. A year later, the assembly in Paris extended to all the colonies what had already been accomplished in St. Domingue, essentially by a slave rebellion.

Emancipation and war brought new leaders to the fore, chief among them a former slave, Toussaint Bréda, later Toussaint L'Ouverture (too-SAN LOO-vehr-tur), meaning "the one who opened the way." Over the course of the next five years, Toussaint and his soldiers, now allied with the French army, emerged victorious over the French planters, the British (in 1798), and the Spanish (in 1801). Toussaint also broke the power of his rival generals in both the mulatto and former slave armies, becoming the statesman of the revolution. In 1801, Toussaint set up a constitution, swearing allegiance to France but denying France any right to interfere in St. Domingue affairs. The constitution abolished slavery, reorganized the military, established Christianity as the state religion (this entailed a rejection of vodoun, a blend of Christian and various West and Central African traditions), and made Toussaint governor for life. It was an extraordinary moment in the revolutionary period: the formation of an authoritarian society but also an utterly unexpected symbol of the universal potential of revolutionary ideas.

Toussaint's accomplishments, however, put him on a collision course with the other French general he admired and whose career was remarkably like his own: Napoleon Bonaparte. St. Domingue stood at the center of Bonaparte's vision of an expanded empire in the New World, an empire that would recoup North American territories France had lost under the Old Regime and pivot around the lucrative combination of the Mississippi, French Louisiana, and the sugar and slave colonies of the Caribbean. In January 1802, Bonaparte dispatched 20,000 troops to bring the island under control. Toussaint, captured when he arrived for discussions with the French, was shipped under heavy guard to a prison in the mountains of eastern France, where he died in 1803. Fighting continued in St. Domingue, however, with fires now fueled by Bonaparte's decree reestablishing slavery where the convention had abolished it. The war turned into a nightmare for the French. Yellow fever killed thousands of French troops, including one of Napoleon's best generals and brother-in-law. Armies on both sides committed atrocities. By December 1803, the French army had collapsed. Napoleon scaled back his vision of an American empire and sold the Louisiana territories to Thomas Jefferson. "I know the value of what I abandon . . . I renounce it with the greatest regret," he told an aide. In St. Domingue, a general in the army of former slaves, Jean-Jacques Dessalines, declared the independent state of Haiti in 1804.

The Haitian revolution remained, in significant ways, an anomaly. It was the only successful slave revolution in history and by far the most radical of the revolutions that occurred in this age. It suggested that the emancipatory ideas of the revolution and Enlightenment might apply to non-Europeans and enslaved peoples—a suggestion that residents of Europe attempted to ignore but one that struck home with planter elites in North and South America. Combined with later rebellions in the British colonies, it contributed to the British decision to end slavery in 1838. And it cast a long shadow over nineteenth-century slave societies from the southern United States to Brazil. The Napoleonic episode, then, had wide-ranging effects across the Atlantic: in North America, the Louisiana purchase; in the Caribbean, the Haitian revolution; in Latin America, the weakening of Spain and Portugal's colonial empires.

Toussaint L'Ouverture. A portrait of L'Ouverture, leader of what would become the Haitian revolution, as a general.

CHRONOLOGY

REIGN OF NAPOLEON, 1799–1815

Napoleon becomes first consul	1799
Concordat with the pope	1801
Napoleon becomes consul for life	1802
Napoleon abolishes the republic and crowns himself emperor	1804
Napoleonic Code	1804
The Continental System	1806
Napoleon invades Spain	1808
Invasion of Russia	1812
Abdication of Napoleon	1814
Return and final exile of Napoleon	1815

Conclusion

The tumultuous events in France formed part of a broad pattern of late-eighteenth-century democratic upheaval. The French Revolution was the most violent, protracted, and contentious of the revolutions of the era; but the dynamics of revolution were much the same everywhere. One of the most important developments of the French Revolution was the emergence of a popular movement, which included political clubs representing people previously excluded from politics, newspapers read by and to the common people, and political leaders who spoke for the sans-culottes. In the French Revolution as in other revolutions, the popular movement challenged the early and moderate revolutionary leadership, pressing for more radical and democratic measures. And as in other revolutions, the popular movement in France was defeated, and authority was reestablished by a quasi-military figure. Likewise, the revolutionary ideas of liberty, equality, and fraternity were not specifically French; their roots lay in the social structures of the eighteenth century and in the ideas and culture of the Enlightenment. Yet French armies brought them, literally, to the doorsteps of many Europeans.

What was the larger impact of the revolution and the Napoleonic era? Its legacy is partly summed up in three key concepts: liberty, equality, and nation. Liberty meant individual rights and responsibilities and, more specifically, freedom from arbitrary authority. By equality, as we have seen, the revolutionaries meant the abolition of legal distinctions of rank among European men. Though their concept of equality was limited, it became a powerful mobilizing force in the nineteenth century. The most important legacy of the revolution may have been the new term *nation*. Nationhood was a political concept. A nation was formed of citizens, not a king's subjects; it was ruled by law and treated citizens as equal before the law; sovereignty did not lie in dynasties or historic fiefdoms but in the nation of citizens. This new form of nation gained legitimacy when citizen armies repelled attacks against their newly won freedoms; the victories of "citizens in arms" lived on in myth and history and provided the most powerful images of the period. As the war continued, military nationhood began to overshadow its political cousin. By the Napoleonic period, this shift became decisive; a new political body of freely associated citizens was most powerfully embodied in a centralized state, its army, its greatest general turned emperor of the French, and a kind of citizenship defined by individual commitment to the needs of the nation at war.

The French did not hesitate to champion their principles abroad. Some of those principles were revolutionary; others, imperial. In the German and Italian principalities the domination of an alien emperor and his unwelcome agents helped forge opposition and a national identity of their own.

When the revolutionary period closed, the three concepts of liberty, equality, and nationality were no longer merely ideas. They had taken shape in new communities and institutions. They had created new alliances among countries. They also polarized Europe and much of the world, giving rise to debates, grievances, and conflict that would shape the nineteenth century.

Key Terms

The Three Estates
Declaration of the Rights of Man and of the Citizen
fall of the Bastille
abolition of feudalism
bourgeoisie
Committee of Public Safety
Civil Constitution of the Clergy
fall and execution of the king
plebiscite
Napoleonic Code

Selected Readings

Applewhite, Harriet B., and Darline G. Levy, eds. *Women and Politics in the Age of the Democratic Revolution.* Ann Arbor, Mich., 1990. Essays on France, Britain, the Netherlands, and the United States.

Bell, David A. *The First Total War: Napoleon's Europe and the Birth of Warfare as We Know It.* Boston and New York, 2007. Lively and concise study of the "cataclysmic intensification" of warfare.

Blackburn, Robin. *The Overthrow of Colonial Slavery.* London and New York, 1988. A longer view of slavery and its abolition.

Blanning, T. C. W. *The French Revolutionary Wars, 1787–1802.* Oxford, 1996. On the revolution and war.

Blum, Carol. *Rousseau and the Republic of Virtue: The Language of Politics in the French Revolution.* Ithaca, N.Y., 1986. Excellent on how Rousseau was read by the revolutionaries.

Cobb, Richard. *The People's Armies.* New Haven, Conn., 1987. Brilliant and detailed analysis of the popular militias.

Connelly, Owen. *The French Revolution and Napoleonic Era.* 3rd ed., New York, 2000. Accessible, lively, one-volume survey.

Darnton, Robert, *The Forbidden Best-Sellers of Pre-Revolutionary France.* New York, 1995. One of Darnton's many imaginative studies of subversive opinion and books on the eve of the revolution.

Doyle, William. *Origins of the French Revolution.* New York, 1988. A revisionist historian surveys recent research on the political and social origins of the revolution and identifies a new consensus.

Doyle, William. *Oxford History of the French Revolution.* New York, 1989.

Dubois, Laurent. *Avengers of the New World. The Story of the Haitian Revolution.* Cambridge, Mass., 2004. Now the best and most accessible study.

Dubois, Laurent, and John D. Garrigus. *Slave Revolution in the Caribbean, 1789–1804: A Brief History with Documents.* New York, 2006. A particularly good collection.

Englund, Steven. *Napoleon, A Political Life.* Cambridge, Mass., 2004. Prize-winning biography, both dramatic and insightful.

Forrest, Alan. *The French Revolution and the Poor.* New York, 1981. A moving and detailed social history of the poor, who fared little better under revolutionary governments than under the Old Regime.

Furet, Francois. *Revolutionary France, 1770–1880.* Trans. Antonia Nerill. Cambridge, Mass., 1992. Overview by the leading revisionist.

Geyl, Pieter. *Napoleon: For and Against.* Rev. ed. New Haven, Conn., 1964. The ways in which Napoleon was interpreted by French historians and political figures.

Hunt, Lynn. *The French Revolution and Human Rights.* Boston, 1996. A collection of documents.

Hunt, Lynn. *Politics, Culture, and Class in the French Revolution.* Berkeley, Calif., 1984. An analysis of the new culture of democracy and republicanism.

Hunt, Lynn, and Jack R. Censer. *Liberty, Equality, Fraternity: Exploring the French Revolution.* University Park, Pa., 2001. Two leading historians of the revolution have written a lively, accessible study, with excellent documents and visual material.

Landes, Joan B. *Women and the Public Sphere in the Age of the French Revolution.* Ithaca, N.Y., 1988. On gender and politics.

Lefebvre, Georges. *The Coming of the French Revolution.* Princeton, N.J., 1947. The classic Marxist analysis.

Lewis, G., and C. Lucas. *Beyond the Terror: Essays in French Regional and Social History, 1794–1815.* New York, 1983. Shifts focus to the understudied period after the Terror.

O'Brien, Connor Cruise. *The Great Melody: A Thematic Biography of Edmund Burke.* Chicago, 1992. Passionate, partisan, and brilliant study of Burke's thoughts about Ireland, India, America, and France.

Palmer, R. R. *The Age of the Democratic Revolution: A Political History of Europe and America, 1760–1800.* 2 vols. Princeton, N.J., 1964. Impressive for its scope; places the French Revolution in the larger context of a worldwide revolutionary movement.

Palmer, R. R., and Isser Woloch. *Twelve Who Ruled: The Year of the Terror in the French Revolution.* Princeton, N.J. 2005. The terrific collective biography of the Committee of Public Safety, now updated.

Schama, Simon. *Citizens: A Chronicle of the French Revolution.* New York, 1989. Particularly good on art, culture, and politics.

Soboul, Albert. *The Sans-Culottes: The Popular Movement and Revolutionary Government, 1793–1794.* Garden City, N.Y., 1972. Dated, but a classic.

Sutherland, D. M. G. *France, 1789–1815: Revolution and Counterrevolution.* Oxford, 1986. An important synthesis of work on the revolution, especially in social history.

Thompson, J. M. *Robespierre and the French Revolution.* London, 1953. An excellent short biography.

Tocqueville, Alexis de. *The Old Regime and the French Revolution.* Garden City, N.Y., 1955. Originally written in 1856, this remains a provocative analysis of the revolution's legacy.

Trouillot, Michel Rolph. *Silencing the Past.* Boston, 1995. Essays on the Haitian revolution.

Woloch, Isser. *The New Regime: Transformations of the French Civic Order, 1789–1820.* New York, 1994. The fate of revolutionary civic reform.

Woolf, Stuart. *Napoleon's Integration of Europe.* New York, 1991. Technical but very thorough.

Chapter Nineteen

Chapter Contents

The Industrial Revolution in Britain, 1760–1850 675

The Industrial Revolution on the Continent 683

The Social Consequences of Industrialization 688

The Middle Classes 696

Conclusion 705

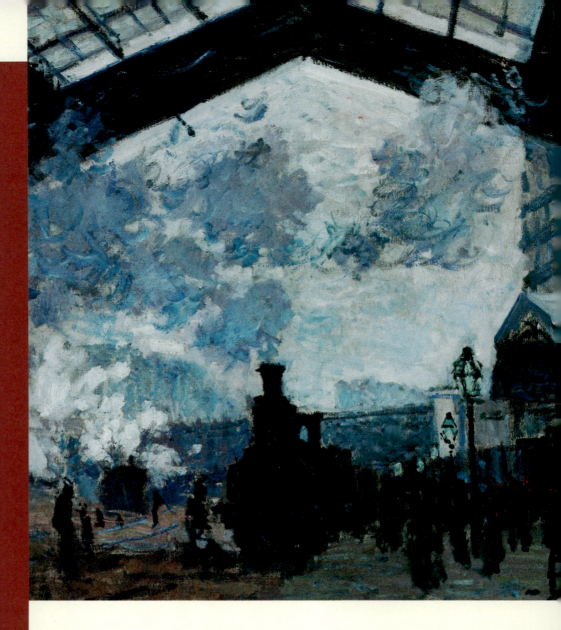

The Industrial Revolution and Nineteenth-Century Society

THE FRENCH REVOLUTION TRANSFORMED the political and diplomatic landscape of Europe suddenly and dramatically. The transformation of industry came more gradually. By the 1830s or 1840s, however, writers and social thinkers were increasingly aware of unexpected and extraordinary changes in their economic world. They spoke of an "industrial revolution," one that seemed to parallel the ongoing revolution in politics. The term has stayed with us. The Industrial Revolution spanned the hundred years after 1780. It represented the first breakthrough from an agricultural, artisanal, and overwhelmingly rural economy to one characterized by larger-scale manufacturing, more capital-intensive enterprises, and urbanization. It involved new sources of energy and power, faster transportation, mechanization, higher productivity, and new ways of organizing human labor. It triggered social changes with revolutionary consequences for the West and its relationship with the world.

Of all the changes, perhaps the most revolutionary came at the very root of human endeavor: new forms of energy. Over the space of two or three generations, a society and an economy that had drawn on water, wind, and wood for most of its energy needs came to depend on steam engines and coal. In 1800, the world produced 10 million tons of coal. In 1900, it produced 1 billion: 100 times more. The Industrial Revolution brought the beginning of the fossil-fuel age. It shattered the constraints of previous times, it opened an era of unprecedented economic growth, and it began to alter irrevocably the balance of humanity and the environment. Within a few more generations, by the end of the nineteenth century, the new energy regime would include oil and electricity—but historians refer to that period as the second industrial revolution.

Machines gripped contemporaries' imaginations, dazzling some observers and disturbing others. The novelist Charles Dickens, for instance, compared the piston of the steam engine working "monotonously up and down" to "the head of an elephant in a state of melancholy madness." Mechanization made possible enormous gains in productivity in some sectors; in so doing it shifted the basis of the economy, in some

FOCUS QUESTIONS

• Why did the Industrial Revolution first take hold in Britain?

• What specific changes did the Industrial Revolution bring?

• How was the Industrial Revolution different on the Continent?

• What were the long- and short-term consequences of industrialization?

• Who were the new middle classes?

CHAPTER 19

INDUSTRIAL REVOLUTION AND NINETEENTH-CENTURY SOCIETY 674

cases creating entirely new livelihoods and industrial regions while rendering others obsolete. Yet to focus on mechanization can be misleading. Especially at the outset, mechanization was limited to a few sectors of the economy and did not always lead to a dramatic break with techniques used in the past. Above all, technology did not dispense with human toil. Historians emphasize that the Industrial Revolution intensified human labor—carrying water or iron rails, digging trenches, harvesting cotton, sewing by hand, or pounding hides—much more often than it eased it.

One historian suggests we speak of an "industrious revolution." The "revolution" did not lie in machines themselves. Instead, it lay in the mushrooming growth of new economic system based on mobilizing capital and labor on a much larger scale. Its sweeping effects redistributed wealth, influence, and power. It created new social classes and produced new social tensions.

> The "revolution" did not lie in machines themselves. Instead, it lay in the mushrooming growth of new economic system based on mobilizing capital and labor on a much larger scale.

It also prompted deep-seated cultural shifts. The English cultural critic Raymond Williams has pointed out that in the eighteenth century, *industry* referred to a human quality: a hardworking woman was "industrious"; an ambitious clerk showed "industry." By the middle of the nineteenth century, *industry* had come to mean an economic system, one that followed its own inner logic and worked on its own—seemingly independent of humans. This is our modern understanding of the term, and it was born during the early nineteenth century. As the Industrial Revolution altered the foundations of the economy, it also changed the very assumptions with which people approached economics and the ways in which they regarded the role of human beings in the economy. These new assumptions could foster a sense of power but also anxieties about powerlessness.

Living as we do in the early twenty-first century, an age of economic and technological transformations, we may identify with the 1840s' sense of extraordinary, far-reaching, and little-understood change. We feel the economic and social world shifting but are unable to grasp the effects, and the changes are simultaneously exhilarating and unsettling. The cascading effects of new technologies, new forms of communication, and new economic imperatives make it difficult to differentiate results from causes. Are new technologies the driving force of change, or are they the effects of other structural transformations? What sectors of the economy and which kinds of employment will expand and which will become obsolete? Will dizzying rises in productivity benefit workers? Will all social groups share in economic growth? These questions and others that haunt us today arose during the first Industrial Revolution. Only in retrospect can we piece together the answers.

The dramatic changes of the late eighteenth and early nineteenth centuries built on developments in earlier times. Overseas commercial exploration and development had opened new territories to European trade. The continents of India, Africa, and North and South America had been woven into the pattern of European economic expansion. Expanding networks of trade and finance created new markets for goods and sources for raw materials; and they made it easier to mobilize capital for investment. All these developments paved the way for industrialization. The seventeenth and eighteenth centuries had seen significant "proto-industrialization," or the spread of manufacturing in rural areas in specific regions (see Chapter Fifteen). Especially in England, as we will see, it had also brought changes in agriculture and property holding with far-reaching ramifications. Population growth, which began in the eighteenth century, was also a key factor. Last, more elusive social and cultural developments, such as more secure property rights or new forms of social mobility, played an essential role in the revolution that created the modern industrial world.

The industrial revolution itself began in northern England and western Scotland during the late eighteenth century and from there moved slowly and unevenly across continental Europe. Various factors (supplies of labor, resources, and capital) and important developments (technological innovations, the emergence of new economic institutions, government subsidies, and legal changes) came together in different ways at different moments. For that reason, industrialization did not follow any single path across the various regions of Europe. Nor did it sweep aside older forms of production. New machines coexisted with intensive, old-fashioned hand labor. Manufacturing regions developed alongside vast areas of seemingly unchanged subsistence agriculture within the same nation. We begin with early industrialization in Great Britain and then turn to the more diverse changes that came later elsewhere.

THE INDUSTRIAL REVOLUTION IN BRITAIN, 1760–1850

Why did the Industrial Revolution first take hold in Britain?

Great Britain in the eighteenth century had a fortunate combination of natural, economic, and cultural resources. It was a small and secure island nation with a robust empire and control over crucial lanes across the oceans. It had ample supplies of coal, rivers, and a well-developed network of canals—all of which proved important at different stages of early industrialization.

Industrialization's roots lay in agriculture. By the middle of the eighteenth century, agriculture in Britain was more thoroughly commercialized than it was elsewhere. British agriculture had been transformed by a combination of new techniques, new crops, and changes in patterns of property holding, especially the "enclosure" of fields and pastures, which turned small holdings, and in many cases commonly held lands, into large fenced tracts that were privately owned and individually managed by commercial landlords. The British Parliament encouraged enclosure with a series of bills in the second half of the eighteenth century. Commercialized agriculture was more productive and yielded more food for a growing and increasingly urban population. The concentration of property in fewer hands drove small farmers off the land, sending them to look for work in other sectors of the economy. Last, commercialized agriculture produced higher profits and more wealth for a class of landed investors, wealth that would be invested in industry.

A key precondition for industrialization was Britain's growing supply of available capital, in the forms of private wealth and well-developed banking and credit institutions. London had become the leading center for international trade, and the city was a headquarters for the transfer of raw material, capital, and manufactured products throughout the world. Portugal alone channeled as much as £50,000 in Brazilian gold per week into London. Nor was banking limited to London; it was well established in the provinces as well. British merchants and financiers had accumulated substantial and well-organized resources, and they had established relatively secure banking. This made capital more readily available to underwrite new economic enterprises and eased the transfer of money and goods—importing, for instance, silks from the East or Egyptian and North American cottons.

Social and cultural conditions also encouraged investment in enterprises. In Britain far more than on the Continent, the pursuit of wealth was perceived to be a worthy goal. Since the Renaissance the nobility of Europe had cultivated the notion of gentlemanly conduct, in part to hold the line against those moving up from below. British aristocrats, whose ancient privileges were meager when compared with those of continental nobles, respected commoners with a talent for making money and did not hesitate to invest themselves. Their scramble to enclose their lands reflected a keen interest in commercialization and investment. Outside the aristocracy, an even lower barrier separated merchants from the rural gentry. Indeed, many of the entrepreneurs of the early Industrial Revolution came from the small gentry or independent (yeoman) farmer class. Eighteenth-century Britain was not by any means free of social snobbery: lords looked down on bankers and bankers looked down on craft workers. But a lord's disdain might well be tempered by the fact that his own grandfather had worked in the counting house.

Growing domestic and international markets made eighteenth-century Britain prosperous. The British were voracious consumers. The court elite followed and bought up yearly fashions, and so did most of Britain's landed and professional society. "Nature may be satisfied with little," one London entrepreneur declared. "But it is the wants of fashion and the desire of novelties that causes trade." The country's small size and the fact that it was an island encouraged the development of a well-integrated domestic market. Unlike continental Europe, Britain did not have a system of internal tolls and tariffs, so goods could be moved freely to wherever they might fetch the best price. A constantly improving transportation system boosted that freedom of movement. So did a favorable political climate. Some members of Parliament were

> Unlike continental Europe, Britain did not have a system of internal tolls and tariffs, so goods could be moved freely to wherever they might fetch the best price. A constantly improving transportation system boosted that freedom of movement. So did a favorable political climate.

businessmen themselves; others were investors. And both groups were eager to encourage by legislation the construction of canals, the establishment of banks, and the enclosure of common lands. In the late eighteenth century Parliament passed acts to finance turnpike building at the rate of forty roads per year, to construct canals, and to open up harbors and navigable streams.

Foreign markets promised even greater returns than domestic ones, though with greater risks. British foreign policy responded to its commercial needs. At the end of every major eighteenth-century war, Britain wrested overseas territories from its enemies. At the same time, Britain was penetrating hitherto unexploited territories, such as India and South America, in search of further potential markets and resources. In 1759, over one third of all British exports went to the colonies; by 1784, if we include the former colonies in North America, that figure had increased to one half. Production for export rose by 80 percent between 1750 and 1770; production for domestic consumption gained just 7 percent over the same period. The British possessed a merchant marine capable of transporting goods around the world and a navy practiced in the art of protecting its commercial fleets. By the 1780s, Britain's markets, together with its fleet and its established position at the center of world commerce, gave

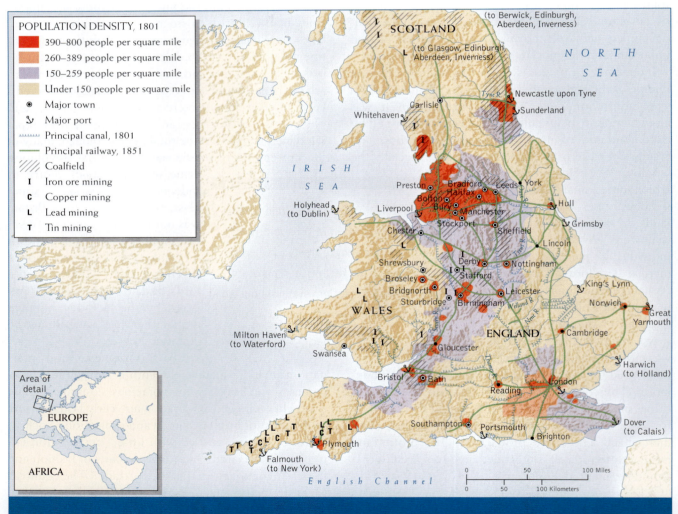

THE FIRST INDUSTRIAL NATION

The Industrial Revolution first took hold in Great Britain. How did its size and status as an island affect industrialization? Why did Great Britain build its first railroad between Durham and Darlington? Why did the railroad system expand more quickly in Great Britain than on the Continent?

its entrepreneurs unrivaled opportunities for trade and profit. These factors enabled Britain to experience the first great changes that would become an industrial revolution.

Innovation in the Textile Industries

The Industrial Revolution began with dramatic technological leaps in a few well-placed industries, the first of which was cotton textiles. The industry was already long established. Tariffs prohibiting imports of East Indian cottons, which Parliament had imposed to protect British woolen goods, had spurred the manufacture of British cotton. British textile manufacturers imported raw materials from India and the American South and borrowed patterns from Indian spinners and weavers. What, then, were the revolutionary breakthroughs?

In 1733, John Kay's invention of the flying shuttle speeded the process of weaving. The task of spinning thread, however, had not kept up. A series of comparatively simple mechanical devices eliminated this spinning-to-weaving bottleneck. The most important device was the spinning jenny, invented by James Hargreaves, a carpenter and hand-loom weaver, in 1764 (patented 1770). The spinning jenny, named after the inventor's wife, was a compound spinning wheel capable of producing sixteen threads at once—though the threads were not strong enough to be used for the longitudinal fibers, or warp, of cotton cloth. The invention of the water frame by Richard Arkwright, a barber, in 1769, made it possible to produce both warp and woof (latitudinal fibers) in great quantity. In 1799 Samuel Compton invented the spinning mule, which combined the features of both the jenny and the frame. All of these important technological changes were accomplished by the end of the eighteenth century.

The water frame and the spinning mule had enormous advantages over the spinning wheel. A jenny could spin from 6 to 24 times more yarn than a hand spinner. By the end of the eighteenth century, a mule could produce 200 to 300 times more. Just as important, the new machines made better-quality—stronger and finer—thread. These machines revolutionized production across the textile industry. Last, the cotton gin, invented by the American Eli Whitney in 1793, mechanized the process of separating cotton seeds from the fiber, thereby speeding up the production of cotton and reducing its price. The supply of cotton fibers could now expand to keep pace with rising demand from cotton cloth manufacturers. This cotton gin had many effects, including, paradoxically, changing the economics of slavery in the United States. The cotton-producing slave plantations in the American South became significantly more profitable, their labor now enmeshed in the very brisk and lucrative trade with merchant exporters of raw cotton and manufacturers who produced cotton textiles in the northern United States and England.

The first textile machines were inexpensive enough to be used by spinners in their own cottages. But as machines grew in size and complexity, they were housed instead in workshops or mills located near water that could be used to power the machines. Eventually, the further development of steam-driven equipment allowed manufacturers to build mills wherever they could be used. Frequently, those mills went up in towns and cities in the north of England, away from the older commercial and seafaring centers, but where local politicians were interested in textile manufacturing and the money and growth it brought in its wake. From 1780 on, British cotton textiles flooded the

Cotton Spinning, 1861. An illustration from a series showing spinning at Walter Evans and Company, cotton manufacturers in Derby, England.

THE FACTORY SYSTEM, SCIENCE, AND MORALITY: TWO VIEWS

Reactions to the Industrial Revolution and the factory system it produced ranged from celebration to horror. Dr. Andrew Ure, a Scottish professor of chemistry, was fascinated with these nineteenth-century applications of Enlightenment science. He believed that the new machinery and its products would create a new society of wealth, abundance, and, ultimately, stability through the useful regimentation of production.

Friedrich Engels (1820–1895) was one of the many socialists to criticize Dr. Ure as shortsighted and complacent in his outlook. Engels was himself part of a factory-owning family and so was able to examine the new industrial cities at close range. He provides a classic nineteenth-century analysis of industrialization. The Condition of the Working Class in England *is compellingly written, angry, and revealing about middle-class concerns of the time, including female labor.*

Dr. Andrew Ure (1835)

This island [Britain] is preeminent among civilized nations for the prodigious development of its factory wealth, and has been therefore long viewed with a jealous admiration by foreign powers. This very pre-eminence, however, has been contemplated in a very different light by many influential members of our own community, and has even been denounced by them as the certain origin of innumerable evils to the people, and of revolutionary convulsions to the state....

The blessings which physico-mechanical science has bestowed on society, and the means it has still in store for ameliorating the lot of mankind, has been too little dwelt upon; while, on the other hand, it has been accused of lending itself to the rich capitalists as an instrument for harassing the poor, and of exacting from the operative an accelerated rate of work. It has been said, for example, that the steam-engine now drives the power-looms with such velocity as to urge on their attendant weavers at the same rapid pace; but that the hand-weaver, not being subjected to this restless agent, can throw his shuttle and move his treddles at his convenience. There is, however, this difference in the two cases, that in the factory, every member of the loom is so adjusted, that the driving force leaves the attendant nearly nothing at all to do, certainly no muscular fatigue to sustain, while it produces for him good, unfailing wages, besides a healthy workshop *gratis*: whereas the non-factory weaver, having everything to execute by muscular exertion, finds the labour irksome, makes in consequence innumerable short pauses, separately of little account, but great when added together; earns therefore proportionally low wages, while he loses his health by poor diet and the dampness of his hovel.

Andrew Ure, *The Philosophy of Manufacturers: Or, An Exposition of the Scientific, Moral and Commercial Economy of the Factory System of Great Britain*, 1835, as cited in J. T. Ward, *The Factory System*, vol. 1 (New York, 1970), pp. 140–141.

FRIEDRICH ENGELS (1844)

Histories of the modern development of the cotton industry, such as those of Ure, Baines, and others, tell on every page of technical innovations. . . . In a well-ordered society such improvements would indeed be welcome, but social war rages unchecked and the benefits derived from these improvements are ruthlessly monopolized by a few persons. . . . Every improvement in machinery leads to unemployment, and the greater the technical improvement the greater the unemployment. Every improvement in machinery affects a number of workers in the same way as a commercial crisis and leads to want, distress, and crime. . . .

Let us examine a little more closely the process whereby machine-labour continually supesedes hand-labour. When spinning or weaving machinery is installed practically all that is left to be done by the hand is the piecing together of broken threads, and the machine does the rest. This task calls for nimble fingers rather than muscular strength. The labour of grown men is not merely unnecessary but actually unsuitable. . . . The greater the degree to which physical labour is displaced by the introduction of machines worked by water- or steam-power, the fewer grown men need be employed. In any case women and children will work for lower wages than men and, as has already been ob-

served, they are more skillful at piecing than grown men. Consequently it is women and children who are employed to do this work. . . . When women work in factories, the most important result is the dissolution of family ties. If a woman works for twelve or thirteen hours a day in a factory and her husband is employed either in the same establishment or in some other works, what is the fate of the children? They lack parental care and control. . . . It is not difficult to imagine that they are left to run wild.

Friedrich Engels, *The Condition of the Working Class in England in 1844*, trans. and ed. W. O. Henderson and W. H. Chaloner (New York, 1958), pp. 150–151, 158, 160.

QUESTIONS FOR ANALYSIS

1. According to Andre Ure, why was industrialization good for Britain? How can the blessings of "physicomechanical science" lead to the improvement of humanity?
2. What criticism did Engels level at Ure and other optimists on industrialization? Why did Engels think conditions for workers were getting worse instead of better?
3. Why do these two writers disagree about the effects of technological change?

world market. Numbers testify to the revolutionary changes in the expanding industry. Between 1760 and 1800, British exports of cotton goods grew from £250,000 worth a year to £5 million. In 1760, Britain imported 2.5 million pounds of raw cotton; in 1787, 22 million pounds; in 1837, 366 million pounds. By 1815, the export of cotton textiles amounted to 40 percent of the value of all domestic goods exported from Great Britain. Although the price of manufactured cotton goods fell dramatically, the market expanded so rapidly that profits continued to increase.

Behind these statistics lay a revolution in clothing. Cotton in the form of muslins and calicos was fine enough to appeal to wealthy consumers. Cotton was also light and washable. For the first time, ordinary people could have sheets, table linens, curtains, and underwear. (Wool was too scratchy.) As one writer commented in 1846, the revolution in textiles had ushered in a "brilliant transformation" in dress. "Every woman used to wear a blue or black dress that she kept

ten years without washing it for fear that it would fall to pieces. Today her husband can cover her in flower-printed cotton for the price of a day's wages."

The explosive growth of textiles also prompted a debate about the benefits and tyranny of the new industries. The British Romantic poet William Blake famously wrote in biblical terms of the textile mills' blight on the English countryside.

> And did the Countenance Divine
> Shine forth upon our clouded hills?
> And was Jerusalem builded here
> Among these dark Satanic mills?

By the 1830s, the British House of Commons was holding hearings on employment and working conditions in factories, recording testimony about working days that stretched from 3:00 A.M. to 10:00 P.M., the employment of very small children, and workers who lost hair and fingers in the mills' machinery. Women

Resisting Industrialization. A crowd attacks a spinning jenny, a symbol of the costs of industrial transformation.

and children counted for roughly two thirds of the labor force in textiles. The principle of regulating any labor (and emphatically that of adult men), however, was controversial. Only gradually did a series of factory acts prohibit hiring children under age nine and limit the labor of workers under age eighteen to ten hours a day.

COAL AND IRON

Meanwhile, decisive changes were transforming the production of iron. As in the textile industry, many important technological changes came during the eighteenth century. A series of innovations (coke smelting, rolling, and puddling) enabled the British to substitute coal (which they had in abundance) for wood (which was scarce and inefficient) to heat molten metal and make iron. The new "pig iron" was higher quality and could be used in building an enormous variety of iron products: machines, engines, railway tracks, agricultural implements, and hardware. Those iron products became, literally, the infrastructure of industrialization. Britain found itself able to export both coal and iron to rapidly expanding markets around the industrializing regions of the world. Between 1814 and 1852, exports of British iron doubled, rising to over 1 million tons of iron, more than half of the world's total production.

Rising demand for coal required mining deeper veins. In 1711, Thomas Newcomen had devised a cumbersome but remarkably effective steam engine for pumping water from mines. Though it was immensely valuable to the coal industry, its usefulness in other industries was limited by the amount of fuel it consumed. In 1763, James Watt, who made scientific instruments at the University of Glasgow, was asked to repair a model of the Newcomen engine. While tinkering with the machine, he hit on a way to improve it: adding a separate chamber to condense the steam eliminated the need to cool the cylinder. Watt patented his first engine incorporating this device in 1769. Watt's genius as an inventor far surpassed his ability as a businessman. He admitted that he would "rather face a loaded cannon than settle a disputed account or make a bargain." As a consequence, he fell into debt in attempting to place his machines on the market. He was rescued by Matthew Boulton, a wealthy hardware manufacturer from Birmingham. The two men formed a partnership, with Boulton providing the capital. By 1800 the firm had sold 289 engines for use in factories and mines. Watt and Boulton made their fortune from their invention's efficiency; they earned a regular percentage of the increased profits from each mine that operated an engine.

Steam power was still energy consuming and expensive and so only slowly replaced traditional water power. A series of improvements over the course of the nineteenth century made steam engines vastly more powerful than they had been in Watt's day. Even in its early form, however, the steam engine decisively transformed the nineteenth-century world with one application: the steam-driven locomotive. Railroads revolutionized industry, markets, public and private financing, and ordinary people's conceptions of space and time.

CHRONOLOGY

THE INDUSTRIAL REVOLUTION IN GREAT BRITAIN, 1733–1825

Invention of the fly shuttle	1733
Invention of the spinning jenny	1764
Invention of the water frame	1769
Invention of the steam engine	1769
Invention of the spinning mule	1779
Invention of the cotton gin	1793
First railroad built	1825

Child Labor in the Mines. This engraving of a young worker pulling a coal cart up through the narrow shaft of a mine accompanied a British Parliamentary report on child labor.

The Coming of Railways

Transportation had improved during the years before 1830, but moving heavy materials, particularly coal, remained a problem. It is significant that the first modern railway, built in England in 1825, ran from the Durham coal field of Stockton to Darlington, near the coast. Coal had traditionally been hauled short distances via tramways, or tracks along which horses pulled coal carts. The Stockton-to-Darlington railway was a logical extension of a tramway, designed to answer the transportation needs produced by constantly expanding industrialization. The man primarily responsible for the design of the first steam railway was George Stephenson, a self-educated engineer who had not learned to read until he was seventeen. The locomotives on the Stockton-Darlington line traveled at fifteen miles per hour, the fastest rate at which machines had yet moved goods overland. Soon they would move people as well, transforming transportation in the process.

Building railways became a massive enterprise and a risky but potentially profitable opportunity for investment. No sooner did the first combined passenger and goods service open in 1830, operating between Liverpool and Manchester, England, than plans were formulated and money pledged to extend rail systems throughout Europe, the Americas, and beyond. In 1830, there were no more than a few dozen miles of railway in the world. By 1840, there were over 4,500 miles; by 1850, over 23,000. British engineers, industrialists, and investors were quick to realize the global opportunities available in constructing railways overseas; a large part of Britain's industrial success in the later nineteenth century came through building other nations' infrastructures. The English contractor Thomas Brassey, for instance, built railways in Italy, Canada, Argentina, India, and Australia.

Throughout the world, a veritable army of construction workers built the railways. In Britain, they were called "navvies," derived from *navigator*, a term first used for the construction workers on Britain's

Manchester to Liverpool, late nineteenth century. Lower class passengers, physically separated from their social superiors, are packed into the rear of the train.

eighteenth-century canals. Navvies were a rough lot, living with a few women in temporary encampments as they migrated across the countryside. Often they were immigrant workers and faced local hostility. A sign posted by local residents outside a mine in Scotland in 1845 warned the Irish navvies to get "off the ground and out of the country" in a week or else be driven out "by the strength of our armes and a good pick shaft." Later in the century railway building projects in Africa and the Americas were lined with camps of immigrant Indian and Chinese laborers, who also became targets of nativist (a term that means "opposed to foreigners") anger.

The magnitude of the navvies' accomplishment was extraordinary. In Britain and in much of the rest of the world, mid-nineteenth-century railways were constructed almost entirely without the aid of machinery. An assistant engineer on the London-to-Birmingham line calculated that the labor involved was the equivalent of lifting 25 billion cubic feet of earth and stone 1 foot high. He compared this feat with building the Great Pyramid, a task he estimated had involved the hoisting of some 16 billion tons. The building of the pyramid, however, had required over 200,000 men and had taken twenty years. The construction of the London-to-Birmingham railway was accomplished by 20,000 men in less than five years. If we translated this into individual terms, a navvy was expected to move an average of 20 tons of earth per day. Railways were produced by toil as much as by technology, by human labor as much as by engineering; they illustrate why some historians prefer to use the term *industrious* revolution.

Steam engines, textile machines, new ways of making iron, and railways—all these were interconnected. Changes in one area endorsed changes in another. Pumps run by steam engines made it possible to mine deeper veins of coal; steam-powered railways made it possible to transport coal. Mechanization fueled the production of iron for machines and the mining of coal to run steam engines. The railway boom multiplied the demand for iron products: rails, locomotives, carriages, signals, switches, and the iron to make all of these. Building railroads called for engineering expertise: scaling mountains, designing bridges and tunnels. Railway construction, which required capital

Navvies and the Steam Excavation Machine. Despite help from new construction technology, much of the work on mid-nineteenth-century railways was manual labor done by navvies, many of whom were immigrant workers.

investment beyond the capacity of any single individual, forged new kinds of public and private financing. The scale of production expanded and the tempo of economic activity quickened, spurring the search for more coal, the production of more iron, the mobilization of more capital, and the recruitment of more labor. Steam and speed were becoming the foundation of the economy and of a new way of life.

THE INDUSTRIAL REVOLUTION ON THE CONTINENT

How was the Industrial Revolution different on the Continent?

Continental Europe, with its different natural, economic, and political resources, followed a different path. Eighteenth-century France, Belgium, and Germany did have manufacturing districts in regions with raw materials, access to markets, and long-standing traditions of craft and skill. Yet for a variety of reasons, changes along the lines seen in Britain did not occur until the 1830s. Britain's transportation system was highly developed; those of France and Germany were not. France was far larger than England: its rivers more difficult to navigate; its seaports, cities, and coal deposits farther apart. Much of central Europe was divided into small principalities, each with its own set of tolls and tariffs, which complicated the transportation of raw materials or manufactured goods over any considerable distance. The Continent had fewer raw materials, coal in particular, than Britain. The abundance and cheapness of wood discouraged exploration that might have resulted in new discoveries of coal. It also meant that high-energy-consuming, coal-run steam engines were less economical on the Continent. Capital, too, was less readily available. Early British industrialization was underwritten by private wealth; this was less feasible elsewhere. Different patterns of landholding formed obstacles to the commercialization of agriculture. In the east, serfdom was a powerful disincentive to labor-saving innovations. In the west, especially in France, the large number of small peasants, or farmers, stayed put on the land.

The wars of the French Revolution and Napoleon did hasten legal changes and the consolidation of state power, but they disrupted economies. During the eighteenth century, the population had grown and mechanization had begun in a few key industries. The ensuing political upheaval, the financial strains of warfare, and the thundering hooves of armies, however, did virtually nothing to help economic development. Napoleon's Continental System and British destruction of French merchant shipping hurt commerce badly. The ban on British-shipped cotton stalled the growth of cotton textiles for decades, though the armies' greater demand for woolen cloth kept that sector of textiles humming. Iron processing increased to satisfy the military's rising needs, but techniques for making iron remained largely unchanged. Probably the revolutionary change most beneficial to industrial advance in Europe was the removal of previous restraints on the movement of capital and labor—for example, the abolition of craft guilds and the reduction of tariff barriers across the Continent.

After 1815, a number of factors combined to change the economic climate. In those regions with a well-established commercial and industrial base—the northeast of France, Belgium, and swaths of territory across the Rhineland, Saxony, Silesa, and northern Bohemia (see map on page 686)—population growth further boosted economic development. Rising population did not by itself produce industrialization, however: in Ireland, where other necessary factors were absent, more people meant less food.

Transportation improved. The Austrian Empire added over 30,000 miles of roads between 1830 and 1847; Belgium almost doubled its road network in the same period; France built not only new roads but 2,000 miles of canals. These improvements, combined with the construction of railroads in the 1830s and 1840s, opened up new markets and encouraged new methods of manufacturing. In many of the Continent's manufacturing regions, however, industrialists could long continue to tap large pools of skilled but inexpensive labor. Thus older methods of putting out

> In many of the Continent's manufacturing regions, however, industrialists could long continue to tap large pools of skilled but inexpensive labor. Thus older methods of putting out industry and handwork persisted alongside new-model factories.

industry and handwork persisted alongside new-model factories.

In what other ways was the continental model of industrialization different? Governments played a considerably more direct role in industrialization. France and Prussia, for instance, granted considerable subsidies to private companies that built railroads. After 1849, the Prussian state took on the task itself, as did Belgium and, later, Russia—an undertaking that required importing material and expertise but that often yielded significant profits. In Prussia, the state also operated a large proportion of that country's mines. Governments on the Continent provided incentives for and laws favorable to industrialization. Limited-liability laws, to take the most important example, allowed investors to own shares in a corporation or company without becoming liable for the company's debts—and they enabled enterprises to recruit many small investors to put together the capital for massive investments in railroads, other forms of industry, and commerce.

Mobilizing capital for industry was one of the challenges of the century. In Great Britain, overseas trade had created well-organized financial markets; on the Continent, capital was dispersed and in short supply. New joint-stock investment banks, unlike private banks, could sell bonds to and take deposits from individuals and smaller companies. They could offer start-up capital in the form of long-term, low-interest commercial loans to aspiring entrepreneurs. The Belgian Société Générale dated from the 1830s, the Austrian Creditanstalt and the French Crédit Mobilier from the 1850s. The Crédit Mobilier, for instance, founded in 1852 by the wealthy and well-connected Périere brothers, assembled enough capital to finance insurance companies; the Parisian bus system; six municipal gas companies; transatlantic shipping; enterprises in other European countries; and, with the patronage of the state, the massive railroad-building spree of the 1850s. The Périeres' success earned them reputations as upstart speculators, and the Crédit Mobilier collapsed in scandal, but the revolution in banking was well under way.

Finally, continental Europeans actively promoted invention and technological development. They were willing for the state to establish educational systems whose aim, among others, was to produce a well-trained elite capable of assisting in the development of industrial technology. In sum, what Britain had produced almost by chance, the Europeans began to reproduce by design.

Industrialization after 1850

Until 1850 Britain remained the preeminent industrial power. Individual British factories were small by the standards set later in the century, let alone those of modern times. Still, their output was tremendous and their ability to sell to home and foreign markets was unrivaled. Between 1850 and 1870, however, France, Germany, Belgium, and the United States emerged as challengers to the power and place of British manufacturers. The British iron industry remained the largest in the world (in 1870 Britain still produced half the world's pig iron), but it grew more slowly than did its counterparts in France or Germany. Most of continental Europe's gains came as a result of continuing changes in those areas we recognize as important for sustained industrial growth: transport, commerce, and government policy. The spread of railways encouraged the free movement of goods. International monetary unions were established and restrictions removed on international waterways such as the Danube. Free trade went hand in hand with removing guild barriers to entering trades and ending restrictions on practicing business. Guild control over artisanal production was abolished in Austria in 1859 and in most of Germany by the mid-1860s. Laws against usury,

Silk Weavers of Lyons, 1850. The first significant working-class uprisings in nineteenth-century France occurred in Lyons in 1831 and 1834. Note the domestic character of the working conditions.

most of which had ceased to be enforced, were officially abandoned in Britain, Holland, Belgium, and in many parts of Germany. Governmental regulation of mining was surrendered by the Prussian state in the 1850s, freeing entrepreneurs to develop resources as they saw fit. Investment banks continued to form, encouraged by an increase in the money supply and an easing of credit after the California gold fields opened in 1849.

The first phase of the industrial revolution, one economic historian reminds us, was confined to a narrow set of industries and can be summed up rather simply: "cheaper and better clothes (mainly made of cotton), cheaper and better metals (pig iron, wrought iron, and steel) and faster travel (mainly by rail)." The second half of the century brought changes farther afield and in areas where Great Britain's early advantages were no longer decisive. Transatlantic cable (starting in 1865) and the telephone (invented in 1876) laid the ground for a revolution in communications. New chemical processes, dyestuffs, and pharmaceuticals emerged. So did new sources of energy: electricity, in which the United States and Germany led both invention and commercial development; and oil, which was being refined in the 1850s and widely used by 1900. Among the early exploiters of Russian oil discoveries were the Swedish Nobel brothers and the French Rothschilds. The developments that eventually converged to make the automobile came primarily from Germany and France. The internal combustion engine, important because it was small, efficient, and could be used in a very wide variety of situations, was developed by Carl Benz and Gottlieb Daimler in the 1880s. The removable pneumatic tire was patented in 1891 by Edouard Michelin, a painter who had joined with his engineer brother in running the family's small agricultural-equipment business. These developments are discussed fully in Chapter Twenty-three, but their pioneers' familiar names illustrate how industry and invention had diversified over the course of the century.

In eastern Europe, the nineteenth century brought different patterns of economic development. Spurred by the ever-growing demand for food and grain, large sections of eastern Europe developed into concentrated, commercialized agriculture regions that played the specific role of exporting food to the west. Many of those large agricultural enterprises were based on serfdom and remained so, in the face of increasing pressure for reform, until 1850. Peasant protest and liberal demands for reform only gradually chipped away at the nobility's determination to hold onto its privilege and system of labor. Serfdom was abolished in most parts of eastern and southern Europe by 1850 and in Poland and Russia in the 1860s.

Although industry continued to take a back seat to agriculture, eastern Europe had several important manufacturing regions. By the 1880s, the number of men and women employed in the cotton industry in the Austrian province of Bohemia exceeded that in the German state of Saxony. In the Czech region, textile industries, developed in the eighteenth century, continued to thrive. By the 1830s, there were machine-powered Czech cotton mills and iron works. In Russia, a factory industry producing coarse textiles—mostly linens—had grown up around Moscow. At mid-century, Russia was purchasing 24 percent of the total British machinery exports to mechanize its own mills. Many who labored in Russian industry actually remained serfs until the 1860s—about 40 percent of them employed in mines. Of the over 800,000 Russians engaged in manufacturing by 1860, however, most were employed in small workshops of about forty persons.

By 1870, then, the core industrial nations of Europe included Great Britain, France, Germany, Italy, the Netherlands, and Switzerland. Austria stood at the margins. Russia, Spain, Bulgaria, Greece, Hungary, Romania, and Serbia formed the industrial periphery— and some regions of these nations seemed virtually untouched by the advance of industry. What was more, even in Great Britain, the most fully industrialized nation, agricultural laborers still constituted the single largest occupational category in 1860 (although they formed only 9 percent of the overall population). In Belgium, the Netherlands, Switzerland, Germany, France, Scandinavia, and Ireland, 25 to 50 percent of the population still worked on the land. In Russia, the number was 80 percent. *Industrial*, moreover, did not mean automation or machine production, which long remained confined to a few sectors of the economy. As machines were introduced in some sectors to do specific tasks, they usually intensified the tempo of handwork in other sectors. Thus even in the industrialized regions, much work was still accomplished in tiny workshops—or at home.

> As machines were introduced in some sectors to do specific tasks, they usually intensified the tempo of handwork in other sectors. Thus, even in the industrialized regions, much work was still accomplished in tiny workshops—or at home.

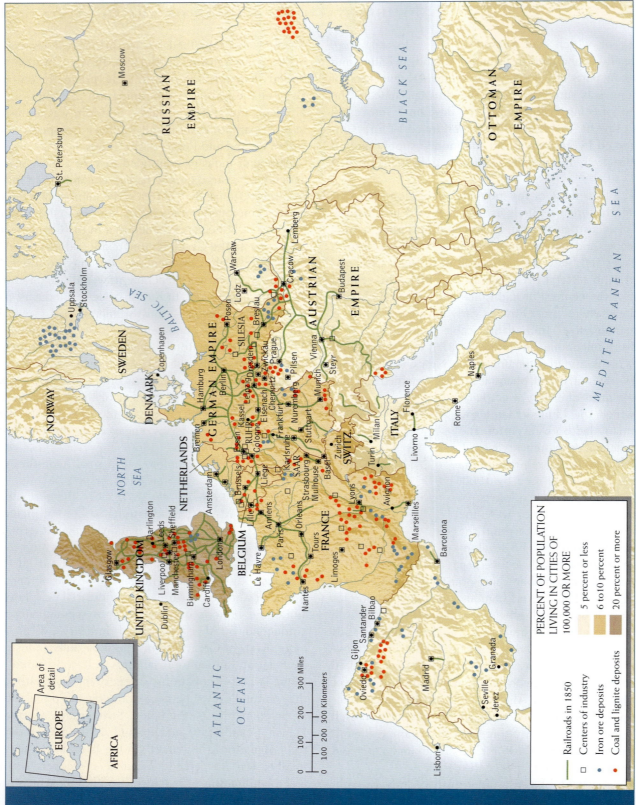

THE INDUSTRIAL REVOLUTION

Why were the effects of the Industrial Revolution more rapidly apparent in Great Britain and in north central Europe? How did an extensive railroad system help accelerate industrialization? What effects did the Industrial Revolution have on urban population densities?

INDUSTRY AND EMPIRE

From an international perspective, nineteenth-century Europe was the most industrial region of the world. Europeans, particularly the British, jealously guarded their international advantages. They preferred to do so through financial leverage. Britain, France, and other European nations gained control of the national debts of China, the Ottoman Empire, Egypt, Brazil, Argentina, and other non-European powers. They also supplied large loans to other states, which bound those nations to their European investors. If the debtor nations expressed discontent, as Egypt did in the 1830s when it attempted to establish its own cotton textile industry, they confronted financial pressure and shows of force. Coercion, however, was not always necessary or even one sided. Social change in other empires—China, Persia, and the Mughal Empire of India, for example—made those empires newly vulnerable and created new opportunities for the European powers and their local partners. Ambitious local elites often reached agreements with Western governments or groups such as the British East India Company. These trade agreements transformed regional economies on terms that sent the greatest profits to Europe after a substantial gratuity to the Europeans' local partners. Where agreements could not be made, force prevailed, and Europe took territory and trade by conquest.

Industrialization tightened global links between Europe and the rest of the world, creating new networks of trade and interdependence. To a certain extent, the world economy divided between the producers of manufactured goods—Europe itself—and suppliers of the necessary raw materials and buyers of finished goods—everyone else. Cotton growers in the southern United States, sugar growers in the Caribbean, and wheat growers in Ukraine accepted their arrangements with the industrialized West and typically profited by them. If there were disputes, however, those suppliers often found that Europe could look elsewhere for the same goods or dictate the terms of trade down the business end of a bank ledger or a cannon barrel.

In 1811 Britain imported 3 percent of the wheat it consumed. By 1891, that portion had risen to 79 percent. Why? In an increasingly urban society, fewer people lived off the land. The commercialization of agriculture, which began early in Britain, had taken even firmer hold elsewhere, turning new regions—

British Clipper Ships in Calcutta Harbor, 1860. Calcutta, a long-established city on the eastern coast of India, was one of the hubs of the British Empire—a center for trade in cotton, jute, opium, and tea. The dazzling new clipper ships, first built in the 1830s and 1840s, were very fast and were central to the global economy of the nineteenth century.

INDUSTRIAL REVOLUTION AND NINETEENTH-CENTURY SOCIETY

Australia, Argentina, and North America (Canada and the United States)—into centers of grain and wheat production. New forms of transportation, finance, and communication made it easier to shuttle commodities and capital through international networks. Those simple percentages, in other words, dramatize the new interdependence of the nineteenth century; they illustrate as well as any statistics can how ordinary Britons' lives—like their counterparts' in other nations—were embedded in an increasingly global economy.

THE SOCIAL CONSEQUENCES OF INDUSTRIALIZATION

What were the long- and short-term consequences of industrialization?

We have mentioned population growth as one factor in industrial development, but it deserves treatment on its own terms. By any measure, the nineteenth century constituted a turning point in European demographic history. In 1800 the population of Europe as a whole was estimated roughly at 205 million. By 1850, it had risen to 274 million; by 1900, 414 million; on the eve of World War I it was 480 million. (Over the same span of time, world population went from about 900 million to 1.6 billion.) Britain, with its comparatively high standard of living, saw its population rise from 16 to 27 million. Increases, however, came in the largely rural regions as well. In Russia, the population rose from 39 to 60 million during the same period.

POPULATION

How do historians explain this population explosion? Some speculate that the cyclical potency of microbes made certain fatal diseases less virulent. From 1796 on, Edward Jenner's technique of vaccinating for smallpox gradually gained acceptance and made the disease less fatal. Improved sanitation helped curb cholera, though not until much later in the nineteenth century. Governments were better able and more determined to

monitor and improve the lives of their people. Less expensive foods of high nutritional value—most notably the potato—and the ability to transport foodstuffs cheaply by railroad meant that many European populations were better nourished and so less susceptible to debilitating illness. But real changes in mortality and life expectancy came only late in the nineteenth or the beginning of the twentieth century. In 1880, the average male life expectancy in the city of Berlin was no more than 30 years, and in rural districts nearby it was 43. Historians now attribute the population growth of the nineteenth century to rising fertility rather than to falling mortality. Men and women married earlier, which raised fertility (the number of births per woman) and family size. Peasants tended to set up households at a younger age. The spread of rural manufacturing allowed couples in the countryside to marry and set up households—even before they inherited any land. Not only did the age of marriage fall but more people married. Population growth has its own dynamic, increasing the number of young and fertile people, thus raising significantly the ratio of births to total population.

LIFE ON THE LAND: THE PEASANTRY

Even as the West grew more industrial, the majority of people continued to live on the land. Conditions in the countryside were harsh. Peasants—as farmers of humble origin were called in Europe—still did most of their sowing and harvesting by hand. Millions of tiny farms produced, at most, a bare subsistence living, and families wove, spun, made knives, and sold butter to make ends meet. The average daily diet for an entire family in a good year might amount to no more than two or three pounds of bread—a total of about 3,000 calories daily. By many measures, living conditions for rural inhabitants of many areas in Europe grew worse in the first half of the nineteenth century, a fact of considerable political importance in the 1840s. Rising population put more pressure on the land. Small holdings and indebtedness were chronic problems in regions where peasants scraped by on their own lands. The uncertainties of the market compounded the unpredictability of the weather and the harvest. Over the course of the century some 37 million people—most of them peasants—left Europe, eloquent testimony to the bleakness of rural life. They

> By many measures, living conditions for rural inhabitants of many areas in Europe grew worse in the first half of the nineteenth century, a fact of considerable political importance in the 1840s.

THOMAS MALTHUS ON POPULATION AND POVERTY

Thomas Malthus's enormously influential Essay on the Principle of Population *(1798) marked a shift away from Enlightenment optimism about the "perfectibility of society" and a break with a long tradition of considering a large population to be a sign of economic strength. The English cleric (1766–1834) argued that hopes for prosperity ran up against a simple and grim law of nature: population grew more rapidly than food supply. Famine, disease, poverty, infant malnutrition—Malthus considered all of these inevitable, indeed "positive," checks on population. Governments could do nothing to alleviate poverty, he argued; instead the poor had to exercise "moral restraint," postpone marriage, and have fewer children.*

I say, that the power of population is indefinitely greater than the power in the earth to produce subsistence for man.

Population, when unchecked, increases in a geometrical ratio. Subsistence increases only in an arithmetical ratio. A slight acquaintance with numbers will shew the immensity of the first power in comparison of the second.

By that law of our nature which makes food necessary to the life of man, the effects of these two unequal powers must be kept equal.

This implies a strong and constantly operating check on population from the difficulty of subsistence. This difficulty must fall somewhere and must necessarily be severely felt by a large portion of mankind.

Through the animal and vegetable kingdoms, nature has scattered the seeds of life abroad with the most profuse and liberal hand. She has been comparatively sparing in the room and the nourishment necessary to rear them. The germs of existence contained in this spot of earth, with ample food, and ample room to expand in, would fill millions of worlds in the course of a few thousand years. Necessity, that imperious all pervading law of nature, restrains them within the prescribed bounds. The race of plants and the race of animals shrink under this great restrictive law. And the race of man cannot, by any efforts of reason, escape from it. Among plants and animals its effects are waste of seed, sickness, and premature death. Among mankind, misery and vice. The former, misery, is an absolutely necessary consequence of it. Vice is a highly probable consequence, and we therefore see it abundantly prevail, but it ought not, perhaps, to be called an absolutely necessary consequence. The ordeal of virtue is to resist all temptation to evil.

This natural inequality of the two powers of population and of production in the earth, and that great law of our nature which must constantly keep their effects equal, form the great difficulty that to me appears insurmountable in the way to the perfectibility of society. All other arguments are of slight and subordinate consideration in comparison of this. I see no way by which man can escape from the weight of this law which pervades all animated nature. No fancied equality, no agrarian regulations in their utmost extent, could remove the pressure of it even for a single century. And it appears, therefore, to be decisive against the possible existence of a society, all the members of which should live in ease, happiness, and comparative leisure; and feel no anxiety about providing the means of subsistence for themselves and families.

Consequently, if the premises are just, the argument is conclusive against the perfectibility of the mass of mankind.

Thomas Malthus, *An Essay on the Principle of Population*, ed. Philip Appleman, Norton Critical Edition, 2nd ed. (New York, 2004), pp. 19–20.

QUESTIONS FOR ANALYSIS

1. How does Malthus's conception of *nature* differ from that of Enlightenment thinkers?
2. Can you detect Malthus's influence in the documents on p. 691 concerning the 1846 Irish famine?

settled where land was plentiful and inexpensive: the vast majority in the United States and others in places from South America, northern Africa, New Zealand, and Australia to Siberia. In many cases, governments encouraged emigration to ease overcrowding.

The most tragic combination of famine, poverty, and population in the nineteenth century came to Ireland in the Great Famine of 1845–1849. Potatoes, which had come to Europe from the New World, fundamentally transformed the diets of European peasants, providing much more nutrition for less money than corn and grain. They also grew more densely, an enormous advantage for peasants scraping a living from small plots of land. Nowhere did they become more important than in Ireland, where the climate and soil made growing grain difficult and both overpopulation and poverty were rising. When a fungus hit the potato crop—first in 1845 and again, fatally, in 1846 and 1847—no alternate foods were at hand. At least 1 million Irish died of starvation; of dysentery from spoiled foods; or of fever, which spread through villages and the overcrowded poorhouses. Before the famine, tens of thousands of Irish were already crossing the Atlantic to North America; they accounted for one third of all voluntary migration to the New World. In the ten years after 1845, 1.5 people million left Ireland for good. The potato blight also struck in Germany, Scotland, and the Netherlands, but with less catastrophic results. Europe had known deadly famines for centuries. The tragic Irish famine came late, however, at a time when many thought that starvation was receding into the past, and it illustrated just how vulnerable the nineteenth-century countryside remained to bad harvests and shortages.

> When a fungus hit the potato crop—first in 1845 and again, fatally, in 1846 and 1847—no alternate foods were at hand. At least 1 million Irish died of starvation; of dysentery from spoiled foods; or of fever, which spread through villages and the overcrowded poorhouses.

Changes in the land depended partly on particular governments. States that were more sympathetic to commercialized agriculture passed legislation making it simpler to transfer and reorganize land, encouraging the elimination of small farms and the creation of larger, more efficient units of production. In Britain, over half the total area of the country, excluding wasteland, was composed of estates of 1,000 acres or more. In Spain, the fortunes of large-scale commercial agriculture fluctuated with changes in the political regime: in 1820, the liberal regime passed legislation encouraging the free transfer of land; when absolutism was restored in 1823 the law was repealed. In Russia land was worked in vast blocks; some of the largest landowners possessed over half a million acres. Until the emancipation of the serfs in the 1860s, landowners claimed the labor of dependent peasant populations for as much as several days per week. But the system of serfdom gave

Potato Fields. A scene from the Irish countryside in the late eighteenth century showing potatoes densely planted on a hillside.

THE IRISH FAMINE: INTERPRETATIONS AND RESPONSES

When the potato blight appeared for the second year in a row in 1846, famine came to Ireland. The first letter excerpted here is from Father Theobald Mathew, a local priest, to Charles Edward Trevelyan, the English official in charge of Irish relief. While Father Mathew attributes the potato blight to "divine providence," he also worries that businessmen opposed to government intervention in a free market will let the Irish starve.

The second and third excerpts are from letters that Trevelyan wrote to other British officials concerned with the crisis. Trevelyan makes clear that, although he does not want the government to bear responsibility for starving its people, he believes that the famine will work to correct "social evils" in Ireland, by which he means everything from families having too many children to farmers failing to plant the right crops. In the nineteenth century, reactions to food crises were reshaped by the rise of new economic doctrines, changing social assumptions, and the shifting relationship between religion and government. These letters provide good examples of those changes and how they affected government officials.

THE REVEREND THEOBALD MATHEW TO TREVELYAN

Cork, 7 August 1846.

Divine providence, in its inscrutable ways, has again poured out upon us the viol [sic] of its wrath. A blot more destructive than the simoom of the desert has passed over the land, and the hopes of the poor potato-cultivators are totally blighted, and the food of a whole nation has perished. On the 27th of last month I passed from Cork to Dublin, and this doomed plant bloomed in all the luxuriance of an abundant harvest. Returning on the 3rd instant, I beheld, with sorrow, one wide waste of putrefying vegetation. In many places the wretched people were seated on the fences of their decaying gardens, wringing their hands and wailing bitterly the destruction that had left them foodless.

It is not to harrow your benevolent feelings, dear Mr. Trevelyan, I tell this tale of woe. No, but to excite your sympathy in behalf of our miserable peasantry. It is rumoured that the capitalists in the corn and flour trade are endeavoring to induce government not to protect the people from famine, but to leave them at their mercy. I consider this a cruel and unjustifiable interference.

TREVELYAN TO ROUTH

Treasury, 3 February 1846.

That indirect permanent advantages will accrue to Ireland from the scarcity and the measures taken for its relief, I entertain no doubt; but if we were to pursue these incidental objects to the neglect of any of the precautions immediately required to save the people from actual starvation, our responsibility would be fearful indeed. Besides, the greatest improvement of all which could take place in Ireland would be to teach the people to depend upon themselves for developing the resources of their country, instead of having recourse to the assistance of the government on every occasion. Much has been done of late years to put this important matter on its proper footing; but if a firm stand is not made against the prevailing disposition to take advantage of this crisis to break down all barriers, the true permanent interest of the country will, I am convinced, suffer in a manner which will be irreparable in our time.

TREVELYAN TO LORD MONTEAGLE

To the Right Hon. Lord Monteagle.

My Dear Lord,

I need not remind your lordship that the ability even of the most powerful government is extremely limited in dealing with a social evil of this description. It forms no part of the functions of government to provide supplies of food or to increase the productive powers of the land. In the great institution of the business of society, it falls to the share of government to protect the merchant and the agriculturist in the free exercise of their respective employments; but not itself to carry on those employments; and the condition of a community depends upon the result of the efforts which each member of it makes in his private and individual capacity. . . .

I must give expression to my feelings by saying that I think I see a bright light shining in the distance through the dark cloud which at present hangs over Ireland. A remedy has been already applied to that portion of the maladies of Ireland which was traceable to political causes, and the morbid habits which still to a certain extent survive are gradually giving way to a more healthy action. The deep and inveterate root of social evil remains, and I hope I am not guilty of irreverence in thinking that, this being altogether beyond the power of man, the cure has been applied by the direct stroke of an all-wise providence in a manner as unexpected and unthought of as it is likely to be effectual. God grant that we may rightly perform our part and not turn into a curse what was intended for a blessing. The ministers of religion and especially the pastors of the Roman Catholic Church, who possess the largest share of influence over the people of Ireland, have well performed their part; and although few indications appear from any proceedings which have yet come before the public that the landed proprietors have even taken the first step of preparing for the conversion of the land now laid down to potatoes to grain cultivation, I do not despair of seeing this class in society still taking the lead which their position requires of them, and preventing the social revolution from being so extensive as it otherwise must become.

Believe me, my dear lord, yours very sincerely,

C. E. Trevelyan. Treasury, 9 October 1846.

Noel Kissane, *The Irish Famine: A Documentary History* (Dublin, 1995), pp. 17, 47, 50–51.

QUESTIONS FOR ANALYSIS

1. Would you agree with Trevelyan that dealing with "social evil" was beyond the function of government? What actions could or should governments take in times of famine?
2. In what ways did new economic doctrines, changing assumptions about society, and a shift in the relationship between religion and government affect British government officials?
3. What, concretely, does each of these individuals propose to do about the famine?

---

neither landowners nor serfs much incentive to improve farming or land-management techniques.

European serfdom, which bound hundreds of thousands of men, women, and children to particular estates for generations, made it difficult to buy and sell land freely and created an obstacle to the commercialization and consolidation of agriculture. Yet the opposite was also the case. In France, peasant landholders who had benefited from the the French Revolution's sale of lands and laws on inheritance stayed in the countryside, continuing to work their small farms. Although French peasants were poor, they could sustain themselves on the land. This had important consequences. France suffered less agricultural distress, even in the 1840s, than did other European countries; migration from country to city was slower than in the other nations; far fewer peasants left France for other countries.

Industrialization came to the countryside in other forms. Improved communication networks not only afforded rural populations a keener sense of events and opportunities elsewhere but also made it possible for governments to intrude into the lives of these men and women to a degree previously impossible. Central bureaucracies now found it easier to collect taxes from the peasantry and to conscript sons of peasant families into armies. Some rural cottage industries faced direct competition from factory-produced goods, which meant less work or lower piece rates and falling incomes for families, especially during winter months. In other sectors of the economy, industry spread out into the countryside, making whole regions producers of shoes, shirts, ribbons, cutlery, and so on in small shops and workers' homes. Changes in the market could usher in prosperity, or they could bring entire regions to the verge of starvation.

Vulnerability often led to political violence. Rural rebellions were common in the early nineteenth century. In southern England in the late 1820s, small farmers and day laborers joined forces to burn barns and haystacks, protesting the introduction of threshing machines, a symbol of the new agricultural capitalism. They masked and otherwise disguised themselves, riding out at night under the banner of their mythical leader, "Captain Swing." Their raids were preceded by anonymous threats, such as the one received by a large-scale farmer in the county of Kent: "Pull down your threshing machine or else [expect] fire without delay. We are five thousand men [a highly inflated figure] and will not be stopped." In the southwest of France, peasants, at night and in disguise, attacked local authorities who had barred them from collecting wood in the forests. Since forest wood was in demand for new furnaces, the peasants' traditional gleaning rights had come to an end. Similar rural disturbances broke out across Europe in the 1830s and 1840s: insurrections against landlords; against tithes, or taxes to the church; against laws curtailing customary rights; against unresponsive governments. In Russia, serf uprisings were a reaction to continued bad harvests and exploitation.

Many onlookers considered the nineteenth-century cities dangerous seedbeds of sedition. Yet conditions in the countryside and frequent flareups of rural protest remained the greatest source of trouble for governments, and rural politics exploded, as we will see, in the 1840s. Peasants were land poor, deep in debt, and precariously dependent on markets. More important, however, a government's inability to contend with rural misery made it look autocratic, indifferent, or inept—all political failings.

THE URBAN LANDSCAPE

The growth of cities was one of the most important facts of nineteenth-century social history, and one with significant cultural reverberations. Over the course of the nineteenth century, as we have seen, the overall population of Europe doubled. The percentage of that population living in cities tripled—that is, urban populations rose sixfold. Like industrialization, urbanization generally moved from the northwest of Europe to the southeast, but it also followed very specific demands for resources, labor, and transportation. In mining and manufacturing areas or along newly built railway lines, it sometimes seemed that cities (like Manchester, Birmingham, and Essen) sprang up from nowhere. Industrialization swelled the size of port cities such as Danzig (modern Gdansk), Le Havre, and Rotterdam. Most striking to contemporaries was the very rapid expansion of Europe's old cities. Sometimes the rates of growth were dizzying. Between 1750 and 1850, London (Europe's largest city) grew from 676,000 to 2.3 million. The population of Paris went from 560,000 to 1.3 million, adding 120,000 new residents between 1841 and 1846 alone! Berlin, which like Paris became the hub of a rapidly expanding railway system, nearly tripled in size during the first half of the century alone. Such rapid expansion was almost necessarily unplanned, and the combination of unregulated growth and the pressure of numbers brought in its wake new social problems.

Almost all nineteenth-century cities were overcrowded and unhealthy, their largely medieval infrastructures strained by the

Agricultural Disturbances. Violence erupted in southern England in 1830 in protest against the introduction of threshing machines.

INDUSTRIAL REVOLUTION AND NINETEENTH-CENTURY SOCIETY   694

burden of new population and the demands of industry. Construction lagged far behind population growth, especially in the working-class districts of the city. In many of the larger cities, old and new, working men and women who had left families behind in the country lived in temporary lodging houses. The poorest workers dwelt in wretched basement or attic rooms, often without any light or drainage. A local committee appointed to investigate conditions in the British manufacturing town of Huddersfield—by no means the worst of that country's urban centers—reported that there were large areas without paving, sewers, or drains, "where garbage and filth of every description are left on the surface to ferment and rot; where pools of stagnant water are almost constant; where dwellings adjoining are thus necessarily caused to be of an inferior and even filthy description; thus where disease is engendered, and the health of the whole town perilled."

Governments gradually adopted measures in an attempt to cure the worst of these ills, if only to prevent the spread of catastrophic epidemics. Legislation was designed to rid cities of their worst slums by tearing them down and to improve sanitary conditions by supplying both water and drainage. Yet by 1850, these projects had only just begun. Paris, perhaps better supplied with water than any other European city, had enough for no more than two baths per person per year; in London, human waste remained uncollected in 250,000 domestic cesspools; in Manchester, fewer than a third of the dwellings were equipped with toilets of any sort.

INDUSTRY AND ENVIRONMENT IN THE NINETEENTH CENTURY

The Industrial Revolution began many of the environmental changes of the modern period. Nowhere were those changes more visible than in the burgeoning cities. Dickens's description of the choking air and polluted water of "Coketown," the fictional city in *Hard Times* (1854) is deservedly well known:

> It was a town of red brick, or of brick that would have been red if the smoke and ashes had allowed it. . . . It was a town of machines and tall chimneys, out of which interminable serpents of smoke trailed themselves forever and ever, and never got uncoiled. It had a black canal in it, and a river that ran purple with ill-smelling dye, and vast piles of building full of windows where there was a rattling and a trembling all day long.

Wood-fired manufacturing and heating for home had long spewed smoke across the skies, but the new concentration of industrial activity and the transition to coal made the air measurably worse. In London especially, where even homes switched to coal early, smoke from factories, railroads, and domestic chimneys hung heavily over the city; and the last third of the century brought the most intense pollution in its history. Over all of England, air pollution took an enormous toll on health, contributing to the bronchitis and tuberculosis that accounted for 25 percent of British deaths. The coal-rich and industrial regions of North America (especially Pittsburgh) and central Europe were other concentrations of pollution; the Ruhr in particular by the end of the century had the most polluted air in Europe.

Toxic water—produced by industrial pollution and human waste—posed the second critical environmenal hazard in urban areas. London and Paris led the way in building municipal sewage systems, though those emptied into the Thames and the Seine. Cholera, typhus, and tuberculosis were natural predators in areas without adequate sewage facilities or fresh water. The Rhine River, which flowed through central Europe's industrial heartland and intersected with the Ruhr, was thick with detritus from coal mining, iron processing, and the chemical industry. Spurred by several epidemics of cholera, in the late nineteenth century the major cities began to purify their water supplies; but conditions in the air, rivers, and land continued to worsen until at least the mid-twentieth century.

SEX IN THE CITY

Prostitution flourished in nineteenth-century cities; in fact it offers a microsom of the nineteenth-century urban economy. At mid-century the number of prostitutes in Vienna was estimated to be 15,000; in Paris, where prostitution was a licensed trade, 50,000; in London, 80,000. London newspaper reports of the 1850s cataloged the elaborate hierarchies of the vast underworld of prostitutes and their customers. Those included entrepreneurs with names like Swindling Sal who ran lodging houses; the pimps and "fancy men" who managed the trade of prostitutes on the street; and the relatively few "prima donnas" or courtesans who enjoyed the protection of rich, upper-middle-class lovers, who entertained lavishly and whose wealth allowed them to move on the fringes of more respectable high society. The heroines of Alexandre Dumas's novel *La Dame aux Camélias* and of Giuseppe

THE SOCIAL CONSEQUENCES OF INDUSTRIALIZATION

View of London with Saint Paul's Cathedral in the Distance, by William Henry Crome. Despite the smog-filled skies and intense pollution, many entrepreneurs and politicians celebrated the new prosperity of the Industrial Revolution. As W. P. Rend, a Chicago businessman, wrote in 1892, "Smoke is the incense burning on the altars of industry. It is beautiful to me. It shows that men are changing the merely potential forces of nature into articles of comfort for humanity."

Verdi's opera *La Traviata* (The Lost One) were modeled on these women. Yet the vast majority of prostitutes were not courtesans but rather women (and some men) who worked long and dangerous hours in port districts of cities or at lodging houses in the overwhelmingly male working-class neighborhoods. Most prostitutes were young women who had just arrived in the city or working women trying to manage during a period of unemployment.

THE SOCIAL QUESTION

Against the backdrop of the French Revolution of 1789 and subsequent revolutions in the nineteenth century (as we will see in the following chapters), the new "shock" cities of the nineteenth century and their swelling multitudes posed urgent questions. Political leaders, social scientists, and public health officials across all of Europe issued thousands of reports—many of them several volumes long—on criminality, water supply, sewers, prostitution, tuberculosis and cholera, alcoholism, wet nursing, wages, and unemployment. Radicals and reformers grouped all these issues under a broad heading known as "the social question." Governments, pressed by reformers and by the omnipresent rumblings of unrest, felt they had to address these issues before complaints swelled into revolution. They did so, in the first social engineering: police forces, public health, sewers and new water supplies, inoculations, elementary schools, Factory Acts (regulating work hours), poor laws (outlining the conditions of receiving relief), and new urban regulation and city

CHAPTER 19

INDUSTRIAL REVOLUTION AND NINETEENTH-CENTURY SOCIETY

planning. Central Paris, for instance, would be almost entirely redesigned in the ninteenth century—the crowded, medieval, and revolutionary poor neighborhoods gutted; markets rebuilt; streets widened and lit (see Chapter Twenty-One). From the 1820s on, the social question hung over Europe like a cloud, and it formed part of the backdrop to the revolutions of 1848 (discussed in Chapter Twenty-One). Surveys and studies, early social science, provided direct inspiration for novelists such as Honoré de Balzac, Charles Dickens, and Victor Hugo. In his novel *Les Misérables* (1862), Hugo even used the sewers of Paris as a central metaphor for the general condition of urban existence. Both Hugo and Dickens wrote sympathetically of the poor, of juvenile delinquency, and of child labor; revolution was never far from their minds. The French writer Balzac had little sympathy for the poor, but he shared his fellow writers' views on the corruption of modern life. His *Human Comedy* (1829–1855) was a series of ninety-five novels and stories, including *Eugenie Grandet, Old Goriot, Lost Illusions,* and *A Harlot High and Low.* Balzac was biting in his observations about ruthless and self-promoting young men and about the cold calculations behind romantic liaisons. And he was but one of many writers to use prostitution as a metaphor for what he considered the deplorable materialism and desperation of his time.

> The middle class was not one homogeneous unit, in terms of occupation or income. Movement within middle-class ranks was often possible in the course of one or two generations.

THE MIDDLE CLASSES

Who were the new middle classes?

Balzac's many novels aimed to be a sweeping portrait of middle-class society in the early to mid-nineteenth century. They are peopled with characters from all walks of life—journalists, courtesans, small-town mayors, mill owners, shopkeepers, and students. Balzac's main argument throughout is clear: he believed the political changes of the French Revolution and the social changes of industrialization had done no more than replace an older aristocracy (for which Balzac was nostalgic) with a new and materialistic middle class (which he disdained). Older hierarchies expressed as rank, status, and privilege, he believed, had given way to gradations based on wealth, or social class. It is not surprising that Balzac

(although he was deeply conservative) was Karl Marx's favorite novelist. Balzac's point was echoed by many others: by Dickens, whose middle-class characters are often heartless, rigid, and obtuse; by the French artist Honoré Daumier, whose famous caricatures of early nineteenth-century lawyers are veritable portraits of power and arrogance; and by the British novelist William Makepeace Thackeray in his similarly panoramic *Vanity Fair* (1847–1848). One of Thackeray's characters observes caustically that "Ours is a ready-money society. We live among bankers and city big-wigs . . . and every man, as he talks to you, is jingling his guineas in his pocket." Works of literature need to be approached cautiously, for their characters express their authors' points of view. Still, literature and art offer an extraordinary source of social historical detail and insight. And we can safely say that the rising visibility of the middle classes and their new political and social power— lamented by some writers but hailed by others—were central facts of nineteenth-century society.

Who were the middle classes? (Another common term for this social group, the *bourgeoisie,* originally meant city [*bourg*] dweller.) The middle class was not one homogeneous unit, in terms of occupation or income. Movement within middle-class ranks was often possible in the course of one or two generations. Very few, however, moved from the working class into the middle class. Most middle-class success stories began in the middle class itself, with the children of relatively well-off farmers, skilled artisans, or professionals. Upward mobility was almost impossible without education, and education was a rare, though not unattainable, luxury for working-class children. Careers open to talents, that goal achieved by the French Revolution, frequently meant opening jobs to middle-class young men who could pass exams. The examination system was an important path upward within government bureaucracies.

The journey from middle class to aristocratic, landed society was equally difficult. In Britain, mobility of this sort was easier to achieve than on the Continent. Sons from wealthy upper-middle-class families, if they were sent to elite schools and universities and if they left the commercial or industrial world for a career in politics, might actually move up. William Gladstone, son of a Liverpool merchant, attended the exclusive educational preserves of Eton (a private boarding school) and Oxford University, married into the aristocratic Grenville family, and became prime

Who were the new middle classes?

The Legislative Belly, by Honore Daumier, 1834. Daumier's caricatures of bourgeois politicians prefigure George Grosz's acerbic drawings and paintings of the twentieth century.

minister of England. Yet Gladstone was an exception to the rule, even in Britain, and most upward mobility was much less spectacular.

Nevertheless, the European middle class helped sustain itself with the belief that it was possible to get ahead by means of intelligence, pluck, and serious devotion to work. The Englishman Samuel Smiles, in his extraordinarily successful how-to-succeed book *Self-Help* (1859), preached a gospel dear to the middle class. "The spirit of self-help is the root of all genuine growth in the individual," Smiles wrote. "Exhibited in the lives of many, it constitutes the true source of national vigor and strength." As Smiles also suggested, those who suceeded were obliged to follow middle-class notions of respectability. The middle-classes' claim to political power and cultural influence rested on arguments that they constituted a new and deserving social elite, superior to the common people yet sharply different from the older aristocracy, and the rightful custodians of the nation's future. Thus middle-class respectability, like a code, stood for many values. It meant financial independence, providing responsibly for one's family, avoiding gambling and debt. It suggested merit and character as opposed to aristocratic privilege and hard work as opposed to living off noble estates. Respectable middle-class gentlemen might be wealthy, but they should live modestly and soberly, avoiding conspicuous consumption, lavish dress, womanizing, and other forms of dandyish behavior associated with the aristocracy. We need to emphasize that these were aspirations and codes, not social realities. They nonetheless remained key to the middle-class sense of self and understanding of the world.

Private Life and Middle-Class Identity

Family and home played a central role in forming middle-class identity. Few themes were more common in nineteenth-century fiction than men and women pursuing mobility and status by or through marriage. Families served intensely practical purposes: sons, nephews, and cousins were expected to assume responsibility in family firms when it came their turn; wives managed accounts; and parents-in-law provided business connections, credit, inheritance, and so on. The family's role in middle-class thought, however, did not arise only from these practical considerations; family was part of a larger worldview. A well-governed household offered a counterpoint to the business and confusion of the world, and families offered continuity and tradition in a time of rapid change.

Gender and the Cult of Domesticity

There was no single type of middle-class family or home. Yet many people held powerful convictions about how a respectable home should be run and about the rituals, hierarchies, and distinctions that should prevail therein. According to advice manuals, poetry, and middle-class journals, wives and mothers were supposed to occupy a "separate sphere" of life, in which they lived in subordination to their spouses. "Man for the field and woman for the hearth; man for the sword and for the needle she. . . . All else confusion," wrote the British poet Alfred Lord Tennyson in 1847. These prescriptions were directly applied to young people. Boys were educated in secondary schools; girls at home. This nineteenth-century conception of separate spheres needs to be understood in relation to much longer-standing traditions of paternal authority, which were codified in law. Throughout

Europe, laws subjected women to their husbands' authority. The Napoleonic Code, a model for other countries after 1815, classified women, children, and the mentally ill together as legally incompetent. In Britain, a woman transferred all her property rights to her husband on marriage. Although unmarried women did enjoy a degree of legal independence in France and Austria, laws generally assigned them to the "protection" of their fathers. Gender relations in the nineteenth century rested on this foundation of legal inequality. Yet the idea or doctrine of separate spheres was meant to underscore that men's and women's spheres complemented each other. Thus, for instance, middle-class writings were full of references to spiritual equality between men and women; and middle-class people wrote, proudly, of marriages in which the wife was a "companion" and "helpmate."

It is helpful to recall that members of the middle class articulated their values in opposition to aristocratic customs on the one hand and the lives of the common people on the other. They argued, for instance, that middle-class marriages did not aim to found aristocratic dynasties and were not arranged to accumulate power and privilege; instead they were to be based on mutual respect and division of responsibilities. A respectable middle-class woman should be free from the unrelenting toil that was the lot of a woman of the people. Called in Victorian Britain the "angel in the house," the middle-class woman was responsible for the moral education of her children. It was understood that being a good wife and mother was a demanding task, requiring an elevated character. This belief, sometimes called the "cult of domesticity," was central to middle-class Victorian thinking about women. Home life, and by extension the woman's role in that life, were infused with new meaning. As one young woman put it after reading a popular book on female education, "What an important sphere a woman fills! How thoroughly she ought to be qualified for it—I think hers the more honourable employment than a man's." In sum, the early nineteenth century brought a general reassessment of femininity. The roots of this reassessment lay in early-nineteenth-century religion and efforts to moralize society, largely to guard against the disorders of the French and Industrial Revolutions.

As a housewife, a middle-class woman had the task of keeping the household functioning smoothly and harmoniously. She maintained the accounts and directed the activities of the servants. Having at least one servant was a mark of middle-class status; and in wealthier families governesses and nannies cared for children, idealized views of motherhood notwithstanding. The middle classes, however, included many gradations of wealth, from a well-housed banker with a governess and five servants to a village preacher with one. Moreover, the work of running and maintaining a home was enormous. Linens and clothes had to be made and mended. Only the wealthy had the luxury of running water, and others had to carry and heat water for cooking, laundry, and cleaning. Heating with coal and lighting with kerosene involved hours of cleaning, and so on. If the "angel in the house" was a cultural ideal, it was partly because she had real economic value.

> Called in Victorian Britain the "angel in the house," the middle-class woman was responsible for the moral education of her children.

Outside the home, women had very few respectable options for earning a living. Unmarried women might act as companions or governesses—the British novelist Charlotte Brontë's heroine Jane Eyre did so and led a generally miserable life until "rescued" by marriage to her difficult employer. But nineteenth-century convictions about women's moral nature, combined as they were with middle-class aspirations to political leadership, encouraged middle-class wives to undertake voluntary charitable work or to campaign for social reform. In Britain and the United States, women

Illustration from a Victorian Book on Manners. Advice books such as this were very popular in the nineteenth century—a mark, perhaps, of preoccupation with status and the emergence of new social groups.

Who were the new middle classes?

played an important role in the struggle to abolish the slave trade and slavery in the British Empire. Many of these movements also drew on the energies of religious, especially Protestant, organizations, committed to the eradication of social evils and moral improvement. Throughout Europe, a wide range of movements to improve conditions for the poor in schools and hospitals, for temperance, against prostitution, or for legislation on factory hours were often run by women. Florence Nightingale, who went to the Crimean Peninsula in Russia to nurse British soldiers fighting there in the 1850s, remains the most famous of those women, whose determination to right social wrongs compelled them to defy conventional notions of woman's "proper" sphere. Equally famous—or infamous, at the time—was the French female novelist George Sand (1804–1876), whose real name was Amandine Aurore Dupin Dudevant. Sand dressed like a man and smoked cigars, and her novels often told the tales of independent women thwarted by convention and unhappy marriage.

Queen Victoria, who came to the British throne in 1837, labored to make her solemn public image reflect contemporary feminine virtues of moral probity and dutiful domesticity. Her court was eminently proper, a marked contrast to that of her uncle George IV, whose cavalier ways had set the style for high life a generation before. Though possessing a bad temper, Victoria trained herself to curb it in deference to her ministers and her public-spirited, ultrarespectable husband, Prince Albert of Saxe-Coburg. She was a successful queen because she embodied the traits important to the middle class, whose triumph she seemed to epitomize and whose habits of mind we have come to call Victorian. Nineteenth-century ideas about gender had an impact on masculinity as well femininity. Soon after the revolutionary and Napoleonic period, men began to dress in sober, practical clothing—and to see as effeminate or dandyish the wigs, ruffled collars, and tight breeches that had earlier been the pride of aristocratic masculinity.

"Passionlessness": Gender and Sexuality

Victorian ideas about sexuality are among the most remarked-on features of nineteenth-century culture. They have become virtually synonymous with anxiety, prudishness, and ignorance. An English mother counseling her daughter about her wedding night is said to have told her to "lie back and think of the Empire." Etiquette apparently required that piano legs be covered. Many of these anxieties and prohibitions, however, have been caricatured. More recently, historians have tried to disentangle the teachings or prescriptions of etiquette books and marriage manuals from the actual beliefs of men and women. Equally important, they have sought to understand each on its own terms. Beliefs about sexuality followed from convictions, described earlier, concerning separate spheres. Indeed, one of the defining aspects of nineteenth-century ideas about men and women is the extent to which they rested on scientific arguments about nature. Codes of morality and methods of science combined to reinforce the certainty that specific characteristics were inherent to each sex. Men and women had different social roles, and those differences were rooted in their bodies. The French social thinker Auguste Comte provides a good example: "Biological philosophy teaches us that, through the whole animal scale, and while the specific type is preserved, radical differences, physical and moral, distinguish the sexes." Comte also spelled out the implications of biological difference: "[T]he equality of the sexes, of which so much is said, is incompatible with all social existence. . . . The economy of the human family could never be inverted without an entire change in our cerebral organism." Women were unsuited for higher education because their brains were smaller or because their bodies were fragile. "Fifteen or 20 days of 28 (we may say nearly always) a woman is not only an invalid, but a wounded one. She ceaselessly suffers from love's eternal wound," wrote the well-known French author Jules Michelet about menstruation.

Finally, scientists and doctors considered women's alleged moral superiority to be literally embodied in an absence of sexual feeling, or "passionlessness." Scientists and doctors considered male sexual desire natural, if not admirable—an unruly force that had to be channeled. Many governments legalized and regulated prostitution—which included the compulsory examination of women for venereal disease—precisely because it provided an outlet for male sexual desire. Doctors disagreed about female sexuality, but the British doctor William Acton stood among those who asserted that women functioned differently:

> I have taken pains to obtain and compare abundant evidence on this subject, and the result of my inquiries I may briefly epitomize as follows:—I should say that the majority of women (happily for society) are not very much troubled with sexual feeling of any kind. What men are habitually, women are only exceptionally.

MARRIAGE, SEXUALITY, AND THE FACTS OF LIFE

In the nineteenth century sexuality became the subject of much anxious debate, largely because it raised other issues: the roles of men and women, morality, and social respectability. Doctors threw themselves into the discussion, offering their expert opinions on the health (including the sexual lives) of the population. Yet doctors did not dictate people's private lives. Nineteenth-century men and women responded to what they experienced as the facts of life more than to expert advice. The first document provides an example of medical knowledge and opinion in 1870. The second offers a glimpse of the daily realities of family life in 1830.

A FRENCH DOCTOR DENOUNCES CONTRACEPTION

One of the most powerful instincts nature has placed in the heart of man is that which has for its object the perpetuation of the human race. But this instinct, this inclination, so active, which attracts one sex towards the other, is liable to be perverted, to deviate from the path nature has laid out. From this arises a number of fatal aberrations which exercise a deplorable influence upon the individual, upon the family and upon society....

We hear constantly that marriages are less fruitful, that the increase of population does not follow its former ratio. I believe that this is mainly attributable to genesiac frauds. It might naturally be supposed that these odious calculations of egotism, these shameful refinements of debauchery, are met with almost entirely in large cities, and among the luxurious classes, and that small towns and country places yet preserve that simplicity of manners attributed to primitive society, when the *pater familias* was proud of exhibiting his numerous offspring. Such, however, is not the case, and I shall show that those who have an unlimited confidence in the patriarchal habits of our country people are deeply in error. At the present time frauds are practiced by all classes....

The laboring classes are generally satisfied with the practice of Onan [withdrawal].... They are seldom familiar with the sheath invented by Dr. Condom, and bearing his name.

Among the wealthy, on the other hand, the use of this preservative is generally known. It favors frauds by rendering them easier; but it does not afford complete security....

Case X.—This couple belongs to two respectable families of vintners. They are both pale, emaciated, downcast, sickly....

They have been married for ten years; they first had two children, one immediately after the other, but in order to avoid an increase of family, they have had recourse to conjugal frauds. Being both very amorous, they have found this practice very convenient to satisfy their inclinations. They have employed it to such an extent, that up to a few months ago, when their health began to fail, the husband had intercourse with his wife habitually two and three times in twenty-four hours.

The following is the condition of the woman: She complains of continual pains in the lower part of the abdomen and kidneys. These pains disturb the functions of the stomach and render her nervous.... By the touch we find a very intense heat, great sensibility to pressure, and all the signs of a chronic metritis. The patient attributes positively her present state to the too frequent approaches of her husband.

The husband does not attempt to exculpate himself, as he also is in a state of extreme suffering. It is not in the genital organs, however, that we find his disorder, but in the whole general nervous system; his history will find its place in the part of this work relative to general disturbances....

Louis-François-Etienne Bergeret. The Preventive Obstacle, or Conjugal Onanism, tr. P. de Marmon (New York, 1870), pp. 3–4, 12, 20–22, 25, 56–57, 100–101, 111–113. Originally published in Paris in 1868.

DEATH IN CHILDBIRTH (1830)

Mrs. Ann B. Pettigrew was taken in Labour after returning from a walk in the garden, at 7 o'clock in the evening of June 30, 1830. At 40 minutes after 11 o'clock, she was delivered of a daughter. A short time after, I was informed that the Placenta was not removed, and, at 10 minutes after 12 was asked into the room. I advanced to my dear wife, and kissing her, asked her how she was, to which she replied, I feel very badly. I went out of the room, and sent for Dr. Warren.

I then returned, and inquired if there was much hemorrhage, and was answered that there was. I then asked the midwife (Mrs. Brickhouse) if she ever used manual exertion to remove the placenta. She said she had more than fifty times. I then, fearing the consequences of hemorrhage, observed, Do, my dear sweet wife, permit Mrs. Brickhouse to remove it: To which she assented. . . . After the second unsuccessful attempt, I desired the midwife to desist. In these two efforts, my dear Nancy suffered exceedingly and frequently exclaimed: "O Mrs Brickhouse you will kill me," and to me, "O I shall die, send for the Doctor." To which I replied, "I have sent."

After this, my feelings were so agonizing that I had to retire from the room and lay down, or fall. Shortly after which, the midwife came to me and, falling upon her knees, prayed most fervently to God and to me to forgive her for saying that she could do what she could not. . . .

The placenta did not come away, and the hemorrhage continued with unabated violence until five o'clock in the morning, when the dear woman breathed her last 20 minutes before the Doctor arrived.

So agonizing a scene as that from one o'clock, I have no words to describe. O My God, My God! have mercy on me. I am undone forever. . . .

Cited in Erna Olafson Hellerstein, Leslie Parker Hume, and Karen M. Offen, eds. *Victorian Women: A Documentary Account of Women's Lives in Nineteenth-Century England, France, and the United States.* (Stanford: Stanford University Press, 1981) pp. 193–94, 219–20.

QUESTIONS FOR ANALYSIS

1. The French doctor believed that an increasing population was a sign of a healthy state. Sex was lawful within marriage for procreation, he argued, and artificial birth contro interfered with nature. How and why does he describe the birth control methods as "conjugal frauds"?
2. What happened to a "very amorous" couple that practiced birth control? Why did the French doctor think excessive sexual indulgence led to physical and mental detericration?
3. What problem or problems concern the French doctor? Why?
4. What might be the effects of the conditions described in the second document?

Like other nineteenth-century men and women, Acton also believed that more open expressions of sexuality were disreputable and, also, that working-class women were less "feminine."

Convictions like these reveal a great deal about Victorian science and medicine, but they did not necessarily dictate people's intimate lives. As far as sexuality was concerned, the absence of any reliable contraception mattered more in people's experiences and feelings than sociologists' or doctors' opinions. Abstinence and withdrawal were the only common techniques for preventing pregnancy. Their effectiveness was limited, since until the 1880s doctors continued to believe that a woman was most fertile during and around her menstrual period. Midwives and prostitutes knew of other forms of contraception and abortifacients (all of them dangerous and most ineffective), and surely some middle-class women did as well, but such information was not respectable middle-class fare. Concretely, then, sexual intercourse was directly related to the very

real dangers of frequent pregnancies. In England, 1 in 100 childbirths ended in the death of the mother; at a time when a woman might become pregnant eight or nine times in her life, this was a sobering prospect. Those dangers varied with social class, but even among wealthy and better-cared-for women, they took a real toll. It is not surprising that middle-class women's diaries and letters are full of their anticipations of childbirth, both joyful and anxious. Queen Victoria, who bore nine children, declared that childbirth was the "shadow side" of marriage—and she was a pioneer in using anesthesia!

MIDDLE-CLASS LIFE IN PUBLIC

The public life of middle-class families literally reshaped the nineteenth-century landscape. Houses and their furnishings were powerful symbols of material security. Solidly built, heavily decorated, they proclaimed the financial worth and social respectability of those who dwelt within. In provincial cities they were often freestanding villas. In London, Paris, Berlin, and Vienna, they might be in rows of five- or six-story townhouses or large apartments. Whatever particular shape they took, they were built to last a long time. The rooms were certain to be crowded with furniture, art objects, carpets, and wall hangings. The size of the rooms, the elegance of the furniture, the number of servants—all depended, of course, on the extent of one's income. A bank clerk did not live as elegantly as a bank director. Yet they shared many standards and aspirations, and those common values helped bind them to the same class, despite the differences in their material way of life.

As cities grew, they became increasingly segregated. Middle-class people lived far from the unpleasant sights and smells of industrialization. Their residential areas, usually built to the west of the cities, out of the path of the prevailing breeze and therefore of industrial pollution, were havens from congestion. The public buildings in the center, many constructed during the nineteenth century, were celebrated as signs of development and prosperity. The middle classes increasingly managed their cities' affairs, although members of the aristocracy retained considerable power, especially in central Europe. And it was these new middle-class civic leaders who provided new industrial cities with many of their architectural landmarks: city halls, stock exchanges, museums, opera houses, outdoor concert halls, and department stores. One historian has called these buildings the new cathedrals of the industrial age; projects intended to express the community's values and represent public culture, they were monuments to social change.

The suburbs changed as well. The advent of the railways made outings to concerts, parks, and bathing spots popular. They made it possible for families of relatively moderate means to take one- or two-week-long trips to the mountains or to the seashore. New resorts opened, offering racetracks, mineral springs baths, and cabanas on the beach. Mass tourism would not come until the twentieth century. But the now familiar Impressionist paintings of the 1870s and 1880s testify to something that was dramatically new in the nineteenth century: a new range of middle-class leisures.

Working-Class Life

Like the middle class, the working class was divided into various subgroups and categories, determined in this case by skill, wages, gender, and workplace. Workers' experiences varied, depending on where they worked, where they lived, and, above all, how much they earned. A skilled textile worker lived a life far different from that of a ditch digger, the former able to afford the food, shelter, and clothing necessary for a decent existence, the latter barely able to scrape by.

Some movement from the ranks of the unskilled to the skilled was possible, if children were provided, or provided themselves, with at least a rudimentary education. Yet education was considered by many parents a luxury, especially since children could be put to work at an early age to supplement a family's meager earnings. Downward mobility from skilled to unskilled was also possible, as technological change—the introduction of the power loom, for example—drove highly paid workers into the ranks of the unskilled and destitute.

Working-class housing was unhealthy and unregulated. In older cities single-family dwellings were

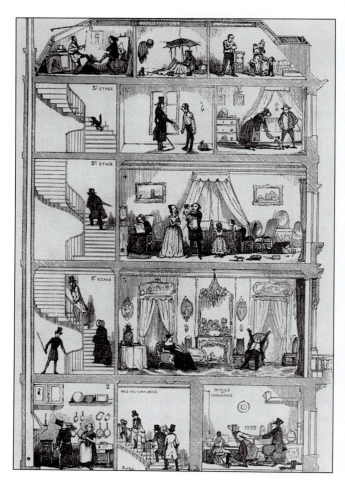

Apartment Living in Paris. This print shows that on the Continent rich and poor often lived in the same buildings, the rich on the lower floors, the poor at the top. This sort of residential mixing was less common in Britain.

broken up into apartments, often of no more than one room per family. In new manufacturing centers, rows of tiny houses, located close by smoking factories, were built back to back, thereby eliminating any cross-ventilation or space for gardens. Crowding was commonplace. A newspaper account from the 1840s noted that in Leeds, a textile center in northern Britain, an ordinary worker's house contained no more than 150 square feet, and that in most cases those houses were "crammed almost to suffocation with human beings both day and night."

Household routines, demanding in the middle classes, were grinding for the poor. The family remained a survival network, in which everyone played a crucial role. In addition to working for wages, wives were expected to house, feed, and clothe the family on the very little money different members of the family earned. A good wife was able to make ends meet even in bad times. Working women's daily lives involved constant rounds of carrying and boiling water, cleaning, cooking, and doing laundry—in one- and two-room crowded, unventilated, poorly lit apartments. Families could not rely on their own gardens to help supply them with food. City markets catered to their needs for cheap goods, but these were regularly stale, nearly rotten, or dangerously adulterated. Formaldehyde was added to milk to prevent spoilage. Pounded rice was mixed into sugar. Fine brown earth was introduced into cocoa.

> Most women labored at home or in small workshops—"sweatshops," as they came to be called—for notoriously low wages, paid not by the hour but by the piece for each shirt stitched or each matchbox glued.

WORKING WOMEN IN THE INDUSTRIAL LANDSCAPE

Few figures raised more public anxiety and outcry in the nineteenth century than the working woman. Contemporaries worried out loud about the "promiscuous mixing of the sexes" in crowded and humid workshops. Nineteenth-century writers, starting in England and France, chronicled what they considered to be the economic and moral horrors of female labor: unattended children running in the streets, small children caught in accidents at the mills or the mines, pregnant women hauling coal, or women laboring alongside men in shops.

Women's work was not new. Industrialization made it more visible. Women and children formed nearly half the labor force in some of the most modern industries, such as textiles. Women workers were paid less and were considered less likely to make trouble; manufacturers sought to recruit women mill hands from neighboring villages, paying good wages by comparison with other jobs open to women; in some cases they asked poor-law officials to find "needy and suitable families" for the mills. Most began to work at the age of ten or eleven years old; and once they had children they either put their children out to wet nurses, brought them to the mills, or continued to earn wages doing piecework (paid by the piece rather than by the hour) at home. One of the common causes of labor protest during the period was the introduction of women workers to do jobs considered the property of men.

Still, most women did not work in factories, and the gender division of labor remained remarkably unchanged. Most women labored at home or in small workshops—"sweatshops," as they came to be called—for notoriously low wages, paid not by the hour but by the piece for each shirt stitched or each matchbox glued. And by far the greatest number of unmarried working-class women worked, less visibly, in domestic service, a job that brought low wages and, to judge by the testimony of many women, coercive sexual relationships with male employers or their sons. Domestic service, however, provided room and board. In a time when a single woman simply could not survive on her own wages, a young woman who had just arrived in the city had few choices: marriage, which was unlikely to happen right away; renting a room in a boardinghouse, many of which were often centers of prostitution; domestic service; or living with someone. How women balanced the demands for money and the time for household work varied with the number and age of their children. Mothers were actually more likely to work when their children were very small, for there were more mouths to feed and the children were not yet old enough to earn wages.

Poverty, the absence of privacy, and the particular vulnerabilities of working-class women made working-class sexuality very different from its middle-class counterpart. Illegitimacy rose dramatically between 1750 and 1850. In Frankfurt, Germany, for example, where the illegitimacy rate had been a mere 2 percent in the early 1700s, it reached 25 percent in 1850. In Bordeaux, France, in 1840, one third of the recorded births were illegitimate. Reasons for this increase are difficult to establish. Greater mobility and urbanization meant weaker family ties, more opportunities for young men and women, and more vulnerabilities. Premarital sex was an accepted practice in preindustrial villages, but because of the social controls that dominated village life, it was almost always followed by marriage. These controls were weaker in the far more anonymous setting of a factory town or commercial city. The economic uncertainties of the early industrial age meant that a young workingman's promise of marriage based on his expectation of a job might frequently be difficult to fulfill. Economic vulnerability drove many single women into temporary relationships that produced children and a continuing cycle of poverty and abandonment. Historians have shown, however, that in the city as in the countryside, many of these temporary relationships became enduring ones: the parents of illegitimate children would marry later. Again, nineteenth-century writers dramatized what they considered the disreputable sexuality of the "dangerous classes" in the cities. Some of them attributed illegitimacy, prostitution, and so on to the moral weakness of working-class people, others to the systematic changes wrought by industrialization. Both sides, however, overstated the collapse of the family and the destruction of traditional morality. Working-class families transmitted expectations about gender roles and sexual behavior: girls should expect to work, daughters were responsible for caring for their younger siblings as well as for earning wages, sexuality was a fact of life, midwives could help desperate pregnant girls, marriage was an avenue to respectability, and so on. The gulf that separated these expectations and codes from those of middle-class women was one of the most important factors in the development of nineteenth-century class identity.

A Life Apart: "Class" Consciousness

The new demands of factory life also created common experiences and difficulties. The factory system, emphasizing as it did standard rather than individual work patterns, denied skilled laborers the pride in craft they

Capital and Labour. In its earliest years, the British magazine *Punch,* though primarily a humorous weekly, manifested a strong social conscience. This 1843 cartoon shows the capitalists enjoying the rewards of their investments while the workers shiver in cold and hunger.

had previously enjoyed. Many workers found themselves stripped of the protections of guilds and formal apprenticeships that had bound their predecessors to a particular trade or place and that were outlawed or sharply curtailed by legislation in France, Germany, and Britain in the first half of the nineteenth century. Factory hours were long; before 1850 workdays were usually twelve to fourteen hours long. Textile mills remained unventilated, so that minute particles of material lodged in workers' lungs. Machines were unfenced and posed a particular danger to child workers, often hired, because of their supposed agility, to clean under and around the moving parts. Surveys by British physicians in the 1840s cataloged the toll that long factory hours and harsh working conditions were taking, particularly on young workers, such as spinal curvature and other bone malformations that resulted from standing hour after hour in unnatural positions at machines. And what was true of factories was true as well of mines, in which over 50,000 children and young people were employed in Britain in 1841. Children were used to haul coal to underground tramways or shafts. The youngest were set to work—often for as long as twelve hours at a stretch—operating doors that regulated the ventilation in the mines. When they fell asleep during long shifts they jeopardized the safety of the entire workforce.

Factories also imposed new routines and disciplines. Artisans in earlier times worked very long hours for very little pay. But at least to some degree, they could set their own hours and structure their own activities, moving from their home workshops to their small garden plots and back again as they wished. In a factory, all "hands" learned the discipline of the whistle. To function efficiently, a factory demanded that all employees begin and end work at the same time. Most workers could not tell time; fewer possessed clocks. None was accustomed to the relentless pace of the machine. To increase production, the factory system encouraged the breaking down of the manufacturing process into specialized steps, each with its own assigned time, an innovation that upset workers accustomed to completing a task at their own pace. Workers began to see machinery itself as the tyrant that had changed their lives and bound them to a kind of industrial slavery. A radical working-class song written in Britain in the 1840s expressed the feeling:

> "There is a king and a ruthless king; / Not a king of the poet's dream; / But a tyrant fell, white slaves know well, / And that ruthless king is steam."

Yet the defining feature of working-class life was vulnerability—to unemployment, sickness, accidents in dangerous jobs, family problems, and spikes in the prices of food. Seasonal unemployment, high in almost all trades, made it impossible to collect regular wages. Markets for manufactured goods were small and unstable, producing cyclical economic depressions; when those came, thousands of workers found themselves laid off with no system of unemployment insurance to sustain them. The early decades of industrialization were also marked by several severe agricultural depressions and economic crises. During the crisis years of the 1840s, half the working population of Britain's industrial cities was unemployed. In Paris, 85,000 went on relief in 1840. Families survived by working several small jobs, pawning their possessions, and getting credit from local wineshops and grocery stores. The chronic insecurity of working-class life helped fuel the creation of workers' self-help societies, fraternal associations, and early socialist organizations. It also meant that economic crises could have explosive consequences (see Chapter Twenty).

By mid-century, various experiences were beginning to make working people conscious of themselves as different from and in opposition to the middle classes. Changes in the workplace—whether the introduction of machines and factory labor, speedups, subcontracting to cheap labor, or the loss of guild protections—were part of the picture. The social segregation of the rapidly expanding nineteenth-century cities also contributed to the sense that working people lived a life apart. Class differences seemed embedded in a very wide array of everyday experiences and beliefs: work, private life, expectations for children, the roles of men and women, and definitions of respectability. Over the course of the nineteenth century all of these different experiences gave concrete, specific meaning to the word *class*.

CONCLUSION

Between 1800 and 1900, the population of Europe doubled. Over that same period, Europe's gross national product more than doubled. Yet even startling statistics on growth only begin to suggest how profoundly Europe's economics, politics, and culture were transformed. The Industrial Revolution was one of the turning points in the history of the world. It did not happen overnight and it did not happen evenly. In

1900 agriculture was still the largest single sector of employment. Villages and farms in vast stretches of Europe could seem virtually untouched by industry. Landowners still exercised enormous political and social clout, even when they had to share power with new elites. Yet the changes were by any measure extraordinary; they reached across the globe and into the private lives of ordinary people. Family structures changed. Industry changed the European landscape and, even more fundamental, humanity's relationship to the environment. As we will see in later chapters, the revolutionary transformations in communication, transportation, and economics had among their many effects the expansion of national states and bureaucracies. Europe's economic surge forward also decisively altered the global balance of power, tilting the scales toward an increasingly industrialized West. Economic development became a new yardstick of value, technology a measure of progress. Increasingly, the West came to be associated with—or even defined as—those nations with advanced industrial economies.

Industrialization created new forms of wealth alongside new kinds of poverty. It also fostered an acute awareness of the disparity between social groups. In the eighteenth century, that disparity would have been described in terms of birth, rank, or privilege. In the nineteenth century, it was increasingly seen in terms of class. Champions and critics of the new order alike spoke of a "class society," and new class identities were another key feature of the period. They were embodied in the growing and overcrowded working-class districts of the new cities, in the daily experiences of work, in new conceptions of respectability, and in middle-class homes. Those new identities would be sharpened in the political events to which we now turn.

Key Terms

enclosure
spinning jenny
Irish potato famine
Charles Dickens
Human Comedy
cult of domesticity
sweatshops
the social question

Selected Readings

Berg, Maxine. *The Age of Manufactures: Industry, Innovation, and Work in Britain,* 1700–1820. Oxford, 1985. Good on new scholarship and on women.

Bridenthal, Renate, Claudia Koonz, and Susan Stuard, eds. *Becoming Visible: Women in European History,* 2d ed. Boston, 1987. Excellent, wide-ranging introduction.

Briggs, Asa. *Victorian Cities.* New York, 1963. A survey of British cities, stressing middle-class attitudes toward the new urban environment.

Cameron, R. E. *France and the Industrial Development of Europe.* Princeton, 1968. Valuable material on the Industrial Revolution outside Britain.

Chevalier, Louis. *Laboring Classes and Dangerous Classes during the First Half of the Nineteenth Century.* New York, 1973. An important, though controversial, account of crime, class, and middle-class perceptions of life in Paris.

Cipolla, Carlo M., ed. *The Industrial Revolution,* 1700–1914. New York, 1976. A collection of essays that emphasizes the wide range of industrializing experiences in Europe.

Cott, Nancy. *The Bonds of Womanhood: "Woman's Sphere" in New England,* 1780–1935. New Haven, Conn., and London, 1977. One of the most influential studies of the paradoxes of domesticity.

Davidoff, Leonore, and Catherine Hall. *Family Fortunes: Men and Women of the English Middle Class,* 1780–1850. Chicago, 1985. A brilliant and detailed study of the lives and ambitions of several English families.

Ferguson, Niall. *The Cash Nexus: Money and Power in the Modern World,* 1700–2000 (New York, 2001). A very stimulating and fresh overview of the period.

Ferguson, Niall. "The European Economy, 1815–1914." In *The Nineteenth Century,* ed. T. C. W. Blanning. Oxford and New York, 2000. A very useful short essay.

Gay, Peter. *The Bourgeois Experience: Victoria to Freud.* New York, 1984. A multivolume, path-breaking study of middle-class life in all its dimensions.

Gay, Peter. *Schnitzler's Century: The Making of Middle-Class Culture,* 1815–1914. New York and London, 2002. A synthesis of some of the arguments presented in *The Bourgeois Experience.*

Hellerstein, Erna, Leslie Hume, and Karen Offen, eds. *Victorian Women: A Documentary Account.* Stanford, Calif., 1981. Good collection of documents, with excellent introductory essays.

Hobsbawm, Eric J. *The Age of Capital, 1848–1875*. London, 1975. Among the best introductions.

Hobsbawm, Eric J. *The Age of Revolution, 1789–1848*. London, 1962.

Hobsbawm, Eric, and George Rudé. *Captain Swing: A Social History of the Great English Agricultural Uprising of 1830*. New York, 1975. Analyzes rural protest and politics.

Kemp, Tom. *Industrialization in Nineteenth-Century Europe*. London, 1985. Good general study.

Kindelberger, Charles. *A Financial History of Western Europe*. London, 1984. Emphasis on finance.

Landes, David S. *The Unbound Prometheus: Technological Change and Industrial Development in Western Europe from 1750 to the Present*. London, 1969. Excellent and thorough on technological change and its social and economic context.

Langer, William L. *Political and Social Upheaval, 1832–1852*. New York, 1969. Comprehensive and detailed survey.

McNeill, J. R. *Something New under the Sun: An Environmental History of the Twentieth-Century World*. New York and London, 2000. Short section on the nineteenth century.

Mokyr, Joel. *The Lever of Riches: Technological Creativity and Economic Progress*. New York, 1992. A world history, from antiquity through the nineteenth century

O'Gráda, Cormac. *Black '47 and Beyond: The Great Irish Famine*. Princeton, N.J., 1999.

O'Gráda, Cormac. *The Great Irish Famine*. Cambridge, 1989. A fascinating and recent assessment of scholarship on the famine.

Rendall, Jane. *The Origins of Modern Feminism: Women in Britain, France and the United States, 1780–1860*. New York, 1984. Helpful overview.

Rose, Sonya O. *Limited Livelihoods: Gender and Class in Nineteenth-Century England*. Berkeley, Calif., 1992. On the intersection of culture and economics.

Sabean, David Warren. *Property, Production, and Family Neckarhausen, 1700–1870*. New York, 1990. Brilliant and very detailed study of gender roles and family.

Sabel, Charles, and Jonathan Zeitlin. "Historical Alternatives to Mass Production." *Past and Present* 108 (August 1985): 133–176. On the many forms of modern industry.

Schivelbusch, Wolfgang. *Disenchanted Night: The Instrialization of Light in the Nineteenth Century*. Berkeley, Calif., 1988.

Schivelbusch, Wolfgang. *The Railway Journey*. Berkeley, 1986. Schivelbusch's imaginative studies are among the best ways to understand how the transformations of the nineteenth century changed daily experiences.

Thompson, E. P. *The Making of the English Working Class*. London, 1963 Shows how the French and Industrial Revolutions fostered the growth of working-class consciousness. A brilliant and important work.

Tilly, Louise, and Joan Scott. *Women, Work and the Family*. New York, 1978. Now the classic study.

Valenze, Deborah. *The First Industrial Woman*. New York, 1995. Excellent and readable on industrialization and economic change in general.

Williams, Raymond. *Keywords: A Vocabulary of Culture and Society*. New York, 1976. Brilliant and indispensable for students of culture, and now updated as *New Keywords: A Revised Vocabulary of Culture and Society* (2005), by Lawrence Grossberg and Meaghan Morris.

Zeldin, Theodore. *France, 1848–1945*, 2 vols. Oxford, 1973–1977. Eclectic and wide-ranging social history.

The Carolingian Dynasty

Pepin of Heristal, Mayor of the Palace, 687–714
Charles Martel, Mayor of the Palace, 715–741
Pepin III, Mayor of the Palace, 741–751; King, 751–768
Charlemagne, King, 768–814; Emperor, 800–814
Louis the Pious, Emperor, 814–840

West Francia
Charles the Bald, King, 840–877; Emperor, 875–877
Louis II, King, 877–879
Louis III, King, 879–882
Carloman, King, 879–884

Middle Kingdoms
Lothair, Emperor, 840–855
Louis (Italy), Emperor, 855–875
Charles (Provence), King, 855–863
Lothair II (Lorraine), King, 855–869

East Francia
Ludwig, King, 840–876
Carloman, King, 876–880
Ludwig, King, 876–882
Charles the Fat, Emperor, 876–887

Holy Roman Emperors

Saxon Dynasty
Otto I, 962–973
Otto II, 973–983
Otto III, 983–1002
Henry II, 1002–1024

Franconian Dynasty
Conrad II, 1024–1039
Henry III, 1039–1056
Henry IV, 1056–1106
Henry V, 1106–1125
Lothair II (Saxony), 1125–1137

Hohenstaufen Dynasty
Conrad III, 1138–1152
Frederick I (Barbarossa), 1152–1190
Henry VI, 1190–1197
Philip of Swabia, 1198–1208 ⎫
Otto IV (Welf), 1198–1215   ⎬ Rivals
Frederick II, 1220–1250
Conrad IV, 1250–1254

Interregnum, 1254–1273

Emperors from Various Dynasties
Rudolf I (Habsburg), 1273–1291
Adolf (Nassau), 1292–1298
Albert I (Habsburg), 1298–1308
Henry VII (Luxemburg), 1308–1313
Ludwig IV (Wittelsbach), 1314–1347
Charles IV (Luxemburg), 1347–1378
Wenceslas (Luxemburg), 1378–1400
Rupert (Wittelsbach), 1400–1410
Sigismund (Luxemburg), 1410–1437

Habsburg Dynasty
Albert II, 1438–1439
Frederick III, 1440–1493
Maximilian I, 1493–1519
Charles V, 1519–1556
Ferdinand I, 1556–1564
Maximilian II, 1564–1576
Rudolf II, 1576–1612

RULERS OF PRINCIPAL STATES

Matthias, 1612–1619
Ferdinand II, 1619–1637
Ferdinand III, 1637–1657
Leopold I, 1658–1705
Joseph I, 1705–1711
Charles VI, 1711–1740

Charles VII (not a Habsburg), 1742–1745
Francis I, 1745–1765
Joseph II, 1765–1790
Leopold II, 1790–1792
Francis II, 1792–1806

RULERS OF FRANCE FROM HUGH CAPET

CAPETIAN DYNASTY
Hugh Capet, 987–996
Robert II, 996–1031
Henry I, 1031–1060
Philip I, 1060–1108
Louis VI, 1108–1137
Louis VII, 1137–1180
Philip II (Augustus), 1180–1223
Louis VIII, 1223–1226
Louis IX (St. Louis), 1226–1270
Philip III, 1270–1285
Philip IV, 1285–1314
Louis X, 1314–1316
Philip V, 1316–1322
Charles IV, 1322–1328

VALOIS DYNASTY
Philip VI, 1328–1350
John, 1350–1364
Charles V, 1364–1380
Charles VI, 1380–1422
Charles VII, 1422–1461
Louis XI, 1461–1483
Charles VIII, 1483–1498
Louis XII, 1498–1515
Francis I, 1515–1547

Henry II, 1547–1559
Francis II, 1559–1560
Charles IX, 1560–1574
Henry III, 1574–1589

BOURBON DYNASTY
Henry IV, 1589–1610
Louis XIII, 1610–1643
Louis XIV, 1643–1715
Louis XV, 1715–1774
Louis XVI, 1774–1792

AFTER 1792
First Republic, 1792–1799
Napoleon Bonaparte, First Consul, 1799–1804
Napoleon I, Emperor, 1804–1814
Louis XVIII (Bourbon dynasty), 1814–1824
Charles X (Bourbon dynasty), 1824–1830
Louis Philippe, 1830–1848
Second Republic, 1848–1852
Napoleon III, Emperor, 1852–1870
Third Republic, 1870–1940
Péain regime, 1940–1944
Provisional government, 1944–1946
Fourth Republic, 1946–1958
Fifth Republic, 1958–

RULERS OF ENGLAND

ANGLO-SAXON DYNASTY
Alfred the Great, 871–899
Edward the Elder, 899–924
Ethelstan, 924–939
Edmund I, 939–946
Edred, 946–955
Edwy, 955–959
Edgar, 959–975
Edward the Martyr, 975–978
Ethelred the Unready, 978–1016

Canute, 1016–1035 (Danish Nationality)
Harold I, 1035–1040
Hardicanute, 1040–1042
Edward the Confessor, 1042–1066
Harold II, 1066

HOUSE OF NORMANDY
William I (the Conqueror), 1066–1087
William II, 1087–1100

Henry I, 1100–1135
Stephen, 1135–1154

HOUSE OF PLANTAGENET
Henry II, 1154–1189
Richard I, 1189–1199
John, 1199–1216
Henry III, 1216–1272
Edward I, 1272–1307
Edward II, 1307–1327
Edward III, 1327–1377
Richard II, 1377–1399

HOUSE OF LANCASTER
Henry IV, 1399–1413
Henry V, 1413–1422
Henry VI, 1422–1461

HOUSE OF YORK
Edward IV, 1461–1483
Edward V, 1483
Richard III, 1483–1485

HOUSE OF TUDOR
Henry VII, 1485–1509
Henry VIII, 1509–1547
Edward VI, 1547–1553
Mary, 1553–1558
Elizabeth I, 1558–1603

HOUSE OF STUART
James I, 1603–1625
Charles I, 1625–1649

COMMONWEALTH AND PROTECTORATE, 1649–1659

HOUSE OF STUART RESTORED
Charles II, 1660–1685
James II, 1685–1688
William III and Mary II, 1689–1694
William III alone, 1694–1702
Anne, 1702–1714

HOUSE OF HANOVER
George I, 1714–1727
George II, 1727–1760
George III, 1760–1820
George IV, 1820–1830
William IV, 1830–1837
Victoria, 1837–1901

HOUSE OF SAXE-COBURG-GOTHA
Edward VI, 1901–1910
George V, 1910–1917

HOUSE OF WINDSOR
George V, 1917–1936
Edward VIII, 1936
George VI, 1936–1952
Elizabeth II, 1952–

RULERS OF AUSTRIA AND AUSTRIA-HUNGARY

*Maximilian I (Archduke), 1493–1519
*Charles V, 1519–1556
*Ferdinand I, 1556–1564
*Maximilian II, 1564–1576
*Rudolf II, 1576–1612
*Matthias, 1612–1619
*Ferdinand II, 1619–1637
*Ferdinand III, 1637–1657
*Leopold I, 1658–1705
*Joseph I, 1705–1711
*Charles VI, 1711–1740
Maria Theresa, 1740–1780

*also bore title of Holy Roman Emperor

*Joseph II, 1780–1790
*Leopold II, 1790–1792
*Francis II, 1792–1835 (Emperor of Austria as Francis I after 1804)
Ferdinand I, 1835–1848
Francis Joseph, 1848–1916 (after 1867 Emperor of Austria and King of Hungary)
Charles I, 1916–1918 (Emperor of Austria and King of Hungary)
Republic of Austria, 1918–1938 (dictatorship after 1934)
Republic restored, under Allied occupation, 1945–1956
Free Republic, 1956–

RULERS OF PRINCIPAL STATES

A4

RULERS OF PRUSSIA AND GERMANY

*Frederick I, 1701–1713
*Frederick William I, 1713–1740
*Frederick II (the Great), 1740–1786
*Frederick William II, 1786–1797
*Frederick William III, 1797–1840
*Frederick William IV, 1840–1861
*William I, 1861–1888 (German Emperor after 1871)
Frederick III, 1888

*Kings of Prussia

*William II, 1888–1918
Weimar Republic, 1918–1933
Third Reich (Nazi Dictatorship), 1933–1945
Allied occupation, 1945–1952
Division into Federal Republic of Germany in west and
    German Democratic Republic in east, 1949–1991
Federal Republic of Germany (united), 1991–

RULERS OF RUSSIA

Ivan III, 1462–1505
Vasily III, 1505–1533
Ivan IV, 1533–1584
Theodore I, 1534–1598
Boris Godunov, 1598–1605
Theodore II, 1605
Vasily IV, 1606–1610
Michael, 1613–1645
Alexius, 1645–1676
Theodore III, 1676–1682
Ivan V and Peter I, 1682–1689
Peter I (the Great), 1689–1725
Catherine I, 1725–1727
Peter II, 1727–1730

Anna, 1730–1740
Ivan VI, 1740–1741
Ellzabeth, 1741–1762
Peter III, 1762
Catherine II (the Great), 1762–1796
Paul, 1796–1801
Alexander I, 1801–1825
Nicholas I, 1825–1855
Alexander II, 1855–1881
Alexander III, 1881–1894
Nicholas II, 1894–1917
Soviet Republic, 1917–1991
Russian Federation, 1991–

RULERS OF SPAIN

Ferdinand { and Isabella, 1479–1504
            and Philip I, 1504–1506
            and Charles I, 1506–1516
Charles I (Holy Roman Emperor Charles V), 1516–1556
Philip II, 1556–1598
Philip III, 1598–1621
Philip IV, 1621–1665
Charles II, 1665–1700
Philip V, 1700–1746
Ferdinand VI, 1746–1759
Charles III, 1759–1788
Charles IV, 1788–1808

Ferdinand VII, 1808
Joseph Bonaparte, 1808–1813
Ferdinand VII (restored), 1814–1833
Isabella II, 1833–1868
Republic, 1868–1870
Amadeo, 1870–1873
Republic, 1873–1874
Alfonso XII, 1874–1885
Alfonso XIII, 1886–1931
Republic, 1931–1939
Fascist Dictatorship, 1939–1975
Juan Carlos I, 1975–

RULERS OF ITALY

Victor Emmanuel II, 1861–1878
Humbert I, 1878–1900
Victor Emmanuel III, 1900–1946

Fascist Dictatorship, 1922-1943 (maintained in northern Italy until 1945)
Humbert II, May 9–June 13, 1946
Republic, 1946–

PROMINENT POPES

Silvester I, 314–335
Leo I, 440–461
Gelasius I, 492–496
Gregory I, 590–604
Nicholas I, 858–867
Silvester II, 999–1003
Leo IX, 1049–1054
Nicholas II, 1058–1061
Gregory VII, 1073–1085
Urban II, 1088–1099
Paschal II, 1099–1118
Alexander III, 1159–1181
Innocent III, 1198–1216
Gregory IX, 1227–1241
Innocent IV, 1243–1254
Boniface VIII, 1294–1303
John XXII, 1316–1334
Nicholas V, 1447–1455
Pius II, 1458–1464

Alexander VI, 1492–1503
Julius II, 1503–1513
Leo X, 1513–1521
Paul III, 1534–1549
Paul IV, 1555–1559
Sixtus V, 1585–1590
Urban VIII, 1623–1644
Gregory XVI, 1831–1846
Pius IX, 1846–1878
Leo XIII, 1878–1903
Pius X, 1903–1914
Benedict XV, 1914–1922
Pius XI, 1922–1939
Pius XII, 1939–1958
John XXIII, 1958–1963
Paul VI, 1963–1978
John Paul I, 1978
John Paul II, 1978–2005
Benedict XVI 2005–

Glossary

Peter Abelard (1079–1142) Famed French theologian, logician, and university lecturer.

abolition of feudalism The end of the feudal system in France, which was brought about by the popular revolts of 1789. Louis XVI and other nobles established the National Assembly, which abolished all forms of privilege, such as the church tax on harvests, the labor requirement of peasants (known as the corvee), the nobility's hunting privileges, and a variety of tax exemptions and monopolies.

absolutism Form of government in which one body, usually the monarch, controls the right to make war, tax, judge, and coin money. The term was often used to refer to the state monarchies in seventeenth- and eighteenth-century Europe.

abstract expressionism The mid-twentieth-century school of art based in New York that included Jackson Pollock, Willem de Kooning, and Franz Kline. It emphasized form, color, gesture, and feeling instead of figurative subjects.

acid rain Precipitation laced with heavy doses of sulfur, mainly from coal-fired plants.

African National Congress (ANC) Multiracial organization founded in 1912 whose goal was to end racial discrimination in South Africa.

Afrikaners Descendants of the original Dutch settlers of South Africa; formerly referred to as Boers.

AIDS Acquired immune deficiency syndrome. AIDS first appeared in the 1970s and has developed into a global health catastrophe; it is spreading most quickly in developing nations in Africa and Asia.

Akhenaten The fourteenth-century B.C.E. pharaoh who developed a sun-oriented religion and ultimately damaged Egypt's position in the ancient world.

Alexander (356–323 B.C.E.) The Macedonian general who conquered northwest Asia Minor, and Persia, and built an empire that stretched as far east as the Indus River.

Algerian War The war in the 1950s and 1960s between France and Algerians seeking independence. Led by the National Liberation Front (FLN), guerrillas fought the French army in the mountains and desert of Algeria. The FLN also initiated a campaign of bombing and terrorism in Algerian cities that led French soldiers to torture Algerians and attract world attention and international scandal.

Allied Powers The World War I coalition of Great Britain, Ireland, Belgium, France, Italy, Russia, Portugal, Greece, Serbia, Montenegro, Albania, and Romania.

al Qaeda The radical Islamic organization founded in the late 1980s by former *mujahedin* who had fought against the Soviet Union in Afghanistan. Al Qaeda carried out the 9/11 terrorist attacks and is responsible as well for attacks in Africa, Southeast Asia, Europe, and the Middle East.

Americanization The fear of many Europeans from the 1920s and on that U.S. cultural products, such as film, television, and music exerted too much influence. Many of the criticisms centered on America's emphasis on mass production and organization. The fears about Americanization were not limited to culture. They extended to corporations, business techniques, global trade, and marketing.

Amnesty International Nongovernmental organization formed in 1961 to defend "prisoners of conscience"—those detained for their beliefs, color, sex, ethnic origin, language, or religion.

Anabaptists Swiss Protestant movement that began in 1521 and insisted that only adults could be baptized Christians. The movement's first generation, who had been baptized as infants according to Catholic practice, was "re-baptized," hence the name.

anarchism The social and political movement that began in the mid-nineteenth century and advocated the destruction of the state through violence and terrorism.

Apartheid The racial segregation policy of the Afrikaner-dominated South African government. Legislated in 1948 by the Afrikaner National Party, it existed in South Africa for many years.

appeasement The policy pursued by Western governments in the face of German, Italian, and Japanese aggression leading up to World War II. The policy, which attempted to accommodate and negotiate peace with the aggressive nations, was based on the belief that another global war like World War I was unimaginable, a belief that Germany and its allies had been mistreated by the terms of the Treaty of Versailles, and a fear that fascist Germany and its allies protected the West from the spread of Soviet Communism.

Glossary

aqueducts Engineering system that brought water from the mountains down to Roman cities.

Saint Thomas Aquinas (1225–1274) Italian Dominican monk and theologian whose intellectual style encouraged the study of ancient philosophers and science as complementary to theology.

Arians The fourth-century followers of a priest named Arius, who rejected the idea that Christ could be equal with God.

Aristotelian The system of thought based on the ideas of the Greek philosopher Aristotle. Aristotelian ideas distinguished between the works of humans and those of nature and posited that as God's creation, nature belonged to a different, higher order.

Asiatic Society A cultural organization founded in 1784 by British Orientalists who lauded native culture but believed in colonial rule.

Assyrians A Semitic-speaking people that emerged around 2400 B.C.E. in northern Mesopotamia. Their highly militarized empire dominated Near-Eastern politics for close to two thousand years.

astrolabe An ancient navigational instrument, thought to have been invented in 150 B.C.E., that was used to find latitude while at sea.

Atlantic system A system of trade and expansion that linked Europe, Africa, and the Americas. It emerged in the sixteenth century in the wake of European voyages across the Atlantic Ocean.

Saint Augustine (c. 354–397) One of the most influential Christian theologians of all time, Saint Augustine described his conversion in his autobiographical *Confessions* and formulated new aspects of Christian theology in *On the City of God*.

Augustus (63 B.C.E.–14 C.E.) The grandnephew and adopted son of Julius Caesar and first emperor of the Roman empire.

Auschwitz-Birkenau The Nazi concentration camp in Poland that was designed to systematically murder Jews and gypsies. Between 1942 and 1944 over one million people were killed in Auschwitz-Birkenau.

Austro-Hungarian empire The dual monarchy established by the Habsburg family in 1867; it collapsed at the end of World War I.

authoritarianism A centralized and dictatorial form of government, proclaimed by its adherents to be superior to parliamentary democracy and especially effective at mobilizing the masses. Authoritarianism was prominent in the 1930s.

Avignon City on the southeastern border of France. Between 305 and 378 it was the seat of the papacy.

Aztecs Native American people of central Mexico; their empire was conquered by the Spanish in the sixteenth century.

baby boom (1950s) The post–World War II upswing in U.S. birth rates; it reversed a century of decline.

Francis Bacon (1561–1626) British philosopher and scientist who pioneered the scientific method and inductive reasoning. In other words, he argued that thinkers should amass observations and then make general observations or theories.

Baghdad Pact (1955) The Middle Eastern military alliance among countries friendly with America who were also willing to align themselves with the Western countries against the Soviet Union.

balance of power Initated by the League of Augsburg in 1689, a new diplomatic goal emerged in western and central Europe to preserve a balance of power to prevent any single country from becoming so powerful as to threaten the position of the other major powers within the European state system.

Balfour Declaration A letter dated November 2, 1917, by Lord Arthur J. Balfour, British Foreign Secretary, that promised a homeland for the Jews in Palestine.

Baroque An ornate style of art and music associated with the Counter Reformation (from the French word for "irregularly shaped pearl").

Battle of the Marne A major World War I battle in September 1914, which stifled German advancement in France and led to protracted trench warfare on the western front.

Bay of Pigs (1961) The unsuccessful invasion of Cuba by Cuban exiles, supported by the U.S. government. The rebels intended to incite an insurrection in Cuba and overthrow the Communist regime of Fidel Castro.

Beer Hall Putsch (1923) The Nazi invasion of a meeting of Bavarian leaders and supporters in a Munich beer hall; Adolf Hitler was imprisoned for a year after the incident.

Saint Benedict of Nursia (c. 480–c. 547) Considered the father of western monasticism, Saint Benedict created the Benedictine rule that became the guide for nearly all western monks. Monks were required to follow the rules laid down by Saint Benedict: poverty, sexual chastity, obedience, labor, and religious devotion.

Berlin Airlift (1948) The supply of vital necessities to West Berlin by air transport primarily under U.S. auspices. It was initiated in response to a blockade of the city that had been instituted by the Soviet Union to force the Allies to abandon West Berlin.

Berlin blockade From June 1948 until May 1949, the Soviets cut all road, train, and river access from the Western zone of Germany to West Berlin. Unwilling to cede control of their portion of the capital, France, Britain, and the United States airlifted supplies over Soviet territory to the Western zone of Berlin.

Berlin Wall The wall built in 1961 by East German Communists to prevent citizens of East Germany from fleeing to West Germany; it was torn down in 1989.

Bill of Rights The first ten amendments to the U.S. Constitution; it was ratified in 1791.

Otto von Bismarck (1815–1890) The prime minister of Prussia and later the first chancellor of Germany, Bismarck helped consolidate the German people's economic and military power.

Black Death The epidemic of bubonic plague that ravaged Europe, East Asia, and North Africa in the fourteenth century, killing one-third of the European population.

Black Jacobins A nickname for the rebels in Saint Domingue, including Toussaint L'Ouverture, a former slave who in 1791 led the slaves of this French colony in the largest and most successful slave insurrection.

Black Panthers A radical African American group that came together in the 1960s; the Black Panthers advocated black separatism and pan-Africanism.

GLOSSARY

Blackshirts The troops of Mussolini's fascist regime; the squads received money from Italian landowners to attack socialist leaders.

Black Tuesday (October 24, 1929) The day on which the U.S. stock market crashed, plunging the U.S. and international trading systems into crisis and leading the world into the "Great Depression."

Blitzkreig The German "lightning war" strategy used during World War II; the Germans invaded Poland, France, Russia, and other countries with fast-moving well-coordinated attacks using aircraft, tanks and other armored vehicles, followed by infantry.

Bloody Sunday On Sunday, January 22, 1905, the Russian tsar's guards killed 130 demonstrators who were protesting the tsar's mistreatment of workers and the middle class.

Giovanni Boccaccio (1313–1375) Italian prose writer famed for his *Decameron*, one hundred short stories about the human condition, mostly from a comic or cynical point of view.

Boer War Conflict between British and ethnically European Afrikaners in South Africa, 1898–1902, with terrible casualties on both sides.

Simon de Bolivar (1783–1830) Venezuelan-born general called "The Liberator" for his assistance in helping Bolivia, Panama, Colombia, Ecuador, Peru, and Venezuela win independence from Spain.

Bolsheviks Former members of the Russian Social Democratic Party who advocated the destruction of capitalist political and economic institutions and started the Russian Revolution. In 1918 the Bolsheviks changed their name to the Russian Communist Party.

Napoleon Bonaparte (1769–1821) Corsican-born French general who seized power and ruled as dictator 1799–1814. After successful conquest of much of Europe, he was defeated by Russian and Prussian forces and died in exile.

bourgeoisie The French term for the middle class, which emerged in Europe during the Middle Ages. The Bourgeoisie sought to be recognized not by birth or title, but by capital and property.

Boxer Rebellion (1899–1900) Chinese peasant movement that opposed foreign influence, especially that of Christian missionaries; it was finally put down after the Boxers were defeated by a foreign army comprised mostly of Japanese, Russian, British, French, and American soldiers.

British Commonwealth of Nations Formed in 1926, the Commonwealth conferred "dominion status" on Britain's white settler colonies in Canada, Australia, and New Zealand.

Brownshirts Troops of young German men who dedicated themselves to the Nazi cause in the early 1930s by holding street marches, mass rallies, and confrontations. They engaged in beatings of Jews and anyone who opposed the Nazis.

bubonic plague An acute infectious disease caused by a bacterium that is transmitted to humans by fleas from infected rats. It ravaged Europe and parts of Asia in the fourteenth century. Sometimes referred to as the "black death."

Julius Caesar (100–44 B.C.E.) The Roman general who conquered the Gauls, invaded Britain, and expanded Rome's territory in Asia Minor. He became the dictator of Rome in 46 B.C.E. and was murdered by Brutus and Cassius, which led to the rise of Augustus and the end of the Roman republic.

caliphs Rulers of the Islamic community who claimed descent from Muhammad.

John Calvin (1509–1564) French-born Protestant theologian who stressed the predestination of all human beings according to God's will.

Canary Islands Islands off the western coast of Africa conquered by Portugal and Spain in the mid-1400s. Used to supply expeditions around the African coast and across the Atlantic.

Canterbury Tales Middle English verse stories by Geoffrey Chaucer (c.1340–1400) that reflect different classes and experiences in late medieval England.

caravans Companies of men who transported and traded goods along overland routes in North Africa and central Asia; large caravans consisted of 600 to 1,000 camels and as many as 400 men.

caravels Sailing vessels suited for nosing in and out of estuaries and navigating in waters with unpredictable currents and winds.

Carthage A great maritime empire that rivaled Rome; at its height, it stretched across the northern coast of Africa from modern-day Tunisia to the Strait of Gibraltar. Carthage fought against Rome in the Punic Wars that began in 264 B.C.E. The wars ended with the destruction of Carthage in 146 B.C.E.

Cassiodorus (490–583) Author of the *Institutes*, which instructed medieval readers on the essential works of literature a monk should know before moving on to more intensive study of theology and the Bible.

caste system A hierarchical system of organizing people and distributing labor, often based on heredity or regional origin.

Baldassare Castiglione (1478–1529) Author of *The Book of the Courtier*, a popular treatise on upper-class social graces.

Catherine the Great (1729–1796) German-born empress of Russia who maintained an absolutist feudal system but encouraged Enlightenment philosophy and the arts at court.

Catholicism Branch of Christianity headed by the pope.

Camillo Benso di Cavour (1810–1861) Anti-papist Italian leader who led the initial stages of revolution against the Habsburgs.

Central Powers The World War I alliance between Germany, Austro-Hungary, Bulgaria, and Turkey.

Charlemagne (742–814) Frankish ruler 767–813 who consolidated much of western Europe by adding Lombardy and Saxony to the Frankish kingdoms. With a strong sense of divine purpose, he forced the Christian conversion of pagan peoples and sponsored arts and learning at court. In 800 he became the first Roman emperor in the west since the 5th century.

Chartist movement (1834–1848) Mass democratic movement to pass the Peoples' Charter in Britain, granting male suffrage, secret ballot, equal electoral districts, and annual Parliaments, and absolving the requirement of property ownership for members of Parliament.

Chernobyl (1986) Site of the world's worst nuclear power accident; in Ukraine, formerly part of the Soviet Union.

chivalry From the word for "horsemanship"; an aristocratic ideology originating with the knights of eleventh-century Europe that encouraged military prowess and social graces.

Glossary A9

Christine de Pisan (c. 1364–c. 1431) Born in Italy and spending her adult life in France, Pisan was the first lay woman to earn her living by her writing. While she wrote treatises on chivalry and warfare, she also wrote popular literature such as *The City of Ladies* and pamphlets debating the misogynistic claims made against women.

Winston Churchill (1874–1965) The British prime minister who led the country during World War II. He also coined the phrase "Iron Curtain" in a speech at Westminster College in 1946.

Church of England Founded by Henry VIII in the 1530s after his excommunication from the Catholic Church by Pope Clement VII, it is the established form of Christianity in England.

Cicero (106–43 B.C.E.) The most famous Stoic philosopher and orator of Rome.

Civil Constitution of the Clergy Issued by the French National Assembly in 1789, the Civil Constitution of the Clergy provided that all bishops and priests should be subject to the authority of the state. Their salaries were to be paid out of the public treasury, and they were required to swear allegiance to the new state, making it clear they served France rather than Rome. The Assembly's aim was to make the Catholic Church of France a truly national and civil institution.

Civil Rights Act (1964) U.S. legislation that banned segregation in public facilities, outlawed racial discrimination in employment, and marked an important step in correcting legal inequality.

Civil War (1861–1865) Conflict between the northern and southern states of America that cost over 600,000 lives; this struggle led to the abolition of slavery in the United States.

Cluny A Benedictine monastery, founded in 910, whose reform ideology tried to separate its network of religious houses from control by lay people.

Cold War (1945–1990) Ideological conflict in which the U.S.S.R. and Eastern Europe opposed the United States and Western Europe.

collectivization The process under Stalin in the 1920s and 1930s where peasants were forced to give up private farmland and join collective farms, which were supported by the state.

Colons French settler population in Algeria that ran the colonial government between 1830 and 1962.

Christopher Columbus (1451–1506) The Italian sailor who persuaded King Ferdinand and Queen Isabella of Spain to fund his expedition across the Atlantic to discover a new trade route to Asia. He miscalculated the size of the Earth and rather than landing in China or Japan, Columbus reached the Bahamas and the island of Hispaniola in 1492.

Committee of Public Safety Political body during the French Revolution that was controlled by the Jacobins, who enforced party rule by executing thousands during the Reign of Terror, September 1793–July 1794.

***The Communist Manifesto* (1818–1883)** Radical pamphlet by Karl Marx that predicted the downfall of the capitalist system and its replacement by a system that operated in the interests of the working class (proletariat).

Compromise of 1867 Agreement between the Habsburgs and the peoples living in Hungarian parts of the empire that the Habsburg state would be officially known as the Austro-Hungarian Empire.

concession areas Territories, usually ports, established by the 1842 Treaty of Nanjing, where Chinese emperors allowed European merchants to trade and European people to settle.

Congo Independent State Large colonial state in Africa created by Leopold II, king of Belgium, during the 1880s, and ruled by him alone. After reports of mass slaughter and enslavement, the Belgian parliament took the land and formed a Belgian colony.

Congress of Vienna (1814–1815) and Restoration International conference to reorganize Europe after the downfall of Napoleon. European monarchies agreed to respect each other's borders and to cooperate in guarding against future revolutions and war.

conquistador Spanish term for "conqueror," applied to European leaders of campaigns against indigenous peoples in central and southern America.

conservatism Reactionary mode of thinking that held that tradition, including hereditary monarchy, would dispel the divisive ideas of the Enlightenment.

Constantinople Former capital of the Byzantine empire, eventually renamed Istanbul after its conquest by the Ottomans in 1453.

Constitutional Convention (1787) Meeting to formulate the Constitution of the United States of America.

Nicholas Copernicus (1473–1543) Polish astronomer who advanced the radical idea that the earth moved around the sun in *De Revolutionibus*.

Corn Laws Laws that imposed tariffs on grain imported to Great Britain, intended to protect British farming interests. The Corn Laws were abolished in 1846 as part of a British movement in favor of free trade.

Council of Trent Intermittent meeting of Catholic leaders (1545–1563) that reaffirmed Catholic doctrine against Protestant criticisms while also reforming the church.

Counter Reformation Movement To counter the spread of the Reformation, the Counter Reformation was initiated by the Catholic Church at the Council of Trent in 1545.

coup d'état Overthrow of established state by a group of conspirators, usually from the military.

courtly love Codes of refined romantic behavior between men and women of high station.

courtly romances Long narrative poems written in vernacular languages based on myths and legends but expressing ideals of medieval aristocratic conduct.

creoles Persons of European descent who were born in the West Indies or Spanish America.

Crimean War (1854–1856) War waged by Russia against Great Britain and France. Spurred by Russia's encroachment on Ottoman territories, the conflict revealed Russia's military weakness when Russian forces fell to British and French troops.

Oliver Cromwell (1599–1658) Puritan leader of the Parliamentary army that defeated the royalist forces in the English Civil War. After the 1649 execution of King Charles I and dispersion of Parliament, Cromwell ruled as self-styled Lord Protector from 1653 until his death.

GLOSSARY

A10

Crusades (1096 to 1291) Series of wars undertaken to free Jerusalem and the Holy Lands from Muslim control.

Cuban Missile Crisis (1962) Diplomatic standoff between the United States and the Soviet Union that was provoked by the Soviet Union's attempt to base nuclear missiles in Cuba; it brought the world closer to nuclear war than ever before or since.

cult of domesticity Concept associated with Victorian England that idealized women as nurturing wives and mothers.

cult of the Virgin Mary A surge in veneration of the mother of Jesus beginning in the twelfth century that seemed to portend a change in how women were regarded as religious and moral beings.

cuneiform One of the earliest writing systems, beginning around 3500 B.C.E., it was the Mesopotamian form of writing on clay tablets using a stylus.

Cyrus (c.585–529 B.C.E.) The ruler of the Persians from circa 559 B.C.E. until 529 B.C.E.

Charles Darwin (1809–1882) British naturalist who wrote *Origin of the Species* and developed the theory of natural selection to explain the evolution of organisms.

David King of the Hebrews from around 1000 B.C.E. to 973 B.C.E. David united Israel and made Jerusalem his capital.

Leonardo da Vinci (1452–1519) Florentine painter, architect, musician, and inventor whose breadth of interests typifies Renaissance ideals.

D-Day (June 6, 1944) Date of the Allied invasion of Normandy under General Dwight Eisenhower to liberate Western Europe from German occupation.

Decembrists Russian army officers who were influenced by events in France and formed secret societies that espoused liberal governance. They were put down by Nicholas I in December 1825.

Declaration of Independence Historic U.S. document stating the principles of government on which America was founded.

Declaration of the Rights of Man and of the Citizen (1789) French charter of liberties formulated by the National Assembly that marked the end of dynastic and aristocratic rule. The seventeen articles later became the preamble to the new constitution, which the Assembly finished in 1791.

Olympe de Gouges (1745–1793) French political radical and feminist whose *Declaration of the Rights of Women* demanded an equal place for women in the new French republic.

Dhimmis "Peoples of the Book"; i.e., Jews and Christians, who were given a protected but subordinate place in Muslim society.

Charles Dickens (1812–1870) Hugely popular English novelist whose fiction exposed urban crime, poverty, and injustice but maintained Victorian domestic ideals.

Dien Bien Phu (1954) Defining battle in the war between French colonialists and the Viet Minh that secured North Vietnam for Ho Chi Minh and his army and left the south to form its own government to be supported by France and the United States.

Diet of Worms Examination of Luther by a church council in 1521. The council condemned him, and Luther was rescued by Frederick of Saxony.

Directory Temporary military committee that took over the affairs of the state of France in 1795 from the radicals and held control until the coup of Napoleon Bonaparte.

Discourse on Method Philosophical treatise by René Descartes (1596–1650) proposing that the path to knowledge was through logical speculation, beginning with one's own self: "I think, therefore I am."

Divine Comedy Italian verse narrative by Dante Alighieri (1265–1321); its complex themes exemplify the concerns of medieval learning.

DNA (deoxyribonucleic acid) Discovered by James Watson and Francis Crick in 1953, DNA contains an organism's genetic information and hereditary characteristics.

Dominican Order Founded by the Spaniard Saint Dominic (1170–1221) and approved by Innocent III in 1216, the order was dedicated to the fight against heresy and the conversion of Jews and Muslims. Many members of the order gained teaching positions in the infant European universities and contributed much to the development of philosophy and theology. The Dominicans always retained their reputation for learning, but they also came to believe that stubborn heretics were best controlled by legal procedures. Accordingly, they became the leading medieval administrators of inquisitorial trials.

Dominion in the British Commonwealth Canadian promise to keep up their fealty to the British crown, even after their independence in 1867. Later applied to Australia and New Zealand.

Don Quixote Comical adventure by Spanish writer Miguel de Cervantes (1547–1616) that mocks chivalric ideas.

Dreyfus Affair The 1894 French scandal surrounding accusations that a Jewish captain, Alfred Dreyfus, sold military secrets to the Germans. Convicted, Dreyfus was sentenced to life in prison. However, after public outcry, it was revealed that the trial documents were forgeries and Dreyfus was released.

Il Duce Term designating the fascist Italian leader Benito Mussolini.

Duma The Russian parliament.

Dunkirk The French port on the English Channel where the British and French forces retreated after sustaining heavy losses against the German military. Between May 27 and June 4, 1940, the Royal Navy evacuated over three hundred thousand troops using commercial and pleasure boats.

Earth Summit (1992) Meeting in Rio de Janeiro between many of the world's governments in an effort to address international environmental problems.

Eastern Front Battlefront between Berlin and Moscow during World War I and World War II.

East India Company (1600–1858) British charter company created to outperform Portuguese and Spanish traders in the Far East; in the eighteenth century the company became, in effect, the ruler of a large part of India. There was also a Dutch East India Company.

Edict of Nantes (1598) Edict issued by Henry IV to end the French Wars of Religion. The edict declared France a Catholic country, but tolerated some Protestant worship.

Eiffel Tower Named after its creator, Gustave Eiffel, the tower was completed in 1889 for the Paris Exposition. This steel monument was twice the height of any other building at the time.

Albert Einstein (1879–1955) German physicist who developed the theory of relativity, which states that space and motion are relative to each other instead of being absolute.

Elizabeth I (1533–1603) Protestant daughter of Henry VIII, Queen of England 1558–1603. During her long reign, the doctrines and services of the Church of England were defined and the Spanish Armada was defeated.

Enabling Act (1933) Emergency act passed by the *Reichstag* (German parliament) that helped transform Hitler from Germany's chancellor, or prime minister, into a dictator, following the suspicious burning of the *Reichstag* building and a suspension of civil liberties.

enclosure Long process of privatizing what had been public agricultural land in the eighteenth century that changed the nature of economic activity in England.

The *Encyclopedia* Joint venture of French *philosophe* writers, helmed by Denis Diderot (1713–1784), which proposed to summarize all modern knowledge.

Endeavor Ship of Captain James Cook, whose widely celebrated voyages to the South Pacific at the end of the eighteenth century supplied Europe with information about the plants, birds, landscapes, and people of this uncharted territory.

Friedrich Engels (1820–1895) German social and political philosopher who collaborated with Karl Marx on many publications.

English Navigation Act of 1651 Act stipulating that only English ships could carry goods between the mother country and its colonies.

Enlightenment Intellectual movement stressing natural laws and classifications in nature, in eighteenth-century Europe.

Epicureanism Greek philosophy that emphasized the individual, denied the existence of spiritual forces, and proposed that the highest good is pleasure.

Desiderius Erasmus (c. 1469–1536) Dutch-born scholar and social commentator who proclaimed his humanist views in lively treatises like *In Praise of Folly* and the *Colloquies*.

Estates-General French quasi-parliamentary body called in 1789 to deal with the financial problems that afflicted France at the time. It had not met since 1614.

Etruscans Non-Indo-European-speaking settlers of the Italian peninsula who dominated the region from the late Bronze Age until the rise of the Romans in the sixth century B.C.E.

Euclid Hellenistic mathematician whose book *Elements of Geometry* was the basis of modern geometry.

eugenics Term, meaning "good birth," referring to the project of "breeding" a superior human race. It was popularly championed by scientists, politicians, and social critics in the late nineteenth and early twentieth centuries.

Eurasia The combined area of Europe and Asia.

European Union (EU) An international political body that was organized after World War II to reconcile Germany and the rest of Europe as well as to forge closer industrial cooperation. Over time, member states of the EU have relinquished some of their sovereignty, and cooperation has evolved into a community with a single currency, the euro, and a common European parliament.

Exclusion Act of 1882 U.S. congressional act prohibiting nearly all immigration from China to the United States; fueled by animosity toward Chinese workers in the American West.

existentialism The philosophy that arose out of World War II and emphasized the human condition. Led by Jean Paul Sartre and Albert Camus, existentialists encouraged humans to take responsibility for their own decisions and dilemmas.

fall of the Bastille On July 14, 1789, the sans culottes, led by the electors of Paris, stormed the Bastille, an ancient fortress, in search of weapons to protect themselves from Louis XVI's troops rumored to be heading toward the city. The fall of the Bastille was the first popular revolt in the French Revolution.

Fascism The doctrine founded by Benito Mussolini. It emphasized three main ideas: statism ("nothing above the state, nothing outside the state, nothing against the state"), nationalism, and militarism.

Fascists Radical right-wing group of the disaffected that formed around Mussolini in 1919 and a few years later came to power in Italy.

February Revolution (1917) The first of two uprisings of the Russian Revolution, which led to the end of the Romanov dynasty.

Federal Deposit Insurance Corporation (FDIC) Created in 1933 to guarantee all bank deposits up to $2,000 as part of the New Deal in the United States.

Federalists Supporters of the ratification of the U.S. Constitution, which was written to replace the Articles of Confederation.

Federal Republic of Germany (1949–1990) Country formed of the areas occupied by the Allies after World War II. Also known as West Germany, this country experienced rapid demilitarization, democratization, and integration into the world economy.

Federal Reserve Act (1913) U.S. legislation that created a series of boards to monitor the supply and demand of the nation's money.

The *Feminine Mystique* Groundbreaking book by feminist Betty Friedan (b. 1921), which tried to define "femininity" and explored how women internalized those definitions.

Fertile Crescent An area of fertile land in what is now Syria, Israel, Turkey, eastern Iraq, and western Iran that was able to sustain settlements due to its wetter climate and abundant natural food resources. Some of the earliest known civilizations emerged there between 9000 and 4500 B.C.E.

feudalism A loose term reflecting the political and economic situation in eleventh- and twelfth-century Europe. In this system, lords were owed agricultural labor and military service by their serfs, and in turn owed allegiance to more powerful lords and kings.

First Crusade (1095–1099) Forces were sent by Pope Urban II to assist Byzantine emperor Alexius Comnenus in fighting Turkish forces in Anatolia. The struggle to recapture Jerusalem for western Christianity was eventually successful. This crusade prompted attacks against Jews throughout Europe and resulted in six subsequent military campaigns to the Holy Land.

GLOSSARY

First World War A total war from August 1914 to November 1918, involving the armies of Britain, France, and Russia (the Allies) against Germany, Austria-Hungary, and the Ottoman empire (the Central Powers). Italy joined the Allies in 1915, and the United States joined them in 1917, helping to tip the balance in favor of the Allies, who also drew upon the populations and material of their colonial possessions. Also known as the Great War.

Five-Year Plan Soviet effort launched under Stalin in 1928 to replace the market with a state-owned and state-managed economy in order to promote rapid economic development over a five-year period and thereby "catch and overtake" the leading capitalist countries. The First Five-Year Plan was followed by the Second Five-Year Plan (1933–1937), and so on, until the collapse of the Soviet Union in 1991.

Flagellants European social group that came into existence during the bubonic plague in the fourteenth century; they believed that the plague was caused by the wrath of God and chose to beat and mutilate themselves as a form of religious penance.

Franciscan order Order of monks established in 1209 by Saint Francis of Assisi (1182–1226); its members strove to imitate the life and example of Jesus.

Frankfurt Assembly An 1848 gathering of delegates from all German states that attempted to unify them into one nation. The liberal agenda and squabbling over whose plan for the nation was best led to the failure of the gathering.

Franz Ferdinand (1863–1914) Archduke of Austria and heir to the Austro-Hungarian empire; his assassination led to the beginning of World War I.

Frederick the Great (1740–1786) Prussian ruler who engaged the nobility in maintaining a strong military and bureaucracy, and led Prussian armies to notable military victories. He also encouraged Enlightenment rationalism and artistic endeavors.

French new wave A group of filmmakers in the 1950s and 1960s that emphasized naturalistic and unsentimental portrayals of ordinary life. Famous new wave directors included Francois Truffaut (1932–1984), Jean-Luc Godard (b. 1930), and Eric Rohmer (b. 1920).

French Revolution of 1830 The French popular revolt against King Charles's July Ordinances of 1830, which dissolved the French Chamber of Deputies and restricted suffrage to exclude almost everyone except the nobility. After several days of violence, Charles abdicated the throne and was replaced by a constitutional monarch, King Louis Philippe.

French Revolution of 1848 Brief uprising caused by economic grievances; it was violently quelled by the government.

Sigmund Freud (1865–1939) The Austrian physician who founded the discipline of psychoanalysis and suggested that human behavior was largely motivated by unconscious and irrational forces.

***Front de Libération Nationale* (FLN)/Algerian Revolutionary National Liberation Front** An anti-colonial, nationalist party that waged an eight-year war, beginning in 1954, against French troops for Algerian independence; the war forced nearly all of the 1 million French colonists to leave.

Galileo Galilei (1564–1642) Italian physicist and inventor. The implications of his ideas raised the ire of the Catholic Church, and he was forced to retract most of his findings.

Mohandas K. (Mahatma) Gandhi (1869–1948) The Indian leader who advocated nonviolent noncooperation and helped win home rule for India in 1947.

Giuseppe Garibaldi (1807–1882) Italian revolutionary leader who led the fight to free Sicily and Naples from the Habsburg empire; the lands were then peaceably annexed by Sardinia.

garrisons Military bases inside cities that were often used for political purposes, such as protecting the rulers and putting down domestic revolt or enforcing colonial rule.

Gaul The region of the Roman empire that is modern Belgium, Germany west of the Rhine, and France.

Gdansk shipyard Site of mass strikes in Poland that led to the formation in 1980 of the first independent trade union, Solidarity, in the Communist bloc.

Geneva Peace Conference (1954) International conference to restore peace in Korea and Indochina. The chief participants were the United States, the Soviet Union, Great Britain, France, the People's Republic of China, North Korea, South Korea, Vietnam, the Viet Minh party, Laos, and Cambodia. The conference resulted in the division of North and South Vietnam.

German Democratic Republic Nation founded from the Soviet zone of occupation of Germany after World War II; also known as East Germany.

German Social Democratic Party Founded in 1875, it was the most powerful Socialist party in Europe before 1917.

Gilgamesh The hero of the Sumerian epic, which was recorded in written form around 2000 B.C.E. Gilgamesh was a powerful ruler who, along with his friend Enkidu, battled monsters and gods and searched for immortality.

Girondins Liberal revolutionary group that supported the creation of a constitutional monarchy during the early stages of the French Revolution.

globalization The term used to describe political, social, and economic networks that span the globe. These global exchanges are not limited by nation states and often rely on new technologies, international laws, and economic imperatives.

Arthur de Gobineau (1816–1882) French writer whose pseudoscientific, racist ideology provided a rationale for European imperialism.

Gold Coast Name that European mariners and merchants gave to that part of West Equatorial Africa from which gold and slaves were exported. Originally controlled by the Portuguese, this area later became the British colony of the Gold Coast.

Gothic style Period of graceful architecture emerging after the Romanesque style in twelfth- and thirteenth-century France. The style is characterized by pointed arches, delicate decoration, and large windows.

Great Depression Period following the U.S. stock market crash on October 29, 1929, and ending in 1941 with America's entry into World War II.

great divide Refers to the division between economically developed nations and less developed nations.

Glossary

Great East Asia Co-Prosperity Sphere Term used by the Japanese during the 1930s and 1940s to refer to Hong Kong, Singapore, Malaya, Burma, and other states that they seized during their run for expansion.

Great Terror The systematic murder of nearly a million people and the deportation of another million and a half to labor camps by Stalin's regime during 1937 in an attempt to consolidate power and remove perceived enemies.

The Great War (1914–1918) World War I.

Greek Civil War (1821–1827) Conflict between Greek Christians and Muslim Ottomans.

Pope Gregory I (540?–604) Roman Catholic Pope 590–604. Used his political influence and theological teachings to separate the western Latin from the eastern Greek church. He also encouraged the Benedictine monastic movement and missionary expeditions.

Guerrillas Portuguese and Spanish peasant bands who resisted the revolutionary and expansion efforts of Napoleon; after the French word for war, *guerre*.

Guernica The Basque town bombed by German planes in April 1937 during the Spanish Civil War. It is also the subject of Pablo Picasso's famous painting from the same year.

guest workers Migrants looking for temporary employment.

guilds Professional organizations in commercial towns that regulated the business conditions and privileges of those practicing a particular craft.

gulag The vast system of forced labor camps under the Soviet regime; it originated in 1919 in a small monastery near the Arctic Circle and spread throughout the Soviet Union and to other Soviet-style socialist countries. Penal labor was required of both ordinary criminals and those accused of political crimes (counterrevolution, anti-Soviet agitation).

Gulf War (1991) Armed conflict between Iraq and a coalition of thirty-two nations, including the United States, Britain, Egypt, France, and Saudi Arabia. The seeds of the war were planted with Iraq's invasion of Kuwait on August 2, 1990.

gunpowder An explosive mixture of nitrates, sulfur, and charcoal that can be used in firearms. The use of gunpowder transformed warfare in the late middle ages and played a major role in the creation of European empires in Africa and the Americas.

Habsburg empire Ruling house of Austria, which once ruled the Netherlands, Spain, and Central Europe but came to settle in lands along the Danube River. It played a prominent role in European affairs for many centuries. In 1867, the Habsburg empire was reorganized into the Austro-Hungarian Dual Monarchy, and in 1918 it collapsed.

Hadith Sayings attributed to the Prophet Muhammad and his early converts. Used to guide the behavior of Muslim peoples.

Hagia Sophia The largest house of worship in all of Christendom, located in Constantinople and built by the emperor Justinian. When Constantinople fell to Ottoman forces in 1453, it was turned into a mosque.

Hajj The pilgrimage to Mecca; an obligation for Muslims.

Hammurabi The ruler of Babylon from 1792 to 1750 B.C.E. Hammurabi issued a collection of laws that were greatly influential in the Near East for centuries.

harem Secluded women's quarters in Muslim households.

Harlem Renaissance Cultural movement in the 1920s that was based in Harlem, a part of New York City where a large African American population resided. The movement gave voice to black novelists, poets, painters, and musicians, many of whom used their art to protest racial subordination; also referred to as the "New Negro Movement."

heliocentric The sun-centered view of the planetary system, which displaced the Earth from the center of the universe.

Henry VII (1491–1547) Oft-married English monarch who broke with the Roman Catholic church when the pope refused to grant him an annulment. The resulting modified version of Christianity became the Church of England, or Anglicanism.

Henry of Navarre (1553–1610) Crowned King Henry IV of France, he renounced his Protestantism but granted limited toleration to Huguenots (French Protestants) with the 1598 Edict of Nantes.

Prince Henry the Navigator (1394–1460) Portuguese noble who encouraged conquest of western Africa and trade in gold and slaves.

hero cults Important ancient Greek families would claim that an impressive Mycenean tomb was that of their own famous ancestor and would practice sacrifices and other observances to strengthen their claim. This devotion could extend to their followers, and eventually whole communities would identify with such local heroes.

Hiroshima Japanese port devastated by an atomic bomb on August 6, 1945.

Adolf Hitler (1889–1945) The author of *Mein Kampf* and leader of the Nazis. Hitler and his Nazi regime started World War II and orchestrated the systematic murder of over five million Jews.

Hittites An Indo-European-speaking people that migrated into Anatolia (now Turkey) around the beginning of the second millennium B.C.E.

Ho Chi Minh (1890–1969) The Vietnamese communist resistance leader who drove the French out of Vietnam and controlled North Vietnam after the Geneva Accords divided the region into four countries.

Holy Roman Empire The collection of lands in central and western Europe ruled over by the kings of Germany (and later Austria) from the twelfth century until 1806.

Holy Russia Name applied to Muscovy, and then to the Russian empire, by Slavic Eastern Orthodox clerics who were appalled by the Muslim conquest in 1453 of Constantinople (the capital of Byzantium and of Eastern Christianity), and who were hopeful that Russia would become the new protector of the faith.

home charges Fees India was forced to pay to Britain as its colonial master; these fees included interest on railroad loans, salaries to colonial officers, and the maintenance of imperial troops outside India.

Homo sapiens Term defined by Linnaeus in 1737 and commonly used to refer to fully modern human beings.

GLOSSARY

hoplite A Greek foot soldier armed with a spear or short sword and protected by a large round shield (a hopla). In battle, hoplites stood shoulder to shoulder in a close formation called a phalanx.

Huguenots French Protestants who endured severe persecution in the sixteenth and seventeenth centuries.

Human Comedy Masterpiece of French novelist Honoré de Balzac (1799–1850) that criticized materialist values.

humanism Medieval program of study built around the seven liberal arts: grammer, logic, rhetoric, arithmetic, music, geometry, and astronomy.

human rights The belief that all people have the right to legal equality, freedom of religion and speech, and the right to participate in government. Human rights laws prohibit torture, cruel punishment, and slavery.

Hundred Years' War (1337–1453) Long conflict, fought mostly on French soil, between England and France, centering on English claims to the throne of France.

Saddam Hussein (b. 1937) The former dictator of Iraq who invaded Iran in 1980 and started the eight-year-long Iran-Iraq War; invaded Kuwait in 1990, which caused the Gulf War of 1991; and was overthrown when the United States invaded Iraq in 2003. Involved in Iraqi politics since the mid-1960s, Hussein became the official head of state in 1979.

Il-khanate Mongol-founded dynasty in thirteenth-century Persia.

Imam Muslim religious leader and also a politico-religious descendant of Ali; believed by some to have a special relationship with Allah.

Imhotep The chief adviser to the Pharaoh Djoser, who ruled in the 27th century B.C.E. Often considered to be the first architect, Imhotep designed tombs and other structures to express the power of the Egyptian pharaohs.

Indian National Congress Formed in 1885, this political party was deeply committed to constitutional methods, industrialization, and cultural nationalism.

Indian Rebellion of 1857 The uprising began near Delhi, when the military disciplined a regiment of Indian soldiers employed by the British for refusing to use rifle cartridges greased with pork fat—unacceptable to either Hindus or Muslims. Rebels attacked law courts and burned tax rolls, protesting debt and corruption. The mutiny spread through large areas of northwest India before being violently suppressed by British troops.

Indo-Europeans A group of people that spoke variations of the same language and moved into the Near East and Mediterranean shortly after 2000 B.C.E.

indulgences Remissions of the penances owed by Catholics as part of the process by which their sins are forgiven.

Inkas The highly centralized South American empire that was toppled by the Spanish conquistador Francisco Pizarro in 1533.

Inquisition Tribunal of the Roman Catholic Church that aimed to enforce religious orthodoxy and conformity.

International Monetary Fund (IMF) Established in 1945 to promote the health of the world economy, the IMF is a specialized agency of the United Nations.

intifada Uprising in the Palestinian occupied territories from 1987 to 1993, in protest against the Israeli occupation and politics. The Oslo Agreement (1993) helped to reduce the tension between the two sides and the Intifada all but ceased by the end of 1993. In early 2000, the Intifada resumed.

Investiture Conflict A disagreement between Pope Gregory VII and Emperor Henry IV of Germany that tested the power of kings over church matters. After years of diplomatic and military hostility, it was settled by the Concordat of Worms in 1122.

invisible hand Described in Adam Smith's *The Wealth of Nations*, the idea that the operations of a free market would produce economic efficiency and economic benefits for all.

Irish home rule The late-nineteenth- and early-twentieth-century movement, led by Sinn Fein (established 1905), for Irish self-government.

Irish potato famine Period of agricultural blight from 1845 to 1849 whose devastating results prompted a mass emigration to America.

Iron Curtain Term coined by Winston Churchill in 1946 to refer to the division of Western Europe, under American influence, from Eastern Europe, under the domination of the Soviet Union.

Ivan the Great (1440–1505) Emperor of Russia who annexed neighboring territories and began Russia's career as a European power.

Jacobins Radical French political group that came into existence during the French Revolution, executed the French king, and sought to remake French culture.

Jacquerie Violent 1358 peasant uprising in northern France, incited by disease, war, and taxes.

James I (1566–1625) Monarch of Scotland and England from 1603 to 1625. He oversaw the English vernacular translation of the Bible known by his name.

Janissaries Corps of enslaved soldiers recruited as children from the Christian provinces of the Ottoman empire and brought up with intense loyalty to the Ottoman state and its sultan. The sultan used these forces to curb local autonomy and to serve as his personal bodyguards.

Jesuits Religious order founded in 1540 by Ignatius Loyola to counter the inroads of the Protestant Reformation; the Jesuits were active in politics, education, and missionary work.

Jihad A struggle and, if need be, a holy war toward the advancement of the cause of Islam.

Joan of Arc (c. 1412–1431) French teenager, supposedly divinely inspired, who led forces against the English during the Hundred Years' War. Burned at the stake for heresy by the English and later made a Catholic saint.

Justinian (527–565) Emperor of eastern Rome. Justinian codified Roman law in the Corpus Juris Civilis and tried to reunify the eastern and western halves of the old Roman empire.

***Das Kapital* (Capital)** The 1867 book by Karl Marx that outlined the theory behind historical materialism and attacked the socioeconomic inequities of capitalism. Mixing economic theory and revolutionary politics, the book became the preeminent socialist critique of capitalism.

Johannes Kepler (1571–1601) Mathematician and astronomer who elaborated on and corrected Copernicus's theory and is chiefly remembered for his discovery of the three laws of planetary motion that bear his name.

Keynesian Revolution Post-Depression economic ideas developed by the British economist John Maynard Keynes, wherein the state took a greater role in managing the economy, stimulating it by increasing the money supply and creating jobs.

KGB Soviet political police and spy agency, first formed as the Cheka not long after the Bolshevik coup in October 1917. It grew to more than 750,000 operatives with military rank by the 1980s.

Chingiz Khan (c. 1167–1227) Title taken by Mongol chief Temujin meaning "The Oceanic Ruler." Began dynasty that conquered much of southern Asia.

Khanate Major political unit of the vast Mongol empire. There were four Khanates, including the Yuan empire in China, forged by Chingiz Khan's grandson Kubilai in the 13th century.

Nikita Khrushchev (1894–1971) Leader of the Soviet Union during the Cuban Missile Crisis, Khrushchev had quickly reached power soon after Stalin's death in 1953. His reforms and criticisms of the excesses of the Stalin regime led to his fall from power in 1964.

Kremlin Once synonymous with the Soviet government, it refers to Moscow's walled city center.

Kristallnacht The Nazi destruction of seventy-five hundred Jewish stores and two hundred synagogues on November 9, 1938.

kulaks Originally a pejorative term used to designate better-off peasants, it was used in the late 1920s and early 1930s to refer to any peasant, rich or poor, perceived as an opponent of the Soviet regime. Russian for "fist."

Labour Party Founded in Britain in 1900, this party represented workers and was based on socialist principles.

League of Nations International organization founded after World War I to solve international disputes through arbitration; it was dissolved in 1946 and transferred its assets to the United Nations.

Vladimir Lenin (1870–1924) Leader of the Bolshevik Revolution in Russia (1917) and the first leader of the Soviet Union.

Leonardo da Vinci (1452–1519) The ultimate Renaissance man, Leonardo was a painter, architect, musician, mathematician, engineer, and inventor. He set up an artist's shop in Florence by the time he was twenty-five and gained the patronage of the Medici ruler of the city, Lorenzo the Magnificent.

Leopold II (1835–1909) Belgian king who sponsored colonizing expeditions into Africa.

Leviathan A book by Thomas Hobbes (1588–1679) that recommended a ruler have unrestricted power.

liberalism Political and social theory that advocates representative government, free trade, and freedom of speech and religion.

lithograph Art form that involves putting writing or design on stone and producing printed impressions.

Long March (1934–1935) Trek of over 10,000 kilometers by Mao Zedong and his Communist followers to establish a new base of operations.

lord Privileged landowner who exercised authority over the people who lived on his land.

lost generation Refers to the 17 million former members of the Red Guard and other Chinese youth who were denied education from the late 1960s to the mid-1970s as part of the Chinese government's attempt to forestall political disruptions.

Louis XIV (1638–1715) The "Sun King," known for his opulent court and absolutist political style.

Louis XVI (1754–1793) Well-meaning but ineffectual king of France, finally deposed and executed with his family by revolutionaries.

Luftwaffe Literally "air weapon," this is the name of the German air force, which was founded during World War I, disbanded in 1945, and reestablished when West Germany joined NATO in 1950.

Lusitania The passenger liner that was secretly carrying war supplies and was sunk by a German U-boat (submarine) on May 7, 1915.

Martin Luther (1483–1546) A German monk who led the Reformation movement. At the center of his ideas is the doctrine, "justification by faith alone," which challenged many of the medieval practices of the Catholic Church and led to the religious wars between Protestants and Catholics.

Lutheranism Branch of Protestantism that followed Martin Luther's (1483–1546) rejection of the Roman Catholic "doctrine of works."

lycées System of high schools instituted by Napoleon as part of his domestic reform campaign.

madrassas Muslim schools devoted to the study of the Quran and Islam.

Magna Carta "Great Charter" of 1215 signed by King John of England, which limited the king's fiscal powers and is seen as a landmark in the political evolution of the West.

Moses Maimonides (1135–1204) Spanish-born Jewish scholar, physician, and scriptural commentator.

mandate system Administered by the League of Nations after the Treaty of Versailles, the mandate system legitimized Europe's dominance of territories in the Middle East, Africa, and the Pacific. Mandate territories were divided into groups based on location and their "level of development."

Nelson Mandela (b. 1918) The South African opponent of *apartheid* who led the African National Congress and was imprisoned from 1962 until 1990. After his release from prison, he worked with Prime Minister Frederik Willem De Klerk to establish majority rule. Mandela became the first black president of South Africa in 1994.

Manhattan Project The secret U.S. government research project in Los Alamos, New Mexico, to develop the first nuclear bomb. The first test of a nuclear bomb was near Los Alamos on July 16, 1945.

manorialism System common to England, northern France, and Germany in the Middle Ages of communal peasant farming under the protection of a landholding lord.

GLOSSARY

Mao Zedong (1893–1976) The leader of the Chinese Revolution who defeated the Nationalists in 1949 and established the Communist regime in China.

Marshall Plan Economic aid package given to Europe after World War II in hopes of a rapid period of reconstruction and economic gain and to secure the countries from a Communist takeover.

Master Eckhart (c. 1260–1327) Dominican monk who preached an introspective and charismatic version of Christian piety.

Karl Marx (1818–1883) German philosopher and economist who believed that a revolution of the working classes would overthrow the capitalist order and create a classless society. Author of *Das Kapital* and *The Communist Manifesto*.

Maxim gun Invented in 1885 by an American, Hiram Maxim, the Maxim gun was the first portable machine gun. Quickly adopted by the majority of European armies and capable of firing 500 rounds per minute, it played a major role in the imperial conquests of the African continent.

Mayans Native American peoples whose culturally and politically sophisticated empire encompassed lands in present-day Mexico and Guatemala.

Giuseppe Mazzini (1805–1872) Founder of Young Italy and an ideological leader of the Italian Nationalist movement.

Mecca Major commercial city of the Arabian peninsula in the sixth century C.E., at which time the founder of Islam, Muhammad, was born and achieved prominence. From the earliest days of the spread of Islam, the city was the destination of the chief religious pilgrimage for Muslims, and it is now considered the holiest site in the Islamic world.

Medici Dynasty of Florentine bankers and politicians known for their patronage of the arts.

Meiji empire Empire created under the leadership of Mutsuhito, emperor of Japan from 1868 until 1912. During the Meiji period Japan became a world industrial and naval power.

Menander (342 B.C.E.?–292 B.C.E.) Ancient Greek dramatist who wrote over 100 plays, many of which were standards of Western literature for hundreds of years. Only one complete surviving play is known, *The Grouch*, which was rediscovered in 1957.

mercantilism A popular Western belief between 1600 and 1800 that a country's wealth and power was based on a favorable balance of trade (more exports and fewer imports) and the accumulation of precious metals.

Michelangelo (1475–1564) Virtuoso artist, best known for the Sistine Chapel ceiling in Rome and his sculptures *David* and *Pieta*.

John Stuart Mill (1806–1873) English radical philosopher whose writings advocated aspects of socialism and civil liberties.

Slobodan Milosevic (b. 1941) The Serbian nationalist politician who took control of the Serb government and orchestrated the genocide of thousands of Croatians, Bosnian Muslims, Albanians, and Kosovars. After ten years of war, he was ousted by a popular revolt in 2000.

Minoans A sea empire that flourished on Crete and in the Aegean Basin from 1900 B.C.E. until the middle of the second millennium B.C.E.

modernism The series of artistic movements, manifestos, innovations, and experiments that redefined art in the first half of the twentieth century. Modernism rejected history and tradition in favor of expressive and experimental freedom.

Michel de Montaigne (1533–1592) French philosopher known for his *Essays*.

mosque Place of worship for the people of Islam.

Wolfgang Amadeus Mozart (1756–1791) Austrian child prodigy and composer of instrumental music and operas.

Muhammad (570–632 C.E.) The founder of Islam, he claimed to be the prophet whom God (Allah) had chosen for his final revelation to mankind.

Mullahs Iranian religious leaders who led the opposition movement against the shah and denounced the depravity of late-twentieth-century American materialism and secularism.

multinational corporations Corporations based in many different countries that have global investment, trading, and distribution goals.

Muslim Brotherhood Egyptian organization founded in 1938 by Hassan al-Banna. It attacked liberal democracy as a façade for middle-class, business, and landowning interests and fought for a return to a purified form of Islam.

Muslim League National Muslim party of India.

Benito Mussolini (1883–1945) The Italian founder of the Fascist party who came to power in Italy in 1922 and allied himself with Hitler and the Nazis during World War II.

Mutiny of 1857 Uprising of Indian soldiers against the ruling British, sometimes called the Sepoy Rebellion.

Mycenaens The ancient Greek civilization that settled in Greece during the second millennium B.C.E. and organized around powerful citadels.

Nagasaki Second Japanese city on which the United States dropped an atomic bomb. The attack took place on August 9, 1945; the Japanese surrendered shortly thereafter, ending World War II.

Napoleonic Code Legal code drafted by Napoleon in 1804; it distilled different legal traditions to create one uniform law. The code confirmed the abolition of feudal privileges of all kinds and set the conditions for exercising property rights.

National Assembly of France Governing body of France that succeeded the Estates-General in 1789 during the French Revolution. It was composed of, and defined by, the delegates of the Third Estate.

National Association for the Advancement of Colored People (NAACP) Founded in 1910, this U.S. civil rights organization was dedicated to ending inequality and segregation for black Americans.

nationalism Movement to unify a country based on a people's common history and social traditions.

NATO The North Atlantic Treaty Organization, which was a 1949 agreement between the United States, Canada, Great Britain, and 8 European countries that declared that an armed attack against any one of the members would be regarded as an attack against all. Other European countries have since joined.

Glossary

"navvies" Slang for laborers who built railroads and canals.

Nazi Party Founded in the early 1920s, the National Socialist German Workers' Party (NDSAP) gained control over Germany under the leadership of Adolf Hitler in 1933 and continued in power until Germany was defeated in 1945.

Nazism The National Socialist Workers Party led by Adolf Hitler which advocated a violent anti-Semitic, anti-Marxist, pan-German ideology.

Nefertiti The wife of Akhenaten, the fourteenth-century B.C.E. Egyptian pharaoh.

Neolithic The "New" Stone Age, which began around 11,000 B.C.E., saw new technological and social developments, including managed food production, the beginnings of semipermanent and permanent settlements, and the rapid intensification of trade.

New Deal President Franklin Delano Roosevelt's package of government reforms that were enacted during the 1930s to provide jobs for the unemployed, social welfare programs for the poor, and security to the financial markets.

new imperialism Expansion of colonial power by Western European nations, especially in Asia, in the last three decades of the nineteenth century.

Isaac Newton (1642–1727) One of the foremost scientists of all time, Newton was an English mathematician and physicist; he is noted for his development of calculus, work on the properties of light, and theory of gravitation.

New World silver The most lucrative export from the Spanish colonies in Central and South America was silver. The massive infusion of New World Silver into the sixteenth-century European economy accelerated inflation and eventually caused the collapse of the Spanish economy and widespread misery for the rest of Europe's poorest inhabitants who could not afford the rising prices of goods.

Nicholas I (1796–1855) Russian tsar who executed the leaders of the 1825 December Revolution and pursued an absolutist reign.

Tsar Nicholas II (1868–1918) The last Russian tsar, who abdicated the throne in 1917. He and his family were executed by the Bolsheviks on July 17, 1918.

Nicomachean Ethics The treatise on moral philosophy by Aristotle, which teaches that the highest good consists of the harmonious functioning of the individual human mind and body.

Friedrich Nietzsche (1844–1900) The German philosopher who denied the possibility of knowing absolute "truth" or "reality," since all knowledge comes filtered through linguistic, scientific, or artistic systems of representation. He also criticized Judeo-Christian morality for instilling a repressive conformity that drained civilization of its vitality.

Non-governmental organizations (NGOs) Private organizations like the Red Cross that play a large role in international affairs.

North American Free Trade Agreement (NAFTA) Treaty negotiated in the early 1990s to promote free trade among Canada, the United States, and Mexico.

Novum Organum Work by English statesman and scientist Francis Bacon (1561–1626) that advanced a philosophy of study through observation.

October Revolution The October 1917 uprising in Russia led by Lenin and the Bolsheviks to overthrow the provisional Russian government, withdraw Russia from the First World War, and establish a one-party Bolshevik state.

OPEC (Organization of Petroleum Exporting Countries) Organization created in 1960 by oil-producing countries in the Middle East, South America, and Africa to regulate the production and pricing of crude oil.

Operation Barbarossa The codename for Hitler's invasion of the Soviet Union.

Opium Wars (1839–1842) War fought between the British and Qing China to protect British trade in opium; resulted in the ceding of Hong Kong to the British.

oracle at Delphi Dating to 1400 B.C.E., the oracle was the most important shrine in ancient Greece. A priestess of Apollo who attended the shrine was believed to be able to predict the future. The shrine ceased to function in the fourth century C.E.

Ottoman slavery Social system of using slave labor for domestic, administrative, and military work that permitted social advancement and religious diversity within the Muslim empire.

Pan-African Conference 1900 assembly in London which sought to draw attention to the sovereignty of African people and their mistreatment by colonial powers.

pan-Slavism Cultural movement that sought to unite native Slavic peoples within the Russian and Habsburg empires.

papal Of, relating to, or issued by a pope.

Patria Latin, meaning "fatherland."

patricians The uppermost elite class of ancient Rome.

Paul One of the twelve apostles of Jesus, Paul spread Christianity throughout the Near East and Greece.

Peace of Paris The 1919 Paris Peace Conference established the terms to end World War I. Great Britain, France, Italy, and the United States signed five treaties with each of the defeated nations: Germany, Austria, Hungary, Turkey, and Bulgaria. The settlement is notable for the territory that Germany had to give up, including large parts of Prussia to the new state of Poland, and Alsace and Lorraine to France; the disarming of Germany; and the "war guilt" provision, which required Germany and its allies to pay massive reparations to the victors.

Pearl Harbor The American Navy base in Hawaii that was bombed by the Japanese on December 7, 1941, which brought the United States into World War II.

Peloponnesian War The ancient Greek war between Sparta and Athens that began in 431 B.C.E. and ended with the destruction of the Athenian fleet in 404 B.C.E.

People's Charter An action of the Chartist Movement (1839–1848); between 1839 and 1842 over 3 million British signed this document calling for universal suffrage for adult males, the secret ballot, electoral districts, and annual parliamentary elections.

perestroika Introduced by Soviet leader Mikhail Gorbachev in June 1987, *Perestroika* was the name given to economic and political reforms begun earlier in his tenure. It restructured the state bureaucracy, reduced the privileges of the political elite, and instituted a shift from the centrally planned economy to a mixed economy, combining planning with the operation of market forces.

GLOSSARY

Pericles The fifth-century B.C.E. Athenian leader who served as strategos for thirty years and pushed through reforms to make Athens more democratic by giving every citizen the right to propose and amend legislation and making it easier for citizens to participate in the assembly and the great appeals court of Athens by paying an average day's wage for attendance.

Peterloo Massacre (1819) The killing of 11 and wounding of 460 following a peaceful demonstration for political reform by workers in Manchester, England.

Peter the Great (1672–1725) Energetic tsar who transformed Russia into a leading European country by centralizing government, modernizing the army, creating a navy, and reforming education and the economy.

Francesco Petrarch (1304–1374) Italian scholar and writer who revived interest in classical writing styles and was famed for his love sonnets.

Pharisees A group of Jewish teachers and preachers that emerged in the third century B.C.E. and insisted that all of Yahweh's (God's) commandments were binding on all Jews.

Philip II (382–336 B.C.E.) The Macedonian king who consolidated the southern Balkans and the Greek city-states; he was the father of Alexander.

Phoenicians The semitic-speaking residents of present-day Lebanon from around 1200 to 800 B.C.E. The Phoenician cities were centers for trade throughout the Mediterranean.

Plato's *Republic* The first systematic treatment of political philosophy ever written, it argued for an elitist state in which most people would be governed by intellectually superior "philosopher-kings."

plebians The citizen population of ancient Rome that included farmers, merchants, and the urban poor; plebians comprised the majority of the population.

plebiscite A common tool of authoritarian leaders where they put a question directly to popular vote. This allows the head of state to bypass politicians or legislative bodies who might disagree with him—as well as permitting local officials to tamper with ballot boxes. For example, in 1802, Napoleon was proclaimed consul for life by a plebiscite.

Plotinus (204–270 C.E.) The neo-Platonist philosopher who taught that everything that exists proceeds from the divine and that the highest goal of life should be the mystic reunion of the soul with the divine, which can be achieved through contemplation and asceticism.

polis One of the major political innovations of the ancient Greeks was the Polis, or city-state. They were independent social and political structures, organized around an urban center, containing markets, meeting places, and a temple; they controlled a limited amount of the surrounding territory.

Marco Polo (1254–1324) Venetian merchant who traveled through Asia for twenty years and published his observations in a widely read memoir, *Travels*.

Populists Members of a political movement that supported U.S. farmers in late nineteenth-century America. The term is often used generically to refer to political groups who appeal to the mass of the population.

potato famine (1845–1850) Severe famine in Ireland that led to the migration of large numbers of Irish to the United States.

Prague Spring A period of political liberalization in Czechoslovakia between January and August 1968 that was initiated by Alexander Dubĉek, the Czech leader. This period of expanding freedom and openness in this Eastern bloc nation ended on August 20, when the USSR and Warsaw Pact countries invaded with 200,000 troops and 5,000 tanks.

The Praise of Folly 1511 satire by Erasmus that attacked the corruption of the papacy.

pre-Socratics A group of philosophers on the Greek island of Miletus, including Thales, Anaximander, and Anaximenes, who raised questions about the relationship between the natural world, the gods, and humans, and formulated rational theories to explain the physical universe they observed.

Primitivism Movement in Western art forms in the late nineteenth and early twentieth centuries that used the so-called primitive art forms of Africa, Oceania, and pre-Columbian America to inspire a break with the established art world.

The Prince Influential treatise by Niccolo Machiavelli (1469–1527) that attempts to lay out methods to secure and maintain political power.

Protestantism Division of Christianity that emerged in sixteenth-century western Europe at the time of the Reformation. It focused on individual spiritual needs and rejected the social authority of the papacy and the Catholic clergy.

Ptolemy (c. 85–165 C.E.) One of the most influential ancient Greeks; he was a leading astronomer, mathematician, and geographer who lived his entire life in Alexandria and helped to transform that city into a center of scientific study and scholarship.

puppet states Governments that have little power in the international arena and follow the dictates of their more powerful neighbors or patrons.

Puritans Seventeenth-century reform group of the Church of England; also known as dissenters or nonconformists.

Qur'an (often ***Koran***) Islam's holy book, comprised of Allah's revelations.

Sayyid Qutb (1906–1966) The Egyptian critic who became one of the most important intellectual leaders of the Muslim Brotherhood and whose writings are often cited as philosophical inspiration for Osama bin Laden and other Islamic radicals.

François Rabelais (c. 1494?–1553) French humanist satirist best known for his crudely comic *Gargantua and Pantagruel*, in which he espouses the "eat, drink, and be merry" lifestyle. Originally a novice in the Franciscan order, later a Benedictine monk who left the order to study medicine, Rabelais spent time in hiding for fear of being labeled a heretic, and some of his books were banned.

radicals Widely used term in nineteenth-century Europe that referred to those individuals and political organizations that favored the total reconfiguration of Europe's old state system.

Raj Term referring to the British crown's administration of India following the end of the East India Company's rule after the Indian Mutiny of 1857.

Ramadan Ninth month of the Muslim year, during which all Muslims must fast during daylight hours.

Raphael (1483–1520) Italian painter noted for his warmly human treatment of religious subjects, particularly his Madonnas and large-figure compositions in the Vatican in Rome.

realism Artistic and literary style which sought to portray common situations as they would appear in reality.

Realpolitik Political strategy advancing power for its own sake.

reason According to thinkers like Descartes, reason is a subjective faculty, or unaided ability, to form concepts.

Rebellion of 1857 Indian rebellion against the English East India Company to bring religious purification, an egalitarian society, and local and communal solidarity without the interference of British rule.

Reds The Bolsheviks.

Reformation Religious and political movement in sixteenth-century Europe that led to the breakaway of Protestant groups from the Catholic Church; notable figures include Martin Luther and John Calvin.

Reich A term for the German state. The first Reich corresponded to the Holy Roman Empire (9th century to 1806), the second Reich was from 1871 to 1919, and the third Reich lasted from 1933 through May 1945.

Reign of Terror Campaign at the height of the French Revolution (1793–1794) in which violence, including systematic executions of opponents of the Revolution, was used to purge France of its "enemies" and to extend the Revolution beyond its borders; radicals executed as many as 40,000 persons who were judged enemies of the state.

Religious Peace of Augsburg 1555 settlement between factions within the Holy Roman Empire that stated a territory would follow the religion of its ruler, whether Catholic or Protestant.

Renaissance Term meaning "rebirth" that historians use to refer to the expanded cultural production of European nations between 1300 and 1600.

Restoration period (1815–1848) European movement after the defeat of Napoleon to restore Europe to its pre-French revolutionary status and to prevent radical movements from arising.

Richard II (1367–1400) King of England (r. 1377–1399), chiefly remembered for his successful resolution of the Peasants' Rebellion (1381) and as a vacillating, yet tyrannical monarch. He was deposed by his cousin Henry Bolingbroke (Henry IV) and assassinated.

Cardinal Richelieu (1585–1642) First minister to French King Louis XIII, who centralized political power and deprived the Huguenots of many rights.

Rights of Man A declaration by the French National Assembly in 1789 that declared property to be a natural right, along with liberty, security, and "resistance to oppression." It declared freedom of speech, religious toleration, and liberty of the press inviolable. All citizens were to be treated equally before the law. No one was to be imprisoned or punished without due process of law. Sovereignty resided in the people, who could depose officers of the government if they abused their powers.

Rembrandt Van Rijn (1606–1669) A Dutch painter famous for his portraits, Biblical scenes, and imaginative experiments with light and shading.

Romanticism Beginning in Germany and England in the late 18th century and continuing up to the end of the 19th century, a movement in art, music, and literature that countered the rationalism of the Enlightenment by stressing a highly emotional response to nature.

Jean-Jacques Rousseau (1718–1778) Philosopher and radical political theorist whose *Social Contract* attacked privilege and inequality. One of the primary principles of Rousseau's political philosophy is that politics and morality should not be separated.

Russification Programs designed to assimilate people of over 146 dialects into the Russian empire by the tsars in the late 19th century.

Rwanda A former Belgian colony in central Africa that has been torn by ethnic violence between the Hutus and the Tutsis since before the country's independence in 1962.

Saint Bartholomew's Day Massacre Massacre of French Protestants (Huguenots) by Catholic crowds that began in Paris on August 24, 1572, spreading to other parts of France and continuing into October of that year. More than 70,000 were killed.

St. Domingue Former French Caribbean colony and site of a slave rebellion in 1791, which embroiled English and French forces until 1804, when St. Domingue was declared the independent nation of Haiti.

salons Informal gatherings of intellectuals and aristocrats that allowed discourse about Enlightenment ideas.

Santa Sophia The Byzantine church in Constantinople, constructed by emperor Justinian I in the sixth century, and famous for its dome, which rested on the keystones of four great arches.

Sappho (c. 620–c. 550 B.C.E.) One of the most famous Greek lyric poets, she wrote beautiful poetry about romantic longing and sexual lust, sometimes about men, but more often about women.

Sargon (r. 2334–2279 B.C.E.) The Akkadian leader who unified Mesopotamia.

Schlieffen Plan Devised by Count Alfred von Schlieffen in 1905 and put into operation on August 2, 1914, the Schlieffen Plan required France to be attacked first through Belgium and a quick victory to be secured so that the German army could fight Russia on the Eastern Front.

scientific societies Organizations that emerged in the seventeenth century to promote the improvement of scientific knowledge, experiments, and collaboration by scientists and philosophers.

Scramble for Africa European rush to colonize parts of Africa at the end of the nineteenth century.

second industrial revolution The technological developments in the last third of the nineteenth century, which included new techniques for refining and producing steel; increased availability of electricity for industrial, commercial, and domestic use; advances in chemical manufacturing; and the creation of the internal combustion engine.

Second World Term invented during the cold war to refer to the Communist countries, as opposed to the West (or First World) and the former colonies (or Third World).

Second World War Worldwide war that began in September 1939 in Europe, and even earlier in Asia (1930s), and that pitted Britain, the United States, and especially the Soviet Union (the Allies) against Nazi Germany, Italy, and Japan (the Axis).

GLOSSARY

A20

Seleucus (d. 280 B.C.E.) The Macedonian general who ruled the Asian territory of Alexander the Great's empire and founded Greek colonies such as Antioch and Selsucia.

Semitic The Semitic language family has the longest recorded history of any linguistic group and is the root language for most of the languages of the Middle and Near East. Ancient Semitic languages include the language of the ancient Babylonians and Assyrians, Phoenician, the classical form of Hebrew, early dialects of Aramaic, and the classical Arabic of the *Quran*.

sepoys Hindu and Muslim recruits of the East India Company's military force.

serfdom Slavery-like system of customs and laws whereby peasants were kept poor and stationary by their manor lords; it had spread throughout the West by the 10th century and its peak was the Middle Ages.

Seven Years War (1756–1763) Worldwide war that ended when Prussia defeated Austria, establishing itself as a European power, and when Britain gained control of India and many of France's colonies through the Treaty of Paris. It is known as the French and Indian War in the United States.

Shah Traditional title of Persian rulers.

William Shakespeare (1564–1616) The greatest Elizabethan playwright, Shakespeare worked as actor before becoming a dramatist. The author of *Hamlet, King Lear,* and *Much Ado About Nothing* wrote nearly 40 plays and over 150 sonnets.

Shiism One of the two main branches of Islam. Shiites recognize Ali, the fourth caliph, and his descendants as rightful rulers of the Islamic world; practiced in the Safavid empire.

Shiites An often-persecuted minority religious party within Islam that insists only descendants of Ali can have any authority over the Muslim community. Today, Shiites rule Iran and are numerous in Iraq but make up only 10 percent of the worldwide population of Islam.

Silicon Valley Valley between California's San Francisco and San Jose, known for its innovative computer and high-technology industry.

Sinn Féin The Irish revolutionary organization that formed in 1900 to fight for Irish independence.

Sino-Japanese War (1894–1895) Conflict over the control of Korea in which China was forced to cede the province of Taiwan to Japan.

Adam Smith (1723–1790) Scottish economist and philosopher who proposed that individual self-interest naturally promoted a healthy national economy. He became famous for his influential book, *The Wealth of Nations* (1776).

Social Darwinism Belief that Charles Darwin's theory of natural selection (evolution) was applicable to human societies and justified the right of the ruling classes or countries to dominate the weak.

social democracy The belief that democracy and social welfare go hand in hand, and that diminishing the sharp inequalities of class society is crucial to fortifying democratic culture.

socialism Political ideology that calls for a classless society with collective ownership of all property.

Social Security Act (1935) New Deal act that instituted old-age pensions and insurance for the unemployed in the United States.

the Social Question In the wake of the Industrial Revolution and rapid urbanization, topics such as criminality, water supply, sewers, prostitution, tuberculosis and cholera, alcoholism, wet nursing, wages, and unemployment were studied by political leaders, social scientists, and public health officials throughout Europe and collectively referred to as the "Social Question." Reformers and politicians believed that these issues needed to be addressed to avoid popular revolts in Europe's cities.

Society of Jesus Also called the Jesuit order, a group of priests influenced by military discipline. The society was founded by Saint Ignatius of Loyola (1491–1556) and is still very active in the field of education.

Socrates (469–399 B.C.E.) The ancient Greek philosopher who emphasized the reexamination of all inherited assumptions and tried to base his philosophical speculations on sound definitions of words. He also wished to advance to a new system of truth by examining ethics rather than by studying the physical world.

Solidarity The communist bloc's first independent trade union; it was established in Poland at the Gdansk shipyard in 1980.

Solon (d. 559 B.C.E.) Elected archon in 594 B.C.E., this ancient Greek aristocrat enacted a series of political and economic reforms that made Athenian democracy possible.

Aleksandr Solzhenitsyn (b. 1918) This Soviet novelist was a critic of the Soviet regime and wrote *The Gulag Archipelago*, which was published in 1974.

Sophists Ancient Greek professional teachers who taught that sense perception was the source of all knowledge and that only particular truths could be valid for the individual knower.

South African War (1899–1902) Often called the Boer War, this conflict between the British and Dutch colonists of South Africa resulted in bringing two Afrikaner republics under the control of the British.

Soviet bloc International alliance that included the East European countries of the Warsaw Pact as well as the Soviet Union, but also came to include Cuba.

Spanish-American War (1898) War between the United States and Spain in Cuba, Puerto Rico, and the Philippines. It ended with a treaty in which the United States took over the Philippines, Guam, and Puerto Rico; Cuba won partial independence.

Spanish Armada Supposedly invincible fleet of warships sent against England by Philip II of Spain in 1588, but routed by the English and bad weather in the English Channel.

Spartiate A full citizen of Sparta who was a professional soldier of the hoplite phalanx.

spinning jenny Invention of James Hargreaves (c. 1720–1774) that revolutionized the British textile industry.

S.S. (*Schutzstaffel*) Formed in 1925 to serve as Hitler's personal security force and to guard Nazi party (NDSAP) meetings, the SS were notorious for their participation in carrying out Nazi policies.

Joseph Stalin (1879–1953) The Bolshevik leader who succeeded Lenin as the leader of the Soviet Union in 1924 and ruled until his death.

Strategic Defense Initiative (Stars Wars) Master plan initiated by President Ronald Reagan that envisioned the deployment of satellites and space missiles to insulate the United States from nuclear bombs missiles.

Stoicism The ancient Greek and Roman philosophy that held that the cosmos is an ordered whole in which all contradictions are resolved for ultimate good. Everything that happens is rigidly determined in accordance with rational purpose, and no individual is master of his or her fate. Founded in the fourth century B.C.E. and still popular well into the fifth century C.E.

Suez Canal Built in 1869 across the Isthmus of Suez to connect the Mediterranean Sea with the Red Sea and to lower the costs of international trade.

Sufism Emotional and mystical form of Islam that appealed to the common people.

sultan An Islamic political leader. In the Ottoman empire, the sultan combined a warrior ethos with an unwavering devotion to Islam.

Sumerians The civilization and people that arose in southern Mesopotamia (modern Iraq and Kuwait) around 4000 B.C.E. and developed one of the first written languages.

Sunnis Orthodox Islam, as opposed to Shiite Islam.

supranational organizations International organizations such as NGOs, the World Bank, and the IMF.

survival of the fittest A main concept of Charles Darwin's theory of natural selection (evolution), which holds that as animal populations grow and resources become scarce, a struggle for existence arises, the outcome of which is that only the "fittest" survive.

sweatshops Textile factories with poor pay and work conditions.

Syndicalism Late-nineteenth-century organization of workplace associations that included unskilled labor.

tabula rasa Term used by John Locke (1632–1704) to describe man's mind before he acquired ideas as a result of experience; Latin for "clean slate."

Testament of Youth The memoir by Vera Brittain about the home front and the changing social norms during World War I.

tetrarchy Diocletian's political reform, which divided the Roman empire into two halves ruled by two rulers and two lieutenants.

Third Estate Delegates from the common class to the Estates General, the French legislature, whose refusal to capitulate to the nobility and clergy in 1789 led to the Revolution.

Third Reich The German state from 1933 to 1945 under Adolf Hitler and the Nazi party.

Third World Nations—mostly in Asia, Latin America, and Africa—that are not highly industrialized and developed.

Thirty Years' War (1618–1648) Beginning as a conflict between Protestants and Catholics in Germany, it escalated into a general European war fought in Germany by Sweden, France, and the Holy Roman Empire.

The Three Estates Eighteenth-century French society was divided into three estates. An individual's status determined his or her legal rights, taxes, and so on. The First Estate was the clergy; the Second was the nobility; and the Third Estate included everyone from wealthy merchants to poor peasants.

Tiananmen Square Largest public square in the world, located in Beijing, the site of the Chinese pro-democracy movement in 1989 that resulted in the killing of as many as 1,000 protesters by the Chinese army.

Timur the Lame (1336–1405) Mongol ruler who was the last leader of the Khans' south Asian empire. Also known as Tamerlane.

total war All-out war involving civilian populations as well as military forces, often used in reference to World War II.

Treaty of Brest-Litovsk (1918) Separate peace between imperial Germany and the new Bolshevik regime in Russia. The treaty acknowledged the German victory on the Eastern Front and withdrew Russia from the war.

Treaty of Nanjing (1842) Treaty between China and Britain following the Opium War; it called for indemnities, the opening of new ports, and the cession of Hong Kong to the British.

Treaty of Utrecht (1713) Resolution to the War of Spanish Succession that redistributed territory among the warring nations of Europe and encouraged England's colonial conquests.

Treaty of Versailles Signed on June 28, 1919, this peace settlement ended World War I and required Germany to surrender a large part of its most valuable territories and to pay huge reparations to the Allies.

trench warfare The twenty-five thousand miles of holes and ditches that stretched across the Western Front during World War I and where most of the fighting took place.

Triangular trade The eighteenth-century commercial Atlantic shipping pattern that took rum from New England to Africa, traded it for slaves taken to the West Indies, and brought sugar back to New England to be processed into rum.

Tripartite Pact (1940) A pact that stated that the countries of Germany, Italy, and Japan would act together in all future military ventures.

Triple Entente Alliance developed before World War I that eventually included Britain, France, and Russia.

Truman Doctrine (1947) Declaration promising U.S. economic and military intervention, whenever and wherever needed, for the sake of preventing further communist expansion.

Truth and Reconciliation Commission Quasi-judicial body established after the overthrow of the apartheid system in South Africa and the election of Nelson Mandela as the country's first black president in 1994. The commission was to take evidence about the crimes committed during the apartheid years. Those who showed remorse could appeal for clemency. The South African leaders believed that an airing of the grievances from this period would promote racial harmony and reconciliation.

tsar Russian translation, similar to the German *kaiser*, of the Roman title "caesar" (emperor), a title claimed by the rulers of medieval Muscovy and then the Russian empire.

Mary Tudor (1516–1558) Catholic daughter of Henry VIII who reinstituted Catholicism in England when she acceded to the throne; she was called "Bloody Mary" for her violent suppression of Protestants during her five-year reign.

Two Treatises on Government Published in 1690, this work by John Locke (1632–1704) defended humans' right to freedom against absolutist ideas and served as one of the underpinnings of the U.S. Constitution.

GLOSSARY

A22

Ubaid This culture flourished in Mesopotamia between 5500 and 4000 B.C.E., characterized by large village settlements and the first temples built in that area. A precursor to the Sumerians and the development of "urban" civilizations.

UFA The German film company that produced films by expressionist directors like F. W. Murnau and Fritz Lang during the 1920s. Under Hitler, it was controlled by the state and began turning out Nazi propaganda.

Universal Declaration of Human Rights (1948) United Nations declaration that laid out the rights to which all human beings were entitled.

Utopia Humanist social critique by English statesman Thomas More (1478–1535).

utopian socialism The most visionary of all Restoration-era movements, Utopian socialists, like Charles Fourier, dreamt of transforming states, workplaces, and human relations, and proposed actual plans to do so.

velvet revolutions The peaceful political revolutions throughout Eastern Europe in 1989.

Versailles Splendid palace outside Paris where Louis XIV and his nobles resided.

Versailles Conference (1919) Peace conference between the victors of World War I; resulted in the Treaty of Versailles, which forced Germany to pay reparations and to give up its colonies to the victors.

Queen Victoria (1819–1901) Influential monarch who reigned from 1837 to her death; she presided over the expansion of the British empire as well as the evolution of English politics and social and economic reforms.

Viet Cong Vietnamese communist group formed in 1954; committed to overthrowing the government of South Vietnam and reunifying North and South Vietnam.

A Vindication of the Rights of Woman Noted work of Mary Wollstonecraft (1759–1797), English republican who applied Enlightenment political ideas to issues of gender.

Virgil (70–19 B.C.E.) One of the most influential Roman authors, his surviving works include the Eclogues and the Roman epic poem, the *Aeneid*.

Visigoths The German "barbarians" who sacked Rome in 410.

Voltaire Pseudonym of French philosopher and satirist Francois Marie Arouet (1694–1797), who championed the cause of human dignity against state and church oppression. Noted Deist and author of *Candide*.

Voting Rights Act (1965) Law that granted universal suffrage in the United States.

Wars of the Roses Fifteenth-century conflict between the English dynastic houses of Lancaster and York (each symbolized in heraldry by the rose), ultimately won by Lancastrian Henry VII.

Warsaw Pact (1955–1991) Military alliance between the U.S.S.R. and other Communist states that was established as a response to the creation of the NATO alliance.

James Watt (1736–1819) Scottish inventor and scientist who developed the steam engine.

The Wealth of Nations 1776 treatise by Adam Smith, whose *laissez-faire* ideas predicted the economic boom of the Industrial Revolution.

Weimar Republic The government of Germany between 1919 and the rise of Hitler and the Nazi party.

Western Front Military front that stretched from the English Channel through Belgium and France to the Alps during World War I.

Whites Refers to the "counterrevolutionaries" of the Bolshevik Revolution (1918–1921) who fought the Bolsheviks (the "Reds"); included former supporters of the tsar, Social Democrats, and large independent peasant armies.

William and Mary (1650–1702 and 1662–1694) Dutch noble couple who supplanted the deposed Catholic King James II in 1688 as monarchs of England.

William of Ockham (d. 1349) An English Franciscan monk, Ockham denied that human reason could prove fundamental theological truths such as the existence of God. He argued that there was no necessary connection between the observable laws of nature and the unknowable essence of divinity, and no hope of reason from the laws of nature to the nature of God. Ockham's ideas encouraged intellectuals to investigate the natural world without reference to the supernatural and encouraged empiricism.

William the Conqueror (1027–1087) Duke of French Normandy who crossed the English Channel and defeated Harold for the English throne in 1066. Imposed a centralized feudal system on England and introduced French as the official language.

woman suffrage The movement to win legal and political rights, including the right to vote for all women.

Works Progress Administration (WPA) New Deal program instituted in 1935 that put nearly 3 million people to work building roads, bridges, airports, and post offices.

World Bank International agency established in 1944 to provide economic assistance to war-torn and poor countries. Its formal title is the International Bank for Reconstruction and Development.

Yalta Accords Meeting between President Franklin D. Roosevelt, Prime Minister Winston Churchill, and Premier Josef Stalin that occurred in the Crimea in 1945 to to prepare for the postwar order.

yellow press Newspapers that sought increased circulation by featuring sensationalist reporting that appealed to the masses.

Boris Yeltsin (1931–2007) The President of Russia who led the country after the disintegration of the Soviet Union in 1991.

Young Turks The 1908 Turkish nationalist movement to depose Sultan Abdul Hamid II.

Yugoslavia The Eastern European country that broke apart after the fall of the Soviet Union. Driven by nationalism and ethnic rivalries, the former Yugoslavia divided into six countries: Bosnia-Herzegovina, Croatia, Macedonia, Montenegro, Serbia, and Slovenia.

Zionism Formally founded in 1897, a political movement holding that the Jewish people constitute a nation and are entitled to a national homeland, originally advocating the reestablishment of a Jewish homeland in Palestine.

Zoroastrians Founded by Zoroaster around 600 B.C.E., this Persian religion urged people to be truthful, to help each other, and to practice hospitality. Those who did would be rewarded in an afterlife after a "judgment day."

Zulus African tribe that, under Shaka, created a ruthless warrior state in southern Africa in the early 1800s.

Ulrich Zwingli (1484–1531) A former Catholic priest from Zurich, Zwingli joined Luther and Calvin in attacking the authority of the Catholic Church. Zwingli's reforms resembled those of Luther's except that Zwingli believed that the Eucharist conferred no grace at all. At his peak, Zwingli converted much of northern Switzerland. After Zwingli's death in a battle with Catholic forces, most of his supporters began following John Calvin.

Text Credits

Leon B. Alberti: "On the Importance of Literature" from *University of Chicago Readings in Western Civilizations*, eds. Cochrane & Krishner. Copyright © 1986, University of Chicago Press. Reprinted by permission. "On the Family" from *The Family in Renaissance Florence*, trans./ed. by Renee Watkins. Copyright © 1969, University of South Carolina Press. Reprinted by permission.

Armand Bellée (ed.): *Cahiers de plaintes & doleances des paroisses de la province du Maine pour les Etats-generaux de 1789*, 4 vols. (Le Mans: Monnoyer, 1881–92), 2: 578–82. Translated by the American Social History Project, "Liberty, Equality, Fraternity: Exploring the French Revolution" by Jack R. Censer and Lynn Hunt.

Henry Bettenson (ed.): "Obedience as a Jesuit Hallmark" from *Documents of the Christian Church*, 2nd Edition. Copyright © 1967, Oxford University Press. Reprinted by permission of Oxford University Press.

Jacques Bossuet: "Bossuet on the Nature of Monarchical Authority" from *Politics Drawn from the Very Words of Holy Scripture*, trans. Patrick Riley. Copyright © 1990, Cambridge University Press.

Boyer, Baker & Kirshner (eds): "Declaration of the Rights of Man and of the Citizen," "Napoleon's Letter to Prince Eugene," and "Circular Letter to Sovereigns" from *University of Chicago Readings in Western Civilizations, Volume 7: The Old Regime and the French Revolution*, pp. 238–239; 419–420; 426–427, Copyright © 1987 University of Chicago Press. Reprinted by permission.

Alexius Comnenus: "The Spurious Letter by Alexius Comnenus to Count Robert" from *Christianity, Social Tolerance and Homosexuality*, ed/trans. John E. Boswell, pp. 367–369. Copyright © 1980 by The University of Chicago. All rights reserved. Reprinted with permission.

David Brion Davis: From *Encyclopédie*, Vol. 16, Neuchâtel, 1765, p. 532 as cited in David Brion Davis, *The Problem of Slavery in Western Culture* (Ithaca, N.Y.: Cornell University Press, 1966), p. 416. Copyright © 1966 by David Brion Davis. Reprinted by permission.

Michel de Montaigne: From *Montaigne: Selections from the Essays*, translated and edited by Donald M. Frame (Harlan Davidson, Inc., 1973). Reprinted by permission of Harlan Davidson, Inc.

Auguste Debay: "Hygiène et physiologie de marriage" from *Victorian Women*, Hellerstein, Hune and Offen, pp. 175–177, Document 37i. Copyright © 1981 by the Board of Trustees of the Leland Stanford Junior University. Reprinted by permission.

Jean Froissart: From *Chronicles* by Froissart, translated by Geoffrey Brereton. Translation © 1968 Geoffrey Brereton. Reproduced by permission of Penguin Books, Ltd.

Galileo Galilei: From *Discoveries and Opinions of Galileo* by Galileo Galilei, translated by Stillman Drake, copyright © 1957 by Stillman Drake. Used by permission of Doubleday, a division of Random House.

Henry Bertram Hill: "Cardinal Richelieu on the Common People of France" from *The Political Testament of Cardinal Richelieu*. Copyright © 1961. Reprinted by permission of The University of Wisconsin Press.

Caroline Larrington: "The Condemnation of Joan of Arc by the University of Paris" from *Women and Writing in Medieval Europe*, Caroline Larrington, Copyright © 1995 Routledge. Reproduced by permission of Taylor & Francis Books UK.

L. R. Loomis (ed. and trans.): *Haec Sancta* and *Frequens* from *The Council of Constance* (New York: Columbia University Press, 1961), pp. 229, 246–247. Copyright © 1962, Columbia University Press. Reprinted by permission of the publisher.

Niccolo Machiavelli: From *The Prince* by Niccolo Machiavelli, translated and edited by Thomas G. Bergin. Copyright © 1947 by Harlan Davidson, Inc. Reprinted by permission of Harlan Davidson, Inc.

Konstantin Mihailovic: *Memoirs of a Janissary*, trans. Benjamin Stolz. Michigan Slavic Translations no. 3 (Ann Arbor: Michigan Slavic Publications, 1975), pp. 157–159. Copyright © 1975, Michigan Slavic Publications. Reprinted by permission.

Heiko Oberman, et al.: Reprinted by permission of the publisher from *Defensorium Obedientiae Apostolicae et Alia Documenta* by Gabriel Biel, edited and translated by Heiko A. Oberman, Daniel E. Zerfoss and William J. Courtenay, pp. 224–227, Cambridge, Mass.: The Belknap Press of Harvard University Press, Copyright © 1968 by the President and Fellows of Harvard College.

Dorinda Outram: "Philosophical and Political History of European Establishments and Commerce" from *The Enlightenment*, p. 73. Copyright © 1995, Cambridge University Press.

Ebenezer Pettigrew: "Notebook containing an account of the death of Ann. B Pettigrew, June 10, 1830," in the Pettigrew Family Papers #592, Southern Historical Collection, Wilson Library, The University of North Carolina at Chapel Hill. Reprinted by permission.

E. M. Plass: "Luther on Celibacy and Women" from *What Luther Says, Vol. II*, (pp. 888–889) © 1959, 1987 Concordia Publishing House. Used with permission of CPH. All rights reserved.

TEXT CREDITS   A25

Jean Rousseau: From *Rousseau's Political Writings: A Norton Critical Edition* by Alan Ritter and Julia Conaway Bondanella, editors, translated by Julia Conaway Bondanella. Copyright © 1988 by W. W. Norton & Company, Inc. Used by permission of W. W. Norton & Company, Inc.

M. C. Seymour (ed.): "The Legend of Prester John" from *Mandeville's Travels* (Oxford: Clarendon Press, 1967), pp. 195–199. Copyright © 1967, Clarendon Press. Reprinted by permission of Oxford University Press.

William H. Woodward (trans.): "Concerning Excellent Traits" and "Concerning the Study of Literature" from *Vittorino da Feltre and Other Humanist Educators*, (Cambridge University Press) pp. 81–82, 96–110, 124–129, 132–133.

Every effort has been made to contact the copyright holder of each of the selections. Rights holders of any selections not credited should contact Permissions Department, W. W. Norton & Company, Inc., 500 Fifth Avenue, New York, NY 10110, in order for a correction to be made in the next reprinting of our work.

Photo Credits

Part IV 366–367: *A Portuguese galleon* (National Maritime Museum, London)

Chapter 10: 370: *Les Grandes Chroniques de France* (Erich Lessing/Art Resource, NY); 372: British Museum. Photo: Snark/Art Resource, NY; 373: Bibliotheque Royale Albert I, Brussels. Photo: Snark/Art Resource, NY; 375 (**top**): Bibliotheque Nationale, Paris. Photo: Archives Charmet/Bridgeman Art Library; 375 (**bottom**): Ann Ronan Picture Library, London. Photo: HIP/Art Resource, NY; 376: British Library. Photo: HIP/Art Resource, NY; 377: Bibliothèque Nationale, Paris. Photo: Snark/Art Resource, NY; 378: Bibliotheque Municipale, Besancon, France. Photo: Erich Lessing/Art Resource, NY; 379 (**top**): Bibliotheque Nationale, Paris. Photo: Giraudon/Art Resource, NY; 379 (**bottom**): Réunion des Musées Nationaux/Art Resource, NY; 380: British Library. Photo: HIP/Art Resource, NY; 381, 389, 402: detail from *The Plague of a Murrain Among the Cattle, c. 1250* (The Pierpont Morgan Library, New York. Photo: The Pierpont Morgan Library/Art Resource, NY); 382: Musee Conde, Chantilly, France. Photo: Réunion des Musées Nationaux/Art Resource, NY; 383: Musee Conde, Chantilly, France. Photo: Réunion des Musées Nationaux/Art Resource, NY; 386: British Library. Photo: HIP/Art Resource, NY; 387: Westminster Abbey, London. Photo: Bridgeman Art Library; 388 (**top**): Bibliotheque Nationale, Paris. Photo: Snark/Art Resource, NY; 388 (**bottom**): Archives Nationales, Paris. Photo: Réunion des Musées Nationaux/Art Resource, NY; 391: The Louvre, Paris. Photo: Erich Lessing/Art Resource, NY; 392 (**left**): King's College, Cambridge. Photo: Bildarchiv Preussischer Kulturbesitz/Art Resource, NY; 392 (**right**): National Portrait Gallery, London; 394: Art Archive/ Museo del Prado, Madrid; 398: Vova Pomortzeff/Alamy; 399: Giraudon/ Bridgeman Art Library; 401: Bibliotheque Nationale, Paris. Photo: Bildarchiv Preussischer Kulturbesitz/Art Resource, NY; 406: The Art Archive/British Library; 408: By permission of the British Library; 410: Scrovegni Chapel, Padua, Italy. Photo: Scala/Art Resource, NY; 411: Bibliothèque Royale Albert I, Brussels; 413: © Bibliotheque Royale Albert I, Brussels, ms. 11209, fol. 3 recto

Chapter 11: 416: *Army of Suleiman the Magnificent conquering Europe* (The Art Archive/Topkapi Museum, Istanbul/Dagli Orti); 420: John Massey Stewart Picture Library; 421, 425, 432, 437: *Persian panel of mosaic tilework, 14th–15th century* (Victoria & Albert Museum, London. Photo: Victoria & Albert Museum/Art Resource, NY); 423: Werner Forman Archive/Topkapi Palace Library, Istanbul/Art Resource, NY; 424: Mansell/TimePix/Getty Images; 431: Royal Armouries Museum; 433: José Pessoa, Arquivo Nacional de Fotografia, Instituto Português de Museus; 435: The Art Archive/Biblioteca Nacional de Madrid/Dagli Orti.

Chapter 12: 440: *The School of Athens,* by Raphael (Scala/Art Resource, NY); 444, 447, 450: detail from *Ceiling of Sala di Giove* (Palazzo Farnese, Caprarola, Italy. Photo: Scala/Art Resource, NY); 446: Art Resource, NY; 448: Réunion des Musées Nationaux /Art Resource, NY; 451: Erich Lessing/Art Resource, NY; 452: Erich Lessing/Art Resource, NY; 453 (**top**): Réunion des Musées Nationaux /Art Resource, NY; 453 (**bottom**): Scala/Art Resource, NY; 454: Thyssen-Bornemisza Collection, Madrid, Spain/Art Resource, NY; 455: Scala/Art Resource, NY; 456: Scala/Art Resource, NY; 457: Nimatallah/Art Resource, NY; 458 (**left**): Scala/Art Resource, NY; 458 (**right**): Erich Lessing/Art Resource, NY; 459: Sandro Vannini/Corbis; 463: © Frick Collection, New York; 464: Réunion des Musées Nationaux /Art Resource, NY; 466: Vanni/Art Resource, NY; 467: Bildarchiv Preussischer Kulturbesitz/Art Resource, NY;

Chapter 13: 472: *Martin Luther preaching to faithful and communion and baptism from altarfront from Torslunde, 1561, Denmark* (The Art Archive / Nationalmuseet Copenhagen Denmark / Dagli Orti (A)); 474: Scala/Art Resource, NY; 476: Gemaldegalerie, Staatliche Museen zu Berlin, Berlin. Photo: Erich Lessing/Art Resource, NY; 477: Alinari/Art Resource, NY; 478: Staatsbibliothek, Bern; 480: Bayerische Staatsgemäldesammlungen/Alte Pinakothek, Munich; 481: (**left**) Staatliche Museen zu Berlin—Preuβischer Kulturbesitz Kupferstichkabinett; 481: (**right**) By permission of the British Library; 483: The Warder Collection, NY; 484: Erich Lessing/Art Resource, NY; 485: The Warder Collection, NY; 489, 492, 498: *Reformation monument on front of Vor Frue Kirke, Copenhagen, Denmark.* Photo: Bridgeman Art Library; 491: National Trust/Art Resource, NY; 494: (**left**) Erich Lessing/Art Resource, NY; 494: (**right**) Scala/Art Resource, NY; 496: Scala/Art Resource, NY; 497: Kunsthistorisches Museum, Vienna; 499: Archivo Iconografico, S.A./Corbis

Chapter 14: 502, 511, 516, 520, 524: *View of Toledo* by El Greco (The Metropolitan Museum of Art, H.O. Havemeyer Collection, Bequest of Mrs. H.O. Havemeyer, 1919 (29.100.6) Photograph © 1992 The Metropolitan Museum of Art); 505: Bettmann/Corbis; 506: Gianni Dagli Orti/Corbis; 507: Archivo Iconografico, S.A./Corbis; 509: The New York Public Library. Astor, Lenox and Tilden Foundations; 514: Archivo Iconografico, S.A./Corbis; 518: Courtesy of the National Portrait Gallery, London; 519:

PHOTO CREDITS   A27

Photo Bulloz Collection, Privèe; **523:** Bibliotheque des Arts Dec-
oratifs, Paris. Photo: Bridgeman Art Library; **528:** Scala/Art Resource, NY; **529:** Museo del Prado, Madrid; **530: (top)** Erich
Lessing/Art Resource, NY; **530: (bottom)** Nimatallah/Art Resource, NY; **531: (left)** © English Heritage Photo Library; **531:
(right)** Gift of Mr. and Mrs. Robert Woods Bliss, © 1997 Board of
Trustees, National Gallery of Art, Washington, D.C.

Part V: 534: *Last Naval Battle in the Dutch-English War. August 11,
1637*, by Backhuyzen Ludolf, 1631–1708 (Erich Lessing/Art Resource, NY)

Chapter 15: 538: *Marriage a la Mode* by William Hogarth (National Gallery Collection; By kind permission of the Trustees of the
National Gallery, London/Corbis); **541, 549, 574** : *A fountain
at Versailles* (Giraudon/Art Resource, NY); **543:** Courtesy of the
National Portrait Gallery, London; **544:** Scottish National Portrait Gallery, Edinburgh, Scotland/Bridgeman Art Library; **545:**
Bridgeman Art Library; **546:** Erich Lessing/Art Resource, NY;
547: Giraudon/Art Resource, NY; **553:** The Art Archive/Musee
du Chateau de Versailles/Dagli Orti; **554:** Erich Lessing/Art Resource, NY; **555:** by Friedrich Wilhelm Kurfürst von Branden-
burg/Ullstein; **557:** The Art Archive/Russian Historical Museum
Moscow/Dagli Orti (A); **560:** Giraudon/Art Resource, NY; **561:**
Giraudon/Art Resource, NY; **564:** Ali Meyer/Corbis; **567:** John
R. Freeman & Co.; **569:** Corbis; **570:** Gianni Dagli Orti/Corbis;
571: The Warder Collection, NY

Chapter 16: 578: *The Comet of December 1680* by Lieve Verschuier
(Courtesy of Historisch Museum, Rotterdam); **582:** Erich Less-
ing/Art Resource, NY; **583:** Bettmann/Corbis; **584: (top)** Staple-
ton Collection/Corbis; **584: (bottom)** Bettmann/Corbis; **587,
590, 596:** *Celestial map of planets by George Christoph Eimmert II.* 17th
century. (O'Shea Gallery, London/Bridgeman Art Library); **588:**
Erich Lessing/Art Resource, NY; **591:** Réunion des Musées Na-
tionaux/Art Resource, NY; **592:** Bodleian Library; **594:**
Bettmann/Corbis; **597:** Bodleian Library; **598:** Chateau de Versailles et de Trianon, Versailles, France. Photo: Erich Lessing/Art
Resource, NY; **599: (left)** Bettmann/Corbis; **599: (right)** The
Print Collector/Alamy

Chapter 17: 602: *The Salon of Madame Geofrin* (Giraudon/Art Resource, NY); **605:** Musee de la Ville de Paris, Musee Carnavalet,
Paris/Giraudon/Bridgeman Art Library; **606:** Bettmann/Corbis;
608: Giraudon/Art Resource, NY; **609:** Bettmann/Corbis; **610:**
Historisches Museum der Stadt Wien; **611:** Moritz Daniel Op-
penheim, *"Lavater and Lessing Visit Moses Mendelssohn."* In the permanent collections, Judah L. Magnes Museum. Photo: Ben Ailes;
613, 615, 618, 622: detail from *Ascent of a Mongelfiere in Gardens of
Aranjuez* by Antonio Carnicero (Museo del Prado, Madrid, Spain.
Photo: Erich Lessing/Art Resource, NY); **616:** Stapletib Collec-
tion/Corbis; **619:** Bibliotheque Nationale, Paris, France/Flammar-
ion/Bridgeman Art Library; **620:** Tate Gallery/Art Resource, NY;
626: Bettmann/Corbis; **629:** Erich Lessing/Art Resource, NY;
630: Erich Lessing/Art Resource, NY

Part VI: 632–33: *The Fall of the Bastille, July 14, 1789* (Giraudon/Art
Resource, NY)

Chapter 18: 636: *The Death of Marat*, by Jacques Louis David (Gi-
raudon/Art Resource, NY); **640: (left)** Bibliothèque Nationale de
France, Paris; **640: (right)** Bibliothèque Nationale de France,
Paris; **642:** Photo Bulloz, Versailles; **643, 647, 649, 652, 667:**
Eighteenth Century print of "Bataille de Gemmape" (Gianni Dagli
Orti/Corbis); **644:** Giraudon/Art Resource, NY; **645:** Gi-
raudon/Art Resource, NY; **651:** Réunion des Musées Na-
tionaux/Art Resource, NY; **654:** Giraudon/Art Resource, NY;
655: (left) Bettmann/Corbis; **655: (right)** Bettmann/Corbis; **656:**
Giraudon/Art Resource, NY; **657:** Giraudon/Art Resource, NY;
662: Archivo Iconografico, S.A./Corbis; **664:** Erich Lessing/Art
Resource, NY; **665:** Museo del Prado, Madrid; **669:** Gianni Dagli
Orti/Corbis

Chapter 19: 672: *The Gare St. Lazare* by Claude Monet. (National
Gallery Collection; by kind permission of the Trustees of the Na-
tional Gallery, London/Corbis); **677:** Stefano Bianchetti/Corbis;
678, 689. 700: *A cotton mill in Lancashire, 1834* (The Granger Col-
lection, New York); **680:** Bettmann/Corbis ; **681: (top)** Hulton-
Deutsch Collection/Corbis; **681: (bottom)** Hulton-Deutsch
Collection/Corbis; **682:** Mary Evans Picture Library; **684:** City
Archives of Lyons; **687:** Hulton-Deutsch Collection/Corbis;
690: National Library of Ireland; **691:** *A soup kitchen in Manchester,
England* (The Warder Collection, NY); **693:** Hulton-Deutsch
Collection/Corbis; **695:** Geoffrey Clements/Corbis; **697:** Gi-
raudon/Art Resource, NY; **698:** North Wind Picture Archives/
Alamy; **702:** cliché Bibliothèque Nationale de France, Paris; **704:**
The Granger Collection, New York

INDEX

Abbasid caliphate, 422
absolutism, 539–43, 574, 576
  alternatives to, 542–46
  in Austria, 540–42, 552–54
  in Austro-Hungarian Empire, 552–54
  autocracy and, 557–61
  Bossuet on, 541
  of Brandenburg-Prussia, 553, 554–56
  Catholic Church and, 540
  in Central and Eastern Europe, 553–61
  definition of, 539
  in England, 518
  "enlightened," 554, 556
  Filmer on, 541–42
  of French monarchy, 539, 540–42, 543
  French Revolution and, 637, 653
  international relations and, 550–53
  justification of, 540–42
  law and, 540, 545–46
  in literature, 525
  mercantilism and, 548–50
  Napoleon and, 660
  opponents of, 540–42, 545–46
  restoration of, 690
  in Russia, 553, 557–61
  satirized, 609
  state systems and, 550–53
  theatricality of, 546–47
Abukir Bay, battle of (1798), 658
Académie Française, 624–25, 660
Acquired Immune Deficiency Syndrome (AIDS), 376
Acre, 417
Act of Succession (England; 1701), 544
Act of Supremacy (England; 1534), 491–92
Act of Supremacy (England; 1559), 494
Act of Toleration (England; 1689), 544
Act of Union (Great Britain; 1707), 544
Acton, William, 699–701
Adam, 527
Africa:
  gold in, 427, 431, 432
  Portuguese exploration of, 417, 430, 431
  slave trade and, 433–34, 569–72
  see also specific countries
Against the Thievish, Murderous Hordes of Peasants
  (Luther), 482
agriculture:
  commercialization of, 690–93
  commercial revolution and, 562
  enclosure of common fields and, 675
  in France, 373, 515
  Industrial Revolution and, 673, 674, 675, 683,
    685, 688–93
  in Late Middle Ages, 371, 372–73, 377

New World crops and, 561
  putting-out system of, 562
  tools and, 504
Ahmed, Siblizade, 423
Alberti, Leon Battista (1404–1472), 443, 444,
  446, 449, 451, 469
Albert of Hohenzollern, archbishop of Mainz
  (1490–1545), 476
Albert of Saxe-Coburg, prince consort of queen
  Victoria (1819–1861), 699
Albret, Jeanne d', queen of Navarre (1562–1572),
  507
Alchemist, The (Jonson), 527
alchemy, 581
Alembert, Jean Le Rond d' (1717–1783), 603,
  608
Alexander I, tsar of Russia (1777–1825), 665, 666
Alexander VI, Pope (1492–1503), 446, 449, 477,
  478
Alexandria, Egypt, 420, 423, 430
Alexis (son of Peter I of Russia), 560
Alexis I, tsar of Russia (1645–1676), 557
Allegory of Spring, The (Botticelli), 452
All's Well that Ends Well (Shakespeare), 527
Alsace, 550
Alva, duke of (1507–1582), 509
Ambrose, Saint (c. 340–397), 463, 487
America:
  discovery of, 417, 434–38
  see also New World; United States
American Philosophical Society of Philadelphia,
  624
American Revolution, 546, 572–75, 637–38
American War of Independence, 572–75
Amiens, 562
Amsterdam, 562
Anabaptism, 482, 483–84, 487, 503
Anatolia, 422
"Anatomie of the World, An" (Donne), 590
Anglicanism (Church of England), 464, 487, 492,
  494, 518, 519, 521, 544
  origins of, 491
Anjou, duke of, 383
Anne, queen of England (1702–1714), 544, 551
Anne of Austria (1601–1666), 517
anti-Semitism:
  of Frederick the Great, 556
  see also Jews
Antwerp, 508, 509
Aragon, 393, 394, 401, 515, 542
Archimedes (c. 287–212 B.C.E.), 581
architecture:
  Baroque, 528–29
  classicism in, 467
  Gothic, 458–59, 467

  Renaissance, 458–59, 466–67
  Romanesque, 458–59
Argentina, 681, 687, 688
Ariosto, Ludovico (1474–1533), 451, 465
aristocrats, *see* nobility
Aristotle (384–322 B.C.E.), 442, 455, 582
Aristotle Contemplating the Bust of Homer (Rembrandt),
  532
Arkwright, Richard (1732–1792), 677
Armada, Spanish, 494, 510, 514, 565
ars nova, 468
art:
  Baroque, 461, 528, 532
  chiaroscuro in, 451
  classicism in, 456–58
  Dutch, 529–32
  of fresco, 409
  late medieval, 409–10
  linear perspective in, 451
  Mannerist, 457, 458, 528
  naturalism in, 409, 454
  of portraiture, 409, 451, 454–55
  realism in, 409
  Renaissance, 409, 445–46, 451–59, 460–61,
    467–68, 469
  Venetian School of, 454–55
  Virgin Mary in, 455
artillery, 430–31
Assembly of Notables (France), 642
astrolabes, 428–30
astrology, 580, 581, 584, 627
astronomy:
  Copernican Revolution in, 582–83
  emergence of, 580–82
  Galileo and, 460
  Kepler's laws and, 585
  Tychonic system of, 584, 586
Astronomy or Celestial Physics (Kepler), 585
As You Like It (Shakespeare), 527
Augsburg, 488–90
  League of, 550–51
  Peace of (1555), 506, 510
Augustine, Saint (354–430), 449, 464, 475
Aurispa, Giovanni (c. 1369–1459), 447
Austen, Jane, 626
Austerlitz, battle of (1805), 661
Australia, 681
Austria, 392, 426–27, 510, 550, 551, 555–56,
  572
  absolutism in, 540–42, 553–54
  French Revolution and, 650, 651, 654, 656
  in Industrial Revolution, 683, 684, 685
  Napoleon vs., 658, 661, 664–68
  partition of Poland and, 560–61
Austro-Hungarian Empire, 553–54

A28

INDEX A29

authority, search for, 523–26
autocracy, absolutism and, 557–61
Avignon, papacy in, 398–401
Azores, 411, 417, 428, 430, 433, 434
Aztecs, 435–36

Bach, Johann Sebastian (1685–1750), 628
Bacon, Francis (1561–1626), 580, 589–92, 593, 599, 604, 606
Bahamas, 434
Bailly, Jean (1736–1793), 643
balance of power, 550–51, 553, 560–61
Balboa, Vasco Nuñez de (1475–1519), 435
Balkans, 422, 423
Balzac, Honoré de (1799–1850), 696
Bamberg, witch hunts in, 523
Banker and His Wife, The (Massys), 379
Bank of England, 572
banks, banking:
    commerce and, 379–80, 572
    Fugger family and, 476
    in Industrial Revolution, 684
    in Italy, 380
    Medici family and, 380, 393, 443
Barbados, 571
Barberini, Cardinal Maffeo, *see* Urban VIII, Pope
Baronius, Cardinal, 586
Basel, 463, 484
    Council of, 401
Bastille, 645–46
Battle of the Nations (1813), 666
Batu, 395
Bavaria, 392, 462, 551
Beauharnais, Eugène, 667
Beaumarchais, Pierre Augustin de, 630
Beccaria, Cesare Bonesana de (1738–1794), 604, 609–10, 611
Beethoven, Ludwig van (1770–1827), 663
Beirut, 421, 423, 430
Belarus, 397–98
"Belfagor" (Machiavelli), 451
Belgium, 508
    in Industrial Revolution, 683, 684–85
Bellay, Joachim du (c. 1522–1560), 465, 467
Bellini, Giovanni (c. 1430–1516), 454
Benz, Carl, 685
Berlin, 548, 554, 562
Berlin Academy of Science, 594, 624
Bernini, Gianlorenzo (1598–1680), 528–29
Berry, duke of, 383
Bible, 405, 475, 496, 503
    printing of, 413
    Vulgate, 448, 497
Bill of Rights, British, 544
birth control, 700–701
Birth of Venus (Botticelli), 452
Black Death (plague), 371, 373–80, 382, 407, 421
    causes of, 376–77, 385
    demographics, 373
    Jews blamed for, 375
    recurrences of, 506, 561–62
    rural areas and, 377–78
Black Gazette, The, 624
Blake, William (1757–1827), 679
Blenheim, battle of (1704), 551
Blind Leading the Blind, The (Brueghel), 531
Boccaccio, Giovanni (1313–1375), 407–8
Bodin, Jean (1530–1596), 525, 545
Bohemia, 510–13, 554
    heretical movements in, 405, 406
Boleyn, Anne (c. 1507–1536), queen of England, 491, 493

Bolingbroke, Henry, 386
Bolivia, 436–37
Bologna, Concordat of (1516), 481
Bologna, University of, 462
Bonaparte, Napoleon, *see* Napoleon I, emperor of France
Boniface VIII, Pope (1294–1303), 398
Book of the Courtier, The (Castiglione), 449–51
books:
    censorship of, 460, 496, 587–88, 623–24
    Enlightenment and, 621–24, 625–27
    nationalism and, 413
    on navigation, 430
    printing of, 412, 413
Bordeaux, siege of (1453), 431
Borgia, Cesare (c. 1475–1507), 449, 477
Borgia, Lucrezia (1480–1519), 477
Borneo, 567
Borodino, battle of (1812), 665
Bossuet, Jacques-Benigne (1627–1704), 541, 545
Boston, 575
Bosworth Field, battle of (1485), 392
Botticelli, Sandro (1445–1510), 448, 452–53
Bougainville, Louis-Anne de (1729–1811), 614, 616
Boulton, Matthew (1728–1809), 680
Bourbon, Antoine de, 507
Bourbon dynasty, 507
Boyle, Robert (1627–1691), 592–93, 597
Boyne, battle of the (1690), 545
Brahe, Tycho (1546–1601), 583–84
Bramante, Donato (c. 1444–1514), 459
Brandenburg, 392
Brandenburg-Prussia, 393, 554–56
Brassey, Thomas, 681
Brazil, 411, 570, 571
Bremen, 379
Britain, *see* Great Britain
British East India Company, 572, 575
Brittany, 548
Brontë, Charlotte (1816–1855), 698
Bronzino, Il (1503–1572), 528
Brueghel, Peter (c. 1525–1569), 410, 529–32
Bruni, Leonardo (1369–1444), 444–45, 446, 449
Bruno, Giordano (1548–1600), 460, 469
Bulgaria, 422
Burgundy, 388, 391, 468, 516
Burgundy, duke of, 383, 386, 387, 388
Burke, Edmund (1729–1797), 651, 652
Burney, Fanny (1752–1840), 626
Byrd, William (1543–1623), 468
Byzantine Empire, 418
    Muscovy and, 397–98

Cadíz, 562, 565, 570
Caesar, Julius (100 B.C.E.–44 B.C.E.), 465
Cairo, 425
Calais, battle of, 385
Calas, Jean, 603–4, 609–10
calculus, 595
Calcutta, 687
calendars:
    French Revolutionary, 654, 658
    Roman, 582
California, 565
Calvin, John (1509–1564), 483–87, 490, 495, 496, 500, 503, 507, 518, 519, 522
    Luther compared with, 485
Calvinism, 482, 483–87, 494, 497, 505
    in France, 487
    Lutheranism and, 485
    Protestant Reformation and, 484–87
    in Switzerland, 485–87

theology of, 484–85
Canada, 515, 572, 575, 681
Canary Islands, 417, 428, 430, 433, 434
Canterbury Tales (Chaucer), 408
Cape of Good Hope, 411, 417, 430, 433, 434, 567
Capetian dynasty, 385
Cape Verde Islands, 411, 430, 434, 436
capitalism:
    Industrial Revolution and, 673–74, 675, 683–84
    railway boom and, 681–83
Carroll, Lewis, 413
Cartesians, 592–93, 595
Castiglione, Baldassare (1478–1529), 449–51
Castile, 393, 394, 401, 428, 515, 542
Catalunya, 427–28, 515, 542
Catherine II (the Great), empress of Russia (1762–1796), 540, 560–61, 624, 627
Catherine of Aragon (1485–1536), queen of England, 491, 493
Catherine of Siena, Saint, 404–5
Catholic Church, 398–406, 506, 509, 613
    absolutism and, 540
    book censorship by, 460, 496
    Council of Trent and, 489
    Counter-Reformation and, 495–99
    France and, 548, 661
    French Revolution and, 648–50
    Galileo's conflict with, 585–89
    heresies and, 405–6
    Jesuits and, 496–97
    Lutheranism and, 474–77
    marriage and, 488, 491
    Roman calendar and, 582–83
    sacraments of, 403–4, 405–6, 477, 483, 492, 493, 494, 496
    scientific revolution and, 582–83, 585–89
    theology of, 474–77
    women and, 499
    see also Christianity; papacy
Cavaliers, 519
Cavendish, Margaret, 593
celibacy, 496, 499
    Protestantism and, 487–90
Central America, 565, 568
Cervantes, Miguel de (1547–1616), 526
Chambord chateau, 466–67
Champlain, Samuel de, 515
charity, doctrine of, 499
Charles I, king of England and Scotland (1625–1649), 519–21, 527, 543
Charles II, king of England (1660–1685), 521–22, 527, 565, 593
    reign of, 543–44, 545
Charles II, king of Spain (1665–1700), 551
Charles III, king of Spain (1759–1788), 540
Charles V, Holy Roman emperor (1506–1556), 435, 460, 478–80, 481, 491, 493, 496, 506, 508–9
Charles V, king of France (1364–1380), 386, 399
Charles VI, Holy Roman emperor (1711–1740), 552
Charles VI, king of France (1380–1422), 386–87, 408
Charles VII, king of France (1422–1461), 387, 388, 391
Charles VIII, king of France (1483–1498), 459
Charles the Bold (1433–1477), duke of Burgundy, 391
Charles University, 462
Chaucer, Geoffrey (c. 1342–1400), 407–8, 462

INDEX   A30

checks and balances, doctrine of, 608, 612, 641
child labor, 679–80, 681, 705
China, 373, 417
   Great Wall of, 418
   Mongol invasion of, 418–19, 420
   trade with, 418, 430, 567
Chingiz, *see* Genghis Khan
chivalric orders, 383–84
Christian humanism, 448, 462–65, 469, 495,
      499, 500
Christianity, 611
   of Counter-Reformation, 497–98
   monasticism in, *see* monasticism
   Ottoman Empire and, 425, 426
   predestination in, 475, 500
   see also specific religions
Christine de Pisan, 407–9
chronometer, 430
Churchill, John, duke of Marlborough, 551
Church of England, *see* Anglicanism
Cicero (106–43 B.C.E.), 442, 443, 462, 463
Ciompi uprising (Florence; 1378), 380
Cistercian order, 469
cities:
   Black Death and, 378–80
   class and, 705
   in eighteenth century, 562, 576
   in Industrial Revolution, 693–96
   of Late Middle Ages, 378–80
   literacy and, 627
   manufacturing and industry in, 562–63
   Protestantism and government of, 488–90
   see also urbanization; *specific cities*
"citizen," use of term, 657
City of Ladies, The (de Pisan), 409
civic humanism, 446, 447
Civil Constitution of the Clergy (1789), 648–50
class, class consciousness:
   French Revolution and, 639–41
   in Industrial Revolution, 674, 704–5, 706
   sexuality and, 699–701
   urban working women and, 703–4
   see also middle class, nineteenth-century;
         working class, nineteenth-century
Clement VI, Pope (1342–1352), 375, 399
Clement VII, Pope (1523–1534), 400, 491
Clement VIII, Pope (1592–1605), 497
clipper ships, 687
clocks, 411–12
"Coercive Acts," 575
coffee houses, 625, 626
Cohn, Samuel, Jr., 380–82
Colbert, Jean Baptiste (1619–1683), 548–50,
      567
Colet, John (c. 1467–1519), 465, 469
College of Cardinals, 399–400, 477, 478
Colloquies (Erasmus), 463
Cologne, 550
Cologne, University of, 465
colonialism, 539, 564–75
   cultural assimilation and, 568–69
   disease and, 569
   empire and, 570–75
   English, 438, 539, 565–67, 568–69
   in Enlightenment era, 612–14, 638
   French, 539, 567
   inflation and, 436–38
   international rivalries and, 570
   maritime technology and, 428–30
   Mediterranean, 427–34
   Netherlands and, 539, 567–68
   Portuguese, 430–34, 438
   slave trade and, 428, 433–34

Spanish, 434–38, 504, 539, 565, 569–72
   see also specific countries
Columbus, Christopher (1451–1506), 392,
      393–94, 417, 420, 428, 434, 435, 581
comedy, *see* theater
commerce:
   accounting practices and, 379–80
   Anglo-French rivalry in, 572, 575
   Atlantic expansion of, 428
   banking industry and, 379–80, 572
   Black Death and, 373
   colonialism and, 539, 564–75
   consumer goods and, 564, 575–76
   consumption and, 561–64
   Continental System and, 663
   eighteenth-century economic growth and,
         562–63, 575–76
   European exploration and, 417–18
   impediments to innovation and, 562–64
   in Industrial Revolution, 674–77, 687
   industry and manufacturing in, 562–63
   laissez-faire policy and, 611
   in Late Middle Ages, 372, 373, 377–80, 382,
         411
   Mediterranean, 427–34
   Mongol Empire and, 420–22
   in Ottoman Empire, 423
   in precious metals, 427, 436–38
   Price Revolution and, 504–5
   protoindustrialization and, 562
   service sector in, 564
   on Silk Road, 418, 420–22
commercial revolution (c. 1600–1800), 539
Committee of Public Safety (France), 654–58
Commons, House of, *see* Parliament, British
communication, 692
   Enlightenment revolution in, 621–24
   Industrial Revolution and, 685
compass, 411, 430, 580
Complaint of Peace (Erasmus), 463
Comte, Auguste (1798–1857), 699
conciliarism, 401, 402–3, 473, 481
Concordat of Bologna (1516), 481
Condé, prince de, 507
Condition of the Working Class in England, The
      (Engels), 678–79
Condorcet, Marie-Jean Caritat, marquis de
      (1743–1794), 620, 648
Confederation of the Rhine, 661
Congregation of the Index, 496
conquistadors, 435–38
Constance, Council of, 401, 402, 406
Constantine I (the Great), Roman emperor
      (306–337), 448
Constantinople, 417, 424, 447
   Turkish capture of, 397, 410, 422–23, 431
Constitution, U.S., 608
constitutions, Enlightenment liberalism and, 608,
      630
constitutions, French:
   of 1789, 643
   of 1791, 646, 650
   of 1795, 658
   of 1799, 659
constitutions, Haitian (1801), 669
consumer goods, 564, 575
Continental Congress, 575
Continental System, 663, 683
contract theory of government, 545–46
Cook, James (1728–1779), 614, 616
Copernicus, Nicholas (1473–1543), 582–85,
      586, 587, 588
Corday, Charlotte (1768–1793), 655, 656

Cortés, Hernando (1485–1547), 435–36
Cosmographic Mystery (Kepler), 585
Cossacks, 557, 560
cotton gin, 677
cotton industry, 677–79, 683, 687
"Council of Blood," 509
Council of Constance, 401, 402, 406
Council of Trent, 489, 495–96, 497
Counter-Reformation, 460
courtier, ideal of, 449–51
Cranach, Lucas (1472–1553), 474
Cranmer, Thomas (1489–1556) archbishop of
      Canterbury, 491, 493
Creation of Adam, The (Michelangelo), 456, 467
Crécy, battle of (1346), 385
Crédit Mobilier, 684
Crimea, 560
Crimean War (1854–1856), 699
Crome, William Henry, 695
Cromwell, Oliver (1599–1658), 519–21, 527,
      543, 565
Cromwell, Thomas, 492
Crotus Rubianus, 464
Crusades, as penance, 404
Curaçao, 567
Czechoslovakia, 685

Daimler, Gottlieb, 685
Dangerous Liaisons (Laclos), 621
Dante Alighieri (1265–1321), 407, 442
Danton, Georges Jacques (1759–1794), 655
Danzig (Gdansk), 554, 561
"Dark Ages," 441
Darnton, Robert, 624
Darwin, Charles (1809–1882), 616–17
Daumier, Honoré (1808–1879), 696, 697
David, Jacques Louis (1748–1825), 643, 656,
      662
David (Bernini), 528
David (Donatello), 457, 528
David (Michelangelo), 457–58, 467, 528
death penalty, 610
Decameron (Boccaccio), 407–8
Declaration of Independence, U.S., 574, 575,
      647
Declaration of the Rights of Man and Citizen, 646–47
Declaration of the Rights of Woman and Citizen
      (Gouges), 648
Defense of Cadiz Against the English, The (Zurbaran),
      570
De Fer, Nicholas, 569
Defoe, Daniel (1660–1731), 626
deism, 610
Denmark, 482, 500
Descartes, René (1596–1650), 499, 589–92, 595
Descent from the Cross (Michelangelo), 458
Dessalines, Jean-Jacques (1758?–1806), 659
d'Holbach, Henri (1723–1789), 610
Dialogue Between the Two Great World Systems, The
      (Galileo), 586, 588
Dias, Bartholomeu (c. 1450–1500), 430, 434
Dickens, Charles (1812–1870), 408, 638, 673,
      694, 696
Diderot, Denis, 605, 608–9, 613, 615, 620
Diet, Polish, 561
Directory, French, 658
Discourse on Method (Descartes), 589–92
Discourse on the Origins of Inequality (Rousseau), 624
Discourses on Livy (Machiavelli), 449
disease, 561–62
Disputà (Raphael), 455
Div, battle of (1509), 431
Doctor Faustus (Marlowe), 526

INDEX A31

Dominican order, 586
Donatello (c. 1386–1466), 457, 528
Donation of Constantine, 448
Don Giovanni (Mozart), 630
Donne, John (1572–1631), 590
Don Quixote (Cervantes), 526
Drake, Sir Francis (c. 1540–1596), 510, 565
drama, *see* theater
du Chatelet, Emile, 597
du Guesclin, Bertrand, 386
Duma, Russian, 558
Dumas, Alexandre (1802–1870), 694
Dürer, Albrecht (1471–1528), 467
Dutch East India Company, 567–68
Dutch Reformed Church, 487
Dutch Republic, 510, 539, 575, 576
dynasticism, 505

East Prussia, 554
Eckhart, Master (c. 1260–c. 1327), 405
Ecuador, 617
Edgeworth, Maria, 626
Edict of Nantes (1598), 508, 510, 515, 516, 548, 607
education:
    in Austro-Hungarian Empire, 554
    in Industrial Revolution, 684
    Jesuits and, 496, 497
    in Late Middle Ages, 407, 414
    Locke's theories of, 604–5
    medieval literature and, 407
    Napoleon and, 660
    Newton and, 594
    Protestantism and, 500
    in Renaissance, 443–46, 462
    Rousseau's view of, 619–21
    state-sponsored, 627
    of women, 414, 443, 500
    of working class, 702
    see also literacy
Edward I, king of England (1272–1307), 384
Edward III, king of England (1327–1377), 385, 386, 387, 391
Edward IV, king of England (1461–1483), 391
Edward VI, king of England (1547–1553), 492, 493
Egypt:
    Mamluk sultanate of, 423, 424, 425
    Napoleon in, 658, 661, 662
electricity, 673
El Greco (Domenikos Theotokopoulos) (1541–1614), 528
Elizabeth I, queen of England (1558–1603), 468, 491, 493–94, 510, 517, 518
Elizabethan theater, 526–27
Elizabeth of York, 391
Emile (Rousseau), 619, 620
Emma (Austen), 626
Emperor Charles V at Muehlberg, The (Titian), 506
empiricism, 407, 414
    Bacon and, 589–91
Encyclopedia (Diderot), 608, 609, 612, 614, 623, 624, 625
Engels, Friedrich (1820–1895), 678, 679
England, 426, 428, 504, 513, 540, 550, 551–52, 557, 562–63
    agriculture in, 561
    American colonies of, 438, 539, 553, 565–67, 568–69
    Bank of, 572
    Black Death in, 373
    Calvinism in, 487
    Civil War in (1642–1649), 517–21
    as Commonwealth, 519–21
    Glorious Revolution in, 544–45
    heretical movements in, 405–6
    in Hundred Years' War, 384–92
    law in, 518–19
    as limited monarchy, 522, 539, 543–44
    literature of, 408
    mercantilism and, 565
    monasticism in, 492
    national identity of, 392, 495, 500
    national language of, 392
    national monarchy in, 391–92, 394–95, 473
    papacy and, 491–93, 494
    Parliament of, *see* Parliament, British
    Peasants' Revolt in, 380–82
    population growth in, 561
    "Protectorate" in, 521, 543
    Protestantism in, 500, 510, 543
    Reformation in, 490–95
    reign of Charles II in, 543–44, 545
    Renaissance in, 461, 463, 468–69
    Spain vs., 510, 513, 565
    in Thirty Years' War, 510
    unification of, 544–45
    War of the Roses in, 391
    see also Great Britain
English language, as national language, 392
English Renaissance, 526
Enlightenment, 602–31
    academies in, 605, 624–25
    books and literacy in, 605–6, 621–24, 625–27
    colonialism and, 612
    economics in, 611–12
    Encyclopedia in, 608, 609
    foundations of, 604–6
    French Revolution and, 618, 619, 620, 630, 639, 641, 646, 647, 648, 662, 669
    humanitarianism as theme of, 609–11
    internationalization of, 609–12
    Jews in, 610–11
    mercantilism in, 611–12
    music in, 627–30
    New World colonialism and, 612–14, 638
    philosophes in, 606–9
    popular culture in, 626–27
    public spheres and, 605, 624–25
    religious toleration as theme of, 610–11
    Rousseau's influence on, 617–21
    salons and learned societies in, 625
    scientific exploration in, 614–17
    slave trade in, 612, 613–14
    society and, 689
    women in, 619–21, 625, 626
    see also scientific revolution
environmental problems, 694, 695–96, 706
Episcopalianism, 519
Erasmus, Desiderius (c. 1466–1536), 462–64, 465, 466, 467–68, 469, 475, 478, 487, 495, 496, 499, 500
Erasmus (Holbein), 463
Erfurt, University of, 474
Eroica symphony (Beethoven), 663
Eschenbach, Wolfram von, 407
Essay Concerning Human Understanding (Locke), 597, 604
Essay on Man (Pope), 605
Essay on the Principle of Population (Malthus), 689
Essays (Montaigne), 523–25
Estates-General, 548, 642–44
Esterházy family, 629
Estonia, 558
Eton, 696
Eucharist, sacrament of, 477, 483, 492, 493, 494

Eugene, prince of Savoy, 551
Euripides (485–406 B.C.E.), 447
Eve, 527
Exclusion Crisis, 543
Execrabilis (1460), 402–3
Execution of the Rebels on 3 May 1808 (Goya), 665
eyeglasses, 411

Faerie Queene (Spenser), 465
famine, 561, 576
Ferdinand II, Holy Roman emperor (1619–1637), 513
Ferdinand V, king of Castile (1474–1516), 393–94, 417, 434, 435, 479, 480, 515
Fiacre, Saint, 404
Ficino, Marsilio (1433–1499), 448, 452, 469
Fielding, Henry, 626
Filmer, Robert (1588–1653), 541–42, 545
First Blast of the Trumpet Against the Monstrous Regiment of Women, The (Knox), 500
flagellation, 375, 376
Fleury, Richard, 588
Flood, The (Michelangelo), 456
Florence, 373, 378, 379, 380, 393, 487
    Ciompi uprising in, 380
    in Renaissance, 446, 448–49, 452–54, 457, 460, 461
Florida, 565, 575
flying shuttle, 677
fossil fuels, 673
Four Apostles (Dürer), 467
France, 426, 443, 445, 449, 459, 461, 462, 465, 466–67, 480, 490, 493, 497, 500, 513, 514–17, 550, 551, 555, 572–75
    absolutism in, 539, 540–42, 543
    academies and salons in, 624–25
    agriculture in, 373, 515
    American Revolution and, 641
    Calvinism in, 487
    Capetian kings of, 385
    Catholic Church and, 660
    colonialism of, 539, 553, 567, 568–69
    commercial agriculture in, 692
    commercial rivalry with Britain, 572, 575
    Fronde revolt in, 517
    Great Schism and, 401
    Haitian Revolution and, 668–69
    in Hundred Years' War, 378, 382–94, 410
    in Industrial Revolution, 683, 684, 685–87, 692
    intolerance in, 607
    mercantilism in, 567, 568–69
    Napoleon's reign in, 658–68
    national monarchy in, 394–95, 473
    New World colonies of, 438, 515, 570, 571
    parlements of, 540, 548
    philosophes of, 606–9
    regionalism in, 507, 547–48
    religious wars of, 506–8
    science academies in, 599
    in Seven Years' War, 572
    slave trade and, 571
    Spain compared with, 515
    in Thirty Years' War, 510, 513, 515, 517
    Valois dynasty in, 385, 387, 391
    War of the Spanish Succession and, 550–52
    see also French Revolution
Francis I, king of France (1515–1547), 454, 466, 481
Franciscan order, 407, 495
Francis de Sales, Saint (1567–1622), 499
Frankfurt, Germany, 703
Franklin, Benjamin (1706–1790), 606, 609

Index

A32

Frederick II (the Wise) elector of Saxony (1544–1556), 478
Frederick II (the Great), king of Prussia (1740–1786), 556, 560, 572, 609, 624, 625
Frederick William, elector of Brandenburg (1640–1688), 554–55
Frederick William I, king of Prussia (1713–1740), 554–56
Frederick William III, king of Prussia (1770–1840), 666
Free Companies, 385–86
free trade, 684
free will, 500
French and Indian War (Seven Years' War) (1756–1763), 572
French East India Company, 572
French Revolution (1789), 539, 546, 575, 636–71
    Austria and, 651, 654, 656
    Burke on, 651
    Catholic Church and, 648–50
    causes of, 639–42
    class and, 639–41
    and concept of nation, 670
    economic hardship and, 641–42
    Enlightenment and, 618, 619, 620, 630, 639, 641, 646, 647, 648, 662–69
    first stages of, 645–48
    "Great Fear" and, 646
    Haitian Revolution and, 668–69
    Industrial Revolution and, 692, 695, 696
    Jacobins in, 653, 658
    legacy of, 657, 670
    national identity forged in, 657
    Oath of the Tennis Court in, 643, 644–45
    October Days uprising in, 646–48
    Old Regime, destruction of, and, 642–50
    onset of, 645
    overview of, 638–39
    popular revolts and, 645–46
    radicalization of, 650–58
    religion and, 646–50, 653–54
    royal counterrevolution in, 650–51, 657
    September massacre in (1792), 653
    taxes and, 641–42
    Terror in, 639, 654–57, 658
    warfare and, 651, 654
    women and, 645, 646–48, 650, 657
Frequens (1417), 402
frescoes, 409
Friedland, battle of (1807), 661
Friedrich II, king of Denmark, 584
Fronde, 517
Fugger, Jacob (1459–1528), 476
Fugger family, 476

Galapagos Islands, 617
Galicia, 554, 561
Galileo Galilei (1564–1642), 460, 499, 579, 581, 585–89, 594
    legacy of, 588–89
Galileo Galilei before the Inquisition (Fleury), 588
Gallicans, 548
Gama, Vasco da (c. 1460–1524), 430, 431
Gargantua and Pantagruel (Rabelais), 466
Gascony, 384, 385, 387
Gdansk (Danzig), 554, 561
gender, *see* middle class, nineteenth-century; sexuality, sexual practice; women; working class, nineteenth-century
General Scholium (Newton), 596
Geneva, 485–87, 490, 507

Genghis Khan, 395, 418, 420–21
Genoa, 373, 379, 393, 420–21, 427–28, 438
Geoffrin, Marie-Thérése, 625
geometry, analytical, 592
George I, king of England (1714–1727), 544
George III, king of England (1760–1820), 574
George IV, king of England (1762–1830), 699
Germany (pre-unification), 419, 426, 443, 461, 463, 487, 497, 500, 506, 550, 551
    Black Death (plague) in, 373
    Enlightenment in, 609, 624, 626
    French Revolution and, 651
    in Industrial Revolution, 683, 684–85, 688
    language of, 500
    Lutheran Reformation in, 473–82
    manufacturing in, 562–63
    Napoleon vs., 663
    nationalism of, 464, 477–78
    national monarchy in, 392–93, 394–95
    in Thirty Years' War, 510, 513
Ghent, 508
Gibbon, Edward (1737–1794), 609
Gibraltar, 551, 553, 575
Ginevra da Benci (Leonardo), 454
Giorgione (1478–1510), 454
Giotto (c. 1266–1337), 409–10, 451
Gladstone, William (1809–1898), 696
Glorious Revolution (1688–1689), 544–45, 550
Gluck, Christoph Willibald von (1714–1787), 629
Goa, 430
God Dividing the Light from Darkness (Michelangelo), 456
Goethe, Johann Wolfgang von (1749–1832), 626
Golden Horde, khanate of the, 395–96, 397–98, 421
Gouges, Olympe de (Marie Gouze), 648
government:
    contract theory of, 545–46
    French Revolution, 648–50
    industrialization and, 683–85
    of Protestant cities, 488–90
    Rousseau and, 617–19
Goya, Francisco (1746–1828), 664, 665
Gracchus (François Babeuf) (1760–1797), 658
Granada, 393, 417, 515
gravity, law of, 595–98
Great Britain, 556, 570, 571
    American Revolution and, 572–75
    child labor in, 705
    commercial rivalry with France, 572
    Continental System and, 663
    education in, 626
    Enlightenment in, 609, 626
    French Revolution and, 651, 654, 655
    Great Famine and, 690, 691–92
    in Industrial Revolution, 674–83, 684–87, 688, 690, 693–94
    Napoleon vs., 658, 661, 664–68
    parliamentary government in, 576
    Parliament in, *see* Parliament, British
    railways in, 681–83
    religious toleration in, 607
    St. Domingue invaded by, 668
    slave trade and, 569, 570–72, 575
    sugar trade and, 565
    textile industry in, 677–80
    Treaty of Utrecht and, 553
    union of, 544–45
    Victorian era in, 696
    see also England
Great Famine, 690–92

Great Instauration (Instauratio Magna) (Bacon), 589, 599
Great Northern War, 555, 558
Great Schism (1378–1417), 393, 398–401, 402, 445
Great Wall, 418
"Great War, The," *see* World War, First (1914–1918)
Greece, 423
Greek New Testament, 464
Greenland, 434
Gregory XI, Pope (1370–1378), 399
Grimmelshausen, Hans Jakob Christoph von, 511
guild system, 550
    commercial revolution and, 562
guild system, Industrial Revolution and, 683, 684
Guise, duke of, 507
gunpowder, 410, 431
Gustavus Adolphus, king of Sweden (1611–1632), 513
Gutenberg, Johann, 413

Habsburg dynasty, 393, 426–27, 508, 513, 517, 542, 550–51, 553–54
    as loose confederation, 554
    see also Austria
Haec Sancto Synodus (1415), 402
Haiti, 567
    slave revolution in, 668–69
Halley, Edmond (1656–1742), 595, 596–97
Hamburg, 562
Hamlet (Shakespeare), 527, 579
Handbook of the Christian Knight (Erasmus), 463
Handel, George Frideric (1685–1759), 628
Hanoverian dynasty, 544, 558
Hanseatic League, 379
Hard Times (Dickens), 694
Hargreaves, James, 677
Harmonies of the World, The (Kepler), 585
Harvesters, The (Brueghel), 531
Harvey, William (1578–1657), 592
Hawaii, 614
Hawkins, John, 510
Haydn, Joseph (1732–1809), 628–29
Henrietta Maria, 518
Henry IV, king of England (1399–1413), 386
Henry IV, king of France (1589–1610), 507–8, 515, 517
Henry the Navigator (1394–1460), prince of Portugal, 431–33
Henry V, king of England (1413–1422), 387, 388, 401
Henry VI, king of England (1422–1461), 387, 388, 391
Henry VII, king of England (1485–1509), 391–92
Henry VIII, king of England (1509–1547), 464, 468, 500
    in break with Rome, 491–93, 494
Herder, Johann Gottfried von (1744–1803), 651
Hermetic Corpus (Ficino), 448
Hippel, Theodor Von, 620
Hispaniola, 434, 436
HIV/AIDS, 376
Hobbes, Thomas (1588–1679), 525, 545, 605
Hogarth, William (1697–1764), 597
Hohenzollern family, 393, 476, 554
Holbein, Hans, the Younger (c. 1497–1543), 463, 464, 468, 491
Holland, 438, 500, 505, 508, 542, 544, 550, 557, 562–63, 654
    agriculture in, 561
    Calvinism in, 487

INDEX

population growth in, 561
see also Netherlands
Holy Roman Empire, 508, 510, 550, 554
Hooke, Robert (1635–1703), 592–93, 595
Horrors of War, The (Rubens), 530, 531
Houdon, Jean Antoine, 604
House of Commons, British, 519, 545
see also Parliament, British
House of Lords, British, 521
see also Parliament, British
House of Orange, 542
Huddersfield, 694
Hugo, Victor (1802–1885), 696
Huguenots, 487, 507
persecution of, 507–8, 516, 548
Huizinga, Johann, 384
Human Comedy (Balzac), 696
humanism:
Christian, 448, 462–65, 469, 495, 499, 500
civic, 446, 447
of Renaissance, 443, 444–45, 446, 447, 462–65, 469
scientific revolution and, 581
humanitarianism, 609–11
Humboldt, Alexander von (1769–1859), 616, 620
Hume, David (1711–1776), 605, 606, 609
Hundred Years' War, 384–92, 393, 410, 431, 508
Hungary, 419, 487, 508, 542, 553–54, 556
Hus, Jan (c. 1373–1415), 405–6, 413
Hussites, 405–6, 473
Hutten, Ulrich von (1488–1523), 464–65
Huygens, Christian (1629–1695), 592

Iberian peninsula, 417, 433
Ibn Majid, 430
Ignatius Loyola, Saint (1491–1556), 496–97
Imitation of Christ, The (Thomas à Kempis), 405, 409
Imperial Diet, German, 482
Incas, 436
Independents, 519
Index of Prohibited Books, 460, 496
India, 411, 418, 420, 423, 430, 431, 565, 567, 570, 572, 681, 687
Anglo-French rivalry in, 572
indulgences, Luther's campaign against, 475, 476
industrialization:
communication in, 685
consumers and, 675–76
environment and, 694, 695–96, 706
government and, 683–85
human beings in, new role of, 674, 706
productivity and, 673–74
railway boom and, 681–83
second industrial revolution and, 673
social consequences of, 684–705
social tensions in, 674
Industrial Revolution, 673–706
after 1850, 684–86
agriculture in, 673, 674, 675, 683, 685, 688–93
banks in, 684
capitalism in, 673–74, 675, 683–84
child labor in, 679–80, 681, 705
class in, 674, 704–5, 706
coal industry in, 673, 680–82, 683
commerce in, 674–77, 687
on Continent, 683–88
education in, 684
entrepreneurship in, 675–77
expanding markets in, 674, 676–77, 683
factory life in, 679–80, 704–5
French Revolution and, 683, 692, 695, 696

in Great Britain, 674–83, 684–87
guild system in, 683, 684
iron industry in, 682, 683, 684, 685
origins of, 674
peasantry in, 688–93
population growth in, 674, 683, 688, 693–94, 705
railways in, 681–83
rural poverty in, 688–93
second (1870–1914), 673
standard of living in, 673, 693–96
steam engine and, 673, 677, 680, 682–83
textile industry in, 677–80, 683, 687
transportation in, 673, 675–76, 681–83, 685, 693
urbanization in, 673, 693–96
women workers in, 674
working class in, 674, 678–80, 681–83, 684, 701–5
world economy in, 685–88
inertia, theory of, 588, 594
inflation:
colonization and, 436–38
Price Revolution and, 504–5
Innocent VIII, Pope (1484–1492), 481, 522
Inquisition, 587–88
Roman, 460, 465, 522
Spanish, 481
Inspiration of Saint Jerome, The (Reni), 497
Institutes of the Christian Religion (Calvin), 484, 496
Instrument of Government (England; 1653), 521
insurance, 379
Iran, 420
Ireland, 495, 517, 545, 550, 569, 683, 685
Great Famine in, 690–92
Isabella, Queen of Aragon and Castile (1479–1504), 393–94, 417, 434, 435, 479, 480, 515
Islam, 556
Enlightenment and, 611
Ottoman Empire and, 425–26
Islamic civilization, 417
Abbasid caliphate of, 423
Istanbul, *see* Constantinople
Italy, 373, 379, 411, 438, 509, 515, 551, 552, 554
banking industry in, 380
Catholic Reformation and, 495
Enlightenment in, 609, 624
French Revolution and, 651, 654, 655
Industrial Revolution in, 681, 685
literature of, 407–9
Napoleon vs., 658, 662
national monarchy in, 393, 394–95
papacy in, 393, 398–401, 478
Renaissance in, 409, 443–46
rise of opera in, 629–30
slavery in, 433
Ivan III (the Great), tsar of Russia (1462–1505), 397–98
Ivan IV (the Terrible), tsar of Russia (1533–1584), 557

Jacobins, 653, 658, 663
Mountain party of, 656
Jacquerie uprising (1358), 380–82
Jadwiga, queen of Poland (1384–1399), 397
Jagiello, grand duke of Lithuania, 397
Jamaica, 570, 571
James I, king of England (1603–1625), 517–18, 544
James II, king of England (1685–1688), 543, 544, 545, 546, 550
Jamestown settlement, 565
Jansen, Cornelius (1585–1638), 548

Jansenism, 525, 548
Japan, 567
Java, 421
Jefferson, Thomas (1743–1826), 609, 614, 625
Jena, battle of (1806), 663
Jenner, Edward (1749–1823), 688
Jerome, Saint (c. 340–420), 448, 463, 497
Jerusalem, 425
Jesuits (Society of Jesus), 496–97, 505, 507, 548, 586
Jesus of Nazareth, 402
Jews:
Enlightenment and, 610–11
French Revolution and, 646
in Ottoman Empire, 424
persecution of, 375, 394, 395, 556
see also anti-Semitism; Judaism
Joan of Arc (c. 1412–1431), 387–88, 389, 401, 404
John II (the Good), king of France (1350–1364), 385–86
John of Leyden, 484
Johnson, Samuel (1709–1784), 630
joint-stock companies, first, 684–85
Jonson, Ben (c. 1572–1637), 526–27
Joseph I, Holy Roman emperor (1705–1711), 552
Joseph II, Holy Roman emperor (1765–1790), 540–42, 554
Josephine, empress of France (1763–1814), 661, 663
Judaism:
Enlightenment and, 610–11
see also anti-Semitism; Jews
Julianna of Norwich, 405
Julie (Rousseau), 619
Julius II, Pope (1502–1513), 446, 459, 477–78
Julius Excluded (Erasmus), 478
Junkers, 555, 556
Jupiter (planet), 586
justification by faith, doctrine of, 475, 476, 493

Kabbalah, 448
Kant, Immanuel (1724–1804), 604, 606, 625
Kay, John (1704–1764), 677
Kempe, Margery, 405
Kepler, Johannes (1571–1630), 579, 581, 583–85
laws of, 585–86
Keynes, John Maynard (1883–1946), 598
Kiev, 395, 397
King Lear (Shakespeare), 527
King William's War (1689–1697), 550
Knights of the Garter, 384
Knox, John (1513–1572), 487, 500
Kosovo, battle of (1389), 423
Kremlin, 398, 557
Kublai Khan, 418, 420–21

Labrador, 434
Laclos, Choderlos de, 621
La Fayette, Countess de, 626
Lafayette, Marquis de (1757–1834), 645
laissez-faire, policy of, 611
Lancastrian dynasty, 386, 391
Landini, Francesco (c. 1325–1397), 468
language:
English, *see* English language
Latin, *see* Latin language
of Mongols, 418
in Renaissance, 442, 443, 446–48
Laocoön group, 529
Lassus, Roland de (1532–1594), 468, 469
Last Judgment (Michelangelo), 456, 460
Last Supper, The (Leonardo), 453, 454

INDEX

A34

Lateran Councils, Fifth (1512–1517), 481
Latin language, in Renaissance, 443, 446
Laud, William, 518
law:
  absolutism and, 540, 545–46
  Napoleonic Code and, 660, 662
  in pre-Enlightenment era, 603–4
League of Augsburg, 550
Leeds, 703
Lefèvre d'Étaples, Jacques (c. 1455–1536), 465
Leibniz, Gottfried, 594
Leipzig, 476
Leo X, Pope (1513–1521), 446, 459, 476, 477, 478, 481
Leonardo da Vinci (1452–1519), 453–54, 455, 457, 469, 581
Leopold I, Holy Roman emperor (1658–1705), 551, 552
Lepanto, battle of (1571), 427
Lescot, Pierre (c. 1515–1578), 467
Lessing, Gotthold (1729–1781), 611
Letters of Obscure Men (Hutten and Crotus Rubianus), 464
Letters on Sunspots (Galileo), 586
Letter to the Grand Duchess Christina di Medici (Galileo), 586, 587
Leviathan (Hobbes), 525
Leyster, Judith (1609–1660), 531
liberalism, French Revolution and, 646–48
Liegnitz, battle of (1241), 419
linear perspective, 451
Lisbon, 433
literacy:
  cities and, 627
  Counter-Reformation and, 499
  in Enlightenment, 605–6, 625–27
  printing and, 413
  see also education
literature:
  on absolutism, 525
  Cervantes and, 526
  education and, 407
  Elizabethan and Jacobean, 526–27
  essay as form of, 523–25
  of Late Middle Ages, 407–9
  national identity and, 407
  naturalism in, 407–9, 466
  of nineteenth-century middle class, 694–96
  novel as form of, 626
  professional authors and, 409
  Renaissance, 442, 443, 445, 446, 449–51, 463–66, 469
  vernacular languages in, 407–9
  women authors of, 626
Lithuania, 396–97, 417, 487, 539, 553, 558, 561
Liverpool, 562
Livonia, 558
Livy (59 B.C.E.–17 C.E.), 442
Locke, John (1632–1704), 541, 545–46, 574, 597, 604–6, 617, 641
logic, 407, 443
Lollards, 405–6, 473, 490
Lombard, Peter (c. 1095–1160), 475
Loménie de Brienne, Étienne Charles (1727–1794), 642
London, 373, 548, 562
  Black Death in, 505
  environmental problems and, 694, 696
  first daily newspapers in, 622
  nineteenth-century population of, 693
Lords, House of, see Parliament, British
Louis IX (Saint Louis), king of France (1226–1270), 420

Louis XI, king of France (1461–1483), 391
Louis XII, king of France (1498–1515), 391, 460
Louis XIII, king of France (1610–1643), 515, 516, 517
Louis XIV (the Sun King), king of France (1643–1675), 517, 539, 567, 576, 607, 641
  absolutism of, 540, 543, 544, 546–52
  administration and centralization under, 547–48
  foreign policy of, 550
  religious policies of, 548
  War of the Spanish Succession and, 550–52
  wars of, 550–52
Louis XV, king of France (1715–1774), 642
Louis XVI, king of France (1774–1792), 639, 642, 643, 645, 646, 651, 653, 658
Louis XVIII, king of France (1795–1814), 666
Louvre, 467
Lübeck, 379, 380
Lucretius (98–55 B.C.E.), 442
Lusiads, The (Camöens), 430
Luther, Martin (1483–1546), 464, 465, 473–82, 483, 487, 488, 489, 495, 496, 500, 503, 522
  Calvin compared with, 485
  conversion experience of, 474–75
  at Diet of Worms, 478–80
  indulgences campaign of, 475, 476
  ninety-five theses of, 476, 495
  printing press and, 413, 477
Lutheranism:
  Calvinism and, 485
  Catholicism vs., 474–77
  marriage and, 477
  monasticism and, 476–77, 481
  papacy and, 476–78, 481
  theological premises of, 474–77
  women and, 487–90
Luxembourg, 550
lycées, 660
Lycidas (Milton), 527

Macaulay, Catherine, 620
Macbeth (Shakespeare), 527
Machaut, Guillaume de (c. 1300–1377), 468
Machiavelli, Niccolò (1469–1527), 448–49, 450, 451, 469
Madeira, 430, 433, 434
Madness of Roland, The (Ariosto), 451
Magellan, Ferdinand (c. 1480–1521), 435
Magic Flute, The (Mozart), 630
Magna Carta, 543
Maids of Honor, The (Velázquez), 529
maize cultivation, 561
Malplaquet, battle of (1709), 551
Malthus, Thomas (1766–1834), 689
Mamluk Egypt, 423, 424, 425
Manchester, 694
Mandragola (Machiavelli), 451
Manila, 565
Maoris, 614, 615
Marat, Jean Paul (1743–1793), 655, 656
Maria Theresa, empress of Austria (1740–1780), 554, 556, 572, 642
Marie Antoinette, queen of France (1755–1793), 629, 642, 650
Marie Louise, empress of France (1791–1847), 663
Marignano, battle of (1515), 460
Marlowe, Christopher (1564–1593), 526
marriage:
  Catholic Church and, 488, 491

cultural assimilation and, 568–69
  in Industrial Revolution, 688
  Lutheranism and, 477
  nineteenth century and, 698, 699–701
  Protestantism and, 487–90
  Wollstonecraft's view of, 620–21
Marriage of Figaro, The (Mozart), 630
Mars (planet), 582
Marseillaise, 657
Martin V, Pope (1417–1431), 401
Marx, Karl (1818–1883), 639
Mary, Queen of Scots (1542–1587), 500
Mary, Virgin, 404
  in art, 455
Mary I, queen of England (1553–1558), 491, 493–94, 500, 510
Mary II, queen of England (1689–1694), 544–45, 546, 550
Maryland, 568
Mary of Modena, queen of England (1658–1718), 544
Masaccio (1401–1428), 451, 452
Masons, 625
Massachusetts Bay colony, 568, 575
Massacre of the Innocents (Brueghel), 530, 531
Massys, Quentin, 379
mathematics:
  calculus and, 595
  Descartes and, 589–92
  Newton and, 594–97
Mathew, Theopold, 691
Mazarin, Cardinal (1602–1661), 517
Measure for Measure (Shakespeare), 527
Mecca, 425
Medici, Catherine de' (1519–1589), 507
Medici, Christina de', grand duchess, 586, 587
Medici, Cosimo de' (1389–1464), 448, 586, 587
Medici, Lorenzo de' (1449–1492), 449, 450, 453
Medici, Piero de' (1414–1469), 449, 450
Medici family, 380, 393, 443, 446, 448, 449, 477, 586, 587
medicine, advances in, 688
Medina, 425
Meeting of Joachim and Anna (Giotto), 410
Mehmet II (the Conqueror), Ottoman sultan (1444–1481), 422–23, 424, 425
Memling, Hans (c. 1430–1494), 409–10
Mendelssohn, Felix (1809–1847), 611
Mendelssohn, Moses (1729–1786), 611, 625
Mennonites, 484
Menno Simons (c. 1496–1561), 484
Menshikov, Alexander (c. 1670–1729), 558
mercantilism, 563–64
  in Enlightenment, 611–12
Mercier, Louis Sebastien, 624
Merian, Maria Sibylla, 594
Messiah (Handel), 628
Mexico, Spanish conquest of, 435–38, 565
Michelangelo (1475–1564), 451, 455–59, 460, 467, 469, 528, 529, 586
Michelet, Jules (1798–1874), 699
Michelin, Edouard, 685
microscope, 592–93
Middle Ages, High:
  classical learning in, 442
  Crusades in, see Crusades
  mechanical engineering in, 581
Middle Ages, Late, 370–407
  agriculture in, 371, 372–73, 377
  aristocracy in, 382–84
  art of, 409–10
  cities in, 378–80
  climate in, 371, 372–73

INDEX A35

commerce in, 372, 373, 377–80, 411
education in, 407, 414
exploration in, 411
literature of, 407–9
mysticism in, 405, 409
national monarchies in, 394–95, 410
natural disasters in, 372–73
natural world and, 414
papacy and, 398–406
philosophy in, 407
plague epidemic in, 371, 373–80
popular rebellions in, 380–82
religion in, 398–406
science and technology in, 410–14
serfdom in, 377–78
slavery in, 378
social change in, 380–84
women in, 414
middle class, eighteenth-century, in Britain, 607
middle class, nineteenth-century, 696–705
  Enlightenment and, 624–26
  French Revolution and, 637, 639–41
  home life of, 697–701
  literature of, 694–96
  Napoleonic rule and, 661–63
  public life in, 701–2
  respectability and, 697, 706
  sexuality of, 699–701
  subdivisions of, 696
Midsummer Night's Dream (Shakespeare), 527
Milan, 379, 393, 454, 460, 461, 552
Milton, John (1608–1674), 408, 527
Ming dynasty, 422
Minorca, 551, 553
Mirabeau, Honoré Gabriel Riqueti, Comte de, 640, 644
"Miracle" symphony (Haydn), 629
Misérables, Les (Hugo), 696
missionaries, 487
Moll Flanders (Defoe), 626
Mona Lisa (Leonardo), 454
monasticism, 473, 487
  Cistercian, 469
  in England, 492
  Lutheranism and, 476–77, 481
money, Price Revolution and, 504–5
Mongol Empire, 418–22
  commerce and, 420–22
  rise of, 418–22
Mongolia, 373, 395, 418
Mongols (Tartars), 394–97
Montaigne, Michel de (1533–1592), 523–25
Montesquieu, Charles-Louis Secondat, baron de (1689–1755), 604, 607–8, 612, 617, 620, 625, 641
Monteverdi, Claudio (1567–1643), 629
Moravia, 554
More, Thomas (1478–1535), 464, 465, 468, 469, 492, 495
Moscow, 395–97
  Napoleon's occupation of, 665
Moses (Michelangelo), 458
Mozart, Wolfgang Amadeus (1756–1791), 625, 627–29, 630
Much Ado about Nothing (Shakespeare), 527
Muhammad (prophet), 424, 425
Münster, 483–84
Müntzer, Thomas (c. 1490–1525), 482
music:
  Baroque, 628–30
  Classical style of, 628–29
  of Enlightenment, 627–30
  Franco-Flemish style of, 468

operatic, 468, 629–30
of Renaissance, 461, 468–69
musical instruments, 468
mysticism, 448, 499
  in Late Middle Ages, 405, 409
  of Quietists, 548

Nantes, Edict of (1598), 508, 510, 515, 516, 548
Naples, 401, 460, 461, 515, 552, 562
Napoleon I, emperor of France (1769–1821), 388
  Continental System of, 663, 683
  crowned emperor, 661
  downfall of, 639, 663–69
  in exile, 666, 667
  as first consul, 659
  papacy and, 661
  rise of, 658–60
  in wars of expansion, 661, 664–68
Napoleonic Code, 660, 662
Nathan the Wise (Lessing), 611
National Assembly (France), 644–45, 646–50, 651, 657, 668
National Convention (France), 653, 658
National Guard (France), 645, 646
nationalism, 503
  English, 494
  German, 464, 477–78
  Protestantism and, 500
  spread of books and, 413
Native Americans, 565, 569
navigation, 428–30
Necker, Jacques (1732–1804), 642
Necker, Madame, 625
Nelson, Horatio (1758–1805), 658, 664
Neoplatonism, 580–81
  in Renaissance, 448, 452, 456, 459
Netherlands, 426, 428, 463, 514, 542–43, 550, 551–52, 554, 571
  art of, 529–32
  colonialism and, 539, 567–68
  French Revolution and, 656
  Industrial Revolution in, 685
  manufacturing in, 562–63
  mercantilism in, 539, 567–68
  Napoleon vs., 663
  religious wars in, 508–9
  see also Holland
New Amsterdam, 567
New Atlantis (Bacon), 589
Newcomen, Thomas (1663–1729), 680
New England, 434, 571
Newfoundland, 434, 553
New Hebrides, 614
New Holland, 614
New Model Army, 520
newspapers, 622
New Testament, 462, 500
  Erasmus's translation of, 464
Newton, Isaac (1642–1727), 580, 594–600, 604, 606, 612
New World:
  European rediscovery of, 417, 434–38, 504
  migration to, 690
  see also colonialism; specific countries
New York, 567
New Zealand, 614
Nicopolis, battle of (1396), 426
Nicot, Jean (c. 1530–1600), 565
Nightingale, Florence (1820–1910), 699
Nijmegen, Treaty of (1678–1679), 550
Niña, 428
Nine Years' War (1689–1697), 550

Nobel family, 685
nobility:
  absolutism and, 540–42, 547–48
  British, 675
  commerce and, 675
  French Revolution and, 637, 639–41, 642, 643
  in Late Middle Ages, 382–84
nominalism, 407
Norway, 482
Notes on the New Testament (Valla), 448, 464, 500
novel, as literary form, 626
Novum Organum (Bacon), 590–91
Nystad, Peace of (1712), 558–60

Oath of the Tennis Court (1789), 643, 644–45, 647
Ockham, William of (c. 1285–1349), 407
Ogé, Vincent, 668
Ögedei, 418–19
oil, 673
Old Goriot (Balzac), 696
Old Testament, 484
"On Cannibals" (Montaigne), 523
On Crimes and Punishment (Beccaria), 610
On Temporal Authority (Luther), 482
On the Family (Alberti), 446
On the Religious Authority of Judaism (M. Mendelssohn), 611
On the Revolutions of the Heavenly Bodies (*De Revolutionibus*) (Copernicus), 579, 583, 586
opera, 468
Oration on the Dignity of Man (Pico della Mirandola), 448
oratorio, 628
Order of the Star, 384
Orlando Furioso (Ariosto), 451, 465
Ottoman Empire, 422–27, 553–54, 558, 560
  Christians in, 425, 426
  commerce and, 423
  Constantinople captured by, 397, 410, 422–23, 431
  in Europe, 422, 426–27
  Islam and, 425–26
  Jews in, 424
  Mongols and, 420
  Persians vs., 426, 427
  religious conflicts in, 425–26
  slavery in, 423–24, 433
Ovid (43 B.C.E.–17 C.E.), 442
Oxford University, 462

Pacific Ocean, 435
Padua, University of, 462
Paine, Thomas (1737–1809), 620, 652, 653
Palatinate, 550
Palestrina, Giovanni Pierluigi da (c. 1525–1594), 468, 469
Palladio, Andrea (1508–1580), 459, 529
papacy:
  in Avignon, 398–401
  Catholic reform and, 495–99
  clergy and, 399, 403
  College of Cardinals and, 399–400, 477, 478
  conciliarism controversy and, 401, 402–3, 473, 481
  east-west rift and, 396–97
  England and, 491–93, 494
  French monarchy and, 398–401
  French Revolution and, 648
  Great Schism in, 393, 398–401, 402, 445
  Henry VIII's break with, 491–93, 494
  Italy and, 393, 398–401

INDEX

A36

papacy (continued)
  in Late Middle Ages, 398–406
  Lutheranism and, 476–78, 481
  as monarchy, 401
  Napoleon's concordat with, 661
  in Renaissance, 442, 445–46
  Russia and, 397
  sale of indulgences by, 475, 476
  witchcraft and, 522
  see also Catholic Church; *specific popes*
Papal States, 393, 398, 403, 446, 460, 461
Paradise Lost (Milton), 527
Paris, 373, 389, 504, 507–8, 525, 563
  September Massacres in (1792), 653
  sewers of, 694, 696
Paris, Treaty of (1763), 572
Paris, Treaty of (1783), 575
Paris, University of, 402, 462, 463, 473
Paris, urbanization of, 562
Parkinson, Sydney, 614
parlements, French, 540, 548, 641, 642
Parliament, British, 391, 491, 513, 517, 544–46
  crown vs., 518–22, 543
Pascal, Blaise (1632–1662), 525–26, 592
Paul, Saint, 475
  Epistles of, 448
Paul III, Pope (1534–1549), 495, 497
Paul IV, Pope (1555–1559), 460, 495
Pavia, battle of (1525), 460
Peace of Augsburg (1555), 506, 510
Peace of Nystad (1712), 558–60
Peace of the Pyrenees (1659), 515
Peace of Westphalia (1648), 513
peasantry, in Industrial Revolution, 688–93
Peasants' Revolt (England; 1381), 380–82
Peasants' Revolt (Germany; 1525), 482
Peasant Wedding (Brueghel), 531
Peasant Wedding Dance (Brueghel), 531
Pennsylvania, 568, 569
Pensées (Pascal), 526
Persian Letters, The (Montesquieu), 607
Personal Narratives of Travels (Humbolt), 616
perspective, linear, 451
Peru, Spanish conquest of, 435–38, 565
Peter, Saint, 402
Peter I (the Great), tsar of Russia (1682–1725), 398, 540, 557–60
Peter III, tsar of Russia (1762), 560
Petition of Right (England; 1628), 519, 522, 543
Petrarch, Francesco (1304–1374), 411, 443, 446, 467, 469
Petrarchan sonnets, 446
Philip II, king of Spain (1556–1598), 493, 509, 510, 514
Philip IV (the Fair), king of France (1285–1314), 385
Philip IV, king of Spain (1621–1665), 550
Philip V, king of Spain (1700–1746), 551, 552
Philip VI, king of France (1328–1350), 385
Philippines, 514, 551
philosophes, 606–9, 617, 619, 627, 630
  definition of, 606
Philosophical Dictionary (Voltaire), 610
Philosophical History . . . of Europeans in the Two Indies (Raynal), 612, 624
Philosophical Letters (Voltaire), 606
Philosophical Transactions (Newton), 595
philosophy:
  deductive method of, 591, 592, 596
  inductive method of, 589
  in Late Middle Ages, 407
  mechanists and, 592, 593
  natural, 579, 586, 588–92, 593–97, 599, 600

religion and, 522
  in Renaissance, 448–49, 460, 462–65
  scientific revolution and, 579, 581, 586, 588–92
physics, Aristotelian, 582, 583
physiocrats, 611, 641
Pico della Mirandola, Giovanni (1463–1494), 448
pilgrimage, 404
Pilgrims, 565
Pilgrim's Progress, The (Bunyan), 627
Pisa, 401
Pius V, Pope (1566–1572), 495
Pizarro, Francisco (c. 1475–1541), 436
plague, *see* Black Death
Plato (c. 429–c. 349 B.C.E.), 442, 447, 448, 455, 469
Platonic Academy (Florence), 448, 469
plebiscite, 659
Plotinus (205–270), 448
Poitiers, battle of (1356), 385, 387
Poland, 373, 419, 424, 461, 473, 487, 497, 539, 553, 554, 556, 558
  partition of, 560–61
  Russia's rivalry with, 397
Polish Rider, The (Rembrandt), 532
Political Testament (Richelieu), 516
Polo, Marco, 420–21
Poltava, battle of (1709), 558
Pomerania, 554, 555
Pontormo, Jacopo da (1494–1557), 528
Pope, Alexander (1688–1744), 597, 605
popular culture, in Enlightenment, 626–27
population growth, 504–5, 575–76
  commercial revolution and, 561–62, 563
population patterns and growth, in Industrial Revolution, 674, 683, 688, 693–94, 705
Portrait of Doge Francesco Venier (Titian), 454
Portugal, 394, 515, 565, 570
  expansion and exploration by, 417, 423, 428, 430–34, 438, 539
  independence of, 514, 515
  slave trade and, 431, 433–34, 570, 571
potato cultivation, 561
Prague, 405, 462
Praise of Folly, The (Erasmus), 463, 478
predestination, doctrine of, 475, 500
Presbyterians, 487
Prester John, legend of, 431, 432
Price Revolution, 437–38, 504–5
Pride and Prejudice (Austen), 626
Prince, The (Machiavelli), 449, 450
Principia Mathematica (Newton), 580, 595–97
printing, 562
  invention of, 412, 413
  Luther's use of, 413, 477
prostitution, 694–96, 701, 703
Protestantism:
  discipline and, 487–88
  education and, 500
  in England, 500, 510, 543
  family and, 487–90
  French Revolution and, 646
  Hussite Revolution and, 406
  marriage and, 487–90
  national identity and, 500
  rise of, 465
  social relationships and, 500
  spread of, 460, 482–88, 491–95
  state power and, 500
  William of Ockham and, 407
  women and, 487–90, 499, 500
  see also specific denominations

Protestant Reformation, 406, 464, 465, 473–500, 522, 582
  Calvinism and, 484–87
  Catholic Reformation and, 495–99
  Christian humanism and, 495, 500
  domestication of, 487–90
  in England, 490–95
  German princes and, 480–82
  in Germany, 473–82
  Lollardy and, 405, 491
  Lutheran Reformation and, 473–82
  onset of, 476–77
  Renaissance and, 499–500
  in Switzerland, 482–87
protoindustrialization, 674
Prussia, 392, 397, 551, 558–60, 562, 572
  absolutism in, 540–42
  French Revolution and, 651
  in Industrial Revolution, 683, 684
  Junker class of, 555, 556
  militarism of, 554–56
  Napoleon vs., 661, 663–64, 665, 666, 667
  partition of Poland and, 560–61
  in Seven Years' War, 572
  Silesia seized by, 556
Psalms, 475
Ptolemy I, king of Egypt (323–285 B.C.E.), 581, 582–83
public opinion, 625
Pugachev, Emelyan (1726–1775), 560
Puritans, 487, 518, 519, 527
  English Civil War and, 519–21
Pyrenees, Peace of (1659), 515

quadrants, 428–30
Quakers, 569
Qubilai Khan, 418, 420–21
Quebec, battle of (1759), 572
Quietists, 548

Rabelais, François (c. 1494–1553), 465–66
Radcliffe, Ann (1764–1823), 626
railways, in Industrial Revolution, 681–83
Raleigh, Sir Walter (1554–1618), 565
Raphael (1483–1520), 446, 455, 460, 469, 477, 528
rationalism, 499
Raynal, Guillaume Thomas François, 612, 613, 624
Razin, Stenka, 557
reading glasses, 580
Reflections on the Revolution in France (Burke), 651, 652
Reformation, *see* Protestant Reformation
Regiomontanus, Johannes, 581
regionalism, 506
  in France, 507, 547–48
religion:
  colonization and, 565, 567
  Encyclopedia and, 608, 609
  Enlightenment and, 610–11
  French Revolution and, 646–50, 653–54
  in Late Middle Ages, 398–406
  Mongol, 420
  in Ottoman Empire, 425–26
  philosophy and, 522
  power of state and, 522–23
  scientific revolution and, 580–82, 585–89
  toleration and, 556
  wars of, 505–13, 532
  see also mysticism; papacy; *specific religions*
Rembrandt van Rijn (1606–1669), 410, 531–32
Renaissance, 440–71
  architecture of, 458–59
  art of, 409, 445–46, 451–59, 467–68, 469

INDEX A37

classical learning and, 442, 443, 445, 462
commerce in, 460
decline of, 459–61
definition of, 441
education in, 443–46, 462
English, 526
in Florence, 446, 448–49, 452–54, 457, 460
High, 454, 455, 457
humanism of, 443, 444–45, 446, 447, 462–65, 469
ideal of courtier in, 449–51
Italian, 409, 443–61
Italian political and military disasters and, 449, 460
Latin in, 443, 446
literature of, 442, 443, 445, 446, 449–51, 463–66, 469
Middle Ages and, 442, 462, 469
music of, 461, 468–69
Neoplatonism in, 448, 452, 456, 459
northern, 462–69
origins of, 443–46
papacy and, 442, 445–46
patronage in, 462
philosophy in, 448–49, 460, 462–65
science in, 460
scientific revolution and, 581
textual scholarship in, 446–48
women in, 443, 447, 451
Rend, W. P., 695
Reni, Guido (1575–1642), 497
Reuchlin, Johann, 464–65
Reynolds, Joshua (1723–1792), 615
rhetoric, 443
Rhineland, 550
Richard II, king of England (1377–1399), 382, 386, 387, 391
Richard III, king of England (1483–1485), 391–92
Richardson, Samuel (1689–1761), 626
Richelieu, Cardinal (1585–1642), 513, 515–17
Rigaud, Hyacinthe, 546
Rights of Man, The (Paine), 652, 653
River Sajo, battle of (1241), 419
Robespierre, Maximilien (1758–1794), 654, 655, 658, 668
Robinson Crusoe (Defoe), 626
Rocroi, battle of (1643), 514
Roman calendar, 582
Romance of the Rose (William of Lorris and Jean de Meung), 409
Romanov dynasty, 557
Romanticism, 620
Rome:
　papacy in, 398–401
　in Renaissance, 445–46, 455–57, 460
Romeo and Juliet (Shakespeare), 527
Ronsard, Pierre de (c. 1524–1585), 465, 467
Rothschild family, 685
Roundheads, 519
Rousseau, Jean-Jacques (1712–1778), 604, 605, 617–21, 624, 626, 630, 647
Royal Academy of Sciences, French, 599
Royal Society (England), 593, 595–96, 599, 624
Rubens, Peter Paul, 530, 531
Rubruck, William de, 420
Rudolf I of Habsburg, Holy Roman emperor (1273–1291), 409
Rudolph II, Holy Roman emperor (1576–1612), 584
Rules for Monasteries (Saint Benedict), 498
Rump Parliament, 519–21

Rus, 395, 397
Russia, 373, 395–98, 555
　absolutism in, 553, 557–61
　autocratic tradition of, 539–40
　Byzantium and, 397–98
　Enlightenment in, 609, 623
　expansion of, 558–61
　Industrial Revolution and, 684, 685, 688, 690
　Mongol invasion of, 395–97, 419
　Napoleon I vs., 661, 664–68
　Orthodox Christianity in, 396–97
　papacy and, 397
　partition of Poland and, 560–61
　peasants' rebellion in, 560
　Poland's rivalry with, 397
　reign of Catherine the Great in, 560–61
　reign of Ivan the Great in, 397–98
　rise of Muscovy and, 395–97
　serfdom in, 558
　in Seven Years' War, 572
　streltsy rebellion in, 557
　textile industry in, 685
　transformation of, under Peter I, 557–58
Russo-Turkish War (1877–1878), 561
Ryswick, Treaty of (1694), 550

St. Bartholomew's Day Massacre (1572), 525
St. Domingue, 567, 571
St. Helena, island of, 667
Saint Jerome in His Study (Dürer), 467
St. Kitts, 553
St. Lo, 378
St. Peter's Basilica, 459, 529
St. Petersburg, 558
Salem, Massachusetts, 523
salons, 625
Salzburg, archbishop of, 629, 630
Sand, George (1804–1876), 699
sans-culottes, 645, 654, 657
Sardinia, 427, 433
Savonarola, Girolamo, 487
Saxony, 550
Scandinavia, 373, 379, 482
Scholasticism, 407, 445, 446, 463, 466, 469, 499
School of Athens (Raphael), 455
science and technology:
　artillery and, 430–31
　colonialism and, 428–31
　in Enlightenment, 604, 614–17, 630
　Industrial Revolution and, 673–74, 684
　in industry and manufacturing, 562–53
　in Late Middle Ages, 410–14
　missions of discovery and, 614–17
　natural philosophy and, 588–92
　navigation and, 428–30
　nominalism in, 407
　textile industry and, 677–80
scientific revolution, 578–601
　academic societies and, 593–94
　in astronomy, 582–89
　intellectual roots of, 580–82
　mechanists and, 581, 592, 593, 597
　philosophy and, 579, 581, 588–92
　religion and, 580–82, 585–89
　Renaissance influence on, 581
　scientific method and, 592–94, 605
Scotland, 391, 394, 395, 401, 539, 544–45, 674
　Calvinism in, 487
　in English Civil War, 517–19
　in Hundred Years' War, 384–85
　national monarchy in, 473
Scott, Walter (1771–1832), 391
Scudéry, Madeleine de, 626

sculpture:
　Baroque, 528–29
　medieval naturalism in, 580
　of Renaissance, 457–58
　see also art; specific cultures
sects, 483–84
Seljuk Turks, 422
seminaries, 496
sensibilité, cult of, 620
Sephardic Jews, 424
Serbia, 553
serfs, serfdom, 683
　abolition of, 685, 690–91, 693
　in Late Middle Ages, 377–78
　Peasants' Revolt and, 380–82
　in Russia, 558
Seven Years' War (French and Indian War) (1756–1763), 572, 574, 642
Seville, 504, 514, 565
sexuality, sexual practice:
　in nineteenth-century cities, 694–96
　of nineteenth-century middle class, 699–701
　of urban working class, 703–5
　of women, 699–701
Seymour, Jane, queen of England, 493
Sforza family, 454
Shakespeare, William (1564–1616), 408, 527, 579
Shapin, Steven, 583
Shiite Moslems, 426
shipbuilding, 428, 431
Sicily, 373, 394, 427–28, 460, 515
Sidney, Philip (1554–1586), 465
Siena, 401
Sieyès, Abbé Emmanuel (1748–1836), 643, 644, 657, 658
Sigismund, Holy Roman emperor (1433–1437), 386, 401
Silesia, 553, 556, 572
Silk Road, 418, 420–22
Simplicissimus (Grimmelshausen), 511
Sir Thomas More (Holbein), 464
Sisters of Charity, 499
Sistine Chapel, 456–57
Six Articles (1539), 492, 493
Six Books of the Commonwealth (Bodin), 525
Sixtus IV, Pope (1471–1484), 480
Sixtus V, Pope (1585–1590), 495
slaves, slavery, 378
　abolition of, 575, 613–14
　antislavery movements and, 613–14
　Atlantic colonization and, 433–34, 436
　colonialism and, 428, 433–34, 575
　commercial revolution and, 570–72
　cotton gin and, 677
　in Enlightenment era, 612, 613–14
　French Revolution and, 648, 653
　in Haitian Revolution, 668–69
　in Italy, 433
　Native Americans and, 569
　in Ottoman Empire, 423–24, 433
　plantation-based, 434, 436
　Portugal and, 433–34, 571
　Treaty of Utrecht and, 553
　triangular trade and, 570–72
Smiles, Samuel (1812–1904), 697
Smith, Adam (1723–1790), 609, 611–12, 614, 620
Social Contract, The (Rousseau), 617–19, 624
Société Générale, 684
Society of Jesus (Jesuits), 496–97, 505, 507
Society of the Friends of Blacks, 614
"Solomon's house," 589

INDEX

A38

Sophia, regent of Russia (1657–1704), 557
Sophocles (496–406 B.C.E.), 447
South America, 565, 567
Spain, 393, 426, 449, 460, 461–62, 480, 493,
    494, 500, 508–9, 517, 518, 532, 542,
    550, 551, 570, 571, 572, 575, 654
  absolutism in, 540–42
  Catholic Reformation in, 494
  Christian reconquest of, 417
  colonialism of, 539, 565, 569–72
  commercial agriculture in, 690
  decline of, 514–15
  England vs., 510, 513, 565
  France compared with, 515
  Inquisition in, 481
  Jews expelled from, 394, 424
  mercantilism in, 565
  Napoleon's invasion of, 664, 665, 666
  national monarchy in, 393–94, 473
  New World and, 392, 393–94, 434–38, 504,
    551, 565
  Portuguese independence and, 514, 515
  St. Domingue invaded by, 668
  slave trade and, 571
  in Thirty Years' War, 510, 513–15
  in War of the Spanish Succession, 550–52
Spanish Armada, 494, 510, 514, 565
Spenser, Edmund (c. 1552–1599), 465
Spice Islands, 418, 420, 423, 430, 553, 567
spinning jenny, 677
spinning mule, 677
Spinoza, Baruch (1632–1677), 592
Spirit of Laws, The (Montesquieu), 607, 608, 620
Spiritual Exercises, The (Loyola), 496
Staël, Madame de (1766–1817), 620, 623
Stanislaus Poniatowski, king of Poland
    (1764–1795), 561
Starry Messenger, The (Galileo), 586
steam engine, 673, 677, 680, 682–83
Steen, Jan, 564
Stephenson, George (1781–1848), 681
Strasbourg, 550, 553
Stuart dynasty, 517, 544
suffrage, French Revolution and, 654, 658, 659
sugar trade, 565
  slave trade and, 570–72
Sully, duke of, 515
Sumatra, 567
Summa Theologica (Aquinas), 484
Sunni Moslems, 425
Supplément au Voyage de Bougainville (Diderot), 615
Surinam, 567
Surrender of Breda (Velázquez), 529
sweatshops, 703
Sweden, 379, 482, 500, 513, 539, 550, 553,
    554–55, 558, 665
Switzerland, 482, 539
  Anabaptists in, 483–84
  Calvinism in, 485–87
  Industrial Revolution in, 685
  Reformation in, 482–87
Syria (ancient), 423

Taborites, 406
Tacitus (c. 56–c. 120), 442
Tahiti, 614
Tale of Two Cities, A (Dickens), 638
Talleyrand, Charles Maurice de (1754–1838),
    661
Talmud, 465
Tamburlaine (Marlowe), 526
Tamerlane (1336–1405), 397, 420, 422

Tannenberg, battle of (1410), 397
tariffs, 550
Tartars, see Mongols
taxes:
  in absolutists states, 547–50, 555, 558
  American Revolution and, 572–75
  "child," 424
  commercialization of agriculture and, 692,
    693
  French Revolution and, 641–42
  Peasants' Revolt and, 380
  Price Revolution and, 504–5
technology, see science and technology
telescope, 580, 585, 595
Tempest, The (Shakespeare), 527
Temüjin, see Genghis Khan
Tennyson, Alfred, Lord (1809–1892), 697
Teresa of Avila, Saint, 499
Tetzel, Johann (c. 1465–1519), 476
Teutonic knights, 397
textile industry, 677–80, 683, 705
textile trade, 562–63
Thackeray, William Makepeace, 696
theater, Elizabethan, 526–27
Third Estate, 639–40, 643–45, 653
Thirty-Nine Articles of Faith (1562), 494
Thirty Years' War (1618–1648), 510–13, 515,
    517, 588
Thomas à Kempis (c. 1379–1471), 405
Thomas Aquinas, Saint (1225–1274), 407, 442,
    469, 475, 484, 499
Thucydides (c. 460–c. 400 B.C.E.), 447
Timur the Lame, see Tamerlane
Tintoretto (c. 1518–1594), 528
Titian (c. 1488–1576), 454, 480, 506
tobacco trade, 565
Tobago, 567
Tom Jones (Fielding), 626
tools, of agriculture, 504
Topsy-Turvy World (Steen), 564
Tory party (Great Britain), 543, 544
To the Christian Nobility of the German Nation
    (Luther), 477
Toulon, 562
Toulouse, 378
Tournai, 373
Toussaint L'Ouverture (c. 1743–1803), 669
Tower of London, 464
towns, see cities
trade, see commerce
Trafalgar, British victory at (1805), 664
tragedy, see theater
transportation, 561
  in Industrial Revolution, 675–76, 683, 685,
    693
  see also railways
transubstantiation, doctrine of, 496
Transylvania, 553
Travels (Polo), 420–21
Travels of Sir John Mandeville, The, 432
Traviata, La (Verdi), 695
Treasury of Merits, 475
Treaty of Bretigny, 385, 386
Treaty of Nijmegen (1678–1679), 550
Treaty of Paris (1763), 572
Treaty of Paris (1783), 575
Treaty of Ryswick (1694), 550
Treaty of Troyes, 387
Treaty of Utrecht (1713), 552–53, 558, 570, 572
Trent, Council of, 489, 495–96, 497
Trevelyan, Charles Edward, 691–92
triangular trade, 570–72

Trinity with the Virgin, The (Masaccio), 451, 452
tsar, use of term, 397
Tudor dynasty, 392
Tunis, 427
Turgot, Anne-Robert-Jacques, 642
Turkey, 561
  see also Ottoman Empire
Twelfth Night (Shakespeare), 527
Two New Sciences, The (Galileo), 588
Two Treatises on Government (Locke), 541, 545

Ukraine, 395, 397–98, 424
United Provinces, 542–43, 551
United States, 575
  cotton industry in, 687
  immigration to, 690
  in Industrial Revolution, 677, 684–85, 687–88
  slavery in, 669, 699
universities:
  Lutheran Reformation and, 476, 478
  see also specific universities
Urban V, Pope (1362–1370), 399–400
Urban VI, Pope (1378–1389), 399–400
Urban VIII, Pope (1623–1644), 586, 588
urbanization, 562, 576
  in Industrial Revolution, 673, 693–96
  see also cities
Ure, Andrew, 678
Ursuline order, 499
Utopia (More), 464
utopianism, 464
Utraquism, 406
Utrecht, Treaty of (1713), 552–53, 558, 570, 572

vaccines, 688
Valla, Lorenzo (1407–1457), 448, 464, 469, 500
Valois dynasty, 385, 387, 391
van der Weyden, Roger (c. 1400–1464), 409
Van Dyck, Anthony, 519
van Eyck, Jan (c. 1395–1441), 409
Vanity Fair (Thackeray), 696
Velázquez, Diego (1599–1660), 529, 531
Venetia, 579
Venetian School, 454–55
Venice, 379, 393, 420, 423, 430, 438, 460, 461,
    539
  colonizing by, 427–28
  government of, 542
  Renaissance painting in, 454–55
Venus (deity), 452
Verdi, Giuseppe (1813–1901), 694–95
Vergerius, P. P. (1370–1444), 444
Versailles, palace at, 546–47, 558, 645, 646
Vespucci, Amerigo (1454–1512), 434, 581
Vico, G. B. (1668–1744), 604
Victoria, queen of England (1819–1901), 699,
    701
Vienna, 427, 552, 553
View of London with Saint Paul's Cathedral in the
    Distance (Crome), 695
View of Toledo (El Greco), 528
Vikings, 395, 434
Villa Rotonda, 459
Vincent de Paul, Saint (1581–1660), 499
Vinci, Leonardo da (1452–1519), 453–54, 455,
    456, 457, 469, 581
Vindication of the Rights of Woman, A
    (Wollstonecraft), 620, 648
Virgil (70–19 B.C.E.), 442, 443, 462
Virginia, 568
Virgin of the Rocks, The (Leonardo), 453, 454
Víves, Juan Luis (1492–1540), 465

INDEX A39

Vladimir, principate of, 395
Volpone (Jonson), 526
Voltaire (1694–1778), 595, 597, 603–4, 605, 606–7, 609, 614, 620, 624, 626, 627, 641
Vulgate Bible, 448, 497

Wagram, battle of (1809), 663
Wales, 391
Wallenstein, Eusebius von, 584
warfare:
    colonialism and, 539
    in Eighteenth Century, 572–75
    guerrilla, 664
    medieval, 378, 380–82, 384–95
    medieval technology and, 410–11, 414
    political instability and, 505–6, 532
    religious, 505–13, 532
    see also specific battles and wars
War of Independence, American, 572–75
War of the Austrian Succession, 572
War of the League of Augsburg, 550
War of the Roses (1455–1485), 391
War of the Spanish Succession (1702–1713), 550–52, 555
water frame, 677
Waterloo, battle of (1815), 667
Watt, James (1736–1819), 680
Wealth of Nations, The (Smith), 611
Webster, John (c. 1580–1625), 526
Wellington, Arthur Wellesley, Lord, 664
West Indies, 411
Westphalia, Peace of (1648), 513
"What is Enlightenment?" (Kant), 604
What Is the Third Estate? (Sieyès), 643, 644

Whig party (Great Britain), 543–44
Whitney, Eli (1765–1825), 677
William I (the Silent), stadholder of Netherlands (1579–1584), 509, 550
William III (of Orange), king of England (1689–1702), 543, 544–45, 546, 550, 551
Williams, Raymond, 674
Winkelmann, Maria, 594
witches, witchcraft, 522–23
Wittenberg, 475
Wittenberg, University of, 476
Wolfenbüttel, witch hunts in, 523
Wollstonecraft, Mary (1759–1797), 617, 620–21, 648
women:
    in abolition movement, 699
    Calvinism and, 507
    Catholic Church and, 499
    education of, 414, 443, 500
    in Enlightenment, 619–21, 625, 626
    French Revolution and, 645, 646–48, 650, 657
    in Industrial Revolution, 674, 679–80
    in Late Middle Ages, 414
    literary accomplishments of, 626
    Lutheranism and, 487–90
    in medieval literature, 409
    Napoleonic Code and, 660, 698
    of nineteenth-century middle class, 697–701
    Protestantism and, 487–90, 499, 500
    in Renaissance, 443, 447, 451
    salons and, 625
    sexuality of, 699–701

    in Victorian thought, 698, 699–701
    working class, 703–5
Wordsworth, William (1770–1850), 408, 651
working class, nineteenth-century, 701–5
    education of, 702
    factory life and, 704–5
    illegitimacy among, 704
    in Industrial Revolution, 674, 678–80, 681–83, 684, 701–5
    living conditions of, 702–3
    sexuality of, 703–5
    subgroups of, 701–5
    women, 703–5
World War, First (1914–1918), 551
Worms:
    Diet of (1521), 478–80
    Edict of (1521), 480
Würzburg, witch hunts in, 523
Wyclif, John (c. 1330–1384), 405

Xavier, Saint Francis (1506–1552), 497
Ximénez de Cisneros, Cardinal Francisco (1436–1517), 465, 495

York, duke of, 391
Yorktown, battle of (1781), 575
Yuan dynasty, 420, 422

Zizka, Jan (c. 1376–1424), 406
Zurbaran, Francisco, 570
Zürich, 483
Zwingli, Ulrich (1484–1531), 482–83, 503
Zwinglianism, 482–83